Editor in Chief Charles Capen McLaughlin is professor of history and American studies at the American University in Washington, D.C. Collaborating with him on the Olmsted Papers project are Charles E. Beveridge (senior editor of volume II), David Schuyler (assistant editor of volume II), Victoria Post Ranney, and Jane Turner Censer.

THE PAPERS OF
FREDERICK LAW OLMSTED

CHARLES CAPEN McLAUGHLIN

Editor in Chief

THE PAPERS OF
FREDERICK LAW OLMSTED

VOLUME II

SLAVERY AND THE SOUTH

1852–1857

CHARLES E. BEVERIDGE

CHARLES CAPEN McLAUGHLIN

Editors

DAVID SCHUYLER

Assistant Editor

THE JOHNS HOPKINS UNIVERSITY PRESS
Baltimore and London

This book has been brought to publication with the generous assistance of the Andrew W. Mellon Foundation and the National Historical Publications and Records Commission.

Copyright © 1981 by The Johns Hopkins University Press
All rights reserved
Printed in the United States of America

The Johns Hopkins University Press, Baltimore, Maryland 21218
The Johns Hopkins Press Ltd., London

Library of Congress Cataloging in Publication Data

Olmsted, Frederick Law, 1822-1903.
    Slavery and the South, 1852-1857.

    (The papers of Frederick Law Olmsted; v. 2)
    Includes bibliographical references and index.
    1. Slavery in the United States—Southern States—Sources.
    2. Southern States—History—1775-1865—Sources.
    3. Olmsted, Frederick Law, 1822-1903.
I. Beveridge, Charles E.   II. McLaughlin, Charles Capen.   III. Title.
SB470.05A2 1977 vol. 2 [E449] 712s   80-8881
ISBN 0-8018-2242-4   [975'.03]

EDITORIAL STAFF

Charles Capen McLaughlin
Editor in Chief

Charles E. Beveridge
Editor

Victoria Post Ranney
Associate Editor

ADVISORY BOARD

Lyman H. Butterfield

Neil Harris

Kenneth S. Lynn

Jon L. Wakelyn

CONTENTS

ILLUSTRATIONS — xv

ACKNOWLEDGMENTS — xix

INTRODUCTION — 1

EDITORIAL POLICY — 41

SHORT TITLES USED IN CITATIONS — 45

BIOGRAPHICAL DIRECTORY — 49

CHAPTER I THE JOURNEY THROUGH THE SEABOARD SLAVE STATES: THE UPPER SOUTH, 1852–1853 — 81

To Frederick Kingsbury, October 17, 1852 — 82

"The South" Number 1, *New-York Daily Times*, February 16, 1853 — 85

To Charles Loring Brace, December 22, [1852] — 92

"The South" Number 2, *New-York Daily Times*, February 19, 1853 — 94

CONTENTS

"THE SOUTH" NUMBER 7, *New-York Daily Times*,
MARCH 17, 1853 — 103

TO JOHN OLMSTED, JANUARY 10, 1853 — 111

"THE SOUTH" NUMBER 8, *New-York Daily Times*,
MARCH 30, 1853 — 115

"THE SOUTH" NUMBER 9, *New-York Daily Times*,
APRIL 5, 1853 — 121

"THE SOUTH" NUMBER 10, *New-York Daily Times*,
APRIL 8, 1853 — 127

"THE SOUTH" NUMBER 11, *New-York Daily Times*,
APRIL 13, 1853 — 132

"THE SOUTH" NUMBER 12, *New-York Daily Times*,
APRIL 20, 1853 — 140

"THE SOUTH" NUMBER 14, *New-York Daily Times*,
APRIL 28, 1853 — 144

"THE SOUTH" NUMBER 19, *New-York Daily Times*,
May 24, 1853 — 152

CHAPTER II   THE JOURNEY THROUGH THE SEABOARD
SLAVE STATES: THE LOWER SOUTH, 1853 — 155

"THE SOUTH" NUMBER 24, *New-York Daily Times*,
June 14, 1853 — 155

"THE SOUTH" NUMBER 26, *New-York Daily Times*,
JUNE 21, 1853 — 164

"THE SOUTH" NUMBER 27, *New-York Daily Times*,
JUNE 30, 1853 — 172

"THE SOUTH" NUMBER 28, *New-York Daily Times*,
JULY 8, 1853 — 182

"THE SOUTH" NUMBER 33, *New-York Daily Times*,
AUGUST 13, 1853 — 189

CONTENTS

"The South" Number 34, *New-York Daily Times,*
August 19, 1853 . . . 198

To Charles Loring Brace, February 8, [1853] . . . 202

"The South" Number 35, *New-York Daily Times,*
August 26, 1853 . . . 204

To Charles Loring Brace, February 23, 1853 . . . 209

To Frederick Kingsbury, February 26, 1853 . . . 212

"The South" Number 44, *New-York Daily Times,*
November 21, 1853 . . . 215

"The South" Number 45, *New-York Daily Times,*
November 26, 1853 . . . 223

Chapter III FIRST CONCLUSIONS: 1853–1854 . . . 231

To Charles Loring Brace, December 1, 1853 . . . 232

"The South" Number 46, *New-York Daily Times,*
January 12, 1854 . . . 238

"The South" Number 47, *New-York Daily Times,*
January 26, 1854 . . . 247

"The South" Number 48, *New-York Daily Times,*
February 13, 1854 . . . 256

Chapter IV THE JOURNEY THROUGH TEXAS
AND THE BACK COUNTRY: 1854 . . . 271

To Anne Charlotte Lynch, March 12, 1854 . . . 271

"A Tour in the Southwest" Number 8,
New-York Daily Times, April 24, 1854 . . . 275

"A Tour in the Southwest" (unnumbered),
New-York Daily Times, May 13, 1854 . . . 281

CONTENTS

"A Tour in the Southwest" Number 10,
  New-York Daily Times, May 18, 1854 288

"From the Southwest," *New-York Daily Times,*
  May 27, 1854 294

"A Tour in the Southwest" Number 12,
  New-York Daily Times, June 3, 1854 299

"The Southerners at Home" Number 1,
  New York Daily Tribune, June 3, 1857 307

Appeal for Funds for the *San Antonio Zeitung,*
  [c. October 1854] 314

"A Few Dollars Wanted to Help the Cause of
  Future Freedom in Texas," [c. October 1854] 319

Chapter V   THE LITERARY REPUBLIC: 1854–1855 . . . 322

"Lessons Concerning Means of Security
  on Ocean Steamers," *New-York Daily Times,*
  October 18, 1854 322

To John Olmsted, November 7, [1854] 331

To Bertha Olmsted and Sophia Stevens Hitchcock,
  [Early 1855] 337

To John Olmsted, March 13, [1855] 347

"Plan of Weekly Magazine," [Spring 1855] 350

To John Olmsted, May 28, 1855 352

To Parke Godwin, July 12, [1855] 356

To Arthur T. Edwards, August 7, [1855] 357

To Edward Everett Hale, August 23, [1855] 361

To Parke Godwin, [September 1855] 363

x

CONTENTS

To James B. Abbott, September 17, [1855] 365

To James B. Abbott, October 4, [1855] 367

To James B. Abbott, October 7, 1855 368

To Edward Everett Hale, October 23, [1855] 371

To Parke Godwin, [c. October 1855] 373

To John Olmsted, November 8, [1855] 373

To John Olmsted, December 9, 1855 375

Chapter VI EUROPEAN INTERLUDE: 1856 377

To John Olmsted, [March] 27, 1856 377

To Bertha Olmsted, June 18, 1856 379

"How Ruffianism in Washington and Kansas Is Regarded in Europe," *New-York Daily Times*, July 10, 1856 381

To Joshua Augustus Dix, August 3, 1856 385

To James Elliot Cabot, August 6, 1856 391

To Bertha Olmsted, September 3, 1856 392

To Bertha Olmsted, November 2, 1856 394

Chapter VII FREE-SOIL CRUSADE: 1857 397

To Edward Everett Hale, January 10, 1857 397

To Edward Everett Hale, January 30, 1857 399

To Edward Everett Hale, February 19, 1857 400

CONTENTS

To Edward Everett Hale, February 20, 1857 — 403

American Editor's Introduction to
*The Englishman in Kansas; Or, Squatter Life
and Border Warfare,* by T. H. Gladstone — 405

Supplement by the American Editor to
The Englishman in Kansas (April 13, 1857) — 424

To Samuel Cabot, Jr., June 29, 1857 — 431

To Samuel Cabot, Jr., June 30, 1857 — 435

To Samuel Cabot, Jr., July 4, 1857 — 436

To Secretaries of the Cotton Supply Associations
of Manchester and Liverpool, July 6, 1857 — 443

To Samuel Cabot, Jr., July 26, 1857 — 445

To Samuel Cabot, Jr., August 18, 1857 — 449

To Samuel Cabot, Jr., September 14, 1857 — 450

To Samuel Cabot, Jr., October 22, 1857 — 452

To Samuel Cabot, Jr., October 27, 1857 — 454

Appendix I   CALENDARS OF OLMSTED'S NEWSPAPER LETTERS ON THE SOUTH — 459

"The South," *New-York Daily Times,*
February 16, 1853, to February 13, 1854 — 459

"A Tour in the Southwest," *New-York Daily Times,*
March 6 to June 7, 1854 — 460

"The Southerners at Home," *New York Daily Tribune,*
June 3 to August 24, 1857 — 461

Appendix II ANNOTATED ITINERARIES OF OLMSTED'S
    SOUTHERN JOURNEYS: 1852–1854   463

Appendix III CHRONOLOGY OF FREDERICK LAW
    OLMSTED: 1852–1857   483

        INDEX   487

ILLUSTRATIONS

SLAVES AT WORK   From *Seaboard Slave States*   *Frontispiece*

CHARLES LORING BRACE IN 1856   From *Life of Brace*   51

GEORGE W. CURTIS   From Olmsted's personal collection of photographs, Society for the Preservation of New England Antiquities, Boston, Mass.   54

EDWARD EVERETT HALE   Courtesy of the Massachusetts Historical Society, Boston, Mass.   65

FRIEDRICH KAPP   From Olmsted's personal collection of photographs, Society for the Preservation of New England Antiquities, Boston, Mass.   68

BERTHA OLMSTED   From Olmsted's personal collection of photographs, Society for the Preservation of New England Antiquities, Boston, Mass.   70

JOHN OLMSTED   (Oil painting by Jared Flagg)   Courtesy of Terry Niles Smith   72

MARY BULL OLMSTED   (Oil painting by Jared Flagg)   Courtesy of Terry Niles Smith   73

JOHN HULL OLMSTED   From Olmsted's personal collection of photographs, Society for the Preservation of New England Antiquities, Boston, Mass.   74

VIEW OF CHARLES BENEDICT CALVERT'S RIVERSDALE   From Anthony St. John Baker, *Memoirs d'un Voyageur Qui se Repose* (London, 1850) Courtesy of The Huntington Library, San Marino, Calif.   87

ILLUSTRATIONS

THE NEW STABLE AT RIVERSDALE "Buildings for Cattle &c. at Riversdale belonging to Chas. B. Calvert, Esq. 1853" (Lithograph by A. Hoen & Co., Baltimore, Md.) Courtesy of the Maryland Historical Society, Baltimore, Md. 88

THE JOURNEY THROUGH THE SEABOARD SLAVE STATES, 1852–1853 112

WOMAN WITH BULL CART ON ROAD OUTSIDE SAVANNAH From *Seaboard Slave States* 157

ELIZA CAROLINE CLAY'S RICHMOND-ON-OGEECHEE Courtesy of Thomas C. Clay 160

RICHARD J. ARNOLD Courtesy of Katherine Talbot 161

LOUISA GINDRAT ARNOLD Courtesy of Katherine Talbot 162

FIRST STAGE OF THE JOURNEY THROUGH TEXAS AND THE BACK COUNTRY, 1853–1854 272

OLMSTED AND HIS BROTHER, JOHN, CAMPING IN TEXAS From *Journey Through Texas* 273

VIEW OF SISTERDALE "Dr. Ernst Kapp's Water Cure Facilities at Sisterdale, Texas" (Lithograph by G. Kraetzer, c. 1855, from drawings by Hermann Lungkwitz, 1853) Courtesy of Paula Ingenhuett, copy from University of Texas, Institute of Texan Cultures, San Antonio, Tex. 277

ERNST KAPP'S HOUSE IN SISTERDALE "Dr. Ernst Kapp's Water Cure Facilities at Sisterdale, Texas" (Lithograph by G. Kraetzer, c. 1855, from drawings by Hermann Lungkwitz, 1853) Courtesy of Paula Ingenhuett, copy from University of Texas Institute of Texan Cultures, San Antonio, Tex. 290

THE JOURNEY THROUGH TEXAS, 1854 296

THE MILITARY PLAZA IN SAN ANTONIO From U.S. Department of the Interior, ... *Report on the United States and Mexican Boundary Survey, Made under the Direction of the Secretary of the Interior, by William H. Emory, Major First Cavalry, and the United States Commissioner,* 2 vols. (Washington, 1857–59) Courtesy of the Library of Congress, Washington, D.C. 298

PROPOSED DIVISION OF TEXAS INTO FIVE STATES 303

THE JOURNEY THROUGH THE BACK COUNTRY, 1854 308

THE WRECK OF THE ARTIC From Henry Howe, *Life and Death on the Ocean: A Collection of Extraordinary Adventures* ... (Cincinnati, 1855) 324

ILLUSTRATIONS

ELLEN BATEMAN AS THE NEWSBOY IN *Young America* ("Miss Ellen Bateman as the Newsboy in the New Drama of Young America," color lithograph by Sarony & Company, New York City) Courtesy of the Harvard Theatre Collection, Harvard College Library, Cambridge, Mass.   333

THE HOTEL DE VILLE, PARIS   From *Paris and Its Environs, Displayed in a Series of Two Hundred Picturesque Views, From Original Drawings; Taken under the Direction of A. Pugin, Esq., the Engravings Executed under the Superintendence of Mr. C. Heath; with Topographical and Historical Descriptions,* 2 vols. in 1 (London, 1831)   343

MOUNTAIN HOWITZER PURCHASED BY OLMSTED FOR THE DEFENSE OF LAWRENCE, KANSAS, IN OCTOBER 1855   Courtesy of the Kansas State Historical Society, Topeka, Kans.   369

EDWARD SHEFFIELD BARTHOLOMEW   From *Connecticut Quarterly* 2, no. 3 (July–September 1896)   379

TITLE PAGE FROM T. H. GLADSTONE, *The Englishman in Kansas; Or, Squatter Life and Border Warfare... With an Introduction by Fred. Law Olmsted...* (New York, 1857)   406

FREE-SOIL TEXAS AND NEOSHO   439

ACKNOWLEDGMENTS

Many people have contributed their time, effort and knowledge to the preparation of this volume. The editors owe a special debt of thanks to three people: Terry Niles Smith, who has generously permitted us to publish letters in her possession from Olmsted to her grandmother Bertha Olmsted, and has also given us permission to publish the portraits of her great-grandparents John Olmsted and Mary Bull Olmsted; Phillip Rutherford, who has been most generous in permitting us to publish letters in his possession from Olmsted to Samuel Cabot, Jr., and to include in the editors' notes excerpts from other letters in his holdings of Cabot's correspondence; and Jane Turner Censer, who provided much valuable assistance to the editors during the year she spent with the project on a National Historical Publications and Records Commission fellowship in editing. She reviewed the final form of the annotations prior to copy-editing, identified several of Olmsted's previously unknown Southern hosts and drew up the annotated itineraries of Olmsted's Southern travels that appear as Appendix II of this volume.

The editors appreciate the assistance of Laura Wood Roper, who provided access to material in her research files. They are grateful to the late Katherine Talbot, who gave permission to publish the portraits of Richard J. Arnold and Louisa Gindrat Arnold. She also made available an invaluable source on Olmsted's visit to the Arnolds—a copy of *Seaboard Slave States* annotated by Mary Cornelia Arnold Talbot, Richard J. Arnold's daughter. We wish to thank Thomas C. Clay for use of his picture of Richmond-on-Ogeechee, the plantation of his great-grandaunt Eliza Caroline Clay. We appreciate Paula Ingenhuett's willingness for us to publish her lithographs of Ernst Kapp's home and the surrounding countryside in Sisterdale, Texas. Susan G. Pearl helped us find illustrations of Charles Benedict Calvert's farm, Riversdale. Mrs. Howard J. Morrison, Shelby Myrick, Jr., and J. L. Sibley Jennings III were of great

ACKNOWLEDGMENTS

assistance to the editors in their search for information on the estates that Olmsted saw in the Savannah region. For the preparation of the maps in this volume the editors are most fortunate to have had the continued services of Stephen Kraft, who drew the maps and other illustrations for volume I of *The Papers of Frederick Law Olmsted*.

Of the many persons who worked with the editors in the long process of transcribing, annotating and checking and rechecking the texts and annotation, the editors wish especially to thank Pamela Hoes Cohen and Ray E. Wilson. Kenneth T. Stringer, Jr., solved many problems of annotation, while Leslie Anne Greene checked the accuracy and form of citations prior to submission of the manuscript to the advisory board of the Papers. The editors also benefited from the assistance of Kathleen Dalton, John Vaughan, Melissa Kirkpatrick and Hank Clark. In the process of transcribing and checking texts, the editors relied on the skills of Martha Murphy, Barbara Lautman, Gail Nolting, Gary Weaver and Rogers Spottswood. Sharon Lew helped proofread galleys and pages and construct the index. For research on Olmsted's relations with the antislavery Germans in the San Antonio area, the editors drew on the research and translating abilities of Mary M. El-Beheri and her students Dawn Davis, Ronald Schneider and Eric Vormelker.

Student interns who provided valuable assistance were Matthew Hamilton, who compared the texts of Olmsted's newspaper letters on the South with the volumes Olmsted later published; Judy Ingram and Sophie Lynn, who established a preliminary itinerary of Olmsted's travels; and Ed Cloos, who undertook the preliminary annotation of Olmsted's introduction and supplement to *The Englishman in Kansas*.

We have received generous aid and comments from the Olmsted Papers' Advisory Board and from other historians, including Alice Crozier, John W. Lozier, Larry Jochims, Ernest Isaacs and Richard H. Abbott. In addition, we owe a special debt of gratitude to the staff of the Manuscript Division of the Library of Congress, which has assisted us so assiduously and for so long. We wish also to thank the staffs of the libraries of Boston University, Brown University, Harvard University, the Rhode Island Historical Society, the Kansas State Historical Society and Smith College for their help in providing information and materials used in the preparation of this volume.

We wish also to express our great appreciation to the individuals and institutions that have sponsored our efforts and have provided the funds for our enterprise. The National Endowment for the Humanities provided major funding for the period 1977–80, during which most of the work on this volume was done. The Rockefeller Foundation and the United States Capitol Historical Society provided substantial grants for work on the volume, and these grants were matched by the National Endowment for the Humanities. The Olmsted Papers project also received generous help in the form of similar matching grants from the Gaylord Donnelley Foundation, the New York Times Foundation, the Continental Trust Company of Illinois, and from Clarence Heller and

ACKNOWLEDGMENTS

Mrs. Thomas R. Coyne. The Andrew W. Mellon Foundation provided funds for the final stages of preparation of the volume. In 1977 the National Historical Publications and Records Commission awarded the editors a substantial grant for research on the volume and in addition has provided The Johns Hopkins University Press with a subvention to help meet the costs of publication.

In the preparation of this volume, Charles McLaughlin did the original letter-search and preliminary annotation of a number of the documents. Charles Beveridge supervised the day-to-day work on the volume and was primarily responsible for the annotation of documents concerning Olmsted and the South. David Schuyler assumed primary responsibility for the annotation of documents relating to Olmsted's literary and publishing career.

THE PAPERS OF
FREDERICK LAW OLMSTED

INTRODUCTION

In 1852, at the age of thirty, Frederick Law Olmsted began the first of several brief public careers that he pursued before 1865, when he finally chose landscape architecture as his profession. During the years 1852–57 he was primarily a literary man, a traveler and writer. In that short span of time he became the most prolific and influential of those travelers who published accounts of their visits to the South. He spent a total of fourteen months on two journeys through the South, and wrote seventy-five long letters of description for the *New-York Daily Times* and the *New York Daily Tribune*. He also completed two large volumes on his Southern travels: *A Journey in the Seaboard Slave States,* published in early 1856, and *A Journey Through Texas; Or, A Saddle-Trip on the Southwestern Frontier,* published in early 1857. In the latter year he published an American edition of *The Englishman in Kansas; Or, Squatter Life and Border Warfare,* by the English newspaper correspondent Thomas H. Gladstone, to which he added a long introduction and a supplement. By the fall of 1857 he had also written most of his third volume on the South, *A Journey in the Back Country.*

Olmsted's role in the literary world during these years was broader than that of a commentator on the South. From the spring of 1855 to the spring of 1857 he was a partner in the New York publishing firm of Dix, Edwards & Company. For the first ten months of that period he served as managing editor of *Putnam's Monthly Magazine,* a liberal patron of American writers and an influential vehicle for moderate antislavery views. He then spent the spring and summer of 1856 in Europe and England, acting as agent for the publishing firm. In August 1857 the successor firm to Dix, Edwards & Company failed, bringing Olmsted's career in the literary world to an abrupt end. At that point, in September 1857, Olmsted secured the post of superintendent of New York's nascent Central Park and took a major step along the path that would lead him to a career in landscape architecture.

Although Olmsted changed in five years from a farmer to a writer and publisher, and then to a park administrator, the single problem of slavery dominated his thinking and gave unity to his various activities. In all his endeavors, he felt that he was engaged in a crucial battle for men's minds. Like his Puritan forebears in New England, he believed that the society of which he was a part was like a "city upon a hill." The free-labor society of the North had a historic mission whose outcome held great significance for the future of both the New World and the Old. Olmsted was firmly convinced that it was the responsibility of the North in the decade of the 1850s to vindicate two concepts: the viability of the republican form of government and the superiority of a society based on free labor to that based on slavery.

The failure of Europe's republican revolutions, which had promised to sweep away the anachronistic institutions of monarchy and aristocracy, troubled him. He was distressed during the 1850s to see monarchists in England and on the Continent pointing to the political turmoil produced in the United States by the slavery question as proof of their claims that a republican political system could not provide stable government. At the same time, he was concerned by the charges of proslavery apologists in the South that the free society of the North was incapable of producing a true civilization. The North, these apologists argued, had no means of creating those cultural institutions and works of art that, historically, had depended on the patronage of a ruling aristocratic class. Such critics could be disproved, Olmsted concluded, only if the society of the North realized its full promise for improving the lot—both economic and intellectual—of the common man. His major professional activities of the 1850s served that end, which required the establishment of popular journals of literature and opinion like *Putnam's Monthly,* and which called for the creation of such communal institutions of popular education and recreation as libraries, museums and parks.

While Olmsted's allegiance to republican government and free-labor society were strong from the beginning of the period, political events during the five years between 1852 and 1857 produced significant changes in his views of the South. The single most important development was the new pressure brought to bear by the South for the expansion of slavery following the passage of the Kansas-Nebraska Act in 1854. Before that event, which occurred in the midst of his second Southern journey, Olmsted's writings dealt primarily with the society of the South and with the prospects for ameliorating the condition of the slaves and preparing them for eventual freedom. After the Kansas-Nebraska Act became law, his writings focused increasingly on the threat posed to free-labor society by the expansion of slavery in the territories. He used his writings to point out the danger of the South to the nation at large, and worked actively to prevent the advance of slavery on the southwestern frontier. To that end, he raised money to arm the free-state settlers in Kansas. He also worked

INTRODUCTION

with both local German residents and the New England Emigrant Aid Company to build a barrier of free-soil colonies across Texas in an attempt to remove slavery from West Texas and to counter any move by the national administration to turn the Indian Territory south of Kansas into a slaveholding state.

The present volume includes many of the personal letters that Olmsted wrote during the five-year period 1852–57, as well as numerous professional letters dealing with questions about publishing and free-labor colonization. It also contains what the editors judge to be all of Olmsted's significant statements on the South, slavery and the sectional crisis that did not appear in his three well-known volumes of travel accounts or in the abridged version that he published in 1861 as *The Cotton Kingdom: A Traveller's Observations on Cotton and Slavery in the American Slave States*. These annotated documents, supplemented by the appended calendars of newspaper letters and the annotated itinerary of Olmsted's two Southern journeys, provide the reader with a chronicle of Olmsted's changing views on the South. They also serve as a guide to the process by which Olmsted wrote his books on the South, and provide identification of persons and places mentioned in those volumes.

Like many members of his generation, Olmsted became concerned about slavery primarily as a result of the controversy over the Mexican War and the Compromise of 1850 that followed it. During the summer of 1846, full of patriotism and what he called a "wonderful taste for the pomp & circumstance of glorious war," Olmsted declared that he was almost ready to go and fight. He said so despite the mounting Northern opposition to a war that would expand slavery in the United States, and despite the fact that he was living with a pacifist, George Geddes, and was reading with approval the antislavery newspaper *True American*, edited by Cassius Clay.[1] He did believe by this time, however, that slavery was one of the great curses of the age, and within a year he admitted to having a strong sense of sectional allegiance. To his friend Frederick Kingsbury, a Connecticut Yankee who had lived for some years in Virginia, he wrote: "You've no sort of sectional feeling—I have the strongest in the world."[2] That sectional feeling and the New England values he had absorbed while growing up would in time influence the way he perceived the South and responded to it; but neither led him to the moral condemnation or immediatism that were the hallmarks of Northern abolitionists. He believed that the process of emancipation would be long and complex and could be carried out effectively only by carefully preparing the slaves for freedom. He saw social change as a slow process and believed that social reform should come about through an educational process that would change the habits as well as the beliefs of men.[3]

Olmsted was also unable to share what he viewed as the abolitionists' conviction of their own moral superiority. He found in them the same lack of Christian charity and the same overweening confidence in the rightness of their beliefs that had dismayed him in the various Protestant denominations he

INTRODUCTION

had examined in his search for religious faith. His inability to achieve an unshakable conviction about various "points of doctrine" had kept him from joining any church and had set him on the road to what he later called "a vague blundering indefensible rationalism." The same emphasis on reason kept him from accepting the doctrines of any reform group without careful thought and much argument. As he argued the issue of slavery with his abolitionist friend Charles Loring Brace, he refused to accept the idea that slaveholders could not be conscientious Christians and should therefore be excluded from church membership.[4]

In defining his view of slave ownership and the role that Northerners could play in bringing about emancipation, Olmsted drew upon a tradition of moderate antislavery thought. Although the specific sources of his views can only be conjectured, they were strikingly similar to the teachings of Horace Bushnell, who was for some years the Olmsted family's minister in Hartford and strongly influenced the thought of the young Olmsted.[5] Like Bushnell, Olmsted believed that since many Southerners had inherited their slaves, they should not be condemned for failing to free their bondsmen immediately. Slaveholders were justified in keeping their slaves, however, only so long as they attempted to make slavery a civilizing and Christianizing institution. This meant that they should at least teach their slaves the basic tenets of Christianity, observe the sanctity of marriage, and refuse to break up families when selling their slaves. Since he viewed slaveholders simply as trustees holding the children of heathen barbarians until they were ready for freedom, Olmsted declared that they should train their slaves in self-reliance and skills that would enable them at some not-too-distant date to survive as free men.

Olmsted also held the view—widely shared in his time—that under the Constitution the federal government had no authority to abolish slavery in the states. Slavery was a state institution founded on state laws. Emancipation could come only by action of state governments or through the manumission of slaves by their owners, in accordance with state laws. Northerners should not—and under the Constitution could not—use coercion to bring about the abolition of slavery. Only by persuasion, by appealing to considerations of economics and morality, Olmsted believed, should those Northerners opposed to slavery attempt to improve the condition of the slaves and bring about emancipation. Like Bushnell, he felt that Northerners should make their appeals as Christian gentlemen; they should reason with their Southern brethren rather than attack and condemn them.

Olmsted's references to the slavery question are infrequent and brief in his early letters, but he made a clear statement of his position in *Walks and Talks of an American Farmer in England,* which he published in 1852. In that book, he justified the continued existence of slavery in the South, saying that it was necessary to educate and civilize the still-barbaric slaves before freeing them. Such education, whereby members of a society were elevated to a position of equal freedom and rights with others, was, he declared, "a very necessary part of all rightful government."[6] Olmsted asserted that society was justified in depriving its weakest and most dangerous members of full freedom until they could be educated to discharge their responsibilities as free men and citizens. By the same token, he believed that it was the solemn duty of those with wealth and education to serve as the trustees of those who could not care for themselves, and to bring them as quickly as possible to full participation in society. This paternalism was the responsibility of Southern slaveholders to their slaves, and there was little that Northerners could do except encourage the Southerners to carry out their responsibilities. "The law of God in our hearts binds us in fidelity to the *principles* of the Constitution," Olmsted concluded. "They are not to be found in 'Abolitionism,' nor are they to be found— oh! remember it, brothers, and forgive these few words—in *hopeless, dawnless, unredeeming* slavery."[7] As the first letter in the present volume indicates, Olmsted still held these views as he prepared to leave for the South in the fall of 1852.

By the time of his departure on his first journey, however, Olmsted's sense of the unpleasant implications of his constitutional responsibility of forbearance concerning southern slavery had been strengthened by events both in America and abroad. During his travels in England and Europe in 1850, he had been dismayed by the shadow that fell between himself and the "most earnestly republican and radically democratic" Englishmen because of the existence of slavery in the United States. They could not grasp the concept, so natural and convenient for him, of a federal system under which slavery was a local institution of individual states that were in no way subject to the political action of the central government. His experience in England made Olmsted wish, whimsically, that the Southerners would send lecturers there to explain that "we at the North have nothing to do with their peculiar institution, and are not to be expected to carry pistols and bowie knives and fight every body that chooses to attack it all over the world."[8]

When he wrote these words, with their overtones of violence, passage of the Fugitive Slave Law of 1850, and the use of federal officials to return runaway slaves under its provisions, had revealed the price the South was to demand under the Constitution for the protection of its slave property. Olmsted was disgusted by Northern defenders of the Fugitive Slave Law and of the Compromise of 1850, of which it was a part, but he saw no reason to adopt more radical views. He resisted the attempts of Charles Loring Brace to convert him to abolitionism, even when his friend arrived for the weekend at his Staten Island farm with such powerful advocates of abolitionist doctrine as Theodore Parker and William Lloyd Garrison.[9] He also resisted the appeals of the rising Free Soil party, remaining a loyal Whig until that party's demise following the elections of 1854. Still, the enmity stirred up by the Fugitive Slave Law left its mark. As he prepared for his first journey through the South, he told his friend Frederick Kingsbury that while he thought himself a "moderate Free Soiler," representing "pretty fairly the average sentiment of good thinking men on our side," he nevertheless "would take in a fugitive slave & shoot a man that was likely to get him."[10]

By the time Olmsted began his Southern tours, his sense of the anachronistic nature of slavery and of the aristocratic principles that underlay slave society had been strengthened by the misfortunes of European republicanism. During his European trip of 1850, the reformers he met strongly impressed him, and he returned to the United States with a keener interest in their struggle. His concern for the Hungarians' attempt to create a republic free of Austrian domination became more personal when Austrian officials in Hungary imprisoned Charles Loring Brace for five weeks in 1851 on suspicion of being an intermediary between Hungarian revolutionaries in England and Hungary.[11]

Although Olmsted's European trip of 1850 gave greater personal meaning to his observation of European politics, his desire for the spread of republicanism had been strong from the beginning of the revolutions of 1848. Responding to the scene in the French Chamber of Deputies in March 1848, when Louis Philippe tried to save his dynasty by abdicating in favor of his grandson, only to be greeted by a cry from the galleries "It is too late," Olmsted exclaimed: "Hear it fools, Hear it slaves, and have Faith. Hear it Nicholas! Hear it, Metternich! Hear it Irish landlords! Hear it Scotch lairds and English hunters. Hear it Slaveholding sons of America and prepare to meet—or avert—your fate."[12] The means were unclear and the end was not in sight, but Olmsted was confident that all vestiges of ancient privilege and injustice—all "relics of barbarism"—were destined to fall before the march of nineteenth-century progress.

That optimism was the brighter side of Olmsted's ideas on social change, the foil to the elitism that was implicit in his view of the role of trustees in improving the condition of the lower classes. He and his close friends believed that it was possible to uplift all elements in American society. They were shocked to find their English counterparts less sanguine, and willing to accept the indefinite existence of a poor, degraded class of laborers. Offended by such a view, Olmsted declared: "We hold that party in England, which regard their labouring class as a permanent providential *institution,* not to be improved in every way, educated, fitted to take an equal share with all Englishmen in the government of the commonwealth of England, to be blasphemers, tyrants, and insolent rebels to humanity."[13]

In addition to his concern for the politics of slavery and his interest in European republicanism dating from the late 1840s, Olmsted carried with him to the South a set of standards of civilization that he had been formulating for a much longer time. These standards were drawn for the most part from the values of the regional culture in which he grew up—the precepts of community and domesticity that were rooted in the Puritan values of the seventeenth-century founders of Connecticut. Many of these ideas were a family inheritance, for he traced his American ancestry back to James Olmsted, one of the original proprietors of Hartford in 1636. Frederick absorbed the values of this society in his childhood, and later gleaned them from the writings of such representatives of the Connecticut mind as Timothy Dwight and Horace Bushnell. It is not surprising that his image of the good society was to a large extent an idealized version of the New England town. Men should live in communities, where they could easily engage in the mutual exchange of ideas and services that was the basis of civilized existence. Drawing directly from Puritan ideology, Olmsted believed that the chief purpose of life was to be of service to other members of society, and he held that a society that permitted extensive division of labor made possible the highest form of community. The more specialized the skill that each member of the work force was able to practice, the more effectively he or she could meet the needs of others. Close settlement in communities was necessary for such an exchange of services, and it brought other benefits as well. Communities were able to support public schools and other institutions of popular learning and recreation, all necessary for the development and perpetuation of civilization, and they fostered the creation of good transportation facilities—roads and bridges—which increased the exchange of both information and goods.[14]

Another prerequisite for the growth of civilization was stability and continuity of settlement. Like many other Connecticut thinkers, Olmsted deplored the decivilizing effects of the American tendency to depopulate old areas and press on to sparsely settled frontiers. Part of his mission as a gentleman-farmer in the late 1840s and early 1850s had been to instruct others in ways to improve their lands and to create farms that were both productive and permanent. In that way, a stable society might be created wherein the work of one generation laid the basis for a higher level of civilization in succeeding generations. The tidy, 200-year-old towns of the Connecticut valley gave Olmsted his first impressions of such a society, and during his trip to England in 1850 he saw how centuries of settlement could merge the dwellings of men with their natural surroundings.[15]

As a gentleman-farmer, Olmsted drew from traditions of the English gentry, with its responsibility to provide leadership for the agricultural community it dominated. At the same time, he felt himself to be a participant in the tradition of the English yeomen, with their care for the land and their sturdy independence. It was in that spirit that he signed himself "Yeoman" in his letters to the *New-York Times* and *New York Tribune*.[16]

While Olmsted's identity in print was a humble one—a "farmer" in his first book and a "yeoman" in his letters from the South—his activity as a farmer showed him to be more the squire than the yeoman. When he decided in 1845 to become a farmer, his purpose was to serve as a gentleman farmer and agricultural reformer. After making the decision, he wrote to a friend: "I suppose it's no very great stretch of ambition to anticipate my being a Country

Squire in Old Connecticut in the course of fifteen years. I should like to help then as far as I could—in the popular mind—generosity, charity, taste &c.—independence of thought, of voting and of acting. The education of the ignobile vulgus ought to be much improved and extended."[17]

It was characteristic of Olmsted that in stating his intentions as a farmer, he chose for himself the role of civilizer and advocate of taste. As a gentleman-farmer, as in his various other professional roles, he sought to realize his concept of civilization in America. He had always before him an image of the society that America should become, and the elements of taste, domesticity and gentility were usually to be found at the heart of his enterprise. The millennium he hoped to achieve was an American society in which people of all classes had the opportunity to acquire the "mental & moral capital of gentlemen" and did so. He looked forward to a time when universal gentility would provide a common cultural bond between people of all income levels and occupations—when, in that sense, America would be a classless society of gentlemen.

The most important means of moving people from barbarism to civilization was cultivation of taste—aesthetic sensibility, orderliness, and a knowledge of what was "fitting" both in the arrangement of physical objects and in conduct. The most effective school for taste was the home, for it was there that both young and old would absorb the values of taste and gentility in the most direct and complete way. In looking to taste and the home for the establishment of new social values, Olmsted drew from the teachings of major figures in New England's past. Timothy Dwight—president of Yale College in Jefferson's time and the "Pope of Connecticut," who opposed Jeffersonian rationalism and Democratic-Republican politics—had taught that taste was the first faculty acted on in the process by which men escaped "from a grovelling, brutish character; a character in which morality is effectually chilled or absolutely frozen." Olmsted had learned the lesson from Dwight's accounts of his travels in New England and New York, and he had learned it again from the writings of the horticulturist, landscape gardener and taste-maker Andrew Jackson Downing, a man of Massachusetts stock who had absorbed Dwight's teachings and gave them far more graceful expression than the old Connecticut divine had ever cared to do. Moreover, the importance of the home as a school for civilization was as old as the Connecticut belief that children should be raised up in an atmosphere of "steady habits." Olmsted's family's own minister, Horace Bushnell, who influenced him in many ways, taught modern versions of the old ways of training youth in his sermons on "Christian Nurture" and "Unconscious Influence."[18]

Olmsted's social values bore a close resemblance to those of his mentors Timothy Dwight and Horace Bushnell—ministers both—but his was a later and more secularized version of their precepts. He did not look to the church to play the same role in the community as did those earlier thinkers. Olmsted believed that the home and public institutions ought to assume the traditional function of the church in the New England community. This shift in emphasis owed something to the secularizing spirit of the times, but Olmsted had personal reasons as well. After the age of five, he had received most of his schooling in the homes of country parsons away from Hartford, and he had seen many things that lowered his opinion of the ministerial profession. He disliked the tyranny that church members exerted over the conduct and thought of individuals in the small New England and New York towns where he lived. He was distressed by the divisive nature of sectarianism and the controversy over "points of doctrine" that it fostered. He was also suspicious of revivalism, as were many others in Connecticut, the "Land of Steady Habits." In his own quest for belief he gave precedence to reason and rationality, and had difficulty accepting the inspiration of the Bible (which he eventually rejected) or the ultimate truth of any particular creed or sectarian set of beliefs. He never joined a church, and he came increasingly to judge religion by the way it affected conduct and contributed to the welfare of society in general.[19] With such a set of social and cultural values, firmly based in the traditions of Connecticut and serving as the basis for his program for civilizing America, it is not surprising that during his travels in the South, Olmsted often judged the society he saw and found it lacking.

Olmsted's opportunity to travel through the South came as an outgrowth of his long-standing argument with Charles Loring Brace about slavery. When Brace discovered in mid-1852 that Henry Raymond was looking for a traveling correspondent to tour the South for his newly founded *New-York Times,* and that the editor had read and admired Olmsted's *Walks and Talks,* he proposed Olmsted for the task. Olmsted had not previously met Raymond, but a single meeting of the two men was sufficient for the editor to offer him the role of correspondent. Olmsted later testified that Raymond asked him nothing about his views on slavery or any other subject, but simply requested that he confine his statements to matters that he observed personally. Raymond had doubtless learned something of his new correspondent's views from Brace, as well as from *Walks and Talks,* and must have been confident that what Olmsted wrote about the South would be compatible with the moderate free-soil stance of the *Times*—and that indeed was the case. Privately, Olmsted said that he hoped to "make a valuable book of observations on Southern Agriculture & general economy as affected by Slavery: the condition of the slaves—prospects—tendencies—& reliable understanding of the sentiments and hopes & fears of sensible planters & gentlemen that I should meet. Matter of fact to come after the deluge of spoony fancy pictures now at its height shall be spent."[20]

Since Olmsted was to be paid only after his letters appeared in the *Times,* he was fortunate that he could once again draw on his father's funds to finance his travels. With that problem easily solved, he departed in early December for his first visit to the South below the District of Columbia. His aim was to travel by public transportation, going through the eastern seaboard and Gulf states to New Orleans, thence up the Red River some distance into Texas, and then back to New York through the interior of those same states. Much of his observation of the South and slavery would therefore come from chance encounters on trains, stagecoaches and steamboats, and in hotels and houses where he stopped for the night.

For access to plantations that did not provide facilities for travelers using public conveyances, however, he had to rely on letters of introduction that he brought with him from the North. His most important contacts of this sort were persons connected with Yale College—the friends and classmates of his brother, John, and the acquaintances of his distant cousin Denison Olmsted, a professor of science at Yale who had many southern connections. By these means Olmsted gained access to seven farms and plantations that provided him with his important exposures to slavery and agriculture in the South. During the first part of his journey, in the region of Washington, D.C., and in Virginia, he visited four of those places: the 2,000-acre, mixed-crop farm of the agricultural reformer Charles Benedict Calvert at Riversdale, just outside the District of Columbia in Maryland, where he spent part of a day; a James River plantation, with 20 to 40 slaves, that produced corn, wheat and clover, where he spent three hours; a free-labor farm, Rocouncy (near Richmond), owned by the Quaker Nathaniel Chapman Crenshaw, where he stayed overnight; and the 1,300-acre tobacco plantation, with 60 slaves, of Thomas W. Gee near Stony Creek, south of Petersburg, Virginia. Olmsted had planned to stay at the Gee plantation overnight, but became lost on the way from the train station, spent the night at a roadside farm and had time for little more than a meal at Gee's before returning to the train.[21]

During the rest of the trip, three of Olmsted's most promising connections failed to gain him access to plantations. He passed by the plantations in Halifax County, North Carolina, of Thomas Pollok Devereux, who had nearly 600 slaves and 4,400 acres in that region, and decided not to retrace his steps when he failed to find Devereux in his Raleigh town house. In Montgomery, Alabama, he spent a week waiting in vain for his friend Jefferson Franklin Jackson to arrange for him to visit a cotton plantation, despite the fact that Jackson's law partners were rapidly becoming large slaveholders. By the time he reached New Orleans, Olmsted complained that he had rarely found people to whom he had letters of introduction and had "been able no more than to glance at the outside of things—occasionally getting peeps in through accidental openings." In New Orleans he also discovered that the plantation of another acquaintance from Yale, Anthony Wayne Baker, with nearly 200 slaves, was a two-day journey away in St. Mary's Parish, and so did not attempt to visit it.[22]

Nevertheless, Olmsted's letters of introduction and his acquaintance with Yale students of the mid-1840s did provide him access to the three large plantations where he was able to gain more than a passing glimpse of slavery: White Hall, a large rice plantation on the Ogeechee River near Savannah—one of several plantations in the area owned by Richard J. Arnold, with a total slave

INTRODUCTION

population of nearly 200—where Olmsted stayed three days; Fashion, the 1,200-acre sugar plantation of Richard Taylor in St. Charles Parish on the Mississippi near New Orleans, with 65 slaves, where he stayed one or two days; and the great cotton plantation of Meredith Calhoun on the Red River in Rapides Parish, Louisiana, consisting of four adjoining farms with a total of 15,000 acres and over 700 slaves, where he spent two to three days. Olmsted visited none of these places long enough to become a part of the daily routine of the plantation, but they did afford him the opportunity to examine closely the regimen of work and the agricultural practices of each.[23]

Olmsted's second trip through the South was even more barren of opportunities to examine plantation slavery, and he seems to have had few letters of introduction for the purpose. His letters introduced him to the newspaper editor George Dennison Prentice and the physician and botanist Charles Wilkins Short in Louisville; and in Nashville he and his brother made a crucially important renewal of acquaintance with Samuel Perkins Allison. None of his introductions gained him access to plantations.[24] Olmsted and his brother stopped overnight at a few places as they rode through East Texas, but he described only the appearance and domestic amenities of those places, and mentioned only the house servants. That was probably all he saw during his visits. He made many friends and spent much time in the German settlements outside San Antonio, but what he discovered there was a free-labor society of recent immigrants, and not the South he had set out to see. On the last stage of the second trip, as he rode alone through the back country from Mississippi to Virginia, he once again saw slaveholding establishments. This time they were off the beaten track, away from railroads and stagecoach routes. The first part of the trip was through the inland cotton districts of Mississippi and Alabama, but even so, he stopped at only one sizable cotton plantation that he was able to examine in detail—a plantation of three square miles with 135 slaves in Claiborne County, Mississippi.[25] In fact, this was the only plantation he investigated during the whole second journey, which lasted nine months. He gained many impressions of interior and piedmont cotton country and of the life of the "Highlanders"; but for the most part his knowledge came from conversation, observation along the road, and what he saw in the houses where he spent the night.

The chief source of information about Olmsted's Southern journeys is the series of letters he wrote for the *New-York Daily Times* between 1852 and 1854. He described his first journey in fifty letters under the heading "The South," which appeared between February 16, 1853, and February 13, 1854. Material from those letters made up a substantial part of the book *A Journey in the Seaboard Slave States,* which he published in early 1856. During his second journey in the South, Olmsted began a second series for the *Times*. Entitled "A Tour of the Southwest," it consisted of fifteen letters that appeared between March 6 and June 7, 1854. The series described his travels with his brother, John, across Texas to the Mexican border, and then stopped abruptly. Most of

INTRODUCTION

the material in these letters later became part of *A Journey Through Texas,* which appeared in early 1857. In 1857, as he was writing *A Journey in the Back Country,* Olmsted published a series of ten letters in the *New York Daily Tribune* entitled "The Southerners at Home," which appeared between June 3 and August 24. The series ended just at the time when he turned his full attention to seeking the position of superintendent of Central Park, to which he was appointed on September 11, 1857. The *Tribune* letters appeared almost verbatim in *Back Country,* which he had nearly completed in 1857 but did not publish until 1860.

Olmsted took extensive notes during his two Southern journeys, but none of them have survived. Presumably they, and all of the original letters he wrote for the New York newspapers, were lost in a fire at his Staten Island farm in 1863 while he was in California managing the Mariposa Estate. Private letters to his friends and family during this period also are scarce. It is therefore impossible to determine with assurance which of his original observations found their way into his writings on the South and which he decided not to use. It is possible, however, to reconstruct part of the evolution of his views in the crucial five years between 1852 and 1857 by comparing the newspaper letters he wrote in 1852–54 with the books he wrote between 1854 and 1857. Both of his series of letters for the *New-York Daily Times* contain several complete letters and portions of numerous others that did not appear in later books. This is especially true, and significant, in the case of the first series of letters, "The South."

In part this is because it was John Hull Olmsted who wrote *A Journey Through Texas,* using Olmsted's newspaper letters and manuscript notes. The material relating to the first Southern journey is also richer because more private letters that Olmsted wrote while in the South have survived, and because of the large number of letters from the series "The South" that he did not republish. Only two full letters and portions of three others from the series "A Tour in the Southwest" were left out of *A Journey Through Texas,* while Olmsted omitted twenty-one (either whole or in part) of the "The South" letters from *Seaboard Slave States* and *Back Country.*

The first four chapters of this volume present the surviving private letters that Olmsted wrote during his two Southern journeys, together with all of the significant material that appeared in his three series of newspaper letters but was not included in his published books. In most cases the newspaper letters are presented here in their entirety, even if some portions did appear in later books. Shorter passages that the editors have judged to be significant are presented in notes to relevant passages in the letters. In this way the three stages of Olmsted's process of publishing his material, as well as the evolution of his views, can be reconstructed. For a listing of which sections of the two-volume compilation *The Cotton Kingdom,* published in 1861, are drawn from which of Olmsted's three books on his Southern travels, the reader should consult the version of that work edited by Arthur M. Schlesinger, Sr.[26]

INTRODUCTION

The personal letters that survive from Olmsted's first Southern tour are useful primarily as a guide to his itinerary and for identifying the individuals he met who were known to his family and friends. The letters from the *New-York Daily Times* included in this volume, however, reveal much about his early reaction to the South. Although Olmsted thought poorly of them as his first efforts at correspondence, letters one and two of "The South" series gave his original statement of intent and his first impressions of slave society as he set them down soon after entering Virginia. Letter two raised an issue that he returned to in later letters—the absurdity of the South's complaints about the predominance of the North in manufactures and trade, and the belief expressed by Southern commercial conventions that the South could legislate a change in that situation. The North had not stolen the legitimate trade and industry of a city like Richmond, Olmsted declared. Rather, the Southerners had let them go to the North by default, in spite of the manifest advantages to be gained by, and the great natural opportunities provided for, trade and manufacturers in Richmond and elsewhere in the South. He developed this theme especially in letter fourteen. Similar themes were the poor farming practices of Virginians, both in the past and in the present day, and Olmsted's anticipation of the success that Northerners would have in restoring the old fields and worn-out land of the state. He dealt with these matters in letters ten and eleven.

Although he claimed that when he set out he did not intend to "give much attention to the subject of Slavery," Olmsted soon decided that "the character of the whole agriculture," and indeed of many crucial aspects of the whole society, stemmed from that institution.[27] He discussed this effect extensively in letters seven and eight, and returned to the subject in letter thirty-three; but even in his first letter he was already firmly convinced of the economic superiority of free labor to slave labor. A good deal of the material in letters seven and eight appeared again in chapter 3 of *Seaboard Slave States*, "The Political Economy of Virginia," but the original treatment was more direct and contained fewer references to the work of others. Simply from his own observations and conversations, Olmsted soon confirmed his first observation. Not only did slaves work slowly and poorly, but their presence resulted in a degradation of labor—the lowering of standards of skill and speed—for the whole laboring community, black and white.

A related topic was the condition of free blacks in the South. Olmsted dealt with this in letters eight and nine, and included much of that material in *Seaboard Slave States*, pages 129–33, but the original treatment was more comprehensive, and more severe in its judgment of the industry and morality of free blacks and slaves, than the later version in the book.

Another concern that was central to Olmsted's interest in slavery was the extent to which the treatment of slaves was humane and civilized, and the extent to which slavery served as a civilizing and Christianizing institution. In discussing Richard J. Arnold's Georgia rice plantation in letter twenty-eight, Olmsted reasserted his belief that paternalistic slavery could move the slaves of

13

the South from their native barbarism to civilization. Unfortunately, he observed, there were few institutions in the South that could help make such enlightened treatment the rule rather than the exception; in fact, there was little to rely on except the individual inclination of planters. He pointed out in particular the weakness of Southern laws restricting the sale of slaves and forbidding the breaking up of families. For the most part, he said, these laws were unenforced and unenforceable. This demonstrated that there was no great disposition among Southerners to bring about the strengthening of the family that gradualist antislavery men considered essential.

All in all, Olmsted concluded, "the mind and higher faculties of the negro are less disciplined and improved in slavery than in the original barbarism of the race." He rejected claims that a large proportion of slaves were practicing Christians, and argued strongly that American slavery had accomplished little in the way of training its subject people in true Christian doctrine and practice. He cited as proof the statements of ministers in that part of the South where missionary activity had been most energetic and supposedly most effective.[28] He saw little evidence in his travels that the slaves had gained a real understanding of Christian doctrine, or that their faith had produced the kind of conduct he felt should be the fruit of conversion. Suspicious of revivalism since his own attempts to experience conversion in his youth, he saw little that was Christian or civilized about the religious excitements that passed for religion among the slaves.

Olmsted repeated in *Seaboard Slave States* some of his conclusions about the regrettable nature of the Christianity practiced by slaves, but he did not repeat his more favorable estimation of their physical treatment. In a spirit of forbearance, and with a willingness to admit the shortcomings of free society that disappeared in his later writings, he conceded in his *Times* letters that American slaves were as well fed, clothed, and housed as the agricultural proletariat of Europe, and were protected from the kind of starvation and suffering that had afflicted Irish peasants during the Great Famine of the previous decade: In his last two letters he devoted much attention to this issue, concluding that the slaves he had seen and heard about experienced approximately the same degree of discomfort and corporal punishment, and did the same amount of hard labor, as sailors in the British navy.

While he apparently did not change his opinion on this question, Olmsted was unwilling in his later writings to emphasize those aspects of Southern society that he had found to be better than traditional wisdom in the North held them to be. By the time he wrote his books, his emphasis had changed. He was less concerned about the condition of slaves, or even about the extent to which the "peculiar institution" was a civilizing and Christianizing one. In the intervening years his attention had moved in the same direction as that of most other moderate antislavery thinkers in the North—to a concern with the threat of "Slave Power" to whites in and outside the South.

The most striking change in Olmsted's writings is the absence in his books on the South of those pleas to Northerners for understanding and forbearance toward their Southern brethren that he had made repeatedly in his newspaper letters. As early as letter eight, he wrote that the North should realize how difficult it would be for the South to make all the changes necessary to rid itself of slavery. He urged an end to Northern denunciations of slaveholders and called for an admission that slavery was something over which the North had no control. In "The South" number ten, he described the evils suffered by free laborers in the North and in Europe and ended with the apostrophe, "Oh, God! who are we to condemn our brother? No slave ever killed its own offspring in cool calculation of saving money by it, as do English free women. No slave is forced to eat of corruption, as are Irish tenants. No slave freezes to death for want of habitation and fuel, as have men in Boston. No slave reels off into the abyss of God, from want of work that shall bring it food, as do men and women in New-York. Remember that, Mrs. Stowe. Remember that, indignant sympathizers."

In his last letter, Olmsted continued the conciliatory theme, reasserting that slaveholding itself was not wrong if the owners would meet their responsibilities as trustees and trainers of their slave-wards. At the same time, he questioned the title of Northerners to property in products produced by sweated labor, or drawn from land originally wrested from the Indians by force and fraud. Moreover, he reminded his Northern readers that they had a responsibility to defend the right of Southern states to permit their citizens to hold slaves. There must be no Northern interference with that right, he averred, and the South would be justified in breaking up the Union should the North seek to use the federal government to abolish slavery in the states. Instead of attempting to interfere where they had no right, Northerners should instead apply themselves where they had both the power and the responsibility to strengthen free society and disprove those who claimed that blacks were incapable of surviving as free men. Northerners should work to secure, in their own section, "FAIR PLAY TO THE NEGRO."[29]

While Olmsted's description of the condition of slaves was in some respects less forbidding than that of many abolitionists, his view of the condition of nonslaveholding whites in the South, and of the effect on them of the institution of slavery, was severe indeed. "So far as they can be treated as a class," he wrote in "The South" number forty-seven, "the non-slaveholders are unambitious, indolent, degraded and illiterate;—are a dead peasantry so far as they affect the industrial position of the South."[30] Such a conclusion was only part of the distressing picture he drew of the condition of the whites—the "master class"— in the South.

Olmsted's analysis concerning the nonslaveholders of the South was similar to that of other Northern observers, but his extensive analysis of the condition of the slaveholders was more original and comprehensive. He had gone to the South believing in the Emersonian doctrine of "compensation"— that evil elements in individuals and societies were compensated by peculiar elements of good. His travels in England and on the Continent had sustained that view, and he embarked on his Southern travels expecting to discover the advantages that Southern society gained from the deplorable disadvantage of slavery. He found none; even the planter slaveocracy failed to produce from within itself, as a result of its wealth and leisure, either a high level of culture or a class of truly cultivated and socially responsible gentlemen. Most of these conclusions Olmsted drew together and set down early in his second tour of the South, as his steamboat worked its way up the Cumberland River toward Nashville during the last days of November 1853.

At this point, Olmsted had the pivotal experience of his decade of involvement with the South. In Nashville he and his brother encountered Samuel Perkins Allison, a native Tennesseean of the planter class and a classmate of John's at Yale. Allison proved to be the conversable Southerner—the man willing to talk through the problem of slavery and its effect on the society of the South—that Olmsted had sought without success during his first journey. Allison was familiar with the societies of both North and South, and strenuously challenged Olmsted's comparison of the two. As a result, the Olmsted brothers spent most of their two days in Nashville locked in argument with their Southern friend and adversary. The experience was a sobering one, as Olmsted recounted to Charles Loring Brace in the remarkable letter of December 1, 1853, which he wrote on his way back down the Cumberland River.

Olmsted's conversations with Allison convinced him that there was a fundamental difference between the gentlemen-planters of the South and the earnest, improvement-minded group of Northern gentlemen of which he and his close friends were members. The Southerners were really aristocrats, he decided, concerned only with perpetuating the economic and political power of their own privileged class. They had no thought that government should promote the education and improvement of the lower classes. Moreover, the ruling conception of the Southern gentleman—that of honor—impressed him as "mere deference to time honored rules & conventionalisms" that left little room for intellectual originality. All in all, he concluded, Allison and his group lacked a "fundamental sense of right," which was something that Olmsted and his friends—"all our earnest fellows," as he called them—shared.

Allison himself demonstrated the inferiority of the Southern "high-toned" gentleman to the Northern gentleman-reformer; but he also forced Olmsted to admit that the fruits of free-labor society, as demonstrated by society at large in the North, were not what he wished them to be. "He silenced us and showed us that our own position was by no means consistent and satisfactory," Olmsted confessed to Brace. Allison argued that there were very few gentlemen worthy of the name in the North, and dismissed Olmsted's claim that that shortcoming was compensated by the "*general* elevation of all classes at the North." Olmsted had to admit the truth of much of Allison's critique, and to acknowledge "the rowdyism, ruffianism, want of high honorable sentiment & chivalry of the common farming & laboring people of the North."[31]

Allison's exposure of the shortcomings of Northern free society made Olmsted "very melancholy," but such a passive state was not one that he could maintain for long. Almost immediately, Allison's challenge led him to reaffirm the mission of reforming and civilizing the North, a mission that he and his friends had already embraced. He now saw more clearly than before the urgency of creating in the North a state of society that elevated all classes and gave the lie to proslavery apologists and their mudsill theory of society. "I must be either an Aristocrat or more of a Democrat than I have been—a Socialist Democrat," he exclaimed to Brace. "We need institutions that shall more directly *assist* the poor and degraded to elevate themselves." Mere *"laisser aller"* was not enough: the power of government must be used in the North to encourage "a democratic condition of society as well as of government...." Defining the purpose that would underlie much of his own activity in the years to come, Olmsted concluded, "The poor need an education to refinement and taste and the mental & moral capital of gentlemen."[32]

Olmsted's first step in his renewed program of education of the North was to write—as his steamboat worked its way back down the Cumberland—letter number forty-six for the *Times* "South" series. In it he vigorously exposed the shortcomings of Southern society as reflected in the kind of gentlemen it produced. In that way he could win at least part of the argument that had gone so badly when he and Allison were face to face.

Olmsted carried away from his confrontation with Allison one further conviction, a belief that would soon be startlingly confirmed in the politics of the nation. Allison convinced him that the South was determined to expand the area of slaveholding both within the United States and into the Caribbean and Central and South America. A month later Stephen A. Douglas introduced the Kansas-Nebraska Bill, which touched off new controversy over the expansion of slavery and set in motion a series of events that would change many of Olmsted's views concerning slavery and the South.

Only one private letter that Olmsted wrote during the rest of his second Southern tour has survived, while five of the fifteen letters in his "Tour of the Southwest" series for the *New-York Daily Times* contain significant material that did not appear in the book *Journey Through Texas*. In one of those letters, which he wrote on April 18, 1854, Olmsted expressed his growing sense of the materialism and selfishness of the South as it sought to expand and protect slavery. Three other letters dealt with his exciting discovery of a number of German settlements in the San Antonio region that he thought could provide a nucleus for the creation of a free-labor society in West Texas.

From the beginning, Olmsted's contact with the Germans of West Texas delighted him. When he and his brother came upon Neu Braunfels, they were gratified to find the signs of enterprise and culture, and the communal setting, that were sadly missing in the rest of the South. The clean German inn where the brothers stayed was a traveler's delight, while the sight of smiling, well-scrubbed children on their way to school the next morning led Olmsted to exclaim, "Nothing so pleasant as that in Texas before, hardly in the South."[33]

Olmsted found stronger grounds for his admiration of the Germans in Texas when he and his brother proceeded to San Antonio. There they met Adolf Douai, the intrepid editor of the antislavery *San Antonio Zeitung.* The brothers traveled with Douai to the German settlements around Sisterdale, north of San Antonio, and by the end of the trip Olmsted recorded, "I never saw a man more cheerful, strong in faith, and full of boundless hopes and aspirations for the elevation of all mankind. . . ."[34] In San Antonio, Olmsted also formed a friendship with one of Douai's closest allies, Charles Riotte, the scion of a prosperous Prussian family and supporter of republicanism in Germany, with whom he carried on a long correspondence about American institutions.

The most pleasant discovery Olmsted made during his stay with the Texas Germans was that of the small "Latin Settlement" of Sisterdale, a tiny collection in the hills north of San Antonio of cultured and politically progressive refugees from the reaction that followed the revolutionary movements of 1848. The group included the noblemen Ottomar von Behre and Baron von Westphal, the scholars Ernst Kapp and August Siemering, and the active antislavery men Julius Dresel and Edouard Degener. During his first evening at Sisterdale, Olmsted was charmed by the musical performances held at Degener's log cabin, which included a waltzing party and the performance, accompanied by a good piano, of ensemble sections of Mozart's *Don Giovanni.*[35]

While in the Sisterdale area, Olmsted found teamsters camped on the prairie who hummed airs from Mozart and recited passages from Dante and Schiller "as they lay on the ground looking up into the infinite heaven of the night." He also had the remarkable experience of engaging in "discussions of the deepest and most metaphysical subjects of human thought, with men who quote with equal familiarity, Hegel, Schleiermacher, Paul and Aristotle, and who live in holes in the rock, in ledges of the Guadalupe, and earn their daily bread by splitting shingles."[36] Such a society offered Olmsted a glimpse of his millennium: men living in communities that overcame the decivilizing effects of immigration and frontier settlement, communities where even those who performed menial tasks and manual labor possessed "refinement and taste and the mental & moral capital of gentlemen."

Olmsted's German friends intended to do more than secure their own economic advancement and preserve their cultural traditions; they were also determined to create in their part of Texas a society free of the incubus of slavery—a society that embodied the republican ideals for which they had fought in Germany. They must have explained their beliefs and immediate plans to Olmsted, since the men of Sisterdale had formed an organization for political action, which they called *Der Freie Verein,* in November 1853, only three months prior to his first visit. They were anxious to formulate a platform that would provide the basis for an alliance of like-minded Texans for the purpose of influencing the presidential elections of 1856. On March 15, 1854, the Sisterdale organization issued a call for a mass meeting of Germans in San Antonio on May 14 and 15, which would coincide with the annual *saengerfest* there. Olmsted may well have been involved in discussions following the call, since he and his brother arrived in Sisterdale for their second visit on March 16 and spent the next week in the vicinity, "visiting and [being] visited by the settlers" there.[37]

The platform that the San Antonio convention drew up contained many of the principles of Olmsted's Sisterdale friends, including such proposals as the direct election of the president, U.S. senators, judges, and most administrative officers; popular recall of representatives; abolition of corporal punishment, capital punishment, and imprisonment for debt; graduated income and inheritance taxes; sale of public land only to actual settlers; a homestead law; creation of free schools and universities open to all; and rigorous separation of church and state.

With its endorsement of many changes that did not receive widespread support in the United States until the Progressive era, the platform gave evidence of the broad range of the reform thought of the Germans, but it was the platform's statement on slavery that had the greatest significance for the future of German political influence in Texas and for the situation of the Germans themselves. The platform declared slavery an evil, affirmed that it was a question for each state to handle without interference by the federal government, and requested federal assistance for any state desiring to bring about abolition of the institution within its boundaries. Soon proslavery Americans and conservative Germans condemned these sentiments and brought down upon the progressive and antislavery Germans, and on Douai's newspaper in particular, the wrath of the rising nativist movement in Texas.[38]

Olmsted was probably unaware of the results of the San Antonio meeting as he rode alone through the back country on his way home, but in late June he did write Charles Riotte from Chattanooga, expressing his desire to provide what assistance he could for the antislavery forces in West Texas. Soon after, Adolf Douai informed him more fully of his own problems. In response, Olmsted undertook to raise funds and guarantee the notes of his friend in order to ensure the survival of the *Zeitung*. During the fall he and his brother collected $200, which they forwarded to Texas as a gift. They also supplied Douai with correspondence for his paper and discussed with him the way to encourage free-soil colonization of West Texas. In return, Douai sent not only his thanks but also a flow of vivid descriptions of the menace to his newspaper, and even to his life, of violent proslavery and nativist elements in the San Antonio region. In late October he reported that he had been "threatened for weeks with lynching, and as I did not care for it, they seem to have organized for lynching the press."[39]

The vehemence of the proslavery response to the *Zeitung* and to the

INTRODUCTION

San Antonio platform of 1854, so graphically portrayed by Douai in his letters (some of which arrived with broken seals), provided Olmsted with a first-hand account of the violent threat to the antislavery cause, and to freedom of thought and press, posed by defenders of the "peculiar institution" in the South. His involvement in the free-soil activities of the Germans in Texas gave him a taste of those problems a few months before similar events in Kansas intruded on the consciousness of the North. It was through this experience in the fall of 1854 that Olmsted began to form an increasingly radical view of the threat posed by the expansion of slavery and Southern violence—a process that reached a crescendo in the summer of 1857.

After he returned to New York at the end of his second journey through the South, Olmsted began to write his first book of travels, *A Journey in the Seaboard Slave States*. For the most part he drew from the letters he had written for the *New-York Times,* but he supplemented that primarily descriptive material with more analytical discussions of the historical background of the society of the seaboard states. To prepare for that task, he spent a considerable amount of time in the libraries of New York City. He was convinced that historians should study the development of society at large, as well as the actions of those with power, wealth and education. As he observed, "The dumb masses have often been so lost in this shadow of egotism, that, in later days, it has been impossible to discern the very real influence their character and condition has had on the fortune and fate of nations." It was in this spirit that he had walked across England and parts of the European continent in 1850. It was also in this spirit that he wrote the chapters of *Seaboard Slave States* on the social history of Virginia, South Carolina and Georgia.

In Virginia, Olmsted found from the beginning the debilitating spirit of aristocracy and the degradation of the laboring class that impressed him so painfully in his own time; in South Carolina he perceived a supercilious aristocratic prejudice at work from the earliest years; and in Georgia he found a contrasting measure of "life, enterprise, skill and industry" that stemmed directly from the nonslaveholding character of the state's original settlers.[40] The writing of *Seaboard Slave States* took Olmsted over a year; he completed it in November 1855 and it was published in January 1856.

During the fall and winter of 1854, Olmsted was still a gentleman-farmer taking advantage of the slack season to follow literary pursuits. In April 1855, however, he left farming and his Staten Island farm behind and moved to New York City to devote himself exclusively to literary work. His father's wealth and generosity made it possible for him to embark on yet another career: John Olmsted provided his son with $5,000 with which he became a partner in the newly formed publishing firm of Dix, Edwards & Company.[41]

Part of Olmsted's work with Dix & Edwards was a direct extension of the writing in which he was already immersed. The firm was to be the publisher of *Seaboard Slave States,* and Olmsted's arrangements as a partner left him time for his own work. His primary role in the firm was to function as managing editor of *Putnam's Monthly Magazine,* which Dix & Edwards had recently acquired from the publisher George Palmer Putnam. Since its founding in 1853, the journal had served as an important patron of American writers and a model of the Victorian journal dedicated to popular education and enlightenment. The original editor of *Putnam's*, Charles Briggs, had turned to other employment, and Olmsted assumed some of his duties. At the time, John Hull Olmsted said that his brother "acts as publisher, i.e. editing publisher, answers letters, receives literary men, and conducts the literary side of the business."[42]

Fortunately, Olmsted did not have to carry all the responsibility himself. He was soon able to enlist the secret support of three leading figures in the New York publishing world, two of whom had been closely associated with *Putnam's Monthly* during its first years. The actual work of choosing and editing manuscripts for publication in *Putnam's* was carried out, incognito, by George W. Curtis, who was on the editorial staff of the *New York Tribune* and wrote articles for the "Easy Chair" column in *Harper's Monthly.* Curtis was also well known by this time as the author of travel tales and social satire. For occasional articles, especially on political topics, Olmsted could turn to Parke Godwin, an editor of William Cullen Bryant's *New York Evening Post,* and the poet's son-in-law. He also received assistance from Charles A. Dana, the city editor of the *Tribune,* who, while not associated with the earlier *Putnam's*, had been a member of Brook Farm with Curtis.[43]

The fact that the role of the other editors of *Putnam's* was kept secret gave Olmsted a better opportunity to gain recognition in the "literary republic of New York," as he called it, without being overshadowed by his better-known associates. This was gratifying, since he was anxious to secure a reputation as a literary man. In undertaking to edit *Putnam's*, his goal was to make it "more than ever the leading magazine and the best outlet of thought in the country." He planned to publish the work of the best American writers and thinkers and to pay them well. It was during his editorship that *Putnam's* published such important works as Herman Melville's *Benito Cereno* and Henry David Thoreau's *Cape Cod.* Other notable figures contributed during that period, among them Longfellow and Whittier. Olmsted's attempts to solicit manuscripts also brought him into communication with Nathaniel Hawthorne, Ralph Waldo Emerson, Harriet Beecher Stowe, and Theodore Parker. The high point of such associations with literary figures came when he gave a luncheon for James Russell Lowell on the eve of the author's departure for Europe in June 1855.[44]

In addition to seeking a reputation for himself, Olmsted sought through his work on *Putnam's Monthly* to use the journal as a vehicle for carrying out one part of the program for improving the society of the North that he had outlined after his debates with Samuel Perkins Allison. In his letter to Charles Loring Brace of December 1, 1853, he had called for the creation of a journal that would mold the thought of the American people, a subject he had clearly discussed with Brace before: "We ought to have that Commentator as an organ of higher Democracy and a higher religion than the popular," he wrote his friend. "And it ought to be great—sure of success—well founded. Bound to succeed by its merit, by its talent. A cross between the Westminster Review & the Tribune, is my idea."

This concern was not new to Olmsted. Even before he had thought about the need for such a journal he had been intrigued by the opportunities for popular education that were open to the religious tract societies. He was dismayed, however, by their approach and by the "flattering sick school-girl sentimentalism" that so often cloyed their publications. "Why in God's name," he had exclaimed to his father in the summer of 1849, "do not great good men, real men who are capable of thinking for others, and are not thought for by all the old women that would fain have a name to live after they have got into their dotage—take hold of this immense engine of good?"[45]

The business of publishing was not all high-minded endeavor, however. Problems of money soon intruded into the arcadia of literary life, represented in their most immediate form by Arthur T. Edwards, the partner with major responsibility for the financial affairs of the firm. One point of contention was the reimbursement of foreign authors for publication of their work in *Putnam's Monthly*. The absence of an international copyright law made such payments legally unnecessary, and *Putnam's* competitor, *Harper's Monthly*, filled much of its space with pirated material. Olmsted objected to such a course and tried to convince Edwards of the "absolute moral right" of foreign authors to payment in return for publication of their works. He also argued that because Dix & Edwards had published an American edition of Charles Dickens's popular magazine, *Household Words*, it should provide some payment to the original English publishers of the magazine, Bradbury & Evans.

While that debate involved somewhat abstract issues of principle and policy, Edwards's own policies hit closer to home when he rescinded an agreement to advance Olmsted the money for publishing *Seaboard Slave States*. Forced to turn to his father once again for financial assistance, Olmsted pondered, "I wonder how I could have been swerved from my repeated resolution not to be a business-man, knowing so well my unaptness for it."[46] By the time his connection with the publishing firm of Dix & Edwards was over (two years later), Olmsted had learned more painfully how great a mistake he had made.

The future still seemed promising, however, when in February 1856 he embarked on an eight-month trip to Europe and England for the firm. His twenty-four-year-old half-sister Mary accompanied him on the first part of the tour. They landed in England, proceeded to Paris, and then went on to Rome to join his half-sister Bertha and her companion, Sophia Stevens Hitchcock. Olmsted and the young women spent some time in Rome, traveled south as far as Amalfi, then toured northern Italy and went on to Vienna, Prague and Leipzig. In Leipzig, Olmsted attended to business with publishing firms and then the group proceeded to Dresden; there they split up. By late May, Olmsted reached London, where he spent most of the next five months seeking consignments from English publishers. At the same time, he gained entrée to the publishing and literary world of London and took much pleasure and some pride in the acquaintances he made. His most pleasing experiences were with the circle of men who owned and wrote for the humorous magazine *Punch*. The high point of his stay in London was the supper party that William Thackeray gave at his house each year for the editors of *Punch* and their close associates.[47]

Although he did not know it, during his European tour of 1856 Olmsted was also laying the basis for the professional activity that would take up far more of his life than the two years he spent as an editor and publisher with Dix & Edwards. While living in London he found himself drawn to the city's parks, and he later recalled that he spent all possible spare time in them. In the process, he learned much about the role that urban parks and public grounds could play in the life of a city. During his tour of Italy, which he had not visited before, he also absorbed images of landscapes, gardens and the settings of buildings that he would draw upon years later when he designed public grounds and college campuses in the semiarid climate of California.[48]

Olmsted's European idyll was short-lived, however. By midsummer 1856 he began to receive worried reports from his partner Joshua A. Dix concerning Arthur Edwards's handling of the firm's finances. In the fall, Olmsted returned to New York prepared to resign as a partner, but instead agreed to remain with the firm. The firm's financial problems continued to mount thereafter, and were complicated by the deterioration of the general economic situation as the Panic of 1857 approached. In April 1857, both Dix and Edwards withdrew from the firm and were replaced by the partnership of Olmsted, George W. Curtis and their printer, J. W. Miller, which took the name of Miller & Company. Olmsted withdrew from the firm in June, and two months later, on August 6, it failed. He had been right in his misgivings about embarking on a business career. He lost all the money his father had loaned him to invest in Dix, Edwards & Company, and found himself morally, if not legally, liable for some of the debts of Dix & Edwards that the firm of Miller & Company had assumed.[49]

Faced anew with the problems of earning a living and recouping his finances, Olmsted hoped to find another niche in the "literary republic" of New York. His best chance, he felt, was to write for the *New-York Times,* but there was no immediate prospect of that. Instead, he retired to a seaside inn near New Haven, Connecticut, to pursue the one literary activity that was still within his power—completion of the third volume of his Southern travels, *A Journey in the Back Country*. While he was there, an opportunity presented itself that eventually led him to a career in landscape architecture. A fellow guest at the hotel was his friend Charles W. Elliott, one of the commissioners of New York's new Central Park. The commission was about to hire a superintendent,

Elliott told Olmsted, and wanted a Republican with few political enemies. When Elliott urged him to apply for the position, Olmsted agreed to leave at once for New York and to decide on the way whether to apply for it.

Faced with the lack of other prospects, Olmsted decided to make the attempt, and set out to rally his friends and acquaintances in support of his candidacy. Although he was about to leave the "literary republic," his membership in it stood him in good stead. Many important literary men signed the petitions he circulated, and the consideration that in the end led the commissioners to select him was the fact that among those who endorsed him was the most respected literary figure in New York, Washington Irving.[50]

During the time of his partnership in the firm of Dix & Edwards and its successor, literary work absorbed most of Olmsted's time. Even so, he remained active in the free-soil cause. By the summer of 1855, a year after he had volunteered to assist Adolf Douai and the Germans in Texas, the situation there had deteriorated badly. Douai's uncompromising antislavery position angered proslavery and nativist elements in the San Antonio area and caused increasing anxiety among conservative Germans. By August 1855 Douai was reporting to Olmsted that an influential group of Germans was attacking him in newspapers and by word of mouth and was circulating rumors that he was on the verge of bankruptcy. Many of his advertisers had left him, he said, and he had lost a sixth of his subscribers. Many others, thinking that his paper would soon fail, refused to pay their bills. By late summer Douai was receiving new threats against himself and his paper, and for two weeks kept his printing office under armed guard.[51]

At the same time that the danger of Douai's position in Texas was increasing, the threat of civil war was growing in the territory of Kansas. On March 30, 1855, the election of members of the territorial legislature was carried for proslavery interests by the fraudulent votes of Missourians. The creation of this "bogus" legislature, which remained the officially recognized lawmaking body during the next few crucial years, presented an ominous threat to the free-soil group in the territory. The free-soil leaders in Lawrence, the western headquarters of the New England Emigrant Aid Company, immediately appealed to their eastern supporters for two hundred Sharps rifles and two field guns. Soon, emissaries of the free-state settlers hurried East to secure arms. Among them was James Burnett Abbott, who sought guns for his company of the free-state militia, which was being formed to counteract any aggressive actions by the "bogus" legislature or by the proslavery territorial militia and bands of armed "border ruffians."

Abbott secured one hundred Sharps rifles from the officers of the New England Emigrant Aid Company in Boston, and then went on to Hartford, Providence and New York, raising enough funds to purchase seventeen more. He returned to Kansas in late September 1855, leaving Olmsted in charge of soliciting funds for more weapons. With the money that he collected, Olmsted bought a mountain howitzer and ammunition. In October he shipped the howitzer—packed in several cases and disguised—to Kansas City. The men from Lawrence who were sent to claim it barely managed to carry the cannon back to their town before proslavery bands closed the roads. The "Sacramento," as it came to be called, was the first free-state cannon in Kansas and was in place at the Free State Hotel in Lawrence by December 1855, when the "Wakarusa War" brought proslavery forces to the verge of invading the town.[52]

As conflict with the "bogus" legislature and proslavery groups increased, the free-state movement gained strength. In December 1855 its supporters ratified the free-state Topeka constitution, and on January 15, 1856, they held elections for a slate of state officers and legislators. They also elected Charles Robinson, an agent of the New England Emigrant Aid Company, as the free-state governor. On March 4 the free-state legislature convened at Topeka, in defiance of Franklin Pierce's administration and the proslavery legislature that it recognized. Soon the official territorial government, led by the newly appointed governor, Wilson Shannon, undertook to suppress the free-state government and to arrest its leaders for treason.

In Texas, the spring of 1856 saw the collapse of the free-soil movement that Olmsted had worked to sustain. The success of the nativist movement in suppressing antislavery agitation had so alienated Olmsted's friend Charles Riotte that in December 1855 he secured a grant of two million acres of land near Monterrey, in the state of Nuevo Leon, Mexico, which he planned to colonize with Germans from their homeland and from the United States. In January he informed Olmsted of his intention to move to Monterrey, and held to that purpose despite Olmsted's objections to his project. At the same time, Adolf Douai was reaching the end of his endurance. In late January he wrote Olmsted that he had lost his influence in the German community because so many blamed him for bringing down on them the fury of the Know-Nothings. At the same time, he refused the Olmsted brothers' offer to raise more money to keep the *Zeitung* alive. In March Douai sold his press to a group of antagonists that he said were about to ruin him. He published the last issue of the *Zeitung* on March 29, 1856, and in early May left Texas for Boston.[53]

By the time of the free-state elections in Kansas and Douai's retreat from Texas, Olmsted was on the other side of the Atlantic. What he learned of events in America, and what he saw of the European response to them, increasingly troubled him.

Soon after his arrival in London for the summer came the news of the "sacking" of Lawrence on May 20 by sheriff Samuel Jones and a force of several hundred men, who had come to the town as a posse for a federal marshal seeking to arrest free-state leaders for treason against the territorial government. Though the invaders killed none of the residents (who offered no resistance), they destroyed the Free State Hotel, the house of free-state "governor"

Robinson, and the presses of the town's two antislavery newspapers. They looted a number of shops and houses and carried off Olmsted's howitzer for their own use. Two days later, Preston Brooks of South Carolina caned Charles Sumner of Massachusetts into insensibility on the floor of the Senate for his insulting references to Brooks's kinsman, Senator Andrew P. Butler, in a speech on Kansas. In Kansas on May 24 came the brutal murder by John Brown and his men of five proslavery men along Pottawatomie Creek. That atrocity unleashed three months of violence in the territory and spawned hundreds of incendiary reports and editorials in Eastern newspapers and the English and European press.

Olmsted left little record of how the events in "Bleeding Kansas" during the summer of 1856 impressed him, but he did express dismay at the ill-repute that they gave the American republican experiment, even among previously sympathetic foreigners. He discovered that the anarchy in Kansas and the other violent signs of the times were playing into the hands of the European forces of aristocracy and reaction epitomized by Emperor Napoleon III, who was building his Second Empire on the ruins of the French republic he had betrayed and overthrown. One indication of Olmsted's concern was the letter "How Ruffianism in Washington and Kansas is Regarded in Europe," which he wrote to the *New-York Daily Times* on June 19, 1856.

Olmsted was too occupied with business and too far from the scene to do much for the free-soil cause during his stay in Europe in 1856. During that time, however, his brother, John, was writing *A Journey Through Texas* from Olmsted's newspaper letters and travel notes. When Olmsted returned to New York in November, the manuscript was all but completed. The notes from which John had written the book, however, were more than two years old, and the volume contained no analytical sections like the historical chapters that Olmsted had added to *Seaboard Slave States*. To remedy this deficiency, Olmsted sat down in December 1856 to write a long "Letter to a Southern Friend" as an introduction to the book.[54] Part of his theme was the superiority of free-labor colonization in establishing society on the frontier. He described in detail the variety of public institutions (from roads to schools) that free-labor settlers quickly established in new communities. He contrasted this process of building a society with the approach of slaveholders, who tied up their capital in slaves and deferred for years the creation of public institutions or even the provision of domestic amenities. In this introduction, Olmsted once again set forth his view that slavery perpetuated a "frontier condition of society."[55]

That theme directly served the purpose for which he wished to use *Journey Through Texas*. As soon as he received proof sheets of the book in January 1857, he set out to use them to promote the cause of free labor in Texas. He authorized Edward Everett Hale and James Elliot Cabot to send copies, at his expense, to any persons they felt should be influenced in favor of free-labor colonization. He hinted to Hale, with no apparent success, that he was looking for an agency that would send a hundred copies of the book, at cost, to settlers who might be interested in "taking Texas next." Hale did agree, however, to forward sets of selected pages of the book to newspaper editors throughout New England, with the suggestion that they use the material to present Texas to their readers in a favorable light.[56]

Olmsted hoped to convince a few hundred New Englanders to form the vanguard of a substantial movement into Texas of Northern and European nonslaveholders. He also wanted to gain the support of influential Englishmen in order to attract their countrymen, and to that end he wrote in January 1857 to George Robinson, second viscount Goderich. At the same time, he was corresponding with the owners of West Texas land that might be desirable for free-labor colonies.

As Olmsted pursued his scheme for free-labor colonization in the Southwest in the spring of 1857, his writings on the South reflected his increasing concern about the consequences of the expansion of slavery. He was particularly alarmed at the willingness of the South to resort to violence in order to expand the area of slaveholding and ensure the safety of slave property in new areas. In examining that subject, he became more and more convinced of the cultural differences between North and South that slavery created. Already in his introduction to *Journey Through Texas* he had declared that slave labor was not as economical as free labor, and that Southerners clung to their "peculiar institution" for other than economic reasons. Ownership of slaves conveyed status in the South, he observed, as did land with the English, horses with the Arabs, and beads and vermilion with Indians. It also trained men to desire absolute command over those working under them: as he phrased it, "slavery educates, or draws out, and strengthens, by example and exercise, to an inordinate degree, the natural lust of authority, common as an element of character in all mankind."[57]

There was danger for the nation, Olmsted decided, in the fact that slavery could expand only if unacceptable demands were made on the nonslaveholding population. The protection of slave property required the enforcement of a whole series of oppressive laws: "When you demand of us to permit slavery in our territory," he had declared to his "southern friend," "we know that you mean to take advantage of our permission, to forbid freedom of discussion, and freedom of election; to prevent an effective public educational system; to interrupt and annoy our commerce, to establish an irresponsible and illegal censorship of the press; and to subject our mails to humiliating surveillance." In consequence, the people of the North were resolved that slavery should expand no further. "They will accept anything else that you may place in the alternative," he warned. "Be it disunion, be it war, foreign or domestic, it will not divert them from their purpose."[58]

The conclusion of Olmsted's December 1856 "Letter to a Southern Friend," with its litany of the ways in which slave society threatened free institutions, was based in part on the history of Southern attempts to suppress antislavery agitation within its borders during the previous twenty years, and in part on what Olmsted had learned of the harassment of Adolf Douai and his other friends in West Texas.

To a large extent, however, Olmsted based his predictions concerning the future demands of the "Slave Power" on what he saw taking shape in Kansas. As soon as it convened for its first session in July 1855, the "bogus" legislature passed a series of severe laws for the protection of slave property in the territory. Particularly harsh and provocative was the "Act to Punish Offenses Against Slave Property," which imposed the death penalty on anyone who assisted a slave insurrection or introduced into the territory any publication for the purpose of inciting revolt among either slaves or free blacks. The act also made it a felony, punishable by at least two years at hard labor, to make any statement denying the right of persons in the territory to hold slaves, or to circulate a document containing such a denial.[59] Olmsted was also distressed by the way territorial officials rode roughshod over the rights of free-state settlers, inciting the "sacking" of Lawrence, as sheriff Samuel Jones had done, and holding free-state men in jail without bond, as had been the case with Charles Robinson and others.

When Olmsted wrote his introduction to *Journey Through Texas,* the worst violence in Kansas was past, owing to governor John W. Geary's "pacification" of the territory just before the presidential election in the fall of 1856. Even in that process, however, the antislavery side had borne the brunt of official actions. Most of those arrested under Geary's regime were free-state men, and the ardently proslavery territorial judges promptly released proslavery men on bail while refusing bail for those on the other side. Moreover, Geary was rebuffed both by the judges and by the legislature when he attempted to promote moderate policies. In December, over Governor Geary's veto, the legislature passed a bill that would have put the whole state-making process firmly in the hands of the proslavery elements. Abandoned by the Pierce administration and increasingly threatened by violence from proslavery ruffians, Geary resigned as governor on March 4, 1857, the day of James Buchanan's inauguration. Olmsted expected that Buchanan would appoint a new governor more sympathetic to the "bogus" legislature, and that attempts to enforce the laws and collect the taxes of the legislature more vigorously would lead to new confrontation and violence in the territory.[60]

On March 6, the U.S. Supreme Court added another ominous ingredient to the sectional controversy. In its decision on the Dred Scott case, the Court declared that slaveholders had the right to carry their property into all territories, and implied that it might be illegal for the states themselves to outlaw slavery within their borders.

In the midst of this controversy, Olmsted undertook to have the firm of Miller & Company, of which he was a partner, publish *The Englishman in Kansas; Or, Squatter Life and Border Warfare,* a highly colored account of the violence of proslavery "border ruffians" in Kansas. The author was Thomas H. Gladstone, a correspondent for the *Times* of London who had visited the territory in the early summer of 1856. Olmsted had presumably read some of Gladstone's letters to the *Times* while still in England in the fall of 1856. As the American editor of the volume, he provided an introduction—probably written in late March and early April 1857—and a supplement that he dated April 13.

The task Olmsted set for himself in his introduction to *The Englishman in Kansas* was to explain the reasons for the violence displayed by the border ruffians in Gladstone's account, and to explore the implications of their conduct for the future of American society. His conclusions were severe, and his predictions dark and foreboding. The contrast the Englishman found in Kansas between the character of men from the North and those from the South—both descended from the same English stock—would be incredible, Olmsted declared, if there were not prior reason to expect men from the slave states to display "a special proneness to violence, and a distrust, or habitual forgetfulness, of law and civilized customs under exciting circumstances." This dangerous quality, he asserted, was inevitably and necessarily bred into the character of Southerners, and grew more ingrained with every passing generation.

The Southerners' lack of respect for human life stemmed from a fundamental instinct for self-preservation: the safety of the master race in a slave society depended on constant schooling of the slaves in habits of obedience, and of the masters in habits of command. It also required the masters to be mentally prepared at all times to respond, with violence, to any sign of insubordination. They must, Olmsted said, "hold themselves always in readiness to chastize, to strike down, to slay, upon what they shall individually judge to be sufficient provocation." This attitude nullified "the usual sentiment of the sacredness of life" where slaves were concerned, and it poisoned the relations of whites as well. Southern newspapers were full of evidence that Southerners acquiesced in violent acts and that juries were most reluctant to convict men for them. The fundamental conditions for the perpetuation of slavery, Olmsted concluded, diminished in the people of the American South "that constitutional and instinctive regard for the sanctity of human life, the growth of which distinguishes every other really advancing people just in proportion to their progress in the scale of Christian civilization."[61]

One perverse effect of the use of violence to safeguard slavery was the barbaric quality it gave to the upper classes in the South. A Southern gentleman might attack and kill a slave for a slight show of insubordination, and indeed the stability of his society required that he do so. This very fact, Olmsted observed, had devastating implications. It exposed a fundamental flaw in Southern gentility and greatly strengthened the case against the Southern gentleman which he had begun to build following his arguments with Samuel Perkins Allison in late 1853. "Thus slavery educates gentlemen in habits," Olmsted concluded with satisfaction, "which, at the North, belong only to bullies and ruffians."

Olmsted's concern in the spring of 1857, however, was the threat of Southern violence against the free-labor society of the North. On this score, the implications of the Kansas experience were painfully clear. It indicated that in the future, slaveholders would require the suppression of all opposition, all questioning of their right to hold slaves, and would demand the right to use both legal process and extralegal violence to protect and strengthen the institution. The safety of the masters in a slave society required that they must be permitted to act "in a spirit of cruel, unconsiderate, illegal, violent, and pitiless vengeance." "To educate the people otherwise," Olmsted declared, "would be suicidal." Therefore, he asserted, "no free press, no free pulpit, nor free politics can be permitted in the South, nor in Kansas, while the South reigns." The acts of the "bogus" legislature, as well as the actions of the border ruffians, had demonstrated the truth of this assertion. Nor was the experience of Kansas an unusual and isolated incident.

The whole tenor of the Democratic party under Pierce, and now under Buchanan, was to provide support by the federal government for the spread of slavery and the suppression of free institutions wherever slaveholders found them dangerous to their interests. And now the Dred Scott decision raised the possibility that slaveholders would demand protection of their ownership of slaves not only in all remaining territories but in the states as well. The power of the federal government, already used to force the return of fugitive slaves from free states, would soon be used to force slaves, as slaves, *into* those states. Wherever the slaveholders went, they would carry with them their traditions of violence and their hostility to the exercise of free speech and free press. The experience of "Bleeding Kansas" would be repeated again and again.

Unless the whole trend of federal policy was reversed, Olmsted anticipated the spread of a life-and-death struggle between slavery and free institutions. In an outburst that showed how much he had been radicalized in five years' time, he exclaimed, "Shall we hereafter exercise our rights as citizens of the United States, which are simply our natural rights as men, only by favor of Sharps rifles and in entrenched villages?"[62]

That question was of immediate importance to Olmsted because he was actively engaged in the attempt to create a barrier of free-labor settlements across the path of advancing slavery from Kansas to Texas. The anticipated policy of the Buchanan administration and the hostility of Texans to his German friends indicated to him that any settlements of free laborers in the Southwest would indeed have to resort to entrenchments, Sharps rifles and mountain howitzers if they were to survive.

By mid-April 1857, the Buchanan administration had promised to continue support for the "bogus" legislature in Kansas. That policy threatened to produce more violence as the free-state settlers strengthened their resolve to resist the authority of officials appointed by the legislature. As Olmsted pointed out, President Buchanan had accepted the laws of the "bogus" legislature as legal, and had not moved to punish the violence of proslavery adherents during the previous year. He had also supported the provision (vetoed by Geary) for a census and for the convening of a constitutional convention that would ensure a proslavery constitution. In early April the appointment of Robert J. Walker as territorial governor gave no encouragement to Olmsted, despite Walker's stated belief that the climate of Kansas would not permit the survival of slavery. It was the agency of man, rather than that of nature, that concerned Olmsted in Kansas, and he judged that Walker would do nothing to oppose the operation of the "bogus" legislature, with its oppressive laws and unjust officials.[63]

The future of Kansas, however, was not Olmsted's primary concern. That was the sphere of action of the New England Emigrant Aid Company and of federal officials, and he could do little to affect the outcome of the conflict there. He looked instead to the regions south of Kansas, where he believed the next struggle would take place, and where he hoped the Emigrant Aid Company would soon concentrate its efforts. He had met with little success when he tried in January and February of 1857 to interest the company in distributing *Journey Through Texas* to potential settlers, but events were moving quickly and by the spring the company's officials were thinking more seriously about Texas. In mid-May, Colonel Daniel Ruggles of the regular army, who had been stationed in Texas for several years, visited Boston and presented the executive committee of the Emigrant Aid Company with a proposal for buying land and founding settlements there. Olmsted talked with Ruggles soon after and during the next month also went to Boston and met with the company's executive committee. On June 19 the committee authorized its "Texas committee" to employ Olmsted and others to gather information and help select land for purchase. Samuel Cabot, Jr., Olmsted's principal correspondent in the committee, asked him to draw up a "good plan of action in a matured form," and on July 4, 1857, Olmsted sent Cabot a long proposal.[64]

The area that Olmsted was most anxious to colonize was along the Red River opposite the Indian Territory between Texas and Kansas. Both Olmsted and the Emigrant Aid Company's officers were apparently convinced that the Buchanan administration intended to open the Indian Territory to settlement in the very near future, and planned to do so in a way that would make it a slave state. Olmsted believed that the next battle against the advance of slavery would be fought in that region, which he called "Neosho." He was anxious to gather along the Red River the armed settlers whose entrenched villages would form the vanguard of free-labor forces when the struggle began. Being the first settlers on the land and well armed, the men from the Texas colonies could move into Neosho in force as soon as the area was opened to settlement, face down proslavery border ruffians, and make it unsafe to move slaves into the territory.[65]

In his outline of the settlement plan, Olmsted proposed that the Emigrant Aid Company create a land company with at least one hundred thousand dollars of capital. Twenty thousand dollars should be invested immediately in twenty thousand acres of land and such improvements as mills, cotton gins and school houses. Two thousand acres of land should be offered without charge to a group of settlers to form the nucleus of the colony. The response to Olmsted's

INTRODUCTION

proposal came quickly, and on July 8, Charles J. Higginson—brother of Thomas Wentworth Higginson and one of the officers of the company—proposed that the venture begin with ten thousand dollars of capital that the newly formed Boston Kansas Company, of which he was a trustee, had ready to invest. The Emigrant Aid Company's officers also wanted to expand Olmsted's role in their Texas scheme. They proposed that he go to Texas to select land and asked if he would go to England to seek support there. They also wanted him to accompany to Texas any representatives that English supporters might send to the United States in the fall. In mid-July the company asked Olmsted to write a statement for them on the feasibility of increasing the cotton supply by creating free-labor settlements in the Southwest. They intended to use the statement in their search for support in England.[66]

Olmsted had already anticipated these requests. On July 6, two days after his letter to Samuel Cabot, Jr., he had written the secretaries of the cotton supply associations of Manchester and Liverpool, giving them the statement on free labor and cotton supply that the Emigrant Aid Company asked him to prepare soon after. He also wrote to several individuals in England, including two members of Parliament—Lord Goderich and C. Fowell Buxton—and to John Delane, the editor of the *Times* of London, urging that they support the sending of English colonists to Texas. Goderich had already replied to Olmsted's earlier letter, saying that he sympathized with the plan to "turn the flank" of slavery by blocking its expansion westward with a ring of free states. But he refused to involve Englishmen in so dangerous an undertaking.

In his letter to the cotton supply associations, Olmsted took Goderich's response into account and made no mention of gaining Texas and other areas for freedom. Instead, he limited himself to describing the way that colonization of Englishmen in the Southwest would help insure a steady supply of cotton. He warned Samuel Cabot, Jr., that there should be no mention to the English of the role that the Emigrant Aid Company would play in creating the Texas settlements. At the same time, he was at work on the more comprehensive proposal he had promised Cabot in July. To that end he secured offers of land in northern Texas, land owned by merchants who had already bought the "free-labor" cotton grown around Neu Braunfels.

Other circumstances intruded before Olmsted could make his final proposal, however, or begin to act on it. The failure of the publishing firm of Miller & Curtis on August 6 ended any possibility of income from his publishing venture and saddled him with debts. He quickly sought other employment and on September 11 received the appointment as superintendent of Central Park. Three days later he announced to Samuel Cabot, Jr., that he could no longer play a major role in organizing free-labor colonization in the Southwest.[67]

For the next two and a half years the Emigrant Aid Company continued to study the project without taking further action. Finally, in March 1860, the executive committee agreed to authorize a subscription of fifty thousand dollars to finance a series of settlements in Texas. Their purpose was to extend the barrier to slavery's expansion that already existed in the form of a hundred-mile-long line of German communities north and south of San Antonio from the Rio Frio to the Rio Llano. To secure the two-hundred-mile stretch northward to the mouth of the Little Wichita, the committee proposed to create six or eight communities on two-thousand-acre tracts set fifteen miles apart. Once the land was purchased, the company planned to send in armed settlers as quickly as possible, "without even letting the settlers themselves (except a few chosen men) know the object in view, until we feel ourselves strong enough to bid defiance to the Slave power."[68]

Despite this brave statement of intent, no effective move was made to carry out the plan before the outbreak of the Civil War. What success Olmsted's friends and associates achieved in fostering free-labor colonies in the slave states came in border states suffering from the emigration of population, rather than on the frontier in the path of slavery's advance. Eli Thayer turned to west Virginia and his stillborn settlement of Ceredo, while Charles Loring Brace and James Hamilton worked with others to settle a few German winegrowers in Missouri.[69]

Olmsted's appointment as superintendent of Central Park marked the virtual end of both his colonization attempts and his writing on the South. During the summer of 1857 he had been writing a series of letters entitled "The Southerners at Home" for the *New York Daily Tribune*. They described his journey on horseback through Mississippi and Alabama during the summer of 1854. The series stopped abruptly on August 24, after only ten installments: failing eyesight had kept him from writing during the first two weeks of August, and at that point he turned his attention to securing the Central Park appointment. The letters he wrote for the *Tribune* became, with little alteration, the first, fourth and fifth chapters of *A Journey in the Back Country*, which he finally published in 1860.

By the fall of 1857, Olmsted had also completed most of the remainder of the manuscript of *Back Country*. The second and third chapters of the book described his journey through the Red River country of Louisiana and across northern Mississippi during his first trip to the South. He had published that account in November and December of 1853, in the last five descriptive letters of "The South" series for the *New-York Daily Times*. The sixth and seventh chapters of *Back Country*, narrative in form and appearing to follow closely the notes that Olmsted made as he traveled, described his journey through the Appalachians in Tennessee and North Carolina, and across Virginia to Richmond.

While those first 290 pages of *Back Country* were drawn primarily from previously published newspaper letters, the final 200-page section was a very different matter. It provided the analysis that was lacking in the first half of the book, and it is significant that Olmsted stated clearly that he wrote almost all of that material, as well, during 1857.

INTRODUCTION

In the preface to *Back Country,* which Olmsted wrote in early 1860, he informed his readers that the book "was prepared for the press nearly in its present form and announced for publication three years ago." He said that at that time he had intended to add a chapter on the "natural history of southern politics," but that before he could do so he was "interrupted by unanticipated duties." This is clearly a reference to his sudden switch from literary work to the superintendency of Central Park in September 1857, and indicates that by that time he had virtually completed the rest of *Back Country,* and not just the material that had appeared in newspapers. He further testified that the narrative part of the book concerning slave insurrection had been printed, and that the material in the last chapter on the subject had been written "some time before the John Brown plot is supposed to have formed." Olmsted's reference in this case is probably to the gathering of men by John Brown at Tabor, Iowa, in the summer of 1857, which was the first stage of his preparation for raids into Missouri and Virginia.[70]

This evidence shows that in 1857, while Olmsted actively worked with the New England Emigrant Aid Company to foster free-labor colonization in the Southwest, he also continued the impassioned analysis of the South and the problems it posed for the country that he had begun earlier in the year with his introductions to *Journey Through Texas* and *Englishman in Kansas.* Much of the last section of *Back Country* dealt with concerns that Olmsted had expressed at the time of his colonization activities: the consequences of the fact that American slavery was peculiarly a system of colonization, due to its constant requirement of new fertile land; the effect that the continued expansion of slavery would have on the slave states and the territories; and the effect that the checking of slavery's expansion would have on the society of the slave states. In *Back Country,* Olmsted also gave much attention to the question of cotton supply, which he had raised with prospective English supporters of free-labor colonization, and he further developed his view that free whites were capable of providing at least as steady a flow of cotton from the South as were enslaved blacks. He also took time to consider further some themes from his earlier writings: answering Southern claims that there had been great improvement in the condition and intelligence of their slaves; casting new aspersions on "Southern Breeding"; and providing new examples, in response to an attack on him by J. D. B. DeBow, of the poor quality of Southern hospitality to strangers.[71]

Internal evidence and the dates of quotations he used suggest that Olmsted wrote only the two most foreboding parts of *Back Country* after 1857: one was his discussion of the increasing demand in the South for resumption of the African slave trade, with his prediction that many Northerners would acquiesce in the resumption of trade even if it remained illegal; the other was his analysis of the comparative military capacities of the North and South in the face of imminent disunion and war.[72]

When *Back Country* was finally published in 1860, it contained brief sections that he must have written after the summer of 1857 and that dealt with the most recent phases of the sectional crisis. Even so, no part of the book contained a more virulent condemnation of the South than the portion of the last chapter, describing murder, mayhem and slave-burning in the South, that Olmsted extracted verbatim from his introduction to *Englishman in Kansas*.[73] By the spring of 1857 his anger about the expansion of slavery and about Southern violence was as strong as it would become until the Civil War itself raised both his thoughts and actions to a new level of intensity.

Secession and the prospect of Civil War did bring Olmsted one more chance to write about the South—the compilation of his three books into the single volume *The Cotton Kingdom*. Although he delegated most of the work of abridgment to a collaborator, the antislavery author and editor Daniel Reaves Goodloe, Olmsted wrote most of the new material himself. The purpose of the longest section, which served as an introduction to the book, was to increase the propaganda value of the work with its intended English audience. Olmsted sought to show in that introduction that although cotton was "King" in the South, the region had gained little real wealth or power from its staple crop. Part of his argument was his old contention that the South's large income from cotton brought the society itself neither the institutions nor the amenities of civilization, but simply went to buy more slaves. He coupled this claim with a reassertion of his belief that a society of free laborers in the South could supply the world with cotton as cheaply and efficiently as could slaves.[74]

The fact that the new sections Olmsted wrote in 1861 for *The Cotton Kingdom* repeated arguments he had already made is one more indication of the extent to which 1857 was the critical year of his involvement with the South, the culmination of five years of intensive travel, study, writing and organizing activity.

The letters Olmsted wrote between 1852 and 1857 provide a remarkable chronicle of the way he experienced and came to interpret the society of the South. They also show how he turned to actions as well as words to strengthen the cause of free labor as the decade of the 1850s advanced. His letters supplement the record that he left in the three famous and influential volumes on the South that were published between 1856 and 1860. They give a far richer setting for the whole drama of his involvement with the issue of slavery than the books alone provide. Equally important, his letters constitute a remarkably full record of one thoughtful observer's response to the growing sectional antagonism that in 1861 exploded into the armed conflict of the Civil War.

Charles E. Beveridge

---

1. FLO to FJK, June 12, 1846 (*Papers of FLO*, 1: 244); FLO to JO, July 1, 1846 (ibid., p. 256); FLO to FJK, Sept. 23, 1847 (ibid., 1: 303).
2. FLO to JO, Aug. 12, 1846 (*Papers of FLO*, 1: 272); FLO to FJK, Sept. 23, 1847 (ibid., p. 304).

3. "The South" no. 28, below; *Walks and Talks,* 2: 104-6.
4. FLO to CLB, March 22, 1847 (*Papers of FLO,* 1: 291-92); FLO to Andrew D. White, June 21, 1873; FLO to JHO, Dec. 13, 1846 (*Papers of FLO,* 1: 278-80).
5. For the fullest statement of Bushnell's views on slavery and the responsibility of Northerners for its amelioration and abolition, see Horace Bushnell, "Discourse on the Slavery Question, Delivered in the North Church, Hartford, Thursday Evening, Jan. 10, 1839..." (Hartford, Conn., 1839).
6. *Walks and Talks,* 2: 106 (see FLO to FJK, Oct. 17, 1852, n. 10, below).
7. *Walks and Talks,* 2: 56-63, 104-6, 188-92.
8. Ibid., 1: 221.
9. *Life of Brace,* p. 182; FLO to Letitia Brace, Jan. 22, 1892.
10. FLO to FJK, Oct. 17, 1852, below.
11. FLO to CLB, Nov. 12, 1850 (*Papers of FLO,* 1: 359); FLO to JO, Dec. 5, 1851 (ibid., pp. 372-73); *Life of Brace,* pp. 134-48.
12. FLO to CLB, March 25, 1848 (*Papers of FLO,* 1: 316-17).
13. *Walks and Talks,* 2: 103-7.
14. *Olmsted Genealogy,* pp. x-xv, 5-10, 106-9; Frederick Law Olmsted, "Public Parks and the Enlargement of Towns," in *Civilizing American Cities: A Selection of Frederick Law Olmsted's Writings on City Landscapes,* ed. S. B. Sutton (Cambridge, Mass., and London, 1971), pp. 59-62; *BC,* pp. 302-5; *JT,* pp. viii-xii; Horace Bushnell, "The Day of Roads," in *Work and Play; Or, Literary Varieties* (New York, 1864), pp. 403-39; Perry Miller, *The New England Mind: From Colony to Province* (Cambridge, Mass., 1953), pp. 40-43; FLO, manuscript treatises, "History of Civilization in the United States," and "Mariposa, a Pioneer Community of the Present Day," both c. 1864-65.
15. FLO, "Appeal to the Citizens of Staten Island" (Dec., 1849) (*Papers of FLO,* 1: 331-34); ibid., pp. 72-74; *Walks and Talks,* 1: 106-8; ibid., 2: 88-95, 156; Horace Bushnell, "Barbarism the First Danger; A Discourse for Home Missions" (New York, 1847); Timothy Dwight, *Travels in New England and New York,* ed. Barbara Miller Solomon and Patricia M. King, 4 vols. (Cambridge, Mass., 1969), 2: 229-33.
16. For some aspects of these traditions, see William Best Hesseltine, "Four American Traditions," *Journal of Southern History* 27, no. 1 (Feb. 1961): 3-32.
17. FLO to FJK, June 12, 1846 (*Papers of FLO,* 1: 243).
18. For Timothy Dwight's classic statement of the function of taste in moving men from barbarism to civilization, see his *Travels in New England and New York,* 2: 346-47. For the influence of Andrew Jackson Downing on Olmsted, see Charles E. Beveridge, "Frederick Law Olmsted: The Formative Years, 1822-1865" (Ph.D. diss., University of Wisconsin, 1966), pp. 143-49; see also *Papers of FLO,* 1: 72-77.
19. Frederick Law Olmsted, autobiographical fragment, "Passages in the Life of an Unpractical Man" (*Papers of FLO,* 1: 100, 105-9); FLO to CLB, March 27, 1846 (ibid., pp. 232-33); FLO to FJK, Aug. 22, 1846 (ibid., pp. 275-76); FLO to CLB, Sept. 20, 1847 (ibid., pp. 299-300); FLO to CLB, March 25, 1848 (ibid., pp. 313-16); FLO to FJK, Nov. 17, 1848 (ibid., pp. 321-22); *Walks and Talks,* 1: 245.
20. FLO to Letitia Brace, Jan. 22, 1892; "The South" no. 48, below; FLO to FJK, Oct. 17, 1852, below.
21. For Charles B. Calvert, see "The South" no. 1, below; and *SSS,* pp. 5-11. For the James River plantation, see "The South" no. 2, below; and *SSS,* pp. 40-47. For Nathaniel Crenshaw, see FLO to CLB, Dec. 22, 1852, below. For Thomas W. Gee, see "The South" no. 2, below; and *SSS,* pp. 88-94.
22. For Thomas P. Devereux, see FLO to JO, Jan. 10, 1852, below. For Olmsted's experience in Montgomery, Ala., see FLO to FJK, Feb. 26, 1853, below. Concerning Anthony Wayne Baker, see FLO to CLB, Feb. 23, 1853, below.
23. For Richard J. Arnold, see "The South" no. 24, below; "The South" no. 28, below; *SSS,* pp. 418-19; and R. J. Arnold, "A List of Persons belonging to me on all the Plantations & their ages Jany 1st, 1858," Talbot Family Papers, Rhode Island Historical Society, Providence, R.I. For Richard Taylor, see FLO to FJK, Feb. 26, 1853, below; and *SSS,* pp. 656-63, 668-69, 673-76. For Meredith Calhoun, see "The South" no. 44, below; "The South" no. 45, below; and *BC,* pp. 72-93.
24. FLO to CLB, Dec. 1, 1853.

INTRODUCTION

25. The plantation that Olmsted visited was probably Evermay, a plantation near Port Gibson in Claiborne County, Mississippi, forty miles north of Natchez. It was owned at the time of Olmsted's visit by the widow of Benjamin Smith (d. 1846), who lived in Louisville, Kentucky. The characteristics of both Evermay and the Smith family closely resemble Olmsted's description. He did not give the precise location of this plantation, but indicated that his visit took place two days after he left Natchez, and that he had traveled thirty miles on the second day. He included his description of the plantation in the chapter of *Back Country* entitled "The Valley of the Lower Mississippi," which suggests that, like Natchez and Woodville, which he also mentioned in the chapter, the plantation was located in a county on the Mississippi River.

    The Smith plantation, with its 2,460 acres (almost four square miles), had the "several square miles" of land that Olmsted noted. The 1,283 acres of "improved" farmland that were listed under its name in the 1850 census made it one of the few plantations in the region to have the 1,300 to 1,400 acres under cultivation that Olmsted reported. The Smith plantation also had the same number of hogs—two hundred—that Olmsted recorded. Finally, the number of slaves on the plantation was close to Olmsted's count. Olmsted reported a total of 135; although the number of slaves on the Smith plantation was 176 in 1850, it had fallen to 120 by 1860, suggesting that a sizable number were sold or transferred to another plantation between 1850 and 1860, and possibly by the time of Olmsted's visit in 1854.

    The detailed information that Olmsted gave about the owner of the plantation he visited also points strongly to the Benjamin Smith family. He indicated that the owner lived "several hundred miles away," which almost certainly placed him outside the state. Landholdings under absentee ownership in the Mississippi River counties of Claiborne, Jefferson, Warren and Adams, however, almost always belonged to planters living on another plantation in the same county or one adjacent to it. (Records of only one other plantation whose owner lived far away have been found by the editors for this area in 1850, and this plantation's holdings of land, livestock and slaves do not fit Olmsted's description.)

    The Smith family, with its ties to Louisville, Kentucky, was a rare exception among Mississippi River planters. Benjamin Smith had made a Louisville mansion his summer home for many years, and after his death in 1846 his widow, Irene, and daughter, Frances, made it their permanent residence. Olmsted referred to the owner as "rich," and the Smiths were immensely wealthy. In 1850, Irene and Frances Smith estimated their real estate alone to be worth $250,000. Although Benjamin Smith died in 1846, there are reasons why Olmsted might have referred to the owner of Evermay in 1854 as a man. To have stated that the owner was female would, in a society where few women possessed real estate, have revealed her identity to a number of readers. Moreover, the Smiths' only child, Frances, married Alexander C. Bullitt, and the overseer may have considered that man to be the owner of the property (clipping, *Louisville Times*, Sept. 16, 1954, and Will of Benjamin Smith, courtesy of the Filson Club, Louisville, Ky.; Katy McCaleb Headley, comp., *Claiborne County, Mississippi: The Promised Land* [Port Gibson, Miss., c. 1976], p. 236; U.S., Census Office, 7th Census, *7th Census 1850. Kentucky* [Washington, D.C., 1850], schedule 1, Jefferson County, p. 232; U.S., Census Office, 7th Census, *7th Census 1850. Mississippi* [Washington, D.C., 1850], schedule 2, Claiborne County, p. 211; ibid., schedule 4, Claiborne County, p. 303; Joseph Karl Menn, "The Large Slaveholders of the Deep South, 1860" [Ph.D. diss., University of Texas, 1964], p. 956).
26. Frederick Law Olmsted, *The Cotton Kingdom: A Traveller's Observations on Cotton and Slavery in the American Slave States... Edited, with an Introduction, by Arthur M. Schlesinger* (New York, 1953), pp. xxxii–xxxiii.
27. "The South" no. 7, below.
28. "The South" no. 26, below.
29. "The South" no. 48, below.
30. "The South" no. 47, below.
31. FLO to CLB, Dec. 1, 1853, below.
32. Ibid.
33. *JT*, pp. 142–47.
34. "Tour in the Southwest" no. 8, below.
35. Rudolph L. Biesele, *The History of the German Settlements in Texas, 1831–1861* (Austin, Tex., 1930), pp. 171–73; Charles Ramsdell, "The Latins of Sisterdale," *San Antonio Express Magazine*, May 8, 1949; *JT*, p. 198.

36. "Tour in the Southwest" no. 8, below.
37. Rudolph L. Biesele, "The Texas State Convention of Germans in 1854," *Southwestern Historical Quarterly* 33, no. 4 (April 1930): 247–55; *JT*, p. 222.
38. Ibid., pp. 252–55.
39. Adolf Douai to JHO, Sept. 4, 1854; Adolf Douai to "Dear Friend!," Nov. 17, 1854; FLO to JO, Dec. 31, 1854; Adolf Douai to FLO, Oct. 28, 1854.
40. *SSS*, pp. 214–23, 489–97, 523–30.
41. Memorandum of Agreement between Dix, Edwards & Co. and FLO, April 2, 1855; JHO to JO, March 19, 1855.
42. Laura Wood Roper, "'Mr. Law,' and *Putnam's Monthly Magazine*: A Note on a Phase in the Career of Frederick Law Olmsted," *American Literature* 26, no. 1 (March 1954): 88–90; JO to Bertha Olmsted, May 6, 1855; FLO to JO, April 27, 1855.
43. Frank Luther Mott, *A History of American Magazines...*, 5 vols. (Cambridge, Mass., 1938–68), 2: 419–28; *DAB*, s.v. "Briggs, Charles"; FLO to JO, March 13, 1855, below.
44. FLO to JO, Dec. 9, 1855, below; FLO to FLO, Jr., Aug. 15, 1891; "Cape Cod," *Putnam's Monthly* 5, no. 30 (June 1855): 632–40; ibid. 6, no. 31 (July 1855): 59–66; ibid., no. 32 (Aug. 1855), pp. 157–64; "Benito Cereno," ibid., no. 34 (Oct. 1855), pp. 353–67; ibid., no. 35 (Nov. 1855), pp. 459–73; ibid., no. 36 (Dec. 1855), pp. 633–44.
45. FLO to JO, June 25, 1849.
46. FLO to Arthur T. Edwards, Aug. 7, 1855, below; FLO to JO, Nov. 24, 1855.
47. Memorandum of Bertha Olmsted Niles on European travel in the early 1850s, n.d.; FLO to Augustus J. Dix, Aug. 3, 1856, below.
48. FLO to Mariana Griswold Van Rensselaer, June 11, 1893; FLO to Leland Stanford, Nov. 27, 1886; FLO to JO, March 27, 1856, below.
49. FLO to Asa Gray, Aug. 20, 1857, in Library of the Gray Herbarium, Harvard University, Cambridge, Mass.; Francis G. Shaw to FLO, May 22, 1860; FLO to Henry W. Bellows, Aug. 15, 1863.
50. Autobiographical fragment, "Passages in the Life of an Unpractical Man"; FLO to JHO, Sept. 11, 1857.
51. Adolf Douai to JHO, Sept. 4, 1854; Adolf Douai, "Autobiography," pp. 118–19.
52. Kansas State Historical Society, *Collections of the Kansas State Historical Society*, 17 vols. in 16 (Topeka, Kans., 1881–1928), 1–2 (1875–81): 214–26; William H. Isely, "The Sharps Rifle Episode in Kansas History," *American Historical Review* 12, no. 3 (April 1907): 551–56 (see FLO to James B. Abbott, Sept. 17, and Oct. 4 and 7, 1855, below).
53. "German Emigration to Mexico," *NYDT*, Jan. 31, 1856, p. 4; Charles Riotte to FLO, Feb. 25, 1856; Adolf Douai to FLO, Jan. 27, 1856; JHO to FLO, May 4, 1856; Adolf Douai, "Autobiography," pp. 124–27.
54. That Olmsted wrote his "Letter to a Southern Friend" in December 1856 is indicated by his reference in it to the fourth annual message of Franklin Pierce (delivered on December 2, 1856) as "the late message of President Pierce to Congress" (*NYDT*, Dec. 3, 1856, p. 2; *JT*, pp. xxiv–xxv).
55. *JT*, pp. vii–xv.
56. FLO to Edward Everett Hale, Jan. 10 and 30, and Feb. 19 and 20, 1857, below.
57. *JT*, p. xvi.
58. Ibid., pp. xix–xx, xxvii–xxviii.
59. Kansas (Territory), *The Statutes of the Territory of Kansas; Passed at the First Session of the Legislative Assembly, One Thousand Eight Hundred and Fifty-five...* (St. Louis, Mo., 1855), pp. 715–17.
60. Allan Nevins, *Ordeal of the Union*, vol. 2, *A House Dividing, 1852–57* (New York, 1947), pp. 484–86; idem, *The Emergence of Lincoln*, vol. 1, *Douglas, Buchanan, and Party Chaos, 1857–1859* (New York, 1950), pp. 133–40; Daniel Webster Wilder, *The Annals of Kansas... New Edition. 1841–1885* (Topeka, Kans., 1886), pp. 135–59; Thomas A. Gladstone, *The Englishman in Kansas; Or, Squatter Life and Border Warfare... With an Introduction, by Fred. Law Olmsted...* (New York, 1857; rpt. ed. with an introduction by James A. Rawley, Lincoln, Neb., 1971), pp. 318–25.
61. See Olmsted's "American Editor's Introduction" to *Englishman in Kansas*, below.
62. Ibid.
63. See Olmsted's "Supplement by the American Editor" to *Englishman in Kansas*, below.

INTRODUCTION

64. Minutes of the Executive Committee of the New England Emigrant Aid Company, May 15 and 22, and June 19, 1857, New England Emigrant Aid Company Papers, Manuscript Department, Kansas State Historical Society, Topeka, Kans.
65. FLO to Samuel Cabot, Jr., July 4, 1857, below.
66. Ibid.; Charles J. Higginson to Samuel Cabot, Jr., July 8, 1857, in the possession of Phillip Rutherford; Samuel Cabot, Jr., to FLO, July 16, 1857.
67. FLO to the Secretaries of the Cotton Supply Associations of Manchester and Liverpool, July 6, 1857, below; FLO to Samuel Cabot, Jr., July 26, 1857, below; Lord Goderich to FLO, May 5, 1857; FLO to JHO, Sept. 11, 1857; FLO to Samuel Cabot, Jr., Sept. 14, 1857, below.
68. New England Emigrant Aid Company, Minutes of Third Quarterly Meeting of Directors, Nov. 23, 1858; Minutes of Second Quarterly Meeting of Directors, Aug. 30, 1859; and Minutes of Special Meeting of Executive Committee, March 16, 1860; all in New England Emigrant Aid Company Papers, Kansas State Historical Society; Samuel Cabot, Jr. to FLO, March 4, 1860.
69. James A. Hamilton, *Reminiscences of James A. Hamilton; or, Men and Events, At Home and Abroad, During Three Quarters of a Century* (New York, 1869), pp. 421–22.
70. BC, p. 5; Stephen B. Oates, *To Purge This Land with Blood: A Biography of John Brown* (New York, Evanston and London, 1970), pp. 210–21.
71. BC, pp. 337–55, 373–80, 381–84, 398–430.
72. Ibid., pp. 358–73, 459–80. The sharp increase in Southern agitation for resumption of the African slave trade occurred in 1859; see A. Nevins, *Emergence of Lincoln*, 1: 432–40.
73. BC, pp. 440–47.
74. CK, pp. 3–23.

EDITORIAL POLICY

The purpose of the Frederick Law Olmsted Papers project is to make generally available, in annotated form, the most significant of Olmsted's letters, unpublished writings, design reports, and newspaper and periodical articles. The letterpress edition will consist of eight volumes of selected documents arranged in chronological order, two volumes of Olmsted's reports to cities on parks, parkways and parkway systems, one volume of his writings on the general theory of landscape design and one volume of plans and illustrations of his work.

Although the choice of letters for a selected edition of papers is to some extent a subjective matter, the editors require that every document published should meet at least one of three criteria: first, it should give the reader insight into Olmsted's character; second, it should present valuable commentary on his times; or third, it should contain an important statement on landscape design.

The editors feel that it is their responsibility to make clear the context within which Olmsted wrote the documents selected and to explain the significance of certain statements that readers not expert in the field might otherwise not adequately comprehend. They feel also that part of their function is to identify the persons, places and events Olmsted mentions, and to explain his relation to them. The annotation in these volumes is fuller than it would be in a complete edition of Olmsted's papers, where the documents would more frequently annotate one another. In order to supply background information and provide continuity within each volume, the editors make use of volume introductions, biographical directories, and chapter headnotes, as well as chronologies, itineraries, genealogies and other aids for the reader.

In transcribing the documents for publication, the intent of the editors was to prepare texts that convey Olmsted's meaning clearly. The complete existing text of each letter is presented. Drafts of letters and other writings appear in what the editors consider to be their final form. All legible words that Olmsted wrote are included except those he inadvertently repeated. Words that he crossed out are omitted unless they are considered to be of particular interest. If included they are accompanied by an explanatory note. The treatment of illegible and missing words is as follows:

1. [...] indicates illegible words or words missing because of mutilation of the manuscript.
2. [*italic*] indicates the editors' reading of partially missing words.
3. [roman] indicates a word supplied by the editors.

Olmsted's erratic spelling—he consistently misspelled words with double consonants, such as "dissapoint," and "loose" for "lose"—is silently corrected unless it is clear that he deliberately misspelled a word for humorous effect or to convey dialect. English variants of standard American spellings are left as he wrote them. Words in languages other than English are rendered as he spelled them. Except for some that are in common use, such as "etc.," contractions and abbreviations are silently expanded.

When the original punctuation leaves the meaning or structure of a sentence unclear, it is altered. Where Olmsted provides a punctuation mark at only one end of a subordinate clause, a matching punctuation mark is added at the other end of the clause. In a long and involved sentence, long appositive phrases are set off by dashes, while shorter interior clauses are indicated by commas. In cases where a sentence is particularly difficult to follow, parentheses are added to enable the reader to perceive more clearly the main flow of the sentence. Paragraphing is supplied within long sections that Olmsted left unparagraphed and where he indicated paragraphing by the use of long dashes or larger than normal spaces between sentences.

Material that Olmsted added in the margins that has no clear place in the text is printed at the end of the document with an explanatory note. Notes or jottings on a document by other persons are not included in the document itself, but if informative, are given in a note. Olmsted's rare footnotes are presented at the end of the document in which they appear.

Dates for documents are given as they appear in the original, but abbreviations are spelled out. If that information is partial, incorrect, or missing, the probable date or time period is supplied in brackets, with an explanatory note if needed. Addresses are given whenever they occur on the original letters.

The documents are presented in chronological order except for occasional pieces like the autobiographical fragments and "The Real China" in volume I, which are reminiscences written at a later time. The latter are presented with the letters from the period they describe.

Full bibliographical data are provided in the first citation of a source in each chapter except when the source is listed in "Short Titles Used in Citations." A full listing of sources on an individual is given in the note accompanying the first mention of that individual in the documents of a volume. In subsequent references, sources are given only for additional information supplied. Birth and death dates of persons mentioned in the text of the letters are given in the first note identifying them and, for selected persons, in the index.

Unless otherwise indicated, all manuscript material referred to is in the Frederick Law Olmsted Papers, Manuscript Division, Library of Congress, Washington, D.C.

SHORT TITLES USED IN CITATIONS

1. Correspondents' Names

    CLB   Charles Loring Brace
    FLO   Frederick Law Olmsted
    FJK   Frederick John Kingsbury
    JHO   John Hull Olmsted
    JO   John Olmsted

2. Standard References

    BDAC   *Biographical Directory of the American Congress, 1774–1971*
    DAB   *Dictionary of American Biography*
    DNB   *Dictionary of National Biography*
    EB   *Encylopaedia Britannica*, 14th ed.
    NCAB   *National Cyclopaedia of American Biography*
    NYDT   *New-York Daily Times*
    OED   *Oxford English Dictionary*

3. Books by Frederick Law Olmsted

    Back Country (BC in citations)   *A Journey in the Back Country...* (New York, 1860).
    Cotton Kingdom (CK in citations)   *The Cotton Kingdom; A Traveller's Observations on Cotton and Slavery in the American Slave States. Based upon Three Former Volumes of Journeys and Investigations by the Same Author.* Edited, with an introduction, by Arthur M. Schlesinger (New York, 1953).
    Journey Through Texas (JT in citations)   *A Journey Through Texas; Or, A*

Saddle-Trip on the Southwestern Frontier... (New York and London, 1857).

Seaboard Slave States (SSS in citations) *A Journey in the Seaboard Slave States, With Remarks on Their Economy*... (New York and London, 1856).

Seaboard Slave States (1904 ed.) *A Journey in the Seaboard Slave States in the Years 1853–1854, With Remarks on Their Economy, by Frederick Law Olmsted, [Originally Issued in 1856] With a Biographical Sketch by Frederick Law Olmsted, Jr., and With an Introduction by William P. Trent...*, 2 vols. (New York and London, 1904).

Walks and Talks   Walks and Talks of an American Farmer in England, 2 vols. in 1 (New York, 1852).

4. Other Published Works

Appleton's Cyc. Am. Biog.   Appleton's Cyclopedia of American Biography, ed. James G. Wilson and John Fiske (New York, 1887–89).

Dictionary of Artists in America   New-York Historical Society, *Dictionary of Artists in America, 1564–1860, by George C. Groce and David H. Wallace* (New Haven and London, 1957).

Eleventh Reunion   The Eleventh Reunion of the Olmsted Family Held at Ridgefield, Connecticut, September 17, 1932 (privately printed, n.d.). Copy in possession of Charles C. McLaughlin.

Forty Years   Frederick Law Olmsted, Jr., and Theodora Kimball, eds., *Frederick Law Olmsted, Landscape Architect, 1822–1903* (*Forty Years of Landscape Architecture*), 2 vols. (New York, 1922–28).

Life of Brace   Charles Loring Brace, *The Life of Charles Loring Brace, Chiefly Told in His Own Letters*, ed. Emma Brace (New York, 1894).

Notable American Women   Notable American Women, 1607–1950: A Biographical Directory, ed. Edward T. James, 3 vols. (Cambridge, Mass., 1971).

Olmsted Genealogy   Henry K. Olmsted and George K. Ward, comps., *Genealogy of the Olmsted Family in America Embracing the Descendants of James and Richard Olmsted and Covering a Period of Nearly Three Centuries 1632–1912* (New York, 1912).

Papers of FLO   The Papers of Frederick Law Olmsted, ed. Charles C. McLaughlin et al. (Baltimore, 1977–).

Putnam's Monthly   Putnam's Magazine. Original Papers on Literature, Science, Art, and National Interests. In 1853–57 was titled *Putnam's Monthly Magazine of American Literature, Science, and Art.*

Schaff-Herzog Encyc.   The New Schaff-Herzog Encyclopedia of Religious Knowledge, Embracing Biblical, Historical, Doctrinal, and Practical Theology and Biblical, Theological, and Ecclesiastical Biography from the Earliest Times to the Present Day, Based on the Third Edition of the Realencyclopädie Founded by J. J. Herzog, and Edited by Albert Hauck, . . . Prepared by More

SHORT TITLES USED IN CITATIONS

Than Six Hundred Scholars and Specialists Under the Supervision of Samuel Macauley Jackson . . . (Editor-in-Chief) With the Assistance of Charles Colebrook Sherman and George William Gilmore . . . (Associate Editors) and [Others], 13 vols. (New York, [1908–c.1914]).

[See Spear ___] Designates the number assigned to a city directory in the microfiche edition of Dorothea N. Spear's *Bibliography of American Directories through 1860* (Worcester, Mass., 1961).

Yale Obit. Rec. Yale University, *Obituary Record of Graduates of Yale University* (New Haven, [1860–]).

5. Unpublished Sources

Adolf Douai, "Autobiography" "Autobiography of Dr. Adolf Douai, Revolutionary of 1848, Texas Pioneer, Introducer of the Kindergarten, Educator, Author, Editor 1819–1888. Translated from the German by Richard H. Douai Boerker his grandson." Typescript, deposited in the Texas State Library, Austin, Texas. Portions of the "Autobiography" were published in the original German in *Die Neue Welt,* nos. 45–58 (Leipzig, 1878), and in *Wochenblatt der New Yorker Volkszeitung* 11, no. 4 (Jan. 28, 1888).

JO Journal A manuscript journal and domestic account book kept by John Olmsted from 1836 to 1873 and continued until 1888 by his widow Mary Ann Bull Olmsted. Three volumes, in the Frederick Law Olmsted Papers, Manuscript Division, Library of Congress, Washington, D.C.

BIOGRAPHICAL DIRECTORY

CHARLES LORING BRACE (1826–1890) introduced Olmsted to a number of influential people during the period 1852–57, and thereby provided him, at least indirectly, with his most important professional opportunities of those years. The two had known each other since childhood, but their friendship had broadened into an intellectual companionship during Olmsted's visits to Yale in the years 1844–46, when Brace, John Hull Olmsted and Frederick Kingsbury were students there.

After graduating from Yale, Brace spent two years studying for the ministry, first at Yale Divinity School and then at Union Theological Seminary in New York. By the time Brace moved to New York City, Olmsted was already working his farm on Staten Island. Brace's frequent visits to the farm kept the old friendship alive, permitting the two friends to continue the intense debates on religion and politics they had begun at Yale. Brace described one such weekend to Frederick Kingsbury as follows: "But the amount of talking done upon that visit! One steady stream from six o'clock Saturday night till twelve the next night, interrupted only by meals and some insane walks on the beach! And this not like ours together, easy, discursive, varied, but a torrent of fierce argument, mixed with diverse oaths on Fred's part, and abuse on both!"[1]

As the letters from Olmsted to Brace in this volume show, some of that habit of abuse carried over into the later correspondence of the two men. In his letters of the 1850s and 1860s, Olmsted was often impatient with Brace and frequently upbraided him. Such treatment apparently did not faze Brace, who was earnest, generous and thick-skinned enough to tolerate the sallies of his combative friend. Olmsted, for his part, appreciated the vigor that enabled Brace to keep pace with him in their long and intense arguments. Years later he offered this description of the Brace he had known in college: "He never showed fatigue, lassitude or ennui; was always disposed to pursue a debate through the night; was always ready to walk ten miles further, wade a quagmire or swim a river, if there was a prospect that it would add to the success of a day's outing. He was simple and sturdy and resolute; not good in finesse but the best of us all in grit and steadfastness. . . ."[2] Those qualities helped to make a success of the six-month walking tour of England and the Continent that Brace took with the Olmsted brothers in the summer of 1850.

Slavery was one of the issues the two friends discussed frequently. Brace attempted unsuccessfully to convert Olmsted to his own abolitionist views. Despite the fact that Brace sometimes brought other abolitionists with him for the weekend to argue his case—including such leaders in the cause as William Lloyd Garrison and Theodore Parker—Olmsted held resolutely to his belief in gradual emancipation. That long-standing debate with Brace was of great importance for Olmsted because it was Brace who arranged for Henry Raymond to propose that Olmsted tour the South as a correspondent for the *New-York Daily Times*. Brace's connections helped as well to make the southern journeys successful: Olmsted received letters of introduction from Asa Gray, husband of Brace's first cousin Jane Loring Gray. It is also likely that it was through Brace's connections with the family of Lyman Beecher that Olmsted came to provide Harriet Beecher Stowe with a description of the Great Dismal Swamp in Virginia during his first journey through the South. (Brace's mother's sister was the stepmother of Harriet Beecher Stowe and Henry Ward Beecher, and the mother of James and Thomas Kinnicut Beecher and Isabella Beecher Hooker). When Olmsted went to England in 1856, Brace himself wrote a letter of introduction to Sir Charles Lyell, the eminent geologist.

Brace's position in the worlds of philanthropy and literature in New York City also was helpful to Olmsted. As head of the Children's Aid Society, Brace worked with many leaders in both fields. He introduced Olmsted to the family of George Schuyler, whose daughter Louisa Lee Schuyler became one of Olmsted's most effective associates when he ran the U.S. Sanitary Commission during the Civil War. Through Brace, Olmsted also met Mrs. Schuyler's father, James Alexander Hamilton, who assisted him in his free-soil colonization activities. And it was Brace who took the lead in cultivating the friendship of the poet Anne Charlotte Lynch Botta, whose literary salon enabled the two young men to meet leading members of the city's "literary republic," which Olmsted sought to enter in the mid-1850s.

Brace's assistance was valuable in Olmsted's literary career and in the work on Central Park that followed it. Joshua Dix, who was primarily responsible for Olmsted's venture into the publishing world as a partner in the firm Dix, Edwards & Company, had become a friend of Brace's before Olmsted began his tours of the South; and it was Charles Wyllys Elliott, another friend who came to Olmsted through Brace, who informed him in August 1857 that the Central Park commission was looking for a superintendent, and urged him to apply for the post. At that time both Asa Gray and James A. Hamilton provided important statements of support for Olmsted's candidacy. Olmsted

CHARLES LORING BRACE

also expected Brace to look after a variety of petty details while he was traveling—from overseeing the publication of his letters in newspapers to dealing with nurserymen and caring for his orchards.

In addition to a skilled opponent in argument and a great source of assistance in his professional activities, Olmsted found in Brace a dedicated, energetic and like-minded social reformer. Whatever reservations he may have felt about the "cant" involved in Brace's religiosity,[3] Olmsted greatly appreciated his friend's reformist and philanthropic activities. As early as 1847 he had viewed Brace as an able comrade in the cause of improving American society and combating the materialism that seemed so universal in it. "There's a great *work* wants doing in this our generation, Charley," he exclaimed; "let us off jacket and go about it."[4] Brace's mission of working with the poor and abandoned children of New York City impressed Olmsted. The methods he employed—providing education for the underprivileged, strengthening domestic institutions, and utilizing the process of "unconscious influence" by which those with better education and culture trained the lower classes in manners and citizenship—were the means that Olmsted himself believed were necessary for improving American society. It is significant that it was to Brace that Olmsted wrote the revealing letter of December 1, 1853, in which he defined the task that lay before Northern reformers if they were to disprove the arguments of proslavery critics. The "moral" he offered in that letter was the course of action that both he and Brace would follow throughout most of the rest of their lives: ". . . go ahead with the Children's Aid," Olmsted counseled, "and get up parks, gardens, music, dancing schools, reunions which will be so attractive as to force into contact the good & bad, the gentlemanly and the rowdy."[5]

During the years 1852-57, Olmsted had reason to envy Brace in his personal life as well as to approve his professional activities. While Olmsted was still smarting from being jilted by Emily Perkins, Brace found himself a wife and helpmate in his Children's Aid Society work. In June 1854 he left for Ireland, intent on winning the hand of Letitia Neill, one of the daughters of Robert Neill of Belfast whom he and Olmsted had met in 1850. At that time, Olmsted had been attracted to the Neill daughters. After his return he had written Brace, remarking how much the people he had met during his six-month tour meant to him and adding: "Even Neill and the ladies I love. I believe I would half marry one of them if she were here. Indeed I do."[6] Instead, it was Brace who did the marrying; Letitia became his wife on August 21, 1854, in Belfast, shortly after Olmsted returned to New York from his solitary ride through the back country of the South.

1. *Life of Brace*, p. 61.
2. FLO, memorandum concerning CLB, Jan. 1, 1892.
3. FLO to JHO, June 23, 1845 (*Papers of FLO*, 1: 217); FLO to FJK, Aug. 27, 1846 (ibid., pp. 275-76); FLO to CLB, March 25, 1848 (ibid., p. 313).
4. FLO to CLB, July 26, 1847.
5. FLO to CLB, Dec. 1, 1853, below.
6. FLO to CLB, Nov. 12, 1850 (*Papers of FLO*, 1: 359).

Additional Sources

Brace, Charles Loring, *The Dangerous Classes of New York, and Twenty Years' Work Among Them* (New York, 1872).
Brace, John Sherman, *Brace Lineage . . .*, 2d ed. (Bloomsburg, Pa., 1927).
DAB, s.v. "Brace, Charles Loring."
Langsam, Miriam, *Children West; A History of the Placing-Out System of the New York Children's Aid Society, 1853-1890* (Madison, Wis., 1964).

SAMUEL CABOT, JR. (1815-1885), a Boston physician, was the son of the prominent Boston merchant Samuel Cabot (a partner of Thomas Handasyd Perkins) and son-in-law of the pioneering Massachusetts textile manufacturer

Patrick Tracy Jackson, Sr.[1] Cabot became a member of the executive committee of the New England Emigrant Aid Company in March 1855, when the company was organized under its Massachusetts charter. Olmsted corresponded with him in 1857 when he was working with the company to promote free-labor colonization in Texas.

Cabot played an important part in sending relief supplies to Kansas, but his most notorious role was that of treasurer of the "rifle committee" organized by some officers of the Emigrant Aid Company. In that capacity he collected funds and purchased arms for free-state settlers in Kansas.[2] Olmsted dealt with Cabot as a member of the Emigrant Aid Company's three-member "Texas Committee," which was formed in May 1857. At Cabot's request he evolved a plan for creating free-labor colonies in Texas and wrote an appeal to cotton-supply associations in England setting forth the advantage they would gain from a supply of cotton grown in the American Southwest by nonslaveholders. Cabot hoped to engage Olmsted to go to Texas to select land for the Emigrant Aid Company to buy, and also to represent the company and its interests in England.[3] Beginning in September 1857, however, Olmsted's involvement with Central Park prevented him from carrying out any missions for the company. By the end of the year he had turned over to Cabot and his associates the task of creating free-soil settlements in Texas.

1. L. Vernon Briggs, *History and Genealogy of the Cabot Family, 1475-1927...*, 2 vols. (Boston, 1927), 2: 685-86; *DAB*, s.v. "Jackson, Patrick Tracy."
2. Samuel A. Johnson, *The Battle Cry of Freedom: The New England Emigrant Aid Company in the Kansas Crusade* (Lawrence, Kans., 1954), pp. 113, 116, 124-28.
3. Samuel Cabot, Jr., to FLO, July 16, 1857.

GEORGE W. CURTIS (1824-1892) became Olmsted's closest friend among the "generation of serious literary men of somewhat earnest semi-political disposition antagonistic to the growing war spirit of the Slave States,"[1] with whom he became associated in the 1850s. As the secret literary editor of *Putnam's Monthly Magazine* in 1855-56, when Olmsted was managing editor, Curtis made available the wealth of his literary and editorial experience. Although he protested against the vagaries of Olmsted's spelling—the "illegal" spelling of "the Law" or "Mr. Law," as he called his friend (a combination of Websterized spelling and Olmsted's idiosyncratic treatment of double consonants)—theirs was a cordial relationship that developed into a lifelong friendship of special warmth.[2] When Olmsted began his work as editor, Curtis readily agreed to his desire to reform the art and music reviews of *Putnam's*

GEORGE W. CURTIS

Monthly by replacing Clarence Cook and Richard Grant White with William Henry Hurlbert. He also allowed Olmsted to play a major role in shaping the political stand of the journal.

By the time he became associated with Olmsted on *Putnam's* staff in the spring of 1855, Curtis had already helped Charles Briggs to edit the magazine for over two years. In 1855 he refused the offer of Dix, Edwards & Company to make him editor and instead assumed, incognito, the role of literary editor. By that time he had established himself as an author, having published two books describing his travels in Egypt and Syria, a volume of whimsical stories and essays entitled *Lotus-Eating,* and the *Potiphar Papers,* a satirical portrayal of New York's high society. He was also writing the "Editor's Easy Chair" column in *Harper's Monthly.*

While the association of Curtis and Olmsted with *Putnam's Monthly* was presumably enjoyable to both men, it was probably their financially disastrous involvement with the publishing firm of Dix, Edwards & Company and its successors that provided the shared experience that most cemented their friendship in later years. In 1856, Curtis became a general partner in the firm. In the spring of 1857, when the firm was on the verge of bankruptcy, its creditors accepted an arrangement whereby Joshua Dix and Arthur T. Edwards left the partnership, and a new firm, Miller and Company, was formed by Olmsted, Curtis and the printer J. W. Miller. Olmsted withdrew from the latter in June 1857, but continued to be responsible for at least his share of the debts accumulated by Dix, Edwards & Company between 1855 and 1857.

Ever since his return from England in the fall of 1856, Olmsted had been hoping to leave the partnership, transform into a loan the money he had put into the firm when he became a partner, and then continue as an employee by advising in literary matters, corresponding with contributors, and looking after the firm's U.S. sales of books originally published in England. He presumably expected to pursue such an arrangement with Miller & Curtis after June 1857, and may have done so briefly.

When the firm of Miller & Curtis failed in August 1857, Olmsted was responsible for some of the debts of its predecessor, and lost both the $5,000 of his father's money that he had invested and any prospect of continued employment with that firm. The situation was even worse for Curtis. In 1856 he had married Anna Shaw, the daughter of the philanthropist Francis George Shaw. Her father had provided funds to strengthen Curtis's publishing firm in 1857; but when the firm failed, Shaw was held by a technicality to be a general partner and to be liable for an unlimited amount of its debts. After a little more than a year of marriage, Curtis faced the loss of all of his own money and the responsibility for his father-in-law's loss of as much as $70,000. Shaw dealt with the creditors of the publishing firm, paying at least $24,000 in settlement of claims. In 1860, Olmsted's lawyer, William Emerson, calculated that he should repay Shaw one-third of that amount, and that Curtis was responsible for an equal sum.

Both Olmsted and Curtis did attempt to repay Shaw. For Curtis, the effort was long and grueling. For the next sixteen years he followed the lecture and lyceum circuit, slowing earning the funds to settle his accounts with Shaw. In 1873, prostrated by illness and exhaustion, he abandoned the effort after accomplishing much of it. Olmsted's attempts at repayment were less extensive and exhausting, but in 1860 he did sign over to Shaw his copyright to *Journey in the Back Country,* at a value of $500. His remaining debt to Shaw presumably made up a large part of his total indebtedness of $12,000, of which he said in 1863: "... though the sheriff is not likely to trouble me about [it], my self-respect is."[3]

While the memory of shared misfortune—and some gratitude on Curtis's part for Olmsted's attempt to repay Shaw—helped to create a special friendship between the two men, there were several aspects of Curtis himself that must have appealed strongly to Olmsted. Curtis was the epitome of the gentleman and scholar who dedicated himself to the pressing social and political issues of the day. During the mid-1850s he preached that doctrine in his writings and in such lectures as "The Duty of the American Scholar" and

"Patriotism," and after the Civil War he devoted himself increasingly to the cause of civil service reform. To this dedication to public service he added a particularly winning manner, attractiveness of person and sweetness of temper.

The two men saw each other infrequently after the 1850s, but frequently exchanged warm greetings through mutual friends. Curtis also promoted Olmsted's interests on occasion. In 1862, he and Francis Shaw urged Secretary of the Treasury Salmon P. Chase to appoint Olmsted to head the Freedman's Bureau when it was created, and he assisted Olmsted and their mutual friend, gentleman-scholar and reformer Charles Eliot Norton in the fight to create the public reservation at Niagara Falls in the 1880s.

1. FLO to Frederick Law Olmsted, Jr., Aug. 15, 1891.
2. Laura Wood Roper, "'Mr. Law' and *Putnam's Monthly Magazine*: A Note on a Phase in the Career of Frederick Law Olmsted," *American Literature* 26, no. 1 (March 1954): 88–93.
3. Francis George Shaw to FLO, May 22, 1860; FLO to Henry W. Bellows, Aug. 15, 1863, Bellows Papers, Massachusetts Historical Society, Boston, Mass.

Additional Sources

DAB, s.v. "Curtis, George William."
Milne, Gordon, *George William Curtis & the Genteel Tradition* (Bloomington, Ind., 1956).
NCAB, 3: 96.

JOSHUA A. DIX (1831–1894) provided Olmsted with the opportunity to enter the field of publishing by joining the firm of Dix, Edwards & Company as a partner.[1] He had become a friend of Charles Loring Brace's in 1852 or earlier, while employed by the New York publisher George Palmer Putnam. In the summer of 1854, Dix left Putnam's establishment and worked with the publisher Thomas McElrath. Soon after, he purchased from McElrath the American publishing rights to *Household Words*, a magazine edited in England by Charles Dickens, and started his own publishing company. On March 1, 1855, he formed a partnership with Arthur T. Edwards and acquired *Putnam's Monthly*. A month later, Olmsted joined the firm as a partner.[2]

Dix felt a "great friendship for Fred," according to John Hull Olmsted, and was a congenial, if ineffective, partner. He caused Olmsted great concern, however, during the summer of 1856. While Olmsted was still in London, Dix began to send him alarming reports of mistakes and irregularities committed by Edwards in the conduct of the firm's finances, indicating as well that he had no control over Edwards and had not attempted to call him to account.[3] Olmsted replied that from the first he had relied on Dix's assurances of Edwards's total honesty and great skill as a businessman. He then proceeded to vent his anxiety and frustration in mock rhetoric:

> Have you not imposed upon me sweetly?—Did you not with honeyed persuasion tempt me from that quiet and blissful philosophic retirement to which I assured you I had surrendered myself for life with the strongest determination never to become the slave of exciting, wearing commerce. . . . Did I not allow myself to be so imposed upon, impelled by a high moral purpose, & be damned to you, namely to save that great engine Putnam's Monthly from the hands of Philistine cowardice . . . ?[4]

After that outburst, Olmsted concluded: "Is it not my duty to be after you with a sharp stick? It is, and I'm coming."

Olmsted attempted to withdraw as a partner in the firm as soon as he returned to New York in October 1856. The partnership dragged on, however, until it faced bankruptcy in the spring of 1857. Then Dix and Edwards withdrew and Olmsted formed a new partnership, with George W. Curtis and J. W. Miller. Dix tried to weather the Panic of 1857 that followed by selling insurance, and in September Olmsted saw him going about "in slightly shabby clothing," distributing his business card.[5] He soon moved to Elizabeth, New Jersey, and after 1880 served as a superintendent of schools for that city. No correspondence between Dix and Olmsted survives for the years after 1857, and it is doubtful that their active friendship lasted beyond that date.

1. New Jersey, Dept. of State, . . . *Index of Wills, Inventories, etc. in the Office of the Secretary of State Prior to 1901* . . . , 3 vols. (Trenton, 1912–13; rpt. ed. entitled *New Jersey Index of Wills* [Baltimore, 1969]), 3: 1352.
2. JHO to Bertha Olmsted, May 6, 1855; Thomas McElrath to Arthur T. Edwards, Feb. 12, 1855, Papers of Dix, Edwards & Co., Houghton Library, Harvard University, Cambridge, Mass.
3. JHO to FLO, July 27, 1856; Dix to FLO, July 29, 1856.
4. FLO to Dix, Sept. 4, 1856, Papers of Dix, Edwards & Co.
5. FLO to JHO, Sept. 11, 1857.

Additional Sources

NCAB, 5: 306.

KARL DANIEL ADOLF DOUAI (1819–1888) was the editor of the antislavery *San Antonio Zeitung* when Olmsted met him in Texas in early 1854. During the next two years he and Olmsted worked closely together in an effort to create a nonslaveholding state in West Texas. The common beliefs they shared and their mutual dedication to the antislavery cause made them fast friends.

Douai was born in Altenburg, Saxony, of French stock. His father was an impoverished schoolteacher and his mother died when he was still a child. By his early teens, according to his own account, he assumed much of the responsibility for supporting himself. He thus began early a life of hard work in the face of pressing necessities and frequent reverses. His difficulties were frequently compounded by his unrelenting independence of thought and intransigent assertion of his beliefs.

Educated at the Altenburg Gymnasium and Jena and Leipzig universities, Douai hoped to teach philosophy and theology at the University of Jena. He earned a doctorate at the University of Koenigsberg in East Prussia with a dissertation on the philosophy of Hegel. Under the influence of the German theologian David Strauss, he began to write a defense of Christianity by applying the principles of historical criticism and Hegelian philosophy to the Bible. In the process he became increasingly unorthodox in belief. During his religious quest he became a friend and disciple of Gustave Adolf Wisclicenus of Halle, whose followers began in the mid-1840s to form free congregations (*freie gemeinden*) independent of the state church of Saxony. Those pietistic groups emphasized the importance of the inner spirit and challenged the ultimate authority of the Scriptures.

By the time Douai emigrated to America in 1852 he was a self-confessed "infidel," or freethinker, insisting that all religious doctrines be capable of rational proof. His own quest led him to believe in an imminent God who imposed spiritual as well as material unity on the universe and acted as a moral force within it.

In 1841, Douai began his lifelong—if intermittent—career as a pedagogue with five years of service as a private tutor in western Russia. In 1843 he married Agnes von Beust, from a noble family of Saxony, and four years later returned to Altenburg and founded a school there.

With the outbreak of revolution in Saxony in 1848, Douai became a political agitator and journalist. He edited a newspaper in Altenburg and wrote pamphlets for the republican cause, for which he was arrested three times and served a total of twelve months in prison. He was also elected to the Reformlandtag of Sachsen-Altenburg. After his third prison term, state officials made it impossible for him to support himself by means of his school, the eight *freie gemeinden* that he formed, or an emigration agency that his father had set up before being imprisoned and exiled for his own role in the revolution of 1848.

Douai emigrated to Texas with his wife, children and father in 1852. He settled first in Neu Braunfels and attempted unsuccessfully to establish a school there. Then, with the encouragement of Charles Riotte and Gustav Theissen, he agreed to edit the *San Antonio Zeitung*. In July 1853 he published the first issue of that weekly newspaper.

Olmsted met Douai in January 1854 and found in him a kindred spirit with whom he could share both political and religious views. During their trip with Douai to Sisterdale in early February, the Olmsted brothers "listened to some details of a varied and stormy life, . . . and were not long in falling into discussions that ran through deep water, and demanded all our skill in navigation."[1] Douai, too, was pleased to find that his new friends shared many of his religious and political views. "It is very agreeable to me to see that your own ideas on the subject of Religion and Morals almost coincide with mine," he wrote some months later.[2]

Douai's political and social beliefs, and his strong allegiance to them, also appealed greatly to Olmsted. The German editor was a European republican who had suffered economic loss, imprisonment and exile for his beliefs. In Texas he was dedicating himself to the program of free-labor colonization that Olmsted believed would solve the problem of the decivilizing effect of frontier settlement and would demonstrate the viability of a free-labor economy in the South. Moreover, the formation of a free state in West Texas would halt the expansion of slavery into the Southwest. Beyond that, Douai was proving once again his willingness to risk his safety and that of his family in the interest of a cause in which he believed.

When Olmsted returned to New York in the fall of 1854, he was ready to help the cause of a free state in West Texas. By that time, the San Antonio Platform of 1854, which Douai had promoted, had divided the German community and the stockholders of the *Zeitung*. Douai's friends among the stockholders prevailed, however, and on September 17, 1854, he became owner as well as editor of the paper. At that point Olmsted began to raise funds to assist him, provided correspondence from the North for the *Zeitung* and solicited subscriptions to it among his acquaintances.

In December 1854, Friedrich Kapp reported to Douai of Olmsted's activities that "not even a brother could do more and in a more appropriate way" for him and his paper. Douai expressed his appreciation to the Olmsted brothers, saying, "I never before witnessed in friends of so short an acquaintance such a readiness to help his friends, and such an untiring energy in overcoming all hindrances, that obstructed their efforts!"[3]

Nonetheless, Douai had to face many difficulties. During the summer of 1854, proslavery gangs threatened him with violence, and the following year rising nativist sentiment in Texas turned against the Germans. Douai's editorial policy fed the flames when in February 1855 he declared that West Texas should be made a free state. The necessity for this declaration, however, he blamed on the injudicious statements of others, citing especially Friedrich Kapp's lecture on the history of the Germans in Texas, published in the *New York Daily Tribune* of January 20, 1855, which included a prediction that the Germans were to play a central role in the creation of the "*Free State of Western Texas.*"[4]

Increasing opposition from within the apprehensive and generally conservative German community also reduced Douai's subscriptions, thereby hurting him financially. By August 1855 he was working far into the nights, setting most of the type for the *Zeitung* himself. At the same time, threats of violence against his press and himself led Douai to sleep armed in his office and at times to mount a guard of his friends. Learning of Douai's problems, Olmsted renewed his assistance, guaranteeing payment of a debt of $150 and soliciting funds for the *Zeitung* from members of peace groups.

By January 1856, however, Douai was nearing the limit of his endurance. There could be no effective free-soil movement in Texas, he warned, without a strong nucleus of from two thousand to four thousand "Northern back-bone people" to strengthen the fading resolve of the Germans. He saw no prospect of such an influx in the near future and declared that in any case he could no longer serve as a leader. "I can not do much in favor of that project," he confessed in discouragement. "In spite of my peaceable character I am almost hated by every one hereabout. Whatever I take in hand, is sure to be lost forever. If this is a fault of mine—I do not know; perhaps I serve rather as a scape-goat for the sins and faults of others."[5] He refused the Olmsted brothers' offers of continued assistance and soon after abandoned his efforts. In April he sold the *Zeitung*'s press and type to his opponents, claiming that otherwise they would have bought their own press and ruined him through competition. In May he left for New York with his wife, father and seven children to start a new life there. His loyal supporter Charles Riotte assumed the still-unpaid original debt of $600 (at 48 percent interest) that Douai had assumed when he purchased the *Zeitung* in the fall of 1854.

Soon after he reached New York, Douai proceeded to Boston, where he had the best prospect of employment. The German community there provided him with private pupils and a teaching position in a school, and raised money for him to give scientific lectures and to campaign for the Republican party. He continued to write, providing articles for several German-language periodicals as well as for the *New American Cyclopedia,* edited by George Ripley and Olmsted's erstwhile co-editor of *Putnam's Monthly,* Charles A. Dana. In 1858, Douai won a prize offered by a St. Louis newspaper with his novel *Fata Morgana,* which described an attempt by a group of Germans who had become disillusioned with the United States to found a colony in Mexico. A major source for Douai's material was clearly the similar project of Charles Riotte in 1856.

Douai continued his pedagogical activities with the publication of a German grammar that went through five editions between 1858 and 1859. In 1859 he helped found a German school in Boston, a school which offered one of the first kindergartens in the United States. He also secured a position from Samuel Gridley Howe at the Perkins Institute for the Blind, in part through the intercession of the Olmsted brothers.

While in Boston, Douai kept alive his interest in establishing a free state in West Texas, advising Howe on the subject and consulting with other members of the New England Emigrant Aid Company. Both he and Olmsted were present at the meeting on November 23, 1858, at which the directors of the company revived the West Texas colonization project and appointed a committee, which included Howe, to devise a plan of action.

Although he prospered in Boston, Douai could not stay clear of controversy for long. At a large meeting held in May 1859 to honor the memory of Alexander Humboldt, he asserted that the great geographer had been a freethinker like himself. This offended many influential persons in Boston and led to a sharp decrease in his sources of income. In July he left Boston for New York.

For the next twenty-eight years Douai remained in the New York region, actively engaging in the fields of education, free thought, and journalism. As an educator he was director of the Hoboken Free Academy and the Green Street School in Newark, New Jersey. He published a manual for kindergartens that was based on the teachings of Friedrich Froebel, a German disciple of Pestalozzi, and edited a series of "rational readers" that combined the methods of the two educational theorists. Still an active freethinker, he was an executive member of a *freie gemeinde* established in Hoboken in 1865 and he participated the next year in the founding of a national *Bund der Freidenker*.

It was in the area of political journalism, however, that Douai was most influential. He campaigned for the Republican party in 1860 and propagandized for it as editor of the *New Yorker Demokrat*. A delegate to the party's national convention, he served as secretary of the German contingent. During the 1860s he became a Marxist, probably having been influenced by Friedrich Adolf Sorge, a member of the staff of the Hoboken Academy and a leading publicist of Marxist theory in the United States (as well as secretary of the First International).

In 1868, Douai became editor of the *Arbeiter Union,* the organ of the central body of German trade unions of the same name in New York City, a post he held until the demise of the paper in 1870. In 1876, with the formation of the Working Men's party (which became the Socialist Labor party the following year), he performed editorial functions for three of its publications. From 1878 until his death ten years later, he was an editor of the influential *New Yorker Volkszeitung,* a daily newspaper published in New York by German socialist and trade union groups.

After their collaboration in the West Texas free-state movement of the 1850s, Olmsted and Douai apparently lost contact with each other. The only extant correspondence between them in later years is a letter of introduction to Olmsted that Douai gave an acquaintance in 1884. Addressing his "Dear old friend," Douai wrote:

> I regret in a lively manner that I was for many years prevented from cultivating intercourse with you which is so desirable to me, by the constant pressure of business on me.
>
> For more than twenty years I could not even see your dear old face.
> But I hope, this will not always be the case.
> Take the assurance of my undying respect for you and let me continue to think that I still have a place in your remembrance.[6]

1. *JT*, pp. 187–88.
2. Douai to FLO and JHO, Dec. 16, 1854.
3. Douai to FLO, Dec. 7 and Nov. 17, 1854.
4. "The History of Texas," *New York Daily Tribune,* Jan. 20, 1855, p. 5.
5. Douai to FLO, Jan. 27, 1856.
6. Douai to FLO, July 23, 1884.

Additional References

Douai, Adolf, "Autobiography."
Friesen, Gerhard K., "Adolf Douai's Literary Activities," *Journal of German-American Studies* 13, no. 2 (Summer 1978): 25–38.

ARTHUR T. EDWARDS (1828–1857) was one of Olmsted's partners in the publishing firm of Dix, Edwards & Company. He had been a clerk in a dry-goods establishment and was reputed to have outstanding financial ability. After Dix and Edwards formed their partnership in March 1855, Dix wished to take Olmsted on as an additional partner. Edwards agreed reluctantly and his relations with Olmsted were strained from the first. Olmsted wanted the firm to practice the kind of liberality that he was used to in his own finances, while Edwards preferred a policy that seemed to him both ungenerous and unwise.

In June 1855 Olmsted and Edwards had a heated argument concerning the obligation of Dix & Edwards to pay English publishers for republication rights in the United States. A rather stiff reconciliation of the two men followed immediately, and they continued to work together. Olmsted's serious difficulties with Edwards developed in the spring and summer of 1856. As soon as he reached England in March 1856, Olmsted purchased more than 150 wood blocks and electrotypes at a cost of over $750. When Edwards received the bill, he promptly protested. "We cannot imagine the reason for making such a purchase," he wrote, "as we were particular in instructing you not to make purchases without consulting us in regard to them. . . . There is no earthly use to which we can possibly put them, and when they arrive we shall if possible sell them for what they will fetch."[1] He then warned Olmsted to make no further purchases without consulting his partners. This attempt by Edwards to discipline him offended Olmsted, and he was angry that his partners would sell the wood blocks without waiting to learn why he had purchased them.

In July 1856 Olmsted became even more concerned about Edwards's policies when Dix informed him that during the previous six months Edwards had twice made errors in his accounts of over $1,500. One of the errors had occurred just before the bill for Olmsted's wood blocks arrived, and was the apparent cause of Edwards's severe response. Olmsted learned further that Edwards was lending the firm's funds to his brothers without informing his partners.

Olmsted at first considered buying out Edwards's interest in the partnership. By the time he returned to New York in October 1856, however, he had decided instead to withdraw as a partner, make a loan of the $5,000 he had provided the firm when he became a partner, and then work for Dix & Edwards as a salaried employee. He remained as a partner, however, until April 1857, when Dix and Edwards themselves left the partnership in the face of impending bankruptcy. The next fall, during the Panic of that year, Olmsted reported to his brother: "I see my friend Edwards, pale, nervous, anxious, proper and evidently *shinning,* in the streets, but avoid meeting or a recognition. He is a bad as well as a foolish man."[2] Hard times and ill health soon took their toll on Edwards: on December 17, 1857, he died in Dubuque, Iowa.[3]

1. Dix & Edwards to FLO, April 30, 1856.
2. FLO to JHO, Sept. 11, 1857.
3. William Henry Edwards, comp., *Timothy and Rhoda Edwards of Stockbridge, Mass., and Their Descendants: A Genealogy* (Cincinnati, Ohio, 1903), p. 99.

PARKE GODWIN (1816–1904) assisted Olmsted in editing *Putnam's Monthly Magazine* during 1855 and early 1856, serving primarily as a writer of articles on political questions. His essays for *Putnam's Monthly* on the South, slavery and nativism express views similar to Olmsted's, indicating the accuracy of the claim Olmsted made in the summer of 1856 that his own proposals concerning the magazine's position on political issues had hitherto been decisive.[1] The letters in this volume indicate, however, that Godwin did not always follow Olmsted's editorial suggestions once he had written an article.

Godwin had collaborated with George W. Curtis and Charles A. Dana from 1853 to 1855, when *Putnam's Monthly* was under the ownership of George Palmer Putnam. He was also an editor of the *New York Evening Post,* whose chief editor was his father-in-law, William Cullen Bryant. Godwin remained connected with the *Post* until 1878—the year that marked the end of Olmsted's involvement in New York City parks—and Olmsted occasionally turned to him for editorial support in park matters. No correspondence of importance between the two men has survived for the years after 1856, and it appears that they saw little of each other after that time.

1. FLO to Parke Godwin, July 29, 1856, Bryant-Godwin Papers, Manuscript Division, New York Public Library, New York City.

Additional Sources

DAB, s.v. "Godwin, Parke."

Wennersten, John Raymond, "A Reformer's Odyssey: The Public Career of Parke Godwin of the New York Evening Post, 1837–1870" (Ph.D. diss., University of Maryland, 1969).

EDWARD EVERETT HALE (1822–1909), author and Unitarian minister, was an important associate of Olmsted's in his free-labor colonization activities. In working with Hale, however, Olmsted had to overcome the natural diffidence that he felt toward the man who had married a woman he himself had planned to wed. In the summer of 1851, following a courtship and correspondence of over two years, Olmsted had become engaged to Emily Baldwin Perkins of Hartford. Almost immediately, she changed her mind and broke off the engagement. A little over a year later, in October 1852, she married Hale. Olmsted's distress even four years later is evident in his admission to Hale that "I can't well write a word to you without much emotion even now, but I am anything but a miserable or even a dissatisfied man...."[1]

In the summer of 1855, Hale was already one of the leading figures in the New England Emigrant Aid Company. By then, Olmsted had already informed Hale about his own free-soil activities and had sent him letters from Adolf Douai and Charles Riotte describing their difficulties with proslavery nativists, letters that Olmsted hoped Hale would use as the basis for articles on the subject.

Olmsted probably came to correspond with Hale in 1855 because of Hale's prominence in the Emigrant Aid Company's fund-raising efforts of that year. During the summer, Amos Lawrence had threatened to resign from the company if he had to continue to finance its operations virtually by himself. Hale then took the lead in soliciting funds: in July he sent a form letter to many of the clergymen in New England, urging them to collect contributions from their parishioners. During October and November 1855, he left his church and devoted all of his time to raising funds for the company.

As early as April 1855 Hale had become involved in the attempts of free-state settlers in Kansas to secure arms. When the "bogus" territorial legislature was elected, Charles Robinson, the Emigrant Aid Company's agent in Lawrence, appealed to him for assistance in sending two hundred Sharps rifles and two field guns to Kansas. Olmsted joined in these efforts later in the year when James B. Abbott toured the East seeking funds. He became Abbott's agent in New York, kept Hale informed of his activities, and purchased the one cannon that was sent to Lawrence.[2]

Early in 1856 Olmsted continued to inform Hale of his activities,

EDWARD EVERETT HALE

reporting on Kansas-related developments in New York and describing the enthusiastic plans that Eli Thayer laid before him while in the city.³ At the same time, he promoted Hale's literary career. In January 1856 he accepted Hale's short story "The Spider's Eye," which appeared in the July 1856 issue of *Putnam's Monthly*. It was the first story that Hale published in a major journal and the first piece of secular fiction that he published outside his brother's ephemeral *Boston Miscellany*. Hale reciprocated by writing an enthusiastic review of *Seaboard Slave States* for the July 1856 issue of the *North American Review*.

Early in 1857 Olmsted once again sought assistance from Hale, who was now a director and member of the executive committee of the New England Emigrant Aid Company. He was anxious to secure Hale's aid in using *A Journey Through Texas* to encourage emigration to the state by New Englanders. Accordingly, Hale sent selected pages of the book to a number of New England editors with the suggestion that they draw from them discreetly in their editorials. He also placed a highly favorable review of the book in his family's newspaper, the *Boston Daily Advertiser*.⁴

Olmsted also discussed with Hale the desirability of convincing textile manufacturers to spin cotton into thread in West Texas and of encouraging expansion of sheepherding in the region. In addition, he solicited Hale's assistance for friends in San Antonio who were anxious to secure the services of a Unitarian minister.[5] After early 1857 the collaboration of Olmsted and Hale on free-soil matters apparently ended. When Olmsted began to work with the Emigrant Aid Company later in the year to promote colonization in Texas, he dealt with Samuel Cabot, Jr., and the "Texas Committee."

After the Civil War, Olmsted and Hale saw little of each other. Even though they lived in adjoining towns near Boston after 1881, their families had no social contact. During 1869 and 1870, when Hale was living near Boston and Olmsted was still in New York, they did assist each other in park and community planning. Around 1869, Hale and a group of Bostonians attempted to create a series of suburban communities for workingmen along railroad lines running out of Boston. Hale outlined such a scheme in "How They Lived at Naguadavick," part of *Sybaris and Other Homes*, which he published in 1869. Olmsted responded to Hale's request for information on the subject by sending him descriptions and plans of the suburban village of Riverside, Illinois, which he and Calvert Vaux were designing at the time. Hale, in turn, indicated that he hoped to secure Olmsted's professional advice if any of the projected communities were actually built. Agitation for a public park in Boston was increasing rapidly at this time and Olmsted provided Hale with his views on that subject as well. Hale used them to argue the case for a park, most notably in his Thanksgiving Day sermon in 1869 entitled "The People's Park."[6]

1. FLO to Hale, Aug. 23, 1855, below.
2. Samuel A. Johnson, *The Battle Cry of Freedom: The New England Emigrant Aid Company in the Kansas Crusade* (Lawrence, Kans., 1954), pp. 112–16.
3. FLO to Hale, Jan. 17, 1856; FLO to Hale, Feb. 4, 1856, New England Emigrant Aid Company Papers, Manuscript Department, Kansas State Historical Society, Topeka, Kans.
4. FLO to Hale, Jan. 30 and Feb. 19, 1857, below.
5. FLO to Hale, Feb. 4, 1857, New England Emigrant Aid Company Papers; FLO to Hale, Feb. 19 and 20, 1857, below.
6. Hale to FLO, Oct. 27, 1869, and Jan. 1, 1870; *Boston Daily Advertiser*, Nov. 20, 1869, p. 1.

Additional Sources

DAB, s.v. "Hale, Edward Everett."
Holloway, Jean, *Edward Everett Hale: A Biography* (Austin, Tex., 1956).

FRIEDRICH KAPP (1824–1884), a leading figure among the Germans in the North in the 1850s and 1860s, became a close friend and valued ally of Olmsted's. Kapp was born in Hamm, Westphalia, where his father was director of the gymnasium. In 1848 he became a newspaper correspondent and took part briefly in the revolution in Germany. He moved to New York City in 1850, where he practiced law and wrote on political topics. His home became the center of a literary and political circle. He was active in the Republican party, played an influential part in gaining German support for it, and was a presidential elector for Lincoln in 1860.

Only an occasional reference in Olmsted's letters tells of his relations with Kapp, but the two men must have been in frequent contact, especially after Olmsted moved to Manhattan in 1855. They first met following Olmsted's second journey in the South, during which he had met Kapp's uncle Ernst Kapp in Sisterdale. By that time Friedrich Kapp had already given careful study to American politics, particularly to the influence of slavery on it. Later in 1854 he published in Germany a book on American slavery entitled *Die Sklavenfrage in den Vereinigten Staaten*. Olmsted reviewed the book in the *New-York Daily Times* of January 15, 1855, and praised it highly. He welcomed Kapp as "the first writer on the United States who views us from the stand-point of European Republicanism," and declared that the book gave "the clearest and most comprehensive introduction to American politics which has yet been written by a foreigner." The similarity of the views of the two men on politics and slavery is indicated by Olmsted's reference in his review to Kapp's assessment of the implications of the Kansas-Nebraska Law:

> The author, in conclusion, intimates that in the passage of the Nebraska bill the supremacy of the South over the North was probably permanently established, and that what is likely to occur hereafter will only consolidate the power of the planting interest; that the theories of Mr. Calhoun will subvert entirely the principles of Jefferson, and that such alterations of the Constitution as will be necessary to change the old Democratic Republic into an Oligarchical, Slaveholding Aristocracy will soon be openly advocated and finally effected.[1]

By January 1855 Kapp had also dedicated himself to the free-soil cause in Texas. On January 18 he delivered an address that was printed in the *New York Daily Tribune*. In it he recounted the history of the Germans in Texas and predicted that they would succeed in creating a free state in its western portion. During the next five years he and Olmsted collaborated in promoting the free-soil cause. Kapp assisted Olmsted in his search for land to purchase for colonies in Texas and helped publicize the idea of creating a free-soil barrier to the expansion of slavery.

As a testimonial to their work together and to the value that he placed on Olmsted's writings, Kapp dedicated to Olmsted the expanded history of American slavery that he published in 1861 as *Geschichte der Sklaverei in den Vereinigten Staaten von Amerika*. "I inscribe these pages to you," ran the printed dedication, "as a proof of my friendship for you, and as a token of my appreciation of your excellent exposition of American slavery." In the dedication he also expressed the conviction that "the conflict now on the eve of a decision in the United States, is neither more nor less than one of the manifold phases of the

FRIEDRICH KAPP

struggle between aristocracy and democracy (in the original sense of the word) which has agitated the civilized world for more than twenty centuries...."[2]

Kapp presented the first bound volume of the book to Olmsted, saying, "I hope that the dedication, as it now reads, will answer your views; I copied the conclusion entirely from you."[3] That conclusion reads as follows:

> In conclusion, my dear Olmsted, let us still cherish the hope that events are preparing, in not only the old country, but in all parts of the continent, for a day when all labor of head and of hand may be as harmoniously and happily combined and as worthily directed in motive, as in the good and beautiful work, which you have the present satisfaction of guiding. It was in scenes of industry such as now surround you, that Faust at the end of his career hoped to find greater happiness than in all human wisdom, causing him to exclaim:
> "Such busy multitudes I fain would see,
> Stand upon free soil with a people free!"

In addition to his antislavery political writing and activities, Kapp also carried on original research and writing concerning the historical relation between Germans and the United States. Between 1858 and 1871 he published biographies of the revolutionary generals Friedrich Wilhelm von Steuben and Johann Kalb, as well as a history of German emigration to the United States and a monograph on Frederick the Great and the United States.

Kapp returned to Germany in 1870 and became a naturalized Prussian. During all but two of his remaining years he was a member of the German Reichstag. In addition to his political career he retained his interest in America, and in 1876 published a two-volume study of the United States entitled *Aus und über Amerika.*

1. [Frederick Law Olmsted], "The Slavery Question Judged by a European Republican," *NYDT,* Jan. 15, 1855, p. 2.
2. Friedrich Kapp, *Geschichte der Sklaverei in den Vereinigten Staaten von Amerika,* (Hamburg, Germany, 1861), dedication.
3. Kapp to FLO, Oct. 19, 1860.

Additional Sources

DAB, s.v. "Kapp, Friedrich."
"Friedrich Kapp," *Nation* 39, no. 1010 (Nov. 6, 1884): 393-94.
Zucker, Adolph Eduard, ed., *The Forty-Eighters: Political Refugees of the German Revolution of 1848* (New York, 1950).

FREDERICK JOHN KINGSBURY (1823-1910) became a close friend of Olmsted's when he, John Hull Olmsted and Charles Loring Brace were fellow students at Yale in 1842-46. During the next few years he and Olmsted kept up a correspondence that focused especially on political issues. Kingsbury had a keen critical sense and conservative attitude that, as Olmsted confessed, punctured many of his favorite theories and taught him "much-needed discipline of mind." By the early 1850s the correspondence waned as the two pursued careers in very different fields.

After graduating from Yale and studying law in Boston and Hartford, Kingsbury had returned to his native Waterbury, Connecticut. There he married Alathea Scovill, heiress to the city's largest manufacturing fortune, and engaged in professional activities and civic service, as had his father and grandfather before him. During the 1850s he practiced law, served twice in the state legislature, and functioned as an officer in local banks—including a savings bank that he helped found in Waterbury. He became increasingly involved with the manufacturing concerns in Waterbury and in 1857 became a director of the Scovill Manufacturing Company.

Olmsted's letters to Kingsbury in this volume are primarily concerned with his first journey to the South and indicate that Kingsbury's uncle Abner Leavenworth of Petersburg, Virginia, was a helpful source of hospitality and information for him when he visited that city.

BIOGRAPHICAL DIRECTORY

Additional Sources

Kingsbury, Frederick John, *The Autobiography of Frederick J. Kingsbury,* Mattatuck Historical Society (Waterbury, Conn.), *Occasional Publications,* n.s., no. 10 (1946), no. 11 (1947), no. 12 (1947) and no. 13 (Oct. 1947).

Kingsbury, Frederick John, and Talcott, Mary Kingsbury, eds., *The Genealogy of Henry Kingsbury of Ipswich and Haverhill, Mass.* (Hartford, Conn., 1905).

NCAB, 12: 208-9.

Yale Obit. Rec., 6th ser., no. 1 (June 1911): 8-10.

BERTHA OLMSTED (1834-1926), Olmsted's youngest half-sister, was apparently in awe of her energetic, older half-brother and looked to him for advice as she entered womanhood in the mid-1850s. She had seen little of him as a child, since he was living outside Hartford during those years. Long afterward, in response to a query concerning her early memory of him, she wrote, "I can only remember him at home for short vacations, which were remarkable to me, because being a timid child, he tried to cultivate my courage by teasing and frightening me."[1] While Olmsted's approach to her had become somewhat subtler by the mid-1850s, he was still ready with advice and counsel of all kinds, as the letters to her in this volume demonstrate.

After attending school in Hartford, Bertha spent six months during 1852 studying French and music at a female seminary in Middlebury, Ver-

BERTHA OLMSTED

mont. The seminary's principal, Stephen W. Hitchcock, had just married Sophia Stevens, who had lived with the Olmsted family while she was teaching at Hartford High School from 1848 to 1851. Hitchcock died in 1852, and in November of that year Sophia left for a long stay in Europe that was financed in part by John Olmsted. In October 1854 he sent Bertha to Europe for over three years of travel and study under Sophia's supervision. The two spent most of 1855 in Paris, where Bertha studied French and music and went sightseeing. Later in the year they moved to Rome, where Olmsted and his half-sister Mary joined them in March 1856. Then followed two months of travel in Italy, after which the group proceeded to Dresden.

While Bertha and Sophia were in Rome they received the constant attentions of Edward Sheffield Bartholomew (1822–1858), a Connecticut-born sculptor who had lived in Hartford from c. 1836 to 1850 and then moved to Rome. Bertha assumed that Sophia was the object of his interest, but when the young women left Italy in the late spring of 1856, Bartholomew presented Bertha with a letter declaring his love for her. Surprised and taken aback by this revelation, she was uncertain for some time what her response should be. She had the dubious benefit of conflicting counsel, since Olmsted urged Bartholomew's qualities while Sophia Hitchcock categorically declared her opposition to the match. In early June, however, Bertha refused Bartholomew's suit. Her decision disappointed Olmsted and provided the occasion for the letters to her on life and love that appear in this volume.

In January 1857 Bertha returned to Hartford with John Olmsted and Mary Bull Olmsted (who had gone to Europe in July 1856). In April 1861 she became engaged to William Woodruff Niles (1832–1914). Still ready with views on what his sister should and should not do, Olmsted observed, "I suppose no man will be allowed to marry during the war but it does not interrupt engagements."[2] Despite Olmsted's views, Bertha and Niles were married in June 1862. Niles had graduated from Berkeley Divinity School in New Haven in 1861 and was ordained an Episcopal priest in 1862. After serving in several small New England parishes, he was elected bishop of the Episcopal church in New Hampshire in 1870, a position he held until his death.[3]

1. Bertha Olmsted to John Charles Olmsted, June 30, 1914, John C. Olmsted Papers, Harvard Graduate School of Design, Cambridge, Mass.
2. FLO to JO, April 17, 1861.
3. *Olmsted Genealogy*, p. 109; *Eleventh Reunion*, p. 9.

JOHN OLMSTED (1791–1873), Olmsted's father, was a successful drygoods merchant in Hartford, Connecticut. He prospered, and was able to sell

JOHN OLMSTED

his interest in his firm in 1851 and live comfortably for the rest of his life. He also provided liberally for the education and travel of the five of his children who lived to maturity. He was especially generous to his two oldest sons, neither of whom showed any marked ability for earning a living. He sent John Hull Olmsted to France for six months in 1840 to study French, paid for his education at Yale and for his medical studies thereafter, and supported him and his family while he traveled in search of his health in Europe in 1851–53 and in Cuba and Europe in 1857. He paid for Frederick Law Olmsted's education away from home and for his apprenticeship with working farmers. He bought Olmsted a farm in Guilford, Connecticut, in 1846 and another on Staten Island in 1848. He also paid for the six-month tour of England and the Continent that Olmsted and his brother took with Charles Loring Brace in 1850.

During the years 1852–57, John Olmsted continued to give his eldest son significant financial help. He advanced funds to cover the cost of the two journeys through the South and supplied substantial sums to meet the expenses of running the Staten Island farm. He also provided large amounts of money to launch Olmsted in his publishing career—including $5,000 to make him a partner of Dix, Edwards & Company, and $500 to pay for the printing of *Seaboard Slave States*. John Olmsted's wealth, generosity and patience made it possible for Olmsted to spend the twenty years from 1837 to 1857 receiving

MARY BULL OLMSTED

training and experimenting with a variety of professional activities without a fixed or reliable income. During the mid-1850s, John Olmsted's support of his son's ventures as farmer, travel-writer and editor-publisher was particularly important, for it gave Olmsted the freedom to broaden his experience in a variety of ways.

Additional Sources
  Papers of FLO, 1: 83–85.

JOHN HULL OLMSTED (1825–1857) was Olmsted's closest friend and confidant. He and Olmsted were the only children born to John Olmsted and his first wife, who died when Olmsted was three and his brother was less than six months old. A year later, their father married Mary Ann Bull, who had been a close friend of their mother's. Between 1832 and 1842, six children were born to the couple, two of whom died in childhood.

JOHN HULL OLMSTED

Although the bond between Olmsted and his brother was strong from their early years, they seldom lived under the same roof for long. When he was seven, Olmsted went away to live with a minister and attend school in a town thirty miles from Hartford. He returned to live with his family for only short periods thereafter. The brothers were both in the New York City region after 1848, and in 1851 the discovery that John was suffering from tuberculosis added a new poignancy to their relationship. Despite his illness, John married Mary Cleveland Bryant Perkins—a Staten Island neighbor of Olmsted's—in the fall of 1851. The couple spent the next year and a half in Europe. They returned in the summer of 1853 with a baby son, soon after Olmsted completed his first southern journey. John and his family then settled with Olmsted on his Staten Island farm. From that time until Olmsted moved to Manhattan in April 1855, the brothers were constantly together. During that period they spent over six months traveling to Texas and exploring that state and part of northern Mexico.

When Olmsted moved to Manhattan in April 1855, John continued to operate the farm, a task he found increasingly difficult and onerous. He therefore welcomed the opportunity for literary activity that came when he undertook to write *A Journey Through Texas* from Olmsted's notes and published letters. The brothers agreed that for that work he was to receive two thirds of the royalties from sales of the volume. John completed the book by the time Olmsted returned from Europe in the fall of 1856. Even before *A Journey*

Through Texas was published in January 1857, however, John left America on a last, vain search for improved health. He and his family went first to Cuba, then to Switzerland, and finally to Nice, where on November 24, 1857, John Hull Olmsted died.

With his brother's death vanished the last glimmers of the humor and vivacity of youth that had flashed so often in the letters Olmsted had written in previous years. John's death left him lonely and faced with new responsibilities. To assuage his grief, Olmsted turned with great energy to his professional responsibilities. From that time on he immersed himself in work. He now had to look after John's widow and three children as well. They returned to the Staten Island farm in the spring of 1858, and he visited them when he could. Soon he arranged to meet those responsibilities in a more complete way: on June 13, 1859, he and Mary were married.

Additional Sources
  Papers of FLO, 1: 86-88.

CHARLES N. RIOTTE was born in St. Wendel, Prussia, in 1814. He was trained in the law and served for some time as a judge in a superior court in Prussia. He also became director of a railroad, anticipating the consistent interest he would show in railroad promotion during his twenty-five years in the New World. He emigrated to the United States in 1849 and settled in San Antonio. While there he gave Adolf Douai both moral and financial support and at times helped edit the *San Antonio Zeitung*. In 1854 he became an American citizen.

Olmsted met Riotte during his journey through Texas in 1854, and tried to convince him to move to New York and practice law. Instead, Riotte remained in the Southwest until he was expelled from Texas by Confederate authorities in the spring of 1861. Olmsted's first discussions with Riotte about the possible future of a free-soil West Texas aroused his enthusiasm, and even before he left the South he wrote his new friend offering his services to the cause. During the fall of 1854, Riotte corresponded with Olmsted concerning the prospects of attracting free-soil settlers to Texas. As part of such a program he urged construction of a railroad from San Antonio to the Gulf Coast along a route similar to the one he had proposed while a director of the San Antonio and Mexican Gulf Railroad.

Increasing difficulties with proslavery nativists and the absence of any prospect of a strong flow of antislavery settlers to West Texas soon led Riotte to resolve to leave the United States. Accordingly, in December 1855 he negotiated an agreement with General Vidaurri, governor of Nuevo Leon and Coahuila in Mexico, for a land grant of two million acres on which he proposed to create a colony of German and Mexican settlers.[1]

In January 1856 he announced to Olmsted that he intended to move to Monterrey, Mexico, with his wife, seven children and two servants. Olmsted objected to his plans, but Riotte replied that the difference in attitude between Americans and Germans, aggravated by the nativist movement in Texas, had convinced him that Germans could not become a part of American society:

> We are judged from the standpoint of an American—indeed a very strange people! We look upon a political society or state as a *congregation* of men; whose aim it is to elevate the wellbeing of the aggregate by the combined exertion, and if required, sacrifice of the individuals, and thus to benefit all. Americans look first upon themselves as *private individuals,* entitled to ask for all rights and benefits of an organized community even to the detriment of the whole and think to secure the wellbeing of the community by the wellbeing of the single individual, even if mostly acquired to the prejudice of the community. To us, the State is a ideal being, whose welfare must be our pride, must be secured by the exertions of our head and the work of our hand and will then redound to the benefit of all—to the Americans it is the *formal* guarantee of certain (inalienable) rights in a loose conglomeration of human beings to secure an internal "bellum intra omnes et contra omnes";—to us honor of the state is that of each citizen,—to you (dont take that personally) the honor of the state has its foundation in the greatness of some men,—we idealize the community—you the individual! How is it possible, that we ever should amalgamate? If you follow the difference of our starting points up through all phases of political and social life you will, I believe, arrive to the same conclusion I came to, that is, a decided: Never![2]

Riotte apparently did not attract a very large group of settlers or stay for long in Mexico himself: he served on the San Antonio Library Committee in 1857, ran a German-American school there in 1859, and in 1860 requested Olmsted's assistance in seeking the position of assistant collector of customs in that city. With the election of Lincoln he applied for the post of U.S. minister in Costa Rica. Olmsted supported his appointment, and in so doing offered Charles Sumner his estimation of Riotte's character and the extent of his contribution to the antislavery cause:

> If he fails to produce upon you the impression of a man of the right stamp for such an office as that to which he aspires, have the goodness to consider that at present he carries with him the effect of ten years of hard fighting with continual defeat, disappointment and increasing poverty—and that he has too good a temper to have been made sour or savage by it. No man comes out of such a battle without some evidence of it in his face or manner. I believe him to be a man of good parts, education, & breeding and in the vain, hopeless and inglorious struggle in which he has been engaged with Slavery on the South-Western frontier, he has acted with great discretion, bravely and nobly.[3]

Riotte secured the Costa Rican post and served there from 1861 until January 1867. During that time he carried on his correspondence with Olmsted, discussing at length the possibility of constructing a railroad across the isthmus in that country. He argued that such a railroad would make Costa Rica a commercial tributary to the United States and would pave the way for annexation. In December 1865, after receiving a letter from Olmsted on the subject, he wrote that he had convinced the president and minister of foreign affairs of Costa Rica to arrange for construction of the railroad. Moreover, he reported, the minister had agreed to Riotte's proposal that Olmsted be one of the two representatives of Costa Rica who would negotiate terms with capitalists in New York. Nothing seems to have come of the plan, however.

After his removal from office by Andrew Johnson in 1867, Riotte spent two years in Hoboken, New Jersey, where Adolph Douai also was living. He then served from April 1869 to January 1873 as U.S. minister to Nicaragua. Failing to secure another diplomatic appointment, he left the United States in mid-1874. He presumably returned to Prussia, a course of action that a decree of amnesty in 1861 had made possible, and that his friend Friedrich Kapp had already followed.

While Olmsted's long correspondence with Riotte did not convince his friend to remain in the United States, it may at least have given him a greater appreciation of Americans and their political institutions. "You have reconciled me with America and the Americans," Riotte wrote Olmsted in early 1857, "at a time when my experience in Texas had led me to believe, I, a republican by principle, had started in the wrong direction when going to the U.S."[4]

1. "German Emigration to Mexico," *NYDT,* Jan. 31, 1856, p. 4; "Die neue Deutsche Colonie in Mexico," *Neu Braunfelser Zeitung,* Feb. 16, 1856, p. 2; *San Antonio Zeitung,* Jan. 12, 1856, pp. 1, 2.
2. Riotte to FLO, Feb. 25, 1856.
3. FLO to Charles Sumner, April 5, 1861, Record Group 59, Letters of Application and Recommendation during the Administrations of Abraham Lincoln and Andrew Johnson, 1861–1869, Diplomatic Branch, Civil Archives Division, National Archives and Records Service, Washington, D.C.
4. Riotte to FLO, Jan. 22, 1867.

SLAVERY AND THE SOUTH

1852–1857

CHAPTER I

THE JOURNEY THROUGH THE SEABOARD SLAVE STATES: THE UPPER SOUTH

1852–1853

THE LETTERS AND ARTICLES in this chapter describe Olmsted's journey from the District of Columbia through eastern Virginia and North Carolina in December 1852 and January 1853. All of the personal letters of that period that have survived are included here. In addition to giving information about the people he visited, they offer statements of his intentions as a traveler and responses to what he saw that he did not include in his published writings. The letters from "The South" series in the *New-York Daily Times* contain his first attempts to analyze the ways in which slavery affected the society of the South.

In "The South" numbers 2 and 14, Olmsted discusses the failure of Virginia to develop the manufacturing that its situation and natural resources made possible, while in numbers 7, 8 and 9 he offers his first assessment of the condition of the slaves and the comparative expense of free and slave labor. Number 11 presents numerous illustrations of the inefficiency of labor resulting from the institution of slavery, while number 14 discusses the prospects for Northerners and Europeans wishing to settle in Virginia.

Although Olmsted soon concluded that the effects of slavery on Southern society were evil and pervasive, his early letters to the *Times* display a spirit of tolerance that was missing from his later writings: he acknowledges the difficulty of abolishing slavery, or even of legislating improvements in the treatment of slaves. In "The South" number 12, in the same spirit, he deplores the treatment of American sailors and suggests that they be considered a fruitful object of Northern philanthropic concern. In number 8 he makes his most impassioned call for Northern forbearance on the slavery question and gives his strongest statement of the evils suffered by the poor in free-labor society.

To Frederick Kingsbury

Tosomock,[1] Oct. 17th 1852

Dear Fred,

    I had it in my mind to write to you immediately, when we heard that John had a boy,[2] but somehow I didn't, & of course somebody else did. And I won't repeat. If Charley[3] didn't, you will have John's letter with all the particulars, mental, moral, physical & medical.

    He has a boy, though, if you didn't know it, & his name by a tyrannical law of the mountain republic is *Charles*. Drink to him at tea time. Fine fellow, very handsome, looks like me & if they could have had their own way they would have called him after us. Has a scowl (of course Charley told you this) "as if he *already found life a bore.*"

    Mary was all right and was eating steaks & chickens enough for two ordinary sized mortals. The baby got mad at her in five minutes after he was born, snatched her up, laid her over his knee, & spanked her so she had to give it up on natural depravity; but thinks there may have been something in the air of *Geneva.*[4]

    My second volume published day before yesterday—& second edition of the first & the two bound in one.[5] The latter a splurgy, thick book—which I will send you if you'll tell me how. The two volumes only take 4 weeks of our summer walk—& I could make another volume or two, better than these are, out of it if I choose to. But I shall not.

    It was at the printer's in July. Ought to have been issued 15th August, but Putnam had others advertized in advance. So it is only just delivered—three months in labor (Mary was some 70 hours; tedious but not very hard).

    I have thoughts of going South this winter. Partly to save my throat the winter's trial here, & mainly with the idea that I could make a valuable book of observations on Southern Agriculture & general economy as affected by Slavery; the condition of the slaves—prospects—tendencies—& reliable understanding of the sentiments and hopes & fears of sensible planters & gentlemen that I should meet. Matter of fact matter to come after the deluge of spoony fancy pictures now at its height shall be spent.[6]

    I should value your advice as much as anybody's I know. And you must give it [to] me extensively. If I should conclude to go I shall try to get up to see you, if you can't & won't come here. Should calculate to leave middle of December & return early in March.

    I made acquaintance of some Virginia families at Philadelphia this fall. Liked them & they liked me & I should want to visit them. Farmersburgh (or ville) Prince Edward, I think, County (I've got it upstairs).[7] Then I should go to see your uncle (with the Scripture name—which I can't think of now—yes) Abner[8] & then—tell me where, will you? Down eastways to South Carolina & the cotton country below? Or by Kentuck, Tennessee to New Orleans? And generally, what do you think of it & what could I do?

JOURNEY THROUGH THE UPPER SOUTH: 1852-1853

I am not a red-hot Abolitionist like Charley, but am a moderate Free Soiler. Going to vote for Scott & would take in a fugitive slave & shoot a man that was likely to get him.[9] On the whole, I guess I represent pretty fairly the average sentiment of good thinking men on our side. The way I look at it you will see in my second volume, page 106, rather awkwardly.[10]

How do you like that chapter & how the chapter on prisons? It is a little beyond me, I am afraid, to do that sort of thing. But the stage coach ride I think I did pretty well out of the whole cloth.[11] Don't you like it?

Land rising rapidly in value on the upper part of the island & much speculation. Great many fine houses building & moving this way.

Farm about as usual. Nursery business good. Have orders for $400 worth of trees already. Pear speculation promises well, too. Have tried the market with all my orchard sorts & been offered 3 to 5 dollars a bushel. Sold a dozen Bartletts for 50 cents to a Broadway confectioner & one Duchess for 25 cents and was offered 12½ cents each for several more.

Trees have grown finely & fruited fairly. Have had larger fruit & finer-flavored than is usual from my varieties in other localities. I understand the business—have a system of cultivation of my own that succeeds well & believe I can beat the world at it.

It appears that only the first section of the original letter is preserved in the Olmsted Papers in the Library of Congress.

1. Tosomock Farm was the name of Olmsted's farm on Staten Island.
2. On September 14, 1852, a son was born at Vandoeuvres Hamlet, Geneva, Switzerland, to John Hull Olmsted and Mary Perkins Olmsted. They wanted to name him Frederick, after Frederick Law Olmsted and Frederick Kingsbury, but local law apparently prevented them from doing so. Instead, they named him Charles John Olmsted. That remained his name until sometime in the 1860s, when his name was changed to John Charles. When in 1859 Olmsted married Mary Perkins Olmsted, his brother's widow, the boy became Olmsted's stepson. Although his parents at first intended that he become a doctor, like his father, John Charles eventually received training in landscape architecture and in 1889 became Olmsted's partner in the firm of F. L. and J. C. Olmsted. He remained a partner until Olmsted's retirement in 1895, and from then until his own death in 1920 was senior partner of the firm (*Olmsted Genealogy*, pp. 154-55; *DAB*; JO Journal, Sept. 30, 1852).
3. Charles Loring Brace.
4. The Reformation theologian John Calvin, one of whose chief doctrines was the natural depravity of man, founded a theocratic city-state at Geneva in the sixteenth century.
5. On February 18, 1852, George P. Putnam and Company of New York published the first volume of Olmsted's *Walks and Talks of an American Farmer in England* as volume 3 of Putnam's Semi-Monthly Library for the Traveller and the Fireside. During that year David Bogue of London published the volume in England. In October 1852 Putnam published the second volume, *Further Walks and Talks of an American Farmer in England*, as volume 19 of the Semi-Monthly Library. At the same time, Putnam issued both volumes bound as one (FLO to JO, Feb. 14, 1852; JO Journal, Feb. 18, 1852).
6. Although Olmsted may be referring to Harriet Beecher Stowe's *Uncle Tom's Cabin: or Life Among the Lowly*, which was published in March 1852, it is more likely that he means the spate of books and writings that immediately followed its publication. *Uncle Tom's Cabin* appeared serially in the *National Era* during the ten months prior to its publication in book form, and imitations and fictional rebuttals of Mrs. Stowe's work began to appear early in 1852. Among

the works published in that year that Olmsted may have considered "spoony fancies" were Baynard Rush Hall, *Frank Freeman's Barber Shop; A Tale;* Caroline Lee Hentz, *Marcus Warland; or, The Long Moss Spring. A Tale of the South;* Mary Eastman, *Aunt Phillis's Cabin: Or, Southern Life As It Is;* Charles Jacobs Peterson, *The Cabin and Parlor; Or, Slaves and Masters. By J. Thornton Randolph* [*pseud.*]; Robert Criswell, "*Uncle Tom's Cabin" Contrasted with Buckingham Hall, The Planter's Home, or, A Fair View of Both Sides of the Slavery Question;* and William Gilmore Simms's series of essays on plantation life entitled "Home Sketches," which appeared in the *New York Literary World* beginning in January 1852. All of these works gave a more favorable picture of the South and slavery than did *Uncle Tom's Cabin* (see William R. Taylor, *Cavalier and Yankee: The Old South and American National Character* [New York, 1961], pp. 307–8).

7. Probably Farmville in Prince Edward County, Virginia, seventy miles southwest of Richmond. Olmsted did not indicate in any of his travel accounts that he visited his friends there, but he did pass through the region of Farmville in July 1854, at the end of his journey through the back country, and may have stayed with them at that time (*BC*, p. 400).

8. Frederick Kingsbury's uncle Abner Johnson Leavenworth (1803–1869) was born in Waterbury, Connecticut, and graduated from Amherst College in 1825 and from Andover Theological Seminary in 1828. He preached in Connecticut for four years and then moved to Charlotte, North Carolina, where he took charge of a young ladies' seminary and became pastor of a Presbyterian church. In 1838 he moved to Warrenton, Virginia, and started a school there. A few years later he moved to Petersburg, Virginia, organized a church, and founded the Leavenworth Academic and Collegiate Seminary for Young Ladies. He also played an important role in the founding of the Virginia Educational Association. Olmsted visited Leavenworth during the Christmas season of 1852, during his first southern trip.

Olmsted's particular reason for asking for advice on the itinerary of his southern trip was that Kingsbury had first-hand knowledge of Virginia. He had lived there with Abner Leavenworth and his family from February 1840 to July 1841—first at Warrenton and then at Petersburg. During that time he had visited many parts of the Virginia piedmont and tidewater (Elias Warner Leavenworth, *A Genealogy of the Leavenworth Family in the United States, with Historical Introduction, etc.* . . . [Syracuse, N.Y., 1873], pp. 222–23; Amherst College, *Biographical Record of the Alumni of Amherst College . . . 1821–1896 Edited by W. L. Montague* . . . , 2 vols. [Amherst, Mass., 1881–1901], 1: 23–24; FLO to FJK, Feb. 26, 1853, below; *The Autobiography of Frederick J. Kingsbury,* Mattatuck Historical Society [Waterbury, Conn.], *Occasional Publications,* n.s., no. 11 [1947]).

9. Although he resisted the abolitionist doctrines urged on him by his friend Charles Loring Brace, Olmsted had opposed the Compromise of 1850, particularly the Fugitive Slave Act. His opposition to the expansion of slavery, however, was not strong enough to make him support the Free Soil party, which in 1852 was running John P. Hale for president on a platform that denounced the Compromise of 1850 and opposed further extension of slavery into the states and federal territories. Instead, Olmsted maintained his allegiance to the Whig party and accepted its candidate, General Winfield Scott. Although a Virginian, Scott was primarily the candidate of the Northern wing of the party and had only scattered support in the South. Even so, the Whig platform of 1852 did not express Olmsted's views on the slavery question; it accepted the Compromise of 1850 as the final settlement of the issues with which it dealt, including that of fugitive slaves (FLO to CLB, Nov. 12, 1850; FLO to CLB, Jan. 11, 1851; Allan Nevins, *Ordeal of the Union,* vol. 2, *A House Dividing, 1852–1857* [New York and London, 1947], pp. 26–34).

10. In the section of *Walks and Talks* to which he refers here, Olmsted discussed American slavery while comparing the American and English conceptions of the lowest classes of society. He was appalled to find so many Englishmen willing to accept the permanence of a large class of poverty-stricken agricultural and industrial laborers. With his American optimism, he viewed these English pessimists as "blasphemers, tyrants and insolent rebels to humanity." He expressed the American approach to the lowest elements of society as follows:

> In America we hold that a slave, a savage, a child, a maniac, and a condemned criminal, are each and all *born,* equally with us, with our President, or with the Queen of England, free and self-governing; that they have the same natural rights with us; but that attached to those natural rights were certain duties, and when we find them, from whatever cause—no matter whether the original cause be with them, or our fathers, or us—

unable to perform those duties, we dispossess them of their rights: we restrain, we confine, we master, and we *govern* them. But in taking upon ourselves to govern them, we take duties upon ourselves, and our first duty is that which is the first duty of every man for himself—improvement, restoration, *regeneration*. By every consideration of justice, by every noble instinct, we are bound to make it our highest and chiefest object to restore them, not the liberty first, but—the capacity for the liberty—for exercising the duties of the liberty—which is their natural right. And so much of the liberty as they are able to use to their own as well as our advantage, we are bound constantly to allow them—nay, more than they show absolute evidence of their ability to use to advantage. We must not wait till a child can walk alone before we put it on its legs; we must not wait till it can swim before we let it go in the water. As faith is necessary to self-improvement, *trust* is necessary to education or restoration of another: as necessary with the slave, the savage, the maniac, the criminal, and the peasant—as necessary, and equally with all necessary—as with the child. (*Walks and Talks,* 2: 104-7.)

Then follows the passage to which Olmsted particularly refers in this letter:

Education, then, with certain systematic exercise or discipline of the governed, having reference to and connected with a gradual elevation to equal freedom with the governing, we hold to be a very necessary part of all rightful government. Where it is not, we say this is no true and rightful government, but a despotism and a sin.

But we shall be at once asked: Is your fugitive law designed for such purposes? Do your slaveholders govern the simple-minded Africans whom they keep in restraint on these principles?

So far as they do not, their claim is "heretical and blasphemous."

Let us never hesitate to acknowledge it—any where and every where to acknowledge it—and before all people mourn over it. Let us, who need not to bear the heavy burden and live in the dark cloud of this responsibility, never, either in brotherly love, national vanity, or subjection to insolence, fear to declare, that, in the misdirection of power by our slaveholders, they are false to the basis of our Union and blasphemous to the Father who, equally and with equal freedom, created all men. Would that they might see, too, that while they continue to manifest before the world, in their legislation upon it, no other than mean, sordid, short-sighted, and barbarian purposes, they must complain, threaten, expostulate, and compromise in vain. If we drive back the truth of God, we must expect ever-recurring, irrestrainable, irresistible *reaction.* The law of God in our hearts binds us in fidelity to the *principles* of the Constitution. They are not to be found in "Abolitionism," nor are they to be found—oh! remember it, brothers, and forgive these few words—in *hopeless, dawnless, unredeeming* slavery. (Ibid., p. 106.)

11. Chapter 8 of volume 2 of *Walks and Talks* contained a description of the model prison at Pentonville, outside London. Chapter 10 consisted of a long discussion, during a stagecoach ride, between Olmsted, an Englishman and a Frenchman about the national characteristics of their countries.

New-York Daily Times, February 16, 1853[1]

THE SOUTH.

LETTERS ON THE PRODUCTIONS, INDUSTRY AND RESOURCES OF THE SLAVE STATES.

NUMBER ONE.

Special Correspondence of the New-York Daily Times

Introduction—from New-York to Washington—Agriculture in the District and Neighboring Country—New England Emigration to Fairfax—Good Effects of it—From Washington to Richmond, Va.—Aspect of the Country—A Prairie Farmer's View of it—Appearance of the People—Style of Planters' Houses—Social Position of Slaves.

This letter will be the first of a series, in which, while travelling at the South, I propose to give you such minutes of the observations that I make as shall seem to me indicative of the wealth and intelligence of the districts through which I pass; of the elements of happiness possessed by their inhabitants; and of the degree in which they are made available. More especially I wish to examine and describe their agricultural character and the manner of the husbandry under which are produced those great staples, the annual magnitude and value of which have become a subject, in our day, of world-wide interest and of vital consequence to our manufactures and commerce.

No man can write of the South and put Slavery entirely in the background. I wish to see for myself, and shall endeavor to report with candor and fidelity, to you, the ordinary condition of the laborers of the South, with respect to material comfort and moral and intellectual happiness. I am disposed to treat the subject with kindness, frankness and candor, and I trust in so doing I may be able to encourage the conviction that it is only in the justice, good sense, and Christian sentiment of the people of the South, that the evils of Slavery will find their end.

I shall endeavor to ascertain the general disposition and purposes of our Southern fellow-citizens with regard to Slavery, and shall look for any indications of a changing character, advance or otherwise, in civilization, religion and intelligence, of the African race under the influence of the circumstances in which it exists at the South. I shall also study as far as I am able, the economical aspect of Slavery, and learn what degree of adaptability is exhibited by the negro for other than agricultural and domestic drudgery.

Twelve hours of travel over exceedingly mismanaged railroads, changing cars four times; a few miles by omnibus, and a few more of horse-draft; no chance to dine or sup, only to snatch a poor mouthful in a ferryboat; left, nevertheless, half an hour at one point, with no one to direct you or explain the delay; obliged to run at another to save your passage; no fires in New-Jersey; roasting ones in Maryland;—so you come from the metropolis to the capital of the United States. Fares high, and speed low. It is too shameful to be passed without grumbling.

In the vicinity of the District of Columbia, the staple crop is tobacco; the land much of the same character, and cultivated most miserably on the same system as has long prevailed in the tobacco districts of the Middle States,

JOURNEY THROUGH THE UPPER SOUTH: 1852–1853

CHARLES BENEDICT CALVERT'S RIVERSDALE

and which I shall describe in Virginia. Wheat culture has lately become profitable by the aid of guano, a very large amount of which has been used this season. The "three crop" system of Virginia is followed where tobacco is not cultivated: maize, wheat and clover (*rest,* or pasture) in constant succession, the fertility of the soil being sustained by dung applied to the hoed crop, and lime, plaster, and of late, guano, to the wheat. The clover is sometimes allowed to remain two years, and the whole crop of the second year plowed in. This, with liming or marling, (the marl being mainly fossil sea-shells, containing about forty per cent. carbonate of lime), is an improving course. On one farm that I visited,[2] there was a large dairy-stock, supplying milk to Washington City, and on this turnips (ruta baga and hybrids) were largely cultivated. The crop of this year was estimated to be 30,000 bushels, grown on about 33 acres. They were sown from the 15th to 25th of July, by drill barrow, flat, the soil enriched by dung and guano. The stock of this farm was excellent, a large proportion being thoroughbred Short-horns, with imported Ayrshires and Alderneys, and some small black and white "Natives."

What the ordinary stock of the region is may be judged on market day at Washington; the most miserable, dwarfish, ugly, lean kine that I ever saw. I do not believe all the Northern States could produce such a scurvy drove. Market day in Washington (it occurs three times a week) is very amusing to the stranger. The horses are as bad as the cattle, and the human stock (negroes) is, if possible, worse than either. I saw but one pair of horses out of over a hundred together, that did not appear to have been foundered or maimed.

There is a good story told by a member of Congress from Pennsylvania, to show the style in which business is often done in these parts. An old negro woman called at his door, having a fine turkey for sale. Struck with her fatigued appearance, he asked her how far she had come, and learned that she had been

THE NEW STABLE AT RIVERSDALE

three days and nights on the road. "Old massa" was in need of some money, and having nothing else convenient to sell, she had been dispatched on foot with the turkey to Washington, to "raise" it for him.[3]

The number of slaves in Maryland has slightly increased during the last ten years. A great many are annually sold out of the State, the purchasers being mainly Jews, who take them first to Richmond, Virginia, and after-wards to New-Orleans. There are many free negroes, and I have heard complaints of kidnappers. One gentleman told me that many more free boys were sent South and made slaves in his District, than there were of slaves that escaped to the free States. In the District of Columbia the *Slave-trade* no longer exists,[4] and the number of slaves has decreased twenty-five per cent. during the last ten years. White servants are employed at some of the hotels, and Irishmen are largely engaged on public works, and considerably in agriculture. At one plantation where I found them digging drains,[5] when I asked the proprietor why he did not employ them more, he asserted that slave-labor was much cheaper, except for certain operations. His main objection to the Irish was, that they would not perform their work faithfully, and that they cheated and lied to him. He thought better of Germans, but thought there was no chance of any other laborers coming in competition with slaves for general agricultural purposes. He was a large hereditory slave-owner. A few German emigrants have settled in Maryland during the last ten years, and are doing very well as farmers.

In Fairfax, the nearest county of Virginia to Washington, a large number of Northern farmers have latterly settled, and are reported to be successful and well satisfied. The Virginians everywhere give a hearty welcome to

Northern immigrants. I understand that these Northern men seldom purchase slaves, but frequently hire them. They are usually small farmers, occupying from fifty to one hundred and fifty acres of land, and tilling it mainly by their own labor and that of their families, in the old New-England way. They are said to have greatly improved the general character of the county, and on this point the following evidence is interesting.

"In appearance the county is so changed in many parts, that a traveler who passed over it ten years ago, would not now recognize it. Thousands and thousands of acres, which had been cultivated in tobacco by the former proprietors, would not pay the cost, and were abandoned as worthless, and became covered with a wilderness of pines. These lands have been purchased by Northern emigrants; the large tracts divided and subdivided, and cleared of pines; and neat farm houses and barns, with smiling fields of grain and grass in the season, salute the delighted gaze of the beholder. Ten years ago, it was a mooted question whether Fairfax lands could be made productive; and if so, would they pay the cost? This problem has been satisfactorily solved by many, and in consequence of the above altered state of things, *school houses and churches have doubled in number.*"—*Report to Com. of Patents,* 1852.[6]

There is one cotton factory in the District of Columbia employing one hundred and fifty hands, male and female; a small foundry; a distillery; and two tanneries—all not giving occupation to fifty men; less than two hundred altogether, out of a resident population of nearly 150,000, being engaged in manufactures. Very few of the remainder are engaged in *producing* occupations.

Leaving Washington at day-light, and breakfasting on the boat as she passed Mount Vernon, I took the cars at Acquia Creek[7] for Richmond, Virginia. Flat rail; distance 75 miles; time, 5½ hours (13 miles an hour); fare, $3.50; 4⅔ cents, a mile. Boat makes 55 miles in 3½ hours, including two stoppages; (12½ miles an hour); fare $2.00; (3.6 cents a mile.)

The country seen by the traveler on the route, is not, I believe, a fair specimen of this part of Virginia. Most of it is wet, swampy; pine and white and red oak forest, now and then an old "clearing;" the fields grown over with thin, dry, coarse grass, young gum trees, pines and sassafras. Rotting log-cabins that you can see the light through the chinks of, are scattered around a shabby board-house without a tree or a bit of grass near it; swine, and black and white children, lounge about; and perhaps a white and a black woman's face are thrust together out at the door, to stare at the train. The only sign of a *production* other than the little live stock, is to be found in the long piles of cord-wood, which line the rail-road.

There will be occasionally a few miles of a more cultivated district. The soil looks poor and there is much water standing in it. Considerable breadths of it are in wheat, which is usually well put in, in narrow bands or *beds,* and carefully water-furrowed; contrasting much with all the other husbandry and indicating that it has been of late a sufficiently profitable crop to rouse some enterprise and skill. This is due to guano. The stubble of maize, three or four feet high, it having been cut above the ear for fodder, is the only sign of any other crop that you can find, except very rarely a small patch of sweet potato ridges. Much the larger share of the fields are "resting" and covered with a tall, dry, coarse and worthless grass, called *broomsedge*. In about three miles of one of the best tracts we passed, I judged there were the proportions of three hundred "at rest"; one hundred, wheat; and twenty, maize.

The planter's house is usually a plain, two-story, clap-boarded building, fifty feet long, and twenty wide, divided in its length by a hall, against each outside door of which is a broad porch. It is more commonly shaded by a few old white-oak trees, left from the original forest growth. Scattering about it, without much order, are from two to a dozen log-cabins for the negroes. The latter you will see, men and women, loading and carting maize to the corn-crib, or "grubbing" the sassafras bushes with great awkward hoes and clumsy axes, loaded with much unnecessary weight of iron. At every cross-road and stopping-place you see plenty of them with mules and long heavy wagons, and with crownless or brimless hats, and rags and grins and incomprehensible outcries to the cattle; all but for their dark, inexpressive faces, exactly like the poorest Irish peasantry. Their masters, you see, too, occasionally, on horseback (very good blood-like horses), or they leave the seat by the side of you, carrying out a pair of saddlebags, and mount a horse that a black boy has brought for them. At twenty such country stations I did not see a spring-carriage.

Many of the planters' mansions are much finer than those I have described. You see these at a distance on the most elevated ground in the vicinity, with more or less of a grove about them and the "negro quarters" at some distance; log huts as before but regularly placed in rows. The house may be of brick and quite large with a verandah, and long low buildings stretching out from it, somewhat after the fashion of the Washington mansion at Mount Vernon; more commonly they are in a compact heavy style, not in particularly bad taste, but never elegant and usually failing in neatness and more or less needing repairs.

We passed in sight of one tannery and two or three saw mills, and at Fredericksburg through the streets of a rather busy, shabbily built town; but altogether the country showed less signs of an active and prospering people, in the distance passed over, than any other I have ever journeyed through either in the old or new world. A coarse rough looking old man sat beside me, and wishing to obtain some information, I asked him if he was acquainted with the country. "No I ain't—don't look very fer*tile*, does it?"

"It does not indeed."

"I've heerd 'em say out West, that old Virginny was the mother o' statesmen—reckon she must be about done, eh? This ere's about the *barrenest* look for a mother, ever I see."

At a way-station a lady entered the car with a family behind her. She looked about, as if seeking a place where they could get together, and I rose and suggested to a gentleman on the next seat that by both of us moving we might

JOURNEY THROUGH THE UPPER SOUTH: 1852-1853

leave her four seats, and offering her my place withdrew; she accepted it without thanking me, and immediately installed in it a great negro-woman, and seated the rest of her party near her. There was a young white girl, probably her daughter, and a bright and very pretty, nearly white, mulatto girl of about the same age; the latter was dressed as expensively, and appeared every way as well as the former, and they talked and laughed together, as if on terms of entire equality and perfect familiarity. Afterwards I noticed that they were all four eating something out of the same paper. Many people at the North would have been indignant or "disgusted" with such proceedings, but they excited no attention here.

YEOMAN.

1. In *Seaboard Slave States*, Olmsted described the period dealt with in this letter in the form of a journal dated December 10, 14 and 16. Presumably he wrote this letter in its basic form at about that time (*SSS*, pp. 1-19).
2. This, the first farm operated by slave labor that Olmsted visited in the South, was Riversdale in Prince George's County, Maryland, owned by Charles Benedict Calvert (1808-1864). Olmsted did not disclose the name of the farm or of its owner, whom he called "Mr. C." in both this letter and in the longer account in *Seaboard Slave States*, but his description fits the available information about both Calvert and Riversdale.

   Olmsted described "Mr. C." as "a large hereditary owner of slaves": Calvert owned 55 slaves in 1850; his father had owned 52 slaves in 1820, while his grandmother Elizabeth, daughter of Charles, fifth Lord Baltimore, had owned 228 in 1790. Olmsted described "Mr. C." as being engaged in agricultural experimentation and the promotion of agricultural reform: Calvert was a nationally important leader in agricultural reform and the leading figure in the founding (on one of his farms) of the Maryland College of Agriculture. The following characteristics were shared by Riversdale and the farm Olmsted visited: an extent of two thousand acres; considerable woodland; bottom lands that were underdrained by v-shaped drains formed by joining two planks together; considerable use of wire fences; wheat and hay as the principal cash crops; extensive cultivation of rutabagas for cattle feed; extensive application of guano as fertilizer; a large herd of milk cows consisting of Durhams ("Short horns"), Alderneys and Ayrshires; and a steam-powered saw mill.

   Charles Benedict Calvert salted the rutabagas that he fed his cows, in order to prevent the milk from tasting of turnip. Olmsted said that "Mr. C." followed this practice, and thought it was an "original discovery" of his. Calvert also believed that milk from Alderney cows made the best butter—a view expressed to Olmsted by "Mr. C."

   The most telling common feature of Riversdale and the farm that Olmsted visited was what he described as a new stable that was "most admirably contrived for convenience, labor-saving, and economy of space," and of which descriptions and illustrations had appeared (by 1856) in several agricultural journals. Calvert constructed at Riversdale a two-story octagonal cow barn one hundred feet in diameter with space for over a hundred cows. It made efficient use of space, had stanchions of innovative design and provided novel means for feeding the cows and disposing of liquid manure. He first described the barn in an article in the *American Farmer* of June 1854. The article was then reprinted in other agricultural journals, along with a plan and views of the structure.

   Olmsted also noted of "Mr. C." that his farm, "from its vicinity to Washington, and its excellent management, as well as from the hospitable habits of its owners, has a national reputation." The Calverts often entertained prominent politicians and visitors to Washington, and Henry Clay was a close friend and frequent visitor. Olmsted described the mansion itself as being a quarter-mile from the highroad and built of brick, and he added that "as seen through the surrounding trees," it had "somewhat the look of an old French chateau." All elements of this description fit the Riversdale mansion, whose central portion was a modified replica of the

Chateau du Mick near Antwerp, Belgium, the residence of Henry Joseph, Baron de Stier, who built Riversdale after fleeing Belgium at the time of the French invasion in 1794. The supposition that Charles Benedict Calvert and "Mr. C." were the same person is supported by a reference in a letter from Olmsted to the sanitary engineer George E. Waring, Jr., of July 19, 1874. Explaining why he planned to prepare the soil of the U.S. Capitol grounds by working peat into the subsoil separately from the topsoil, he wrote: "I work the subsoil independently because Calvert, who is a very intelligent and scientific farmer with large capital and varied experience, told me that after repeated trials of bringing up subsoil both moderately and thoroughly with lime and manure, a few miles from Washington, he had never any but bad results." Presumably, this is a reference to Olmsted's visit to Riversdale in December 1852 (*DAB*; *SSS*, pp. 5–11; Katherine Scarborough, *Homes of the Cavaliers* [New York, 1930], pp. 73–81, 86; Eugenia Calvert Holland, "Riversdale, The Stier-Calvert Home," *Maryland Historical Magazine* 45, no. 4 [Dec. 1950]: 271–93; "Visit to Riversdale," *American Farmer*, 4th ser. 4, no. 2 [Aug. 1848]: 52–55; "Prize Essay on Farm Buildings," ibid. 9, no. 11 [May 1854]: 352; Charles B. Calvert, "Essay on Farm Buildings," ibid., no. 12 [June 1854], pp. 369–71; "Plan of Farm Buildings for Animals," *Country Gentleman* 4, no. 7 [Aug. 17, 1854]: 108–9; "Riversdale," ibid. 10, no. 10 [Sept. 3, 1857]: 161–62; "Editorial Correspondence—II," ibid. 11, no. 22 [June 3, 1858]: 353; "Editorial Correspondence—III," ibid., no. 23 [June 10, 1858], pp. 361–62).

3. The *New-York Daily Times* mistakenly printed this phrase as "to 'guise' it for him." In *Seaboard Slave States*, Olmsted called the man who told this anecdote "Mr. F.," indicating that he might have been Thomas B. Florence, a Democratic congressman from Philadelphia, or Henry M. Fuller, a Whig from Wilkes-Barre (FLO to CLB, Feb. 23, 1853, below; *SSS*, p. 12; *BDAC*, p. 238).

4. The Compromise of 1850 outlawed the slave trade in the District of Columbia as of January 1, 1851 (Henry Steele Commager, ed., *Documents of American History*, 9th ed. [New York, 1973], no. 174).

5. Charles Benedict Calvert's farm Riversdale (see *SSS*, pp. 10–11).

6. Olmsted quotes here from a letter dated February 20, 1852, from Thomas Crux of Fairfax, Virginia, to Thomas Ewbank, the U.S. Commissioner of Patents. The italics in the quotation are Olmsted's (U.S., Patent Office, *Report of the Commissioner of Patents for the Year 1851*, H.R. Exec. Doc. no. 102, 32d Cong., 1st sess., 1851–52, pp. 274–75; see also Richard H. Abbott, "Yankee Farmers in Northern Virginia, 1840–1860," *Virginia Magazine of History and Biography* 76, no. 1 [Jan. 1968]: 56–63).

7. Acquia Creek, on the Potomac River forty-five miles below Washington, was the railhead of the Richmond, Fredericksburg and Potomac Railroad.

To Charles Loring Brace

Richmond, Virginia
Thursday, 22nd December [1852]

Dear C.,

I spent the night with a pair of Friends who both cultivate farms with free labor,[1] and got much valuable matter from them. I shall be able to show conclusively, I think, that free labor is cheaper than slave (I have a two page letter on it now).[2] The difficulty only consists in the want of hands (white) and the bad effect of slave faithlessness, corrupting them.

I told Thomas Hayes, my old foreman, I would try to procure him a place here. The younger Quaker may want him after New Year's. If he does, he will write you and you must find Thomas. If at the island before, ask if Thomas is there; see him and if he will be prepared to come.

They are very good people. The place is healthy and there are no Negroes, but two Irishmen & two Irishwomen in the family. He will pay him $120.00 a year & board. It is five miles only from Richmond, and a wagon goes in every morning—plenty of Catholic churches in R. Distance from New York, 21 hours by rail, no time by telegraph. But he will best come by sea, which by steamer will take I suppose 2 days. Probably cost 6 or 7 dollars by steamer & 2 or 3 by sailing vessel. Business of the farm; wheat & hay growing, and a milk dairy. I think it a first rate place and advise him to come at once.

I told friends Crenshaw that whenever they or anyone else who was disposed to make trial of free labor wanted hands, male or female, to write to you, and you or Pease[3] would be glad to find some for them. There are no better people; kind, charitable, sensible and earnest.

I can not see my way out of Virginia. I think I shall make seven letters out of her.[4] Don't see how I can do the subject justice with less. It takes much more time to write and study than I had anticipated. More a great deal than to observe. I could spend a week more in Richmond, I think, profitably, but shall try to cut and get further South in a day or two.

I would rather give $50 than go to Dismal Swamp.[5] It disarranges everything and takes time. I doubt if I can get so far as New Orleans, but may find as I get south that thorough study of one district saves much with another & I shall cover my ground faster. (Over to 4th [page])

I want you to call at Putnam's and leave the enclosed memo. Or give it to your chum Mr. (what *is* his name?) to send for my Friend, copy Walks & Talks by next parcel they are sending to Adolphus Morris, Bookseller.[6]

I shall write to him that you have done so.

Give me some other address than Tribune Office.[7]

Fog, damp, drizzle. Rheumatism. Not very well, but can write all day.

Yours

Fred.

Olmsted misdated this letter: December 22, 1852, was a Wednesday. He often made such errors in dating letters while traveling, and seems usually to have given the correct day of the week and the wrong day of the month. He should probably have dated this letter Thursday, December 23, 1852.

1. The Quakers Nathaniel Chapman Crenshaw (d. 1866) and his son John Bacon Crenshaw (1820–1889). The elder Crenshaw had owned slaves, but after his conversion to the Quaker faith he freed them and persuaded some other slaveholders to do likewise. His farm, Rocouncy, was in Henrico County, Virginia, six miles north of Richmond. John Bacon Crenshaw took up a farm nearby in 1846, and in 1852 he set up a dairy and sold milk to hotels and restaurants in Richmond. The next year he helped promote construction of a plank road between Richmond and the neighborhood of Rocouncy. Olmsted's description of "A Free-Labor Farm" in "The South" number 4 and in *Seaboard Slave States*, pages 94–101, apparently deals with his visit to Rocouncy (*NYDT*, March 4, 1853; Margaret E. Crenshaw, "John Bacon Crenshaw," in Soci-

ety of Friends, Philadelphia Yearly Meeting, Book Committee, *Quaker Biographies, Series 2. Brief Biographical Sketches Concerning Certain Members of the Religious Society of Friends* . . . , 5 vols. [Philadelpha, 1917–192?], 3: 167–71; [James P. P. Bell], *Our Quaker Friends of ye Olden Time* . . . [Lynchburg, Va., 1905], pp. 7, 266).
2. This letter on the expensiveness of slave labor probably comprises part of "The South" number 7 (*NYDT,* March 17, 1853).
3. Lewis Morris Pease (1818–1897), the former head of the Five Points House of Industry in New York, with whom Brace worked for a time before beginning his career with the Children's Aid Society (*Monthly Record of the Five Points House of Industry* 41, no. 3 [July 1897]: 33–34; *Life of Brace,* p. 153).
4. Olmsted devoted twice as many letters to the state of Virginia as he anticipated at this time. His first fourteen letters to the *Times* all dealt with the subject.
5. The Great Dismal Swamp in southeastern Virginia and northeastern North Carolina. Olmsted had apparently promised Harriet Beecher Stowe that he would visit the area and send her descriptions of it (see FLO to JO, Jan. 10, 1853, below).
6. Olmsted wanted to have a copy of his book *Walks and Talks* (published by G. P. Putnam & Co. of New York) sent to John Bacon Crenshaw through the Richmond bookseller Adolphus Morris. Brace's friend at Putnam's was Joshua A. Dix, later Olmsted's partner in the publishing firm of Dix, Edwards & Company (*The Richmond Directory and Business Advertiser, for 1852. by Wm. L. Montague, Number Two* . . . [Richmond, Va., 1852], p. 91; FLO to JO, May 19, 1853).
7. That is, the office of the *New York Tribune,* to which Olmsted was apparently reluctant to send letters destined for the rival *New-York Daily Times.*

New-York Daily Times, February 19, 1853[1]

THE SOUTH.

LETTERS ON THE PRODUCTIONS, INDUSTRY AND RESOURCES OF THE SLAVE STATES.

NUMBER TWO.

Special Correspondence of the New-York Daily Times

The City of Richmond—Personal Appearance and Character of the Virginians—Manufactures and Commerce—Competition with New-York—Notes of a Visit to a James River Farm—Soils—Course of Cropping—Forage in Virginia—Manures—Guano—Value of Guano as an Agent in Restoring Fertility to Exhausted Soils—The Horse Reapers—Claim of the Scotch for Precedence in Their Invention—Slaves—Their Character, Condition and Treatment—Overseers—Their General Bad Character—Comparison of Slave and Free Labor.

Richmond, the capital city of Virginia, is very picturesquely situated upon and among several hills, and viewed from the adjacent high ground, through the bituminous smoke it creates, reminds the traveler of Edinburgh. It is generally well built, but, with the exception of a few modern mansions, entirely without elegance. The streets are unpaved, and but a few of them are provided with sidewalks other than of gravel. The city is well lighted with gas, and supplied with water by an aqueduct. The population is about 28,000. The Capitol, standing on elevated ground, so that as you approach the city you see it well above the surrounding roofs, has a very imposing appearance. It is modeled after the *Maison Quarrée* of Nismes,[2] and like most public edifices copied from the ancients, is very inconvenient in its interior arrangements. There is a statue of Washington, by Houdon, a French sculptor, in the Rotunda, which was obtained by Mr. Jefferson in Paris.[3] The grounds about the Capitol are naturally admirable, and have lately been improved with neatness and taste. A fine monument, to be surmounted by an equestrian statue of Washington, by Crawford,[4] is now building in them. Their beauty and interest would be greatly increased if some of the fine native trees and shrubs of Virginia, particularly the holly and the evergreen magnolias, were planted in them. I noticed these, as well as the Irish and palmated ivy, showing great vigor and beauty, in the private gardens of the town. On some high, sterile lands, of which there are several thousand acres, *uninclosed and uncultivated,* near the city, I saw a group of exceedingly beautiful trees, having the lively green and all the lightness, gracefulness and beauty of foliage in the Winter of the finest deciduous trees. I could not believe, until I came near them, that they were what I found them to be, our common red cedar. I have before observed that the beauty of this tree was greatly affected by the soil it stood in; in certain localities, on the Hudson River for instance, and in the lower part of New-Jersey, it grows in a perfectly dense, conical, cypress-like form. These, on the other hand, were square-headed, dense, flattened at the top, like the cedar of Lebanon, and with a light, graceful, slightly drooping spray, wherever they cut the light. They stood in *gravel;* small quartz gravel, slightly bound with red clay. The red cedar is very much more beautiful here generally than I have often observed it at the North, and probably enjoys the climate more.

    The Legislature was in session, and the city filled with a respectable representation of the whole State. The hotel that I stayed at was a very excellent one, hardly excelled in the country; the proprietor had served an apprenticeship at the North. I went to the theatre one night while those delightful pets, the "Bateman children,"[5] were performing. Long before the curtain rose every seat was occupied. I have rarely seen a better looking assembly, or one in which there was so large a proportion of fine, *tall,* spirited men and beautiful, cultivated-looking women. The men, however, were greatly deficient in robustness, and the women in stateliness and grace, so that they had by no means an aristocratic or *high-bred* air. Everybody in Richmond seemed to be always in *high dress.* You would meet ladies early of a drizzly day, creeping along their muddy streets in light silk dresses and satin hats; and never a gentleman seemed to relieve himself of the close-fitting, shiny, black, full evening suit, and indulge in the luxury of a loose morning coat. Their manners, too, seemed to me to partake of the same character. I acknowledge I found it otherwise in the country. The Virginia gentleman on his plantation drops town restraints, and enjoys a rough shooting-jacket life. Here you find him, for all the world like an English squire, independent, wayward, extravagant, truth-speaking, hearty and frank, though holding hard to some ceremony; sport-loving, and affecting roughness, but really courteous, simple minded, and hospitable to all men and all things that come well introduced or respectably connected.[6]

There is probably no part of the world where great wealth confers so little rank, or is attended with so few advantages over a moderate competency; nevertheless wealth is much concentrated in Virginia, and while there is an immense poverty-stricken community, there are also many very great estates. One young gentleman was pointed out to me as having an annual income of $50,000, entirely from landed property. I remarked that I should think he would dispose of some of it and invest in other ways; as agricultural property, beyond what a man can personally superintend, is rarely profitable. "On the contrary he is constantly buying new plantations to stock with the natural increase of his niggers." Another, I was told, was the owner of half a dozen parks, all stocked with deer, in different parts of the State.

Richmond is now rapidly increasing and greatly-prospering commercially. It is the market for a great wheat, tobacco and maize-producing country, which is fast being brought closer to it and much extending by the canals and railroads running west and southwest, and which will soon be pushed through the blue ridge to the valleys of the Ohio and the Tennessee, with the competing lines from Boston, New-York, Philadelphia, Baltimore, Charleston and Savannah for the produce of the West. It is situated at the Falls of the James River, which give it great manufacturing capabilities, and at the head of navigation on that river for sea-going vessels drawing not over ten feet water. The river channel is narrow and crooked, however, and much injured by bars that a comparatively small sum would remove. Virginia, with an admirable spunk, has, until lately, refused, from laziness or from feebleness to act about this little job for herself, or from her peculiar political notions to ask, or allow the right of, the Federal Government to do it for the good of the nation. An appropriation of $40,000 was made by the last Congress for it, and operations are about commencing, which she shows no disposition at present to interrupt. The commerce of Richmond, by the sea, is trifling; principally with New-York, where nearly all the materials of her trade, whether of export or import, are transshipped. A line of steamers is now running regularly between the two ports.

The flouring mills of Richmond are among the largest in the world, perhaps the largest. Those of one house, I was told, are capable of turning out 1,000 barrels of flour a day. The whole amount of flour made here was, in 1850, 336,120 barrels. Very large new mills are now building.

Tobacco manufacturing is also a very large, extensive business. I am not able to give the amount of it, but it is a mere trifle compared with the amount of tobacco manufactured elsewhere, at the North and in Europe, from the raw leaf that is collected and shipped at this market.

There are also extensive distilleries, one or two paper mills, &c.

There are several large Cotton manufactories. A stockholder in one of these told me, that although manufactories at the East were now paying well that had the same sort of machinery, made similar goods, and that paid about the same rates of wages, *these* were not. I asked him if he could explain the cause; he answered: "I suppose it must be want of good management." The cotton used here is mainly produced in the State; some comes up by railroad from North Carolina. It must cost less than to the Eastern manufacturer.

In the Cotton factories the hands employed are white, mainly women; and are paid by the piece at the same rates as in New-England, or a little lower. In the tobacco factories, blacks, both slaves and free, are engaged. They are also paid according to their expertness and activity, earning from fifty cents to two dollars a day.

The water power is unlimited and most convenient.

Bituminous coal is plentifully supplied from mines near the city. It is the same coal that is used in all our Eastern cities for gas manufacture and is retailed at 12½ cents a bushel—a bushel weighing from 70 to 90 lbs. Anthracite comes by sea from Philadelphia. Pine and oak wood $2.50 per cord, or any amount of either, I suppose, for little more than the expense of cutting and hauling a dozen miles. Staple articles of food, the produce of the country, 16 per cent. cheaper than in New-England. Anything foreign, and most manufactured articles, 10 per cent. above Eastern prices. The climate is represented by Northern men and Europeans to be agreeable, but little if any greater extremes of heat than at New-York in Summer, and much milder in Winter. The mean temperature in July and August is about 80° Fahrenheit, and in January, 44°. The city is mainly built on elevated ground and has a porous and dry foundation. It is also well supplied with water. Its health statistics, as might be expected, compare favorably with those of other cities. The deaths are 1 in 70 of the population, while in Philadelphia they are 1 in 45; Boston, 1 in 40; Charleston, 1 in 36; Liverpool, 1 in 19.

Excepting at New-York, I do not know of a situation in the Northern States having natural advantages for manufacturing purposes and trade equal to these. There are, however, no advantages for foreign commerce. The citizens talk of it much as if there were, and they have proposed, by aid of Government, to establish a line of steamers to Europe; but in the present era of ocean conveyance, it is simply absurd. Glasgow is much better situated for foreign commerce, but has not, by most energetic and persevering attempts, succeeded in becoming a port of any consequence to the world beyond Great Britain. She has been obliged to give it up to Liverpool. She can build steamers and ships for other ports, but never can sail them profitably herself. But Richmond has a hundred times the advantages of New-York or of Glasgow, or of any Northern or European city for manufacturing, much greater than some of the largest in the world for inland and domestic commerce. Glasgow has none to compare with her, and yet Glasgow is running neck and neck with New-York in population and wealth and beating her in the ratio of her increase.

Will you not stop quarreling with New-York for "stealing your legitimate trade" and give a moment's thought to this, Virginians?

This morning I visited a farm, some account of which will give you a good idea of the more advanced style of agriculture in Eastern Virginia. It is situated on the bank of James' River, and has ready access by water or land-carriage to the city of Richmond. The soil of the greater part, is a red, plastic clay—loam of a medium or low fertility, with a large intermixture of small quartz pebbles. On the river bank is a tract of low alluvial land, varying from an eighth to a quarter of a mile in breadth. The soil of this is a sandy loam of the very finest quality in every respect, and it has been discovered in some places to be over ten feet in thickness; at which depth the sound trunk of a white oak has been found, showing it to be a recent deposit. I was assured that good crops of corn, wheat and clover had been taken from it, without its giving any indications of "wearing out," although no manure, except an occasional dressing of lime, had been returned to it; for forty years a corn-crop of 50 bushels an acre had been grown, without manure except the plowed-in clover upon it, this year.

The rotation, corn, wheat, and clover two years, is followed on both upland and lowland, herd's grass (red-top of New-York) sometimes taking the place of the clover, or grown with it, and mowed for hay for a series of years.

Hay always brings a high price in Richmond, and is usually shipped to that market from the eastward. This year, however, it is but a trifle above New-York prices, and the whole supply is drawn from this vicinity.

Oats in the straw are brought in considerable quantity to Richmond for horse feed, from the surrounding country. It is often pressed in bales like hay, and sells for about the same price. Thus at present, Hay (Northern bale) is $1.25 to $1.50; Oats in straw the same; while Oats, clean, (threshed) are 40¢ to 50¢. Wheat straw, 75¢; Corn 56¢ to 70¢; "Shucks," the sheaths of the ears of Maize, are also sold here for horse-feed, generally at half the price of Northern Hay, which is evidently below their comparative value.

Lime is used largely, being applied at the wheat-sowing, at the rate of 25 to 50 bushels the acre. The lime for this is stone-lime, *bought at Haverstraw, New-York,* costing, delivered here, 7¼¢ to 7½¢ a bushel.

Plaster (gypsum) has been tried with little or no profit.

Dung is largely accumulated from the farmstock, and is applied to the corn-crop.

Guano is largely used. After trying greater and less quantities, the proprietor arrived at the conclusion that 200 lbs. the acre was the most profitable. It is now applied at that rate to all the wheat, and is also used for turnips. For corn it was not thought of much value; the greatest advantage had been obtained by applying it to the poorest land of the farm, some of which was of so small fertility and at such a distance from the cattle quarters and the river, that it could not be profitably cultivated, and had been at waste for many years. Two hundred weight of Peruvian Guano to the acre brought 15 bushels of wheat; and a good crop of clover was perfectly sure to follow, by which the permanent improvement of the soil could be secured. This the proprietor esteemed to be the greatest benefit he derived from Guano, and he was pushing a regular plan for bringing all his more sterile upland into the system of convertible husbandry by its aid.

This plan is, to prepare the ground by fallowing for wheat, spread 200 pounds Guano broadcast, on the harrowed surface, and turn it under as closely as possible after the sowers, with a two-shovel plow (a sort of large two-shared cultivator), the wheat either being sowed and covered with the guano or immediately afterwards drilled-in with a horse-machine. In the Spring clover is sown. After the wheat is harvested, the clover is allowed to grow, without being pastured or mown, for twelve months. The ground is then limed, clover plowed in, and in October again guanoed 200 cwt. to the acre, and wheat sowed, with clover to follow. The clover may be pastured the following year, but in the year succeeding that, it is allowed to grow unchecked until August, when it is plowed in, the ground again limed, guanoed, and wheat sowed with herd's-grass (red-top) and clover, which is to remain for mowing and pasture as long as the ground will profitably sustain it. The lime is not allowed to come in contact with the guano.

A horse-drill was used for wheat-sowing, and Hussey's reaper for harvesting it; the proprietor preferring it to McCormick's, on account of its greater strength and durability.[7] He had used both, and found McCormick's often occasioned delays at harvest from getting out of order. I have heard a similar report from others, and found Hussey's generally in use on the larger plantations. I will say here, that the Scotch claim of precedence in the invention of Horse Reapers is, without doubt, correct. I understand there is a Scotchman in Richmond, who states that he saw Bell's Reaper in operation in that country many years ago. I myself saw a model of a Horse Reaper in Scotland the year before the Great Fair.[8] It is nevertheless no doubt true, that both the inventions of Hussey and McCormick, were original, and that the credit of first bringing horse-power into extensive practical operation in cutting wheat, both in this country and in Great Britain, belongs to them.

The labor of this farm was entirely performed by slaves. Their "quarters" lined the approach road to the mansion, and were well-made, comfortable log cabins, about thirty feet long by twenty wide, and eight feet tall, with a high loft and shingle roof; each divided in the middle, and occupied by two families, having a brick chimney outside the wall at each end. There were square windows, closed by wooden ports, having a single pane of glass in the centre. The house servants were neatly dressed, but the field hands wore very coarse and ragged garments.

I was in company with the proprietor at least three hours, and I don't think there were ten consecutive minutes of that time uninterrupted by some of the slaves requiring his direction or assistance. He was obliged to leave the dinner-table three times. Truly remarked he, "A farmer's life here is no sinecure."

He was a very generous-minded, good-hearted man, as was indicated, among other ways, by his interest in the efforts to introduce Christianity among the degraded poor of New-York. When there, he had visited the Five Points, and his admiration and respect for Mr. Pease, the missionary whose exceedingly sensible and noble labors have been frequently the subject of commendation in your paper,[9] was almost unbounded. "I consider that man a hero," said he, "worthy to rank among the great and brave men of the world." With regard to Slavery, he said, "I only wish you philanthropists could contrive any way to relieve us of it. But what can we do? The free blacks are, almost all—there are some exceptions—here, and at the North, as well, miserable vagabonds, drunken, vicious, worse off, I candidly believe, than those in slavery. I am satisfied, too, that our slaves *in Virginia* are in a happier condition than most of the poor laborers of the North, certainly than those of England, or almost any other Christian country. I am not sure that free labor would not be more profitable; the slaves are wasteful, careless, and in various ways subject me to provoking losses.

"This is a hard life. You see how constantly I am called on, often at night as well as day. I did not sleep a wink last night till near morning; my health is failing and my wife is feeble, but I cannot rid myself of it. I cannot trust an overseer. I had one, and paid him four hundred dollars a year, and I had almost as much work and anxiety in looking after him as in overseeing for myself."

I asked what was the general character of the overseers. "They are the curse of the country, the worst men in our community, Sir. But the other day, I had another sort of one offer, a fellow like a dancing master, with kid gloves and wristbands turned neatly over his sleeves, and all so nice that I almost was ashamed to talk to him in my old coat and slouch hat; half a bushel of recommendations, too, he had with him. Well, he was not the man for me; not half the gentleman, with all his airs, that Ned, here," (a black boy) "is."

Afterwards he said to me of the slaves: "Oh, they are interesting creatures, Sir, and, with all their faults, have many beautiful traits. I can't help being attached to them, and I am sure they love us." I did not doubt it; his manner towards them was parental—familiar and kind; and they came to him like children who have been given some task, and constantly are wanting to be encouraged and guided, simply and confidently. At dinner, he frequently addressed the servant who waited on us familiarly, and drew him into our conversation as if he were a family friend, better informed on some local and domestic points than himself.

He informed me that *able-bodied field-hands* were hired out in this vicinity at the rate of one hundred dollars a year and their board and clothing.

Four able-bodied men that I have employed the last year, on my farm in New-York, I pay on an average one hundred and five dollars each, and board them; they clothe themselves (at an expense, I think, of twenty dollars a year; probably slave's clothing costs five dollars). They constitute all the force of my farm hired by the year, except a boy, who goes to school in Winter, and have no overseer, but one of themselves, in my absence. I pay the fair wages of the market, more than any of my neighbors, I believe, and these are no lower than the average of what I have paid for the last five years. This, then, probably offers a fair comparison of the proportionate cost of free and slave labor. I have little doubt that mine is most economical.

It is difficult to measure the labor performed in a day by one with that of the other, on account of undefined differences in the soil and in the bulk and weight of articles operated with and upon. But here I am shown tools that no man in his senses with us would allow a laborer he was paying wages to, to be encumbered with; and the excessive weight and clumsiness of which, I should judge, would make work at least ten percent. greater than with those ordinarily used with us, and I am assured that in the careless and clumsy way that they must be used by the slaves, anything lighter or less rude would not be good economy, and that such tools as we constantly give our laborers and find our profit in giving them, would not last out a day in a Virginia corn field—much lighter and more free from stones though it be than ours.

So, too, I ask why mules are so universally substituted for horses on the farm! The *first* reason, and confessedly the most conclusive one, is, that horses cannot bear the treatment that they always *must* get from slaves; horses are always soon foundered or crippled by them, while mules will bear cudgelling, and lose a meal or two now and then, and not be materially injured, and they do not take cold or get sick if neglected or overworked; but I do not need to go further than to the window of the room in which I am writing to see, at almost any time, treatment of cattle that would insure the immediate discharge of the driver by almost any farmer owning them at the North.

Before leaving Virginia, I hope to be able to examine this subject more thoroughly.

YEOMAN.

---

1. Olmsted wrote this letter sometime between December 16 and 25, 1852. The account of his visit to a James River farm appears in a different version in *Seaboard Slave States*, pages 40–47 (*SSS*, p. 16; "The South" no. 5, *NYDT*, March 10, 1853).
2. Thomas Jefferson, the designer of the Virginia Capitol in Richmond, modeled his plan after the Maison Carrée (or Quarrée) at Nîmes in southern France, a Roman temple patterned after the Parthenon of Athens and dating from the first century A.D. (Dumas Malone, *Jefferson and His Time*, vol. 2, *Jefferson and the Rights of Man* [Boston, 1951], pp. 89–92).
3. A full-length standing statue of George Washington by the French sculptor Jean Antoine Houdon (1741–1828). The statue was authorized by the Virginia Assembly in 1784, and Thomas Jefferson selected Houdon to carry it out (*Dictionary of Artists in America*; Gilbert

Chinard, ed., *Houdon in America: A Collection of Documents in the Jefferson Papers in the Library of Congress* . . . [Baltimore and London, 1930], pp. xiv–xxiii).

4. Thomas Crawford (1813?–1857), American sculptor. Crawford won the design competition for the monument held by the city of Richmond in 1849, and completed the work just before his death. Consisting of a colossal equestrian statue of Washington surrounded on a lower level by six statues of famous Virginians and four allegorical figures, and standing over sixty feet high, it was intended to be the largest monument of its kind then in existence (*DAB*; *Richmond Enquirer*, Dec. 31, 1852, p. 1; Sylvia E. Crane, *White Silence: Greenough, Powers, and Crawford, American Sculptors in Nineteenth-Century Italy* [Coral Gables, Fla., 1972], pp. 342–44; Lorado Taft, *The History of American Sculpture* [New York and London, 1903], pp. 76–79, 390).

5. The child actresses Kate Bateman (1843?–1917) and Ellen Bateman (1844–1936), who were touring the United States following a triumphant tour of the British Isles in 1851 under the sponsorship of P. T. Barnum (*Notable American Women; DAB*; for Olmsted's later experience with the Batemans, see FLO to JO, Nov. 7, 1854, below).

6. Olmsted apparently had no experience of the life of the Virginia country squire before he visited Richmond, and the statement here seems to have been the result of his visit, after Christmas 1852, to the plantation of "Thomas W." south of Petersburg, Virginia. In his description of that visit in *Seaboard Slave States*, Olmsted observed: "On their plantations, generally, the Virginia gentlemen seem to drop their full-dress and constrained town-habits, and to live a free, rustic, shooting-jacket life."

"Thomas W." was probably Thomas William Gee (b. 1819), who lived on a plantation in Sussex County, Virginia, in the vicinity of the village of Stony Creek. Although Olmsted gave a long description in *Seaboard Slave States* of his horseback ride from a country railroad station to the plantation of "Thomas W." and back, he did not say where the station was, and simply dated the passage "Petersburg, Dec. 28." In "The South" number fourteen, however, he did reveal, in another connection, that a few days after reaching Petersburg he took a train twenty miles into the country on the railroad running to Wilmington, North Carolina, and that the train reached his station with only one "cross-road stoppage." This means that he left the train at Stony Creek.

In *Seaboard Slave States,* Olmsted wrote that "Thomas W." was very wealthy, lived in an "old family mansion" and was "one of the few large planters, of his vicinity, who still made the culture of tobacco their principal business." He was also an extensive slaveholder, as indicated by slave quarters of a dozen "small and dilapidated" cabins near the public road, and a second group of large cabins near his mansion. Olmsted indicated that his host had owned the plantation long enough to make some improvements to the mansion and grounds: he had cut down the oak trees near the house and planted ailanthus trees in parallel rows, and had added a "large wooden portico" to the building. The fact that Olmsted specified the material of the portico suggests that the building itself was not made of wood.

All of these features support the conclusion that "Thomas W." was Thomas W. Gee. He had inherited the ancestral 1,358-acre "brick house plantation" from his father, Thomas Gee (b. 1793), around 1850. He may have represented the fifth generation of the family to live in the house. In 1860, Thomas W. Gee owned sixty-five slaves, who lived in seven houses (presumably having abandoned the small cabins near the road for the larger and "comfortable-looking" group that Olmsted noted near the house). In that year, Gee was the third-largest producer of tobacco in Sussex County, with an 18,735-pound crop. Only five planters in the county produced over 15,000 pounds of tobacco annually. Gee's farm was valued at $17,000, and he had 53 cattle and oxen, 73 sheep and 200 hogs.

Olmsted's source for an introduction to Thomas W. Gee is not known, but Thomas's sister, Caroline M. Gee (b. 1829), would have been twelve years old when Abner Leavenworth founded his seminary in Petersburg in 1841, and could have attended that institution (*SSS*, pp. 88–91; U.S., Census Office, 7th Census, *7th Census 1850. Virginia* [Washington, D.C., 1850], schedule 1, Sussex County, p. 132; idem, 8th Census, *8th Census 1860. Virginia* [Washington, D.C., 1860], schedule 1, Sussex County, p. 528; schedule 2, p. 393; William James Fletcher, *The Gee Family: Descendants of Charles Gee [d. 1709] and Hannah Gee [d. 1728] of Virginia* . . . [Rutland, Vt., 1937], pp. 18–19, 28–29).

7. A reference to the horse-drawn reapers invented by the Americans Obed Hussey and Cyrus McCormick and patented in 1833 and 1834, respectively (Lewis Cecil Gray, *History of Agriculture in the Southern United States to 1860* . . ., 2 vols. [Washington, D.C., 1933], 2: 798–800).

8. That is, during Olmsted's walking tour of the British Isles in 1850, the year before the International Exhibition was held in London.
9. Lewis Morris Pease, former head of the Five Points House of Industry in New York.

New-York Daily Times, March 17, 1853[1]

THE SOUTH.

LETTERS ON THE PRODUCTIONS, INDUSTRY AND RESOURCES OF THE SOUTHERN STATES.

NUMBER SEVEN.

Special Correspondence of the New-York Daily Times

The Connection of Slavery with Agricultural Prosperity in Virginia—Discussion of the Comparative Value of Free and Slave Labor—The Amount Accomplished in a Day by a Slave and by a Free Laborer Compared—Labor and Wealth—The Humiliating Position of Virginia—Its Probable Cause.

To the Editor of the New-York Daily Times:

I did not intend when I commenced writing these letters to give much attention to the subject of Slavery; but the truth is, the character of the whole agriculture of the country depends upon it. In every department of industry I see its influence, vitally affecting the question of profit, and I must add that everywhere, and constantly, the conviction is forced upon me, to a degree entirely unanticipated, that its effect is universally ruinous. My first impression upon crossing the country was, that to account for the general superior prosperity asserted of the North, we need go no further than to examine the soil; the main source of wealth at the South being agriculture, no cheapness of labor could make profitable the culture of such poor soil as that which at first fell under my observation. It did, indeed, occur to me that only by the low value of slave labor, could such land have been so long retained in cultivation. Would you think it possible that a man could live by cultivating ground that only produced three bushels of wheat to the acre? The very slightest possible cultivation of the soil, and the mere seed and sowing of it without the slightest tillage, would cost a northern farmer as much as the value of the crop. Such crops are common in Virginia. I do not exaggerate in saying so. I have heard of repeated instances where the crop of a whole, large plantation was not over three bushels to the acre! Without asserting, as, however, I am much inclined to think, and as many Virginians confess to me they are themselves convinced, that the system of slavery is responsible, by its enervating effects upon the minds of the superior race, for this beggarly farming; there is not room for the shadow of a doubt across my mind, that slave labor makes the cost of cultivating such lands greater, and the profit (!) less, than it would be under free labor.

But the soils from which I derived the impression I have spoken of, are by no means to be taken as a criterion of the ordinary lands of this country; I have since seen large tracts of as fine wheat land, deep and rich upland of clayey loam; or alluvial meadows of the best description of soil for general cropping, that I ever saw in any country, and even on the same old piney land—or worn out tobacco fields—under a system of agriculture of moderate enterprise and skill, I have found that fair crops of all sorts can be made. And under free labor, and the direction of men exercising the ordinary intelligence and skill applied to Northern farms, I am wholly convinced that there is not in all the Northern States, or in all of Europe, a district of country where the business of farming would be so profitable, as in Eastern Virginia. I shall hereafter discuss the inducements offered under present circumstances to emigration. As to the capability of the soil, I heard this morning that a Northern man last year purchased a farm in Southern Virginia, but a few miles from a railroad, and but twenty from a seaport, for which he paid $5 an acre. It had not ordinarily produced wheat at the rate of five bushels the acre, and had never been plowed over four inches in depth; upon which, by plowing eight inches, turning up not only virgin soil, but clay to mix with the sand of the surface, and applying 150 barrels of guano, costing $3.75 to the acre, he obtained a crop averaging twenty bushels an acre, and from which he realized much more than sufficient money to pay for the cost of the land it grew upon, and the expense of growing it. I have seen land of a similar description, which has been sold, with its improvements, during the last year, for $2.25 an acre.

As I may hereafter wish sometimes to assume the superior cheapness or economy of free labor, I will in addition to the reasons I have before given for it, state here a few more.

I have compared notes with several farmers, planters and manufacturers, capitalists and contractors, and I arrive at the conclusion to which they have without one exception conceded, that the wages of laborers, measuring them merely by power of muscle, or brute force, without regard to energy or will, are at this time at least 25 per cent. higher in Eastern Virginia, than in the State of New-York.

In addition to this difference there is to be deducted from the profit of the slave the loss of time occasioned by his sickness (or absence from any cause); which loss does not fall upon the proprietor under the free labor system, and the temptation to counterfeit which is not offered to the laborer. The loss of this to the slave farmer is of various consequence, sometimes small, often excessively embarrassing, always a subject of anxiety and suspicion. A farmer told me for the purpose of showing me the weakness of the family tie and the promiscuous intercourse among slaves, that having allowed one of his men, a mechanic, to work some time in a shipyard at a city, soon after his return, and at a time when he was pressed for labor, he suddenly found twelve hands, male and female, and all of them married parties, laid up with a disgusting disease, and was obliged to procure, at a great expense, a physician to come from town twice a week to examine the whole force, to prevent its spread among them. After all, an old "nigger doctor," a slave in the neighborhood, was more successful in curing them with an empirical remedy, than the regular practitioner. I mention this as indicating that this complaint is not unfrequent among them. A decoction of pine leaves is one of the negro remedies.

As to sham-sickness or "playing 'possum" I heard much complaint of it, and it is said to be nearly as hard to treat negroes in sickness as it is children, because they use their imagination so much, greatly puzzle the doctors by lying as to their symptoms, and from their neglect or refusal to take the remedies left for them. They will generally conceal pills in their mouth, declare they have swallowed them, and it is only discovered that they have not by their failing to have any effect. This is a general custom, but probably arose from the fact that unless very disagreeably ill they are loth to recover from that which exempts them from labor.

Amusing incidents illustrating this difficulty I have heard, showing that the slave rather enjoys getting a severe wound that lays him up. He has his hand smashed by accident, and says: "Bless de Lord—de hand b'long to massa. I don't reckon I'se got no more corn to hoe dis year, for sartin."

On the other hand the suspicion that when a hand complains he is "playing 'possum" and the refusal to allow him to "knock off" often aggravates what might be otherwise a slight and temporary indisposition, into a long and serious illness. From this reason, the labor of women on a plantation, as a large planter assured me, "actually does not pay for their salt." After they get to the "breeding age" they do no more work of any account. "They are forever complaining of 'irregularities.' They don't come to the field, and you ask what's the matter, and the old nurse always nods her head and says, 'Oh, *she's not well, sir; she's not fit to work, sir,*'—and you have to take her word for it."

I believe that the slaves are generally very kindly and considerately treated in sickness, but the profit of slave labor is all the less from this, from the encouragement to the slave to make the most of sickness and so to withdraw his labor and be a mere "bill of expense" to his master.

Then the slaves sometimes *refuse* to labor, or "balk," from mere "rascality," which, as I have before shown, is sufficiently common and inexplicable as to be considered a disease.[2] They are then inconceivably stubborn, and can barely be driven to work by the lash, and in no way restrained from recklessly or malevolently doing much injury to their master's property.

"How do *you* manage, then, when a man misbehaves, or is sick?" I have been asked at this point of the discussion.

"If he is sick, I simply charge against him every half day of the time he is off work, and deduct it from his wages. If he is careless, or refuses to do what in reason I demand of him, I discharge him, paying him wages to the time he leaves. With new men in whom I have not confidence, I make a written agreement, before witnesses, on engaging them, that will permit me to do this. As for "rascality," I never had but one case of anything approaching to what you call so. A man contradicted me in the field; I told him to leave his job and go to the house, took hold and finished it myself; then went to the house, made out a written statement of account, counted out the balance in money due him, gave him the statement and the money, and told him he must go, and had not another word with him. I've no doubt he was a good and respectful man to his next employer."

The slave master, in case he finds he has a "tartar" on his hands, has no remedy, if he has hired him, but to ask a deduction of what he has paid from his owner, on the same ground that you would if you had hired a vicious horse, and instead of helping you on your journey he had broken your leg; or, if he is an owner, to *sell* him "to go South."

That the slaves have to be "humored" a great deal, and often cannot be made to do their master's will, is very evident,—I do not think they will do from fear nearly as much as Northern laborers will simply from respect to their contract or regard to their duty. The gentleman I before spoke of as employing white laborers on a farm,[3] had been especially struck with this. A dam had given way, and it was necessary to do a good deal of work very promptly in the water. He was greatly surprised to find how much more readily than negroes his white men would obey his orders, jumping into the water waist deep in the midst of winter without the slightest hesitation or grumbling. He had noticed the same on all emergencies, when it was desirable to work late at night, &c., or to do any very disagreeable job. A farmer in England told me that he had once, in a very bad harvest season, had laborers at work without a wink of sleep for sixty hours, himself heading them, and eating and drinking with them.

Finally, to come to the point of the amount of work which will be done under the Northern and the Southern system. I regret that I cannot get more exact data here. The only close observation of the work done in a day by slaves that can be fairly compared with that by free laborers, that I have been able to obtain, was made by Mr. T. R. Griscom, of Petersburg;[4] a man remarkable for the accuracy and preciseness of his information on all subjects. I was recommended to call upon him, as a man possessing very intimate knowledge with regard to the agriculture of the district in which he lives, by as strong a pro-Slavery man as I have met. He formerly resided in New-Jersey, and has had the superintendence of very extensive and varied agricultural operations in Virginia.

He tells me he once very carefully observed how much labor was expended in securing a crop of very thin wheat, and found that it took four negroes one day to cradle, rake, and bind one acre. (That is, this was the rate at which the field was harvested.) In the wheat-growing districts of Western New-York, four men would be expected to do five acres of a similar crop.

Mr. Griscom further states, as his opinion, that four negroes do not, in the ordinary agricultural operations of this State, accomplish as much as one laborer in New-Jersey. Upon my expressing my astonishment, he repeated it, as his deliberately formed opinion.

I have since, again called on Mr. Griscom, and obtained permission to give his name with the above statement. He also wishes me to add, that the ordinary waste in harvesting, by the carelessness of the negroes, above that which occurs in the hands of Northern laborers, is large enough to equal what a Northern farmer would consider a satisfactory profit on the crop.

I do not think there is a man in Virginia whose information on this point would be more reliable or whose opinion would be formed with less prejudice to either side and is entitled to greater respect than Mr. Griscom's.

I have at second hand the result of the experience of another man who has superintended extended labors of a similar character, both at the North and in Virginia, which precisely agrees with Mr. Griscom's. I am not able now to see him and obtain the facts directly, but have been promised a statement of them by him in writing.

In a late article by H. M. Brackenridge, in the *National Intelligencer,* copied in the New-York Times of Dec. 29, reproving the spirit of *Uncle Tom's Cabin,* and containing many very sensible observations on Slavery,[5] the result, the writer says, of ten years observation and much reflection, it is stated that "the day's labor of the slave is notoriously not more than half that of the white man; and if left to himself (it would be) not more than half that."

Another gentleman here, who formerly resided in Connecticut, told me that he believed that a Northern laborer would finish a negro's day's work by 11 o'clock in the forenoon.

I have stated that I had met no farmer that was not convinced of the superior economy of free-labor (if the slaves were not on their hands and in some way to be provided for), but few however are willing to concede or can believe the difference to be as great as the above opinions would indicate. On mentioning them to one, he remarked, that although the four men might not have done more than at the rate of an acre a day, it must have been because they were not well driven. He thought that if driven hard enough, threatened with punishment, and *punished* if necessary, they would do as much work as it was *possible* for any white man to do. The same man, however, has told me that slaves were very rarely punished—he thought not more than apprentices were at the North—that the driving was almost always left to overseers, who were the laziest and most inefficient dogs in the world—frequently not worth half so much as the slaves they pretended to manage—and that the wages of an overseer were often not more than half as much as one of the negroes put under his control could be hired out for.

A planter on the coast, whom I asked to examine these statements, and my conclusions with regard to this subject, that he might, if he could, refute them, or give me any facts of an opposite character, replied: "Why, I have no doubt you are right, Sir; in general, a slave does not do half the work he easily might, and which, by being harsh enough with him, he can be made to do. When I came into possession of my plantation, I found the overseer was good for nothing, and I soon told him I had no further occasion for his services, and I went to driving the negroes myself. In the morning, when I went out one of them came up to me saying, 'Well, massa, what'll you hab me go at dis mornin'?' 'Well, ole man,' said I, 'you may go to the swamps and cut wood.' 'Well, massa,' said he, 's'pose you wants me to do kordins we's been use to doin' here: ebery niggar cut a cord o' wood a day.' 'A cord! that's what you have been used to doing, is it?' said I. 'Yes, massa, dat's wot dey always makes a niggar do roun' heah—a cord a day, dat's allers de job.' 'Well, now, ole man,' said I, 'you go and cut me two cords to-day.' 'Oh, massa! two cords! Nobody couldn do dat. Oh! massa, dat's too hard! Nebber heard nobody's cuttin' more 'n a cord in a day roun' heah. No niggar couldn do it.' 'Well, ole man, you have two cords of wood cut to-night, or to-morrow morning you shall get two hundred lashes. Now, go off and be about it.' And he did it, and ever since no negro has ever cut less than two cords a day for me, though my neighbors never get but one cord. It was just so with a great many other things—mauling rails—I always have twice as many rails mauled in a day as it is the custom of the country to expect of a negro, and just twice as many as my negroes always had been made to do before I managed them myself."

Allowing that the opinions of the practical men who have had experience at the North and the South, that I have given, somewhat exaggerate the difference in the amount of work accomplished by a slave and a Northern free laborer (though I did not give them because they were extreme, but because they were the only exact statements that I could obtain)—allowing that I have been unfortunate in this way, and that a longer residence in the State would give me information that would much modify these estimates, there still remains, beyond a doubt, a very great loss in using the labor of the slave. These statements would make the loss between three and four hundred *per cent.* Now although they were the calculations and deliberate estimates of men who had enjoyed a liberal education, and who had unusual facilities for observing both at the North and South—men who employ slaves, and who sustain Southern opinions on the political questions arising from slavery—I am not disposed to insist upon full credit for them. *Cut them down one-half,* and we still have a loss of nearly *one hundred per cent.* Even if you will have them to be utterly mistaken, and calculate that the slaves accomplish equally as much—man for man—as Irishmen under wages contract, yet consider how large a sum would pay for clothes, time lost by sickness or otherwise—five or more additional holidays, which custom gives them, and for all that they pilfer or damage and destroy through carelessness, improvidence, recklessness and rascality!

Can there be a reasonable doubt that the State of Virginia loses fifty per cent. on the cost of labor, in employing slaves in preference to freemen!

Suppose that half the cost of a crop is expended in the human labor given to it, the profits of the farmers of Virginia would then be increased 25 per cent. per annum, if they could substitute the labor of freemen for that of slaves.

Labor is the creator of wealth. There can be no honest wealth, no true prosperity without it, and in exact proportion to the economy of labor is the cost of production and the accumulation of profit.[6]

Remembering this, I cannot but ask the people of Virginia to read again the facts that follow, which I extract from the leading article of the Richmond *Enquirer* of this date (Dec. 29), and seriously and candidly reflect for themselves with regard to them.[7]

> Virginia, anterior to the Revolution and up to the adoption of the Federal Constitution, contained more wealth and a larger population than other States of this Confederacy.
>
> * * *
>
> Virginia, from being first in point of wealth and political power, has come down to the fifth in the former, and the fourth in the latter. New-York, Pennsylvania, Massachusetts and Ohio stand above her in wealth, and all, but Massachusetts, in population and political power. Three of these States are literally chequered over with Railroads and canals, and the fourth (Massachusetts) with Railroads alone.
>
> But when we find that the population of the single city of New-York and its environs exceeds the whole free population of Eastern Virginia, and the valley between the Blue Ridge and Alleghany, we have cause to feel deeply for our situation. Philadelphia herself contains a population far greater than the whole free population of Eastern Virginia.
>
> —The little State of Massachusetts has an aggregate wealth exceeding that of Virginia by more than one hundred and twenty-six millions of dollars—a State, too, which is incapable of subsisting its inhabitants from the production of its soil. And New-York, which was as much below Massachusetts, at the adoption of the Federal Constitution, in wealth and power, as the latter was below Virginia, now exceeds the wealth of both. While the aggregate wealth of New-York, in 1850, amounted to $1,080,309,216, that of Virginia was $436,701,082—a difference in favor of the former of $643,608,134. The unwrought mineral wealth of Virginia exceeds that of New-York. The climate and soil are better; the back country, with equal improvements, would contribute as much.

All true, and facts and contrasts more striking and far more humiliating might have been shown you. Why be driven by fanaticism and bigotry to shut your eyes to the most simple and evident explanation of them?

I shall next show why it is not possible for any single farmer or manufacturer to relieve himself of his proportion of this tax to support slavery and increase his products and profits in a corresponding ratio, and make it evident that only by the general action of the people, their "commercial vassalage" can be remedied.

1. Internal evidence indicates that Olmsted wrote part of this letter on December 29, 1852, while in Petersburg, Virginia. It also appears that part of the letter is the two pages on the relative cost of free and slave labor that he wrote before December 22. Another section refers to an article in the *New-York Daily Times* of December 29, 1852, which indicates that he completed the letter after that date. Portions of this letter appear in *Seaboard Slave States,* pages 186–208 (FLO to CLB, Dec. 22, 1852).
2. In "The South" number 4, Olmsted presented the findings of Samuel Cartwright, a New Orleans physician and author of numerous articles offering a scientific justification for slavery, concerning diseases that seemed peculiar to black slaves. One was *"Drapetomania,"* a disease that caused slaves to run away for no apparent reason; another was "*Dysaesthesia Aethiopica,"* or "Hebetude of Mind and Obtuse Sensibility of Body." Cartwright described its symptoms, and the traditional misinterpretation of them by overseers, as follows (italics supplied by Olmsted):

> When roused from sloth by the stimulus of hunger, he takes anything he can lay his hands on, and tramples on the rights as well as on the property of others, with perfect indifference. When driven to labor by the compulsive power of the white man, *he performs the task assigned to him in a headlong, careless manner, treading down with his feet or cutting with his hoe the plants he is put to cultivate—breaking the tools he works with, and spoiling everything he touches that can be injured by careless handling.* Hence *the overseers* call it "rascality," *supposing that the mischief is intentionally done.*
>
>   The term "rascality" given to this disease by overseers, is founded on an erroneous hypothesis, and leads to an incorrect empirical treatment, which seldom or never cures it.

Olmsted then contributed, in a passage he did not include in *Seaboard Slave States,* his own observation of a slave apparently suffering from *Dysaesthesia Aethiopica:*

> I must assure you again that this is no joke. Just imagine the disease to have got into the printing office, Messrs. Editors: think what a mess, what a pie there would be. I think I have seen indications in one of your little contemporaries, occasionally, that compositors were subject to a mild type of it. I do not believe, however, it ever very seriously affects white men. "Green" Irishmen sometimes have symptoms of it; and the practice with all Northern farmers is to immediately discharge them as soon as anything of the sort ("breaking, wasting, destroying." &c.,) is noticed. This almost always affects a cure, and the second "boss" has no trouble of the kind with them. It would be deemed ironical, I fear, to suggest this mode of dealing with *dysaesthesian* patients to our Southern friends. The disease is too virulent in the slave constitution.
>
>   From my own observations, I should judge *dysaesthesia,* in a comparatively mild type, at least, to be quite common here; and I am informed that it not unfrequently becomes chronic and incurable. I just now saw a good instance of that insensibility of body and hebetude of mind that characterize it. Hearing a loud swearing in the street, I rose and saw that a young negro, who was still carelessly suffered to go at large, and who was driving three mules attached to a load of coal, had allowed them to bring the cart-wheel in contact with the wheel of another cart belonging to a white man, who was carting sand. It was the loud voice of the latter that had attracted my notice to the case, calling upon the dysaesthesiated black, with some profanity and much energy of gesture, to remedy the evil occasioned by his carelessness. The subject, with a beautiful exhibition of the stupidity of mind peculiar to the disease, immediately began slashing his mules with his whip, and these springing forward, only increased the difficulty—upon which the white man, intending, I suppose, to withdraw a portion of the highly carbonized blood that lay at the seat of the *dysaesthesia,* sprang hastily towards him and jammed the sharp edge of a shovel violently into his face. The subject withdrew backwards, with considerable rapidity, and raised his hands to his face, as if this had had the effect of reviving sensation in the locality of the operation. A disengagement of the wheels was effected, by the interposition of a third party, and, after a

moment's pause, the negro again lashed his mules, and they started. Before proceeding a rod, however, they again brought the hub of a wheel in collision with a milk wagon.

The liability to such complaints, must take considerably from the value of slave labor. There are also many other diseases to which the blacks in Virginia are subject, and which, especially under "the usual empirical treatment of overseers," and Dr. Cartwright says they rarely get any other, must occasion much inconvenience and frequent losses. For instance, I observe that a correspondent of a Richmond Agricultural paper says that "the typhoid fever, in a very malignant form, has been very fatal in his family this Fall, and his loss of hands from death and sickness (during the last two months), has been such as greatly to retard his plantation operations." "The disease is still progressing in a milder form," he afterwards says, "and we cannot foreshow the result."

("The South" no. 4, *NYDT*, March 4, 1853; *SSS*, pp. 191-94; Samuel Adolphus Cartwright, "Report on the Diseases and Physical Peculiarities of the Negro Race...," *New Orleans Medical and Surgical Journal* 7 [May 1851]: 691-715, reprinted in *DeBow's Review* 11, no. 1 [July 1851]: 64-69; ibid., no. 2 [Aug. 1851], pp. 209-13; ibid., no. 3 [Sept. 1851], pp. 331-36; William Stanton, *The Leopard's Spots: Scientific Attitudes toward Race in America, 1815-59* [Chicago and London, 1960], pp. 160, 232).

3. Charles Benedict Calvert (see "The South" no. 1, n. 5, above).
4. The name in the *New-York Daily Times* version is J. R. Griscom, but Olmsted corrected it in *Seaboard Slave States* to read T. R. Griscom. The first city directory of Petersburg, Virginia, listed a Thomas Griscomb, surveyor (*SSS*, p. 203; *First Annual Directory for the City of Petersburg. To Which is Added a Business Directory for 1859. Compiled by W. Eugene Ferlew* [Petersburg, Va., (1859)], p. 69 [see Spear 272]).
5. An article entitled "Uncle Tom's Cabin," by Henry Marie Brackenridge (1786-1871), a Pennsylvania-born lawyer, politician and writer. Brackenridge lived for several years in Missouri, Louisiana, Maryland, and spent eleven years in Florida—first as secretary to the territorial governor, Andrew Jackson, and then as a judge. In the newspaper article to which Olmsted refers, Brackenridge said: "The day's labor of the slave is notoriously not more than half that of the white man; and, if left to himself, it would not be half of that" ("Slavery in the South," *NYDT*, Dec. 29, 1852, p. 3; *DAB*).
6. Most political economists whose writings were current at this time conceived of labor, in some sense, as being the most important source of wealth. This was true of classical economists like Adam Smith and David Ricardo, later modifiers of their theories like John Stuart Mill, and such socialists as Marx, St. Simon and Fourier. Although Olmsted uses the terms of political economy here, he seems to be drawing rather from a New England tradition that stressed the economic and moral value of hard work and the desirability of efficient application of labor.
7. The editorial that Olmsted quotes appeared on page 3 of the *Richmond Enquirer* of December 29, 1852. In it the editor castigated Virginians for letting the North gain control of their international trade. Only the first and fourth paragraphs that Olmsted quotes appear in the article.

To John Olmsted

Raleigh, N.C., January 10th 1853

Dear Father,

I arrived here Saturday, 8th, after a rather dismal week at Norfolk—stormy, wet & chilly, but my health good.

In coming from Weldon to Gaston (see my letter that will be published, giving amusing account of it),[1] coach turned over; was not hurt any, but

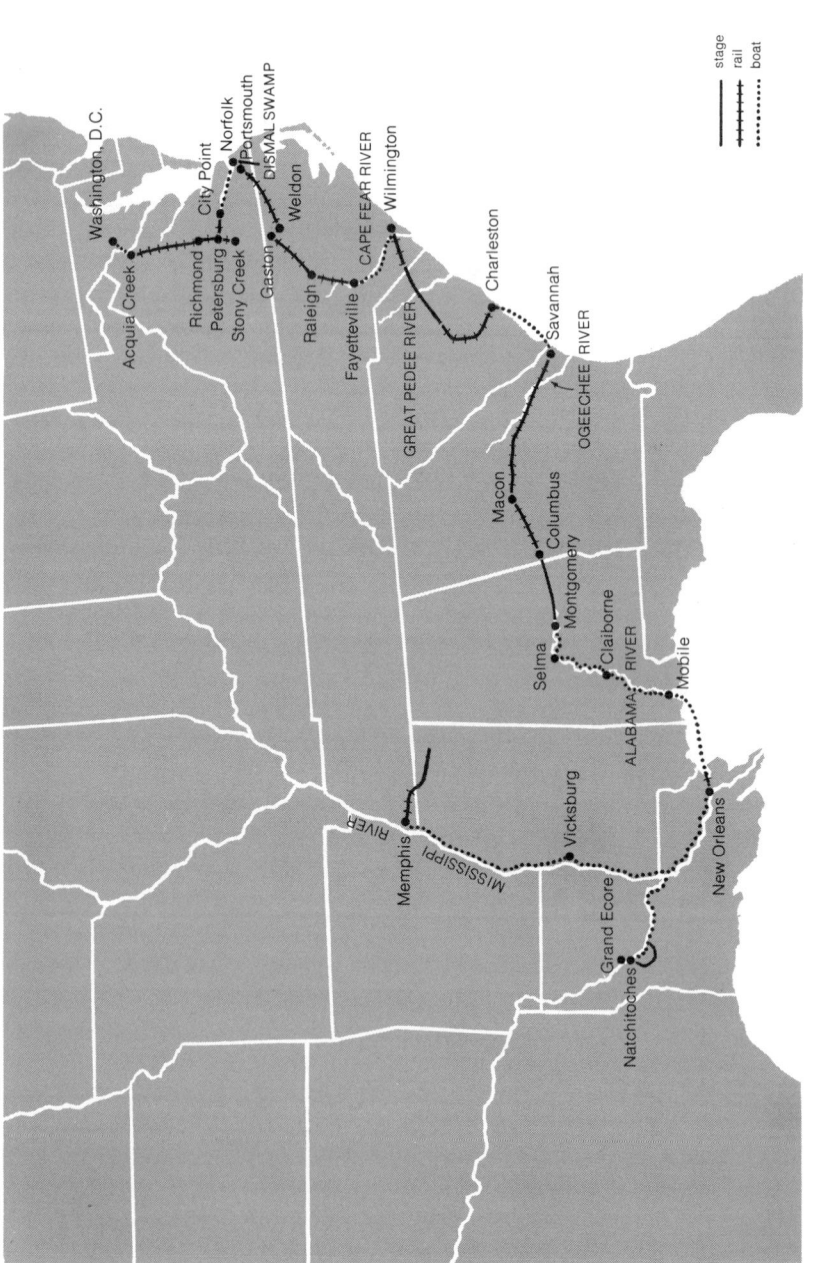

The Journey through the Seaboard Slave States, 1852–1853

From northern Mississippi, Olmsted returned to the North "along the eastern base of the Appalachian Chain in the upper parts of the States of Mississippi, Alabama, Georgia, the Carolinas and Virginia..." ("The South" number 44).

my bag (valise trunk) some damaged, torn; bottle of arnica[2] in dressing case broke, no great harm. A regular swindle the whole route.

I have spent all my money and drew on McC. A. & S.[3] this morning for $50 to take me to Charleston. It has cost me $2.00 a day, besides travelling expenses, ever since I left N.Y.

I have found but one man at home that I had letters to—(Fred Kingsbury's uncle, the school teacher at Petersburg.)[4] Here I expected to have a good acquaintance in Mr. Deveroux?[5] The landlord says he lives a hundred miles from here—only occasionally here, & not now.

I shall stay here several days, writing, and shall finish as many as twelve letters, so I shall pay my expenses. I think I have done pretty well. I have not fully determined my route—the roads never were so bad & lots of people here mud bound. Think I shall leave here Thursday and go by Guilford Co. House, Greensboro, Lexington, Salisbury to Charlotte, the gold district. Have a letter to Superintendent of Mint, there.[6] I should like to go across from there to Chattanooga, Tennessee—North Alabama—Memphis (New Orleans) so as to return by Savannah & Charleston. Because if I get behindhand, I can return by Steamer at any time direct to New York.

I would rather lose South Carolina—than any other state—as I can examine both cotton & rice before I get there. Then I would be very glad to get more time if I could afford it in the Spring to look over this section & the Atlantic shore more thoroughly than I dare to now, lest I shouldn't have time for Louisiana.

But this plan makes necessary 400 miles of stage coaching night & day. Hazardous & awfully tiresome and 8 cents a mile. So it's *hardly* likely I shall adopt it. If not, I go by Columbia, S.C., to Charleston & shall try to arrive there by Sunday week (23rd January).[7]

I gave Mrs. Andover[8] two long, heavy letters about Dismal Swamp, &c., & shall make two of it for Times.[9]

I shall make a book of 500 pages octavo—and shall want Mary or Bertha[10] to copy and collate for me next summer. I shall take at least $300 from Raymond,[11] which will just about cover my expenses. I omit several letters, not having time now to take up the topics—shall add them after I return (out of place).

I shall be very anxious when the letters begin to be printed to have my friends' opinion of them. I wish you would buy an extra copy every day when they appear, make remarks along the margin, or on slips pinned in—indicating doubtful assertions, opinions, errors of fact or calculation, infelicities of expression &c., that I may have the advantage of them in revising.

The first two letters[12] are the poorest of the lot. Those most interesting are those that cost me the least labor. Most of them are written very rapidly, as fast as I have written this.

I received letter from you at Norfolk. Robert, William, & C.L.B.[13] are all charged to take care of the trees. I can not make more definite arrangements. C.L.B. must call on Bossange.[14] It would take a sheet to tell him, what, his judgment is as good as mine for—and that is worth $4 to me.

Yours very affectionately,

Fred.

1. "The South" number 15 (*NYDT*, May 4, 1853).
2. A medicine applied externally for bruises and sprains.
3. The New York firm of M'Curdy, Aldrich & Spencer, commission merchants (*The New-York City Directory, for 1853-1854. Twelfth Publication*... [New York, (1853)], p. 407 [see Spear 1000]).
4. Abner Leavenworth (see FLO to FJK, Oct. 17, 1852, above).
5. Thomas Pollok Devereux (1793-1869), son of John Devereux, a planter and merchant, and of Frances Pollok Devereux, a granddaughter of Jonathan Edwards. Devereux graduated from Yale College in 1813. He practiced law and served as U.S. district attorney and court reporter of the North Carolina Supreme Court from 1826 to 1839. He then retired from law to manage his parents' plantations, which he inherited during the 1840s. By 1850 he possessed 580 slaves and real estate worth $52,000 in Halifax and Northampton counties, North Carolina, and in Raleigh. He made his home at Conacanarra Plantation in Halifax County.

    In marriage, Devereux followed the pattern of New England connections established by his father. His first wife was Catherine Ann Johnson (1796?-1836), daughter of Robert and Catherine Bayard Johnson of Stratford, Connecticut, and the granddaughter of William Samuel Johnson, member of the Federal Convention of 1787 and U.S. senator from Connecticut. His brother George followed the same pattern, marrying Sarah Elizabeth Johnson of Stratford, Connecticut—who returned to that state after George's death in the mid-1830s.

    Olmsted probably carried a letter of introduction to Devereux from his cousin Denison Olmsted (1791-1859), a Yale classmate of Devereux's. He may also have been acquainted with Devereux's son John Devereux (1819-1893), who graduated from Yale College in 1840 and at this time was a planter in Bertie County, North Carolina (*DAB*, s.v. "Olmsted, Denison"; Catherine Devereux Edmondston, *Journal of a Secesh Lady: The Diary of Catherine Ann Devereux Edmondston, 1860-1866*, ed. Beth G. Crabtree and James W. Patton [Raleigh, N.C., 1979], pp. xxii-xxiii; U.S., Census Office, 7th Census, *7th Census 1850. North Carolina* [Washington, D.C., 1850], schedule 1, Halifax County, p. 41B, no. 773; schedule 2, Halifax County, p. 175, Northampton County, p. 935, and Wake County, p. 667; Margaret Devereux, *Plantation Sketches* [Cambridge, Mass., 1946], pp. 1-4; Yale University, Class of 1840, *Historical Record of the Class of 1840, Yale College*, comp. John C. Hollister [New Haven, 1897], pp. 17-18; information on the Devereux family supplied by Jane Turner Censer).
6. James W. Osborne (1811-1869) was superintendent of the U.S. Mint at Charlotte, North Carolina. Olmsted probably had a letter of introduction to Osborne from his cousin Denison Olmsted, who had been a professor of chemistry and mineralogy at the University of North Carolina from 1817 to 1825 and during that time had served as director of the state's geological survey. Osborne may have studied briefly under Denison before he left North Carolina in 1825 to become a professor at Yale.

    Denison Olmsted's successor in the North Carolina geological survey was his Yale classmate Elisha Mitchell, who also taught at the University of North Carolina while Osborne was a student there (D. A. Tompkins, *History of Mecklenburg County and the City of Charlotte, from 1740 to 1903*, 2 vols. [Charlotte, N.C., 1903], 2: 78, 124-30; *Cyclopedia of Eminent and Representative Men of the Carolinas of the Nineteenth Century*... , 2 vols. [Madison, Wis., 1892], 2: 201-3; Kemp P. Battle, *History of the University of North Carolina*... , 2 vols. [Raleigh, N.C., 1907-12], 1: 250-53, 289).
7. As Olmsted anticipated, he went directly to Charleston from Raleigh, instead of heading west; his route was not through Columbia, but rather through Fayetteville and Wilmington, North Carolina (*SSS*, pp. 374-403).
8. "Mrs. Andover" was apparently Harriet Beecher Stowe, and it appears that Olmsted had agreed, before leaving for the South, that he would visit the Great Dismal Swamp in Virginia

and send her a description of it. Charles Loring Brace may have secured the assignment for Olmsted: at least, he was aware that Olmsted had agreed to visit the Great Dismal Swamp, since in a letter of December 22, 1852, Olmsted complained to him about having to go there, saying that it "disarranges everything and takes time." Brace had close connections with Mrs. Stowe and her family: his mother was a sister of her stepmother, Harriet Porter Beecher, and his father was her teacher at the Misses Pierces' School in Litchfield, Connecticut, where her father, Lyman Beecher, was minister from 1810 to 1826. She later spoke of the elder Brace as "one of the most stimulating and inspiring instructors I ever knew." Olmsted also knew, or at least was known to, Mrs. Stowe, since he had been engaged to her niece Emily Perkins in the summer of 1851.

Olmsted seems to have been afraid, in a letter mailed from the South, to make a clear reference to his connection with Mrs. Stowe. Accordingly, he referred to her by her place of residence—Andover, Massachusetts, where her husband, Calvin Stowe, had recently accepted a professorship at the Andover Theological Seminary.

It is not clear that Mrs. Stowe made use of Olmsted's letters on the Great Dismal Swamp; but in 1856—when she was writing *Dred, A Tale of the Great Dismal Swamp*—she asked him to visit her, read what she had written and advise her about various questions concerning the topography and flora of North Carolina. She made this request in a letter thanking Olmsted for sending her a copy of *Seaboard Slave States*, which contained a description of the Great Dismal Swamp and other parts of eastern North Carolina (*Notable American Women; DAB*, s.v. "Brace, John Pierce"; *Life of Brace*, pp. 1–3; *Papers of FLO*, 1: 89–91; Harriet Beecher Stowe to FLO, n.d. [Jan. 1856]; FLO to JO, Jan. 31, 1856).

9. "The South" numbers 12 and 13 (*NYDT*, April 20 and 23, 1853).
10. Olmsted's half-sisters Mary Olmsted (1832–1875) and Bertha Olmsted (1834–1926) (*Olmsted Genealogy*, pp. 60, 109; *Eleventh Reunion*, p. 9).
11. Henry Jarvis Raymond (1820–1869), editor of the *New-York Daily Times* (*DAB*).
12. "The South" numbers 1 and 2 (*NYDT*, Feb. 16 and 19, 1853).
13. Two of the hired men on Olmsted's Staten Island farm and Charles Loring Brace.
14. Edouard Bossange, an importer of French nursery stock ("The Horticulturist Advertiser," *Horticulturist* 10 [1855], bound at the end of the volume without pagination; *The New York Directory, for 1852–1853. Eleventh Publication . . .* [New York, 1852], p. 65 [see Spear 995]).

New-York Daily Times, March 30, 1853[1]

THE SOUTH.

LETTERS ON THE PRODUCTIONS, INDUSTRY AND RESOURCES OF THE SOUTHERN STATES.

NUMBER EIGHT.

Special Correspondence of the New-York Daily Times

Why Free Labor is not more Profitable than Slave Labor, Now, in Virginia—The Difficult Question of Disposing of the Slaves—Their Condition—The Condition of the Free Blacks at the South.

To the Editor of the New-York Daily Times:

In my last, it was made to appear that the cost of employing Slave labor in Virginia over free labor in New-York, was equal to an addition of one dollar to every dollar now expended for labor. This loss, be it remembered, is not a loss merely to the employer, but is a loss to the whole body politic—an abstraction from the general wealth of Virginia, of the United States, and of the world.

And it by no means follows, that, by disposing of his slaves, as things are at present, and hiring free laborers, any farmer in Virginia can make a saving of 100 per cent. The principle of demand and supply here comes in. The laborer that, in New-York, gives a certain amount of exertion for a certain price, soon finds that for that price here a less amount of work is customarily expected. He adopts slave habits of labor—he suits his wares to the market. He sees that the capitalists of Virginia give a high price for a poor article—he furnishes the poor article. But there are also other laws, besides this of demand and supply, that affect this matter.

"Man is a social being." The large amount of labor performed in Virginia is and long has been done by negroes. The negroes are a degraded people; degraded not merely by position, but actually immoral, low-lived; without healthy ambition, but little influenced by high moral considerations, and in regard to labor not [at] all affected by regard for duty. This is always recognized, and debasing fear, not cheering hope, is in general allowed to be the only stimulant to exertion. A capitalist was having a building erected in Petersburg, and his slaves were employed in carrying up the brick and mortar for the masons on their heads; a Northern man standing near remarked to him that they moved so indolently it seemed as if they were trying to see how long they could be in mounting the ladder without actually stopping. The builder started to reprove them, but after moving a step turned back and said, "It would only make them move more slowly still when I am not looking at them, if I should hurry them now—and what motive have they to do better? It's no concern of theirs how long the masons wait. I am sure if I was in their place I shouldn't move as fast as they do."

Now let the white laborer come here from the North or from Europe; his nature demands a social life; shall he associate with the poor, slavish, degraded, low-lived, despised, unambitious negro, with whom labor and punishment are almost synonymous, or shall he be the friend and companion of the white man in whose mind labor is associated with no ideas of duty, responsibility, comfort, luxury, cultivation or elevation and expansion either of mind or estate—as it is, where the ordinary laborer is a free man, free to use his labor as a means of obtaining all these and all else that is to be respected, honored or envied in the world?

Associating with either or both is it possible that he will not be demoralized, hate labor, give as little of it for his hire as he can, become base, cowardly, faithless—"worse than a nigger."

I ask *you, Virginians,* if this is not so—if you do not know it to be so? Is not this a simple, reasonable, satisfactory explanation of those failures in the substitution of free laborers for slaves to which you are in the habit of referring as settling this question?

See you not that it is Slavery still, that, like the ship-worm, is noiselessly and imperceptibly ever opening the leaks by which your state, the greatest of all, the vanguard of the fleet, rolls helplessly water-logged far astern of all?

Nine out of ten of the thinking men of Virginia are so convinced, and whisper among themselves, what is to be done? And the rest of the crew double-shot the starboard battery, and loudly threaten what they *will do* if we of the North don't mind our business, and quit advising and pitying them, and send back the rats that swim away from them.

Well, it's all very true that we can't help them, and that our attempts to do so only embarrass them, and that we have among us plenty of bad and more weak and foolish people that would do better to mind their own business and leave them to their fate; that we have beams enough in our own eyes; that the condition of *some* of our laborers is bad, as bad as theirs, worse than theirs; that this shows a rottenness in the planks of our system which we would do well to probe and study to mend. I am convinced of it all—the more so, the more sadly and earnestly so, for what I see here. There is wrong in both systems. Too much competition and self-seeking in our labor as there is too little in theirs. They prove it to me; I thank them for it; they cannot object if I, with no unkind or invidious purpose, frankly describe the nature of the evils they themselves have to deal with.

And they must understand that we have an interest and a certain responsibility in whatever of evil belongs to them, as we have in all that concerns the human family. That with a fair understanding of the nature of this evil, and of all its relations, we shall find that we have little or nothing to do about it ourselves, but to quietly wait and pray, for them in wisdom to move, is not improbable; and I hope and believe, that what I shall have occasion to write in regard to it, will favor such an understanding.

A proper appreciation of the difficulties that embarrass the people of the South in connection with the subject of Slavery, that lie in the way of any action favorable to even the amelioration of the condition of the slave by the action of law, would do more to restore friendly feeling and confidence between the two great sections of our country, than all the compromise measures that could be contrived, however strictly and conscientiously carried out. Only let it be known at the North in addition to a slight appreciation of these difficulties, that there was a general disposition to boldly, manfully, look them in the face, and to deal with them in a broad, Statesmanlike and Christianlike spirit, and the fanaticism of Abolition is dead and buried.

Only let the North show a disposition in future to regard the subject of Slavery as one *over which she has no control*, let indignation be quieted and turned to the injustice, and barbarism in her midst, let fierce denunciation and exciting appeals and even senselessly unpractical counsels be silenced, and I rejoice to state my conviction that in Virginia at least, hosts of great, good, and talented men, are all ready and earnestly purposed to give themselves with all their energies to the mighty task.

Even the men who have no concern above dollars and cents are well convinced this day, and it is commonly calculated among them, that if the Slaves could be quietly removed from their limits, the State would fill up so rapidly with free-men, and its sources of wealth would be so much more speedily and economically developed, that in five years' time the increase in the value of all real estate would more than pay for the value that the Slaves are now reckoned by their masters to be worth.

I am ready to give it as my present opinion, after what I have seen already of Slavery, that the African race whether it has been elevated or degraded by subjection to the whites of the South, is in many respects, and shows itself in the majority of instances to be, happier, intellectually, morally and physically, in Slavery than in what passes at the South under the name of Freedom, and that almost is the only freedom that it is practicable at present to be permitted to it.

Slavery in Virginia, up to the present time, however it has improved the general character and circumstances of the race of miserable black barbarians that several generations since were introduced here, has done nothing to prepare it, and is yet doing nothing to prepare it, for the free and enlightened exercise of individual independence and responsibility. THEREFORE, is Slavery the greatest sin and shame upon any nation or people on God's earth. The slaveholders say that we and others, by our impracticable interference, are responsible for this sin and shame. Let God judge, and let us keep silence.

I wish now to give you some idea of the condition of the freed blacks at the South; in Virginia. I shall incidentally refer to the condition of those at the North.

In one county of Virginia, a few years ago, an inventory and estimate of the value of the property of all the free blacks was made by order of the magistracy. With one exception the highest value placed upon the property of an individual was two dollars and a half ($2.50.) The person excepted owned one hundred and fifty acres of land, a cabin upon it, a mule and some implements. He had a family, including only his wife and children, of nine. Of provisions for their support, there were in the house, at the time of the visit of the appraisers, a peck and a half of Indian meal and part of a herring. The man was then absent to purchase some more meal, but had no money, and was to give his promise to pay in wood, which he was to cut from his farm. And this was in Winter.

This shows their general poverty. That this poverty is not the result of want of facilities or security for accumulating property, is proved by the exceptional instances of considerable wealth existing among them. An account of the death of a free colored man who devised by will property to the amount of thirty thousand dollars, has been lately in the newspapers. I have ascertained the general accuracy of the narration though one somewhat important circumstance was omitted. It was stated that the man preferred that his children should continue in the condition of slaves, and gave his property to a man who was to be their master. He gave as a reason for this that he had personally examined the condition of the free blacks in Philadelphia and Boston, as well as in Virginia, and he preferred that his children should remain slaves, knowing that their master would take better care of them than they were capable of exercising for themselves. This was substantially correct, and I have conversed with a gentleman who tried to persuade him to act otherwise, to whom he gave these reasons. He had been, however, for a long time before his death, in a low state of health, and I know not how sound, or uninfluenced by others, his mind might have been. The circumstance omitted was, that these were illegitimate children, by a slave woman, although he had a wife that was a free woman, and had had a child by her—which, however, died young. It is a general custom of white people here to leave their illegitimate children, by slaves (and they are *very* common) in slavery. The man was himself a mulatto.[2] I know of a very respectable and very wealthy man who sold his own half-brother to the traders to go South, because he attempted to run away.

I have heard of another case of a free negro in Virginia, supposed to be worth at least $5,000.

At the present rate of wages, any free colored man can accumulate property more rapidly in Virginia than almost any man, depending solely on his labor, can at the North. In the tobacco factories in Richmond and Petersburg slaves are at this time in great demand, and are paid one hundred and fifty to two hundred dollars, and all expenses, for a year. These slaves are expected to work only to a certain extent for their employers; it having been found that they could not be "driven" to do a fair day's work so easily as they could be stimulated to it by the offer of a bonus for all they would manufacture above a certain number of pounds. This quantity is so easily exceeded that the slaves earn for themselves from five to twenty dollars a month. *Freemen* are paid for all they do at rates which make their labor equally profitable, and *can* earn, if they give but moderate attention and diligence to the labor, very large sums. The barber under the Bollingbroke Hotel[3] has a younger brother, who works in a tobacco factory, whose wages last year amounted to over nine hundred dollars. Of this he has laid up not one cent, and such is the case with nearly all the hands so employed in the town; they spend their wages as do the slaves their "over money," almost as rapidly as they receive it, and as foolishly and as much to their own injury as do sailors, or the manufacturing workmen in England. Of the truth of this, I have assurances from every quarter, and from men of all opinions.

Formerly, I am told, the slaves were accustomed to recreate themselves in the evening and on holidays a great deal in dancing, and that they took great enjoyment in this exercise. It was at length, however, preached against, and the "professors" so generally induced to use their influence against it as an immoral practice, that it has greatly gone "out of fashion," and in place of it the young ones have got into the habit of gambling, and worse occupations, for the pastime of their holidays and leisure hours. I have not seen any dancing during these holidays, nor any amusement engaged in by the blacks that was not essentially gross, dissipating or wasteful, unless I except firing of crackers.

Improvidence is generally considered here a natural trait of African character; and by none is it more so than by the negroes themselves. I think it is a mistake. Negroes, as far as I have observed at the North, although suffering from the contamination of habits acquired by themselves or their fathers in Slavery, unless they are intemperate, are more provident than whites of equal educational advantages. Much more so than the newly-arrived Irish, though the Irish are soon infected with the desire of accumulating wealth and acquiring permanent means of comfort. This opinion is confirmed by the experience of the City Missionaries—one of whom has informed me that where the very poorest classes of New-York reside, black and white in the same house, the rooms occupied by the blacks are generally much less bare of furniture and the means of subsistence than those of the whites.[4]

I observed that the negroes themselves follow the notion of the whites here, and look upon the people of their race as naturally unfitted to provide for themselves far ahead. Accustomed like children to have all their necessary wants provided for, their whole energies and powers of mind are habitually given to obtaining the means of temporary ease and enjoyment. Their masters and the poor or "mean" whites acquire somewhat of the same habits from early association with them, calculate on it in them, do not wish to cure it, and by constant practices encourage it. The negroes depend much for the means of enjoying themselves on presents. Their good-natured masters (and their masters are very good-natured, though capricious and quick-tempered) like to gratify them, and are ashamed to disappoint them—to be thought mean. So it follows that with the free negroes, habit is upon them; the habits of their associates, slaves, make the custom of society—that strongest of agents upon weak minds. The whites think improvidence a natural defect of character with them, expect it of them as they grow old, or as they lose easy means of gaining a livelihood, charitably furnish it to them; expect them to pilfer; do not look upon it as a crime; if they do, at least, consider them but slightly to blame, as, indeed, they are; and so every influence of association is unfavorable to providence, forethought, economy. I shall continue this subject in my next.

YEOMAN.

1. Olmsted probably wrote this letter during his stay in Norfolk, Virginia, between January 3 and 7, 1853, or in Raleigh, North Carolina, between January 8 and 14 (FLO to JO, Jan. 10, 1853, above).

2. The *Richmond Enquirer* of December 28, 1852, carried an article from the *Martinsburg* [Virginia] *Gazette* telling of the recent death in a lower county of Virginia of a free mulatto whose story fits Olmsted's description. His master left him "a respectable property," and he then accumulated an estate of $25,000 and bought his wife and children (since freeing them would have required removing them from Virginia). Being in poor health, he went to Philadelphia for medical advice in the summer of 1852. There he learned that he was close to death, and prevailed on a relative of his old master to take him back to Virginia. He died soon after, and left all his property, including his wife and children, to that man. The editor of the *Enquirer* presented this information as "facts for the next edition of Uncle Tom's Cabin"—facts that would "put to shame the exaggerated fictions of Mrs. Stowe and her adherents" ("Southern Facts," *Richmond Enquirer*, Dec. 28, 1852, p. 2).
3. The Bollingbrook Hotel in Petersburg, Virginia (Edward A. Wyatt IV, *Along Petersburg Streets: Historic Sites and Buildings of Petersburg, Virginia* [Richmond, Va., 1943], p. 14).
4. By city missionaries, Olmsted means ministers who attempted to reach those of the city's poor who were neglected by existing churches. His informant may well have been Charles Loring Brace, who worked during 1852 at the Five Points House of Industry in one of the worst slum sections of New York City (*Life of Brace*, p. 153).

New-York Daily Times, April 5, 1853[1]

THE SOUTH.

LETTERS ON THE PRODUCTIONS, INDUSTRY AND RESOURCES OF THE SLAVE STATES.

NUMBER NINE.

Special Correspondence of the New-York Daily Times

Condition of Free Blacks at the South—Free Blacks at the North—Evils of Enfranchisement—Aversion to Colonization—Dependence of Negroes on the Whites—General Sentiment on Slavery in Virginia.

To the Editor of the New-York Daily Times:

With such influences upon them, with such a character, with such education, with such associations, as I described in my last letter, it is not surprising that Southerners say that the condition of the slave who is subject to some wholesome restraint, and notwithstanding his improvidence is *systematically* provided for, is preferable to that of the free black. The free black does not in general feel himself superior to the slave, and the slaves of the wealthy and aristocratic families consider themselves in a much better and more honorable position than the free blacks. I have heard their view of the matter expressed thus "_____ *dirty free niggers!—got no body to take care of 'em.*"

It is for this reason that slaves of gentlemen of high character, who are treated with judicious indulgence, and who can rely with confidence on the permanence of their position, knowing that they will be kindly cared for as they grow old, and feeling their own incapacity to take care of themselves, do often voluntarily remain in slavery when freedom is offered them, whether it be at the South, or North, or in Africa. A great many slaves that have been freed and sent to the North, after remaining there for a time, have of their own accord, returned to Virginia, and their report of the manner in which negroes are treated there, the difficulty of earning enough to provide themselves with the luxuries to which they have been accustomed, the unkindness of the white people to them, and the want of that thoughtless liberality in payments to them which they expect here from their superiors, has not been such as to lead others to pine for the life of an outcast at the North. Among those so returning, have been many of Mr. Randolph's slaves, I understand.[2]

And here let me say, as I am most happy to do, that I am convinced that the real kindness of heart and generosity of the people of Virginia, makes practically of no effect their unjust, cruel and cowardly laws with regard to free negroes—unjust, because they interfere with a man's quiet possession of the rewards of his own labor—cruel, because they separate friends, break up families, and make men homeless outcasts among strangers—cowardly, because they attempt to throw upon others a danger and evil which is the natural result of the peculiar constitution of their own society.[3]

The spread of intelligence of all kinds among the slaves is remarkable. A planter told me that he had frequently known of his slaves going twenty miles from home and back during the night, without their being missed at all from work, or known at the time to be off the plantation. Another told me that he had been frequently informed by his slaves of occurrences in a town forty miles distant, where he spent part of the year with his family, in advance of the mail, or any means of communication that he could command the use of. Also, when in town, his servants would sometimes give him important news from the plantation, several hours before a messenger dispatched by his overseer arrived.

I do not wish to be understood as intimating that the slaves generally would not like to be freed and sent to the North, or that they are ever really contented or satisfied with slavery; only that as having been deprived of the use of their limbs from infancy, as it were, they are not such fools as to wish now suddenly to be set upon their feet, and left to shift for themselves. They prefer, if they have sufficient worldly wisdom, to secure at least plain food and clothing, and comfortable lodging, at their owner's expense, while they will return as little for it as they can, and have only the luxuries of life to work for on their own account. It is not easy to deprive them of the means of securing a good share of these.

These luxuries to be sure, may be of very degrading character, and such as, according to our ideas, they would be better without. But their tastes and habits are formed to enjoy them, and they are not likely to be content without them.

But, to live either on their own means, or the charitable assistance of others, at the North, they must dispense with many of them. It is as much as most of them—more than some of them, with us—can do, by their labor, to obtain the means of subsistence, such as they have been used to being provided with, without a thought of their own, at the South. And if they are known to indulge in practices that are habitual with them, they will not only lose the charity, but even the custom, of most of their philanthropical friends; and then they must turn to pilfering again, or meet that most pitiful of all extremities—poverty from want of work. Again: Suppose them to wish to indulge in their old habits of sensual pleasure, they can only do so by forsaking the better class of even their own color, or by drawing them down to their own level. In this way, Slavery, even now, day by day, is greatly responsible for the degraded and immoral condition of the free blacks of our cities, and especially of Philadelphia. It is, perhaps, necessary that I should explain that licentiousness and almost indiscriminate sexual connection among the young is very general, and is a necessity of the system of Slavery. A Northern family that employs slave domestics, and insists upon a life of physical chastity in its female servants, is always greatly detested; and they frequently come to their owners and beg to be taken away, or not hired again, though acknowledging themselves to be kindly treated in all other respects. A slave owner told me this of his own girls hired to Northern people.[4]

That the character and condition of some is improved by coming to the North, it is impossible to deny. From a miserable half barbarous, half brutal state they have been brought to the highest civilization. From slaves they have sometimes come to be intelligent, cultivated, free-thinking, independent-minded, and good and even great men. Frederick Douglass[5] is a *great* man, if poetry, eloquence and vigorous original thought make greatness. He is but little less great that the vindictive energy with which he pursues the enemy that prevents his being recognized as so, that even *taboos* him from the society of the cultivated and refined, sometimes carries him beyond the bounds of calm reason and good taste.

It is minds of such character originally that slavery is most galling to, and in which the intelligence and energy necessary to obtain freedom is most likely to reside. For this reason the condition and character of the fugitive slaves does not give a fair indication of that of the mass, and yet it surely is not such, take them all in all, as to make it appear that if the great body of slaves should be sent to free States they would be better off than they are now. I doubt if we have reason to think their children would. In my opinion, this is the greatest reproach to slavery, but the fact remains against *hasty* measures to destroy it.

As to slaves set free by the masters, without any previous education for it and sent to the free States, I have no doubt they often come to great suffering; and if it should be a frequent or general practice, the result would be anything but desirable. I know of one case in which seven were thus permitted to go to

Philadelphia, of which five died in three years, two returned to Virginia, and only one remains—of whose condition I am uninformed, but have no reason to think, and do not believe it at all better in any way than when he was a slave.

As to Liberia,[6] it is certainly true that the negroes, either slave or free, are not generally disposed to go there. It is a distant country, of which they can have but very little reliable information, they do not like the idea any more than other people do of emigrating from their native country. But I really think that the best reason for their not being more anxious to go there is that they are sincerely attached in a certain way to the *white race*. At all events they do not incline to live in communities entirely separate from the whites and do not long for entire independence from them. They have been so long accustomed to trusting the government of all weighty matters to the whites, that they would not feel at home where they did not have them to "take care of them." As I pointed out before, they do not feel inclined to take great responsibilities on themselves, and have no confidence in the talent of their race for self-government. A gentleman told me that he owned a very intelligent negro who had acquired some property, and that he had more than once offered him his freedom, but he would always reply that he did not feel able to fall entirely upon his own resources, and preferred to have a master. He once offered him his freedom to go to Liberia, and urged him to go there. His reply was to the effect that he would have no objections if the Government was in the hands of white folks, but that he had no confidence in the ability of black people to undertake the control of public affairs.

To conclude this letter, I will tell you what I think the continued existence of Slavery in Virginia depends upon. First—

Upon the very low and degraded condition of the mass of the people. The proportion of those who cannot read and write in the State is *more than thirty times as great as in Connecticut.*[7] From their want of intelligence they are duped, frightened, excited, prejudiced and made to betray their most direct and evident interests by the more cultivated and talented, spendthrift and unprincipled of the wealthy class. These, who, without the slightest prudence or care for the future of the Commonwealth, live dependent for the means of their selfish extravagance on the slave labor of today, form "public opinion" by their reckless energy.

Meanwhile the truly wise and good men of the State suffer themselves to be left in the background, suffer themselves to appear in a false position, even aid by their apparent countenance of the wicked and foolish, the general expression of attachment to Slavery, because the question, What can be done, is too great for them, and because they really think the only remedy that is proposed would be productive of greater evil than the disease.

No one speaks a word aloud of it, but not a sober, thinking man of the State is there that does not know that Slavery is a Curse upon him and his, and that if it were possible to remove the effect of causes that are not alone in the future or the present, Virginia would be a hundred times richer, a thousand times happier, if Slavery were not.

P. S.—Since I wrote this letter I have been convinced that the sentiment I have described in the last paragraph is even deeper and more general with the mass of the people than I then imagined. I must mention an incident indicative of it. I was standing on the platform of a railroad car at a station where a gang of slaves had been waiting to take our train to proceed South, but the "servant's car" being full they were left behind. Two men, one of whom I afterwards learned to be a bar-keeper, the other an overseer, stood with me on the platform. As we moved off one said to the other:

"That's a good lot of niggers."

"Good! I only wish they belonged to me, I wouldn't ask for anything else."

They continued in conversation, *starting* with this, for some time, though I heard but little of what they said. They were talking of their different occupations, and grumbling that they succeeded no better. One, I heard say, that the highest wages he had ever had was two hundred dollars a year, and that year he did not lay up a cent. Soon after, one of them spoke with much vehemence and bitterness of tone, so I do not doubt their whole previous conversation had had reference to the point.

"I wish to God, old Virginny was free of all the niggers!"

"It would be a d——d good thing if she was."

"Yes, and I tell you, it would be a—d——d *good thing for us poor fellows.*"

"Well, I reckon it would, myself."

But, mind you, these same "poor fellows" understand the impracticability of instantly abolishing Slavery and having on their hands a vast population of freed slaves—more degraded and impressible with exciting prejudices than even themselves—as well as any body, and would be the very first to tar and feather an "Abolitionist" if he came to advise them to it.

YEOMAN.

---

1. Olmsted probably wrote this letter during his stay in Raleigh, North Carolina, from January 8 to 13, 1853.
2. John Randolph of Roanoke (1773–1833) freed his slaves in his will and provided for his executor, Benjamin Watkins Leigh, to settle them in the North. In 1846, Leigh arranged the purchase of land in Mercer County, Ohio, and had buildings constructed. When the 385 freedmen arrived in July 1846, however, armed citizens of the region refused to let them settle and forced their removal within three days (*DAB*; John H. Russell, *The Free Negro in Virginia, 1619–1865* [Baltimore, 1913], p. 72; "John Randolph's Negroes," *Liberator*, August 7, 1846, p. 1; *Richmond Enquirer*, July 7, 1846, p. 2; ibid., July 28, 1846, p. 3).
3. Free blacks in Virginia were subject to numerous legal disabilities. They had to carry papers proving their free status, and in any challenge the burden of proof of freedom rested with them

rather than with the challenger. Any free black found in a county or town other than the one in which he had the right of legal residence could be arrested and hired out to labor as a vagrant. No free black could change his residence without permission from the county or town to which he proposed to move. Free blacks could not leave the state for education, and could not go to a free state and return to Virginia. They were denied trial by jury and were subject, like slaves, to corporal punishment for a variety of misdemeanors. They were also forbidden to have firearms.

Olmsted appears to be referring in particular to the law of 1806 that required all emancipated slaves to leave the state within twelve months, on pain of being sold back into slavery. Enforcement of the law was lax, however, and a growing proportion of the free blacks in the state—perhaps as many as one-third of the total by 1860—were illegal residents. They stood to suffer from forced sale of their property should the law be enforced. Olmsted is also saying here that by coupling manumission with the requirement of removal from the state, Virginians threw onto others the problems resulting from their own failure to make a place for the free black in their society or to prepare slaves properly for freedom (J. H. Russell, *Free Negro in Virginia*, pp. 70–77, 152–53, 174–77).

4. Olmsted regretted writing this assertion of the inevitability of licentiousness among slaves, and within a month urged Charles Loring Brace to excise it before the letter went to press (see FLO to CLB, Feb. 8, 1853, below).

Much of this letter up to this point appears in *Seaboard Slave States*, pages 129–33; the remainder of the letter does not appear in Olmsted's later publications.

5. The black abolitionist orator and journalist Frederick Douglass (1817–1895), at this time editor of the weekly *Frederick Douglass' Paper*, which he had founded in 1847 as the *North Star* (Benjamin Quarles, *Frederick Douglass* [Washingtin, D.C., 1948], pp. 80–91).

6. A colony for American free blacks and emancipated slaves, founded by the American Colonization Society in 1820. By 1852 the Society had sent some 7,335 colonists there (Philip J. Staudenraus, *The African Colonization Movement, 1816–1865* [New York, 1961], pp. 48–68, 251).

7. At the time that Olmsted wrote this letter, the statistics on illiteracy gathered for the census of 1850 had not yet been published. His source was probably the census of 1840, which provided figures on the number of white illiterates over the age of twenty in the total white population of each state. Connecticut had 526 such illiterates in a white population of 301,856, while Virginia had 58,787 in a white population of 740,858—a proportion nearly 44 times as great.

By 1850 the situation had changed markedly, however, due primarily to the influx of foreign-born immigrants into Connecticut during the latter part of the 1840s. The census of 1850 revealed that Connecticut now had 4,739 adult white illiterates in a white population of 363,099, while Virginia had 77,005 in a white population of 894,800—a proportion only 7 times as great.

Faced with this rapid decline in the relative superiority of the North in literacy, Northerners often continued to consider only the native-born white illiteracy rate when comparing the two sections. In their comprehensive statistical study of the North and the South of 1856, for instance, Henry Chase and C. H. Sanborn calculated the illiteracy rate as the proportion of native-born adult illiterates in the adult white population. This yielded a figure of 1 in 277 for Connecticut and 1 in 5 for Virginia—a proportion 55 times as great (U.S., Census Office, 7th Census, *The Seventh Census. Report of the Superintendent of the Census for December 1, 1852; To Which is Appended the Report for December 1, 1851* [Washington, D.C., 1853], p. 27; idem, 7th Census, *The Seventh Census of the United States: 1850. Embracing a Statistical View of Each of the States and Territories . . .* J. D. B. DeBow, Superintendent of the United States Census [Washington, D.C., 1853[, pp, ix, xxxiii, lxi; Henry Chase and C. H. Sanborn, *The North and the South: Being a Statistical View of the Condition of the Free and Slave States*, 2d ed. [Boston and Cleveland, 1857], pp. 103–4).

JOURNEY THROUGH THE UPPER SOUTH: 1852–1853

New-York Daily Times, April 8, 1853[1]

THE SOUTH.

LETTERS ON THE PRODUCTIONS, INDUSTRY AND
RESOURCES OF THE SOUTHERN STATES.

NUMBER TEN.

Special Correspondence of the New-York Daily Times

General View of the Physical Character and Agricultural History of Eastern Virginia and Region adjoining—Aristocracy and Slavery—Ireland and Virginia.

To the Editor of the New-York Times:

I remained a fortnight at Richmond and Petersburg, making excursions by the railroads, on horseback, or on foot, to plantations of different character, and that were recommended to me, as illustrating the different systems of culture prevailing in Eastern Virginia; and I now proceed to give you a general sketch of this district.

It extends from the base of the Blue Ridge to the sea at Chesapeake Bay, being about 175 miles in width, and the same in length. It has no distinct physical boundary on the north and south; and my observations may be considered applicable—allowing for some modification of climate, owing to difference of latitude—to the greater part of Maryland and the northern and eastern part of North Carolina.

It is so divided by streams, that but a small part of it is more than fifteen miles from water navigable by sea-going vessels or bateaus. Ships of the largest class ascend several of the rivers more than fifty miles, and sloops much further. These rivers and their tributaries also afford, at convenient intervals, excellent milling power.

About one hundred miles from, and parallel to, the shore, but with frequent irregular spurs, a granite steppe, or ledge, subdivides the district—the country below it being alluvial, generally level, and frequently low and marshy. In geological phrase, the upper region is primary, the low country of tertiary formation. The rivers are subject to the influence of tides up to this ledge, which occasions "rapids" in them, precluding further ascent of vessels from the sea. There is a general tendency of descent in a southeasterly direction from the Blue Ridge to the shore; but this is more rapid, and the surface is much more undulating and varied above than below the ledge.

In the tide-water region the summers are long and debilitating, though the extremes of heat are no greater than at New-York—the mercury seldom, if ever, rising to 100°F. As you ascend towards the mountains the summer is shorter, and in their immediate vicinity, or in what is known as the *piedmont* country, the climate is peculiarly healthful and invigorating.

Most of the plants of the temperate zone flourish—a few fruits and agricultural productions slightly changing the character they have in New-York. It is more favorable to Indian corn than the climate of New-York, less so to oats, which grain has a peculiar adaptability to flourish and increase in weight in regions of short summers and bleak surfaces. Apples, of varieties that mature in February in New-York, here ripen on the tree. There were formerly apples that were probably seedlings of the district that ripened late in the winter; but with the characteristic habit of the people they have been allowed to become nearly or quite extinct. Winter apples, therefore, are extensively imported from the North.

The climate would permit the culture of many valuable plants which cannot exist at New-York, and the indigenous productions of the soil are much more varied. But little advantage has, however, been taken of this opportunity; the productions of agriculture being *less*-varied in general than in the free states. The difficulty of introducing anything new into the routine of labor where slaves are employed, is the first reason of this.

Near Norfolk, the culture of semi-tropical vegetables for the Northern markets has commenced. It is mainly a free-labor enterprise. In the southern part, for about fifty miles north from the south line of Virginia, cotton is cultivated on many plantations, not however to any great extent for other than the local demand. By some attention to varieties, and a gradual improvement under careful culture, it would be profitably extended much further, if the demand for it should continue as at present.

Rice is cultivated by the negroes in the swamps for their own use and for sale, but nowhere is any attention paid to it by the planters. Under a small proprietory, enough would be raised for the home demand and its consumption be increased.

The fig and the olive can be grown anywhere with cotton. The fig is cultivated in gardens in Norfolk, and single trees of considerable age may be found on exposed sites in all the southern half of the district. The olive is not cultivated or known here at all. There is no grape culture or wine making, except experimentally. There is a reasonable prospect that it might be a successful business.

An experimental plantation in the vicinity of Washington, in which the fitness of the climate to the culture of various foreign agricultural productions should be tested, would add greatly to the wealth and commerical independence of the country if there were sufficient enterprise in the people of this district to make use of the results.

The soil of both the upper and lower regions is greatly varied, and often every description will be found on a single small farm. The local names made use of to distinguish the different varieties ("mulatto," "chinquapin," &c.) have reference only to the color of the surface. In the lower region, there is a large proportion of poor sandy land, but on the border of the rivers, the soil is in every respect of excellent quality and suitable to the culture of all the most valuable agricultural productions. In the upper region, a clayey soil of good natural quality, predominates, though it is often covered with sand. This sandy surface soil varies in texture and quality, but most generally is so thin where it is poor, that it can be broken through and clay mingled with it by a four-horse plow.

Beds of fossil sea-shells underlay many counties of the lower region, the application of which to the surface-soil is of very great advantage. Of this improvement I shall again speak.

The earlier settlers of Virginia naturally located themselves on the banks of the broad navigable streams, and first brought the rich meadows on their borders into cultivation. I think there is no evidence that these meadows have declined in productive capacity from that time to this. A gradual, slight deepening of the tillage, with the addition, in late years, of a little lime to the soil, to hasten and make more complete the process of disintegration and decomposition, has sufficed to supply abundant material for the crops removed from it during nearly two centuries.

The great profits of the Tobacco growing, on *new soils,* however, when this plant became the staple of the Colony, as it soon did, led to the rapid removal of the natural forests of oak, beech, and other deciduous trees, on the naturally poor soils of the upland. As fast as the newly cleared land failed to make a profitable return under the careless culture of the exhausting tobacco, it was given up and new breadths of the forest cleared.

In the *"old field,"*[2] in place of the former growth of deciduous trees, the wronged soil sent up a thick growth of pines, which were eventually, when all the aboriginal forest within convenient reach had been gone over, themselves felled and burned on the ground, and the land was again subjected to a course of tobacco. Thus the rotation was first, tobacco; second, pine, until after a few generations the tobacco crop became so light that it ceased to be profitably cultivated. Then the planter, if he had sufficient enterprise, would gather together his flocks and herds of African slaves and European "bondsmen or *redemptioners;*"[3] and settle himself again upon some previously unoccupied tract, fell the oaks, and put it through the same process, pine succeeding tobacco, and tobacco, pine.

Thus gradually the plantations were advanced across all the light soils of the lower region, and into the stiffer and better soils above the rapids of the rivers, until at length these became almost exclusively dovoted to the tobacco culture, and so continue to the present day, little or no tobacco being cultivated in the tide-water district, while it continues the staple of most of the counties above.

It would be naturally supposed that after a time the light lands would sufficiently recover to tempt their owners again to resume tobacco planting, and you would certainly see no reason why it should not prevail on the river-meadows, the soils of which are entirely unexhausted, and admirably adapted to support its heavy demands. The reason given is that they are more profitably employed in bearing corn and wheat. But knowing that soils of a similar description in the more Northern States, equally well adapted to wheat and corn, have lately increased in value from its having been discovered that tobacco could be matured upon them, it is evident that this is not a sufficient explanation.

A great depression of the *price* of tobacco occurred at the period of our second war with England, owing to the interruption of commerce, and was sustained by the continued political agitations in Europe and the subsequent financial distress in our own country up to a late period. At this time, tobacco, being an article of compact value and cheaply transported, could still be much more profitably raised and brought to market from the back country than corn and wheat, there being then no facilities of communication from these districts superior to horse draft over the rudest roads, while crops raised on the river bank could be readily and cheaply transported by shipping to any desired market. Thus tobacco was entirely lost as a crop below the rapids that obstructed a higher navigation, the possessors of the land only retaining a holy horror of it as the scourge that had rendered the greater part of the land within their reach utterly valueless for the general purposes of husbandry.

The reason the culture is not resumed at the present day, when tobacco is again high and wheat low (and when tobacco is taking the place of corn crops on land no better and in climate much less adapted to it than on the soils of the river intervals) is probably this. The cultivation and curing, sorting, packing, &c., of tobacco, are processes entirely different from any the laborers of the present day in the low country are familiar with, and slave labor is so exceedingly unintelligent and prejudiced that it is next to impossible to introduce any new process requiring skill or the use of unaccustomed instruments where it is employed.

The utter poverty of the soil, and the sorry, disgraceful, bankrupt condition of the proprietors of it in lower Virginia, at the period in which tobacco culture became no longer profitable, can only be compared to the misery of a sot who is deprived of the means of obtaining his accustomed stimulus. Up to this period the Virginia proprietors had been a race of lords. Of the mode of life and the character of the agriculture then prevailing, a Virginian writer of our day thus gives a picture:[4]

> No man of wealth, or with a moderate estate, thought of attending personally to his farming. Every detail of management was entrusted to the overseers, who rarely were stimulated by even the general superintendence and control of their employers. Overseers' wages were generally paid in a certain share or proportion of the crops they made. Thus, they had a direct interest in drawing from the land and labor as much as possible during the current year of their engagement; and none whatever in preserving or increasing the productive power of the land for later times. It came to be recognised as a maxim of agricultural

morals, that "it was not *just* for a proprietor to interfere with and change his overseer's designed direction of the labors of the farm, inasmuch as any abstraction from immediate product, for the sake of future improvement, operated to lessen the overseer's profits for the present year." This doctrine accorded so well with the disposition of every indolent, careless, and wasteful proprietor, then it is no wonder that it came to be generally received, and conformed to in practice.

The more wealthy proprietors, having no occupation of industry, spent their time mostly in seeking pleasure. Visits to each other were frequent and protracted. It was rare that any one of this class was without some company, either at home or abroad. Besides such exercises of reciprocal hospitality, every idle or homeless "gentleman" of the whole country found in every mansion a comfortable sojourning place, and, at least the outward show, if not the reality, of welcome, so long as he might choose to stay. Of course, visits from such persons were ordinary occurrences—and were sometimes protracted for weeks or months. That this particular neighborhood was not "eaten out" by this class of genteel and honorable vagrants and spongers, was not because of their deficiency of numbers, or of active use of their facilities—but because they had like privileges in every part of the country. This race, fortunately, is now nearly extinct. But many such individuals are still remembered, who for many years of their adult life, and some for their whole life, pursued no other business, and had no other means of support, except visiting their friends. Of course they counted their friends by hundreds.

The wealthier proprietors were not only hospitable and kind hosts, but also refined and pleasing companions. Their fathers' wealth had served to give to them education and manners of good society. With many excellent social and moral qualities, their habits of idleness and pleasure-seeking naturally led to the attendant and consequent vices. Social drinking was often carried to excess; and card-playing was sure to be introduced whenever as many neighbors dined together as served to make up a game of loo.[5] Horse-racing was a favorite amusement of all classes; some of the farmers owned and ran race-horses, and nearly all reared horses of the high blood, and at the high cost required for the turf.

How like the *"true gentlemen" of Ireland!*
But let us not forget in passing that when the time of retribution came, the slaves suffered not—*the peasants starved!* I have seen the one intimately,[6] and from what I have at present seen of the other, I must declare that the Virginia slave is more happy, more comfortable, in some sense more *free;* and in better and more manly relation to his masters, than the Irish peasant or the English agricultural laborer is to the "higher classes" of those countries.

I wonder not that the London *Times* moves against "Uncle Tom."[7] It has a cut backward which its hundreds of thousands of English readers will not lose. Slavery will not die until the world has humbled itself to learn a lesson from it.

Oh, God! who are we that condemn our brother? No slave ever killed its own offspring in cool calculation of saving money by it, as do English free women. No slave is forced to eat of corruption, as are Irish tenants.[8] No slave freezes to death for want of habitation and fuel, as have men in Boston. No slave reels off into the abyss of God, from want of work that shall bring it food, as do men and women in New-York. Remember that, Mrs. Stowe. Remember that, indignant sympathizers.

Oh, Christian capitalists, free traders in labor, there is somewhat to be built up, as well as somewhat to be abolished before we repose in the millennium.

YEOMAN.

1. Olmsted probably wrote this letter between January 8 and 14, 1853, during his stay in Raleigh, North Carolina.
2. An "old field" was a field formerly under cultivation that had been abandoned and left to revert to natural growth.
3. Redemptioners were immigrants to the American colonies who worked as indentured servants in order to pay (or "redeem") the cost of their passage.
4. The article from which Olmsted quotes appeared in the *Southern Planter,* a journal published in Richmond, Virginia. In it the anonymous author, who called himself "Calx.," described the historical stages of agriculture and society in a tidewater county of Virginia where he had spent his youth ("Four Eras of Agricultural Condition, in a Particular Locality," *Southern Planter, Devoted to Agriculture, Horticulture, and the Household Arts* 12, no. 5 [May 1852]: 133–37).
5. A game of cards played for stakes.
6. When he visited Ireland in 1850, Olmsted saw the effect of the famine of 1845 and succeeding years. In some instances the suffering and starvation at that time were aggravated by the refusal of the local landlords to assist in relief efforts and by the wholesale eviction of tenants who could not pay their rent (Cecil Blanche Woodham-Smith, *The Great Hunger, Ireland 1845–9* [London, 1962], pp. 160–64).
7. On September 3, 1852, the *Times* of London carried a long editorial entitled "Uncle Tom's Cabin," which criticized Harriet Beecher Stowe for giving Uncle Tom such a faultless character and for raising anger and resentment that would impede both the gradual amelioration of the condition of slaves and their preparation for freedom (see "American Slavery. English Opinion of 'Uncle Tom's Cabin,'" *NYDT,* Sept. 18, 1852, p. 6).
8. During the potato famine in Ireland in the 1840s, the peasants in some places were reduced to eating food "from which . . . so putrid and offensive an effluvia issued that in consuming it they were obliged to leave the doors and windows of their cabins open" (C. B. Woodham-Smith, *The Great Hunger,* pp. 70–71).

New-York Daily Times, April 13, 1853[1]

THE SOUTH.

LETTERS ON THE PRODUCTIONS, INDUSTRY AND RESOURCES OF THE SOUTHERN STATES.

NUMBER ELEVEN.

Special Correspondence of the New-York Daily Times

JOURNEY THROUGH THE UPPER SOUTH: 1852-1853

General Sketch of Virginia Husbandry, Continued—Corn Farming—The Ordinary and the Improving Modes of Agriculture—Calcareous Manures—The Usual Rotations—Guano—The Future—New-Englanders Advised to Emigrate—A World for Old England.

To the Editor of the New-York Daily Times:

With the low prices for tobacco consequent upon the War of 1812, the distress and poverty resulting from the previous extravagance and pride, reached its climax. The Virginia aristocracy had come to the end of their rope. The writer from whom I have previously quoted thus describes the period of humility that followed:

> After more or less time, every farm was greatly impoverished—almost every estate was seriously impaired—and some were involved in debt to nearly their value. Most of the proprietors had died, leaving families in reduced circumstances, and in some cases in great straits. No farm, whether of a rich or a poor proprietor, had escaped great exhaustion; and no property great dilapidation, unless because the proprietor had at first been too poor to join the former expensive habits of his wealthier neighbors.
>
> * * * *There was nothing left to waste, but time and labor;* and these continued to be wasted in the now fruitless efforts to cultivate to profit, or to replace the fertility of soil which had been destroyed. Luxury and expense had been greatly lessened. But on that account the universal prostration was even the more apparent. Many mansions were falling into decay. Few received any but trivial and indispensable repairs. No new mansion was erected, and rarely any other farm building of value. There was still generally prevailing idleness among proprietors; and also an abandonment of hope, which made every one desirous to sell his land and move to the fertile and far West, and a general emigration and dispersion only was prevented by the impossibility of finding purchasers for the lands, even at half the then low estimate of market prices.[2]

All was not sufficient. The virus still remained in the system and was transmitted from father to son. Two generations have passed and still Virginians all draw the distinct line between *gentleman* and *workman*. Still it is their creed, "so far as the mere laborer has the pride, the knowledge or the aspirations of a freeman, he is unfitted for his situation." Still they liken the man who worketh with his own hands to "the horse or the ox;" and ask sneeringly, "Would you do *him* a benefit to give him a cultivated understanding or fine feelings?"[3]

The land has very generally passed out of the families of the ancient proprietors, whose descendants are now in a large part to be found among the low whites; low because poor—poverty and degradation being synonymous in a slave country. The tendency is still much more to the concentration of property than at the North, and the land is held generally in much larger parcels than can be efficiently superintended by the owner. There is a monstrous proportion of the people, even beside the negroes, that are living most miserably—

uneducated, unintelligent and unambitious—but comparatively few in the condition most favorable to the development of the resources and increase of the wealth of a State—that in which they are raised above the hopeless depression of poverty, and stimulated by both their needs and their opportunities to the constant exercise of observation and intelligent reflection, and to ever hopeful, active, well-rewarded industry.

I should judge that a large proportion of the plantations in Eastern Virginia had been, to this day, conducted with precisely the same purposes and with very similar consequences that they were one hundred years ago. The proprietors or landholders, as long as it is possible, occupy themselves with "hospitality" and "abstractions," and are practically *absentees;* leaving the details of management to overseers; cultivating their estates with reference entirely to the greatest immediate return; putting away from their thoughts the evil days that must result from such a system.

But there are now many exceptions. Here and there a farm has been improved, its productions increased, and the proprietor is adding to his wealth. You find some few whole counties or districts that have caught the spirit of enterprise; and the means of improvement being simple, obvious and well established in their effects, everywhere that this is the case, there is a glow of prosperity strongly contrasting with the deadness and poverty which generally prevails. Of late, the statistics of the State begin to be influenced, and the arch-abstractionists lay back in their chairs and rub their hands, and proudly tell you Virginia is beginning to live again.

The best farms and the most profitable in Virginia are on the banks of the James River. Nearly all these are in the hands of comparatively new proprietors, and are managed with the skill, energy, forethought and enterprise acquired in other and less "aristocratic" occupations.

On the lighter lands of Eastern Virginia maize has been the staple crop and in many parts the only crop that has paid for cultivation. On many farms, to this day, *the sole crop raised* is corn, the only produce of the land, bacon and corn. Swine live mainly in the woods on herbage and nuts; the cleared land is all planted with corn, what little manure is made is all applied to it, and the force of the farm is almost wholly employed in its cultivation. Much more labor is given to it than at the North, and though very uneconomically, owing to rude implements and shallow ideas of plowing up the subsoil, generally the crop is better "tended," the surface kept mellower and more free from weeds than at the North. This is partly because the season of cultivation is longer and because the hands are not obliged to be taken off for harvest. The crop on new land may be twenty-five bushels from an acre, but, of course, greatly varies with the soil, the manure and the season; generally there will be enough to provide the slaves with an abundant allowance of meal, something more for the swine, and a surplus that will, according to the season, provide the proprietor with the means of a greater or less degree of comfort or luxury in his family. Often, however, bacon and meal will be almost the sole food of the household from year's end to year's end. And this where the capital stock would be considered a fortune, and the owner of it rank as one of "our first men," and live like a prince in a New-England village; the property consisting of four or five hundred acres of land, worth from one to ten dollars an acre, and twenty or thirty slaves, worth $500 a-piece. Rarely, though, would it not be heavily encumbered. Certainly if it were not, there could have been during the present possession, but little of "old-fashioned Virginia hospitality." I speak now only of the worst-managed "corn, corn, corn" plantations.

After corn, comes corn; and then, corn, again; and so on, until it will hardly pay for the labor, when the poor, worn out land is dropped—left at last to rest, and Nature, with almighty pity, immediately clothes it with a thick growth of pines. This invariable sequence is most singular, and has long been the subject of a discussion among naturalists. The original growth was almost as universally of deciduous trees—oak, gum, chinquapin, &c.

As the oldest tilled land of the farm is thus dropped behind, every year a piece of the pine wood ("old field," of thirty years standing, perhaps) is cleared, the wood burned mainly on the ground, and that in heaps, and the ashes seldom spread; and after some little grubbing of the smaller roots, during the winter, planted again with corn. This first crop of the new land, seldom exceeds twenty-five bushels to the acre, on the oldest land, it is often not over five bushels. The greatest part of the land, perhaps the whole, has received no manure. The farmer, like the leech, cries constantly give! give! give! and bestows only as an inducement, a rude tillage some three or four inches deep.

I do not like to say that such is the general style of farming now in Virginia, but it certainly, even at this day, is not rare, and as far as my observation goes, is quite as common as any other.

The next step is to introduce wheat, and to leave the land to rest for a year or two after it, during which time there is a natural growth of coarse grass, weeds, and bushes, sometimes of clover (which is then called "volunteer clover"). This on being turned in with the plow affords a slight green manuring. In some soils plaster is sowed with wheat to encourage clover; better farmers buy clover seed and sow; better still, apply lime or marl. But supposing none of these aids are employed, the crop of wheat seldom exceeds five bushels, and of corn twenty-five bushels; oftener three will measure the wheat, and ten the corn, under this system.

I have seen oats put between corn and wheat, and in that case the land was regularly left three or four years to rest, as Heaven knows it had need to be, for a severer rotation could hardly be contrived. A three years' rest made necessary a regular "grubbing" of the field, the bushes getting too strong for the plow to "rip" through them.

Thirty years ago there was very little farming better than this in Eastern Virginia, there is a great deal no better now.

About 1826 the value of marl, an inexhaustible deposit of which exists not far from the surface of a large part of this district, as an agent to restore the fertility of the worn-out lands, began to be understood among the more intelligent and enterprising agriculturists. The publication of Mr. Edmund Ruffin's "Treatise on Calcareous Manures,"[4] probably the most valuable original agricultural work ever published in the United States, assisted greatly to diffuse a knowledge of its value, and of the principles and most economical methods of its application, among the reading men of the State as well as elsewhere.

It was ascertained that the value of marl (except in certain cases where it contained sulphate of lime) was very nearly proportionate to the per centage of carbonate of lime contained in it, and thus it was cheaper in many cases to obtain lime made from oyster-shells or from lime-stone than to open marl pits. Lime has been generally procured from New-York; it is just beginning to be brought by the new communications opening through the Blue Ridge from Western Virginia. Of course, it varies in quality according to the purity of the lime-stone or the proportion of magnesia or phosphate of lime entering into its composition. Lime has been sometimes brought here and sold to the farmers that contained so large a part of magnesia as to be an injury to the crops that it was applied to improve. Formerly, stone-lime was preferred; of late, farmers find shell-lime more rapidly beneficial. Theoretically, we should expect shell-lime to be of the most advantage on the most sandy soils, these being usually more particularly deficient in the phosphates.

The effect of the application of lime, whether in purity or in the form of marl, the latter being merely half decomposed shells, on nearly all the soils of Eastern Virginia is great and immediate. The crops of the second following rotation have been sometimes increased by it two hundred *per cent.,* and the texture of the land and its susceptibility to other agricultural improvement, is also greatly improved. In a few soils, containing but little vegetable matter, the effect is sometimes not seen for several years, and yet it will continue to increase and may be distinctly observed for twenty years. Marl generally costs $1.25 per hundred bushels, spread on the field, and 300 bushels is the usual dressing for an acre. Lime from New-York costs seven to eight cents a bushel, and fifty bushels is a usual application for an acre.

By means of lime, wheat may be raised profitably; the straw is converted into manure, and as large stocks of cattle are scarcely kept here, straw is often applied directly to the land; heavy stands of clover are soon made to follow; this is but lightly pastured, and sometimes not at all; usually remains two years and is turned in, supplying large additional food for future crops. By these means and deeper plowing, and sometimes longer and more ameliorating courses of cropping, the soil very greatly improves in its productive capacity. The land is generally light, of easy tillage, and very frequently on the better class of farms a four-horse-plow (of heavier draught than it should be) is used, which overturns the surface to a depth of from six to twelve inches.

There are large districts (and out of them, many single plantations) where the above described practices, together with some one of the rotations, which will be given below, have for many years been systematically followed, and which might boast, if it were not for their wretched and uneconomical labor system, of being the best cultivated districts in the United States. By best, I mean the most scientific and profitable, cultivation under all existing circumstances.

Within four years another wonderfully effective agent of production has come into use and under the increased demand for it of this season, it is impossible to predict what its effect will be. I mean, of course, *guano*. The enormous profits frequently arising from the use which has been made of it during the last two years, have startled even the old "corn, corn, corn" planters. It would seem now as if a revolution in Virginia Agriculture had commenced.

The following systems of cropping, or Rotations, are commonly used on the better class of farms in the tide-water district:

The Four-field System—1. Corn—2. Wheat—3. Clover, plowed in and sowed after, for—4. Wheat.

The Five-field or "Pamunkey" System—1. Corn—2. Wheat—3. Clover—4. Wheat—5. Clover, or—4. or 5. Pasture.

The five-field system is also varied very judiciously sometimes, by introducing Peas, which are sowed in the intervals between the rows of maize the first year. They are sown at the last tillage and, without subtracting at all perceptibly from the crop of growing corn (forming their seed after that is nearly ripe, or has been removed), often make a valuable crop of seeds and of haulm for fodder.

The "peas" are of a variety unknown at the North, and should rather be called beans.

The veteran Ruffin, who has done so much for the agriculture of Virginia, and who is still almost as actively and as usefully as ever engaged both in the field and at the desk in his more honorable labors, has lately adopted on his farm, and recommended to the public the following:[5]

Six-Field System.—1. Corn; 2. Peas—Sowed broadcast, and plowed under in Autumn for; 3. Wheat—Clover sown, grazed after harvest; 4. Clover—1st crop mown or grazed; 2d, plowed under for; 5. Wheat; 6. Clover, grazed.

Just at present, *good farming* is a very profitable business in Eastern Virginia; and there is an unusual life and animation pervading the Agricultural community. It is probable that in a few years the aspect of the country will be much changed from that I have described. The general use of guano must effect great results, used discreetly. As an agent of improvement as well as of immediate money-getting, it will add vastly to the permanent value of land; otherwise, it is not improbable that its effects will be like that of hearty stimulating viands rashly devoured by a famished man—a wild flush of life and quick following death. Thus, judicious farmers will be enriched; poor farmers soon utterly impoverished. But this is conjecture, and guano thus far laughs at all the prophets.

I do not feel able, at present, to speak confidently of Eastern Virginia as a field for emigration. Slavery, and bilious and intermittent fevers, are the main objections. If it were not for these, there are two classes whom I should have no hesitation in recommending to come here; and as it is, I must call their attention more particularly to the inducements offered.

The first class I refer to are the hundreds of thousands of New-England families, who may know, by the simplest calculation of chances, that if they remain where they are they are bound to be divided, broken up and brought to an end by that terrible New-England pestilence, *Consumption*. In southern Virginia my inquiries lead me to hope they will be *comparatively* safe from this most fearful danger. I have heard of many cases of New-Englanders predisposed to it, and exhibiting its warning marks, who have lived long and become permanently well after removing here; one or two such, on returning to New-England to reside after many years' absence, have speedily fallen. New-Englanders, with steady, persevering, working habits, if they can retain them, and will buy small farms and till them well after the best New-England fashion, will prosper much more in a worldly way than at home. They can rear healthful families; and if they will but come, several together, and settle in communities, they can so secure good moral and intellectual training for them. They can only do this by controlling the school in which they are educated. I mean, of course, in general.

The great error made by Northern farmers moving here has been that they have allowed themselves, tempted by the almost frivolous prices of land to undertake too much. Calculate closely how much you can manage with your own family force, or the labor of those only to whom you can give pecuniary interest in the result. Do not *plant* a rood more than you can be sure of taking good care of all the way to harvest; better care than it is customary to give in New-England; more tillage is necessary here and is well repaid because the plants of all kinds suited to the climate are longer growing and grow larger and bear more heavily. Sell your farms for a little below what they would be appraised at, and come half a dozen together, and buy one Virginia plantation. If you have means enough to live in New-England, you have more than enough to buy it, build on it, fence and stock it in good style. Come together, stick together, and work together, and hold fast to the honorable calling of free men, working with their own hands, and you can find no better country for you this side heaven.

The other class whose attention should be called to Virginia is that of young English farmers. Since the repeal of the corn laws, no young man can live by renting land at anything like the present rates without either plenty of capital or plenty of credit and *good luck*. There are thousands of farmers' sons in England, who, trained for a farmer's life and fitted for no other, and having no inclination for any other, crowd the market and take farms at exorbitant rents, because they must do that or become mere pauper laborers. The style of farming in which they were educated, which did very well under the corn laws, is altogether *too slow* under the reign of the houses of Manchester and Birmingham, and they are constantly breaking down and throwing up their rents.[6]

They had better, it strikes me, come to Virginia. The climate and the slave system they must consider, but for the present leave these objections, and remark the advantages offered there.

They can own a farm in fee simple, for what they pay for a year's use of one in England. To be sure, there will be no comparison in their quality. The soil of these farms is extremely poor—but little better than the midland heaths—but under the ordinary old-fashioned English farming, they would become rapidly of very fair quality; good for fifteen or twenty bushels of wheat. They are naturally very good light turnip soils. I have seen two crops of Swedes[7] this year on them as good as any in Norfolk. Sheep enjoy the climate quite as well as that of England; they need less care than they do there, and less provision of food. Ranges for them could be erected for the merest trifle, in which, with a shepherd and dogs to protect them from other dogs and the negroes, they would find food through the Summer under the pines of the "old fields" I have described. Late in the Autumn there springs up in these also a mushroom, that sheep eat greedily, and on which they will get almost fat. With such a range for their general keeping, you could have a large stock to feed off clover and [to feed] turnips to, and rapidly and cheaply make your soil rich and firm enough for wheat. Indeed, the turnip and sheep husbandry of England (with some modification to admit Indian corn and sweet potatoes as an auxiliary to turnips), as it was carried on ten years ago, or before thorough drainage[8] became general, seems to me just suited in every way to the soils and climate of Virginia. The crops suffer excessively from surface water, but it would not at all pay to thorough-drain in the present English fashion; narrow *butts* and deep water furrows as still used by the poor old-style farmers, would answer admirably well. Wheat may be presumed to be worth, on the farm, 90 cents, or 3s. 6d. to 3s. 9d. sterling, per bushel. It has commonly been better than this. Mutton and wool are worth within 10 per cent. here what they are in England. For the rest, the same advice that I gave to New-Englanders applies to all the world.

Wool-growing as a distinct business is likely to be very profitable in some parts of Virginia, especially in the counties near the Blue Ridge. But of this I am not at present prepared to speak particularly.

YEOMAN.

---

1. Olmsted probably drafted this letter between January 8 and 14, 1853, during his stay in Raleigh, North Carolina, and completed it after his return to Staten Island on April 6.
2. The passages that Olmsted quotes here, with italics that he added, are in the *Southern Planter* article on Virginia agriculture that he quoted in "The South" number 10 ("Four Eras of Agricultural Condition," pp. 134–35).

3. Olmsted identified the author of these two statements as "Chancellor Harper"—that is, William Harper (1790–1847), chancellor of the state of South Carolina from 1828 to 1830 and from 1835 until his death. Olmsted's quotations are from Harper's *Memoir on Slavery,* published in 1837:

> Is it not better that the character and intellect of the individual should be suited to the station which he is to occupy? Would you do a benefit to the horse or the ox, by giving him a cultivated understanding or fine feelings? So far as the mere laborer has the pride, the knowledge, or the aspirations of a freeman, he is unfitted for his situation, and must doubly feel its infelicity. If there are sordid, servile, and laborious offices to be performed, is it not better that there should be sordid, servile, and laborious beings to perform them?

(*The Pro-slavery Argument; As Maintained by the Most Distinguished Writers of the Southern States, Containing the Several Essays on the Subject, of Chancellor Harper, Governor Hammond, Dr. Simms, and Professor Dew* [Charleston, 1852], p. 51; *DAB.*)

4. *An Essay on Calcareous Manures,* published in 1832 by the Virginia agricultural reformer Edmund Ruffin (1794–1865).
5. Perhaps a reference to a communication from Ruffin to the Virginia State Agricultural Society, entitled "New Views of the Theory and Laws of Rotation of Crops, and their Practical Application" (Edmund Ruffin, "Southern Agricultural Exhaustion, and Its Remedy," U.S., Patent Office, *Report of the Commissioner of Patents for the Year 1852. Part 2. Agriculture,* H. R. Exec. Doc. no. 65, 32d Cong., 2d sess., 1853, p. 381n).
6. The repeal of the Corn Laws by the British Parliament in 1846 removed the barrier of tariffs that had protected English farmers, and exposed them to competition from other countries. Farmers with whom Olmsted talked during his walking tour of England in 1850 complained bitterly about the effect on them of the repeal (*Walks and Talks,* 1: 89).
7. The Swede turnip—*brassica campestris,* or rutabaga.
8. Thorough drainage of wet land by means of an underground system of drains was an important part of the agricultural reform movement in England during the early nineteenth century. Olmsted read extensively on the subject, and met its leading advocate, Josiah Parkes, in England in 1850 (*Papers of FLO,* 1: 121, 341, 343, 354).

New-York Daily Times, April 20, 1853[1]

THE SOUTH.

LETTERS ON THE PRODUCTIONS, INDUSTRY AND RESOURCES OF THE SOUTHERN STATES.

NUMBER TWELVE.

Special Correspondence of the New-York Daily Times

Bad Traveling Arrangements—James River Scenery—Hampton Roads—Seamen of the Naval Service—A Field for Northern Philanthropy—The Ethnological Question—The Town of Norfolk.

JOURNEY THROUGH THE UPPER SOUTH: 1852–1853

In going from Petersburg to Norfolk, I was first taken, with two cars full of other people, to City Point,[2] where we were all discharged under a dirty shed, from which projected a wharf into the James River. After waiting an hour, sitting on a pile of baggage upon the wharf, or, when it rained, walking up and down the dirty shed, I ventured to ask what we were waiting for? For a steamboat to take us down the river. What is the cause of her detention? Oh, there was no detention—*no more than usual, yet;* it was *about time* for her to be along now, I was answered. After waiting an hour and twenty-five minutes, having had a "hasty" breakfast before the usual time in Petersburg, that we might take this train, the boat did come, and this is what they call a "connection." Nobody showed any surprise, or seemed to have any objection to the arrangement, though it must have been exceedingly disagreeable to the ladies, who had not even a chair or a clean bench to sit upon, and one would suppose might be a little provoking to the men of business.

The shores of the James River are low and level—the scenery uninteresting; but frequent planters' mansions, often of great size and of some elegance, stand upon the bank, and sometimes these have pretty and well-kept grounds about them—finer than any other I have seen at the South—and the plantations surrounding them are cultivated with neatness and skill. Many men distinguished in law and politics here have their homes.

I arrived in Norfolk on the eve of a terrific gale,[3] during which vessels went down at their anchors in the Roads,[4] and the City and Country were much excited by various disasters, both on shore and at sea.

Several men-of-war were waiting at the Navy-Yard for crews, and the officers were in great trouble from the difficulty experienced in getting men. What crews the ships are and must be manned with, you may imagine, when the highest wages the law allows to be paid are $12 a month, and merchantmen are paying $25 for able seamen.

And, at the same time, the usual means of discipline are forbidden to be exercised. I am the last man that would advocate a return to the *cat,*[5] and the old terrifying discipline. I would not, because I believe that it is good policy to train, even at great temporary inconvenience and expense, a new species of seamen, both in the navy and the merchant service; men, not slaves; men, who should, from sensible understanding of their relation to their officers, and manly considerations of duty and republican respect for law, be a thousand times more efficient and reliable, and honorable to the country, than these slaves of choice for a time, who need officers trained as bullies to command them—who are only strong from want of faith in their strength—who simply do their duty, because they *dare* not refuse to do it.

The national naval service should be the school of good seamen, not the harbor for bad ones, miserable sots, broken down "sogers" and insolent ruffians, that cannot or dare not take employment with decent men, at the market rate of wages. But this is the system we are at present trying; and they tell you, seriously, *it is a failure,* and you must restore the *cat!*

Oh! why do we hear so little of the wrongs and the sufferings of the sailor. There is no cruelty, no tyranny, no suffering, no murdering of the spirit of men, and no murder of body or soul either, on Southern plantations that will compare with all this in nine out of ten ships that sail this year from New-York. Search the whole South, study all the noisome records of torture and villainy connected with Slavery, and if you could but sober all the sailors that dance in Cherry-street[6] to night, you might learn of vastly more atrocity and barbarity. The first officer you meet, if you can but get him to calmly and candidly think back over his life, will tell you of cruelty to seamen that will make you turn from him with horror; and yet he will probably confess to you, brother in the Church, kind father, loving husband, mild and courteous gentleman though he be, that he himself has sanctioned or directed such cruelty; and he will defend it, and will be satisfied before God and man that it was right and necessary. On the principles everywhere recognized by seamen themselves, it *is* necessary. As sailors are, it *is* necessary. And yet nothing is doing at the North to give a better character to them, to make a better *breed* of sailors.

Unless these high wages of seamen induce a different class of men to go to sea, and promote men to command in the merchant service before they have been ruined in temper by incessant bullying, and all rational ideas of the principles of administration and execution forever made impossible to be habitual, by long slavery, there is no prospect that our sea-service will ever grow better, ever be less disgraceful or more Christianlike.

I repeat; this curse and shame upon the world is constantly passing in and out of our doorways, and no prospect of its ever being in the least reformed or mitigated, for all that Northern philanthropists are doing or thinking about it. God bless the Bethel people, and the "Seamen's friend" people, and the Tract people, for their good purposes.[7] Sailors' Homes, I confess, have done good, more good a thousand times, than all other agencies that are employed for them; but *all* are as nothing. They count up their *converts,* they *do not* count the *backsliders,* and all who do not backslide never go to sea again while they are sober. If they do they are crazy.

One thing more I am reminded of in conversing with these naval gentlemen. It is a great deal harder for an officer to realize that sailors— common rope-haulers—are not of a lower grade than themselves of God's original creation, than it is for slaveholders to believe that negroes are of the same race with white people.

Norfolk is a dirty, low, ill-arranged town, nearly divided by a morass. It has a single creditable public building, a number of fine private residences, and the polite society is reputed to be very agreeable, refined and cultivated, receiving a character from the families residing here. It has all the immoral and disagreeable characteristics of a large seaport, with very few of the advantages that we should expect to find in connection with, and as relief to them. No lyceum or public libraries, no public gardens, no galleries of art, and though there are two "Bethels," no *"home"* for its seamen; no public resorts of healthful and refining amusement, no place better than a filthy tobacco-impregnated bar-room or a licentious dance-cellar for the stranger of high or low degree to pass the hours unoccupied by business. If there are, they are so out of the way that, during a week in which I had a damp, foul lodging in its best hotel, I was unable, by diligent inquiry, to find them. I must add that one hotel, of good reputation, was temporarily closed, and the others were overcrowded. Norfolk has a safe and convenient harbor, forty feet in depth, and is every way favorably situated for a great commercial port.

Two objects of interest there are near Norfolk, the "Dismal Swamp," the riches of which here find their main outlet, and the Naval Station of Gosport, with now the beautiful steamer *Powhatan*[8]—the finest war-steamer I think she is in the world—and that big, blundering, useless line-of-battle-ship, the *Pennsylvania*.[9] The market farms that supply "early truck" to you in New-York further demand some attention from the Agriculturist.[10]

1. Olmsted probably wrote a draft of this letter during his stay in Raleigh, North Carolina, between January 8 and 14, 1853, and wrote the final version after his return to Staten Island on April 6. Only the first half of the letter is presented here; the rest, on the Great Dismal Swamp, appears in *Seaboard Slave States*, pages 149–52.
2. City Point is on the south shore of the James River below Richmond.
3. A heavy gale and snowstorm that commenced on the evening of Monday, January 3, 1853 (*Norfolk & Portsmouth Herald*, Jan. 5, 1853, p. 2).
4. Hampton Roads, the great natural harbor near Norfolk, Virginia, formed by the confluence of the James, Nansemond and Elizabeth rivers as they enter Chesapeake Bay.
5. The cat-of-nine-tails whip.
6. Cherry Street, near the waterfront of lower Manhattan.
7. Seamen's bethels were houses of worship provided in ports for sailors, while organizations like the American Seamen's Friends Society ran "sailors' homes," which were boarding houses that stressed temperance, cleanliness and Christianity. Tract societies, led by the American Tract Society, distributed religious publications to seamen.
8. The 254-foot, 2,400-ton, bark-rigged sidewheel steamer *Powhatan*, launched at Gosport, Virginia, in 1850 (George Foster Emmons, *The Navy of the United States, From the Commencement, 1775 to 1853; With a Brief History of Each Vessel's Service and Fate* . . . [Washington, D.C., 1853], pp. 32–4).
9. The 212-foot, 120-gun ship-of-the-line *Pennsylvania*, launched in 1837 (ibid, pp. 24–25; William A. Fairburn, *Merchant Sail*, 6 vols. [Center Lovell, Me., 1945–55], 6: 3695).
10. The *American Agriculturist*, one of the leading agricultural journals of the time, founded in 1842 by Anthony Benezet Allen and his brother Richard Lamb Allen, and published in New York City. The Allens ceased publishing the journal as a monthly at the end of 1851 and revived it as a weekly in September 1853. At the time this letter was written, they were publishing a weekly, the *New York Agricultor*. Olmsted apparently had an opportunity to write for that journal the articles he calls for here; soon after returning to New York he wrote his father, "Allen told me he had credited me with $100 and wanted me to work it out in first rate editorials for the Agricultor—leading elaborate articles at my own price" (*DAB*; Albert Lowther Demaree, *The American Agricultural Press, 1819–1860* [New York, 1941], pp. 348–49; FLO to JO, n.d. [Spring, 1853]).

New-York Daily Times, April 28, 1853[1]

THE SOUTH.

LETTERS ON THE PRODUCTIONS, INDUSTRY AND RESOURCES OF THE SLAVE STATES.

NUMBER FOURTEEN.

Special Correspondence of the New-York Daily Times

The Mercantile Character and Commercial Position of Eastern Virginia—Railroads—Richmond, Petersburg and Norfolk—Ocean Steamers to Norfolk—Lieut. Maury—Effect of Slavery—Incidents—Tradespeople and Mechanics as affected by Slavery—Jealousy of New York.

Richmond, Petersburg and Norfolk are the chief mercantile centres of Eastern Virginia. They are the termini of railroads crossing large agricultural districts, the produce of which is delivered at these points to the cheaper means of transit towards the consumers on the navigable waters. The railroads do not appear to have been designed upon any grand system of giving the greatest facilities to the general commerce of the country, but more with reference to local interest, for, on one side or the other of the direction of their ultimate destination, one gets the impression, by a mere glance at the roads, that the Virginia railroads have been built upon a system of *log-rolling*. The towns I have mentioned are situated at the natural points for exchange of commodities, and owe their importance simply to this circumstance. In the early colony days it was attempted to force trade to other points than these by legal enactments—privileges and monopolies. Of some of these government-made towns hardly one stone is now left on another, and none of them are places of importance. It is curious to see how the same crude and farcical notions of nullifying the natural laws of trade possessed the minds of the noble fathers of Virginia, as has lately been displayed in the proceedings of Southern Conventions.[2]

The natural advantages of the position of Richmond, with reference to manufactures and trade, I have already described. They were not exceeded any where on the Continent. It was inevitable that there should be an important town on its site, though as yet it is hardly known, except as the Capital of the State. If it had been the recognized policy of its citizens to restrict its growth, it could hardly have been prevented from being a more prosperous town than it is.

Petersburg, half your readers have probably never heard of since they were at school. It is situated at the fall and head of navigation of the Appomattox, as Richmond is on the James, both these rivers having a common outlet to the ocean. Its milling power is great and readily applicable, and it has a very large and productive back country, to which it offers the only outlet or easy place of exchange for the commodities of the rest of the world. It has somewhat the advantage of its rival in directness of communication with the ocean.

Norfolk is the name of the town that the necessities of the maritime world require to exist at the head of Hampton Roads. It was not possible to prevent the existence of some agency here for the transshipment of goods and for supplying the needs of vessels forced to resort to the harbor. Beyond this, and what results from the adjoining naval rendezvous of the nation, there is nothing of Norfolk. Lieut. Maury has lately very well shown what advantages were originally possessed for profitable commerce at this point, in a report the intention of which is to advocate the establishment of a line of steamers hence to Para, the port of the mouth of the Amazon; I have the best wishes for the success of the project in its most important features, and the highest respect for the judgment of Lieut. Maury but it seems to me pertinent to inquire why are the British Government steamers not sent exclusively to Halifax, the nearest port to England, instead of to the more distant and foreign port of New-York? If a Government line of steamers should be established between Para and Norfolk, and should be found in the least degree commercially profitable, how long would it be before another line would be established between New-York and Para, by private enterprise, and then how much business would be left for the Government steamers while they continued to end their voyage at Norfolk? So, too, with regard to a line from Antwerp to Norfolk. Says Lieutenant Maury, however:

> Norfolk is in a position to *have* commanded the business of the Atlantic seaboard. It is midway the Coast. It has a back country of great fertility and resources, and as to approaches to the ocean, there is no harbor from the St. Johns to the Rio Grande that has the same facilities of ingress and egress at all times and in all weathers. * * * * The back country of Norfolk is all that which is drained by the Chesapeake Bay—embracing a line drawn along the ridge between the Delaware and the Chesapeake, thence northerly, including all of Pennsylvania that is in the Valley of the Susquehanna, all of Maryland this side of the mountains, the Valleys of the Potomac, Rappahannock, York and James Rivers, with the Valley of the Roanoke, and a great part of the State of North Carolina, whose *only* outlet to the sea is by way of Norfolk.[3]

Undoubtedly the original natural advantages of Norfolk were superior to those of New-York, yet if the citizens had always been subject to deadly enervating pestilence, it could not be a more miserable, sorry little seaport town than it is. What little life it has is communicated to it by New-York. A poor whining, ungrateful invalid it is while New-York is a giant, growing in strength, whose prosperity is the prosperity of the country, whose adversity would be felt throughout the land. But you find singularly simple, childlike ideas about commercial success among the people, even the merchants themselves here. The agency by which commodities are transferred from the producer to the consumer, they seem to look upon as a kind of swindling operation;

they do not see that the merchant acts a useful part in the community, or that his labor can be other than selfish and malevolent. They speak angrily of New-York, as if it fattened on the country without doing the country any good in return. They have no idea that it is *their* business that the New-Yorkers are doing, and that whatever tends to facilitate it and make it simple and secure, is an increase of their wealth by diminishing the costs and lessening the losses upon it. They gravely demand of each other why the Government mail steamers should be sent to New-York when New-York has so much business already, and why the nation should build costly Custom Houses, and Post-Offices, and Mints, and sea defences, and collect stores and equipments there, and not at Norfolk, and Petersburg, and Richmond and Danville, and Lynchburg, and Smithtown, and Jones-Cross-Roads? It never seems to occur to them that it is because *the country needs* them there—because the skill, enterprise and energy of New-York merchants, the confidence of capitalists in New-York merchants, the various facilities for trade offered by New-York merchants, enable them to do the business of the country cheaper and better than it can be done anywhere else (and that thus they can *command* commerce, and need not petition their legislature or appeal to mean sectional prejudice to obtain it), but all imagine it is by some shrewd Yankee trickery it is done. By the bones of their noble fathers they will set their faces against it, and their faces are not of dough, so they bully their local merchants into buying in dearer markets, and make the country tote its gold on to Philadelphia to be coined, and their Conventions resolve that the world shall come to Norfolk or Richmond, or Smithtown, and that no more cotton shall be sent to England until England will pay a price for it that shall let negroes be worth a thousand dollars a head, &c., &c., &c.

Then, if it is asked why Norfolk, with its immense natural advantages for commerce, has not been able to do their business for them as well as New-York; or why Richmond, with its great natural superiority for manufacturing, has not prospered like Glasgow, or Petersburg like Lowell:—why Virginia is not like Pennsylvania, or Kentucky like Ohio?—they will perhaps answer that it is owing to the peculiar tastes they have inherited; "settled mainly (as was Virginia) by the sons of country gentlemen, who brought the love of country life with them across the Atlantic and infused it into the mass of the population, they have ever preferred that life; and the title of a country gentleman, implying the possession of landed estates, has always been esteemed more honorable than any other." It is simply a matter of taste—an answer which reminds us of Aesop's fox.

Ask any honest stranger who has been brought into intimate intercourse for a short time with the people, why it is that here has been stagnation and there constant, healthy progress, and he will answer that these people are less enterprising, energetic and sensible in the conduct of their affairs—that they live less in harmony with the laws that govern the accumulation of wealth than those. Ask him how this difference of character should have arisen and he will tell you it is not from the blood but from the education they have received;

from the institutions and circumstances they have inherited. It is the old, fettered, barbarian labor system, in relation with which they have been brought up, against which all their enterprise must struggle, and with the chains of which all their amibition must be bound. This conviction is universal in the minds of strangers, and is forced upon one more strongly than it is possible to make you comprehend by a mere statement of isolated facts. You could as well convey an idea of the effect of mist on a landscape by enumerating the number of particles of vapor that obscure it. Give Virginia blood fair play, remove it from the atmosphere of Slavery, and it shows no lack of energy and good sense. What were the pioneers of Kentucky?

It is strange what cowards the Virginians are, that they dare not look this in the face. Strange how contemptibly they bluster in their legislative debates, in their newspapers, and in their bar-rooms, about the "Yankees," and the "Yorkers," declaring that they are "*swindled* out of their legitimate trade," when the simple truth is, that the Northern merchants do that for them that they are unable to do for themselves. As well might the Chinese be angry with us for sending our clipper ships for their tea, because it is a business that would be more "legitimately" (however less profitably) carried on in *junks*.

"I have raised hay, potatoes, and cabbages, on my farm in New-York, that found a market in Richmond," I said to a planter, "but here you have a capital soil for such crops; how is it you don't supply your own market?" "Well, I should be laughed at if I bothered with such little crops," he replied. So it is—they leave such little crops to the niggers and Yankees, and then grumble because all the profits of their business go to build "Fifth-avenue palaces," and "down-east school houses." They will not bear it any longer, they are going straightway to do something for themselves—what? Establish a dignified State line of steamers to—Antwerp![4] There's nothing to be laughed at in that, you observe.

I think the evidence I laid before you in a previous letter will have convinced you that the direct effect of slavery is to increase the cost of production of the most important articles of Virginia commerce, fifty per cent. I will take this opportunity to say what I should have expressed then, that there are not unfrequent instances in which slaves are made to perform agricultural operations in a very admirable and apparently economical manner. But these are rare exceptions and generally occur where but few slaves are kept together, and where they enjoy the confidence of their owner so much as to have acquired something of his interest and pride in their work. In these cases the slave is always noticeably superior to the great mass of his class, and according to the general opinion it would be dangerous to permit any large collected number of them to be equally improved. But I much doubt if the general popular opinion, and the Legislative theory of the State as to this, is correct.

Another great check upon enterprise and most strong bar to all progressive improvement in the State is the absorption of capital in the slave property. This I shall further explain at another time.

The *indirect* effect of slavery upon the business character of the State is seen in the general dilatory, unsystematic, indefinite, indistinct and unreliable character of the people as exhibited—on every side.

I have shown you some instances of it on the public conveyances. I recall a few more.[5]

When I took the railroad train at Richmond for Petersburg, the cars were crowded with passengers, and at the time advertised for departure, there was a shriek from the locomotive to intimate it was ready to be off; the train was presently jerked on a few rods; stopped; soon was shoved back; then ahead again, and so we continued "backing and filling" upon the bridge for a half-hour. There was a loss of time, amounting in value, at ordinary men's wages, to not less than one hundred dollars, to say nothing of broken engagements, and plans interrupted by it among all the passengers, and those who were expecting them. All unnecessary and simply the worst of bad management. And the worst part of it was nobody seemed to care at all about it. Nobody seemed to have calculated on the railroad company's promises being kept.

There was one man (intoxicated) who was disposed to hold an "indignation meeting" in the car I was in, not, however, with reference to the delay of the train, but to some "unconstitutional" proceedings that he apprehended the House of Delegates was engaged in. At every stoppage of the train, as it was jerked to and fro on the bridge, he would inquire what station we had reached, and how long it would be before we should arrive at Petersburg. As the car was full when he entered, he tried to take a seat in my lap, and when a seat was at length given to him, he put his feet upon the shoulder of the gentleman before him. He made a great disturbance, and at the North would have been immediately expelled from the car; but nobody here seemed to think they had a right to object to such a nuisance, and the conductor, though he several times passed through the car while he was defending the Constitution at the top of his voice, paid no attention to him.

After getting finally off, we were an hour and thirty-five minutes running twenty miles (advertised *fast,* mail train)—thirteen miles an hour; about twenty minutes being lost at way-stations. At one of these stoppages, smoke was seen issuing from the box of one of the carwheels. The conductor, on observing it, nodded his head sagely, took a chew of tobacco, spat at it, and then shouting "All right—go ahead!" stepped upon the platform. At the next station it was burning furiously; the conductor examined it and called for some water. As the negro brought it to him, he asked him, "Hasn't got no oil, Columbus?" "No, Sir." "Well, go ask Mr. _____ for some; this is a screaking so I durstn't go on. Scott, get some salt, and some of you boys fetch some more water, d'ye hear?" Oil, water and salt were crowded into the box, and after a few minutes we went on again, the box still smoking furiously, and the oil and water boiling in it, till we reached Petersburg. This occurred, I suppose, because it had not been sufficiently or timely oiled. Afterwards, I saw a Negro at the railroad station in Petersburg oiling the wheels of a train, and noticed that after finishing with one, he passed on to the next without elevating the spout of his oiler, so that a stream of fine sperm oil, worth probably $1.50 a gallon, was poured upon the ground all around the train.

A few days after, I was going a short distance into the country, south from Petersburg, by the Wilmington road.[6] Train started ten minutes after time—was an hour and a half running twenty miles, with but one mere crossroad stoppage. I asked the station master about the return train, and was informed that it did not generally get along until half an hour after the advertised time, though lately, *sometimes* they had been more punctual, and it would not do to calculate on it. It is not bad management necessarily, that the trains are run slowly, for that *might* be apologized for on the ground of economy, or, on some roads, of safety; but it is, that they are not run with regularity—that nothing can be relied upon with regard to them.

I wished to go from Norfolk on the train, advertised to leave at half-past eight, of the Seaboard and Roanoke Railroad; was called up an hour too early, and given a cold breakfast with coffee without milk, that I might be in time. A negro was sent to carry my baggage. The station is across the harbor; the ferry boat came in soon after we reached the wharf, but the fires had been neglected, and it took twenty minutes to get up steam enough to cross again. I was anxious lest I should be detained till after the train had left, as the landlord had told me at breakfast there was no time to lose. "Oh, no danger, masser, Baltimore boat aint ben arrive yet—dey wont go widout dat be, suah." There were several ladies and gentlemen *waiting* at the station when I reached it, but no signs of a departing train. The ticket-office did not open till after half-past eight. When I had been waiting half an hour longer, I asked a man in the employment of the Company, "Does not this train usually leave before nine o'clock?" "Oh, no sir, 'tis'nt often she starts before ten." The Baltimore boat arrived at half-past nine, and at five minutes of ten—nearly an hour and a half after the time advertised—the train began to move.

Incidents, trifling in themselves, instantly betray to a stranger the bad economy of using enslaved servants. The catastrophe of one such occurred since I began to write this letter. I ordered a fire to be made in my room, as I was going out this morning. On my return, I found a grand fire—the room door having been closed and locked upon it, and, by the way, I had to obtain assistance to open it, the lock being "out of order." Just now, while I was writing, down tumbled upon the floor and rolled away close to the valance of the bed half a hod-full of ignited coal, that had been so piled up on the diminutive grate, and left without a fender or any guard, that this result was almost inevitable. If I had not returned at the time I did, the house would have been fired and probably an incendiary charged with it, and some Northern Insurance Company made good the loss to the owner. And such carelessness of servants you have constantly to notice. But the constantly occurring delays, and the waste of time and labor that you encounter everywhere, are most annoying and provoking to a stranger.

The utter want of system and order, almost essential, as it would appear, where slaves are your instruments, is amazing—and when you are not in haste, often amusing. At a hotel, for instance, you go to your room and find no conveniences for washing; ring and ring again, and hear the office-keeper ring again and again. At length two servants appear at your door, get orders and go away. Quarter of an hour afterwards, perhaps, one returns with a pitcher of water, but no towels; and so on. Yet the servants are attentive and anxious to please, (expecting to be "remembered" when you leave). It only results from the want of system and order.

Again, I have had a servant come into my room and make a fire for me to dress by in the morning, then open the window to throw out the slops from the washstands, and walk off with my boots, leaving the window and door both wide open, and forgetting to return my boots until I go down to breakfast without them, the bell-wire being broken. Except in Richmond, I have not seen a negro yet shut a door on leaving a room with a fire in it, unless he was called back to do it.

Until the negro is big enough for his labor to be calculably profitable to his master, he has no training to application or method, but only to idleness and carelessness. Until the children arrive at a working age, they hardly come under the notice of their owner. An inventory of them is taken on the plantations at Christmas; and a planter told me that he had sometimes had them brought in at twelve or thirteen years old, that had escaped the vigilance of the overseer up to that age. The only whipping I have seen in Virginia, has been of these wild, lazy children, as they are being broke in to work at that age. They cannot be depended upon a minute out of sight. You will see how difficult it would be, if it were attempted, to eradicate the indolent, careless, listless habits so formed in youth. The influences that continue to act upon a slave in the same direction, cultivating every quality at variance with industry, precision, forethought, and providence, I have before sufficiently described to you.

It is impossible that the habits of the whole community should not be influenced by, and be made to accommodate to, these habits of its laborers. It inevitably affects the whole industrial character of the people. You may see it in the habits and manners of the mechanics and trades-people. All of these must have dealings or be in competition with slaves, and so have their standard of excellence made lower, and become accustomed to, until they are content with slight, false, unsound workmanship. You notice in all classes, vagueness in ideas of cost and value, and injudicious and unnecessary expenditure of labor by thoughtless manner of setting about work. To give you an instance: I had an umbrella broken. I noticed it as I was going out from my hotel during a shower, and stepped into an adjoining locksmith's to have it repaired. He asked where he should send it when he had done it. "I intended to wait for it," I answered; "how long is it going to take you, and how much shall you charge?"

"I can't do it in less than half an hour, Sir, and it will be worth a quarter."

JOURNEY THROUGH THE UPPER SOUTH: 1852-1853

"I shouldn't think it need take you so long, it is merely a rivet to be tightened."

"I shall have to take it all to pieces, and it will take me all of half an hour."

"I don't think you need take it to pieces."

"Yes I shall—there's no other way to do it."

"Then, as I can't well wait so long, I will not trouble you with it," and I went into the hotel, and with the fire-poker, did the job myself in less than a minute, as well as he could have done it in a week, and went on my way; saving half an hour and quarter of a dollar, like a "Yankee."

Virginians laugh at us for such things; but it is plainly because they are indifferent to and *above* regarding these fractions, that they cannot do their own business with the rest of the world, and all their commerce, as they are constantly most absurdly complaining, only goes to enrich Northern men.

Indolence, inconstancy of will, improvidence, extravagance and reckless carelessness, are almost necessities of their labor system. Is it too much to say, that they are the diseases of their whole body coroporate? With the greatest admiration for their many noble qualities, and with gratitude for the hospitality I have received from them, I must say that a stranger visiting them cannot avoid such a conviction.

So it is that Virginia has gone backwards, particularly where the slave system has operated most freely and purely—so that, in the midst of the first settlements, on lands that were once cultivated and richly productive, you may now be invited to hunt, with assurance that there is no lack of wild-turkeys and venison.

YEOMAN.

---

1. Olmsted probably wrote a draft of this letter during his stay in Raleigh, North Carolina, between January 8 and 14, 1853, and wrote the final version after his return to Staten Island on April 6.
2. A reference to the Southern commercial conventions, which met occasionally before 1852 and at least once a year for the rest of the decade. They called for national and state legislation that would make the South economically independent of the North through the establishment of direct steamship lines to Europe, encouragement of manufacturing in the South, and provision of internal improvements in the form of roads, canals, railroads and the dredging of rivers and harbors (Robert R. Russel, *Economic Aspects of Southern Sectionalism, 1840–1861* [Urbana, Ill., 1924], pp. 123–30).
3. A paraphrase, with italics added by Olmsted, of a passage in an article by the oceanographer Matthew Fontaine Maury (1806–1873) ("Direct Foreign Trade of the South," *DeBow's Review* 12, no. 2 [Feb. 1852]: 128; *DAB*).
4. A reference to the Old Point Comfort Convention, held in Virginia on July 4, 1850, and its aftermath. Attended by politicians from Virginia and nearby slaveholding states, the convention called for federal and state aid for the creation of direct steamship lines between the South and Europe. Later in the year legislation was introduced into the Thirty-first Congress to provide federal aid for a steamship line between Antwerp, Belgium, and (alternately) Philadelphia and

Norfolk. Supporters of the scheme made various attempts, through 1852, to secure aid from the Virginia Assembly (R. R. Russel, *Economic Aspects,* pp. 114–18).
5. The rest of this letter, presenting illustrations of the unfortunate effect of slavery on habits of industry and workmanship in Virginia, appears in somewhat different form in *Seaboard Slave States,* pages 52–54, 145–58.
6. Probably a reference to Olmsted's trip to visit the plantation of "Thomas W." (Thomas W. Gee), in Sussex County, south of Petersburg, Virginia, c. December 28, 1852 (ibid., pp. 59–94).

New-York Daily Times, May 24, 1853[1]

THE SOUTH.

LETTERS OF THE PRODUCTIONS, INDUSTRY AND RESOURCES OF THE SLAVE STATES.

NUMBER NINETEEN.

Special Correspondence of the New-York Daily Times

Remarks on the Character of the People of North Carolina—The Aspect of Slavery—Prosperity opposed to Humanity in Slavery—Education—The "Poor Whites."

North Carolina has a proverbial reputation for the ignorance and torpidity of her people, being in this respect at the head of the Slave States. I do not find the reason of this in any innate quality of the popular mind, but rather in the physical circumstances under which it finds its development. Owing to the poverty of the soil in the Eastern part of the State, and to the difficulty and expense of reaching market with bulky produce from the interior and western districts, population and wealth is smaller and more divided than in the other Atlantic States, industry is almost entirely rural, and there is but little communication or concert of action among the small and scattered proprietors of capital. For the same reason the advantages of education are more difficult to be enjoyed, the distance at which families reside apart preventing children from coming together in such numbers as to give remunerative employment to a teacher. The teachers are generally totally unfitted for their business—young men, as a clergyman informed me, themselves not only unadvanced beyond the lowest knowledge of the elements of primary school learning, but often coarse, vulgar and profane in their language and behavior, who take up teaching as a temporary business to supply the demand of a neighborhood of people as ignorant and uncultivated as themselves.

The aspect of North Carolina with regard to slavery, as I have intimated in previous letters, is less offensive than that of Virginia. Slavery has more of the *patriarchal* character which is claimed for it; the slave is more generally a family servant, a member of this master's family, sharing with him, and therefore interested with him, in his fortune, good or bad. This is the result of less concentration of wealth in families or individuals, which is occasioned by the circumstances I have described. Slavery thus loses much of its inhumanity, and, like feudalism in its latter days, is more nearly compatible with civilization. It is still questionable, however, if, as the subject race approaches civilization, the dominant race is not proportionately detained in its progress. One is forced often to question too, in viewing slavery in this aspect, whether humanity and the accumulation of wealth—the prosperity of the master and the happiness and improvement of the subject—are not incompatible. So far as my observation goes, facts would favor such a conclusion, with, of course, such exceptions and modifications as result from individual character.

As wealth naturally devolves upon the more intelligent and enterprising, the slaves, from association with their owners, are often, and (when living in the familiarity I have described as common on the farms in a country where, at the best, wealth must accumulate slowly) generally, a superior class to the poor whites, who from influences of the institution which I sufficiently explained in Virginia, are made to have an imprudent and reckless character. At the same time they seem to acquire generosity, boldness, a certain independence or originality of mind and all those peculiar virtues that distinguish the Indian and other vagabond and wandering tribes of the uncivilized world. They will make a valuable kind of soldier, while their quick insight of character, their respect for real dignity of worth when presented to them in the stump candidate for their suffrages, and their own absence of ambition, make them, as experience proves, conservative and sage, though not honorable citizens to the Republic. North Carolina has furnished more than her proportion of true statesmen to our National Councils, and though eminently prudent and conservative, her political influence has always been of a broader, more generous and catholic character than that of either of her two self-important neighbors. There is no State in the Union whose elements of wealth and usefulness are so varied and interesting as those of North Carolina, and there is reason to hope that while her people move with their accustomed prudence and deliberation, they will not be wanting the sagacity, enterprize and energy necessary to secure from these resources their own private prosperity by making them available to the needs of her country and the world.

The northern parts of North Carolina offer inducements to emigration similar to those I enumerated in Virginia, her political character is more honorable, there seems to be more freedom of thought on the subject of Slavery and the inquisition of public opinion upon its expression is less tyrannical. The State is less cursed with demagogues and self-seeking politicians, and the moral and social atmosphere is less enervating.

YEOMAN.

1. Olmsted probably wrote this letter in early May 1853. Only the concluding section, assessing the general character of slavery in North Carolina and its influence on society there, is presented here. The material in the rest of the letter appears, much of it verbatim, in *Seaboard Slave States,* pages 357–66 (FLO to JO, May 19, 1853).

CHAPTER II
THE JOURNEY THROUGH THE SEABOARD SLAVE STATES: THE LOWER SOUTH

1853

THE LETTERS IN THIS CHAPTER describe Olmsted's trip from Savannah, Georgia, through Montgomery and Mobile, Alabama, to New Orleans, and from there up the Red River. In "The South" numbers 44 and 45, Olmsted discusses his visit to the sugar plantation of his friend Richard Taylor, son of the late president, near New Orleans, and his stay on the great 15,000-acre plantation of Meredith Calhoun on the Red River in Louisiana. In number 28 he describes those aspects of the Northerner Richard J. Arnold's plantation outside Savannah which made it a model of what he believed slavery should be in America—a benevolent, patriarchal and civilizing institution.

Numbers 26 and 27 offer Olmsted's most extensive discussion of the religion practiced by the slaves and explore the effect of slavery on their moral condition and mental capacity. In these letters, Olmsted also passes severe judgment on the ineffectiveness of Southern laws designed to protect slaves from harsh punishment and to regulate the internal slave trade.

Number 34 gives a general picture of the society of Georgia, and number 35 provides a description of Alabama, including a classic characterization of the frontiersmen of the region.

New-York Daily Times, June 14, 1853[1]

THE SOUTH.

LETTERS ON THE PRODUCTIONS, INDUSTRY AND
RESOURCES OF THE SLAVE STATES.

NUMBER TWENTY-FOUR.

Special Correspondence of the New-York Daily Times

A Ride on the Rice Coast—The Crackers—Southern Household Markets—Birds of the Swamps—Plantations—Negro Settlements—Fine Trees.

  Having been provided by a kind friend with an excellent saddle horse, I rode out one fine morning to see the district in which the sea-island cotton is cultivated, and visit a rice plantation.
  Passing a mere belt of "vacant lots" about the town, I again entered the great pine forest that, with only small and widely separated dots of corn and cotton fields and broader blots of malarious marshes, covers the whole country one hundred miles in width from Baltimore to the Gulf of Mexico. Instead of the fine silvery, silicious powder, which, south of Virginia, constitutes most of the surface, the soil here bordering the coast varies from a dark brown, sandy loam to a coarse, clean, yellow sand. The long-leafed pine is displaced by a shorter leafed variety, less resinous and close grained, and of more rapid growth, showing that the land has nearly all at some time been under culture, and it thus lost its primeval fertility. At intervals, there are comfortable cabins with small corn or cotton patches in their vicinity, but not more than one mile in twenty of the road is bordered by land that had recently been under tillage.
  A stage-coach whirled along in a suffocating cloud of dust, drawn rapidly through the heavy sand by six horses; long teams of mules, driven by a negro on the back of one of them, toiled slowly towards the town with waggons laden with cotton or rice, and twice I met stylish turn-outs that would not have seemed out of place in the *Bois de Boulogne*,[2] with stiff and primly-dressed black servants in the rumble—gentlemen rice planters heavily bearded and fashionably clad driving in from their country estates; the only other vehicles were the carts of the "crackers"—the poor and uneducated peasantry. I was surprised at the number of these until I learned that my road was a great thoroughfare, in which all the travel and inland commerce of some hundred miles was collected.
  Many of the carts had been two days on the road; these generally came several together, a small caravan, for mutual assistance on the way. Women and children—often whole households—traveled with them, camping at night. Once I met two women without any man, one riding in the cart 'tending two babies, the other mounted (not astride as you see women in Italy) on the horse which drew it. Some of the carts coming in had in them a single bale of cotton, but generally they were loaded with corn, sweet potatoes, poultry, game, hides and peltry, with a few bundles of "shucks" to feed the horse, always thrown on top. A low semi-circular cover of white cotton is stretched over the cart on hoops or twigs to protect the load from sun and rain, the wheels are purchased, being made at the North for this market, the rest of the cart seems generally to have been made by the owner in the woods, with no better tools than an ax and a jack-knife; very little iron is used in its construction—pins of wood and thongs

of hide holding it together. The harness matches the vehicle, a large part of it commonly being made of ropes and undressed hides; but there is always a riding saddle, high-peaked in the Mexican style, made at the North, in which the driver commonly sits—more commonly he walks by the side of the horse, proceeding at a smart walk, but never trotting. From the axletree of some of the carts there hung a gourd of grease for the wheels, and a kettle for the camp-cooking. One man carried a rifle on the pommel of his saddle, ready to drop any deer or turkey that should chance within range while he was on the road. It is said that turkeys, though the shyest of game to a man approaching on foot, will often allow a cart to be driven very near them.

The household markets of most of the Southern towns seem to be mainly supplied by the poor country people, who, driving in this style bring all sorts of produce to exchange for such small stores and articles of apparel as they must needs obtain from the shops. Sometimes, owing to the great extent of the back country from which the supplies are gathered, they are offered in great abundance and variety; at other times, from the want of regular market men, there will be a scarcity, and prices will be very high.

A stranger can not but express surprise and amusement at the appearance and language of these country traffickers in the market-places. The "wild Irish" hardly differ more from the English gentry than these rustics from the better class of planters and towns-people with whom the traveler more commonly comes in contact. One figure I shall never forget. I was riding into a village with a gentleman who resided in it, when we met a little low cart or truck, having no body, but a few boards nailed into the axle-tree, on which sat

WOMAN WITH BULL CART ON ROAD OUTSIDE SAVANNAH

bolt upright, her legs rectangular with her trunk, her feet straight before her, a little brown woman with an old hat on her head and a pipe in her mouth, who turned and bowed to us very elegantly and with the most amiable and self-satisfied expression of face imaginable. She was driving a little black dwarf of a bull, who was buckled between shafts, with a bit in his mouth, and driven with reins like a horse. My companion said that she had been in the habit of coming to town for twenty years, and until lately always on foot, toting in half a bushel of potatoes or a peck of meal, a fowl or two, or half a dozen eggs: she often stopped at his house to light her pipe after she had sold out, and always seemed to be as contented and cheerful, and since she had got the bull and cart, as proud and rich, as it was possible for mortal woman to be.

The women commonly smoke, and I have seen one while nursing a baby, sitting three rods from a fire, repeatedly take a pipe from her mouth and spit upon a particular brand with a precision and force which was truly wonderful. I am happy to say that I never saw a woman put tobacco in her mouth, but the practice of chewing among men of all classes is nearly universal. I shall never be able to say again that Englishmen exaggerate in their strictures upon this filthy American habit: being much more common, the nuisance it occasions is even less restricted by regard to decency at the South than at the North. No elegance or careful neatness and no conventional sacredness restrains the nauseating expectoration.

The people with the carts were generally dressed in long-skirted homespun coats, heavy boots over the pantaloons and slouched hats. They were thin and gaunt, with very sallow complexion, sunken eyes, sharp high cheek bones, and were of less than the usual stature of the Anglo-Saxon race. The hair of the children was generally white or yellowish, growing darker as they grow older, always remaining dry and towy and commonly allowed to grow so as to cover the neck. Usually they bowed to me as we met, and often made a remark about the weather in a bold but courteous manner, frankly and distinctly, which gave one a good impression of their character and at all events showed that they were free from the servility and self-degradation which speaks in every action of the European peasant to a well-dressed stranger.

I rode slowly, occasionally stopping to sketch, or to satisfy my curiosity with regard to some vegetable novelty, or my admiration of the noble magnolias that stood here and there among the pines. Twice during the day I crossed streams with broad reedy Savannahs and Cypress swamps on their margins some miles in width. At one point on these there were large rice fields; and negroes, men and women, were engaged in burning off the woods and making ditches and dykes, to extend them: on their dryer borders were fields covered with the large black stalks of the sea-island cotton plant.

The feathered inhabitants of these low fields and Savannahs were interesting and wonderfully numerous. Immense clouds of the red-winged black-birds would float down, covering half an acre at once of the rice stubble, as with a black pall. Jackdaws, the first I have seen in this country, and crows occupied by hundreds the top of the trees that had grown upon the causeway, croaking and cawing incessantly. Clear and cheerful through the clamor you would hear the piping of the dapper Mocking-bird, and then he would spring out from the bushes, and with grisette-like vivacity and grace, dance along on the ground before you. The Blue-bird flutters from bush to bush and greets you with his Spring-time notes, and the gay Cardinal flashes in his flaming jacket through the lights and shadows of the foliage. Pearl white cranes lift their heads inquiringly above the rushes and rise with long sweeps of their wings, their plumage glistening in the sun light, as if there were silver in it. Gulls and ospreys with active flight follow the river's course, and over them poises a watchful, keen-eyed eagle; at a higher elevation, far up, dim and dreary in the upper sky, slow and majestic sail great hawks and buzzards.

Mark the close of the day. I reached a district of rich, dark, fine soil, much of it reclaimed from the swamp, cultivated with rather more than usual care for corn and sea-island cotton. At a distance from the road, white houses could be seen with dark trees about them, and long rows of negro-cabins and large barns, beyond these, in one direction, uninterrupted to the horizon, were flat Holland-like rice-lands, with a silver thread of glistening water winding through them.

After passing several gates and lanes, I entered one,[3] and rode through a narrow grove bordered by cultivated ground. At the end of the grove, a quarter of a mile from the road, was a negro "settlement," as what is in Virginia termed the "quarters," and in England would be the laborers' *hamlet*. It was an avenue of the Pride of China trees, fifty feet wide, with the approach road to the proprietor's mansion running through the midst, and thirty neat white-washed cottages on the outside, in the shade of the trees. The cottages were framed buildings, boarded on the exterior, with shingle roofs and brick chimneys; they stood fifty feet apart, with gardens and pig-yards enclosed by palings between them. At one of them, which I knew to be the "sick house" or hospital, there were several negroes of both sexes, wrapped in blankets, and reclining on the door steps or lying on the ground basking in the sunshine. Some of them were evidently ill, but they were all chatting and laughing as I rode up to make an enquiry. I learned from them that this was not the plantation I was intending to visit, and received a direction, as usual so indistinct and incorrect that it led me wrong.

At the next plantation I entered[4] I found the "settlement" arranged the same way, the cabins being only a slightly different form. In the middle of one row was a well-house and opposite it, on the other row was a mill-house, with stones, at which the negroes grind their corn. It is a kind of pestle and mortar, and I learned afterwards that the negroes prefer to take their allowance of corn and "crack" it for themselves, rather than to receive meal, because they think the mill-ground meal does not make as sweet bread.

At the head of the settlements, in a garden looking down the street, was an overseer's house, and here the road divided, running each way at right

ELIZA CAROLINE CLAY'S RICHMOND

angles; on one side to the barns and the landing on the river, on the other toward the mansion of the proprietor. A negro boy opened the gate of this and I entered.

On the other side, at fifty feet distant were rows of old live oak trees, their branches and twigs slightly hung with a delicate fringe of grey moss, and their dark, shining, green foliage meeting and intermingling naturally but densely overhead. The sunlight streamed through and played aslant the lustrous leaves and waving, fluttering, quivering, palpitating, pendulous moss: the arch was low and broad; the trunks were huge and gnarled, and there was a heavy groining of strong, dark, rough, knotty branches. I stopped my horse, bowed my head, and held my breath. I have hardly in all my life seen anything so impressively grand and beautiful: "Light, shade, shelter, coolness, freshness, music, dew, and dreams dropping through their unbrageous twilight—dropping direct, soft, sweet, soothing, and restorative from heaven."[5]

Alas! there were no fairies, only little black babies toddling about with an older child or two to watch them. At the upper end of the avenue was the house, with a circular court-yard around it, and surrounded by an irregular plantation of great trees, one of the oaks, as I afterwards learned, seven feet in diameter of trunk, and covering with its branches a circle of one hundred and twenty feet in diameter. As I approached it, a servant came out to take my horse. I obtained from him a direction to the residence of the gentleman I was searching for, and rode away, thankful that I had stumbled into so charming a place.

At the next plantation I entered I reached my destination.[6] The approach to the house was a quarter of a mile long, and very broad, with the pine forest on either side lined with a dense screen of water oaks, wild olives and cedars. This led to a grove of large evergreen oaks and magnolias, in the middle of which, surrounded by a little court of japonicas, oranges, wild olives and roses, stood the mansion. It was a structure of wood, with double roof, dormers and belvedere gallery; the principal apartments on the second floor, with the doors and windows opening upon broad piazzas. In a rear court was a detached kitchen, servants' house and other offices, of brick, and behind this a garden. A little way one side were the stables. The negro settlement was at no great distance, at the end of a cedar avenue, but could not be seen from the house.

About a quarter of a mile from the house, but entirely hidden from it by the grove, were rice-fields, subject to be irrigated from a large sewer, which, a few miles below, mingled its waters with those of the ocean.

It was the residence of a gentleman who was born and bred on a New-England farm, and who had been a very successful merchant, and was still largely interested in manufactures at the North. His wife was a Southern lady, and this plantation had been for several generations the property of her family. She had inherited with it the slaves upon it; her children had been born

RICHARD J. ARNOLD

LOUISA GINDRAT ARNOLD

and brought up with them; so that all the happy influences which attend early domestic association existed between them. The gentleman brought to the management of the estate all the keen talent for organization and administration, and the exact business habits of a man trained in the rugged fields of New-Hampshire, among the looms of Lowell and in the counting rooms of Boston. He was also a religious, generous and humane-minded man. As was to be anticipated, I here found Slavery under its most favorable circumstances, and the agriculture with which it was conducted under the most economical and profitable management.

YEOMAN.

1. In this letter Olmsted describes his horseback ride from Savannah to an outlying plantation around Saturday, January 29, 1853. He wrote the final version of the letter during early June (see "The South" no. 26, n. 1, below).
2. The Bois de Boulogne, a park near Paris, which Olmsted had visited in 1850.

JOURNEY THROUGH THE LOWER SOUTH: 1853

3. Unidentified plantation.
4. The plantation Richmond-on-Ogeechee, owned by Eliza Caroline Clay (1809–1895) (Robert Manson Myers, ed., *The Children of Pride: A True Story of Georgia and the Civil War* [New Haven, Conn., 1972], p. 1491; see also n. 6 below).
5. In *Seaboard Slave States*, Olmsted added the following sentence before this quotation: "I thought of old Kit North's rhapsody on trees; and it was no rhapsody—it was all here and real." Christopher North was the pseudonym of the Scottish writer John Wilson (1785–1854), whose works Olmsted read as early as February 1849, when, during a visit to Hartford, he read Wilson's *Noctes Ambrosianae* with Sophia Stevens (*SSS,* pp. 417–18; *EB,* s.v. "Wilson, John"; FLO to JHO, Feb. 10, 1849).

Olmsted's description here is reminiscent of his response to the scenery near Charleston, South Carolina, which he recorded in "The South" number 22:

Some twenty miles from Charleston we passed from the pine-barrens into low ground, covered mostly by deciduous trees and often marshy. This was broken by a beautiful park-like ground, with a planter's mansion and then a rice field.

As we came nearer the coast the landscape was more and more tropical and for a few miles from the city it was more green and warm and cheerfully rural (1st February) as June at home. Large market gardens with men and women pulling radishes and hoeing turnips and cabbages and earthing up the half-grown celery, plowing the mellow brown soil and *mowing* some tall green crop; and all about, moving in a pleasantly cooling breeze off the sea, large trees, green as England's greenest, old oaks, ever green old oaks, and hollies and great, dark, glossy-leafed magnolias, and many other smooth leafed trees that I never saw before; roses twining among palmettos and chippering birds and the hum of insects!—the sensation was strange and delightful; it was dream-like; but as dreams sometimes startle one to wakefulness, so I suddenly roused myself. There was a mosquito singing at my ear.

The humorous, self-deprecating return to reality that concludes each of these passages was characteristic of Olmsted's infrequent rhapsodic descriptions of scenery ("The South" no. 22, *NYDT,* June 7, 1853; *Papers of FLO,* 1: 128, 201).

6. This plantation, which Olmsted visited longer and examined more closely than any other that he saw during either of his southern trips, was a rice plantation owned by a man whom he referred to as "Mr. A." in his letter to the *New-York Daily Times* and as "Mr. X." in *Seaboard Slave States*. That man was Richard James Arnold (1796–1873), a native of Providence, Rhode Island, and son of one of the city's leading merchants, Welcome Arnold. After graduating from Brown University (College) in 1814, Richard Arnold studied law and then became a merchant, forming a partnership with his brother Samuel Greene Arnold (1778–1826), who was already engaged in the China trade. His business activities changed abruptly when in 1823 he married Louisa Caroline Gindrat (1804–1871), who was of South Carolina Huguenot descent, and had inherited the plantation White Hall on the Ogeechee River in Bryan County, Georgia. Following his marriage, Arnold devoted himself primarily to managing White Hall and the other nearby plantations that he acquired. By the time of Olmsted's visit in 1853, these included Cherry Hill, Mulberry Hill, Sedgefield and Silk Hope. Arnold also owned other land in Georgia and North Carolina, and remained active in Providence, where he developed suburban land and built screw docks, wharves and other improvements on his shore-front property. He and his family passed the winter at White Hall and spent the larger part of the year in Rhode Island—at a town house in Providence and an estate at Newport.

Positive identification of Arnold as Olmsted's host is possible because of annotations made in a copy of *Seaboard Slave States* (1904 edition) by Richard James Arnold's daughter Mary Cornelia Arnold Talbot (1841–1928). She identified "Mr. X." as "my father Richard J. Arnold"; Arnold's smaller plantation and winter residence on the Ogeechee River, as White Hall. His larger plantation on that river, which had over 500 acres of rice land fitted for irrigation, and what Olmsted called the "largest negro settlement," near which the overseer made his winter residence, she identified as Cherry Hill. The overseer, she noted, was "Mr. Ferguson." Arnold's factor in Savannah she identified as Robert Habersham—a neighbor who had extensive holdings of land and slaves in Chatham County and ran a factorage and commission business. The plantation that Olmsted ventured onto just before reaching White Hall, and on which he saw the old live oaks, she identified as "Aunt Eliza Clay's 'Richmond.'"

At the bottom of page 35 of volume 2 of the Talbot family copy of *Seaboard Slave States* there is the following notation by Mary Cornelia Talbot (1862-1939), daughter of Mary Cornelia Arnold Talbot: "Mr. Olmsted came South & visited R. J. A., & he was so much liked. He went everywhere & stayed a month. Later he sent Mr. Arnold his book saying he had so enjoyed his visit & that in his book he had always called him Mr. X. Mother added the side notes on my copy. Mary Cornelia Talbot 2nd."

In fact, Olmsted's visit to the Arnolds could not have been nearly as long as family tradition held it to be: he probably arrived on the evening of Saturday, January 29, and left on Tuesday, February 1, or at the latest, early on Wednesday, February 2. By his own account it took him twenty-four hours to reach Columbus, Georgia, from Savannah, and on February 8 his father received a letter from him that had been mailed in Columbus: it took about a week for a letter to go from there to Hartford, Connecticut.

Olmsted described his visit to the Arnolds in "The South" numbers 28 through 30, and in *Seaboard Slave States*, pages 418-49 (George Sears Greene, *The Greenes of Rhode Island, with Historical Records of English Ancestry, 1534-1902*... [New York, 1903], pp. 289-93; *The Biographical Cyclopedia of Representative Men of Rhode Island* [Providence, R.I., 1881]; typescript of the Arnold family genealogy in Talbot Family Papers, Rhode Island Historical Society, Providence, R.I.; Joseph Karl Menn, "The Large Slaveholders of the Deep South, 1860" [Ph.D. diss., University of Texas, 1964], p. 589; Writers' Program, Georgia, *Savannah River Plantations: Savannah Writers' Project*, ed. Mary Granger [Savannah, 1947], pp. 17-19, 37-38; JO Journal, Feb. 8, 1853).

New-York Daily Times, June 21, 1853[1]

THE SOUTH.

LETTERS ON THE PRODUCTIONS, INDUSTRY AND RESOURCES OF THE SOUTHERN STATES.

NUMBER TWENTY-SIX.

Special Correspondence of the New-York Daily Times

On the Religious, Moral and Intellectual Improvement of Negroes in Slavery.

As I remarked in my last letter, the largest part of the negroes making a religious profession are classed under the denomination of Baptists. They insist upon immersion as necessary to salvation; and I have heard one of them argue the point with his master with no less confidence, wit and pertinacity than doctors of divinity commonly employ in theological discussions; it will not be disrespectful to those who intelligently embrace this doctrine, to nevertheless suppose that the mass of negroes accept it because it makes more of an event of the baptismal ceremony, thus gratifying their passionate fondness for excitement. All who write upon this dogma, and act upon it, are considered to be within the reach of God's mercy, and are held in fellowship by them, but within this they also split into numerous parties or sects, each designated by a title which is generally expressive of the degree of loyalty to some standard of orthodoxy attributed to each, such as "Hard Shell," "Soft Shell," &c.

On almost every large plantation, and in every neighborhood of small ones, there is one man who has come to be considered the head or pastor of the local church. The office among the negroes, as among all other people, confers a certain importance and power. A part of the reverence attaching to the duties is given to the person; vanity and self-confidence is cultivated, and a higher ambition aroused than usually can enter the mind of a slave. The self-respect of the preacher is also increased by the consideration in which he is held by his masters as well as his fellows; thus, the preachers generally have an air of superiority to other negroes; they acquire a remarkable memory of words, phrases and forms—a sort of curious poetic talent is developed—a habit is obtained of rhapsodizing and exciting furious emotions, to a great degree spurious and temporary, in themselves and others, through the imagination. I was once introduced to a preacher, who was represented to be quite distinguished among them. I took his hand respectfully, and said I was happy to meet him. He seemed to take this for a joke, and laughed heartily. He was a "driver," and my friend said, "He drives the negroes at the cotton all the week, and Sundays he drives them at the Gospel—don't you, John?" He commenced to reply in some Scriptural phrase, soberly, but before he could say three words, began to laugh again, and reeled off like a drunken man—entirely overcome with merriment. He recovered himself in a moment and came up to us again. "They say he preaches very powerfully, too." "Yah, Massa! 'kordin to der grace—*yah! yah!*" and he staggered off again with the peculiar hearty negro guffaw. My friend's tone was, I suppose, slightly humorous, but I was grave, and really meant to treat him respectfully, wishing to draw him into conversation; but he had started upon a merry mood, and I found it impossible to get the better of it.[2]

There is no element in the difficult problem of Slavery which we of the North so little comprehend and leave out of view in our theorizing, as the exceedingly low moral and intellectual condition of the slaves. In one of my earliest letters after entering Virginia, I conveyed to you the impressions which I had received on this point from the general appearance, language, and conversation of the negroes.[3] These impressions have been strengthened and confirmed by further observation of them as I have proceeded South. I described to you the influences which, by destroying ambition and elevated aims, and by cultivating improvidence and carelessness, and by stimulating only the lowest impulses of a man, combine to keep the negro in a condition of mental childishness and moral debasement.

In considering a great system, we cannot be too careful not to be deceived by its exceptional appearances. Individual instances, in which various Christian virtues and graces are beautifully exhibited by slaves, are constantly cited on both sides, by Southerners as well as Northerners, which can only properly be considered as eddies in the general current of slave life. Give the system fair play, where no sheltering point of an unusually indulgent and sensible master, or a peculiar natural drift of mind (such as in a higher class, according to the proverb, produces the poet), and you see only a dark, deep tide of stupidity and superstition. Mungo Park[4] found exquisite benevolence touchingly displayed among the negroes of the darkest wilds of Africa. I can say myself of a certain heathen I have known, that I scarce ever saw evidence of a character more full of meekness, patience and affection, and I have had an East Indian idolator preach to me with an earnestness, candor and logical ability that deserved my gratitude and respect.[5]

Such cases are to Paganism what such a character as "Uncle Tom" is to slavery, or the religion of slaves. "Such a character is impossible in a negro" (slave) is the most common criticism on "the greatest story of the age," by Southerners, though once or twice, when I remarked that this was evidence unfavorable to slavery, I have been assured by others that they had known slaves wonderfully like "Uncle Tom." I confess the character does not seem to me to be altogether consistent or natural under the circumstances.

The mind and higher faculties of the negro are less disciplined and improved in slavery than in the original barbarism of the race, because in the latter state he has at least to exercise them under the necessity of contriving to procure food, raiment, and habitation; in providing for his offspring, in the consequently necessary acquisition of property, exciting cautious enterprise, having reference to the chances of the future, and in the defence of personal liberty. I do not believe there is a body of men in the world that have so stupid, unmanly, and animal an existence as the *rank and file plantation negroes* of our Southern States. I have never been on the Slave Coast of Africa, but I have been among the essentially savage natives of the Malay Archipelago,[6] and the latter, according to my observation, were as fully developed men by the side of babes, compared with the mass of these plantation slaves. The agricultural laborer in those districts of England in which land is held in the largest parcels, such as Wiltshire, being in a large degree dependent on their immediate employer, more nearly resemble the negroes in this respect than any other people I have known.[7] The number of these is small, their condition is improving, and so far as it is the result of a system of government or law, this is being yearly modified favorably to their elevation. This condition of the negro, which it seems to me is the main, and sufficient reason, against unconditional, immediate abolition of the relation of master and dependent, is not simply a circumstance attending his perpetual slavery, but is its result. I cannot see how this conclusion is avoidable by a candid and sensible observer. I therefore take ground against the writer of a recent article in *Hunt's Merchant's Magazine,*[8] who maintains that slavery is the (only) true, speedy, and successful method for civilizing and christianizing the heathen; and am constrained to say that my judgment, and my observation of facts, *a priori,* would by no means lead me to recommend any such scheme for preaching the Gospel as he favors.

I do not admit, in evidence upon this subject, the statistics that are usually cited, of the number of slaves counted as religious by their owners or by themselves. A profession or name for a religious character among them appears to be founded upon the exhibition of certain phrensied states of the imagination, excitable at will in any mind not habitually disciplined to the control of reason, and in the direction of words and actions according to certain precepts and formulas.

Delirium, madness, and even catalepsy, are often produced by the excited imagination in certain sects of the Mahometans, and in many idolaters, at their festivals and meetings for public worship; and blind obedience to certain rules of conduct which they have been taught to consider of supernatural importance, and slavish reverence to certain days and words and things, are as habitual among the Fetish worshippers of Africa as among their transplanted cousins, the baptized and enrolled church-members of America. That the morality and the superstition of these latter is in all cases better than theirs, that it is much *more like* what Christianity prompts a man to, is very true, but it is no more the same thing than a rush light is a sunbeam.

On two of the rice plantations that I visited there were neat buildings set apart and fitted up as chapels, (called by the negroes "Prayer houses"). In one of these were rows of seats with backs to them, and I was told that the negroes objected to these because they did not leave them *room enough to pray*. It was explained to me that it was their custom in social worship to work themselves up to a great pitch of excitement, in which they yell and cry aloud, and finally shriek and leap up, clapping their hands and dancing, as it is done at heathen festivals—the seats were too close together to admit of this exercise. Mr. A., the rice planter spoken of in a previous letter,[9] told me that he had forbidden his negroes this shouting and jumping at their plantation meeting, from a conviction that there was not the slightest element of religious sentiment in it. He considered it to be engaged in more as an exciting amusement than from any really religious impulse. In the town churches, except, perhaps, those managed and conducted almost exclusively by negroes, they commonly engage in religious exercises in a sober and decorous manner, yet a member of a Presbyterian Church in a Southern city told me that he had seen the negroes in his own house of worship, during "a season of revival," leap from their seats, throw their arms wildly in the air, shout vehemently and unintelligibly, cry, groan, rend their clothes, and fall into cataleptic trances.[10]

In conversation with a very worthy and intelligent gentleman on this subject, I asked if he had often known religion to effect any very great elevation of character among slaves. He replied that he had, and mentioned the following as a case in point. A cook came into his possession, who was generally a very good and valuable servant, but who would sometimes get intoxicated, and then do and say a great deal that was wrong. He several times expostulated with her, but effected no good; at length, knowing that she was a member of a colored church (it was in a city), he threatened to complain to the officers of it of her conduct. This threat had more effect upon her than all the previous means he had used, but, at length, she had a drunken fit again, and he did call on the officers of her church, and told them her conduct was such as was inconsistent with the professions of a church-member, and they ought to warn her. He found the officers—colored men—very respectable, intelligent and obliging persons. They thanked him for advising them of the case, and forthwith called upon the cook, and threatened her with suspension or excommunication if she did not reform. She was very much frightened and *mortified,* and since that time she had been constantly sober, and her moral character in every respect excellent. Now, such a case as this plainly shows the power for good (or evil) of an ecclesiastical inquisition, not the power of religion.

There was an improved morality, or rather, here was an improved self-control, a better degree of self-government, arising not from an elevated moral sense and love of the All Good, but from little better than a base, irreligious, and unmanly principle of heart—the fear or worship of man; or, if it be deemed rather the worship or fear of God, manifested in reverence and obedience to his human representatives or ministers, you simply elevate it from Infidelity to Idolatry. I make these observations with reference to a subject of frequent discussion—how far compensation for the evils, or palliation for the wrong of the perpetual Slavery of the Negroes of the South is to be found in the good it is doing in the way of christianizing them. Christianity can only be practically defined, in considering this question, as a principle of the heart which manifests itself in the constantly progressive, moral elevation of the individual. In my judgment, the general degradation of manhood, the training to cowardice and imbecility, or duplicity of mind, the constraint upon the free development of individuality of character, and the destruction of the sense of high individual responsibility, which is demanded by an established system of perpetual Slavery, is most strongly opposed to the reception in the hearts of its subjects of anything that can be reverently dignified with the holy name of Christianity.

I do not question, that there are many slaves whose lives are radiant with the light of the simple and pure faith of Christianity, nor that there has been a considerable improvement in their moral condition, as a people, since they have been removed from the savage and cannibal state of society and been held in the restraint of American civilization and law; but I think this improvement limited and restricted by the necessities of Slavery; that Slavery, in its effects on slaves, is at war with progress, with enlightenment, with Christianity.

I think the native manly spirit and capacity of the savage is but poorly compensated for by the pseudo-religion and civilization of the slave.

This opinion is not common or popular, but my very first observation of the manners, language and conversation of the slaves in Virginia, as I then expressed to you, favored it, and my continued investigation of this subject has surprisingly established it in my mind. I, therefore, wish to state it frankly and distinctly.

Out of respect to the generous spirit of the correspondent of the Daily Times, "A Native Southerner,"[11] I will refer especially to his views. In my judgment, Slavery as it is intended to be perpetuated at the South, in its general and legitimate operations upon the character of the slaves, *is* "inconsistent with a beautiful type of humanity." He admits that the South is not faithful to the task of regenerating the slaves, but thinks that it is not for want of anxious solicitude and much steady, earnest labor on the part of the whites. So far as my knowledge extends, there is very little of such earnest, steady labor; the labor is isolated, intermittent, and, in the minds of most sensible men engaged in it that I have met, is far from encouraging in its results.

It is always difficult for us to distinctly understand the moral effect of institutions to which we are accustomed, and with which our whole lives are associated, but I think it is because it is felt how impracticable it is to free the slave's mind without freeing his body, and how little he can be improved morally while his mind is left fettered in darkness, that so little is attempted; that so much is by law forbidden at the South in this field of Christian and benevolent labor. A clergyman confessed to me that after seven years' daily intercourse with and labors among slaves, he was deeply grieved to find how little hold upon them he had gained, how small his influence was, and how little real confidence they had in him. He said they seemed to be always suspicious of his motives and to be unable to repose an unfeigned trust in him. A Northern clergyman who had resided for two years in a Southern city, told me that he thought that not more than one in seven of the negroes who were members of the churches in it had a sensible understanding of what they professed.

When "A Native Southerner" speaks of "the largest and most effective missionary operation in the world in steady earnest action on the negro mind," I suppose he uses a figure of speech. There are no associated, systematic, special operations to improve the religious or moral character of the slaves, worth mentioning. Very rarely the planters of a small district may unite to support a missionary or white clergyman to preach in circuit, on their plantations, on Sundays. I have heard of three such, and I also know of one very large slave owner who keeps a white preacher employed upon his own property alone. I have been on plantations where Sunday-schools were formerly kept, and I presume they are not uncommon. In these the children are taught to repeat catechisms, creeds, hymns, and passages of scripture. A lady from Kentucky, on attending such a school while on a visit in Georgia, remarked that she had never seen a Sabbath-school for colored children before. But I will continue this subject in another letter.

YEOMAN.

---

1. Olmsted wrote this letter between June 16 and 20, 1853. In it and "The South" number 27, he pursues the line of thought raised by his observation of the slaves at the "cracker meeting" near Richard Arnold's plantation and discusses the quality of the Christian faith that the slaves had acquired under their masters. The subject had called for more research than had his earlier

letters, however, and had slowed his writing pace considerably. Since his return to Staten Island on April 6, he had been completing two letters a week. This was true up to May 19, when he wrote his father that he was two letters ahead of the *Times*. This would mean that he had completed "The South" number 20, since number 18 was published on that day. He was probably well along with numbers 21 and 22, since in his letter to his father he went on to say, "I have now got rather to a sticking point and after three or four more shall be at my worst place, requiring hardest study." Numbers 21 and 22 were simply a continuation of the narrative of his trip from Portsmouth, Virginia, to Charleston, South Carolina, and presumably contained a good deal of the material he had written on the road prior to February 23, 1853. With number 23 he evidently reached his "sticking point," as well as the end of the material he had written up in somewhat finished form while on his journey. He broke off his travel narrative at this point, skipped over his stay of several days in Charleston, and wrote a general description of rice planting. In number 24 he related his day-long trip from Savannah to the outlying plantation of Richard Arnold, and in number 25 he described the "cracker meeting" that took place nearby on the following Sunday. This brought Olmsted to his doubly "worst place," since on June 16, the day on which number 25 appeared in the *Times*, he wrote his father, "I have not now a single letter for the Times—they printed the last today." How much the research necessary for preparing numbers 26 and 27 slowed him is indicated by the fact that he completed only five letters during the four weeks between May 19 and June 16. During the next two weeks he worked his way out of his predicament, publishing number 26 on June 21 and number 27 on June 30.
2. This paragraph appears in *Seaboard Slave States*, pages 450-51.
3. In "The South" number 3, Olmsted described the slaves he saw in the vicinity of Richmond, Virginia, and offered his first conclusions about their condition and the effects of slavery on them. "With regard to the moral and religious condition of the Slaves," he wrote, "I cannot, either from what I observe, or from what is told me, consider it in any way gratifying." Elaborating on this question, he observed:

> A goodly proportion of them, I am told, "profess religion," and are received into the fellowship of the churches; but it is evident, of the greater part even of these, that their idea of religion, and the standard of morality which they deem consistent with a "profession" of it, is painfully degrading and unelevating. That they are subject to intense excitements, often really maniacal, which they consider to be religious, is true; but as these are described, I cannot see that they indicate anything but a miserable system of superstition, the more painful that it employs some forms and words ordinarily connected with true Christianity.

Although Olmsted offered these conclusions as the result of first impressions only, he repeated them almost verbatim in *Seaboard Slave States*, pages 113-17 and 123-25.

In "The South" number 3, Olmsted also discussed the slaves' belief that there was nothing wrong in stealing from their masters. He then went on to suggest that such cultural traits became, in time, inherited characteristics:

> That such *educational characteristics* are reproduced, I have no doubt. I have a Newfoundland dog, that the first time he saw a man in the water, sprang in after him and attempted to seize him and bring him ashore; and I have had much difficulty in learning him to restrain this impulse. The first time a duck was shot in his presence, (I think the first time he had ever seen a gun fired), he at once dashed in and brought it ashore, without any order or indication that it was expected of him. ("The South" no. 3, *NYDT*, Feb. 25, 1853.)

4. Mungo Park (1771-1806), British explorer, who led an expedition in 1795-97 to discover the course of the Niger River. He described his experience in *Travels in the Interior Districts of Africa* (*DNB*).
5. Probably the incident that Olmsted described in his article "The Real China," in which a clerk at Whampoa, the trading port of Canton, urged him to pray to joss (that is, idols, usually of household deities) before starting the voyage home:

> I had made a friendly acquaintance with a merchant's clerk by giving him some lessons in the English alphabet. Shortly before we went to sea he came on board and remarked to me that when Chinamen ventured upon the ocean they set up Joss in their

JOURNEY THROUGH THE LOWER SOUTH: 1853

cabin before which from time to time they set cups of tea and burned joss sticks and paper prayers. He did not see any Joss in our cabin and he asked me if I would not be more comfortable when a great storm arose if such a recognition of our dependence upon the good will of a Superior Being has been observed? It was a simple friendly inquiry made in a perfectly well-bred way. (*Papers of FLO,* 1: 188.)

6. Olmsted had seen the natives of the Malay Archipelago when his ship stopped at Anjer, Java, during his voyage to China in 1843 (ibid., p. 142).
7. Olmsted had walked across Salisbury Plain in Wiltshire in 1850, and described the labor system there as follows: "The farms are all very large, often including a thousand acres of tillage land, and two, three, or four thousand of down. A farm of less than a thousand acres is spoken of as small, and it often appears that one farmer, renting all the land in the vicinity, gives employment to all the people of a village. Whether it is owing to this (to me) most repugnant state of things, or not, it is certainly just what I had expected to hear in connection with it, that labourers' wages are lower than any where else in England." (*"Walks and Talks,* 2: 140–41).
8. William S. Price's "Moral Benefits of Slavery," which appeared in the April 1853 issue of *Hunt's Merchants' Magazine.* Price, an Alabamian, contended that only through the discipline of slavery could the heathen be civilized and Christianized. He declared that the God of Israel intentionally brought about the enslavement of the Jews to the Egyptians, since "in their native condition they were not suitable material to make a great and useful people of, nor until they were taught subordination and the civilized arts by the enlightened Egyptians." The failure of efforts to civilize the native Indians of America was due, Price asserted, to the failure to enslave them first (*Hunt's Merchants' Magazine* 28, no. 4 [April 1853]: 454–56).
9. Richard J. Arnold.
10. This paragraph and the one that follows it appear in *Seaboard Slave States,* pages 449–50. Olmsted witnessed the revivalistic style of black church worship in New Orleans in February or March 1853. He described the scene in "The South" number 43 and in *Back Country,* pages 187–96; in the book he omitted the last two paragraphs of the newspaper letter:

> About one-twentieth of the congregation were mulattoes, the proportion being less than I had expected to find it. All were dressed cleanly and comfortably, with the greatest variety in quality and fashion of apparel. I perceived no disagreeable odor. There was a greater variety noticeable in the form of the cranium, and in the character and degree of cultivation of mind and taste marked in the faces of the audience, than I ever saw in an equal gathering of whites. The natural politeness of the negro was remarkably shown, as I have always observed it to be in negro assemblies, from the church to the lowest dance-house of New-York in the restraint of all impertinent manifestation of curiosity and uncalled-for attention to a stranger. Nor did the presence of whites appear to have the least effect to check the excitement of those who sat near them. This excitement, throughout, as evidently as possible, was wholly unintellectual, not at all the result of a reflective action of the mind, and, in my opinion, no more appropriate worship of God than would be a similar excitement obtained by drinking intoxicating liquors in the name of Worship.
>
> Would we not despise the human monarch who would be gratified by such senseless homage from his subjects; the human father who would teach his children such debasing and unmanly modes of respect and service to himself? How much higher conception of God, then, does it indicate; how much more enlightened a religion than that of the uninstructed and unenslaved, but reverent and superstitious, savage? The woman in the gallery seemed to me to have really abdicated self-control, and forced herself into something like a hysterical state. The man in the pulpit I judged to be deliberately acting an imposition, not on himself, but the audience. ("The South" no. 43, *NYDT,* Nov. 9, 1853.)

11. The *New-York Daily Times* of June 6, 1853, carried a letter from "A Native Southerner" from "South Alabama" entitled "The South and Slavery," which commented on Olmsted's series of letters on the South and replied to an earlier letter of a Northerner to the *Times* in which the South was criticized for failing to civilize its black slaves. Olmsted identified the author as "the Reverend Mr. Lipscombe, an Alabamian"—probably Andrew Adgate Lipscomb (1816–1890), an Episcopalian minister who at this time was in charge of the Metropolitan Institute for Young Ladies in Montgomery, Alabama.

In his letter to the *Times,* Lipscomb claimed that during the past few years there had been rapid moral and social progress in the South. Improved public opinion had produced greater protection and comfort for the slaves and the application to them nearly everywhere of "Christian modes of thought and action." Moreover, it was moral life under the slavery system, sustained by philanthropic and religious sentiments, that gave the system its strength. "If slavery was not consistent with a beautiful type of humanity," he queried, "if it allowed no virtues to flourish . . . think you, that we would tolerate it another moment?"

In response to the earlier letter in the *Times* by a Northerner (who signed himself "B."), Lipscomb admitted that there was a good deal of truth in the assertion that the South had not educated and Christianized its slaves as thoroughly as it should have. He asserted, however, that much good work had been accomplished. "Does 'B.' know," he asked, "that there is at this day, the largest and most effective missionary operation in the world, in steady, and earnest action on the negro mind of these States?"

Olmsted's reference to the "generous spirit" of "A Native Southerner" was due to the friendly way in which Lipscomb assessed Olmsted's "The South" series in the *Times* (through letter number 16 or 17). "The general tone of his articles is acceptable to unbiased Southerners," Lipscomb wrote, "but nevertheless, we can see very clearly that he is looking at things through a pair of sharp Northern eyes. . . . I am much pleased with his candor and intelligence, and I hope that he will render essential service to the opinions of both sections of the country" ("The South and Slavery, Letters of Yeoman and B.—Views of a Southerner," *NYDT*, June 6, 1853, p. 2; "The South, Condition and Capacities of the Slave, A Letter to the Travelling Correspondent of the New-York Daily Times," *NYDT*, May 18, 1853, p. 2; FLO to JO, June 16, 1853; *DAB*, s.v. "Lipscomb, Andrew Adgate").

New-York Daily Times, June 30, 1853[1]

THE SOUTH.

LETTERS ON THE PRODUCTIONS, INDUSTRY AND RESOURCES OF THE SLAVE STATES.

NUMBER TWENTY-SEVEN.

Special Correspondence of the New-York Daily Times

The Moral and Intellectual Culture of the Negro in Slavery—Evidence of a Missionary—How the South Has Failed of Its Duty—What Business This [Is] of Ours.

In discussing the views presented in my last letter with Southerners, the labors of a society for the religious instruction of negroes in *Liberty* County, Georgia, have frequently been referred to as an instance of the great privileges which the negroes may be blessed with in Slavery. This Society has been in operation for many years, though I believe its operations were interrupted, as were nearly all public efforts to improve the condition of negroes at the South, during the periods of extreme sectional excitement. The Thirteenth Annual

Report of the Society, which has been sent me, conveys to a stranger abundant evidence of the general debased moral and intellectual condition of the slaves. It demonstrates that the tendency of the circumstances of ordinary slave life is exceedingly debasing and demoralizing, and it fails to show that the means used by the Society are generally effectual to counteract this tendency.

The view presented in my last, of the difficulties in the way of the elevation of the negro, inherent in the system of Slavery, is strikingly confirmed by the Missionary of the Society,[2] in some remarks on the proposition that "the moral discipline and culture of the negroes is a duty equally binding upon all who hold the responsible relation of masters and managers with the improvement of their physical condition."[3]

As it is a point upon which many of your Southern readers will, I fear, have disagreed with me, and in which I may be thought to have observed superficially and judged with prejudice, I shall quote several passages, which will indicate the result of thirteen years' experience in the duties of a special instructor and pastor of negroes, by a Southern Presbyterian clergyman (since appointed Professor of Theology at Columbia, S.C.):[4]

> A right estimation of servants as immortal and accountable beings, lies at the foundation of attention to their moral discipline and culture. And I am free to confess that while it is hard, in our corrupt and imperfect state, to estimate rightly even our children and relations as immortal and accountable beings, and to treat them accordingly, *there are difficulties in the way of forming such an estimation of servants, because they are servants,* (i.e. slaves.)[5] You inquire why it is so? I presume your experience, if you have watched your own thoughts and feelings, will suggest the reply.
>
> They are, in the language of Scripture, *"your money."* They are the source, the means of your wealth; by their labor do you obtain the necessaries, the conveniences and comforts of life. The increase of them is the general standard of your worldly prosperity; without them, you would be comparatively poor. *They are consequently sought after and desired as property, and when possessed, must be so taken care of and managed as to be made profitable.*
>
> Now it is *exceedingly difficult to use them as money; to treat them as property, and at the same time render to them that which is just and equal as immortal and accountable beings,* and as heirs of the grace of life, equally with ourselves. They are associated in our business, and thoughts, and feelings, with labor, and interest, and gain, and wealth. Under the influence of the powerful feeling of self-interest, *there is a tendency to view and to treat them as instruments of labor,* as a means of wealth, and to forget, or pass over lightly, the fact that they are what they are, under the eye and government of God. *There is a tendency to rest satisfied with very small and miserable efforts for their moral improvement, and to give one's self but little trouble to correct immoralities and reform wicked practices and habits, should they do their work quietly and profitably, and enjoy health, and go on to multiply and increase upon the earth."*[6]

This is addressed to a body of professing evangelical Christians, in a district in which more is done for the elevation of the slaves than in any other of the South. What they are called to witness from their own experience, as the tendency of a system, which recognizes slaves as absolute property, mere instruments of labor and means of wealth, *"exceedingly difficult"* for them to resist, it is evident to me, is the *entirely irresistible effect* upon the mass of slave holders. In general, I assert that they rest satisfied with "very small and miserable efforts (if they make any at all) for their moral improvement," that they give themselves "but little (if any) trouble to correct immoralities and reform wicked practices and habits," caring for little, if for anything, else but that "they do their work quietly and profitably, and enjoy health, and go on to multiply and increase upon earth." More even than this. Fearing that moral and intellectual culture may injure their value as property, they oftener interfere to prevent, than they endeavor to assist, their slaves from using the poor opportunities that chance may throw in their way. Without referring to state enactments of this character, I could mention some instances of individuals so doing that have come within my personal observation.

But beside this direct influence of the system, it is remarked that there is, indirectly, an additional effect:

> The current of the conversation and of business in society, in respect to negroes, runs in the channel of interest, and thus increases the blindness and insensibility of owners. We have a right to their *obedience* and service, it is true; but it is equally true that they have a right to our *consideration,* and care, and government, as immortal and accountable beings.[7]

Now, see what effect the Christian missionary laboring among slaves has discovered this tendency of the system to have on their moral elevation, aside from its denying them the means of improvement:

> The negroes themselves, seeing, and more than seeing, *feeling and knowing,* that their owners regard and treat them as their money—as property only—*are inclined to lose sight of their better character* and higher interests, and, in their ignorance and depravity, *to estimate themselves,* and religion, and virtue, no higher than their owners do.[8]

Consider, with such an influence constantly acting upon them from all sides (and impossible to be counteracted by any one or two masters, if it were desired), what advance it is probable the slaves are making, as men, and personally accountable beings. Does it not wholly bear out the judgment expressed in my last letter?

Many of the difficulties in the way of the progressive elevation of the negroes, while they continue to be considered as property, are mentioned. Owners are likely to provide them with only such accommodations for spending the time in which they are not actively employed, as shall be favorable to their bodily health, and enable them most rapidly to comply with the commandment, obedience to which will be most profitable to them, to "increase and multiply upon the earth," without regard to their moral health, without caring much for their obedience to the more pure and spiritual commands of the Scriptures.

JOURNEY THROUGH THE LOWER SOUTH: 1853

> The mingling up of husbands and wives, children and youths, banishes the privacy and modesty essential to domestic peace and purity, and opens wide the door to dishonesty, oppression, violence, and profligacy. The owner may see or hear, or know little of it. His servants may appear cheerful, and go on in their usual way, and enjoy health and do his will, yet their actual moral state may be miserable. * * *If family relations are not preserved and protected, we cannot look for any considerable degree of moral and religious improvement.* [9]

No one can doubt the truth of this last proposition, and it must be acknowledged of slavery, as a system, as that system finds the expression of the theory on which it is based in the laws of every Southern State, that family relations are *not* preserved and protected under it, as we should therefore expect. The missionary finds that:

> One of the chief causes of the immorality of negroes, arises from the indifference both of themselves, and of owners, to their family relations. [10]

The rice planters generally, and some others owning a large number of slaves, do not allow their negroes to marry off the plantation to which they belong, conceiving "that their own convenience and interest, and," the missionary thinks, "the comfort and *real* happiness of their people, are promoted by such a regulation." He disagrees with them, and in endeavoring to convince them of their error, asks a few questions practical to his duty as their agent to Christianize their property, which they could hardly answer in a way that would justify them in continuing the restriction. One of these questions is this:

> Admitting that they are people having their preferences as well as others, and there be a supply, can that love which is the foundation and essence of the marriage state, be forced? [11]

Did a missionary in "infidel France" ever have occasion to seriously ask such a question? And is the system defensible under the name of "the largest and most effective missionary operation in the world, in steady, earnest action,"[12] which the combined legislative wisdom of every Slave State has always thought to require, that any poor, depraved mortal of a white citizen should possess power like this over numbers of such people, in the ratio of his talent for the acquisition of property? And while this is the case, does it seem likely that it will exert a beneficent moral influence upon the race? Is Slavery, for them, a reforming, civilizing, Christianizing process? Is the whole world wrong, and the Christian Church of the Southern United States of America alone right, in its theory and practice on this point? If so, then truly has it found godliness, great gain.

> It is not denied that an owner's people may be healthy and increase, and do their work, and be in a manner cheerful, and that, externally, things may wear a good appearance—but what is the actual morality of the people? That is the question. [13]

And so I understand "B.," whom a native Southerner undertakes to answer,[14] to wish to know of the South—not denying that its people are healthy and multiplying in the most exemplary manner, that they are well fed and sufficiently well clothed, soft-bedded and lovingly cared for, and that *externally* things wear a good aspect—but now what is the actual Christianity they are acquiring? That is the question. And I must answer, from all I have heard and seen, that the great body of them are only dragged bodily along, as it were, in the path of Christianity, because they are attached to the skirts of the civilization and social customs that attend it.

"It is said by some," continues the missionary, "that laws and regulations and punishments, in matters of this kind, can effect no good; that they amount to nothing; and the best, and least troublesome, plan, is to let the people alone."[15] He contends against this indolent view of the difficulty with some warmth of language, and evident bitterness of feeling, but finally acknowledges—"It may not be possible effectually to restrain immorality, even by the best and wisest regulations. Yet much will be accomplished. 'We speak what we do know, and testify to that which we have seen.'"[16] How far a people may be made to swallow religion, or wear morality by "laws, regulations and punishments," Spain, Italy, Prussia and New-England have given greater or less testimony precisely in proportion to the duration of the experiment in each.

The missionary calls attention to the character and conduct of the negro drivers, who, he says, "have it amply in their power to oppress and corrupt the people intrusted to their supervision."

> Yea, such may be the influence of these men, and the fear inspired by them, that they may carry on their immoralities among the people to a great extent, and the owner be kept in profound ignorance of the fact.[17]

What, then, is the power, and how great the evil influence, of a corrupt and immoral owner! Is it right to give such power to any human beings?

Touching honesty and thrift among the negroes, the missionary observes:

> While some discipline their people for every act of theft committed against their interests, they have no care whatever what amount of pilfering and stealing the people carry on *among themselves*. Hence, in some places, thieves thrive and honest men suffer, until it becomes a practice "to keep if you can what is your own, and get all you can besides that is your neighbor's." Things come to such a pass, that the saying of the negroes is literally true, "the people live upon one another."[18]

Recommending the authority of the master to be used to restrain quarrelling, fighting and profanity, the "*custom* of husbands whipping and beating their wives"[19] is referred to as a common thing, as I have otherwise learned it to be. "The negro always plays the nabob in his own cabin," an old planter observed to me; his wife is the slave of a slave, and respects her husband the more if he is a tyrant.

Referring to the evil of Intemperance, it is observed:

> Whatever toleration masters use towards ardent spirits in others, they are generally inclined to use none in respect to their servants; and in effecting this reformation, masters and mistresses should set the example; for without example, precepts and persuasions are powerless. Nor can force effect this reformation as surely and perfectly as persuasion—*appealing to the character and happiness of the servant himself,* the appeal recognizes him *in such a manner as to produce self-respect, and it tends to give elevation of conduct and character.* I will not dwell upon this point.[20]

Unfortunately this is the very point that needs to be dwelt upon. Here lies the whole insurmountable difficulty, and I will close the subject by reiterating it. Slavery, in itself, rendering impossible a strong appeal to the character and happiness of its subject, recognizing him solely in such a manner as produces self-*humiliation,* can tend only to *degradation* of conduct and character.

The present moral and intellectual condition of the majority of the plantation slaves at the South, as I have understood it, is such as must be explained on one of two theories: either that the original capacity of the race for improvement is very limited (in other words, that they constitute a distinct and inferior race), or that the effect of the system under which they live, is to reduce their natural capacity in some respects, to limit and forbid improvement in others, and is generally demoralizing and debasing. The latter effect may be counteracted by peculiar local and personal circumstances, such as confidential relations with cultivated whites, as often where the negroes reside in active trading communities, where they are family servants, or where they are the slaves of comparatively poor men, who, owning but a few of them, are brought into more intimate and constant personal association with them. The great contrast between the negroes living under these circumstances and the ordinary laboring plantation slaves, cannot but be manifest to the most superficial observer; it is much greater a degree than the difference between the corresponding classes of the white laboring people of the Free States. The character and intellectual condition of the more privileged negroes is so superior, that I deem it in itself the strongest evidence against the first hypothesis—which affirms that the negro race has but very little capacity for improvement.

This theory is that which was held by Mr. Calhoun,[21] and which I find is sustained by most men of logical minds at the South—not so much, I imagine, because they have been convinced by evidence before them, as because only on this theory can Slavery be logically defended. An esteemed friend at the South writes to me: "Slavery has always existed about me, and without reasoning, I have accepted it as the natural condition of the black population." Such is the situation of nearly all Southern-born men, and when called upon to reason about it, they must admit Slavery to be unjust, unnatural and cruel, or take the position that the negro is naturally incapacitated for personal freedom, for the attainment of such civilization or elevated moral character, or argue that the negro race needs training, cultivation and discipline to fit it for freedom;

and that to give it this education, it must be held in restraint as in a self-sustaining manual labor school. The argument for the first position is sustained on a strong basis of facts, in Ethnological science, by the present and past condition of the negroes in Africa, compared with other races of men;[22] and it is supposed to be sustained by Scripture. It is simple, strong and consistent. At a future time, I will consider it more particularly, and examine whether, if it were admitted, the conclusions with regard to Slavery which are commonly based upon it are justifiable. At present, I take the hypothesis more generally accepted by the world, and more popular even at the South, especially among religious people, that the race is capable of indefinite elevation; that the same general laws of progress apply to it that are admitted for our own race; that all are descended from one parent stock, and that difference of physique is due to outward circumstances, and has followed rather than caused the difference of mental character which has distinguished the races.

Admitting this, Slavery can only be justifiable temporarily—for so long a time, namely, be it for years, generations, or centuries, as shall suffice to elevate the subjects of it, or their descendants, to a mental and moral position in which they can be trusted to their own guidance with safety to themselves and others, and until their forced labor shall have paid fair tuition fees to their masters; admitting this, it follows that the system of restraint (for it should no longer be revolting to the ear of a freeman under the odious name, even, of Slavery) should be carefully adapted, not only to the one purpose of self-sustentation, but to the other, namely, education.

In accordance with this theory, the state of bondage of the negroes is a painful but justifiable system, and under the circumstances in which they had to be dealt with at the Revolution, is no more inconsistent with republicanism, than the bondage of children or of the insane.[23]

Such were the views and expectations of the earlier patriots and statesmen of the south; it was with such views and expectations, expressed by them and by many popular assemblies and legislative bodies at the South, that the compact of our Union was formed. Such views and purposes are still held by thousands of our fellow citizens of the South, who, holding slaves and sustaining Slavery on this theory, are, it is not to be doubted, consistent followers of Christ and true Democrats.

But this theory has never been accepted by the strength of the South. Popular legislation, custom, feeling and avowed purpose have not been in accordance with it. The negro is held in a state of pure and unmitigated slavery incompatible with his elevation, and only to be in the least degree defended as justifiable, on the theory on which our Government is based, on the ground that the negro is a brute, or on the plea of necessity for self-preservation. And in point of fact, all arguments for Slavery as it exists are reducible to one of these two. All other arguments which we hear from Southerners are in defence of Slavery as it should be—as I deny that it is. But I do not undertake to prove that Slavery, intertwined with the most effective institutions for popular elevation in the world, can absolutely make the negro more degraded and debased in all points of character than heathen barbarism.

Along with the immense improvements of all other classes of the people, which the democratic and republican form of Government has occasioned, Slavery could not prevent an improvement of the physical condition of the negroes. They are better fed, better clothed and housed, and less often cruelly punished. This, in itself, would insure a better exercise of their moral and intellectual faculties. Admitting, therefore, in a certain sense, the better intellectual and moral aspect of the class, I deny that this shows that Slavery is an educating process. Under Slavery as it is now legalized by legislation and established in custom, I affirm that the negroes are *instructed* merely, that they acquire from without certain habits and forms, but that they are not *educated* in the primary and higher sense of the word; that their mind is not *drawn out,* that their capabilities are not developed, and that what is deemed their intellectual improvement is like the intellectual improvement of a parrot, who, once knowing only enough to croak when it was hungry, has now learned to call for food in a form of words.

I think it is obvious that the laws and customs of Slave States are such as to interfere with and prevent any general elevation of the negro. They are plainly and often avowedly contrived with reference to this end. The power of the master to govern his slaves with sole reference to his own profit, is not at all restricted by regulations to insure their intellectual elevation and eventual *capacity for* emancipation.

The order of society and the customs of the people, with exceptions that I have mentioned favorable to a moiety, are entirely opposed to the elevation of the negroes. Slaves are looked upon in law and in custom as property solely, and not in any sense in a state of pupilage. They are generally treated as property, and the restrictions upon the power of their masters, or the penalties for abusing it, enforced by law or in social usage, are of the same nature as those which restrict the power, or punish the abuse of power, of a man over his brutes in free countries. There are but few and unimportant exceptions to this rule.

The only defence for this course is the necessity which the danger of insurrection and anarchy is imagined or assumed, by those who are influenced by only low, cowardly and selfish views, to occasion. How far it is justifiable on this ground, it is difficult for a stranger to know. One thing I am certain of—if the slaves are satisfied with their present condition and prospects, they are more degraded and debased than I have described them to be. There is no reason why, in the future, the danger of treating them justly (by which I do not mean freeing them from the control of their masters) should be less than at present. If there is any such danger at present, it would seem likely to increase as their numbers increase and concentrate, unless this danger may be averted by measures favorable to their improvement and elevation. Up to this time, there has been no disposition shown by the South to remove the difficulty before her in this way. On the contrary, the policy which most intelligent men of the more free and enlightened countries of the world consider suicidal in the despots of Austria and Sicily—the policy of restricting, holding down and keeping dark the minds of the dangerous class—is yet constantly adhered to. The laws of the South for this purpose are of precisely the same title, purport, tendency and effect (so far as a stranger in each can judge) with those of Russia, Germany, Italy and France. It would be equally dangerous for me to publish and circulate this letter in Charleston, Paris, or Naples. In Russia, I might do it—for I have but to insert this clause, reminding the serfs that only the power and goodness of the Emperor prevents them from being subject to the mere cupidity of their natural masters, equally with the American slaves, to obtain for it the approval of the censor. The only measure having reference to the difficulty, besides those of this character, generally and energetically advocated and pursued by the South, has been, and is, that of enlarging the area of the country which may be occupied by slaves—thus putting off the danger which their concentration will occasion.

Up to this point we of the North have politically nothing to do with it. Here we have much to do. Here we must be consulted, here we must assist; here, at least, we must permit, or here we must prevent.

Therefore, it is not impertinent for us to inquire if there is not a better way. There is nothing impracticable, nothing fanatical, nothing unconstitutional, in our holding and expressing the belief that there is.

For us to cry out for Abolition, the direct sundering of the tie of master and dependent, may be impracticable, fanatical, mischievous and unjust. For Amelioration, the improvement and elevation of the negro, it seems to me, in view of the honor, safety and future prosperity of the country whose institutions we unite to govern and protect, there is no impropriety for us to ask.

YEOMAN.

1. Olmsted probably wrote this letter between June 21 and 29, 1853.
2. Charles Colcock Jones (1804–1863), Presbyterian clergyman and a native of Liberty County, Georgia. He spent the years 1825–1830 in the North, attending Phillips Andover Academy, Andover Theological Seminary and Princeton Theological Seminary. After graduating from Princeton, he spent one year as pastor of the First Presbyterian Church, Savannah. He then returned to Liberty County and devoted himself to missionary work among the slaves there. From 1837 to 1838, and again from 1848 to 1850, he was professor of ecclesiastical history and church polity at Columbia Theological Seminary in Columbia, South Carolina (R. M. Myers, *Children of Pride*, p. 1567).
3. [Charles Colcock Jones], "Moral Discipline and Culture of the Negroes," in *Thirteenth Annual Report of the Association for the Religious Instruction of the Negroes, in Liberty County, Georgia* (Savannah, Ga., 1848), pages 13–23.
4. Charles Colcock Jones.

5. Parenthetical phrase added by Olmsted.
6. [C. C. Jones], "Moral Discipline and Culture," page 14. The italics in this passage, except for the phrase "your money" in the second paragraph, are Olmsted's.
7. Ibid., page 15 (Olmsted's italics).
8. Ibid. (Olmsted's italics).
9. Ibid., pages 16, 17 (Olmsted's italics).
10. Ibid., page 17.
11. Ibid.
12. The quoted phrase is from a letter from "A Native Southerner" to the *New-York Daily Times* (see "The South" no. 26, n. 11, above).
13. [C. C. Jones], "Moral Discipline and Culture," page 18.
14. See "The South" number 26, note 11, above.
15. [C. C. Jones], "Moral Discipline and Culture," page 18.
16. Ibid., page 19.
17. Ibid.
18. Ibid., page 20.
19. Ibid., page 21.
20. Ibid., pages 21-22 (Olmsted's italics).
21. Perhaps a reference to the views expressed by John C. Calhoun while serving as secretary of state in 1844, in a letter to the British envoy Richard Pakenham. Responding to the stated intention of the British government to work for the abolition of slavery throughout the world, Calhoun declared that the condition of free blacks in the North clearly demonstrated their inability to improve or prosper in other than a servile state. Citing the findings of the 1840 census on the high incidence of vice, pauperism, deafness, blindness, insanity and idiocy among free blacks in the North, sixty years or less after emancipation in those states, Calhoun asserted that "in all instances in which the States have changed the former relation between the two races, the condition of the African, instead of being improved, has become worse." The relationship of the races in the slaveholding states, in contrast, he found to be "consistent with the peace and safety of both, with great improvement to the inferior." Even at the time that Calhoun cited the census of 1840 on the condition of free blacks in the North, however, those findings were under attack, and Northern critics soon demonstrated their great inaccuracy (John C. Calhoun, *The Works of John C. Calhoun* . . . , ed. Richard K. Crallé, 6 vols. [New York, 1851-56], 5: 333-39; William Stanton, *The Leopard's Spots: Scientific Attitudes toward Race in America, 1815-59* [Chicago and London, 1960], pp. 58-65).
22. The most important ethnological work dealing with the ancient history of blacks in Africa was *Crania Aegyptiaca; or Observations on Egyptian Ethnography, Derived from Anatomy, History and the Monuments*, published in 1844 by the Philadelphia ethnologist Samuel George Morton. By painstakingly measuring twenty embalmed heads from the Egyptian catacombs, he determined that the mean cranial capacity of Caucasians among them was eighty-five cubic inches, while that of Negroes was seventy-one inches. This was the same relative brain size that he had found in measuring contemporary skulls. Morton also concluded, from the depiction of different races on monuments, that the social position of Negroes in ancient Egypt had been the same as it was in the nineteenth century—that of servants and slaves. While Olmsted may not have read *Crania Aegyptiaca*, he did refer in *Back Country* to the work of two other men, both friends and co-workers of Morton's. One was the Scotsman George R. Gliddon, who had anticipated Morton's findings about ancient Egypt and supplied him with the Egyptian skulls. The other was Josiah C. Nott, a Mobile physician who drew from the evidence of ancient Egypt in constructing a theory of the separate origin and inferiority of the Negro race. Both men published works on the subject in 1844.

    While Olmsted's reference in this letter to the findings of ethnological science seems to be respectful, his reference to Gliddon, Nott—and Samuel Cartwright—in *Back Country* was not: he compared their purposes unfavorably with those of the English philosophers James John Garth Wilkinson and Hugh Doherty, both of whom he had met in England in 1850 (W. Stanton, *The Leopard's Spots*, pp. 45-53, 65-72; BC, pp. 93-97; *Papers of FLO*, 1: 355, 357).
23. For Olmsted's views on this question, see FLO to Frederick Kingsbury, October 17, 1852, note 10, above.

New-York Daily Times, July 8, 1853[1]

THE SOUTH.

LETTERS ON THE PRODUCTIONS, INDUSTRY AND RESOURCES OF THE SOUTHERN STATES.

NUMBER TWENTY-EIGHT.

Special Correspondence of the New-York Daily Times

Slaves Owning Horses, Guns, and Dogs—The New Code of Alabama—Illicit Trade with Negroes—Pilfering—The Socialistic Aspect of Slavery—The Paternal Aspect of Slavery.

In returning from the "Cracker meeting"[2] to the plantation, we passed a man on horseback, who had the appearance of one of the civilized native East Indian gentlemen; his complexion dark olive, with good features, and a thick moustache. He was well-dressed, and raised his hat in bowing to us with a courteous and well-bred air. I asked who it was.

"He is one of our people—Robert—a very valuable servant. He is the watchman, and has charge of the engine and all the stores."[3]

We met a wagon with a pleasant family party of common fieldhand negroes. They also belonged to Mr. A. I inquired if they usually let them have horses to go to Church.

"Oh, no; that horse belongs to the old man."[4]

"Belongs to him! Why, do they own horses?"

"Oh, yes; William (the House servant)[5] owns two, and Robert, I believe, has three now; that was one of them he was riding."

"How do they get them?"

"Oh, they buy them."

"But can they have money enough to buy horses?"

"Oh, yes; William makes a good deal of money; so does Robert. You see he is such a valuable fellow, father makes him a good many presents. He gave him a hundred dollars only a little while ago. The old man was getting infirm, and could not get about very well, so father gave him a horse."

I afterwards met the man, Robert, at the mill, where he lived as "watchman," or steward, in a cabin by himself, at a distance from the quarters of the other negroes. His language and manner was confident, frank, and manly; contrasting as much as possible with that of the negroes or mulattoes of ordinary circumstances. He wore a belt, on which were hung a large number of keys, and he walked about with his owner and me, to open the doors of the mill, barns, storehouses, and stables, conversing freely, and explaining a variety of matters with much intelligence.

I learned that he was employed while a boy as a house-servant, until, at his own request, he was put in the plantation blacksmith's shop; after acquiring this craft, he learned to make cotton-gins, and then, as he wanted to become a machinist, his master took him to Savannah, where he remained living at his own pleasure for several years. At length his owner, finding that he was acquiring dissipated habits and wasting all his earnings, brought him back to his plantation, and by giving him duties flattering to his self-respect, and allowing him peculiar privileges, made him content to remain there. He had made all the alterations and repairs necessary in running a steam-engine and extensive machinery during seven years, and his work was admirable, both in contrivance and execution.

Elsewhere I saw another negro engineer of remarkable intelligence; the gentleman in whose employment he had been for many years, esteemed him very highly, and desired to make him free. His owner, a large capitalist, a gentleman moving in our best society, and a church-member, resides at the North. He does not think it a good plan to emancipate slaves, and refuses to sell him at even a great price for that purpose. He (the owner) receives two hundred dollars a year as the wages for his services.

Though in reality a slave, being himself the property of another, cannot possess property, yet in the same way that our children and minors have things "*for* their own," they acquire many articles which few masters would be mean enough to take from them, except they were of a character to hurt them—such as ardent spirits—or such as they might be afraid of their using to the injury or annoyance of others.

The new code of Alabama, which, in one or two particulars, is less inhumane than the laws of any other Southern State, except Louisiana, in its provisions with regard to the negroes, has one article forbidding slaves to own dogs. As it seemed to me by the incessant yelping at night that every negro in the State must keep half a dozen curs, I asked a legal friend what was the object of the law. He could not tell me, but assured me that it would never be enforced. I presume it was intended to abate the great destruction of sheep by negroes' dogs (or rather the destruction which the negroes attribute to dogs, to shield a theft of one of themselves), an evil which is everywhere complained of at the South, and which operates to prevent more extensive wool-growing there. It will probably not be enforced except on extraordinary occasions.

Other provisions of this code, enumerated by a writer in the *Times* a few days since,[6] as examples of the humane amelioration of the laws of the South in favor of the negroes, seem to me of value only as expressing the views of the enactors on certain minor moralities of Slavery, such as that forbidding the separation from their mothers (*mothers* only) of children, before they are ten years old, in sheriff's sales, unless their owner deems that his interests require it (for this is all it amounts to), and to prevent the separation of relatives in mortgagee's sales, where they can just as well be sold together in family lots. The gratification which "Walpole" finds in such provisions for the more humane use of negroes, in a State which he considers to be "rapidly advancing in all that constitutes true civilization," and as "leading the way" by such measures in a glorious work of reformation, well shows with how much smaller a progress than most Northern men would have been apt to suppose safe and practicable, even the most intelligent, liberal, humane, and hopeful Southerners would be content—bearing out the views I have before expressed upon this point.

I fear many of your readers will have been surprised to find such a man touching upon it as a great thing—a reformation to be pointed to as an honor to the civilization of the good people of Alabama—that the law does not violently separate, for the fault or indiscretion of another person (their owner, as it deems him), a child under five years of age from its mother, under any circumstances, nor remove a child under ten years old from its mother, unless the said owner will make and deliver to an officer in charge an affidavit that his (the said owner's) interests will be materially prejudiced by the sale of them together. The law does not even propose to hinder, by so much as requiring an affidavit to be made that he will make money by it, the owner of a mother and child who pays his debts, from selling one to go to Texas, and retaining the other. This would be thought exceeding the appropriate duties of legistation—too great an interference with the natural laws of commerce.

I have often suggested the propriety of such laws as "Walpole" refers to, to prevent the internal slave trade, and have been answered that it was impossible to make such laws efficient. In Georgia, I was told, there is a law forbidding the introduction of slaves from abroad to be sold within the State;[7] but it is constantly evaded. The law does not forbid persons without the State selling to those within, nor the transfer of slave property between resident citizens. The slave trader, therefore, has merely to have a partner, or confederate resident, execute bills of sale of his Virginia importation to him, and the latter may then resell without let or hindrance. I entirely agree with "Walpole" in his views of the principles on which Southern Statesmanship should be guided on this subject, and if I had the least ability to influence the South, I would not wish to use it in any other direction than that in which his enthusiasm flows.[8]

If I err in my statement of facts, or if I have misapprehended public sentiment at the South, on this or any other subject, I shall consider it a favor to be corrected by those whose residence at the South gives them means of more reliable information and better judgment, than I can hope to have enjoyed. But I ask you, Southern readers, to remember, that a stranger to their habits and proceedings in connection with Slavery, must reflect from so different and distant a standpoint from that in which familiarity places them, that it will not be strange if what appears light to them, sometimes remains dark to him, and that a movement which to them is great and important, is to him almost imperceptible.

The watchman, Robert, besides owning three horses, had in his possession *three guns*—one of them a valuable fowling piece of a noted London make. Upon further inquiry, I found that several of the field hands also owned guns, which they kept in their cabins. Nothing could show better than this how small is the fear of insurrection where the negroes are managed discreetly, and treated with a moderate degree of confidence and kindness. I have not examined the laws of the State upon the subject, but it was probably illegal, as I know it would be in Alabama and Louisiana for them to be possessed of these weapons. The negroes had purchased them or, in some cases, received them as presents from their owner.

On inquiring of him what were their privileges in buying and selling, he informed me that during a large part of the year all the industrious hands finish the regular tasks required of them by one or two o'clock in the afternoon, and during the remainder of the day are at liberty, if they choose, to labor for themselves. Each family has a half-acre of land allotted to it, for a garden, besides which there is a large vegetable garden, cultivated by a gardener for the plantation, from which they are supplied, to a greater or lesser extent. They are at liberty to sell whatever they choose from the products of their own garden, and to make what they can by keeping swine and fowls. His family had no other supply of poultry and eggs, except what was obtained by purchase from his own negroes; they frequently, also purchase game from them.

The only restriction upon their traffic was a "liquor law." They were not allowed to buy or sell ardent spirits.[9] This prohibition, like liquor laws elsewhere, unfortunately could not be enforced, and of late years, Irishmen moving into the country and opening small shops, buying stolen goods from the negroes, and selling them poisonous washes under the name of grog, had become a very great evil; and the planters, although it was illegal, were not able to prevent it. They had combined to do so, and had brought several offenders to trial; but as it was a penitentiary offence, the culprit would spare no pains or expense to save himself from it, and it was almost impossible, in a community constituted as theirs was, to find a jury that would convict.

A remarkable illustration of this evil had just occurred. A planter, discovering that a considerable quantity of cotton had been stolen from him, and suspecting one of his negroes to have taken it, from finding him drunk and very sick from the effects of liquor soon after, informed the patrol of the neighboring planters of it. A lot of cotton was prepared by mixing hair with it, and put in a tempting place. The negro was seen to take it, and was followed to a grog-shop, several miles distant, where he sold it, its real value being nearly ten dollars, for ten cents, taking his pay in liquor. The man was arrested, and the theft being made to appear, by the hair, before a justice, obtained bail in $2,000 to answer at the higher Court.

In a community where the greater number of families live miles apart, and have but rare intercourse with one another, where occasion for Law and Government is almost unknown, where one part of the people, poor, untrained, illiterate, recklessly and improvidently live almost from day to day on the bounty of Nature, making rude log huts, every man for himself; of restless disposition, and frequently, from mere caprice, leaving them and moving away to make new homes; habitually a law to themselves, while they are accustomed, from childhood, to the use of the most certain deadly weapon; and where, in the other part of the people, a barbarous, patriarchal system of government exists, within another Government—as far as possible, with this circumstance, of the most republican and enlightened form—it is really wonderful that Law has so much power, and its deliberate movements and provisions for justice to accused parties are so much respected, as, spite of calumny and occasional exceptions, is usually the case in our Slave States. Why are not these villainous scamps scourged out of the district, and their dens burned, where the Law is so slow and uncertain with them?

This evil of the grog shops, and other illicit and criminal business with negroes, is a great and increasing one at the South. Everywhere that I have been, I have found the planters provoked and angry about it. A great swarm of Jews, within the last ten years, has settled in nearly every Southern town, many of them men of no character, opening cheap clothing and trinket shops, ruining or driving out of business many of the old retailers, and engaging in a clandestine trade with the simple negroes, which is found very profitable. The law which prevents the reception of the evidence of a negro in Courts,[10] here strikes back with a most annoying force upon the dominant power itself. In the mischief thus arising, we see a striking illustration of the danger which stands before the South, whenever its prosperity shall invite extensive immigration, and lead what would otherwise be a healthy competition to flow through its channels of industry.

Mr. A. remarked that his arrangements allowed his servants no excuse for dealing with these fellows. He made it a rule to purchase everything they had to sell, and to give them a high price for it himself. Eggs constituted a circulating medium on the plantation; their par value was considered to be twelve for a dime, at which they would be exchanged for cash or taken on deposit at his kitchen.

Whatever he took of them that he could not use in his own family, or had not occasion to give to others of his servants, was sent to town to be resold. The negroes would not commonly take money for the articles he had of them, but would have the value of them put to their credit, and a regular account was kept with them. He had a store, well supplied with articles that they most wanted, which were purchased in large quantities and sold to them at wholesale prices; thus giving them a great advantage in dealing with him rather than with the grog shops. His slaves were sometimes his creditors to large amounts; at the present time he owed them about five hundred dollars. A woman had charge of the store, and when there was anything called for that she could not supply, it was usually ordered by the next conveyance of his factors in town.

Here you see an illustration of what, I believe, I have before suggested:

Slavery is a grand, practical, working system of *Socialism*. It brings up, too, another aspect of Slavery—its happiest and best.

The negroes came to us from barbarism as from a cradle, with a confused, half-developed mind, with strong and simple appetites and impulses, but whimsical and unreliable; forming attachments quickly, and cleaving closely to their protectors and superiors; but, if removed from one, forming the same relations quickly, and with equal strength, with another; subject to violent and uncontrollable passions, and altogether undisciplined, uneducated, unchristianized.

Here I see their master, dealing with them as a father might with such children; guarding them sedulously against dangerous temptations, forbidding them to indulge in bad practices, rewarding the diligent and obedient, and chastising the perverse and indolent; anticipating and providing for their wants; encouraging them in the provident use of their little means of amusement, and comfort, and luxury; all the time furnishing them the necessary support of life; caring diligently for them in sickness; and only when they are of good age and strength, so long as he is their guardian, demanding of them a certain amount of their labor and assistance, to increase his own comforts, provide for his age.

Were but all Slavery this, and were but this all of Slavery!

Yeoman.

---

1. Olmsted may have written a draft of this letter late in January 1853 while visiting Richard J. Arnold. He probably wrote the final version in early July, since "The South" number 27 was published on June 30 and he refers in this letter to an article in the *Times* of June 28 as having appeared "a few days since."
2. Olmsted described this service in *Seaboard Slave States*, pages 454–61, but he did not reprint the introductory remarks that he included in "The South" number 25:

   > The family of my host ... regularly attended the services of a Presbyterian church, a few miles from the plantation; twelve miles in an opposite direction there was another house of worship, in which to-day a Baptist preacher was to officiate. This was spoken of as a "Cracker meeting," and as the negroes were generally Baptists, and as a white preacher of that persuasion did not often come within their reach, it was thought they would generally go to hear him. I preferred to attend the "Cracker meeting," and a son of Mr. A. drove me to it....
   >
   > The preacher we found, was an uneducated man, a butcher by trade, and he had been preaching at this house for three days successively; no clergyman being regularly attached to it. I suppose it was thought best to make up in quantity what was lacked in—frequency.

   It is the son of Richard J. Arnold—either Thomas Clay Arnold (1836–1875), Richard James Arnold (1834–1899) or William Eliot Arnold (1838–1883)—with whom Olmsted converses in the first section of "The South" number twenty-eight ("The South" no. 25, *NYDT*, June 16, 1853; typescript Arnold family genealogy in Talbot Family Papers; R. M. Myers, *Children of Pride*, p. 1455).
3. This was Amos Morel (or Morrell) (b. c. 1820), whom Olmsted describes at length in this letter and in *Seaboard Slave States*, pages 426–29. His mother, "Mum Phoebe," was one of the favorite house servants at White Hall and allegedly accompanied the Arnold family in their seasonal migration to the North for nineteen years. In *Seaboard Slave States*, Olmsted quotes

Arnold's son as saying that Amos probably received more pay, in wages and gifts, than did the white overseer. Extant letters that Amos wrote to Richard J. Arnold in Rhode Island show that he kept his master informed of what occurred on the plantation and did not hesitate to criticize the actions of the overseer. He also exercised considerable authority on the plantation when Arnold was absent; during the summer before Olmsted visited White Hall, for instance, Morel wrote to Arnold:

> I am sorry to inform you that I have had to break William of his driver ship and have given him his hoe, since you have left. William has got in debt to the other drivers 35 days and gets along very badly with his work on account of having too many favorites in the field. I have put big Peter in his place to drive and would be glad to hear from you if you approve of what I have done. The carpenters are getting along very badly with their work, they have not got the flat house done as yet. I am satisfied that it would be to your interest to get some white person to take charge of the work, as there is a great deal to be done, and am fearful that the mill will not be repaired time enough to receive the rice.

(Talbot family annotated copy of *SSS*, 2: 55; *SSS*, p. 429; [Richard J. Arnold], "A list of Persons belonging to me on all the Plantations & their ages Jany 1st 1858," Talbot Family Papers; Amos Morel to Richard J. Arnold, June 20, 1852, Talbot Family Papers.)

4. Richard J. Arnold's slave Jacob (Talbot family annotated copy of *SSS*, 2: 57).
5. Tom (b. c. 1813), the brother of the steward Amos Morel. Olmsted wrote the following about him in "The South" number 25, in a description of the departure of the slaves for the "Cracker meeting" at the Baptist church the Sunday after he reached Arnold's plantation: "After we had all left, some on horseback and some in carriages, I noticed that another saddle-horse remained, and as I turned to see how it was to be disposed of, the head servant (a slave), very smartly but not vulgarly dressed, came out and mounted it—as he took the reins, slipping a coin into the hands of the boy who had held it." Another version of the scene is in *Seaboard Slave States*, page 428 ([R. J. Arnold], "List of Persons belonging to me . . . Jany 1st 1858," Talbot Family Papers; Talbot family annotated copy of *SSS*, 2: 56–57; "The South" no. 25, *NYDT*, June 16, 1853).
6. An article in the *New-York Daily Times* of June 28, 1853, page 2, entitled "Southern Slavery. A Glance at Uncle Tom's Cabin. By a Southerner. Second Paper," and signed "Walpole." The section dealing with the Alabama Slave Code reads as follows:

> Already great modifications have been introduced into the laws of some of the Southern States. Take, for example, the State of Alabama. This noble State, now rapidly advancing, not only in wealth, but in all that constitutes true civilization, is leading the way in that work of reformation, which promises to make the system of Slavery, within its limits, a model of productive and cheerful labor.
>
> Its new code contains some excellent provisions in regard to the separation of slave families. No execution can be levied on a child under the age of ten years, without including the mother; or upon the mother, without including the child; and they belong to the same person, unless the owner will make, and deliver to the officer who has them in charge, an affidavit, that his interests will be materially prejudiced by selling the slaves together; but no levy or sale can be made, by which a child under five years of age shall be separated from its mother, under any circumstances.
>
> It is also provided, that in all sales of slaves under the decree of a Chancery Court, or under any deed of trust, or power of sale in a mortgage, the slaves must, if practicable, be sold in families.

7. The Georgia state constitution of 1798 forbade the importation of slaves from any foreign country, and in the same year the legislature outlawed interstate slave trade. Persons moving to Georgia to live were, however, permitted to bring their slaves with them. The prohibition against interstate slave trade was repealed in 1824, re-enacted in 1829, repealed again in 1842 and again re-enacted with some changes in 1851 (Ralph Betts Flanders, *Plantation Slavery in Georgia* [Chapel Hill, N.C., 1933], pp. 182–88).
8. "Walpole" looked forward to the development of public opposition in the South to the evils of the slave trade, which would make it possible "to control and shape Legislation, until a thorough reformation can be effected, and the true principles of Christian statesmanship find a place in the code of every Southern State." His specific proposals for regulation of the slave trade were as follows:

We venture to say, too, that we think that the laws of the Slaveholding States ought to be so amended, as to prevent slaves from being sold under executions for debts. We believe that the day is not distant, when the benign spirit of that Christianity which is destined to restore the world to its pristine purity, will effect this change in our laws. Slaves will then be protected in those social relations which ought never to be broken up;—the sanctity of home, the indestructible marrige tie, the tender attachment which binds parent and child, the reciprocal confidence between master and slave,—all will be respected, and Slavery will lose some of those features which give to the whole system a most unhappy aspect. We might hope, too, to see the traffic in slaves still further restricted, by putting it out of the power of the master to separate those who are connected by ties which ought never to be broken. ("Southern Slavery," *NYDT*, June 28, 1853, p. 2.)

9. In fact, Georgia law forbade slaves to purchase any articles for themselves without their masters' permission. There were numerous laws regulating the sale of liquor to slaves and free blacks, and liquor-dealers had to give bond and take an oath not to sell to slaves without the permission of their masters (R. B. Flanders, *Plantation Slavery in Georgia*, p. 238).
10. The Georgia Slave Code declared testimony of a black against a white to be inadmissible (ibid., p. 236).

New-York Daily Times, August 13, 1853[1]

THE SOUTH.

LETTERS ON THE PRODUCTION, INDUSTRY AND RESOURCES OF THE SLAVE STATES.

NUMBER THIRTY-THREE.

Special Correspondence of the New-York Daily Times

The Agriculture of the Southern Atlantic States—Inevitable Waste and Bad Economy of Slave Labor—Effect of Slavery on Character—Sentiments of Slaveholders Themselves on this Subject—Backward State of Farming—Slave Marriages—Burials—Inscriptions on the Tombs of Slaves, &c. &c.

It may appear, to those of your readers who have had the patience to follow me thus far in this series of letters, that I have dwelt at an unwarrantable length upon the industry of the Atlantic tier of the Southern States, while there remains before me the so much greater field of the Southwest, with its so much greater fertility and promise of consequence, industrial and political; but it should be considered that the application of labor—the means of wealth—are at present much less diversified and interesting in details in the latter, than in the former; being confined entirely—so far, at least, as they will come within the range of my observation—to the production of cotton and sugar. I will, however, in my next, proceed westward in an account of my traveling observations, and return to the Atlantic States only as I have occasion to in describing the culture of and commerce in cotton. In this letter I will write of the economy of slave labor, as observed more especially in the district lately described, and add a few miscellaneous notes illustrating the general condition and habits of the negroes.

I have shown the advantages of the "task" system of working slaves, which is generally followed on the Atlantic plantations south of Virginia.[2] It evidently has the effect to make the negroes ordinarily more active and energetic in their work than I represented them to be in my earlier letters, and probably tends to encourage a high degree of skill within certain narrow limits. Could the hope of reward for faithfulness, instead of the fear of punishment for negligence, be added to it, and some encouragement be given to the application of the mind of the laborer, to a more distant and elevated result than the release from his day's toil—as, it seems to me, there easily might be—it would, inevitably, have an improving effect upon his character. But, on the contrary, the tasked laborer is always watched as closely as possible—a driver standing by, often with a whip in his hand, that he may be *afraid* to do work slightingly. He is trusted as little as possible to use his own discretion, and it is taken for granted that he will never do anything that he *dares* avoid. In short, he is treated as a slave—the body of a man, moved only by outward force; a mind, acted upon only by fear; a soul, without responsibility.

Take men of any original character of mind, and use them as mere animal machines, to be driven by the motive-power of base fear; provide the necessities of animal life in such a way that the want of them shall afford no stimulus to contrivance, labor and providence; work them mechanically under a task-master, so that they shall have no occasion to use discretion, except to avoid the imposition of additional labor, or other punishment; deny them as much as possible the means of enlarged information and of high mental culture—and would they not, as a matter of course, be stupid, indolent, wasteful and treacherous—and constantly become of less and less value as producers, and more and more expensive as consumers? Put the best race of men under heavens into the land where all industry was obliged to bear the weight of such a system, and inevitably their ingenuity, enterprise and skill would be paralyzed, the land would be impoverished, its resources of wealth would remain undeveloped, or they would be wasted; and only by the favor of some extraordinary advantage, could it compare in prosperity with countries adjoining, in which a more simple, natural and healthy system of labor prevailed.

Such *is* the case with the Slave States. On what does their wealth and prosperity, such as it is, depend? On certain circumstances of topography, climate and soil, that give them almost a monopoly of the supply of the most important article of the world's commerce.

Conventions of planters, met to consider preposterous propositions for "regulating the Cotton Market,"[3] annually confess that if the price of this staple should be very greatly reduced by its extended culture in other parts of the world, or by any cause greatly diminishing its consumption, every proprietor at the South would be ruined. If this humiliating state of things, extending over so large a region, and yet so distinctly defined by the identical lines that separate the Slave from the free States, is not caused by the unfortunate system of labor which distinguishes the former, I know not what it can be attributed to.

That such is the effect of Slavery, is the opinion of every foreigner or Northern man, of respectable powers of observation and impartial judgment, who has resided long at the South, that I have met. An eminent merchant of New-York, who has long had intimate commercial and friendly relations with all parts of the South, and who has spent weeks on some of the best plantations, lately expressed his conviction of this to me, in the strongest manner. I know a gentleman in Georgia, a slaveholder himself, and a man of great and increasing wealth, who is so well convinced of the fallacious basis of all Southern schemes of improvement, that he invests his capital wholly in Northern securities, and who is educating his children at the North, especially to free them from the influence of slavery; and has expressed to them his wish that they should determine never to own a slave. I have heard of more than one wealthy Georgian who has sent his son to spend several years in some Northern manufacturing establishment, that he might acquire Northern habits of industry, self-discipline, and quiet energy.

I have described at length the rice plantation of a gentleman born at the North, and with the business habits of a large and successful Northern manufacturing proprietor.[4] I do not believe there is a plantation at the South managed more discreetly and judiciously with reference to profit, at the same time with Christian humanity towards the negroes; nevertheless I saw, during my visit of a few days, repeated instances of the waste and loss that must be connected with an extensive employment of slave labor: gates left open and bars left down, against standing orders; rails removed from fences, supposed to be to kindle fires with; mules lamed, and implements broken carelessly; a flat-boat, carelessly secured, going adrift into the river; men ordered to cart rails for a new fence, depositing them so that a double expense of labor would be required to lay them, more than would have been needed if they had been placed as they might almost as easily have been, by a slight exercise of forethought; men ordered to fill up holes made by alligators or craw-fish, in an important embankment, discovered to have merely patched over the outside, having taken pains only to make it *appear* that they had executed their task, not having been overlooked by a driver; men not having performed duties that were entrusted to them, making statements which their master was obliged to receive as sufficient excuse, though he believed them to be false—all going to show the carelessness, indolence, and mere eye-service of the slave.

The habitual misapplication and waste of labor on many of the rice plantations, is inconceivably great. Owing to the proverbial stupidity and dogged prejudice of the negro (but peculiar to him only as he is more carefully poisoned with ignorance than the laborer of other countries), it is exceedingly difficult to introduce new and improved methods of applying his labor. He always strongly objects to all new-fashioned implements, and if they are forced into his hands, will contrive to break them, or make them only do such work as shall compare unfavorably with what he has been accustomed to do without them. It is a common thing to see a large gang of negroes, each carrying about four shovelsfull of earth upon a board balanced on his head, walking slowly along on the embankment, so as to travel around two sides of a large field, perhaps for a mile, to fill a breach—a job which an equal number of Irishmen would accomplish, by laying planks across the field and running wheelbarrows upon them, in a tenth of the time. The clumsy iron hoe is everywhere made to do the work of pick, spade, shovel and plow. I have seen it used to dig a grave. On many plantations a plow has never been used, the land being prepared for the crop by *chopping* with the hoe, as I described in my last. There is reason for this on the newly-cleared rice-ground, perhaps, encumbered as it is with the close-standing stumps and strong roots and protuberances of the late cypress swamps,[5] though I should suppose it would be more economical to grub these by hand sufficiently to admit of the use of a strong plow, before attempting to get a crop. On old plantations, where the stumps have been removed, the surface is like a garden-bed, the soil a dark, rich, mellow, and exceedingly fine loam, the proportion of sand varying very much in different districts, but always considerable, and sufficient, I should suppose, to prevent an injurious glazing from the plow, unless the land was very poorly drained. Yet even on these the plow is not in general use.

Trials have been made on some of the South Carolina plantations of English horse-drills, I understood, without satisfactory success; but I can hardly doubt that some modification of them might be substituted advantageously for the very laborious hoe and hand process of planting. I should think, too, the horse-hoe, now coming into use in England, for cleaning wheat, which is drilled nearly or quite one-half closer than rice usually is, might be adapted to rice-culture with much saving of labor over the present method of hand-hoeing. Half an acre a day is the usual task of a negro at this operation. Garrett's horse-hoe,[6] on light land, will easily go over ten acres, employing one horse and one man and a boy. The Judges of the Royal Agricultural Society, at a trial in 1851, reported that the work done by it was far superior to any hand-hoeing. It requires to be guided, of course, with great carefulness, and, perhaps, could not be entrusted to ordinary negro field-hands.

I am not aware that any application of the reaping machines, now in use on every large grain farm at the North, has been made in the rice harvest. By the use of a portable tramway for them to run upon, I should think they might be substituted for the present exceedingly slow and toilsome method of reaping with the sickle, with economy and great relief to the laborers. Such portable tramways are in use in England for removing the turnip crop from moist fields in Winter, and it is found that men can earn 60 cents a day contracting to remove heavy crops at the rate of $1.50 an acre, shifting the trams themselves. It is probable, therefore, that the rice crop might be taken out of the wet ground and carried much more rapidly, and at less expense, to the stack-yard, in this way, than by the really cruel method now employed.

Could these, and other labor-saving appliances, in general use elsewhere, be introduced, and competition of labor be obtained by the introduction of coolies, laboring freely, as they may be had, accustomed to labor in their native rice-fields, at exceedingly low wages, the price of rice might be very greatly reduced without diminishing the profit of its culture.[7]

SLAVE MARRIAGES AND BURIALS.

Slave marriages: I have a few notes on this subject, made in Georgia, but your pleasant correspondent, "*Nein,*" has taken the wind out of my sails by her happy description of a wedding in high negro life, and, with a few appropriate anecdotes, has given you a better understanding of the nature of the relation that is formed between husband and wife, under the institution of Slavery, than I should have been able to.[8] I will, therefore, only add another instance in point to her remarks, with a few observations on the weddings of plantation slaves, and finish this letter upon the opposite tack, of *negro funerals*.

A slave, who was hired (not owned) by a friend of mine in Savannah, called upon him one morning while I was there, to say that he wished to marry a woman in the evening, and wanted a ticket from him to authorize the ceremony. "I thought you were married," said my friend.

"Yes, master, but that woman hab leave me and go 'long wid nodder man."

"Indeed! Why, you had several children by her, did not you?"

"Yes, master, we hab *thirteen,* but now she gone 'long wid 'nodder man."

"But will your church permit you to marry another woman so soon?"

"Yes, master, I tell 'em the woman I had leave me and go 'long wid 'nodder man, and she say she don't mean to come back, and I can't be 'spected to lib widout any woman at all, so dey say dey grant me de divorce."

On the plantations the ceremony of marriage varied very much; sometimes there is none at all, the parties merely asking leave of their master, and as soon as a cabin is provided for them, going to live together; sometimes it is performed by their master, generally by the negro-preacher, often by a white clergy-man.

I was standing with my friend, Mr. A.,[9] looking at a gang of negroes engaged in listing a cotton-field, when he said to a girl who was vigorously plying the hoe near us, "Is that Lucy?—Ah, Lucy, what's this I hear about you?"

The girl simpered, but did not answer or discontinue her work.

"What is this I hear about you and Sam, eh?"

The girl grinned, and whispered, "Yes, sir."

"Sam came to see me this morning."

"If master pleases."

"Very well, you may come up to the house Saturday night, and your mistress will have something for you."

There was no law on this plantation that the negroes should not marry off the place, but intercourse with other plantations was discouraged, and they seldom did so.

When a man and woman wished to live with each other, they were required to *ask leave* of their master, and unless there was some very obvious objection this was always granted, and a cabin was allotted to them, and presents were made of dresses and housekeeping articles. A marriage ceremony, in the same form as that used by free people, was conducted by the negro preacher, and they were encouraged to make the occasion memorable and gratifying to all by general festivity. The master and mistress, when on the plantation, always honored the parties by their attendance, and if they were favorite servants, the wedding was held in the house, and the ceremony performed by a white minister.

There was a beautiful, dense, evergreen grove on Mr. A.'s plantation, which was used as the burial-ground of the negroes. The funerals were always at night, and were described to be very quaint and picturesque. All the negroes, not only of the plantation, but of the neighborhood, marching in procession from the cabin of the deceased person to the grave, by the way of the mansion, carrying light-wood torches and singing hymns in their sad, wailing, chanting manner. At the head of each recent grave a wooden post was placed.

I described a negro funeral that I witnessed in Richmond, Va. In Charleston I saw one of a very different character.[10] Those in attendance were mainly women, and they all proceeded on foot to the grave, following the corpse, carried in a hearse. The exercises were simple and decorous, after the form used in the Presbyterian Church, and were conducted by a well-dressed and gentlemanly-looking elderly negro. The women were generally dressed in white, and wore bonnets which were temporarily covered with a kind of hood, made of dark cambric. There was no show whatever of feeling, emotion, or excitement. The grave was filled by the negroes before the crowd, which was quite large, dispersed. Only one white man, probably the undertaker,[11] was in attendance. The burying-ground was a rough "vacant lot" in the midst of the town. The only monuments were a few wooden posts, and one small marble tablet with a simple inscription.

In a ride in the suburbs of Savannah, I accidentally came upon a piece of ground partially enclosed by a dilapidated paling, which I found to be a large negro grave-yard. There were many monuments; some were billets of wood, others of brick and marble, and some of plank cut in the ordinary form of tombstones. Many family-lots were enclosed with railings, and a few flowers or evergreen shrubs had sometimes been planted on the graves; but these were generally broken down and withered, and the ground was overgrown with weeds and briars. The whole was shaded by an old pine grove. Riding in, I fastened my horse to a tree, and spent some time in examining the inscriptions, the greater number of which were evidently painted by self-taught negroes, and were curiously illustrative both of their condition and character. I transcribed a few of them as literally as possible.

SACRED
TO THE MEMORY
OF HENRY. Gleve, ho
Dide JANUARY 19 1849
Age 44.

BALDWING
In men of Charles
who died NOV
20. THE 1846
aged 62 years Blessed are the
dead who dieth
in the LORD
Even so said
the SPerit. For
the Rest From
Thair

[The remainder rotted off.]

DEAR
WIFE OF
JAMES DELBUG
BORN 1814 DIED 1852

In Memr
y, of,
Ma
gare
-t. Born
August
29 and
died oc
tober 29 1852

[The following on marble.]

To record the worth fidelity and virtue of Reynolda Watts, (who died on the 2d day of May 1829 at the age of 24 years, in giving birth to her 3d child).

Reared from infancy by an affectionate mistress and trained by her in the paths of virtue, She was strictly moral in her deportment, faithful and devoted in her duty and heart and soul a

[Sand drifted over the remainder.]

There were a few others, of similar character to the above, erected by whites to the memory of favorite servants. The following was on a large brick tomb:

> This table is erected to record the demise of Rev. HENRY CUNNINGHAM, Founder and subsequent pastor of the 2d African Church for 39 years, who yielded his spirit to its master the 29 of March 1842, aged 83 years.

An inscription to his wife follows:

> This vault is erected by the 2d African Church, as a token of respect.

The following is upon a large stone table. The reader will observe its date; but I must add that I heard of two occasions in which public religious services were interrupted, and the preachers—very estimable colored men—were publicly whipped, within a few years ("during the recent Abolition excitement") in North Carolina:[12]

> Sacred to the memory of Andrew Brian pastor of 1st colored Baptist church in Savannah. God was Pleased to lay his honour near his heart and impress the worth and weight of souls upon his mind that he was constrained to Preach the Gospel to dieng world, particularly to the sable sons of africa. though he labored under many disadvantage yet thought in the school of Christ, he was able to bring out new and old out of the treasury And he has done more good among the poor slaves than all the learned Doctors in America. He was imprisoned for the Gospel without any ceremony was severely whipped. But while under the lash he told his prosecutor he rejoiced not only to be whipped but he was willing for to suffer death for the cause of CHRIST.
>
> He continued preaching the Gospel until Oct. 6 1812. He was supposed to be 96 years of age, his remains were interd with peculiar respect an address was delivered by the Rev. Mr. Johnston Dr. Kolluck Thomas Williams & Henry Cunningham He was an honour to human nature an ornament to religion and a friend to mankind. His memory is still precious in the (hearts) of the living.
>
> Afflicted long he bore the rod
> With calm submission to his maker God.
> His mind was tranquil and serene
> No terrors in his looks was seen
> A SAVIOURS smile dispelled the gloom
> And smoothed the passage to the tomb.
>
> I heard a voice from Heaven saying unto me, Write, Blessed are the dead which die in the Lord from henceforth! Yea saith the Spirit that they may rest from the labours.
>
> This stone is erected by the First Colored Church as a token of love for their most faithful pastor. A.D. 1821."

YEOMAN

---

1. Olmsted probably wrote this letter between August 9 and 12, 1853. The last section, on slave funerals, appears in *Seaboard Slave States*, pages 405–9.

2. In "The South" number 30, Olmsted described the task system of slave labor, by which each slave was given each day a specified amount of work to accomplish. Olmsted stated that the task system was used for nearly all ordinary work on the larger plantations of eastern Georgia and South Carolina. He concluded that "under this 'Organization of Labor,' it must be that most of the slaves work rapidly and well" ("The South" no. 30, *NYDT*, July 21, 1853; *SSS*, pp. 434–36).
3. A reference to the Southern commercial convention that met annually from 1852 to 1859 to discuss ways to improve the economic position of the South vis-à-vis the North. The second meeting of the convention was held in Memphis in June 1853. It passed resolutions requesting Congress to improve the harbors of Southern coastal cities, called for direct trade and steamship communication with Europe and created a committee to prepare a description of the advantages offered by the American South and West for cotton manufacturing, to be circulated in the manufacturing centers of England and Europe (Robert R. Russel, *Economic Aspects of Southern Sectionalism, 1840–1861* [Urbana, Ill., 1924], pp. 123–30; see also "The South" no. 14, n. 4, above).
4. Richard J. Arnold.
5. Elsewhere, Olmsted described the process of preparing new ground—still full of stumps and roots—for rice planting "with a company of clumsy and uncouth black women, armed with axes, shovels and hoes, and directed by a stalwart black man, armed with a whip, all slopping about in the black, unctuous mire at the bottom of the ditches" ("The South" no. 30 [the second so numbered], *NYDT*, July 27, 1853; *SSS*, pp. 469–70).
6. Garrett's horse-hoe, made in England, was wide enough to hoe nine rows of wheat at once (Ph. Pusey, "Report to H.R.H. the President of the Commission for the Exhibition of the Works of all Nations. On Agricultural Implements, Class IX," *Journal of the Royal Agricultural Society of England* 12 [1851]: 610–11).
7. Olmsted did not sustain the interest he shows here in the use of Chinese coolies as a free-labor alternative to slave labor in rice culture. His discussion of the question here may have been stimulated by Henry Raymond's enthusiastic belief, set forth in several editorials during the year before Olmsted began his Southern tour, that Chinese immigrants were fated to replace Negro slaves as the labor force of the American South. Raymond pointed out that the Chinese in California worked well for low wages, and had social habits that produced few criminals, drunkards or paupers. The Chinese had already proved their superiority to Negro slaves as agricultural laborers in Jamaica and Cuba, Raymond claimed, and he believed that the imminent annexation of Cuba to the United States would soon accelerate the revolution that he anticipated in the labor force of the South ("Orientals in America," *NYDT*, April 15, 1852, p. 2; "Cotton, Cane and the Coolies," *NYDT*, May 3, 1852, p. 2; "China-men in America," *NYDT*, June 9, 1852, p. 2).
8. "A Letter from a Southern Matron—The Domestic Aspect of Slavery" (*NYDT*, June 6, 1853, p. 2).
9. Richard J. Arnold.
10. Olmsted described the Richmond funeral in "The South" number three. He saw the Charleston funeral during his visit there in late January 1853 (*NYDT*, Feb. 25, 1853, p. 2).
11. In *Seaboard Slave States*, Olmsted changed this clause to "probably a policeman" (*SSS*, p. 406).
12. After 1831 it was illegal in North Carolina for blacks—slave or free—to preach in public or to officiate "in any prayer meeting or other association where slaves of different families are collected together." Fear of insurrection led whites to disapprove of any activity by a free black that would bring a large number of Negroes together, and this facilitated enforcement of the prohibition against preaching (John Hope Franklin, *The Free Negro in North Carolina, 1790–1860* [Chapel Hill, N.C., 1943], pp. 179–82).

New-York Daily Times, August 19, 1853[1]

THE SOUTH.

LETTERS ON THE PRODUCTIONS, INDUSTRY AND RESOURCES OF THE SLAVE STATES.

NUMBER THIRTY-FOUR.

Correspondence of the New-York Daily Times

Georgia Railroads—The Resources and Prosperity of the State—Soils, Agriculture, Manufactures—Character of the People—Needs of the State.

I left Savannah for the West by the Macon road; the train started punctually to a second, at its advertised time: the speed was not great, but regular, and less time was lost unnecessarily at way-stations than there usually is on Northern roads.

I have traveled more than five hundred miles on the Georgia roads, and I am glad to say that all of them seemed to be exceedingly well managed—much better than any others at the South. The speed upon them is not generally more than from fifteen to twenty miles an hour, but it is made, as advertised, with considerable punctuality; the roads are admirably engineered and constructed, and their equipment will compare favorably with that of any other road on the continent. There are very nearly, if not quite one thousand miles of completed railroads in the State. The Savannah and Macon line was the first built, having been commenced in 1834. The most untiring energy only could have secured its completion, running, as it does, for the greater part of its course, through an almost absolute desert.

The first President of the company was William W. Gordon,[2] a name that will be remembered with gratitude as a father of the prosperity of the State, by all Georgians. He died before success crowned his labors, but not before it was secured. The enterprise was perhaps equally indebted for its success to the judicious and economical management of the first Superintendent, Lorin G. Reynolds (a Connecticut man), who is now President of the Georgia Southwestern Railroad.[3]

The increased commerce of the city of Savannah which followed the completion of this road stimulated many other railroad enterprises, not only within the State, but elsewhere at the South, particularly in South Carolina. Many of these were rashly pushed forward by men of no experience, and but little commercial judgment; the roads were injudiciously laid out, and have been badly managed, and, of course, have occasioned disastrous losses. The Savannah and Macon Road has, however, been very successful. The receipts are now over $1,000,000 annually—the road is well stocked, is out of debt, and its business is constantly increasing; the stock is above par, and the stockholders are receiving eight per cent. dividends, with a handsome surplus on hand.

Georgia is by far the most prosperous of the Eastern Southern States, and I cannot see that this can be ascribed to anything else than the superior talent and enterprise, and better directed industry of her people. In the eastern and southern part of the State, above the recent alluvion of the coast (the "sea-island" and rice region) the soil, at the best, is thin and very rapidly exhausted of fertility under cultivation. The river bottoms are generally so liable to overflow that they cannot be settled upon, and the "pine-barrens," which constitute a large portion of this region, are of not the slightest agricultural value, except for grazing. The only food for cattle is a wire-grass, which grows in tufts, very thinly, affords but very poor pasturage. To encourage a fresh shooting of it, it is burned over every Spring. The law fixes a day, previous to which it is an offense to fire the grass; but this law it is impossible to enforce, and unexpected fires frequently do a great deal of damage, first catching the dry pine wood of the fences, and running on these to stacks and buildings. The cattle are, so far as I observed, without exception, small and gaunt. The hides from them are considered superior to Western hides, and the business of tanning is somewhat extensive in the oak-land districts of the State; but little tallow is obtained from the carcass, and the beef is very poor. Wealthy people, and the best hotels in Savannah, procure their beef from New-York. The *climate* is generally thought to be unfavorable to neat-stock. I would suppose that sheep-grazing would be more profitable, but the land is almost worthless for any purpose.

In what is known as the Cherokee Country, in the northwestern part of the State, there is much land of excellent quality, but owing to its great elevation, the climate is unfavorable to the extensive culture of cotton. Corn, oats, and fruits, are largely and profitably cultivated. This region of the State, which has been in the hands of the Indians until within a comparatively recent period, is being very largely settled upon by working white farmers, with but a few or no slaves. I am very sorry that I cannot give a good account of their moral and educational condition. From what I saw and heard, I fear that they are very generally exceedingly ignorant and intemperate. In the southwestern part of the State, there is also much unimproved land, of considerable fertility, and suitable for cotton culture to which, so far as settled, its agriculture is wholly devoted. The soil is thin, however, and will be rapidly exhausted. There is a scarcity of wholesome drinking-water, and the climate is not very favorable to health.

In the central region of the State, on the southeastern slope of the Alleghanies, above the pine barrens, the soil is generally argillaceous, often with a very tenacious subsoil. It was originally of considerable fertility, bearing oak and hickory. The surface is exceedingly undulating, a continual succession of very steep-sided hills and dells.

This has formerly been a very important cotton-producing district, but with the wretched and most un-husbandman-like agriculture—cotton being grown every year, without any cessation, until the profits of raising it would no longer pay for the labor expended upon it—the soil has been all washed from the hilltops, and, in years of low prices, a great many planters have been ruined and obligated to move to Alabama or Texas. The system of agriculture is lately improving, parallel open drains being now extensively made in the hill-sides to arrest the washing off of the soil, and although emigration still continues, I was glad to see, especially in the vicinity of the Railroads, many indications of increasing wealth in the community at large. The old plantations present a more desolate picture to the traveler, if possible, than those of Eastern Virginia, the hill-sides deeply gullied, with no vegetation but stunted pine shrubs to hide the barren red surface. As in Virginia, under the tobacco culture, whenever the old deciduous forests have been destroyed, and the soil deprived of its original fertility by an exhausting course of cotton, pines have sprung up, and now cover a large portion of the district.

The greater part of the State is abundantly provided with running water, frequently affording excellent milling power. The mineral wealth of the State is said by geologists to be very great, but at present almost entirely underdeveloped. More attention has been given to manufacturing, thus far with but indifferent success, I fear; but I cannot doubt that if the same judgment, skill, and close scrutiny of details, were given to cotton manufacturing that is now evidently applied to the management of railroads in Georgia, it would be well rewarded. The cost of the raw material must be from ten to twenty per cent. less than in Massachusetts, yet I found Lowell cottons, both fine and coarse, for sale almost under the roof of Georgia factories. I learned also, a curious illustration of the tendency of commerce to centralization: Georgia cottons are sent to New-York for sale, and are there sold by New-York jobbers to Georgia retailers, who retransport them to the vicinity in which the cotton was grown, spun and manufactured, to be sold by the yard or piece to the planter. A Georgia merchant returning from New-York, informed me of this.

Land-rent, water-power, timber, fuel and raw material for cotton manufacturing are all much cheaper in Georgia than in New-England. Provisions are somewhat higher: slave-labor can only be profitably applied to cotton culture and corn—breadstuffs and meat are heavily imported—but free labor in the Cherokee district will soon change this. The only other item of importance in estimating the cost of manufacturing must be the cost of labor; which includes, of course, the efficiency of the laborers. By the census, it appears that the average wages of the female operatives in the Georgia cotton factories was, in 1850, $7.39 a month; in Massachusetts, $14.57 a month. Negroes were worth $180 a year, and found in[4] clothes, food and medical attendance by the hirer, to work on Railroads, where I was in Georgia. This summer a Georgia planter sent to New-York for Irish laborers to work on his plantation (being able to hire them, at $10 a month, and found in food only, losing their own time when ill)—a very significant fact. New-England factory girls have been induced to go to Georgia to work in newly-established cotton factories, by the offer of higher wages, but have found their position so unpleasant, owing to the general degradation of the laboring class produced by Slavery, as very soon to force them to return.

I spent several days at Columbus, the most extensive manufacturing town, not only of Georgia, but of the South, below Virginia. The information I received with regard to the prosperity of the manufacturers was so contradictory, that I shall not repeat any of it. The city is at the falls, and head of steamboat navigation at high water of the Chattahoochee; the water-power is sufficient to drive 200,000 spindles, with a proportionate number of looms. There are probably at present from fifteen to twenty thousand spindles running. The operatives in the cotton-mills are said to be mainly "cracker girls" (poor whites from the country) who earn from $8 to $12 a month. There are, besides the cotton-mills, one woolen-mill, one paper-mill, a foundry, a cotton-gin factory, a machine-shop, &c. The laborers are mainly whites, and they are in such a condition that if temporarily thrown out of employment (as they were altogther, at the time of my visit, by a freshet of the river) they are at once reduced to a state almost of destitution, and are dependent very extensively upon credit or charity for their daily food.

I have seen in no place since I left Washington so much gambling, intoxication, and cruel treatment of servants in public as in Columbus. This, possibly, was accidental; but I must caution persons traveling for health or pleasure to avoid stopping in the town. The inn in which I lodged was disgustingly dirty, the table revolting, the waiters stupid, inattentive, and annoying. It was the stagehouse; and fellow-travelers who went to the other principal public house declared that it was, if possible, worse. There are very good hotels at Macon and at Montgomery, Alabama; and it will be best in proceeding from Savannah westward, if possible, not to spend a night between these towns. Let me add that nowhere have I found more genuine courtesy, or met with so unostentatious and hearty hospitality in private, from strangers, as in Western Georgia and Eastern Alabama, in the vicinity of Columbus. Fortunately for the State of Georgia, a very large class of her population is composed of moral, intelligent, and industrious men, of moderate means; her Constitution is much more democratic, and her legislation has been of a much more democratic, liberal, and progressive character, than that of her rival, South Carolina.

A much more rapid material advance, and a much higher position in the respect of the country is the consequence, not withstanding the embarrassments and inconvenience occasioned by the want of capital, of her merchants and men of business—a difficulty which still gives Charleston a commanding advantage over Savannah, even within the natural back country of the latter. There are two very great drawbacks upon the progress of the State. One is the want of a deep, safe, and easily accessible commercial port. The expense, delays and dangers attending the shipment of cotton at Savannah are very great, owing to loss and obstructions in the river below the town. Every means should be resorted to to remove these. The Government appropriations for the purpose are insignificant, in view of the extent of the interests affected. The other point to which I refer, is the dead weight of a numerous unproductive class of exceedingly ignorant, unambitious, indolent people. Increased attention to mining and manufactures, and to all branches of industry, which, by stimulating labor with the hope of immediate reward, encouraging undissipating social association, and demanding activity of mind and body, will infuse new life and spirit among the poor; a greater respect for the profession of teaching in its humblest sphere; a better compensation and a higher standard of capacity for teachers, and a much more liberal expenditure and greater extension of the facilities for general popular instruction by the State, *in loco parentis* to the innumerable white-headed children, that themselves will soon be a part of the State ("*L'Etat c'est moi*"), will have a very strong tendency to remove the latter and most strong impediment. This the intelligence of the State is beginning to appreciate.

YEOMAN.

1. Olmsted probably wrote this letter between August 13 and 18, 1853.
2. William Washington Gordon (1796–1842), lawyer and railroad entrepreneur, whose father moved to Georgia from New Jersey around 1790. Gordon was the first Georgian to graduate from West Point. He became the president of the Central Railroad of Georgia, between Savannah and Macon, which obtained a charter in 1833 and was completed the year before his death (*DAB*).
3. Reynolds began the survey for the route of the Central Railroad of Georgia in 1836 and became president of the Southwestern Railroad Company in 1849 (John Campbell Butler, *Historical Record of Macon and Central Georgia*... [Macon, Ga., 1958], pp. 138, 208).
4. That is, "provided with."

To Charles Loring Brace

February 8th, [1853]

Another confounded illegible problematical letter from you. Who is "Cousin Hal" and what is the N.Y.'s Club?

I *did* get a "friend" in Petersburg and in Norfolk and in Savannah &c., to call at office for me. I've no doubt at all your letters have gone up town. Ask Miss Lynch?[1] Mr. Leavenworth[2] I got a letter from this morning. He says he went to Post Office a dozen times for me & is sure nothing ever came there for me.

The devil take you for leaving it all to Raymond.[3] My letters are not fit to be used in that way. He will be confoundedly disappointed if he thinks they will, and I'm afraid will refuse them when he comes to read them. I would have given a hundred dollars if you had attended to my request. It just throws a wet blanket over me and I am afraid to write at all and am regularly flummoxed. You say you fear so & so. Why the devil not look and see and then tell me?

I never talked of assaying North Carolina gold—but Negro labor as applied to gold raising is a subject of interest and in my legitimate way.[4] So is Negro labor applied to farming—to a mountain agriculture. So is the upper country of the South, for my tour to this time has been confined to a comparatively desert country—except a few small planting districts. I have seen nothing but the Atlantic shore of Virginia, North Carolina, South Carolina & Georgia. On my return I propose to survey upper and interior of all these as well as of the gulf states—and if I am not ruined by it, next year to take the frontier & Southwest slave states. It is but a bird's eye glance I take, at best.

Am I right or not?

Confound you again, I say—you tell me the same thing over & over and it is evident without the slightest thought.

If you can get time to forget Theodore Parker[5] and Miss Lynch, try to tell me in your next if Henry & Eliza Neill[6] are not in this country. Both you and Father have intimated as much. If so where are they & what are they about?

I am very glad to learn that Mrs. Field[7] has a son and is well. Express my most sincere congratulations. Sorry Mr. Field is no better. I advise him to think of moving South. Florida is the best place for summer. But of that I must talk with him and John[8] extensively when I can.

There is an expression with regard to profligacy among slaves, declaring it to be universal and necessary—even among family servants—in one of my Virginia letters, I should think the 7th, perhaps 9th (8, 10.) I much regret it as I am convinced it is too sweeping and will excite indignation. It refers to slaves employed by northern families at the South. I wish it could be tempered down or removed, only without destroying the argument or breaking the connection.[9]

I think you are most fortunately placed as Boys' friend.[10] I have already given you my ideas of your dangers and your opportunities. Cultivate confidence & beware of straining for effect. Be true to your reality.

I have a letter to Baine.[11] Who is Bane?

I *can't* "go to meetings."

I can't write [a] different sort of letters. If Raymond wanted statesmanship and generalizations he is at the wrong shop. He can take my wares at his own price, but it will cost me $450 and every minute given to the work.

---

1. Anne Charlotte Lynch (1815–1891), Hartford-born author, teacher and hostess of an influential literary salon in New York City. Brace came to know and admire her through his work with

poor and vagrant children in New York, where she was one of the sponsors of the Wilson Industrial School (*Notable American Women,* s.v. "Botta, Anne Charlotte Lynch"; Vicenzo Botta, ed., *Memoirs of Anne C. L. Bott, Written by Her Friends. With Selections from Her Correspondence and from Her Writings in Prose and Poetry* [New York, 1894], pp. 345–46; see also FLO to Anne Charlotte Lynch, March 12, 1854, n. 1, below).
2. Abner Leavenworth, whom Olmsted visited in Petersburg, Virginia, in late December 1852 (see FLO to FJK, Feb. 26, 1853, below).
3. Henry Raymond, editor of the *New-York Daily Times.*
4. Olmsted had earlier intended to visit the gold-mining district in central North Carolina, but did not do so (see FLO to JO, Jan. 10, 1853, above).
5. Theodore Parker (1810–1860), Unitarian theologian and abolitionist. Brace had recently visited Boston and had been exhilarated by talks with Parker and his friends, which made him "feel a new spring and impulse at seeing men so free and true" (*DAB;* CLB to Theodore Parker, Feb. 16, 1853, in *Life of Brace,* p. 175).
6. Henry M. Neill (1838–1906) and Eliza Neill, brother and sister of Brace's future wife, Letitia Neill. Olmsted had met them at their home in Belfast, Ireland, in the summer of 1850 (*NYDT,* Sept. 13, 1906, p. 7).
7. Charlotte Errington Field (c. 1817–1880), wife of Olmsted's Staten Island neighbor Alfred Field (1814–1884). Their newly born son was Henry Cromwell Field (1853–1929) (Alfred Field to FLO, May 11, 1880; *Times* (London), May 12, 1880, p. 1; ibid., May 23, 1929, p. 166; *NYDT,* May 28, 1884, p. 4; *Papers of FLO,* 1: 342, n. 11).
8. John Hull Olmsted.
9. Brace apparently failed to make the revision that Olmsted requested of him. "The South" number 9 as it appeared in the *New-York Daily Times* of April 5, 1853, contained the following passage, which must be the one that Olmsted wanted excised:

> Slavery, even now, day by day, is greatly responsible for the degraded and immoral condition of the free blacks of our cities, and especially of Philadelphia. It is, perhaps, necessary that I should explain that licentiousness and almost indiscriminate sexual connection among the young is very general, and is a necessity of the system of Slavery. A Northern family that employs slave domestics, and insists upon a life of physical chastity in its female servants, is always greatly detested; and they frequently come to their owners and beg to be taken away, or not hired again, though acknowledging themselves to be kindly treated in all other respects. A slave owner told me this of his own girls hired to Northern people.

10. On January 9, 1853, a group of New York philanthropists offered Brace a position as "city missionary to vagrant boys." This was the first step in a process that led by March to the creation of the Children's Aid Society, with Brace as its executive head (*Life of Brace,* pp. 156–57, 489–92).
11. Thomas Levingston Bayne (1826–1891), a native of Georgia who graduated from Yale in 1847, went to New Orleans the next year to study law, and in 1849 began to practice law there. Olmsted saw him on at least two occasions during his visit to New Orleans in February 1853 (*Yale Obit. Rec.,* 4th ser. 2 [June 1892]: 106–7; FLO to FJK, Feb. 26, 1853, below).

New-York Daily Times, August 26, 1853[1]

THE SOUTH.

LETTERS ON THE PRODUCTIONS, INDUSTRY AND RESOURCES OF THE SOUTHERN STATES.

NUMBER THIRTY-FIVE.

JOURNEY THROUGH THE LOWER SOUTH: 1853

Special Correspondence of the New-York Daily Times

Alabama—Surface—Soils—Agriculture—Frontier—Character of the State and of the People—Size of Plantations—The Cotton Crop—Immigration and Emigration—Mines, Rivers and Railroads.

The eastern part of Alabama resembles the western part of Georgia, which I have described. In the North, there are rugged lime stone ridges; below these, there is much rich and new land, until lately occupied by the Creek Indians, which is now being rapidly brought into civilization, mainly by emigrants from Carolina and Georgia, who purchase it in small parcels, and labor upon it with their own hands. In the central part of the State, the surface is undulating, and the soil of various character; the best is a dark brown clayey loam called "mulatto land;" there is also a light, gravelly loam, resting on clay, on which I noticed a great deal of cotton that was very small, not more than three feet high, but which was said to produce an extraordinary proportion of wool to the weed. A large amount of land here is, however, a very thin gray soil, over stiff red clay, and is rapidly exhausted under cultivation. Much of this has been worn out and moved away from.

Through all the southern part of the State, for from fifty to one hundred miles from the Gulf shore, the land is sandy, bearing pine, with live-oak and cypress, in the low grounds. The valleys of the rivers only have any agricultural importance; these are broad and very productive and profitable where they are tolerably secure from overflow, but they are very unhealthy, whites being subject to bilious fevers in Summer, and negroes and those who are acclimated, to fatal lung complaints in the Winter. There is a great extent of land of this kind yet to be brought into cultivation by leveeing the river banks. The climate is suitable to the sugar-cane, which is not yet cultivated, except for plantation use.

The valley of the Tennessee in the north is very fertile and better cultivated than any other part of the State. In the west, the soils are calcareous, and of every degree of fertility. On the river borders, there are large tracts of a very dark, unctuous, clayey soil, on which is produced the best "Mobile" cotton. It is called "black land." "Cane-brake" soil is very similar.

Alabama is a young State, with very little exhausted land. Her ordinary crop of cotton is estimated to be over 500,000 bales, not less than $20,000,000 in value. New land is being constantly brought into cultivation, and the demand for negroes is very great—occasioning a constant importation from Virginia and Maryland. The first house I saw, on re-entering the State, had painted on its front, in large letters: "J. & W. McKee, Slave-Dealers;" and one of the curiosities to every Northerner visiting Montgomery—the capital of the State—is the parade of negroes, dressed up attractively (the smallest boys provided with the thickest heeled shoes and the tallest hats), which is made every day through the principal streets.

205

The plantations are not generally large; I should think the greater number of planters owned from ten to twenty slaves only, though plantations on which from fifty to a hundred are employed are not uncommon; and on the rich alluvial soils of the southern part of the State, these are, perhaps, more common than any other. Many of the largest and most productive plantations are extremely unhealthy in Summer, and their owners seldom reside upon them except temporarily. Several of the larger towns in Alabama, remarkable in the midst of wilderness which surrounds them, for the neatness and tasteful character of many of the houses and gardens which they contain, are in a considerable degree made up of the residences of gentlemen who own large plantations in the hotter and less healthful part of the State; many of these have been educated in the older States, and with minds enlarged and liberalized by travel, they form, with their families, a society of high cultivation and of the most attractive social character.

Much the larger proportion of the planters of the State live in log-houses, some of them very neat and comfortable, but frequently rude in construction, un-*chinked,* with windows unglazed, and wanting in many of the commonest conveniences possessed by the poorest class of Northern farmers of the older States. This is not for want of means; at least, many living in this way will be surrounded by servants living in a cluster of cabins, only less comfortable than their own by being a little less in size.

The territorial Government of Alabama was established in 1816, and in 1818 she was admitted as a State into the Union. In 1820, her population was 126,000; in 1850, it had increased to 772,000; the increase of the previous ten years having been 30 per cent. (that of South Carolina was 5 per cent.; of Georgia, 31; Mississippi, 60; Michigan, 87; Wisconsin, 890.) A large part of Alabama has yet a strikingly frontier character. Even from the State-house in the fine and promising young city of Montgomery, the eye falls in every direction upon a dense forest, boundless as the sea, and producing the some solemn sensation of reverence for infinitude. You find towns on the map, and hear them frequently referred to as important points in the stages of your journey, which you are surprised and amused to find, when you reach them consist, perhaps, of not more than three or four cabins, a tavern or grocery, a blacksmith's shop and a stable. A stranger once meeting a coach that I was on, asked the driver whether it would be prudent for him to pass through one of these towns that we had just come from; he had heard that there were more than fifty cases of small pox in the town. "Thar ain't fifty people in the town, nor within ten miles on't it," answered the driver.

The best of the country roads are but little better than open passages for strong vehicles through the woods, made by cutting away the trees, being scarcely "worked" at all. There was, nevertheless, when I was in them, a great deal of travel of heavy wagons, loaded either with the household goods of emigrants, or carrying cotton from the plantation to market;—from two to six bales making a load, which would be drawn by as many mules or horses, or pairs of cattle, as there were bales. At night, the roads were lined at frequent intervals with the camp-fires of the teamsters. There were often three or four wagons proceeding in company, driven by negroes, with their owner on horseback.

I once turned off one of these main-roads to visit a plantation, about half a mile from it. I found my way to it with some difficulty, following an obscure track, which ran very circuitously among the trees, up hill and down, and sometimes in the bed of a stream. In returning, a negro was sent to put me upon a shorter path; soon after he left me, I lost it altogether, and wandered about, giving my horse leave to choose his way, for hours, without coming in sight of a fence or clearing or cabin, till at last I came out on the main road again, four miles from the place I had intended to; and this was within a mile of a town of several thousand inhabitants.[2]

The people, too, have a remarkably frontier character; almost every man you meet talks of "when he first came to Alabama." They generally commence a conversation with a stranger by asking him to "drink" with them. There is a rudeness, and a heartiness, and a truthfulness, and a working-out of characteristic individual purposes, whether disagreeable or gratifying to the tastes of others, a disuse of ordinary conveniences, and an ignorance and neglect of ordinary mannerisms and conventionalities of older communities, in the majority of the people you accidentally fall in with, which indicates that they have lived much in solitude, and have been accustomed to consider very little what other people thought of them. They are inclined to social experiments—"fights," gambling, camp-meetings, &c.; their knowledge and their curiosity is practical and material, and ninety-nine times out of a hundred, if you overhear a conversation, you will find the subject of it closely connected with cotton, or the advantages offered to emigrants in this or that region.

There is evidently, with all the individual independence, a certain homogeneousness of character, distinguishing the manners and habits of the people and the state of society from any that I had before observed. It was impossible to *classify* people as one does elsewhere, by their dress, their tastes, their manners, or their expenditures. These were incomprehensibly united in the same man—the self-possessed, generous and *commanding* gentleman, the coarse and uncivilized boor, and the reckless ruffian; alternately offending taste, affording amusement, and commanding respect. Evidently, here was a new phase and style of civilization, peculiar to Anglo-Saxon development in the Southwest.

Most of these people had been born in the eastern Southern States— Virginia, the Carolinas, and Georgia. Some had moved forward from exhausted plantations in those States, to retrieve or better their fortunes on new lands; many, I am told, had been overseers until they had been able to purchase a few negroes for themselves, and on new, cheap, and productive land to plant for themselves. It is their first thought to buy land to the best advantage for growing cotton upon, without regard to neighbors or surroundings, then to make the most cotton possible, whereby to pay the interest of the debts they have incurred, or to increase their force. For the present they will make shift to live without comfort; they roll the logs into cabins, wherever and in such shape as is easiest. Everything is done roughly, and in [a] make-shift way. Comforts they have been accustomed to are dispensed with until they are forgotten, and they have learned to do as well without them. Hoping everything of luck, they are always short-handed for the work they undertake; they must take hold themselves with the negroes. There's no time to cook two dinners—the same pot boils for white and black; they are forced into companionship until their numbers increase by birth and purchase, so that new quarters for them, and more system and division of labor is necessarily arrived at. But before this, habits are formed that are never to be lost—old habits are lost, never to be regained.

Such men have had no time to loiter away, and they have lost all taste for mild recreations, or for sober, quiet, and contemplative employment of the mind. Their amusements must be exciting, their festivities are exhaustive, as if they were trials of muscular agility and wind and bottom; if they engage in politics, it is as if they were in a battle. Religion, too, is a matter of excitement—of spasms and experiences—of fights with Apollyon[3] and wrestling with Jehovah—of maddening despair, and of ecstatic hope and triumph. Until their heart is engaged for the higher life, they are careless and reckless. They may be scoffers, but they are seldom sceptics. So, too, their whole organization has become strong and tough; their appetites require something coarse and harsh to satisfy them; they like not delicate meats and wheaten bread, or succulent vegetables;—they are satisfied with no repast in which smoked and salted bacon, and hard corn-dodgers and bitter coffee, or fiery whiskey, have not played important parts.

One thing more I must not omit, in speaking of the character and manners of this class. I never met with any unkindness or uncivility from them, or among them. Roughness of manner, and something of surliness, was not uncommon; but rudeness I never witnessed. They are a vastly higher type of mankind than what we call "rowdies"—a too-numerous class at the North. I believe that they are generally kind masters, and that their slaves seldom are deprived of privileges or comforts of which they are capable of rightly appreciating the value. Their greatest wants are unknown to themselves.

Notwithstanding the youth of the State, there is a constant and extensive emigration from it, as well as immigration to it. The profits of planting are in a considerable degree dependent upon the extent of the force engaged, expenditures not increasing in the ratio of numbers of slave property. Large planters, as their stock increases, are always anxious to enlarge the area of their land, and will often pay a high price for that of any poor neighbor, who, embarrassed by debt, can be tempted to move on to cheaper and more productive new land. The tendency in Alabama, and all the Eastern and Southern

States, is the enlargement of plantations. The small farmers are constantly going ahead. Western Texas is their promised land. Of course, the emigration is not wholly confined to this class. The owners of large plantations that have been "worn out," particularly from the thin-soiled hill districts, often emigrate, carrying with them large bodies of slaves.

There are large and rich deposits of coal and iron within the State, which, lying as they do on navigable streams and in a limestone district, if manufacturing and a dense population should ever create a home demand, would be worked with great cheapness and profit.

The State is remarkably well supplied by rivers, with the means of a sufficiently convenient and cheap means of transportation of cotton to the sea, during the usual season of its shipment. In Summer these streams are navigable by only a very small class of steamboats, and that with difficulty and danger. Freights at this season are often very high, and traveling very slow and expensive. There are but a few railroads within the State, and the great Northern and Southern Mail, regularity in the arrival of which is of more importance to commerce than that of any other in the country, is carried through Alabama in stage-coaches, which subjects it to most vexatious delays—no mail from New-York often reaching Mobile and New-Orleans for three or four days in succession. The Mobile and Cincinnati Railroad, now building, is a very important line, and will doubtless, be of the greatest service to Mobile and the western part of the State.

YEOMAN.

1. Olmsted probably wrote this letter between August 19 and 25, 1853.
2. This incident probably occurred near Montgomery, Alabama, where Olmsted spent a week in February 1853.
3. An allusion to *The Pilgrim's Progress,* by John Bunyan, in which the hero, Christian, is forced to do battle with Apollyon, the king and god of the City of Destruction. In the Book of Revelation, Apollyon is the angel of the bottomless pit (Revelation 9:11).

To CHARLES LORING BRACE

New Orleans, February 23d, 1853

Dear Charley,

I received yours of 16th January just now. I have seen my first letter in "Times." There is but one misprint in it: "guise" (italicized) for *raise*.[1] Thank you for your criticisms, but it wouldn't have taken so long to have corrected the errors before printing as after. Why didn't you see that the simple heading

South was made as I told you, instead of the long one that I may not come up to—as you say in your last letter, too, would be better? I have not [*seen*][2] letters sent to H. Neill.[3] He was to direct [them] to [the] office of a friend where I am now writ[ing].[4] I don't know why they don't come, except that they don't give them up on account of the direction "to be called for."

I have called on <u>Bain</u>[5] 8 or 10 times & haven't found him in. He left a card for me also at "St. Charles."[6] I met him once in City Hall & was introduced to him. He will do nothing. The prospect you may judge from his remark, half enquiringly, "I believe your brother was a member of my class."

"Yes."

"*But* only for a short time—he entered it from another."[7]

He seemed to have forgotten that he ever had known John—is it possible? He is over full of business & I doubt if I shall have a talk with him. But I think of employing him in his lawyer capacity to make a digest of *Code Noir* of Louisiana[8] for me—that is if it don't cost too much.

You can't imagine how hard it is to get hold of a conversable man—and when you find, he will talk about anything else but slavery &c. *Music* I am surfeited with, that is, *talk* on music.

Raymond's introduction is very handsome and well expressed, but I can't live up to it.[9] I am very much discouraged. Since Virginia, I have written nothing—but 4 letters merely describing roads and taverns and conveyances.[10] I am in doubt whether to publish them at all. But I have a good deal of material by which I can dress up a general view, description, of the S.E. Slave States. I know all about Red River sort of folks, there's nothing to be said that can't be put into one letter. They are all the same—just the half-brutes, half-gentlemen that John[11] describes the medical students of Paris. And as to domestic life or negro plantation life, I can not see it. The negroes are at work—anywhere the same all day—and you can't go into their cabins at night any more than you could into English cabins—not so much, because their master might shoot you. He himself won't go into them, from delicacy, unless with especial purpose—and such purpose as he wouldn't let another man meddle in. They are jealous of observation of things that would tell against slavery, not only as to northern men but as to southern neighbors.

A letter I wrote father yesterday will show you how I feel—also inform you of my plans. Mr. Duncan,[12] an arrogant, vain, pompous humbug, told me Dick Taylor[13] was nearly dead and there seemed to be no chance of my getting onto a plantation, as Baker's[14] was 2 days distant down toward the gulf, and nobody else seemed willing to help me to see one. But calling on Taylor's factor yesterday to make sure, I learned that he was sufficiently well to walk about & would probably be glad to have me come, so I go tonight. I believe old Duncan purposely deceived me to prevent me seeing [a] slave plantation, for he knew my purpose & told me I was too young and enthusiastic to examine [the] subject, moreover it was nobody's business but their own & the North did [not] need the information &c.—cursed old fogey.

JOURNEY THROUGH THE LOWER SOUTH: 1853

I think you are too damned busy Charley—this is another sprawling note, spun out on 1½ pages of small paper & 2/3ds merely a repetition for the 50th time of what you had said to me several hundred times before I left—or what I have said to you. And about yourself personally, this paragraph is all: "Working like smoke in the Children's"—something illegible and I don't know, having never been informed, what.[15]

Don't advise me any more to go up Red River or to look up *Bane* or to write to J. W. Skinner[16]—(I have done so.) If you can't think of anything else to fill up with—put your signature.

I received John's letter of January 17th, enclosed by father, this morning. It is melancholy.[17] I have not received Eliza Neill's or H. Barnes',[18] though I still continue writing back for them. They are in the tomb of Washington before now.

H. Neill I enjoyed and there is an Englishman here that I didn't find till yesterday—to whom I [am] introduced by him—that promises to be [a] very pleasant if not useful acquaintance.

Look sharp about the trees. $500 risk in their exposure.

Write immediately, last chance, to New Orleans. Next to Tuscaloosa, Alabama.

Yours affectionately

---

1. See "The South" number 1, note 3, above.
2. Editors' reading of a word partially obliterated by a tear in the letter.
3. Presumably Henry Neill, Brace's future brother-in-law, who was traveling in the United States and who within four years founded the firm of Neill Brothers of Mobile, New Orleans and London, cotton merchants (see FLO to CLB, Feb. 8, 1853, above).
4. Editors' reading of letters obliterated by a tear in the letter.
5. Thomas Levingston Bayne (1826–1891), New Orleans lawyer and graduate of Yale in 1847 (*Yale Obit. Rec.*, 4th ser. 2 [June 1892]: 106–7; see FLO to FJK, Feb. 26, 1853, n. 4, below).
6. The St. Charles Hotel in New Orleans.
7. John Hull Olmsted had been forced by ill health to leave Yale College during his sophomore year (1843–44), but he returned as a member of the class of 1847 (Franklin Bowditch Dexter, *Biographical Notices of Graduates of Yale College, Including Those Graduated in Classes Later Than 1815, Who Are Not Commemorated in the Annual Obituary Records* . . . [New Haven, Conn., 1913], p. 373).
8. The *Code Noir* of Louisiana was a set of regulations governing the status, control and treatment of free and enslaved blacks and was patterned after a code instituted by the French in Lousiana in 1724 (Alcée Fortier, ed., *Louisiana: Comprising Sketches of Counties, Towns, Events, Institutions, and Persons, Arranged in Cyclopedic Form* . . ., 2 vols. [Atlanta, Ga., 1909–], 1: 91–97).
9. In an editorial introducing Olmsted's series of letters "The South" in the *New-York Daily Times*, the editor, Henry Raymond, predicted that the letters would meet the great need for "an accurate, complete and dispassionate statement of *facts* concerning the industrial, social, educational, religious and general interests of the Southern States." He continued:

> We can find in abundance pictures claiming to be representations of Southern life and character—dissertations upon the bearing and influence of Southern institutions—and arguments assailing and defending Slavery. But nearly everything written concerning the South hitherto, has been written to sustain some "foregone conclusion"—to fortify some

preconceived opinion—to aid the attainment of some political purpose, or to promote, in some way, the views or interests of the parties concerned.... they do not furnish the *facts* upon which alone a just and dispassionate judgment should be based. And in that respect we trust these letters will supply a defect which every unprejudiced person, at all interested in such inquiries, cannot fail to have felt. ("Facts from the South," *NYDT*, Feb. 16, 1853, p. 4.)

10. Probably the account of his journey from Portsmouth, Virginia, to Charleston, South Carolina, that Olmsted published in "The South" numbers 15, 16, 20, 21 and 22. He wrote the final version of those letters in April and May after his return to Staten Island and supplemented the material he mentions here with letters describing various aspects of the society and economy of North Carolina (FLO to JO, May 19, 1853).
11. John Hull Olmsted.
12. Probably Lucius Campbell Duncan (1801–1855), a graduate of Yale in 1821 and partner with his brother Greer B. Duncan in a New Orleans law firm. His nephew Lucius Campbell Duncan (1830–1902), the adopted son of Greer Duncan, graduated from Yale in 1852. Denison Olmsted may have known Duncan and been the source of Olmsted's introduction to him: he named his youngest son, born in 1827, Lucius Duncan Olmsted (F. B. Dexter, *Biographical Notices of Graduates of Yale College*, pp. 72–73; *Yale Obit. Rec.*, Supplement [June 1900–June 1910], [New Haven, Conn., 1910], p. 1345; *Olmsted Genealogy*, pp. 73, 122).
13. Richard Taylor, only son of President Zachary Taylor and a graduate of Yale College in 1845 (see FLO to FJK, Feb. 26, 1853, n. 2, below).
14. Anthony Wayne Baker (1826–1854), a graduate of Yale College in 1847 who lived on a plantation in St. Mary Parish, Louisiana (F. B. Dexter, *Biographical Notices of Graduates of Yale College*, p. 366).
15. Olmsted was probably unaware that Brace's organization had taken the name "Children's Aid Society" (see FLO to CLB, Feb. 8, 1853, n. 10, above).
16. John Warburton Skinner (1818–1889), a lawyer in St. Louis and graduate of Yale in 1843 who had married Brace's sister Mary in December 1852 (*Yale Obit. Rec.*, 3d ser. 9 [June 1889]: 515–16).
17. John Hull Olmsted was spending the winter in Paris, seeking improved health in the climate of Europe, and was depressed by the weather. As his father reported at this time, "John says the winter in Paris this season is horrible... constant rain & fog; but one pleasant day in a week." He was probably discouraged as well by his failure to gain any marked improvement in the tuberculosis that within five years would cause his death (JO to Sophia Stevens Hitchcock, Feb. 11, 1853, Page Papers, Detroit Institute of Art, Detroit, Mich.).
18. Brace's future sister-in-law Eliza Neill and his Yale classmate Albert Henry Barnes, Jr. (1826–1878), a Presbyterian minister and teacher (*Yale Obit. Rec.*, 2d ser. 8 [June 1878]: 302).

To Frederick Kingsbury

Address: F. J. Kingsbury Esq./Waterbury/Connecticut
Postmark: New Orleans/February 27

New Orleans, February 26th, 1853

Dear Fred,

I saw a good deal of your uncle[1] and his family when at Petersburg and was very pleasantly entertained by them. It was Christmas holidays and the girls were enjoying themselves, and I did some of the same.

JOURNEY THROUGH THE LOWER SOUTH: 1853

I have seen but little of Southern Society or domestic life. I go over too much ground and too hastily for that. I spend but a week at a town: it takes half that to find any body at home and the rest to begin an acquaintance. I have been unfortunate, too, in rarely finding any body to whom I had letters and have been able no more than to glance at the outside of things—occasionally getting peeps in through accidental openings. For 4 days after I reached here I didn't find a soul at home & nobody called or if they did their cards missed coming to me.

However, since then—I've been up to Dick Taylor's.[2] He has been lately taken all aback by a paralysis of right side—all his limbs powerless. He has a capital plantation and a devil of a Creole wife—young, childish, whimsical, comical;[3] with a baby of her own. A capital manager he is and is making money—nearly paid off a debt of $100,000 contracted in purchase of plantation—3 good years. It is the most complete gambling—cotton & sugar planting. Negroes well taken care of and comfortable as possible.

Bayne was immensely busy at law and I couldn't get near him till yesterday when he dined with me at St. Charles. Today he is going to take me out to a plantation & in the evening to a Quadroon circle of friends.[4]

To-morrow I go up Red River on the "*St. Charles*," how high I don't know. It depends on the water & the boiler, which my berth is directly over. I hope it will be to Texas and not to Heaven.[5]

Lost all my baggage—taken by mistake while I was dining out and sent up the river. Can't get it back till I am gone—have to get a new outfit. All my papers, books, &c., in it.

It's jolly hot.

I haven't experienced any remarkable amount of Southern hospitality. What I have met with has been mainly from Northern people & English.

Jackson[6] has been and is making a fortune. Built a fine house, fine as yours (in Southern style), and was too busy to let me see much of him or be of any service to me. I wasted a week waiting for him to get me onto an Alabama cotton plantation; which he didn't after all. Nice woman, his wife, & they were kind to me at home. I had the run of the house, dined & tea'd twice or thrice. He said he would write to you & if you were within reach would strike you for writing him such a letter, you aggravatin' wretch. He hadn't thought much about Slavery—if he had he didn't like to say what he thought, beyond the simple material view. Owns some capital niggers.[7]

Bayne has come in to take me away, so goodbye.
Yours Truly

                  Fred. Law Olmsted

Olmsted must have written this letter on Sunday, February 27, 1853, rather than on the 26th. In *Seaboard Slave States* he stated that he secured his berth on the steamboat *St. Charles* on Saturday, and was assured that the boat would not leave for its trip up the Red River until Monday (*SSS*, pp. 603-4).

1. Abner Leavenworth of Petersburg, Virginia.
2. Richard Taylor (1826-1879), only son of President Zachary Taylor and a student at Yale from 1843 until his graduation in 1845. After graduating from Yale, Richard managed his father's Mississippi cotton plantation and spent considerable time seeking a cure for his chronic rheumatism. In May 1850 Zachary authorized him to purchase and manage a sugar plantation in Louisiana. Richard then purchased the plantation where Olmsted visited him—the 1,200-acre Fashion Plantation in St. Charles Parish on the Mississippi River twenty miles north of New Orleans. For the plantation and the sixty-four slaves on it he paid $115,000 in the form of a cash payment of $19,500 and notes for the remainder payable over the next three years. He also bought eleven more adult slaves for $16,200, paying one third of the amount in cash and receiving credit for the remainder.

    Richard Taylor soon became active in politics, serving in the state senate from 1855 to 1861, and as delegate to the Southern commercial convention of 1858-59. He was a delegate to the Democratic national convention at both Charleston and Baltimore in 1860, and was a disunionist member of the Louisiana secession convention of 1861. With the outbreak of the Civil War he was elected colonel of a Louisiana regiment and soon after was made brigadier general by Jefferson Davis, his ex-brother-in-law. In 1862 he was given command of the District of West Louisiana, where he fought effectively against heavy odds and in 1864 frustrated Nathaniel Banks's Red River campaign. In January 1865 he took command of the demoralized Army of the Tennessee and in May surrendered it, the last Confederate army east of the Mississippi. During the war, Fashion Plantation was confiscated and looted by Union troops.

    In the Reconstruction period, Taylor several times used his national political connections to promote the interests of conservative ex-Confederates: immediately after the war he worked to free Jefferson Davis and the war governors of Mississippi and Alabama, and in 1872 he briefly convinced President Grant to recognize the conservative McEnery faction in Louisiana. In the meantime, his local connections gave him access to economic opportunities: in 1866 he secured a fifteen-year lease of the New Basin Canal in New Orleans. In 1873, after the triumph of the radical Kellogg faction, the state annulled his lease and attempted to recover more than $300,000 in unpaid rent. At that point Taylor traveled to Europe, where he was lionized by powerful members of the ruling class in England, France and Germany, most notably by the Prince of Wales. After returning to the United States he lived in Virginia and followed literary pursuits, including the writing of his memoirs, *Destruction and Reconstruction* (*DAB*; *Yale Obit. Rec.*, 2d ser. 9 [June 1879]: 357-58; Jackson Beauregard Davis, "The Life of Richard Taylor," *Louisiana Historical Quarterly* 24, no. 1 [Jan. 1941]: 50-60, 112-19; Brainerd Dyer, *Zachary Taylor* [Baton Rouge, La., 1946], pp. 262-63).
3. In February 1851, Taylor married Louise Marie Myrthe Bringier (1834-1875), daughter of a Creole planter of Ascension Parish (Stanley C. Arthur and George C. H. deKernion, *Old Families of Louisiana* [New Orleans, La., 1931], p. 430).
4. Bayne was presumably the "gentleman, of New England education," who gave Olmsted the account of his experience with quadroon women that appears in *Seaboard Slave States*. After moving to New Orleans, that gentleman was introduced to a quadroon family in which there were three pretty young women, cultivated and intelligent. He was strongly attracted to them and for a time visited them frequently, but his future plans prevented him from taking one of them to live (or "placer") with, as was a common practice in New Orleans (*SSS*, p. 597).
5. Olmsted expected to leave New Orleans on the steamboat *St. Charles* on Saturday, February 26, 1853, but he was informed that its departure had been postponed until Monday, the 28th. It was not until Wednesday, March 2, however, that the steamboat finally left, and by that time Olmsted's berth had been occupied in his absence by "a very strong man, who was not very polite, when I informed him that I believed there was some mistake—that the berth he was using had been engaged to me." The late start and slow progress of the *St. Charles* up the Red River forced Olmsted to abandon his plan to follow the river far into Texas, and he went only as far as Grand Ecore, Louisiana (ibid., pp. 603-20).
6. Jefferson Franklin Jackson (1821-1862), a lawyer in Montgomery, Alabama, and graduate of Yale in 1846. Jackson was a good friend of Frederick Kingsbury, and Olmsted came to know him while he was at Yale. After graduating from Yale, Jackson studied law in Cambridge, Massachusetts, and in February 1848 married Ellenor Noyes (1823-1887) of Boston. Returning to his native Alabama, he served as U.S. district attorney. He also gained recognition for representing Alabama in negotiations that led to the payment of over ten million dollars to the state by the federal government.

JOURNEY THROUGH THE LOWER SOUTH: 1853

By the time of Olmsted's visit in February 1853, Jackson was well on the way to making his fortune. As Olmsted notes in this letter, he had just built an impressive fourteen-room house in Montgomery. He was also a law partner with two rapidly rising young men, T. J. Judge and Thomas H. Watts. The latter accumulated a fortune of over half a million dollars by 1860 and during the Civil War served as attorney general of the Confederacy and war governor of Alabama. In 1875 he married Jackson's widow, Ellenor (*Yale Obit. Rec.,* 1st ser. 3 [July 1862]: 73; Thomas M. Owen, *History of Alabama and Dictionary of Alabama Biography,* 4 vols. [Chicago, 1921], 3: 893; Henry E. Noyes and Harriette E. Noyes, *Genealogical Record of Some of the Noyes Descendants of James, Nicholas and Peter Noyes...,* 2 vols. [Boston, 1904], 1: 103; *Papers of FLO,* 1: 207, 302; NCAB, 10: 432–33; *Montgomery Advertiser,* May 18, 1941, p. 2-A; J. K. Menn, "Large Slaveholders of the Deep South," p. 452).

7. At this time Jackson owned at least five slaves, whom he had bought during the previous fourteen months. They were valuable: he paid $1,500 for Henry, aged twenty-eight, and $1,200 for Charles, a carpenter, aged twenty-three. He also paid $800 and $850 for two women, aged thirty-seven and thirty-five. By 1860 he had bought a total of at least fifty-four slaves, most of whom he still owned at that time.

The slave Charles was probably the man whose mathematical and muscial abilities Olmsted described in *Seaboard Slave States,* pages 553–54 (bills of sale and list of slaves owned by Jackson c. 1860, Jefferson Franklin Jackson Papers, State of Alabama Department of Archives and History, Montgomery, Ala.).

New-York Daily Times, November 21, 1853[1]

THE SOUTH.

LETTERS ON THE PRODUCTIONS, INDUSTRY AND RESOURCES OF THE SLAVE STATES.

NUMBER FORTY-FOUR.

Special Correspondence of the New-York Daily Times

Return towards the North—Life on a Large Plantation—Treatment of Negroes—Shooting Slaves—Conversation with an Overseer—Flogging a Slave for Shirking Work.

After a voyage up Red River, and a week spent in some of the cotton plantations of that district, I proceeded to Vicksburg, with the intention of visiting Central Mississippi and the Yazoo cotton region. Owing to long continued rains, however, and the consequent floods which had covered and frequently torn up and removed the bridges and log causeways, I found traveling entirely interrupted on the route I had intended to pursue, and was obliged to change my purpose and go up the river to Memphis. Thence I returned to the North, along the eastern base of the Appalachian Chain in the upper parts of the States of Mississippi, Alabama, Georgia, the Carolinas and Virginia, having the intention to make another visit to the South, in which I might examine more thoroughly than I had then been able to, the most important cotton districts and those prospectively the most important.

I shall therefore defer for the present a particular account of the culture and commerce of cotton, as it is that which has come within my personal observation, with regard to the industry of the South which is received with the greatest interest by your readers. I shall occupy my next two or three letters with notes having reference to the condition of the slaves belonging to the proprietors living in circumstances widely different, which will represent the extremes, most favorable and least so, to the well-being and improvement of the laboring class of the South that I encountered.

Other things being equal, the condition of the laborer at the South is least happy, as is that of the free agricultural laborer everywhere, when he is connected with large estates. The evil results from the monopoly of land possession, to the laborer, may be more palpable in a free community, because of the greater mercenary interest of the slave proprietor in the health and adequate physical sustenance of his laborers. The discipline and constant incitement to improvement, however, arising from self-dependence and personal responsibility—constantly calling into action, as it does, industry, patience, and economy—remain much stronger with the free dependent of the large proprietor than with the slave, and greater with the slave of the small proprietor than the large.

At the same time, the benefit arising to the inferior race, from its forced relation to and intercourse with the superior, which is the main advantage claimed for slavery, amounts to nothing on the larger plantations. Each laborer is such an inconsiderable unit in the mass of laborers, that he may even not be known by name, or personally recognizable by his master. At the same time, for the white persons to retain adequate control, and keep the order in so large a body of negroes, necessary to their own personal safety, and the profitable employment of their labor, a *discipline* which, if applied to the free laborer, would be resisted as barbarously cruel, is necessary, and (the righteousness of slavery as a system being granted) is justifiable. The condition of the slaves under such circumstances will be more apparent from what I shall now relate of my observations upon a very large estate on which I spent several days.[2]

There were on this estate nearly one thousand negroes, living in four settlements, some miles apart. It was divided into four plantations, with an overseer to each, and the whole was directed by a manager. The owner had another, smaller, and more healthful estate, and seldom resided on this. The manager was a gentleman of university education, energetic and thorough in his business, but of generous and poetic temperament, and with an enjoyment of nature and the *bucolic* life rarely found in an American. The gang of busy negroes were, to him, as natural and requisite an element of the poetry of nature as flocks of peaceful sheep and herds of lowing kine, and he would no more appreciate the aspect in which an Abolitionist would see them than would

Virgil have honored the feelings of a vegetarian, who would only sigh at the sight of flocks and herds destined to feed the depraved appetite of the carnivorous savage of modern civilization.

The overseers were superior to most of their class, that I have seen; frank, honest, temperate and industrious, but their feelings towards negroes were such as would naturally result from their employment. They were all married, and lived with their families, each in a cabin or cottage, in the settlement of the negroes of which they had especial charge. Their wages were from $500 to $1,000 each. These five men, each living more than a mile distant from either of the others, were the only white men on the estate, and the only others within ten miles were a few vagabonds, who were looked upon with suspicion as likely to corrupt and demoralize the negroes.

Of course, to secure personal safety and the efficient use of the labor of such a large number of ignorant and indolent vicious negroes, rules, or rather habits and customs of discipline were necessary, that would in particular cases be liable to operate unjustly and cruelly. It will be seen, also, as the testimony of negroes is not received as evidence in courts, that there was very little probability that any amount of even illegal cruelty would be restrained by regard to the law. A provision of the law intended to secure a certain privilege to slaves was indeed disregarded under my own observation, and such infraction of the law was confessedly customary with one of the overseers, and not interfered with by the manager, because it seemed to him to be, in a certain degree, justifiable and expedient under the circumstances.

In the main, the negroes were well taken care of and abundantly supplied with the necessaries of vigorous physical existence. A large part of them lived in commodious and well built cottages, with broad piazzas in front, so that each family of five had two rooms on the lower floor and a loft. The remainder lived in log cabins, contracted and mean in appearance, but their overseers lived in very similar cabins, and preparations were being made to replace all of these by handsome boarded cottages. Each family had a fowl-house and hog-sty (constructed by the negroes themselves) and kept an unlimited number of fowls and swine, feeding the latter during the Summer on weeds and fattening them in the Autumn on corn *stolen* (this was mentioned by all the overseers as a matter of course) from their master's corn fields. I saw gangs of them eating their dinner in the field several times, and observed that they generally had plenty, and often some left, of bacon, eggs, corn-bread, and molasses. The following rations were weighed and measured under the eye of the manager by the drivers, and distributed to the head of each family, for each person weekly: 3 lbs. pork, 1 peck meal, and from January to July, 1 quart molasses; monthly, in addition, 1 lb. tobacco, and 4 pints salt. No drink is ever served but water, except after unusual exposure or to ditchers when working in water, who get a glass of whisky at night. All hands cook for themselves after work, at night, each family in its own cabin.

Each family had a garden, the vegetables in which, together with eggs, fowls and bacon, they frequently sold. Most of the families bought a barrel of flour every year. The manager endeavored to encourage this practice, and that they might rather spend their money for flour than for liquor, he furnished it to them at rather less than what it cost him at wholesale, namely, at $4 a barrel. Many poor whites within a few miles would always sell liquor to the negroes and encourage them to steal to obtain the means to buy it of them. These vagabond whites were always spoken of with anger by the overseers, and they had a constant offer of much more than the intrinsic value of their land from the managers to induce them to move away. The negroes also obtain a good deal of game. They set traps for coons, rabbits and turkeys, and I once heard a negro complaining to his overseer, that he had detected one of the vagabond whites in stealing a turkey which had been caught in his pen. I several times partook of excellent game while on the plantation, that had been purchased of the negroes.

The "stock-tender," an old negro, whose business it was to ride about in the woods to keep an eye on the stock cattle that were pastured in them, and who thus was likely to know where the deer ran, had an ingenious way of supplying himself with venison. He lashed a scythe blade or butchers' knife to the end of a pole so that it formed a lance: this he set near a fence or fallen tree which obstructed a path in which the deer habitually ran, and the deer in leaping over the obstacle would leap directly on the knife. In this manner he had killed two deer the week before my visit.

The overseers regulated the hours of work, each for his own gang. I saw the negroes at work before sunrise and after sunset; at about 8 o'clock, they were allowed to stop to breakfast, and again about noon to dine. The lengths of these rests were at the discretion of the overseer or drivers, and I should think, were from half an hour to an hour. There was no rule. The number of hands directed by each overseer was from 150 to 250. The manager told me that he thought it would be better economy to have a white man over every fifty hands, but for the difficulty of obtaining trustworthy overseers. Three of those he had, were the best he had ever known. The majority of overseers he described, as they have always been represented to me, to be drunkards, or passionate, careless, inefficient men, totally unfitted for their duties. The best overseers ordinarily are young men, the sons of planters of moderate means—who take up the business with no intention of following it permanently.

During my visit, the hands were employed in plowing for corn and cotton, in planting corn, in grubbing newly cleared land, and in ditching. The driver of the ditching gang was an Irishman, who was furnished with a cabin, a cow and pasturage, some vegetables and $10 a month wages. The task of the ditchers was to dig thirty feet a day per man of a drain 5 feet wide at top, 4 feet at bottom, and 4 feet deep, clayey soil, with a few roots, but no picking. Coming to somewhat lighter land, the manager one day directed the task to be increased to 40 feet. The plowing, both with single and double mule team, was generally performed by women, and very well performed. I watched them with some interest to see if there was any indication that their sex unfitted them for the occupation. Twenty of them were plowing together with double teams and heavy plows. They were superintended by a male negro driver, who carried a whip, and allowed no delay or hesitation at the turning, and they twitched their plows around on the head land, jerking the rein and yelling to their mules with surprising ease, energy and rapidity. No man could have excelled them with less apparent exertion.

Generally in the Southwest the negroes appeared to be worked much harder than in the eastern and northern Slave States. I do not think they accomplish so much, but they certainly labored much harder than agricultural laborers at the North usually do. They are obliged to keep constantly and steadily moving, and the stupid, plodding, machine-like manner in which they move is painful to witness. This was most the case in the corn-planting. A gang of children dropped the corn at suitable distances, and another gang followed covering it with hoes; there would thus be a hundred or two engaged together, moving across the field in two parallel lines with a considerable degree of precision.

I frequently rode at a canter, with several other horsemen, across and between these lines, often coming suddenly upon them without in the slightest degree interrupting or changing the dogged action of the laborers, or causing one of them to lift an eye from the ground. A strong driver walked to and fro in the rear of the line, frequently cracking his whip and calling out in the surliest manner, to one and another, "Shove your hoe there!" But I never saw him strike any one with the whip except very lightly, and as a caution to smaller children when they did not move fast enough.

Corporeal punishment was evidently frequent, however, on the estate, and often, I have no doubt, severe. There were no rules about it that I learned; the overseers and the drivers used the whip whenever they deemed there was occasion, and in such manner and in such degree as they thought fit. The discipline of the plantation is precisely the same as that of the army and navy; the negroes are privates, enlisted for their lives in the service of their masters; the lash is constantly held over them as the remedy for all wrong-doing, whether of indolence or indiscretion, while they are subject to be shot for insubordination. "If you don't work faster," or "If you don't work better," or "If you don't mind me better—I will have you flogged," I have heard frequently. I have heard a girl not more than seven years old say to an old negro, "If you don't do as I bid you, quick, I will tell the overseer to have you flogged," and the negro then, sullenly and without an answer, obeyed her.

I said to one of the overseers—"It must be very disagreeable to have to punish them so much as you do?" "Yes, it would be to those who were not used to it—but it's my business, and I think nothing of it. Why, Sir, I wouldn't mind killing a negro more than I would a dog." I asked if he had ever killed a negro? He never had quite killed one, but overseers were often obliged to; he had known of several shot. There are some negroes that are determined never to let a white man whip them, and who will fight when you attempt to whip them; of course, you must kill them in that case. He, himself, was once going to whip a negro in the field, when he struck at his head with his hoe; he guarded off the blow with his whip, and drew a pistol and tried to shoot him, but the pistol missed fire, and he rushed in and knocked him down with it. At another time, a negro that he was punishing, grossly insulted and threatened him; he went to his house to get his gun; when he was coming back, the negro thought he would not fire at him and when he got within a few rods, *broke* for the woods. He fired at once, and put six buck shot into his hips. He always carried a bowie knife with him, but did not carry a pistol, unless he anticipated unusual insubordination. He always kept a pair of pistols loaded, however, on his mantel piece.

It was only when he first came into a place that he ever had much trouble. There were a great many overseers that were unfit for their business, and who were too easy and slack with the negroes. When he first came into a place after such a man, he had hard work for a time to break the negroes in, but it did not take long to learn them their place.

His conversation on this subject was exactly like what I have heard again and again, *ad nauseam,* from Northern ship-masters and officers, only he had a less brutal disposition, and more respect for the negroes than those fellows have for the seamen that temporarily subject themselves to the atrocious tyranny and insolence they boast of exercising.

The only instance of very severe corporeal punishment of a negro that I witnessed at the South occurred on this estate.[3] I suppose, however, that equally severe punishment is common—in fact, it must be necessary, to sustain adequate discipline, on every large plantation. The manner of the overseer who inflicted the punishment, and his subsequent conversation with me about it, indicated that it was a common-place occurrence to him.

This overseer was showing me his plantation. In going from one part to the other we had twice crossed a deep gully, in the bottom of which was a thick covert of brush-wood. We were crossing it a third time, and had nearly passed through the brush, when the overseer suddenly stopped his horse, exclaiming, "What's that? Hallo!—who are you there?" A negro girl was lying at full length on the ground at the bottom of the gully, evidently intending to hide herself from us in the bushes. "Who are you there?" "Sam's Sall, Sir." "What are you skulking here for?" The girl half rose, but gave no answer. "Where have you been all day?" Answer unintelligible. After a few more questions, she said her father locked her into the room she slept in, when he went out in the morning, she not having woke up. "How did it happen that he locked you in alone?" "Nobody sleep wid me, Sir, in de room." "How did you manage to get out?" "Pushed a plank off, Sir, and crawl out."

The overseer was now silent for a minute, looking at the girl, and then said, "That won't do—come out here." The girl rose at once and walked up to him. She was a perfectly black girl, about 18 years old. A bunch of keys hung at her waist. These caught the overseer's eye, and he said, "Ah! your father locked you in; but you have got the keys." After a little hesitation the girl replied that those were the keys of some other locks, not of her own room. "That won't do," said the overseer: "you must take some—kneel down." The girl knelt on the ground, he got off his horse, and holding him with his left hand, struck her thirty or forty blows across the shoulders with his *rawhide* riding whip. They were well laid on, as a man would flog a vicious horse or a thievish dog, or a boatswain would lay it on to a skulking sailor. There was not, however, any appearance of angry excitement in the overseer. At every stroke the girl winced and exclaimed, "Yes, Sir!" or "Ah, Sir!" or "Please, Sir!"—not groaning or screaming.

At length he stopped and said, "Now tell me the truth." The girl repeated the same story. "You have not got enough yet," he said; "pull up your clothes—lie down." The girl, without any hesitation or delay, drew all her garments up to her waist and laid down on the ground upon her side, with her face towards the overseer, and he continued to whip her with the rawhide across her naked back and thigh, with as much strength as before. The girl cried out, "Oh, don't; Sir, oh, please stop, master; please, Sir, please, Sir! oh, that's enough, master; oh, Lord! oh, master! master!"[4]

I could not wait to see the end, and after a dozen or twenty blows, I turned my horse's head, and he burst through the bushes, bounding straight up the steep bank, seemingly as excited and impatient to be doing something as I was. I must say, however, the girl did not seem to suffer the intense pain that I should have supposed she would.[5]

I rode on along the top of the bank until I reached the place where the road came out of the gully, and waited until the overseer joined me. He laughed, and said, "She meant to cheat me out of a day's work—and she has done it, too." "Did you succeed in getting another story from her?" "No; she stuck to it." "It wasn't true?" "No; she slipped out of the gang when they were going to work, and she's been dodging about all day, going from one place to another as she saw me coming. She saw us crossing there a little while ago, and thought we had gone to the quarters, but we turned back so quick, we came into the gully before she knew it, and she could do nothing but lay down in the bush." "I suppose they often slip off so." "No, Sir; I never had one do so before—not like this; they often run away to the woods and are gone some time, but I never had a dodge-off like this before." "Was it necessary to punish her so hard?" "If I had not, she would have done the same thing to-morrow, and half the negroes on the plantation would have followed her example, Sir. Oh, you've no idea how lazy these negroes are; you Northern people don't know anything about it. They'd never do any work at all if they were not afraid of being whipped."

We soon after met an old man, who, after being questioned, said that he had seen the girl slip out of the gang as they went to work after dinner. It appeared that she had been at work during the forenoon, but at dinner time the gang moved across the gully, and she slipped out. The driver had not missed her.

The overseer said that when he first took charge of the plantation, the negroes ran away a great deal—they disliked him so much. They used to say 'twas hell to be on his place; but after a few months they got used to his ways, and liked him as well as any of the rest. He had not had any run away now in some time. When they ran away they would generally come in in course of a fortnight. When some of them had been off for some-time, he would make the rest of the force work Sundays, or restrict them in some of their privileges until they returned. The negroes on the plantation could always bring them in if they chose to. They depended on them for their food, and they had only to refuse to supply them, and they would come in.

YEOMAN.

1. Olmsted probably wrote this letter between November 9 and 20, 1853; much of the letter appears in *Back Country,* pages 72–76, 80–88.
2. In *Back Country,* Olmsted added this introductory description of the plantation:

> The estate I am now about to describe, was situated upon a tributary of the Mississippi, and accessible only by occasional steamboats; even this mode of communication being frequently interrupted at low stages of the rivers. The slaves upon it formed about one twentieth of the whole population of the county, in which the blacks considerably outnumber the whites. At the time of my visit, the owner was sojourning upon it, with his family and several invited guests, but his usual residence was upon a small plantation, of little productive value, situated in a neighborhood somewhat noted for the luxury and hospitality of its citizens, and having a daily mail, and direct railroad and telegraphic communication with New York. This was, if I am not mistaken, his second visit in five years. (*BC,* p. 72.)

> The only possible time for Olmsted to have made the visit he describes here was during the week in early March 1853 that he said he spent on some of the cotton plantations of the Red River district in Louisiana. His itinerary indicates that the plantations he visited were in the vicinity of Natchitoches. The only proprietor in that region who fits his description was Meredith Calhoun, born in South Carolina, c. 1805, and one of the largest slaveholders and cotton-growers in the South. Calhoun's plantation was at the present site of Colfax, Louisiana, thirty miles southeast of Natchitoches on the left bank of the Red River near the mouth of the Cane River.

> In a number of ways, Calhoun's plantation corresponds to the one described by Olmsted. First, it was on a tributary of the Mississippi River, accessible only by steamboat and subject to the interruption of communication with other places when the river was low. The 719 slaves on Calhoun's plantation made up approximately one-twentieth of the population of 16,561 in Rapides Parish. In 1850 the blacks in the parish outnumbered the whites by 11,000 to 5,000, and a large number of the whites were day-laborers. Calhoun's plantation was divided into four separate farms—the Smithfield, Farenzi, Mirabeau and Meredith places—each of which had its own slave quarters. These settlements could easily have been over a mile distant from each other, since Calhoun's property of 15,000 acres (over twenty-three square miles) had seven miles of frontage on the Red River, and so must have averaged over three miles in depth back from the river. Both corn and cotton were grown on the plantation: the crop in 1860 was 30,000 bushels of corn and 3,800 four-hundred-pound bales of cotton. The value of the cotton crop in 1860 was $167,000, which suggests that Calhoun's profits in 1852 could well have been as high as the $100,000 Olmsted mentions. The total value of the real and personal property on the plantation by 1860 was over $1,100,000.

Calhoun's plantation had "huge barns, mills, gins, stables," and "countless farming implements, including plows for the use of his 50 horses, 140 mules and 64 working oxen. The large blacksmithing and wheelwright shop that Olmsted visited, where mechanics were putting 50 plows in order for cotton-planting, could well have been the large "ante bellum equipment shed" on Mirabeau plantation that is pictured on page 104 of *Grant Parish, Louisiana,* by Mabel F. Harrison and Lavinia M. McNeely.

The U.S. census of 1850 suggests that Calhoun was an absentee owner, since he, but none of his family, is listed as residing on his plantation in Rapides Parish. Like the proprietor of the plantation Olmsted describes, Calhoun had spent some time in Europe: his son, William, was born in France c. 1834. Calhoun's usual residence was probably in Huntsville, Alabama, where his wife, Mary Smith Calhoun, owned an estate inherited from her grandfather, William Smith, U.S. senator from South Carolina (Joseph K. Menn, *The Large Slaveholders of Louisiana, 1860* [New Orleans, La., 1964], pp. 104, 105, 108, 233, 243–44, 327–28; U.S., Census Office, 7th Census, *7th Census 1850. Louisiana* [Washington, D.C., 1850], schedule 1, Natchitoches Parish, p. 59; schedule 2, Natchitoches Parish, pp. 949–51, and Rapides Parish, pp. 843, 939–51; U.S., Census Office, 8th Census, *8th Census 1860. Louisiana* [Washington, D.C., 1860], schedule 1, Rapides Parish, p. 251; idem, 7th Census, *The Seventh Census of the United States: 1850. Embracing a Statistical View of Each of the States and Territories... J. D. B. DeBow, Superintendent of the United States Census* [Washington, D.C., 1853], p. 473; Mabel Fletcher Harrison and Lavinia McGuire McNeely, *Grant Parish, Louisiana; A History Published to Celebrate Grant Parish Centennial and Louisiana Pecan Festival, 1969* [Baton Rouge, La., 1969], pp. 30–34, 102–9; American Association of University Women, Huntsville Branch, *Huntsville Branch, American Association of University Women Presents Glimpses into Ante-Bellum Homes of Historic Huntsville, Alabama—Bicentennial Ed.* [Huntsville, Ala., c. 1976], p. 34; William Garrett, *Reminiscences of Public Men in Alabama, for Thirty Years* [Atlanta, Ga., 1872], p. 114; *DAB,* s.v. "Smith, William [c. 1762–June 1840]").

3. In *Back Country,* Olmsted changed this sentence to read: "The severest corporeal punishment of a negro that I witnessed at the South, occurred while I was visiting this estate" (*BC,* p. 83).
4. In *Back Country,* Olmsted altered his description of the second stage of the whipping of the girl to read as follows:

> The girl without any hesitation, without a word or look of remonstrance or entreaty, drew closely all her garments under her shoulders, and lay down upon the ground with her face toward the overseer, who continued to flog her with the rawhide, across her naked loins and thigh, with as much strength as before. She now shrunk away from him, not rising, but writhing, groveling, and screaming, "Oh, don't, Sir! oh, please stop, master! please, sir! oh, that's enough, master! oh, Lord! oh, master, master! oh, God, master, do stop! oh, God, master! oh, God, master!" (Ibid., pp. 85–86.)

5. In *Back Country,* Olmsted deleted this sentence and replaced it with the following: "The screaming yells and the whip strokes had ceased when I reached the top of the bank. Choking, sobbing, spasmodic groans only were heard" (ibid, p. 86).

New-York Daily Times, November 26, 1853[1]

THE SOUTH.

LETTERS ON THE PRODUCTIONS, INDUSTRY AND RESOURCES OF THE SOUTHERN STATES.

NUMBER FORTY-FIVE.

Special Correspondence of the New-York Daily Times

Description of a Large Estate continued—Manufactures—The Sick List—No Physician—Child Birth—The Mechanics—Runaways—Field-hands—Cleanliness—Clothing—Adultery—Licentiousness—Mulattoes and Mixed Blood; Are They Mules, as held by the Calhoun School?—Religion on the Estate—The Proprietor's Views of Slavery, and of a Free Laboring Class.

The first morning I was on the estate, while at breakfast with the manager, an old negro woman came into the room and said to him, "Dat gal's bin bleedin' agin dis mornin'."

"Ah, has she? How much did she bleed?"

"About a pint, Sir."

"Very well; I'll call and see her after breakfast."

"I come up for some sugar of lead, master; I gin her some powdered alum 'fore I come away."

"Very well; you can have some."

After breakfast the manager invited me to ride with him on his usual round through the plantations. On reaching the nearest "quarters," we stopped at a house, a little larger than the ordinary cabins, which was called the loom-house, in which a dozen negroes were at work making shoes, and manufacturing coarse cotton stuff for negro clothing. One of the hands so employed was insane, and most of the others were cripples, or invalids with chronic complaints, unfitting them for field-work. From this we went to one of the cabins—where we found the sick woman that had been bleeding at the lungs, with the old nurse in attendance upon her. The manager examined and prescribed for her in a kind manner. When we came out he asked the nurse if there was any one else sick.

"Dere's oney dat woman Caroline."

"What do you think is the matter with her?"

"Well, I don't tink dere's anyting de matter wid her, masser; I mus answer you for true, I don't tink anyting de matter wid her, oney she's a little sore from dat wippin' she had."

We went to another cabin and entered a room where a woman lay on a bed, groaning. It was a very dirty, comfortless room, but there was a mosquito bar, much-patched and very dirty, covering the bed. The manager asked several times what was the matter, but could get no distinct reply. The woman appeared to be suffering very great pain. The manager felt of her pulse and looked at her tongue, and after making a few more inquiries, to which no intelligible reply was given, told her he did not believe she was ill at all; at this the woman's groans redoubled. "I have heard of your tricks," continued the manager, "you had a chill when I came to see you yesterday morning; you had a chill when the mistress came here, and you had a chill when the master came. I never heard of

JOURNEY THROUGH THE LOWER SOUTH: 1853

a chill that lasted a whole day. So you'll just get up now and go to the field, and if you don't work smart, you'll get a dressing; do you hear?"

The manager said they rarely—almost never—had occasion to employ a physician for the people. Never for accouchements; the women, from their labor in the field, became strong and roomy, and were not subject to the difficulty, danger and pain which attended women of the better classes in child-birth.

Near the first quarters we visited was a large blacksmithing and wheelwright shop, and a number of mechanics at work. Most of them were eating their breakfast, which they warmed at their fires, as we rode up. They had about fifty plows which they were putting in order for cotton-planting. The manager inspected the work, found some of it faulty, reprimanded the workmen for not getting on faster, and threatened one of them with a whipping for not paying closer attention to the directions which had been given him. He told me that he had employed a white man from the North who professed to be a first-class workman, but he soon found he could not do nearly as good work as the negro mechanics on the estate, and the latter despised him so much that he had been obliged to discharge him in the midst of his engagement.

One of the overseers rode up while we were at the shop, and reported to the manager how all his hands were employed. There were so many at this and so many at that, and they had done so much since yesterday. "There's Caroline," said the manager; "she's not sick, and I told her she must go to work; put her to the hoeing; there's nothing the matter with her, except she's sore from the whipping she got;—you must go and get her out." The overseer did not seem to like the job. A woman was passing at the time, and the manager told her to go and tell Caroline she must get up and go to work, or the overseer should come and start her. She returned in a few minutes, and reported that Caroline said she could not get up. The overseer and manager rode towards the cabin, but before they reached it the girl came out and went to the field with her hoe. They then returned to me and continued their conversation. Just before we left the overseer, he said, "That girl that ran away last week was in her cabin last night."

The manager told me as we rode on that their people often ran away after they have been whipped, or something else has happened to make them angry. They hide in the swamp and come into the cabins at night to get food. They seldom staid off longer than a fortnight. When they returned they were punished. The woman, Caroline, he said, had been delivered of a dead child about six weeks before, and had been complaining and getting rid of work ever since. She was the laziest woman on the estate. This shamming illness occasioned him the most disagreeable duty he had to perform. Negroes were famous for it. "If it was not for her bad character," he continued, "I should not make her go to work to-day; but her pulse is steady and her tongue perfectly smooth. We have to be sharp with them; if we were not, every negro in the estate would be abed."

I was afterwards told that there had been a girl on one of the plantations that cheated her owner out of nearly two years' work as she was supposed all the time to by dying of consumption. At length, there being some reason to suspect her, she was watched in her cabin, and it was ascertained that she was constantly employed as a milliner and dress-maker, working for pay for the other negroes. She had always previously to her supposed illness, been employed as a field hand, but she was now taken to the house and employed as a seamstress, and it was found that she had acquired a very wonderful degree of skill; so that without further instruction she was able to cut dresses for her mistress with nicety and taste. She was soon after hired out to a fashionable dress-maker in the city at high wages (to be paid, of course, to her owner).

We rode on to where the different gangs of laborers were at work, and inspected them one after another. The manner in which they worked and the way they were driven I have previously described. I observed, as we were looking at one of the gangs, that they were very dirty. "The negroes are the filthiest people in the world," said the manager; "there are some of them that would never look clean twenty-four hours at a time if you gave them thirty suits a year."

I ascertained that they were furnished with two suits of Summer clothing, and one of Winter each year. Besides which most of them get presents of some fine clothing, and purchase more for themselves, at Christmas. It is not unfrequent to see negroes dressed in military clothing. One of the drivers had on a splendid coat of an officer of the flying artillery. I was told that after the Mexican war, a great deal of military clothing was sold at auction in New-Orleans, and much of it was bought by planters at a low price, and given to their negroes, who were greatly pleased with it.

I asked if there were any plantation rules to maintain cleanliness. There were not, but sometimes the negroes were told at night that any one who came into the field the next morning without being clean would be whipped. This gave no trouble to those who were habitually clean, while it was in itself a punishment to those who were not, as they were obliged to spend the night in washing.

Afterwards, as we were sitting near a gang with an overseer, he would occasionally call out to one and another by name. I asked if he knew them all by name. He did, but the manager did not know one-fifth of them. The overseer said he generally could call most of the negroes by their names in two weeks after he came on to a plantation, but it was difficult to learn them on account of their being so many of the same name, distinguished from each other by a prefix. "There's a big Jim here, and a little Jim, and Eliza's Jim, and Jim Bob, and Jim Clarisy."

"What's Jim Clarisy!—how does he get that name?"

"He's Clarisy's child, and Bob is Jim Bob's father. That fellow's name is Swamp; he always goes by that name, but his real name is Abraham, I believe, is it not, Mr. (Manager)?"

"His name is Swamp on the plantation register—that's all I know of him."

"I believe his name is Abraham," said the overseer; "he told me so. He was bought of Judge ____, and he told me his master called him Swamp because he ran away so much. He is the worst run-away on the place."

I inquired about the increase of the negroes on the estate, and the manager having told me the number of deaths and births the previous year, I asked if the negroes began to have children at a very early age. "Sometimes at sixteen," said the manager. "Yes, and at fourteen," said the overseer; "that girl's had a child"—pointing to a girl that did not appear older than fourteen.

"Is she married?"

"No. You see," said the manager, "negro girls are not remarkable for chastity; and it rather hinders them from having children. They'd have them younger than they do, if they would marry and live with but one man sooner than they do. They often do not have children till they are 25 years old."

"Are these that are married true to each other?" I asked. The overseer laughed heartily at the idea, and described the state of things.

"Do you not try to discourage this?"

"No, not unless they quarrel. They get quarreling among themselves sometimes about it," the manager explained, "or come to the overseer and complain, and he has them punished.

"Give all hands a d____d good hiding," said the overseer.

"You punish for adultery, then, but not for fornication?"

"Yes," answered the manager.

"No," replied the overseer, "I punish them for quarreling; if they don't quarrel I don't mind anything about it. But if they make a muss about it, I give all four of 'em a warming."

Riding through a gang afterwards, with two of the overseers in company, I observed that a large proportion of those before us were thorough-bred Africans. Both of them thought that the proportion of pure-blooded negroes was about three to four of the whole number, and that this would hold as an average in Mississippi and Louisiana. One of them pointed out a girl—"That one is pure white; you see her hair?" (it was straight and sandy.) "She is the only one we have got."

It was not uncommon to see slaves as white as that; so white that they could not be distinguished from pure-blooded whites. He had never been on a plantation before, that had not more than one on it.

"Now," said I, "If that girl should dress herself well, and run away, would she be suspected of being a slave?"

"Oh, yes; you might not know her if she got to the North, but any of us would know her."

"How?"

"By her language and manners."

"But if she had been brought up as a house-servant?"

"Perhaps not in that case."

I asked if they thought the mulattoes or white slaves were weaker, or less valuable than the pure negroes.

"Oh, no; I'd rather have them a great deal," said one.

"Well, I had not," said the other; "the blacker the better for me."

"The white ones," added the first, "are more active, and know more, and I think do a good deal the most work."

"Are they more subject to illness, or do they appear to be of weaker constitution?"

One said they were not, the other that they did not seem to bear the heat so well.

The first thought that this might be so, but that, nevertheless, they would do more work. I asked the manager's opinion. He thought they did not stand excessive heat as well as the pure negroes, but that, from their greater activity and willingness, they would do more work. He was confident they were equally strong, and no more liable to illness; had never had reason to think them of weaker constitution. They often had large families, and he had *not* noticed that their children were weaker or more subject to disease than others. He thought that perhaps they did not have so many children as the pure negroes, but the reason evidently was that they did not begin bearing so young as the others, and this was because they were more attractive to the men, and perhaps more amorous themselves. He knew a great many mulattoes married together, and they generally had large and healthy families.

Afterwards, at one of the plantation nurseries, where there were some twenty or thirty infants and young children, a number of which were mulattoes. I asked the nurse to point out the healthiest children to me, and she indicated more of the pure than of the mixed breed. I then asked her to show me which were the sickliest, and she did not point to any of these. I then asked her if she had noticed any difference in this respect between the black and the yellow children. "Well, dey do *say,* master, dat de yellow ones is de sickliest, but I can't tell for true dat I ever see as dey were." I shall endeavor to investigate this subject further before giving the result of my own observations upon it.

In the evening I met the proprietor, and being seated with him and the manager, I asked about the religious condition of the slaves. There were "preachers" on the plantations, and they had some religious observances on a Sunday; but the preachers and the religious negroes were the worst characters among them, and, they thought, only made their religion a cloak to hide their greater immorality of life. They were, at all events, the most deceitful and dishonest slaves on the plantation, and oftenest required punishment. They had some negroes who called themselves Roman Catholics, but were so only in name. They paid no respect to the ordinances of the Church. The negroes of all denominations would join together in exciting religious observances, and even those who ordinarily made no religious pretensions.

These gentlemen considered the public religious exercises of the negroes to be exactly similar, in their intellectual and moral character, to the Indian feasts and war-dances, and did not encourage them. Neither did they like to have a white man preach on the estate, because the negroes were good for nothing for a week afterwards. It excited them so much as to greatly interfere with the subordination and order which was necessary to obtain the profitable use of their labor. They would be singing and dancing every night in their cabins, and so utterly unfit themselves for work.

I remarked that I had been told that a religious negro was considered to be worth a third more, because of his greater honesty and reliability. "Quite the contrary," they both assured me, for a religious negro generally made mischief and trouble, and they were glad to get rid of him. Though there were, to be sure, some negroes who were *truly* religious, and who were orderly, obedient and industrious. But these were seldom found among the field-hands. They were more common in the town negroes, or among house-servants, such as from their position had acquired better habits and more intelligence than were often found on the plantations.

The proprietor[2] believed the negro race was expressly designed by Providence for servitude, and in discussing the subject referred to the condition of the negroes where they were allowed their freedom. Everywhere at the North and in the West Indies they were in a most melancholy condition, except where they were employed as servants, while on the other hand their condition when in Slavery he thought to be superior to that of any white laboring class in the world. Everywhere the laborer was degraded, stupid, unable to take care of himself. In Slavery he had a master, who, unlike a free laborer's master, had a direct pecuniary interest in taking care of him, in protecting him and supporting him in his rights.

In England, he said, the laborer was entirely at the mercy of any bad man who chose to obtain his own emolument or secure his private ends by his ruin, and no matter how much he was defrauded, outraged or ill-used, owing to his own stupidity and poverty, he could obtain no redress or satisfaction, and no one else had any interest to obtain it for him.

At the North, owing to the general prosperity, the evil might not appear so prominently as in England, but in the constitution of society it was worse, because the laborer, being less dependent on his master, the interest of the latter was less like that of an owner. In fact, in the good old times in England, when the relation between master and laborer, or the landlord and his tenants, was more nearly similar to that of master and slave, there was a much more kindly and happy condition of things than at present. In Russia, he had seen his own Russian servant throw one of the laboring class upon the ground and whip him severely, because he had not got horses ready for them when they arrived. No man would dare do so to a slave in the South. His owner would resent it at law as an injury and outrage upon his property.

As to the moral condition of the slaves, he asked me who there was to throw a stone. Look at the condition of things in New-York, where thousands of virtuously disposed women were forced by the state of society and their inability to take care of themselves, to most loathsome prostitution—a state of things that had no parallel, and never could have, in a slave country. In England laborers of all sorts were forced to crime and then punished for it. For a breach of the law to which they were most excusably driven by the destitution in which their master allowed them to live—for a crime, often, that could not be deemed an immorality—their whole future was irretrievably blighted. Even without the action of the law and for no crime, and while their masters were possessed of most sumptuous abundance, millions of them were driven into a dreary exile, voluntarily destroying their social happiness by sundering their family ties, and withdrawing themselves from all they loved, to gratify the meanest and most material wants. What kind of morality was such a state of society likely to produce?

A slave was rarely separated from his family, or deprived of those comforts which he most valued—not even for a crime. When he did wrong, his punishment did not degrade him or lead him to a worse life than before: it did not destroy the happiness of his innocent family and friends, and did not in the least remove their means of support. As to the licentiousness of slaves, it was, at all events, voluntary with them. It was not attended with the horrid consequences which resulted from the pestilential and destructive system into which the laboring class were forced in the North and in England, and it was no worse than the licentiousness which existed, as he asserted that he knew from his personal observation during several years' intercourse with them, among the *higher classes* of the Continent.

YEOMAN.

1. Olmsted probably wrote this letter between November 21 and 25, 1853. The first section appears almost verbatim in *Back Country,* pages 76–80, 88–93.
2. Meredith Calhoun (see "The South" no. 44, above).

CHAPTER III
FIRST CONCLUSIONS

1853–1854

As He Set Out on his second tour of the South in December 1853, Olmsted experienced his crucial encounter with Samuel Perkins Allison, a Yale classmate of his brother, John. A slaveholder and southern gentleman, Allison successfully challenged Olmsted's defense of free-labor society by pointing out the shortcomings of the North. His arguments convinced Olmsted that he should dedicate himself to improving the civilization of the North in order to show the error of Southern proslavery critics and European defenders of aristocracy. At the same time, the encounter with Allison persuaded Olmsted that even the gentlemen of the South were sadly lacking in what he felt were fundamentally important attitudes and virtues. His talks with Allison also convinced him that the South would persist in a craven materialism that would require, for profit's sake, the limitless expansion of slavery into new areas of the Western Hemisphere. His remarkable letter to Charles Loring Brace of December 1, 1853, sums up the conclusions he reached as a result of this meeting with Allison.

The rest of the chapter consists of the three letters of synthesis with which Olmsted closed his first series for the *New-York Daily Times*. In them he examines all elements of Southern society—slaves, nonslaveholding yeomen and slaveholding gentry—with a clarity and perception never exceeded in his later writings on the South. He explains his concept of property as a form of stewardship that entails responsibility, and he defines what the responsibilities of Southern slaveholders would have to be if slavery were to be permitted to exist for even a limited time. He spells out, in that context, what the role of the North should be concerning the amelioration and abolition of the institution of slavery.

To Charles Loring Brace

Address: Mr. C.—Elliott or Brace/104 Waverly Place New York City/N.Y.
Postmark: Cincinnati O./Dec. 13

Cumberland River, December 1st, 1853[1]

Dear Charley
 At Louisville we called on Prentice[2] with a letter from C. M. Clay[3]—an elderly, bright, keen, sorrowed looking man. He said he had written to Greeley[4] and to Raymond to know if they could recommend any talented young man to him to assist in editorship of the Journal. He much wanted to find one. Probably would pay well. Raymond had not replied to him at all.
 We also called on Dr. Short,[5] a wealthy old hunker at a beautiful place 5 miles out of town—introduced to him by Dr. Grey.[6]
 From Louisville, rather than start two nights' coaching, we came to Nashville by the river down Ohio & Cumberland. Were laid up *every* night by fogs and were aground two days, so were a week getting to Nashville. Very tedious & disappointing.
 At Nashville [we met] a classmate of John's, *Allison*.[7] A good specimen of the first class gentleman of the South. We spent nearly all our time in Nashville, two days, in conversation with him, and he gave us a dinner at the hotel. He is wealthy, a bachelor, connected with the largest slaveholding in Tennessee: chivalric and believes in pistols and bowie knives. His argument being similar to Cooper's.[8]
 We confess to each other that he silenced us and showed us that our own position was by no means consistent and satisfactory. He has lately been running for Congress and though running very honorably ahead of his ticket, was beaten by Zollicoffer,[9] a Whig and veteran politician who last year shot a man across the street at his office door. He gave us an amusing account of the canvass.
 He and Z. went in company to all parts of the district, each speaking twice at a place in opposition to each other (such places as "T. Golb's Grocery," "the second gate on the Tobroke 'pike") &c., the crowd varying from 50 to 2000 in number—men, women, children & niggers, all excited and betting. His own body servant came to him after the election and asked him to lend him $10, as he had lost his watch on the election & he could get it back for that.
 He carried a pair of pistols loaded in his pocket for a few days as Zollicoffer had the reputation of a fighting man. But he found them such a bore to carry that he put them in his saddlebags and he got through without any "difficulty."
 In the cars in Kentucky a modest young man was walking through with the hand[le] of a Colt out of his pocket-skirt behind. It made some laugh &

a gentleman with us called out, "You'll lose your Colt, Sir." The man turned and after a moment joined the laugh and pushed the handle into the pocket.[10]

John said, "There might be danger in laughing at him." "Oh no," replied our companion, evidently supposing him serious, "he would not mind a laugh." "It's the best place to carry your pistol, after all," said he. "It's less in your way than anywhere else. And as good a place for your knife as anywhere else is down your back, so you can draw over your shoulder."

"Are pistols and knives generally carried here?"

"Yes, very generally."

Allison said *commonly,* but he thought not generally.

Allison declared himself a Democrat very strongly, but we confused him by proving to him that he was not; that he believed in two distinct and widely separated classes of society. He afterwards defined his Democracy to consist in holding to a strict construction of the Constitution (nevertheless he favored the building of Pacific R.R. by the government) and following the views of Jefferson rather than the Federalists. He admitted that practically there was no difference between the parties at the present time.

He and other gentlemen in Nashville hated Seward as "a devil incarnate." He thought he ought to be hung as a traitor. He was guilty of treason in the Senate—the gravest of all crimes.[11] He thought it a deep misfortune to the country that he could be reelected to the Senate. D. S. Dickinson[12] he thought a true Statesman and the only prominent man at the North who had been true at all times to the country—consistent, reliable, patriotic and unselfish, free from demagogism. He remarked at another time regarding the next President that he had been in correspondence with leading Southern Democrats upon the subject and that there was a general disposition to look to Dickinson as the Democratic candidate for next President. At any rate there was no other northern man the Southern Democrats would support.

Allison and other gentlemen I have seen in Nashville & Kentucky have changed the views I had with regard to the feelings of the South about extension of territory. Allison said they *must* have more slave territory. It was a necessity upon the South which every one saw. He thought California would be a Slave State. He also looked to the Amazon as a promising field for Slave labor. There was no disposition to hasten the matter.

There was a general dislike on the part of the South to a general war in Europe such as was now imminent[13] because it would injure the value of cotton & of course of negroes & everything else. But on some accounts they would like it. In case of a general war which would involve France & England & perhaps Spain, advantage would be taken of it to get possession of Cuba and perhaps of Mexico, as England & France could not then interfere. He hated England & liked France & thought the South did generally. It seems to me probable that the Government at Washington is acting on similar views. He evidently supposed so. He wouldn't go to fighting without some honorable excuse.

His whole idea of honor is of this sort. Mere deference to time honored rules and conventionalisms it seems to me, though he thinks them spontaneous honorable impulses. Oddly enough, with all his hodge podge of honor & morality, he was reading secretly (as he confessed to us) Strauss' life of Christ[14] and some of Parker's[15] books.

Most moral people at the South were Church members. Not that they believed much in particular, but thought that was on the whole the best way. Every man could not expect to [have] his individual opinions accommodated in systems, & systems were necessary. He was not a church member himself. He thought there was a happy gentlemanly medium in which a man would be sufficiently religious (that is, sufficiently to satisfy his poetical nature, I suppose) and yet not deny himself sensual and social pleasures—"spree moderately," I think he expressed it.

He did not believe there was a gentleman in the whole Northwest (the western free states), especially including Cincinnati. And he evidently thought there were very few, and they but poorly developed, anywhere at the North. There was not a man in Yale College who had anything of the appearance or manners of a gentleman, from the North, except a few sons of professional and commercial people who had been brought up in the large towns. There were no gentlemen at the North out of the large towns. He had once met some of the old Dutch aristocracy of New York (your Schuylers,[16] &c.) and he did think them thoroughly well bred people.

There is a great deal of truth in his view. I tried to show him that there were compensations in the *general* elevation of all classes at the North, but he did not seem to care for it. He is, in fact, a thorough Aristocrat. And altogether, the conversation making me acknowledge the rowdyism, ruffianism, want of high honorable sentiment & chivalry of the common farming & laboring people of the North, as I was obliged to, made me very melancholy. With such low, material, and selfish aims in statesmanship [*as the best men of the South have*] and with such a low, prejudiced, party enslaved and material people [*at the North*],[17] what does the success of our Democratic nationality amount to—and what is to become of us. Of course, I have told you but little of the whole conversation that so impressed me.

I must be either an Aristocrat or more of a Democrat than I have been—a Socialist Democrat. We need institutions that shall more directly *assist* the poor and degraded to elevate themselves. Our educational principle must be enlarged and made to include more than these miserable common schools. The poor & wicked need more than to be let alone.

It seemed to me that what had made these Southern gentlemen Democrats was the perception that mere Democracy as they understand it (no checks or laws upon the country more than can be helped) was the best system for their class. It gave capital every advantage in the pursuit of wealth—and money gave wisdom & power. They could do what they liked. It was only necessary for them, the gentlemen, to settle what they wanted. Or if they disagreed, the best *commander* of the people carried his way. The people doing nothing but choose between them. He had no conception of higher than material interests entering into politics. All that these sort of free traders want is protection to capital. Agrarianism would suit them better if they could protect that and use what they consider their rights.

But I do very much [feel] inclined to believe that Government should have in view the encouragement of a democratic condition of society as well as of government—that the two need to go together as they do at the North in much greater degree than at the South or I suppose anywhere else. But I don't think our state of society is sufficiently Democratic at the North or likely to be by mere *laisser aller*. The poor need an education to refinement and taste and the mental & moral capital of gentlemen.

I have been blundering over this and have not, I think, expressed at all what I wanted to. In a steamboat cabin—dark, shaking, and gamesters and others talking about the table—I can't collect my ideas. But to put some shape to it. Hurrah for Peter Cooper[18] and Hurrah for the Reds.[19]

The great difference I feel between such fellows as these gentlemanly, well informed, true and brave Southern gentlemen, whom I admire in spite of my Democratic determination, whom I respect in spite of my general loathing of humbugging dignity; the great difference between them & those I like and wish to live among & wish to be is the deficiency in one & the sense in the other of what I must call Religion (the intrinsic religious sense) as a distinct thing from Belief, Obedience, Reverence, and Love to Personal Deity. The quality which God must have himself. They do not seem to have a fundamental sense of right. Their moving power and the only motives which they can comprehend are materialistic or Heavenalistic—regard for good (to themselves or others or to God) in this world or in another.

I have something which distinguishes me from them, whether the above explains it or not. So have you. So has Field, Elliott,[20] all our earnest fellows. Allison couldn't approach to it and therefore he is a Conservative and a Democrat of the American School.

I am a Democrat of the European School—of the school of my brave porter of Bingen.[21] And these so-called Democrats are not. They are of another sort; material, temporary, temporizing, conservative. I wish I had Victor Hugo's speech[22] now to read you.

The Southern sort are perhaps larger—more generous and braver minds than ours—and they act up to their capabilities better. But ours are more expansive and have need to be more humble as being less true to their principles and feelings.

Allison & his friends evidently had no power of comprehending a hatred of Slavery in itself—no I can't think that. Put themselves in the place of the slave and they would cut their own throats, if there was no other way out, without hesitation. But they didn't & I believe couldn't imagine that the North would be governed by any purpose beyond a regard for self interest (including the gratification of pride, envy, spiritual pride, &c.) with regard to slavery. They could not see how the North could be so *foolish* as to determinedly prevent the extension of Slavery. Its own interest would suffer so much—commerce be injured, market for manufactures not enlarged, &c. Individuals might profit, but the whole would so certainly be injured by this injury for commerce, and beyond this they could not be got. So completely had they swallowed the whole hog of Free Trade. Admitting commerce & trade on the whole to be benefitted, it was a corollary that the measure would be for the highest good. What on the whole injured capital, consols, niggers, State credit, was wicked. What benefitted it, was Godlike. This was the end of their track.

Well, the moral of this damnedly drawn out letter is, I believe, go ahead with the Children's Aid[23] and get up parks, gardens, music, dancing schools, reunions which will be so attractive as to force into contact the good & bad, the gentlemanly and the rowdy.

And the state ought to assist these sort of things *as* it does Schools and Agricultural Societies—on the same plan, with the same precaution that the State of New York now does.[24] I believe that it can do so safely. I *don't* believe the friction compensates for the increased power of the machinery.

And we ought to have that Commentator as an organ of a higher Democracy and a higher religion than the popular. And it ought to be great—sure of success—well founded. Bound to succeed by its merit, by its talent. A cross between the Westminster Review & the Tribune,[25] is my idea. Weekly, I think, to give it variety & scope enough for this great country & this cursedly little people. Keep it before you.

Yours affectionately,

Fred.

1. Olmsted wrote this letter on board the steamboat that took him from Nashville to Paducah, on his way to New Orleans on his second journey through the South. Although he addressed the letter to either Charles Loring Brace or Charles Wyllys Elliott at 104 Waverly Place in New York City, where both were living at the time, internal evidence—including a reference to Elliott in the third person—indicates that he wrote it to Brace (*JT*, p. 37).
2. George Dennison Prentice (1802–1870), Connecticut-born editor of the *Louisville Daily Journal*, an influential Whig newspaper (*DAB*).
3. Cassius M. Clay (1810–1903), editor of *True American*, an antislavery newspaper (*DAB*).
4. Horace Greeley, editor of the *New York Tribune*, and Henry Raymond, editor of the *New-York Daily Times*.
5. Charles Wilkins Short (1794–1863), physician and botanist, who in 1848 had retired from teaching and was engaged in botanical research at his estate, Hayfield, near Louisville, Kentucky (*DAB*).
6. Asa Gray (1810–1888), professor of botany at Harvard. His wife, Jane Loring Gray, was a cousin of Charles Loring Brace (*DAB*; Charles Henry Pope and Katharine Peabody Loring, eds., *Loring Genealogy* ... [Cambridge, Mass., 1917], pp. 166–68).
7. Samuel Perkins Allison (1827–1858), a member of the Yale class of 1847. After graduation he studied law in Nashville and was admitted to the bar there in 1849. Allison had many prosperous relatives in the Nashville region: in 1850, nine members of the Perkins and Allison families in Williamson County owned fifteen or more slaves, and five of them owned more than

FIRST CONCLUSIONS: 1853-1854

fifty slaves. His uncle Thomas F. Perkins owned 106 slaves and was one of the twenty-two largest slaveholders in the state. In 1850, Samuel P. Allison himself owned fifteen slaves (Franklin Bowditch Dexter, *Biographical Notices of Graduates of Yale College, Including Those Graduated in Classes Later Than 1815, Who Are Not Commemorated in the Annual Obituary Records*... [New Haven, Conn., 1913], p. 365; Virginia McDaniel Bowman, *Historic Williamson County: Old Homes and Sites* [Nashville, Tenn., c. 1971], pp. 6-8, 30-32; U.S., Census Office, 7th Census, *7th Census 1850. Tennessee* [Washington, D.C., 1850], schedule 2, Williamson County, pp. 617, 641, 671, 819, 827, 853, 1003, 1033; idem, 8th Census, *Agriculture of the United States in 1860*... [1864; rpt. ed., Wilmington, Del., 1973], p. 248).

8. James Fenimore Cooper.
9. Felix Kirk Zollicoffer (1812-1862), editor of the *Nashville Banner* and one of the most powerful Whig politicians in Tennessee. Zollicoffer easily defeated Allison for a congressional seat in 1852, despite the fact that he devoted most of his energy during the campaign to securing Tennessee's electoral votes for Winfield Scott (*DAB*).
10. This incident took place while Olmsted was traveling by train from Lexington to Louisville, Kentucky. A short description of it appears in *Journey Through Texas*, page 20.
11. On March 11, 1850, William H. Seward delivered a speech in the U.S. Senate in which he opposed the Compromise of 1850 and called on the Senate to follow a "higher law than the Constitution" in its treatment of slavery. Many interpreted this as a call for the use of force, and the speech created a furor. Seward was re-elected to the Senate in 1855 (*DAB*).
12. Daniel Stevens Dickinson (1800-1866), a New York Democratic politician. While U.S. senator from 1844 to 1851 he had supported the Mexican War and the Compromise of 1850, and as early as 1847 had proposed to apply the doctrine of "squatter sovereignty" to the question of slaveholding in the territories (ibid).
13. In October 1853, Turkey had declared war against Russia, and various European powers were about to come to her aid in what was to become the Crimean War.
14. The *Life of Jesus* by the German theologian David Friedrich Strauss (1808-1874), was published in German in 1835-36 and in an English translation in 1846. In the book Strauss applied principles of historical criticism and Hegelian philosophy to the scriptural accounts of the life of Christ (*Schaff-Herzog Encyc.*).
15. Theodore Parker (1810-1860) of Massachusetts, Unitarian theologian and abolitionist and an acquaintance of Charles Loring Brace (*DAB*; *Life of Brace*, p. 175).
16. A reference to the family of the philanthropist and yachtsman George Lee Schuyler (1811-1890) of Dobbs Ferry, New York. Brace came to know them in 1853 as a result of their early support of the Children's Aid Society. Describing two overnight visits that he made to their home in October 1853, Brace recounted that the place was "beautifully situated, commanding a long view up the Hudson, with a large house and old trees, and servants and horses in style." He found the Schuylers to be "altogether a most simple, interesting family, highly cultivated and free in thought." He was much taken by Mrs. Schuyler, the former Eliza Hamilton, daughter of James Alexander Hamilton and granddaughter of both Alexander Hamilton and Robert Morris. He called her "one of the most cultivated and lovely women I ever knew." In early February 1855 Brace took Olmsted with him for a two-day visit with the Schuylers and Hamiltons, "with whom," according to John Hull Olmsted, "he was much pleased—and apparently they with him." Recounting the visit to his father, Olmsted described the Schuylers as "most capital people—the most finished people that I ever saw."

The family became important allies for Olmsted in his own activities: James Alexander Hamilton assisted him in his free-soil colonization schemes of the later 1850s, and all of the women of the Schuyler family—Eliza Schuyler and her daughters Louisa and Georgina—were active in Sanitary Commission affairs during the Civil War. Louisa Lee Schuyler, in particular, was an important friend and colleague of Olmsted's. As corresponding secretary of the Women's Central Association for Relief, she made that organization a nationally effective auxiliary of the U.S. Sanitary Commission, and after the Civil War she enlisted Olmsted's help in forming the New York State Charities Aid Society (*Life of Brace*, pp. 183-85; JHO to JO, Feb. 7, 1855; FLO to JO, Feb. 7, 1855; NCAB, 1: 447-48; *Notable American Women*, s.v. "Schuyler, Louisa Lee"; *New York Genealogical and Biographical Record* 58, no. 1 [Jan. 1927]: 1-2; *DAB*, s.v. "Hamilton, James Alexander").
17. Olmsted drew a line through the two phrases in this sentence that the editors have rendered in brackets and italicized.

18. On September 13, 1853, less than three months before Olmsted wrote this letter, the manufacturer and philanthropist Peter Cooper (1791–1883) had laid the cornerstone of his major philanthropic endeavor, the Cooper Union for the Advancement of Science and Art, in New York City. The Union was to provide a variety of free facilities for popular education and culture, including vocational training for both men and women in the mechanical arts and sciences. The building contained reading rooms, an art gallery, scientific collections, a cosmorama, and the Great Hall for lectures, debates, and concerts (Edward Clarence Mack, *Peter Cooper: Citizen of New York* [New York, 1949], pp. 243–61).
19. The phrase "red republican" was applied at this time to those who held radically republican views and were willing to use force in order to secure political reform. Olmsted apparently is referring here to those who fought in the European revolutions of 1848 and against the *coup d'état* of Louis Napoleon in 1851 (William Alexander Craigie, ed., *A Dictionary of American English on Historical Principles* . . ., 4 vols. [Chicago, 1938–44], 4: 1918).
20. Olmsted's friends Alfred Field and Charles Wyllys Elliott.
21. Probably a man with republican beliefs that Olmsted, Brace and John Hull Olmsted met in Bingen, Hesse-Darmstadt, during their trip to Europe and England in 1850 (*Papers of FLO*, 1: 360, n. 2).
22. Probably a speech delivered by Victor Hugo in the French Assembly on July 18, 1851, in which he defended the idea of a French republic against monarchist critics and warned of the impending overthrow of the Second Republic by Louis Napoleon (Elliott Mansfield Grant, . . . *Victor Hugo during the Second Republic*, Smith College Studies in Modern Languages, 17, no. 1 [Northampton, Mass., 1935]: 63–65; *New York Daily Tribune*, Aug. 4, 1851, p. 6).
23. The Children's Aid Society, of which Brace had been the executive head since March (*Life of Brace*, pp. 157, 492).
24. The New York State Board of Regents granted charters for the formation of academies whose sponsors could show evidence of sufficient funds, suitable buildings, and public need. The Regents then assisted the academies with grants apportioned to the number of students pursuing advanced studies, and made special grants for the purchase of books and maps. In 1832 the state of New York created a state agricultural society, for which it thereafter provided funds, and after 1841 the state also subsidized county agricultural societies and a state fair (David M. Ellis et al., *A Short History of New York State* [Ithaca, N.Y., 1957], pp. 276, 320–21).
25. The *Westminster Review* was a quarterly journal founded in 1824 by Jeremy Bentham and John Stuart Mill to disseminate Utilitarian doctrine. At the time of this letter it was experiencing a resurgence of quality and influence under the editorship of John Chapman and the novelist George Eliot. The Tribune that Olmsted refers to was the *New York Daily Tribune*, edited by Horace Greeley (Daniel N. Fader and George Bornstein, *Two Centuries of British Periodicals* [Ann Arbor, Mich., 1974], pp. 73–85).

New-York Daily Times, January 12, 1854[1]

THE SOUTH.

LETTERS ON THE PRODUCTIONS, INDUSTRY AND RESOURCES OF THE SOUTHERN STATES.

NUMBER FORTY-SIX.

Special Correspondence of the New-York Daily Times

FIRST CONCLUSIONS: 1853–1854

Slavery and its Effects on Character, and the Social Relations of the Master Class.

The wealthy and educated, and especially the fashionable people of all civilized countries, are now so nearly alike in their ordinary manners and customs, that the observations of a passing traveler upon them must commonly be of much too superficial a character to warrant him in deducing from them, with confidence, any important conclusions. I have spent an evening at the plantation residence of a gentleman in Louisiana, in which there was very little in the conversation or customs and manners of the family to distinguish them from others whom I have visited in Massachusetts, England and Germany. I shall, therefore, undertake with diffidence to describe certain apparently general and fundamental peculiarities of character in the people, which it is a part of my duty to notice, from their importance with reference to the condition and prospects of the Slave States and their institution.

Slavery exerts an immense quiet influence upon the character of the master, and the condition of the slave is greatly affected by the modifications of character thus effected. I do not believe there are any other people in the world with whom the negro would be as contented, and, if contentment is happiness, so happy, as with those who are now his masters. The hopeless perpetuation of such an intolerable nuisance as this labor-system, it is, however, also apparent, depends mainly upon the careless, temporizing, *shiftless* disposition, to which the negro is indebted for this mitigation of the natural wretchedness of Slavery.

The calculating, indefatigable New-Englander, the go-ahead Western man, the exact and stern Englishman, the active Frenchman, the studious, observing, economical German would all and each lose patience with the frequent disobedience and constant indolence, forgetfulness and carelessness, and the blundering, awkward, brute-like manner of work of the plantation-slave. The Southerner, if he sees anything of it, generally disregards it and neglects to punish it. Although he is naturally excitable and passionate, he is less subject to impatience and passionate anger with the slave, than is, I believe, generally supposed, because he is habituated to regard him so completely as his inferior, dependent and subject. For the same reason, his anger, when aroused, is usually easily and quickly appeased, and he forgives him readily and entirely, as we do a child or a dog who has annoyed us. And, in general, the relation of master and slave on small farms, and the relations of the family and its household servants everywhere, may be considered a happy one, developing, at the expense of decision, energy, self-reliance and self-control, some of the most beautiful traits of human nature. But it is a great error—although one nearly universal with Southerners themselves—to judge Slavery by the light alone of the master's fireside.

The direct influence of Slavery is, I think, to make the Southerner indifferent to small things; in some relations, we should say rightly, *superior* to small things; prodigal, improvident, and ostentatiously generous. His ordinarily uncontrolled authority (and from infancy the Southerner is more free from control, in all respects, I should judge, than any other person in the world), leads him to be habitually impulsive, impetuous, and enthusiastic; gives him self-respect and dignity of character, and makes him bold, confident, and true. Yet it has not appeared to me that the Southerner was [as] frank as he is, I believe, commonly thought to be. He seems to me to be very secretive, or at least reserved on topics which most nearly concern himself. He minds his own business, and lets alone that of others; not in the English way, but in a way peculiarly his own; resulting partly, perhaps, from want of curiosity, in part from habits formed by such a constant intercourse as he has with his inferiors (negroes) and partly from the caution in conversation which the "rules of honor" are calculated to give. Not, I said, in the English way, because he meets a stranger easily, and without timidity, or thought of how he is himself appearing, and is ready and usually accomplished in conversation. He is much given to vague and careless generalization; and greatly disinclined to exact and careful reasoning. He follows his natural impulses nobly, has nothing to be ashamed of, and is, therefore, habitually truthful; but his carelessness, impulsiveness, vagueness, and want of exactness in everything, make him speak from his mouth that which is in point of fact untrue, rather oftener than anyone else.

From early intimacy with the negro (an association fruitful in other respects of evil) he has acquired much of his ready, artless and superficial benevolence, good nature and geniality. The comparatively solitary nature and somewhat monotonous duties of plantation life, make guests usually exceedingly welcome, while the abundance of servants at command, and other circumstances, make the ordinary duties of hospitality very light. The Southerner, however, is greatly wanting in hospitality of mind, closing his doors to all opinions and schemes to which he has been bred a stranger, with a contempt and bigotry which sometimes seems incompatible with his character as a gentleman. He has a large but unexpansive mind.

The Southerner has no pleasure in labor except with reference to a result. He enjoys life in itself. He is content with being. Here is the grand distinction between him and the Northerner; for the Northerner enjoys progress in itself. He finds his happiness in doing. Rest, in itself, is irksome and offensive to him, and however graceful or beatific that rest may be, he values it only with reference to the power of future progress it will bring him. Heaven itself will be dull and stupid to him, if there is no work to be done in it—nothing to struggle for—if he reaches perfection at a jump, and has no chance to make an improvement.

The Southerner cares for the end only; he is impatient of the means. He is passionate, and labors passionately, fitfully, with the energy and strength of anger, rather than of resolute will. He fights rather than works to carry his purpose. He has the intensity of character which belongs to Americans in general, and therefore enjoys excitement and is fond of novelty. But he has much less curiosity than the Northerner; less originating genius, less inventive talent, less patient and persevering energy. And I think this all comes from his want of aptitude for close observation and his dislike for application to small details. And this, I think, may be reasonably supposed to be mainly the result of habitually leaving all matters not either of grand and exciting importance, or of immediate consequence to his comfort, to his slaves, and of being accustomed to see them slighted or neglected as much as he will, in his indolence, allow them to be by them.

Of course, I have been speaking of the general tendencies only of character in the North and the South. There are individuals in both communities in whom these extreme characteristics are reversed, as there are graceful Englishmen and awkward Frenchmen. There are, also, in each, those in whom they are more or less harmoniously blended. Those in whom they are most enviably so—the happiest and the most useful in the social sphere—are equally common, so far as I know, in both; and the grand distinction remains in the mass—manifesting itself, by strikingly contrasting symptoms, in our religion, politics and social life.

In no way more than this: The South endeavors to close its eyes to every evil the removal of which will require self-denial, labor and skill. If, however, an evil is too glaring to be passed by unnoticed, it is immediately declared to be constitutional, or providential, and its removal is declared to be either treasonable or impious—usually both; and what is worse, it is improper, impolite, ungentlemanly, unmanlike. And so it is ended at the South. But, at the North this sort of opposition only serves to develop the reform, by ridding it of useless weight and drapery.

Northern social life usually leaves a rather melancholy and disagreeable feeling upon the minds of our Southern friends, as many have confessed to me. I think the different tendency of life at the North from that of existence at the South, which I have asserted, will give a key to this unfavorable impression which the Southerner obtains of our social character.

The aspect in which Northern society, even apparently of the more sensible sort, appears to the Southern gentlemen, was clearly shown by a candid and plain-spoken but not unfriendly hand in an article originally published last year in the *Daily Times* and since issued by the Appletons in a pamphlet, under the title of *North and South*,[2] which has deservedly attracted much more attention, and probably been effective of good. I am not disposed to deny the general truth of the allegations of the writer against Northern society. I think he is wholly right in his descriptions of symptoms. His inferences as to the nature and causes of the disease are more questionable.

The people of the North are generally well aware of their social deficiencies, and of the unfitness of many of the customs and mannerisms, required by conventional politeness, to their character and duties. A man comes to our house, and custom requires that our countenance should brighten, and that we should say we are glad to see him. Thus custom makes it unkind in us towards him not to do so. We have no unkindness in our hearts to the man, but entirely the contrary; yet it happens that we are *not* glad to see him, and such is our constitution that we have no impulsive and natural brightening up under hardly any circumstances. Now we have to choose between a forced, artificial, formal and false expression of a true kindness, and truth and simplicity. Amiable people take sides with kindness—the silent and reliable sort, with truth. Each are constantly aware, to a greater or less degree, of the difficulty they are engaged with. Some attach an absurd importance to the value of expression, and become "affected;" others rebel against the falseness of the conventional forms of expression, and become supercilious or sour and forbidding. Both classes are constantly led to make awkward attempts to compromise their quarrel with themselves.

The Southerner can understand nothing of all this. He naturally accepts the institutions, manners and customs in which he is educated, as necessities imposed upon him by Providence. He is loyal to "Society," and it is opposed to his fundamental idea of a gentleman to essentially deduct from them or add to them. This "clothes philosophy"[3] of the North he does not in the least comprehend, or if he does he sees nothing in it but impudent and vulgar quackery. And yet I think there is, perhaps, good to come out of it. We believe not, in our day, in good William of Wickham's maxim.[4] This new Democratic man is not "made of manners;" it may be best he should make manners to suit himself. Between this slavish conformity and anarchical non-conformity, it is to be hoped that the good sense of our society is drifting towards both a nobler and a happier social life.

But, at the present, the social intercourse of the wealthy people of the South is certainly more agreeable, rational, and to be respected, than that of the nearest corresponding class at the North. I should be sorry to think this the highest compliment it deserved.

The wealthy class is the commanding class in most districts of the South, and gives character to all the slaveholding class. Wealth is less distributed, and is more retained in families at the South than the North. With the slaveholding class there is a pride of birth and social position, much more than in any class at the North. This affects the character and conduct of individuals, and reacts on their associates, and on the whole community—in some respects perniciously, but in many respects favorably.

The "high-toned gentleman" (a Southern expression) of the South is rare at the North. He is not an article of city manufacture, as the most cultivated people of the North are. He has a peculiar character, and peculiar habits—more like those of the "old English gentleman" than any class to be found now, perhaps, even in England itself. He rides much, and hunts, and is given to field sports and never knows the want of oxygen; for, even in Winter, his windows and doors are always forgotten to be closed. Accordingly, though his diet is detestable, he is generally well physically developed—lighter and more delicate of frame than the English squires, but tall and sinewy. His face would commonly be handsome but that his mouth is made gross, lifeless, and inexpressive, by his habit of using tobacco excessively. He has a peculiar pride and romance, and, though he often appears laughably Quixotic, he is, in the best sense of the word, also chivalrous. He is brave and magnanimous, courteous and polite, to all white people. If he often values his comfort, or the success of his designs, or the gratification of his passions, more than he does a strict adherence to the received rules of Christian morality, he never values life or aught else more than he does his honor. This "honor"—though if you analyze it, it comes to be little else than a conventional standard of feelings and actions, which must be habitual to entitle a man to consider himself a gentleman—is often really far nobler, and makes a nobler man than what *often* passes for religion at the *North*—at least in this world.

There is, however, a quality, or perhaps it is a faculty of the soul, which is distinct, though seldom separate, from love to the person of God and love to man, or in our time from the Christian faith, which is most nearly defined by the term, an enlightened conscience—a spontaneous requisite perception and loyal love of the fundamental laws of Right—the laws that God himself is subject to. This quality or faculty is the noblest endowment of man, and is essential to the noblest character. I think it is strongly developed in more individuals at the North than at the South, and I think there are obvious causes for its absence at the South. The habitual reference of the Southerner in his judgment of conduct, whether of himself or another, whether past or contemplated, to the conventional standard of honor, prevents the ascendancy of a higher standard. This habitual contemplation of a relation so essentially wrong as that of slavery, as a permanent and necessary one not reformable, not in progress of removal and abolition, destroys or prevents the development of his sense of any standard of right and wrong above a mere code of laws, or conventional rules.

But to the Southern gentleman, by distinction, as I have often met him, I wish to pay great respect. The honest and unstudied dignity of character, the generosity and the real nobleness of habitual impulses, and the well-bred, manly courtesy which distinguish him in all the relations and occupations of life, equally in his business, in his family, and in general society, are sadly rare at the North—much more rare at the North than the South. I acknowledge it freely but with deep regret and melancholy. There are qualities of character (not of deportment, merely) which are common among the planters of many parts of the South, as they are among the aristocratic classes of Europe, which are incompatible with the possession of nothing else that a man should glory in, which the mass of the people of the North have merely lost, or have failed to gain.

This has been often observed by intelligent travelers visiting us, and is sometimes thought sufficient to condemn our democratic form of government, and our approximately democratic state of society. This is the judgment of many Southerners (for the government and society of the South is the most essentially aristocratic in the world), and I have reason to believe that there are many whose confidence in the democracy of the North is so small that they anticipate, and are acting politically with reference to, a division of the present Union and the formation of another great Southern republic—that is, a republic of white capitalists, in which the slavery of the working classes shall be provided for, and every means taken to make it complete and permanent.

But acknowledging the rarity of the thorough-bred gentleman at the North, is an inference to be drawn from it unfavorable to Democratic Institutions? I think not. Without regard to the future, and to what we may yet become under Democracy, the condition and the character of our people *as a whole,* to the best of my judgment, is better, more gentlemanly even, far more entitled to respect than that of the people, *including all classes,* of any other nation. Very much more so than of the South. I do not say more happy. The people of the Northern States, as a whole, probably enjoy life less than any other civilized people. Perhaps it would be equally true to add—or than any uncivilized people. Those who consider that, if so, the uncivilized people (perchance slaves) are to be envied, will do right to condemn Democracy.

But the only conclusion which the fact seems to me to suggest, with regard to our Democratic Government, is perhaps this: that simple protection to capital and letting-alone to native genius and talent is not the whole duty of Government; possibly that patent laws, and the common schools, with their common teachers, and common instruction (not education) such as our institutions as yet give to the people, are not enough. That the aesthetic faculties need to be educated—drawn out; that taste and refinement need to be encouraged as well as the useful arts. That there need to be places and times for *re-unions,* which shall be so attractive to the nature of all but the most depraved men, that the rich and the poor, the cultivated and *well bred,* and the sturdy and self-made people shall be attracted together and encouraged to assimilate.

I think there is no sufficient reason why the aid of the State should not be given to assist corporations and voluntary associations for such purposes, on the same principle, and with the same restrictions, that it is in New York to schools, to colleges, and to agricultural societies. Thus, I think, with a necessity for scarcely any additional governmental offices, or increase of the friction of governmental machinery, might be encouraged and sustained, at points so frequent and convenient that they would exert an elevating influence upon all the people, public parks and gardens, galleries of art and instruction in art, music, athletic sports and healthful recreations, and other means of cultivating taste and lessening that excessive materialism of purpose in which we are, as a people, so cursedly absorbed, that even the natural capacity for domestic happiness, and, more obviously, for the employment of simple and sensible social life in our community, seems likely to be entirely destroyed. The enemies of Democracy could bring no charge more severe against it, than that such is its tendency, and that it has no means of counteracting it.

Slavery is claimed at the South to be the remedy for this evil. In some respects it is a remedy. But (disregarding the slaves and the poor whites) where there is one true gentleman, and to be respected, at the South, there are two whose whole life seems to be absorbed in sensualism and sickly excitements. Everywhere you meet them, well dressed and spending money freely, constantly drinking, smoking and chewing; card-playing and betting; and unable to converse upon anything that is not either grossly sensual or exciting, such as street encounters, filibustering schemes, or projects of disunion or war. These persons are, however, gentlemen, in the sense that they are familiar with the forms and usages of the best society, that they are deferential to women, and that (except in money matters) their word is to be implicitly relied upon. They far exceed in numbers any class of at all similar habits that we yet have at the North.

They are invariably politicians, and they generally rule in all political conventions and caucuses. They are brave, in the sense that they are reckless of life, and they are exceedingly fond of the excitement of the hazard of life. They are as careless of the life of others as of themselves. They are especially ambitious of military renown, and in the Mexican war they volunteered almost to a man, many of those who went as privates taking with them several negro servants. If they were not dependent on the price of cotton for the means of their idleness, they would keep the country incessantly at war. Being so, however, they are as conversative in the policy they favor towards any powerful nation as the cotton lords of England or the land lords of Austria. They hate and despise the Democrats of Europe as much as Francis Joseph himself.[5] They glorify Napoleon,[6] and they boast of the contempt with which they were able to treat the humbug Kossuth.[7]

They call themselves Democrats, and sometimes Democratic Whigs. Call them what you will, they are a mischievous class—the dangerous class at the present of the United States. They are not the legitimate offspring of Democracy, thanks to God, but of Slavery under a Democracy.

YEOMAN.

---

1. Internal evidence suggests that Olmsted wrote this letter in early December 1853, soon after his meeting with Samuel Perkins Allison in Nashville and after he wrote "The South" number 47. In it Olmsted seems to be answering Allison's critique of Northern society and his assertion that it was incapable of producing a class of true gentlemen. In the proposals he makes in this letter for creating institutions of popular culture and education in the North, Olmsted appears to be continuing a train of thought that received strong impetus from his debates with Allison (see FLO to CLB, Dec. 1, 1853, above).
2. Entitled "North and South. Impressions of Northern Society upon a Southerner," and signed "A Southerner," the article appeared in the *New-York Daily Times* of October 16, 1852, pages 2 and 3, and was published separately in 1853 by D. Appleton and Company.

    "A Southerner" asserted that in New England the individual was subservient to society and found his realization only in "unreserved obedience to social organization" and public opinion. The consequence was that "mechnical uniformity, is the mighty law," and spontaneous individuality was suppressed. Social pressure produced much "spurious virtue," with the result that New Englanders were particularly likely to lapse into vice when freed from the control of the community. Although Olmsted found the South to be more conformist in thought and social relations than the North, he had complained earlier about pressure for conformity in the New England society in which he grew up, and may have sympathized with this critique. The author of the *Times* article also complained, as did Olmsted, about the shortcomings of Northern domesticity and the deficiency of the Northern concept of home. New England lacked the home life that was a necessary counterbalance to the demands of society at large, "A Southerner" asserted: as organized, New England could not meet the needs of the "social nature" of its inhabitants.

One direct result of the weakness of domesticity in the North, the author continued, was that New Englanders turned their reformist energies into the only forum available to them—society at large. "Nothing is more common," he observed, "than for a strong sentiment of humanity, denied its rightful scope of activity, to seek another sphere, and to compensate its loss by extravagant and fictitious displays. The world of Philanthropy is too often the counterfeit of the home. Ungratified desires, embittered tempers, unrepaid love, and all the usual concomitants of social affections, unmet and unoccupied at home, rush into the open field of general life, and labor to acquire the happiness which is lost in more genial scenes." This accounted, he said, for the large number of New England women who had become strident reformers. Movements like the one for women's rights were "the natural resistance which sensitive and wronged natures make to the harsh features of severe society."

"A Southerner" discerned another source of New England's reformist impulse: New Englanders carried an "exaggerated idea of human agency" into all their activities and left little room for the action of Providence. Their region, he admitted, had been a testing ground of the human will and they had accomplished wonders in mastering nature. When they turned from physical to moral evils, however, they became abstract, and imposed on social institutions and relations the "absolute law," the "perfect standard." In the uncompromising reformism of New England, and especially of its women, he saw at work the stern spirit of Puritanism, operating as a social law and "incarnating its repulsive dogmas in the structural elements of society."

The section of the *Times* letter that Olmsted believed had been "effective of good" was probably the author's appeal for mutual forbearance and good will by both sides of the debate over slavery. He complained of the fanatical and demagogic way that the abolitionists attacked their adversaries, and declared, "We have a right to demand that men should be gentlemen in everything." He also pointed out that Northerners had many social problems to solve at home, and should learn from that circumstance to be more understanding of their Southern brethren. "Is it not time that you had learned," he asked, "the sad conflict in this deranged world, between ideal visions and absolute circumstances? Is it not time for you to understand, that society adjusts itself slowly to its best imaginable state?" One of the problems that Northerners should solve in their own society, he declared, was that of the free blacks—a field for philanthropy that he found strangely neglected. In this he concurred with Olmsted's call in "The South" number 48 for "fair play for the Negro" (*Papers of FLO*, 1: 246, 272, 276–77, 278–80, 288, 322; see "The South" no. 48, below).

3. An allusion to Thomas Carlyle's *Sartor Resartus* and the "clothes philosophy" of its protagonist, Herr Teufelsdröckh.
4. The maxim "manners maketh the man," of William of Wykeham (1324–1404), Bishop of Winchester, Chancellor of England and founder of New College, Oxford (*DNB*).
5. Francis Joseph I (1830–1916), who became emperor of Austria-Hungary in the midst of the revolutions of 1848 and presided over the restoration of autocratic rule within the empire, including the suppression of the Hungarian revolution with the help of Russian troops.
6. Louis Napoleon (Charles Louis Napoleon Bonaparte) (1808–1873), who in December 1851 overthrew the French Second Republic by coup d'état and proclaimed himself Emperor Napoleon III.
7. Lajos Kossuth (1802–1894), who led the unsuccessful Hungarian revolt against Austrian rule in 1848 and continued thereafter to champion the cause of Hungarian independence and of republican government. The contemptuous treatment of Kossuth to which Olmsted refers was probably the furor touched off in Congress and the press by the bill for $4,600 that Kossuth, as a guest of the United States government, left behind after his celebrated visit in 1851–52. The House of Representatives meticulously examined the bill, and some members took exception to its size and the amount of liquor that had been consumed at taxpayers' expense (James Ford Rhodes, *History of the United States from the Compromise of 1850... New ed. in nine volumes* ... [New York and London, 1928], 1: 242–43).

FIRST CONCLUSIONS: 1853-1854

New-York Daily Times, January 26, 1854[1]

THE SOUTH.

LETTERS ON THE PRODUCTIONS, INDUSTRY AND RESOURCES OF THE SOUTHERN STATES.

NUMBER FORTY-SEVEN.

Special Correspondence of the New-York Daily Times

General Conclusions—The Condition of the Slaves—The Condition of the Non-Slaveholding Whites.

  Southerners often represent the condition of their slaves to be so happy and desirable that we might wonder that they do not sometimes take measures to be made slaves themselves, or at least occasionally offer their children for sale to the highest bidder. Yet there are many among us who always assume these accounts to be the only reliable information that we have upon the subject. On the other hand, there [are] many who always picture the slave as a martyr, with his hands folded in supplication, naked, faint with hunger, dragging a chain, and constantly driven to extremity of human exertion by a monster flourishing a cart-whip.
  A Scotchman, who had been employed at home as foreman of a large stock farm, came, a year or two since, to America, to better his condition. He spent some months in Canada and afterwards in New-England, looking in vain for a situation suited to his capabilities and habits. His little capital being nearly expended, he used what remained in paying his passage to Richmond, Va., learning that the proprietors of farms in the Slave States generally employed overseers, as in Scotland. On arriving at Richmond he immediately walked into the country, and at nightfall came to the plantation of the gentleman who related his story to me. He informed the proprietor of his circumstances and solicited employment, presenting, at the same time, a recommendation from his last employer in Scotland, and a testimonial of his piety, good character and education from the pastor of the church he had belonged to in the old country. Before, however, the gentleman had read these, he said to him, "By the way, Sir, there are a number of your niggers loose in the lane."
  "What?"
  "As I was coming up the lane to the house, Sir, I met a number of niggers just going off loose, without anybody to look after them."
  "Yes, I suppose they have got through their work, and are going to their quarters."

"But they were *loose*, Sir; just straying off, nobody looking after them. If you wish, Sir, I'll run down and catch them."

The Scotchman had always been informed, as he afterwards told the gentleman, that the slaves were treated exactly like cattle, and probably would not have been much surprised if he had been ordered to put half a dozen of them into stalls to be fattened for the butcher.

I think that any one who has read the accounts I have given of the negroes upon the different plantations I have visited, and the chance-observations I have made on others, will have obtained a correct and reliable idea of the *customary* manner in which the slaves are treated by the whites. It may be desired of me, however, to give the conclusions at which I have arrived upon certain points which have been most fruitful of unprofitable controversy.

Are the slaves hard-worked, poorly fed, miserably lodged and clothed, and subject to frequent brutal punishment?

Any sensible man, at all familiar with the Black-laws of the Southern States, can anticipate the true answer to these questions from his general knowledge of human nature. There is all the difference in the treatment of slaves by different masters that there is of horses by their riders, or of children by their parents. The laws have very little power to restrain cruelty or to enforce care and provide adequate sustenance for the negroes. They have less effect than the laws to secure humane treatment of animals at the North, because the violations of the laws at the South would be much more seldom witnessed by persons anxious to secure their enforcement, and because Southerners respect the individuality of each other more than Northerners, and are more loth to meddle in matters that do not *especially* concern themselves. Public Opinion is favorable to humanity and care—in some districts very strongly and effectually so. In general its influence is not very valuable to the negro, for the same reasons that the laws are not. What power has Public Opinion on the treatment of domestics and farm laborers at the North? Except in extreme cases, none. Competition is the balance wheel of cupidity.

But as I have said, in describing the character of the people of the South, they are as kind to their slaves as any people could be imagined to be—much more kind than one whose whole experience of human nature had been obtained at the Northern States would be likely to imagine them to be.

If the labor of the slaves were voluntary—if he were exhilarated with the spirit of the ambitious free laborer, with a loved wife and children to enjoy the fruits of his toil in proportion to its amount, his work would in nearly every case, as far as I could judge, be light. As it is, on the far Southern large plantations especially, it seemed to me that the negro was *driven* at his work more tediously and fatiguingly than agricultural laborers often are in any other part of the world that I have visited.

The negroes, I should think, were *generally abundantly* provided with coarse food[2]—more so than the agricultural laborers of any part of Europe.

They are sufficiently clothed, *in general*, to enable them, if they are at all pains-taking, which they seldom are in this particular, to appear decently, and to protect them from any degree of cold weather to which in the mild climate of the South they are subject. Their habitations are *generally* very deficient in comfort, and are much too small for the number of occupants that are crowded into them. Rapid improvement in this respect, however, is now making; neat (exteriorly) quarters for the negroes having become a fashionable part of every gentleman's plantation.[3] The negroes seldom or never want for fuel.

There are but few plantations in which the negroes are not frequently punished by being whipped, and that not seldom with what I should think would be generally considered at the North, severity. In this respect I think the condition of the negroes is just about what that of the seamen has formerly been in our Navy, and still is in the English service, varying on different plantations as in different ships. Cases of disgusting cruelty are not very rare. I never asked a middle aged Southerner the question (and I put it perhaps twenty times) who was not able to tell me a case within his own knowledge, and occurring, probably, in the near vicinity of his residence, of a slave killed by severe punishment from its master. I do not believe slaves are killed by their masters one tenth as often as sailors are by the cruelty or carelessness of their masters. I believe very few overseers punish their slaves entrusted to them so wantonly, brutally, passionately and cruelly as I have seen a clergyman in New-England punish boys entrusted to him for education.[4] On some few plantations punishment of adult and well-broken negroes is very rare. But it requires a man of peculiar temperament and governing abilities, to efficiently control and direct a large body of persons, dependent on him and subject to his uncontrolled authority, whether they are negroes or sailors, or peasants or children, without the use of the lash or other humiliating punishments.[5]

Are the slaves "happy?"

Any one who thinks that a drunkard can be made happy by supplying him to his full content with the only thing in the world that he craves, might answer this question as it generally is answered by Southern writers and their Northern disciples. And, in this sense, I believe it is true that the negro in Southern slavery is sufficiently degraded to be as happy on an average, as most men are in the world; as happy (in this sense) as the majority of the negroes who enjoy the freedom to live, if they can, in contempt and obloquy at the North.

Are the slaves often separated against their will from their families?

It is astonishing that any one can be so careless as to deny it. In every State of the South, except Florida, Missouri, Delaware, and in Texas, which I have not yet visited, I have known of slaves separated from their families without the slightest indication that it was not a frequent and almost an everyday occurrence. I can show evidence that would satisfy any court that it is a common practice in every Slave State. If any one says that they have never known such a case in their own neighborhood, as our Southern friends often do, and, no doubt, believing that they speak truly, the chances are that if you ask them to let you look at the newspaper published nearest their residence, you will find an advertisement in it of slaves, in which some half dozen will be noted as the children of another, all to be sold singly and with no more restriction as to their future fate than if they were cattle, and at public auction. In a paper now before me there are nine mentioned as of one family, to be sold separately, but the suckling infants of two of them, and the child aged 3 years, and infant aged two months, of a girl aged 19, are to be sold with their mothers. Public opinion is opposed to the sale of old family servants, yet they not unfrequently are sold. I have several friends at the South who have each purchased more than one such, from mere humanity, to save them from being "sold away"—that is, from being separated from their wives and children. It is not a very common thing to sell a slave except "for fault," unless the owner has especial need of money. But this reason for selling a servant will be held over him as a threat, at every trifling occasion for blaming him. It is not common in most communities to sell a single slave, particularly if he is married, without mentioning the intention to do so, to him some time previously, and giving him leave to look about to find some person that he will like for a master, to purchase him. A price is often mentioned at which he is warned to sell himself, or after a certain time he will be sold to the traders. At almost every slave auction, however, the anxiety of the negroes to be purchased by some person living near their old master and their families, and their grief, if they are disappointed, is painfully evident.

    The trade of a slave-dealer is about as reputable at the South as that of a horse jockey is at the North. They are generally considered knaves, and I think *therefore* are not admitted into the society of honorable gentlemen. To say that they are not so, merely because they buy and sell human flesh, is thoughtless, because there are very few of the honorable gentlemen of the South that have not themselves either bought or sold servants.

    I have heard respectable planters speak of their friends as having borrowed money to speculate in negroes. "Negroes are the *consols*[6] of the South," is a proverbial expression with Southerners—certainly indicating the frequent and general transfer of this species of stock. Virginians who visit the North, often angrily deny that any one in that State makes a business of breeding negroes for market. Perhaps not, but I have heard men in Virginia speak publicly of purchasing women with reference to their breeding qualities, and of taking the most suitable care of them for this end. Men speak in railroad cars of "turning off" so many negroes every year, precisely as a Connecticut farmer speaks of "turning off" so many head of neat stock to the drovers every Spring.

    A gentleman whom I visited in Mississippi, to show me that the condition of the negroes in that State was much more desirable than that of those in the Atlantic Slave States—after enumerating certain luxuries and privileges that were generally allowed them there, such as an allowance of molasses and better variety of food generally, a perquisite of money in proportion to the cotton sold, and permission to cultivate cotton, for sale themselves, on Saturday afternoons and holidays—added that the negroes were very much less frequently sold off the plantation and separated from their friends.

"A cotton planter here," he said, "buys all the negroes his credit is good for, and keeps all he can get. Why, in Virginia, if a youngster wants to get a fine horse, or a young lady wants a piano, they teaze their father to sell one of the young negroes to get the money for it; a negro is reckoned just the same as cash." It is undeniable that the human life, sold and exported every year from Virginia, far exceeds in value that of the total of all other of its productions. It is always gratifying to find Virginians ashamed of this, as the cultivated gentlemen and the religious people generally are. The sale and purchase of men, women and children, regarding them so distinctly as property, and property entirely, is such an insult to the human race, that nothing else that disgraces the name of man more demands the shame and the indignant protest of all men who claim to be gentlemen of honor and chivalry.

Are the negroes in Slavery improving and being christianized and becoming fitted gradually for freedom, as was anticipated and expected by the founders of the Republic, both of the North and South, at the time of the Revolution?

Beyond a doubt, the men who signed the Declaration of Independence, and who formed the Constitution of the United States (to judge from the expressions which the most prominent among them are recorded to have made), would be exceedingly disappointed with the present state of things. Not less so would be the men who composed various provincial Conventions in Virginia and North Carolina. Most disappointed would be Jefferson, who even at that early day pronounced in the gravest and most formal manner, in his history of Virginia, that Slavery was a great and dreadful curse upon his native State, the speedy end of which was to be demanded by every consideration of Justice, Humanity and Expediency.[7]

The condition of the slaves is doubtless improving, and has greatly improved since the Revolution, in all the long settled parts of the country, in respect to the kindness with which they are treated. I mean that they are better fed, clothed and lodged, and are less subject to brutal punishment. The present tendency in the Cotton States to the enlargement of plantations, and to gathering negroes in larger bodies, I deem exceedingly unfavorable to their happiness.

The negroes are necessarily acquiring more of the outward forms and habits of civilization and Christianity every day, and many of those engaged in the domestic service of white households, and those living in towns, and the denser and more commercial communities, are growing intelligent, religious and moral. I must doubt if this is the case with the mass. I think they lose as much that is desirable of their original savage virtue from the influence of Slavery, as they gain in character from the influence of Christianity. Manliness, reliability, natural sense of and respect for that which is noble, self-respect and responsibility to conscience, and the natural affections, are all dissipated under the influence of Slavery, and are poorly compensated for by the mixture of formalism and irrational, idolatrous mysticisms, which generally passes with them for Christianity. I am aware that the opinion of most of the religious people of the South does not agree with that which I have been led to form. That of the majority of slaveholders and of all classes, however, so far as I could judge, does so.

There are very, very few Southerners who are not determinedly opposed to the indefinite improvement and elevation of the negroes. If this is doubted, ask any Southerner what is his private opinion with regard to the destiny in the future of the Gulf States, and ten to one, if his answer is made freely and candidly, he will be obliged to admit that his view is incompatible with any great degree of intelligence on the part of the negroes. It is the general belief that in the great cotton, sugar and rice districts, Slavery will, and should, be indefinitely perpetuated. Ignorance and indolence of mind, and want of ambition, energy and intellectual capacity to struggle for freedom, are rightly considered necessary to Slavery.

With regard to the instruction of Slaves, it is well known that in the majority of the States it is forbidden by law to teach them to read and write. Nevertheless, with women and children, higher law notions seem to prevail, and it is not uncommon to find that some of the domestic servants of a family have been taught to read by their mistresses or white playfellows. To express my information as definitely as possible, I should roughly guess that one in five of all the household servants, and that one in one hundred of the field-hands on the plantations of the South, might be able to read haltingly. Half of this number might be able to write intelligibly to themselves. In certain Districts the proportion is much larger.

In this series of letters (which will be concluded with the next number) it has been a minor object with me to show the peculiarities of character and the habits of the Southerners, by describing what appeared to me remarkable in their manner of life and conversation. This class of my observations has been confined, in a great degree, to the less intelligent and cultivated people. It remains for me only to give my conclusions with regard to their condition in general.

It is estimated by a Southern writer, that five-sevenths of the whole white population of the South are non-slaveholders. Of course, this body has the political power to entirely control the destiny of the Slave States. Less information has, nevertheless, been usually given by travelers with regard to them, than the wealthy and hospitable proprietary—and their condition and character is nearly always entirely ignored by Southerners themselves in arguing the advantages of their slave system.

So far as they can be treated of as a class, the non-slaveholders are unambitious, indolent, degraded and illiterate—are a dead peasantry so far as they affect the industrial position of the South. That they are illiterate, will not only have been evident to the readers of the Times, from observations I have given, but may be proved from official statistics. Notwithstanding the constant and immense influx of an uneducated pauper class from Europe into the

FIRST CONCLUSIONS: 1853–1854

Northern States, the proportion of those who cannot sign their names to marriage contracts and other legal papers, is much greater in every Slave State than in any Northern State—so far as the facts have been made known.[8] I am writing in a steamboat, fast aground in the Cumberland River, and cannot refer to the authorities—but they are to be found in all good libraries, and are essentially accurate and reliable.

With regard to their moral condition, I have several times made inquiries of physicians—who almost alone of the educated class, have any valuable knowledge of them—and have invariably been informed that the number of illegitimate children among them was very great; and that many of those living together as man and wife, are never ceremonially married.

That they are non-producers, except of the necessaries of their own existence, is evident from their miserable habitations and other indications of hopeless poverty. I have just been in conversation with a gentleman of Georgia (much the most enterprising of the Southern States) who is returning home after spending the Summer at the North. He observes with regard to the white laboring class: "Poor people in our country seem to care for nothing more than to just get a living. We cannot get them to work steady, even if we give them high wages. As soon as they have earned any money, they quit, and will not go to work again until they have spent it." Of course, as he says, there are some exceptions, but what is the exception at the South is the rule where labor in general is voluntary and not forced.

I have heretofore explained the reason of this—the degradation of all labor which is affected by Slavery. It was very concisely explained to me by a white working mechanic to-day—a foreigner, who had worked at the North, and lately moved to the South to obtain higher wages, but who was returning to the North again, dissatisfied. "Why, you see, Sir, no man will work along side of a nigger, if he can help it. It's too much like as if he was a slave himself."

The mode of life of the greater part of the non-slaveholders—the poor white people in the country—at the South, seems to be much the same. Some of them are mere *squatters*, living by sufferance on the land of others; many own a small body of unproductive land, and in the Eastern Slave States especially, a large part of them occupy a few acres of forest land, which is let to them by the owner for a term of years, on condition that they clear it and perhaps otherwise improve it. They build a small cabin or shanty, of logs, upon the ground, in which to live, with the simplest housekeeping utensils. They raise swine in the forest, and generally own a horse or a pair of cattle, and perhaps a cow—all of the meanest description. They raise on their clearing a meagre crop of corn and a few potatoes, and this, with the game they shoot, furnishes them with food. The women spin and weave, and make most of their clothing. When the land reverts to the owner, they may continue to occupy it by paying him a share (usually one-third) of the corn they raise. They are very seldom observed at work, but are often seen, like young Rip Van Winkle, lounging at the door of a grocery, or sauntering, with a gun and a dog, in the woods.

I speak not less from what I have almost everywhere seen, than from accounts given me by planters of the non-slaveholding class of their own neighborhood, in almost every district I have visited. I may be wrong in supposing such to be the condition of the larger part of the class, when the farmers of the mountain regions and some frontier districts, where few slaves are owned, are included among them; but setting these aside, the condition of the majority of the remainder cannot be much, if any superior, to that indicated in my description.

I think I have had as good means of knowing, and of painfully appreciating the evils which arise from excessive competition, to the laborers of the North, as any man, and I cannot hesitate in affirming that there is no class in the Free States, with the exception of recent immigrants and victims of intemperance, whose condition is not far better than that of the non-slaveholding population of the South. I do not forget the occasional distress of factory hands and mechanics, crowded in large towns. I have been informed of similar distress reaching to an equally painful point in manufacturing towns of the South. The real difference seems to be that the Southern work-people, hoping for less, are less demonstrative of their suffering. The only apology that I can find for the assumption constantly made by almost all Southern gentlemen and by Mrs. Tyler,[9] that evils similar to those arising from over-competition are never found in Slave countries, is the fact of the very slight acquaintance they usually have with the vagabonds that surround them. I have hardly visited a single planter, however, who did not complain of the annoyance which the vagrant and dishonest habits of some of his poor neighbors gave him.

The unfortunate condition and character of these people, so far as they differ from those of the laboring class of the North, is mainly the direct effect of Slavery, and their material, moral and intellectual elevation will be commensurate with that of the negroes. Their ignorance and the vulgar prejudice and jealousy of low minds at present generally prevent their perception of this fact. They may, however, at some future time become a "dangerous class," as they now are a useful one to Southern legislators. Railroads, Manufactures and other enterprises, necessary to be encouraged for the prosperity of the South, will be of more value to them than would be even the gift of common schools. There is no life without intelligence—no intelligence without ambition.

YEOMAN.

---

1. Olmsted wrote this letter c. November 26–27, 1853, while the steamboat carrying him to Nashville, Tennessee, was aground in the Cumberland River (*JT*, p. 29).
2. Olmsted expanded on this subject in an earlier letter:

    The general impression among planters is that the negroes work much better for being supplied with three or four pounds of bacon a week. It seems to me quite probable, that a wholly vegetable diet would be more favorable to health, even with hard-working men, in

FIRST CONCLUSIONS: 1853–1854

this climate, especially in Summer. The above rations, with from two to four pounds of bacon, are what are usually furnished each hand on well-conducted plantations, so far as I am informed. On small plantations, I have been several times told, the negroes sometimes do not have food enough; not so much from the penuriousness of the owner, as because he forgets or neglects to provide in time for them; because his arrangements are not systematic, or because, when from bad calculation, or no calculation, his stores run short, he has no money to replenish them. To anything like a famished condition, it is hardly possible that the negroes can ever be brought. The abundance of poultry they almost always have, the game they take, and the profuse spontaneous vegetable productions of this region in Summer, insure them against famine. ("The South" no. 29, *NYDT*, July 13, 1853.)

3. In an earlier letter, Olmsted had observed:

On the James River plantations, larger houses, boarded and made ornamental, are more common. In these eight families, each having a distinct sleeping room and lock-up closets and every two having a common kitchen or living-room, are accommodated. The single people of the plantation are all attached to some of the families and live in the cabins with them. Generally the cabins of the slaves that I have looked into have been neat and well furnished, and have had an aspect of cheerfulness and comfort that I have rarely found in the dwellings of the poor laboring peasantry of any other part of the world. They are far superior to huts in the Highlands of Scotland in which I have found living very intelligent and well-informed people. ("The South" no. 5, ibid., March 10, 1853.)

4. Whether Olmsted is speaking of punishment that he himself received is unclear, but in later autobiographical reminiscences he mentioned two instances that he may have had in mind when he wrote this letter (*Papers of FLO*, 1: 105–6, 109).
5. In an earlier letter, Olmsted offered the following further discussion of punishment of slaves on the plantation of Richard J. Arnold:

Punishment for slight offenses was administered with the whip, upon the back of the man or woman, without removing their clothes; the whip is a short stick, with a flatlash of leather. For graver offences, the negroes were placed in solitary confinement in a small, dark house or jail kept for that purpose; and of this they had great dread, and much preferred being whipped. I asked how often punishment in any way was inflicted. "Perhaps there will be none at all for three or four weeks; then it will seem as if the devil had got among them, and there is a good deal of it."

In Virginia, punishment is inflicted with a rod or switch of brushwood. In the Carolinas, a "paddle" or ferrule is the common instrument. Overseers are generally instructed not to strike a slave with an instrument which shall materially bruise or injure the skin, as this would seriously affect his salable value, bearing evidence of some bad quality, making severe punishment necessary. Very severe punishment is given, however, with the ferrule or strap, so that the skin is blistered without being broken. ("The South" no. 30, *NYDT*, July 21, 1853.)

6. "Consols" (short for "consolidated annuities") were funded government securities of Great Britain.
7. Thomas Jefferson's classic lament concerning the effect of slavery on the "customs and manners" of Virginia society appears in Query 18 of his *Notes on the State of Virginia*.
8. Since Olmsted is discussing here the condition of nonslaveholding southern whites, he is presumably comparing the rate of illiteracy of whites in the North and the South, as shown by the proportion of adult white illiterates in the total white population. His claim for the absolute superiority of all northern states is inaccurate, but not far from the findings of the seventh census. In 1850 only the two slaveholding states with the lowest white illiteracy rates—Mississippi and Maryland, with 1 in 22 and 1 in 20, respectively—had lower rates than the two free states with the *highest* rates—Indiana and California, with 1 in 14 and 1 in 18, respectively. The free state with the best record was New Hampshire, with 1 in 107, while the slaveholding state with the poorest record was North Carolina, with 1 in 7.5 (U.S., Census Office, 7th Census, *The Seventh Census of the United States: 1850. Embracing a Statistical View of Each of the States and Territories...* J. D. B. DeBow, Superintendent of the United States Census [Washington, D.C., 1853], pp. xxxiii, lxi).

9. Julia Gardiner Tyler (1820–1889), the New York-born wife of ex-president John Tyler, who became an outspoken defender of slavery. Olmsted refers here to a rejoinder that she wrote to a memorial drawn up in November 1852 by the Duchess of Sutherland and a group of English women urging American women to work "for the removal of this affliction from the Christian world." Julia Tyler's reply, addressed "To the Duchess of Sutherland and Ladies of England," appeared in the February 1853 issue of the *Southern Literary Messenger*. In it she pointed to the sufferings of 100,000 persons in the city of London "who rose in the morning without knowing where or how they were to obtain their 'daily bread,'" to the sufferings of the Irish and to the hard lot of British seamen. These were more fitting objects of the concern of English ladies, she averred, than the Negro of the American South, who lived "sumptuously in comparison with the 100,000 of the white population of England" (*Notable American Women*; *DNB*, s.v. "Leveson-Gower, Harriet Elizabeth Georgiana, Duchess of Sutherland"; "Slavery in the United States," *NYDT*, Dec. 15, 1852, p. 1; Robert Seager II, *and Tyler too: A Biography of John & Julia Gardiner Tyler* [New York, Toronto and London, 1963], pp. 402–5).

New-York Daily Times, February 13, 1854[1]

THE SOUTH.

LETTERS ON THE PRODUCTIONS, INDUSTRY AND RESOURCES OF THE SOUTHERN STATES.

NUMBER FORTY-EIGHT—THE LAST.

Special Correspondence of the New-York Daily Times

The Economical, Moral and Political Relations of Slavery

The present number will conclude this series of letters. I have already given a *resumé* of my observations and the conclusions of my judgment with regard to the condition of the slaves and of the poor or non-slaveholding whites of the South, and my impressions, as a traveler, of the character of the people both in the social aspect and as an element in the material condition and prospects of the Slave States. In the present number I shall draw together in a similar way my observations and the conclusions to which they tend, upon the institution of Slavery in its economical and its moral and political relations.

It has been my principal object to inquire into the causes of the great difference known to exist in the industrial condition of the Free and Slave States.

The opinion has been universally formed by previous travelers in the South, and from its inherent probability is commonly received by those who have reflected upon the subject at all, throughout the world, that the institution of Slavery is unfavorable to the success of enterprises involving manual labor as a considerable element of expense. This opinion has, however, of late, been strenuously and confidently opposed by Southern writers on political and industrial economy. The contrary opinion is assumed as an established axiom in a long article on the agriculture of the South in the Government publication called the Patent Office Report recently issued.[2]

The advantages which are to be obtained by the combination of the force of many hands, when efficiently controlled and judiciously directed by a central administration, cannot be doubted. Such advantages are obtained to a greater degree under the Southern system of labor than in that of the Free States, as I have frequently been able to point out, in describing the large cotton, sugar and rice plantations. I have, however, also related many occurrences, of which I was a chance witness on these plantations, which went very strongly to show that where labor is not voluntarily and cheerfully applied to the intended purpose, it is not possible to combine and direct it without either great cruelty to the laborer, or very great (and probably compensating) economical *disadvantages*. I communicated, also, early in the series, a mass of facts and statistical results of actual experience of men interested in sustaining the value of slaves, from which it was demonstrable, in connection with results of my own experience and that of others, some of them also slave-owners, that where this description of labor is brought most closely and distinctly in competition with the free labor in the market, the former actually costs much the most, while it produces much the least.[3] Except in a few cases where slaves were dealt with, measurably, as free men, being virtually paid wages, according to the excellence or amount of their labor, I have almost everywhere observed a depreciation of the standards of labor which obtain at the North, both as to quality and measure.

If, therefore, I have written with discrimination and faithfulness of what I have seen in the South, I am confident that those who have honored my letters with a perusal must have seen convincing reasons for the conclusion, that there are, in the system of labor, with which the South is unfortunately saddled, sufficient economical disadvantages to account for any difference there may be in its industrial prosperity, and that of the adjoining States in which a free competitive system of labor prevails.

The Southern States, in respect to every important branch of industry, are, at the present time, in a peculiarly prosperous condition. In the face of the largest production of Cotton ever known, prices have been sustained at an unusually high point. The case is nearly similar with Tobacco and several other slave labor staples of minor importance. The profits of Cotton growing, however, regulate the prosperity of the South, because the value of nearly all other Southern productions is regulated by the demand of them by the Cotton planters. Especially is this the case with labor, and the price of negroes was never so high, or the trade in them so brisk, as it has been this year. Prime field hands (described as "No. 1, cotton-pickers; guaranteed free from vice or *malady*") are selling in Louisiana as high as $1,400. At a public sale this fall, a large lot of negroes of all descriptions were sold at an average price of $1,800; probably on long credits. A gentleman disposed to be economical, told me lately that being about to marry, it would cost him at least $4,000 to provide himself with house servants. This will illustrate one great cause of difficulty of obtaining capital at the South for associative enterprises. A young man starting in business in the South has a large capital to invest in Slaves. At the North he obtains an equal number of servants, paying them wages by small amounts monthly or yearly out of the profits of his business. He can invest any capital not immediately needed in his stock in trade, in railroads or other public improvements likely to add to his business; and this more especially applies to agriculturists or others requiring a large force of laborers, as servants in limited number can generally be hired at the South, but always only at much higher wages than at the North.

Among the chances of the future I have always looked with confident expectation to a considerable competition with slave labor to arise out of the Chinese emigration to California. I have just observed a newspaper report that the Cumberland Iron Company, on [the] Tennessee River,[4] are about to try an experiment by employing twenty Chinese Coolies in mining and foundry labor. I was at the works of this Company a short time since and heard nothing of it, but I presume the report is true, as the extreme difficulty of procuring laborers and their great cost at present, would be likely to stimulate inquiry and experiment. This Company, as I was informed, own seven hundred negroes, the possession of which doubtless absorbs more than seven hundred thousand dollars of their capital stock, besides which they employ many hired laborers—some free men and some slaves. A million laborers could probably be recruited in China under a contract for a series of years, to be paid one-quarter the wages now paid for the slaves. No such arrangement, however, will be needed to draw a great Chinese emigration after the revolution in China[5] is concluded, the California railroad completed, and lines of packets between San Francisco and Shanghai established.

But every sensible man in the Northern Slave States knows that there would be an immediate profit in abolishing Slavery in those States, even to the owners, if it were not for the profit of breeding slaves. The great question is whether it will ever be possible to substitute any other labor, or bring any other labor in competition with slave labor in the cotton-growing States—whether any other laborers can stand the climate. This is no question to me, for I have myself seen Coolies working steadily and briskly, without a driver, in paddy fields (rice marshes) all day long in a worse climate and in hotter weather than is ever known in cotton-growing districts.[6]

I have not space to enumerate the immense natural privileges and advantages possessed by the South. If the general enterprise and close application, the industry and skill which is used at the North could be applied to their development (as they never can where the mass of the laboring class are hopeless slaves) I have no question that wealth would be accumulated far more rapidly than anywhere else in the world, and in no other land could a dense population exist with more comfort.

A proper appreciation of these natural advantages for the accumulation of wealth, the immigration a knowledge of them will induce, the obstacles in the way of making a profitable use of them (which the destructive system of slave labor, when brought in competition with similar enterprises under free labor, will be more distinctly ascertained to occasion), it is to be hoped, will eventually force the South itself to earnestly search for a solution to the difficulties in the way of the abolition of Slavery. Notwithstanding the apparently overwhelming nature of these difficulties, I have very little doubt that when the South sincerely desires to effect this revolution, and is willing to make the necessary temporary sacrifice to obtain the permanent advantages of it, it will very soon be able to find proper and adequate means to accomplish it.

What the nature of these measures will be, it would be premature and useless at present to hazard a conjecture. In the progress of discovery and invention, in the political changes of the world, and in the changes in the distribution of wealth that may be expected to occur in the future, there will doubtless arise elements affecting the subject of which it would now be idle to endeavor to form an idea. *All* the ordinary machinery of progress is unfavorable to the customs of Slavery. As it was based on injustice it can hardly come to an end without injustice, and the advantage of the mass will have to be secured by the suffering of individuals. These seem to be reasonable anticipations to be formed from the nature of the Institution, and I can think of no other clues offered in the present to unravel its future.

That, in the words of the central organ of the Anti-Slavery party,[7] "the only hope of the peaceful redemption and improvement of the slave population of the South (meaning the abolition of Slavery) is in the South itself," I need hardly declare my conviction—a conviction I believe to be shared by all men who have given the subject any calm consideration.

It has not come within my especial duty as correspondent of the Daily Times on the condition of the South, to consider the moral and political bearings of the institution of Slavery, yet it will be proper for me in this concluding letter to indicate the views I have been led to form on these relations of my subject.

I cannot see how it can be doubted that the beings called negroes are endowed with a faculty, which distinguishes them from brutes, of perceiving the moral distinction of good and evil; of loving the good and regretting the evil which is in themselves. They are, beyond a question, I think, also possessed of independent reasoning faculties. This being the case, it seems to me evident that it was not designed that the mental labor necessary to provide the means of subsistence of themselves and their offspring should be performed mainly by others, or that the responsibility of making such provisions should be taken from them and assumed by others. When it is so, as great a wrong—a much greater wrong—is done than there would be if they were blindfolded and guided through life by another, and as the eye would suffer and be rendered nearly unfit to perform its natural functions by such usurpation, so I believe the soul and mind suffer in Slavery. And as the tyrant who was guilty of such cruelty would not be justified by showing that the man when freed from his tyranny was but poorly able to make his way over a mountain, so I think the condition of the negroes at the North is no justification of permanent Slavery at the South.

Such a condition of things seems to me to be unnatural and unhealthy, and I do not believe that it can ever be made favorable to the objects which Christians believe to be the end for which such beings were created, except by changes which shall be preliminary to and preparatory for its abolition. However, therefore, the exercise of kindness and of uncommon abilities by the master, may, and does temporarily, modify the evils of Slavery, I believe, from the unfitness of the nature of man to live rightly in either of its important relations, it not only is, but always must be, a fearful cause of degradation of manhood, immorality, superstitution and all the evils which in this world attend a disobedience of the laws of Nature and of God.

This theoretic view of the institution of Slavery is confirmed, in my judgment, by the condition of the negroes and of the great mass of the whites at the South. Let any right minded and closely-observant man pass through the South and ask himself what he would sacrifice to save his son or his daughter or his sister from being placed under the moral influence of Slavery, either as a slave or as a self-dependent white, and however charitably or even gratefully disposed he may be, he will hardly think the expression of Wesley, after his visit to Georgia, in the last century, too strong: "Slavery is the sum of all villainies."[8]

But I do not consider slaveholding—the simple exercise of the authority of a master over the negroes who have so wickedly been enslaved—in itself, necessarily wrong, any more than all forcible constraint of a child or lunatic is wrong. And I think the constant assumption of many in speaking on this topic, that it is so, greatly hinders the progress of right and natural sentiment, by arousing prejudice and diverting discussion from the essential and practical wickedness which exists under Slavery.

As a vague charge against all the Southerners, frequently made or implied in Northern publications, it has a bad effect by obscuring the important practical question, whether the South, in its legislation with regard to the negroes which past generations have left in a state of slavery, is doing its duty, and whether individuals who have obtained, or been entrusted with, the control and mastership of these slaves, are governing and using them on principles of justice and Christianity.

Few of those who think it a sin to enjoy the wealth obtained by the labor of purchased or inherited slaves, are very careful to search the channels through which have come to themselves what they term their property, to see whether perchance there be not some taint of dishonesty or cruelty that shall destroy their title.

If we tell the Southerner he steals the labor of his negro, may he not point to our cotton shirts and tell us we wear stolen goods with equal truth; may he not regard the titles under which we hold our own landed property, originally obtained surreptitiously of the Indians, as hardly less sufficient than those under which he enjoys the labor of his negro property?

The term property does not ordinarily convey any other idea than stewardship over certain things which God has chosen to place, under the law of the State, in our hands. Leaving the inquiry as to the limits within which the State can, in the nature of things, construct property, I am willing for the present, to look upon the relation of the master to the negro as that of a stewardship, and am willing that the law should allow the master a reasonable use of the labor of the negro, as the wages of his stewardship. Then comes, I think, the question which the South should ask itself, the true point of the charge which humanity makes against the South, and to which Southerners seldom reply, being wholly taken up in showing the impracticability and unnecessary cruelty of the immediate abolition of all mastership of the weak, ignorant and childish race which Slavery has connected with their property and their homes.

So far as my testimony goes, it cannot be stated too strongly that the government of the negroes of the South, in the present, and independent of all necessities imposed by the past—independent of all necessities arising from the character and capacities of the negro—*Slavery as it is*, in the vast majority of cases, is shamefully cruel, selfish and wicked. It is incredible that the tyrannical laws and customs to which the slave is *everywhere,* and *under every master*, subject, are necessary for any but the most meanly selfish and wholly ungenerous purposes; though individual masters are not always themselves in the least to blame for this. That these laws and everywhere prevalent customs are even favorable to the meanest and most temporarily selfish ends of the cowardly legislators and men of influence in society who make and sustain them, I have not the least degree of faith. On the contrary, I point to the condition of South Carolina, where their unmanly and shameful character is most distinct and notorious,[9] as evidence of the miserable shortsightedness of their policy. Rather it is no policy but the policy of the man, insane with imbecile pride and anger, who inflicts wounds upon his own body. These wicked laws, these accursed privileges given to beings that disgrace the name of man, are wholly inexcusable and can never be justified by outcries at the folly and wickedness of fanatics and demagogues. That the condition of the slaves, as a body, might be immensely ameliorated without the least loss, but with great gain, in a merely heathenish view, to the whites as a body, I have not the slightest doubt.

Why, then, are not these ameliorations accomplished? No one will ask why common, vulgar, narrow-minded, low-lived, proud, selfish and self-willed men oppose them as they are known to, by the characteristic manner of the opposition to them, which is so painfully notorious to the world; but why they are not at least boldly and earnestly advocated, by all the truly sensible, thinking men of the South, if my views are correct, it may be thought hard to answer. The explanation, however, is simple, and to anyone familiar with the thoughts of capitalists and members of the privileged classes throughout the world, will be sufficient. They fear to tamper with the "Rights" of Property.

What is Property? What may be its rights? And what then are its duties? It is not in the South alone that men are found reluctant to have these questions discussed.

But the evil of Slavery to its immediate subjects, is transient and comparatively unimportant. It would be a small thing to prove, were that possible (which I by no means believe), that all this evil to the individual were compensated for by the elevation of the mass. When we trace the influence which Slavery is indirectly exerting, not alone upon the public morals and mind of the South, but upon the moral, intellectual, and material advance of the whole country; when we further watch the reaction of this influence upon the mind of other peoples, and the fate of other nations the world over, we feel that we cannot too much deplore its existence, or struggle too hard to palliate its evils and resist its demoralization.

In my judgment of its ultimate influence, there is no institution in the world, no form of tyranny or custom of society, that is so great an injury, so great a curse upon the whole family of man; nothing that so darkens the evangelical light of Christ, that so obstructs the path of civilization, that so hideously distorts the fair features and manacles the noble form of just, manly, and beneficent Democracy.

Is free discussion of our duty with regard to this system, existing in the States with which our own are incorporated as a nation, with which we are connected by bonds that give our patriotism the same ends, as it has the same memories, to be feared or to be neglected? I cannot believe it. It is our duty, as it is every man's in the world, to oppose Slavery, to weaken it, to destroy it. How and by what means we can rightly do this, it becomes us to study—not in the spirit of cowards, but as sensible and trustworthy men.

Can we abolish Slavery by the direct action of the Federal Government? No more than we can the State Church of England. No more than Great Britain can abolish our Revenue laws, or Austria our Naturalization system. It would not be the right, merely, but the duty, of any Southern State to withdraw from the confederacy if we should attempt it. The act would in itself be revolutionary, and institute a state of war, as would the act of Austria, were she to land a squad of gens d'armes on the Battery, to apprehend Koszta.[10] It may at any time be our duty, and no doubt we shall perform it with alacrity and energy, to defend the independent sovereignty of the Southern States against all *outside force*. It is equally our duty to allow and maintain their clear constitutional right to continue their peculiar institution of Slavery, as it is, and where it is, till they shall themselves see fit to change or abolish it. These are the constitutional duties of the North; duties consistent with our nationality.

There is also a moral duty, one that may at any time involve a political duty, imposed upon the North, with regard to Slavery, by the nature of our Government; and that is to guard against the danger of the power and prestige of our Union with the Slave States being used to extend and perpetuate their unfortunate local system. No one can, I think, honestly believe that such was in the least degree a purpose had in view in the formation of the instrument which defines our mutual political duties. And I for one would rather the Union should be dissolved by the reckless men of the South than that its power should again be perverted to prolong and invigorate this blight upon industry, this disgrace of our country, this curse upon the world. So far as I have been able to judge, the thoughtful and patriotic people of the South are not disposed to allow the attempt to be made. It can never be made except by the most unrighteous abuse of the discipline and organized power of parties. The first duty of every man, therefore, who does not wish to destroy the Union, or to increase the evil of Slavery, is to war against the unfortunate tyranny of parties—not of old parties, only, but of new parties—of parties that are to be.

I think a large majority of the people of the North are opposed to Slavery; not that they are ready in any untimely and unconstitutional manner to destroy this description of property; but that they are altogether unwilling to have the power of the National Government used to improve its value. If such is the case, I think it is not fanatical, treasonable, or impolitic, but exceedingly proper and desirable, both with regard to the designs of Southern politicians and to their own position before mankind, that they should in every appropriate and courteous manner distinctly make it known. Why should we not rather desire to appear before the world as a nation ready, if proper occasion offers, to combat in aid of Liberty, than for the extension of Slavery? In which position have we seemed most desirous to place ourselves during the last ten years?

But is there no active duty in which we can engage at the North, beyond this of forbearance and watchfulness merely? I have declared myself not to be an Abolitionist. The abolition of Slavery must, I judge, be gradual, and must be accomplished by the free determination of the people of the South. Yet the North has a duty to perform and that directly tending to the abolition of Slavery—a duty which every consideration of honor, self-respect, justice and humanity demands of it to perform, and yet to which it is shamefully recreant—a duty in which there is field and scope enough not only for political and social action, but for the most enthusiastic, devoted and self-sacrificing individual labor.

It is *the duty which lies nearest to us.* [11]

It is to deal justly and mercifully with the colored people in our midst, the victims of Slavery, past and present, Southern that is, Northern that was. Everywhere at the South it is asked: "How is it Northern people think us cruel to the negroes? They are only fitted for servitude and are plainly better off in Slavery, where they are taken care of by competent persons, than in the miserable freedom, in the name of which they are persecuted at the North. Look at their condition in the Free States; surely these people are joking when they talk of their being cruelly treated here, or else they are despicable hypocrites. Negroes are not excluded from public conveyances at the South, as we often see them, with violence, at the North. We do not taboo ourselves from them as unclean things with whom contact is pollution. We do not set a second table for them at our Sacramental suppers. We respect their religious organizations, without hesitation, as true churches. We make them our companions and friends; they are our playmates in childhood, the sharers of our joys and our sorrows in age. Our prosperity is to them as their prosperity, and they suffer in our adversity. In the North, although they allow them a certain liberty, as they do wild beasts, they hate them and despise them and loathe them—they neglect them, and cast them out. We look upon them as an ignorant, feeble and incapable people, not to be hated and thrown from us as filthy things, but to be pitied and protected and taken care of as children and idiots. The task is not a pleasant one, and we put them to work to recompense us for doing it, as well as to force them to earn their own living."

In this way of talking, so common with Southerners, there is a great deal of cant, as regards themselves, but the rebuke to us is appropriate and most deserved. South Carolina might with less than her usual absurdity determine to withdraw from the Union, rather than have her name associated before the world with that of such unchristian States as the "Black-laws" of some of those of the North prove them to be. On the Statute book of no Southern State are there to be found laws so disgraceful, so inhuman, so barbarous, so heathenish, under the circumstances, as those of Indiana with reference to negroes— Indiana, which has formerly been reckoned a Free State and a Democratic State![12]

The hopefullest thing that I have seen for the negroes of the United States, slave and free (quasi), was the Rochester Convention last Summer.[13] While we are questioning the possible development of the negro race to an intellectual equality with our own, there meets voluntarily, and at the suggestion of themselves, without any aid or publicly expressed countenance or encouragement of a white man, a large Congress of men of this race, and they remain in session many days, debating and taking grand measures to promote the elevation and improvement of themselves and their brethren, and to obtain their rights as men. It may be doubted if there has ever met a Convention of white men in our country in which more common sense, more talent, more power of eloquence, a higher civilization, more manliness, or more of the virtues and graces of the Christian and the gentleman, were evidenced than in that Convention of the despised Northern negroes. Thank God, at last it proved the negro to be better off in "freedom" at the North than either in "freedom" or slavery at the South; for who thinks that such a Convention could or would be held at the South? Nay, who thinks that a Convention like that, every word of the proceedings of which was a bitter and cutting yet good tempered and appropriate sarcasm, and treasonable defiance of the laws and the customs by which they were oppressed, could be publicly and peaceably held in any country in Europe?

And if it could have been done, would we not respect and love the men who had the will and the courage to prove it?

FIRST CONCLUSIONS: 1853-1854

The supposed inherent inability of the negro to take care of himself, is one of the theoretic legs upon which Slavery stands. There is another almost equally important. It is the same as that on which the social and political degradation of the great mass of the people of Europe is maintained. This is the conviction, very general at the South, that there is something in manual labor, in itself, demoralizing and enervating to the mind, and that there must be, in every country, a large class that is unfitted, by the necessity that is imposed upon them to labor, for the forethought and reflection necessary for the comfortable support of their families, much more for taking any part in the control of their commonwealth.[14] These think that the laboring class is better off in slavery, where it is furnished with masters who have a mercenary as well as a humane interest in providing the necessities of a vigorous physical existence to their instruments of labor, than it is in Europe, or than it will be in the North, when the peculiar advantages to the laboring class which exist in a new country are lost by the increased density of population. These theorists, identical with the aristocratic party of the Old World, point with animation to every instance occurring in our cities or older communities, in which there is evidence either of crime and suffering among the laboring class of people, or of the prevalence among them of ideas, purposes and plans which they conceive to be absurd, radical, dangerous, and likely to interfere with morality or money making.

These people are, at least as often as otherwise, professedly Democrats, and have a consistent democratic theory, in which alone they differ from the aristocratic party of Europe. They do not wish to see any superior classes in our country to their own. A perfect equality of rank of all above the laboring class is what they mean by Democracy, and they will not believe that any *gentleman* seriously approves and desires to uphold anything more than this.

It is not true, then, that the North has no power to hasten the end of Slavery at the South? It can and will (for Hunkerism[15] cannot live) do everything to remove the main hindrances to the liberation of the slave. It can do this by making the best possible use of free labor, by demonstrating that the condition of the laborer is *not* necessarily a servile one; that the occupation of the laborer does *not* necessarily prevent a high intellectual and moral development, does not necessarily separate a man from great material comfort, and that all those blessings to the laborer are attended with no real disadvantages to other classes, but consist with the greatest material prosperity, and the highest good of the whole community.

Yet, mainly, the North must demolish the bulwark of this stronghold of evil by demonstrating that the negro is endowed with the natural capacities to make a good use of the blessing of freedom; by letting the negro have a fair chance to prove his own case, to prove himself a man, entitled to the inalienable rights of a man. Let all who do not think Slavery right, or who do not desire to assist in perpetuating it, whether right or wrong, demand first of their own minds, and then of their neighbors, FAIR PLAY FOR THE NEGRO.

The object of these letters has been to report facts without regard to the opinions of the writer, or of the Editor of the paper in which they have appeared, or of the readers of the paper.

I cannot conclude without expressing my obligations to the Editor of the *Times,* for the perfect freedom with which I have been permitted to give my observations to the public, on a subject which occasions so much bitter and opposing feeling. I allude to this the rather because certain editors at the South were moved soon after the publication of my letters was commenced, to refer to them in a manner which indicated that they were themselves entirely unworthy of the most honorable and responsible calling in which they had engaged themselves.[16]

The Press in our country is so free, and consequently so immeasurably powerful, that it is of the greatest consequence to elevate and sustain the standard of its moral character. I deem this to be greatly injured by insinuations of venality and want of faithfulness of editors of newspapers to the trust which they have assumed, especially of their first duty, to furnish the public according to the best means in their power with true, reliable and accurate information on subjects of public interest. I may be excused, therefore, for stating how very different, how entirely honorable to the Editor of the *Times,* and consistent with the highest view of his duty to his subscribers, was the engagement made with me for the business in which I have been employed.

The Editor of the *Times* had for some time, as I have understood, contemplated sending a Correspondent to the South to perform the duties which have fallen to me. A friend[17] suggested his applying to me for this purpose; at his request I called upon him. The most liberal terms were offered me to go to the South and write a series of letters for the *Times,* under a caption similar to that which has been employed. The Editor did not ask my sentiments on Slavery or any other subject; and the only intimation I received of his expectations as to the matter that I should write, was a request that it should be confined to personal observations, and the expression of a wish that I would not feel myself at all restricted or constrained, by regard to consistency with the general position of the paper or anything else. Full confidence was expressed in my honesty of observation and faithfulness of communication, and no desire or hope or expectation of anything else than this was in any way expressed or intimated. I had never seen the Editor before, but the simplicity of his proposal was so gratifying and flattering to me that I accepted it, without occupying in our whole conversation more than five minutes of his time. I had no other interview or communication with him until after my return, and after the greater number of the letters had been completed. The prominence given to my letters was unexpected.

I do not believe the Editor had any knowledge of my private sentiments on the subject of Slavery, beyond the assurance that they were not such as would prevent my candid observation. He knew me as an agriculturist, as an

FIRST CONCLUSIONS: 1853-1854

employer of laborers at the North, as a traveler, and as an occasional writer for the public, mainly on matters of agricultural interest.

It has been my constant purpose to observe as fairly and accurately, and to report as freely and honestly, as the Editor of the *Times* honored me by supposing that I would.

YEOMAN.

1. Olmsted probably wrote this letter in early December 1853 as he traveled by steamboat from Nashville to New Orleans on his way to Texas. He refers in the letter to his visit "a short time since" to the Cumberland River Iron Works: that visit took place during his trip up the Cumberland River to Nashville, shortly before his arrival in that city c. November 28, 1853 (*JT*, pp. 32-33).
2. "Southern Agricultural Exhaustion, and Its Remedy," the text of a talk delivered at a fair of the South Carolina Institute in Charleston, South Carolina, by the Virginia agricultural reformer and proslavery apologist Edmund Ruffin (1794-1865). Ruffin devoted most of his talk to a discussion of soil exhaustion in the South and ways to remedy it, but he took pains to make sure that his criticism of traditional agricultural practices would not be used to question the efficiency of slave labor (*DAB*; U.S., Patent Office, *Report of the Commissioner of Patents for the Year 1852. Part 2. Agriculture,* H.R. Exec. Doc. no. 65, 32d Cong., 2d Sess., 1853, pp. 373-89).
3. See "The South" numbers eight, nine and ten, above.
4. The extensive Cumberland River Iron Works on the Cumberland River in Dickson County, Tennessee. In *Journey Through Texas*, Olmsted mentioned passing near the works on his trip up the Cumberland River in late November 1853. He related what passengers on his steamboat said about the mining industry, including the fact that one company—presumably the Cumberland River Iron Works—employed a capital of $700,000 and owned 700 of the slaves who worked there (Robert Ewing Corlew, *A History of Dickson County, Tennessee* [Nashville, Tenn., 1945], p. 70; Robert S. Starobin, *Industrial Slavery in the Old South* [New York, 1970], pp. 14-15, 140; *JT*, pp. 32-33).
5. The T'ai P'ing Rebellion (1850-64), a revolt against the Manchu dynasty in China.
6. Olmsted is presumably referring to coolies he saw working on the shores of Whampoa Reach, near Canton, China, in the fall of 1843 (*Papers of FLO*, 1: 56).
7. Presumably the *National Era*, founded in 1847 by the anti-Garrisonian American and Foreign Antislavery Society. At the time of this letter the paper had a circulation of some 25,000 (nearly ten times that of Garrison's *Liberator*), in part because of its serialization of *Uncle Tom's Cabin* in 1851-52. In speaking of the ultra antislavery group in the North, an editorial that Olmsted read in the *New-York Daily Times* of December 29, 1852, called the *National Era* "the central organ of its advocates" ("The Slavery Question," NYDT, Dec. 29, 1852, p. 4; Eric Foner, *Free Soil, Free Labor, Free Men: The Ideology of the Republican Party Before the Civil War* [New York, 1970], p. 105; Russel B. Nye, *William Lloyd Garrison and the Humanitarian Reformers* [Boston, 1955], pp. 135-36).
8. While returning to England from Georgia in 1772, the Methodist preacher John Wesley noted in his journal that he had read a book "on that execrable sum of all villanies, commonly called the Slave-trade." His statements concerning slavery itself were almost as severe. In response to the claim that slavery was necessary, he declared: "I deny that villany is ever necessary, It is impossible that it should ever be necessary for any reasonable creature . . . to burst in sunder all the ties of humanity" (John Wesley, *The Journal of the Rev. John Wesley . . . Enlarged from Original Mss., with Notes from Unpublished Diaries, Annotations, Maps, and Illustrations.* Standard Ed. Edited by Nehemiah Curnock . . . , 8 vols. [London, 1938-], 5: 446-47; John Wesley, *Thoughts Upon Slavery* [London; reprinted in Philadelphia, with notes, and sold by Joseph Cruckshank, 1774], p. 35).
9. By the 1850s the Slave Code of South Carolina was, in fact, not appreciably more severe than

that of other slaveholding states, and was one of only two codes that set minimum standards for the food and clothing furnished to slaves. Olmsted seems here to be adopting the views of Richard Hildreth, whose history of the United States, published in 1849, he cited in his discussion of early South Carolina slave codes in *Seaboard Slave States*. Hildreth described at length the severity of the restrictions and punishments established by the Slave Code of 1712 and concluded that "South Carolina, it thus appears, assumed at the beginning the same bad preeminence on the subject of slave legislation which she still maintains." Hildreth admitted that the Slave Code of 1740, which with revisions remained in effect until the Civil War, dropped some of the harsh provisions of the 1712 statute and added some new safeguards for slaves. Still, he asserted that the new code, "on the whole, was harder than before."

Olmsted's prime sources concerning South Carolina customs in the treatment of slaves were apparently the statements made to him by individuals from other Southern states, as the following passage from *Seaboard Slave States* indicates:

> To this time, whether with justice, I know not, South Carolinians have a reputation generally, at the South, not only of being the most bigoted and fanatical conservators of Slavery, but also of being hard masters to their slaves. I have, several times, been cautioned by other Southerners, not to draw general conclusions with regard to the condition of slaves in the South at large, from what I saw and heard of those belonging to persons born in South Carolina. If this report is unjust to the South Carolinians, I think it probably is not without foundation in some truth; and probably this: that the South Carolina planters have more faith in the Divine right of masters over subjects than those of other origin and education, and consequently are more determined and thorough in the exercise of despotic power. None will deny, at any rate, that there is a difference of this kind between South Carolina planters and all others, nor doubt that it has had considerable influence on the economy, public and private, of the State.

In referring in this letter to the "condition" of South Carolina, Olmsted seems to have in mind the general condition of society there and the implications it held for the fortunes of both the slaveholding class and white society as a whole, but he does not elaborate on the point in this letter. The best indication of his thought appears in the chapter he wrote for *Seaboard Slave States* on the "experimental political economy" and history of South Carolina. In that chapter he made it clear that he viewed society there as one with rigid caste and class boundaries in which a small group of wealthy slaveholders held fast to their political power and property rights, while many nonslaveholders sank into poverty and ignorance. Already the political economy of the state had brought the majority of whites to the point of stagnation. Improvement and progress could come only from outside: either through immigration into the state by free laborers, which would require the end of slavery, or through resumption of the foreign slave trade and the further degradation of free laborers. "South Carolina must meet her destiny," he concluded, and "either be democratized or barbarized." In a final query, he drew together the several themes concerning the present and future condition of the state:

> One hundred years hence, the men whose wealth and talent will rule South Carolina, will be, in large part, the descendants of those now living in poverty, ignorance, and the vices of stupid and imbecile minds. Will they still be taking counsel of their pride, cramming their children with the ancient sophistries of tyranny, and harden their hearts to resist the demands of vulgar Humanity?

(George M. Stroud, *A Sketch of the Laws Relating to Slavery in the Several States of the United States of America. With Some Alterations and Considerable Additions*, 2d ed. [Philadelphia, 1856], p. 17; H. H. Henry, *The Police Control of the Slave in South Carolina* [Emory, Va., 1914], pp. 3-6; Richard Hildreth, *The History of the United States of America, from the Discovery of the Continent to the Organization of Government under the Federal Constitution*, 3 vols. [New York, 1849], 2: 271-75, 421-22; *SSS*, pp. 499-500, 523.)

10. Martin Koszta, whose kidnapping by Austrian officials at Smyrna in June 1853 led to a diplomatic incident between Austria and the United States. The Hungarian-born Koszta took part in his country's revolt against Austria in 1848 and then took refuge in Turkey. In 1852 he accompanied Kossuth to the United States and declared his intention to become a U.S. citizen. Before the process of naturalization was completed, however, he returned temporarily to

FIRST CONCLUSIONS: 1853-1854

Turkey, where he put himself under the protection of the U.S. Consul. Nevertheless, the Austrians there had him seized and imprisoned him on an Austrian warship. The commander of an American warship at Smyrna secured Koszta's release only after threatening to free him by force (Francis B. C. Bradlee, *A Forgotten Chapter in Our Naval History: A Sketch of the Career of Duncan Nathaniel Ingraham, Commander U.S.N. and Commodore C.S.N.* [Essex, Mass., 1923], pp. 7-9; J. F. Rhodes, *History of the United States*, 1: 416-19).

11. An echo of the teachings of Thomas Carlyle in *Sartor Resartus*, which strongly influenced Olmsted. Toward the end of the climactic chapter describing the protagonist's spiritual quest, Carlyle wrote:

> Most true is it, as a wise man teaches us, that "Doubt of any sort cannot be removed except by Action." On which ground too let him who gropes painfully in darkness or uncertain light, and prays vehemently that the dawn may ripen into day, lay this other precept well to heart, which to me was of invaluable service: "*Do the Duty which lies nearest thee,*" which thou knowest to be a Duty! Thy second Duty will already have become clearer. (*Sartor Resartus*, bk. 2, chap. 9.)

12. The Indiana Constitution of 1850 forbade any Negro or mulatto to enter the state, and anyone employing such newcomers or encouraging them to stay was subject to a fine. All fines so collected were to be used for the colonization of any blacks who were willing to emigrate from the state. Those who remained in the state were forbidden to vote or hold office (Emma Lou Thornborough, *The Negro in Indiana; A Study of a Minority* [Indianapolis, Ind., 1957], pp. 68-73).

13. The Rochester Colored National Convention, held in Rochester, New York, on July 6, 7 and 8, 1853. The convention adopted a series of resolutions on means of improving the lot of free blacks, including rejection of colonization and approval of a plan for creating a manual-labor college. The convention also set up four permanent standing committees: one on the manual-labor college, another to protect the civil liberties of blacks, a third to expand the employment opportunities of blacks and a fourth to create a bibliography of writings by and about American blacks and to answer attacks on their character and condition (Benjamin Quarles, *Frederick Douglass* [Washington, D.C., 1948], pp. 123-27).

14. This sentence is presented here in the form that seems to make most sense. The last phrase of the sentence as it appeared in the *Times* is as follows: "that there must be, in every country, a large class that is unfitted for the necessity that is imposed upon them to labor, for the forethought and reflection necessary by the comfortable support of their families, much more for taking any part in the control of their commonwealth."

15. The "Hunkers" were members of the New York Democratic party in the 1840s and early 1850s who sought to suppress antislavery agitation within the party. Their opponents accused them of "hunkering" (hankering) after office and caring more for that than for principles or conscience (James Truslow Adams, ed., *Dictionary of American History...*, 5 vols. [New York, 1940], s.v. "Hunkers").

16. One such instance—and the only one of which the *Times* specifically took notice—was an editorial in the *Savannah Republican* of February 22, 1853, responding to Olmsted's first letter in "The South" series and to the *Times* editorial announcing the beginning of the series. The *Republican* asserted that no Northerner could do justice to the South on the basis of a rapid trip through the section, and deplored any discussion of the slavery question by Northerners:

> We had hoped that the controversy about Slavery was not to be an everlasting one. The Compromise has been adopted—the general judgment of the country has been given in its favor—and there we trusted it would be permitted to rest. The *Times*, however, is not content with the present calm. It sends a stranger among us "to spy out the nakedness of the land." What is its object, if it be not an evil one? If it seeks to render the Northern people hostile to the institution, its labor is thrown away, as that has already been accomplished. If its aim be to make an impression upon Southern minds, its labor is worse than thrown away. Why not attend to your own business, and relieve the misery at your own doors? What good can come of this interminable discussion? You are not responsible for the institution, either as men or as citizens. All your efforts have only bound the chains of the slave still closer to his limbs. You complain that he is not permitted to learn to read and to write, and yet you forced the restriction upon him by scattering incendiary publications

through the State. Many of the disabilities under which he labors have been imposed in consequence of your impertinent interference. This, any well informed man will tell you.

There is one truth which may as well be told now as at any other time. It is this;—*It is not in the power of the North either to abolish Slavery, or to hasten or postpone its extinction. The Union may be destroyed, the land may be drenched with fraternal blood, and laid waste with fire and sword, but the institution can never be removed by any agency of the North. The South alone can give the Negro freedom, and the extinction of the institution, if ever accomplished, will be the deliberate and well matured act of the Southern people.* The Northern people should learn to reflect upon this fact—They may destroy the Government, but not Slavery.

Why, then, continue to agitate the subject? If they are not responsible for slavery—if they can neither hasten or retard its abolishment—if their interference thus far has been a positive injury to the slave—why not drop the subject, and leave us to take care of ourselves? We put this question to the editor of the *Times*, and call upon him and all other Northern agitators to answer it upon their consciences. ("Facts from the South," *Savannah Republican*, Feb. 22, 1853, reprinted in *NYDT*, March 9, 1853, p. 2.)

17. Charles Loring Brace (FLO to Letitia Brace, Jan. 22, 1892).

CHAPTER IV

THE JOURNEY THROUGH TEXAS AND THE BACK COUNTRY

1854

THE LETTERS IN THIS CHAPTER, which Olmsted wrote while traveling in Texas from January through May 1854, deal with the three concerns that were then most immediate for him. One was the Kansas-Nebraska Bill and its implications for the relationship of the South to the rest of the country. Another was his delight with the German settlements near San Antonio and with the friends he made while visiting them. A third was the exciting prospect of the creation of one or more free states in West Texas. The letter from Olmsted's "The Southerners at Home" series for the *New York Daily Tribune* presents the one passage from that series that he did not publish in virtually identical form in *A Journey in the Back Country*. The chapter closes with two of the letters that he and his brother wrote in early October 1854 as they solicited funds with which to aid their new friend Adolf Douai and his antislavery newspaper, the *San Antonio Zeitung*.

To ANNE CHARLOTTE LYNCH[1]

San Antonio de Bexar, March 12th 1854

My Dear Friend,
     I hear from Brace of your return from your European tour and that you have "evidently enjoyed yourself very much." I am very glad to know that, and hope that you also gained health and the foundation for a higher enjoyment of your life at home.
     You probably know of the long tour I had intended to make and how our plans have been in some degree frustrated, causing our long detention in this region.[2] Our journey through Eastern Texas was disagreeable in the extreme—an unpleasant country and a wretched people—bad supplies and bad weather. With Western Texas, however, we have been greatly pleased. The

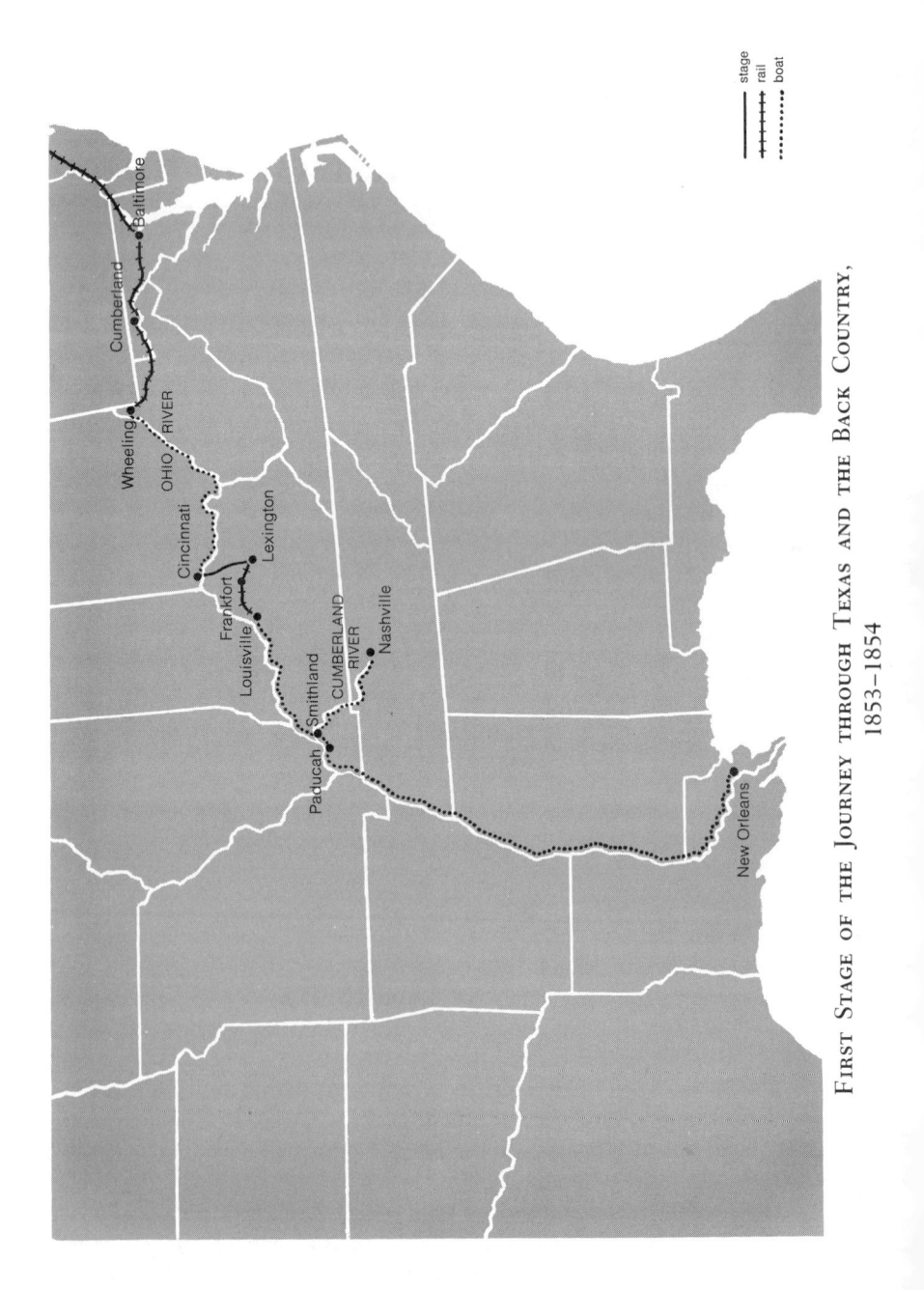

First Stage of the Journey through Texas and the Back Country, 1853–1854

OLMSTED AND HIS BROTHER, JOHN, CAMPING IN TEXAS

country has a great deal of natural beauty and we have fallen among a German population very agreeable to meet; free-thinking, cultivated brave men. We have, indeed, been so much pleased that we have been considerably inclined to cast our lot among them, the doctor[3] especially so. And we now await advices from his wife and the other folks at home, upon which he may determine to become a settler. In that case we remain making the preliminary arrangements, during the summer. Otherwise, we expect to go on to California.

Meantime we are travelling about, without definite aim, in an original but on the whole, very pleasant fashion. The spring here is very beautiful. The prairies are not mere seas of coarse grass, but are of varied surface with thick wooded borders and many trees and shrubs, standing singly and in small islands. Having been generally burnt over or the rank grass fed closely down, they have very frequently a fine, close, lawn-like turf, making an extremely rich landscape. At this season, moreover, there are a very great variety of pretty, small, modest flowers, such as I send you, growing, often very thickly, in the grass.[4] There is an evergreen shrub, rare, and new to me, which is the finest shrub I have ever seen. Its leaves are Acacia-like, but evergreen, bright and glossy like Laurel, and it bears clusters, like those of the Horse Chestnut, of deep blue and lilac bloom, which have a perfume like that of grapes.[5]

We ride and take along with us a pack-mule which carries our tent, bedding and stores. Always in the evening we search out a pleasant spot by some water-side and take plenty of time to pitch our tent securely & make every thing comfortable about us. So we have had from fifty to a hundred pleasant homes of our own selection, construction & furnishing in the most beautiful spots we could find in this great wilderness. It gives me an entirely new appreciation of the attachment of nomad tribes to their mode of life. I was always however much of a vagabond.

As the spring comes on at New York, I hope you may find it agreeable to visit the island.

Your friend

Fred. Law Olmsted

1. The recipient of this letter was probably Anne Charlotte Lynch (1815–1891), a poet who at this time conducted a famous literary salon in New York City.

    The contents of this letter indicate that Olmsted wrote it to an American living in New York City who had recently completed a European trip. The formal tone of the letter indicates that it was written to someone who was not an intimate friend. The expression of aesthetic pleasure in plants and scenery suggests that it was written to a woman, and the fact that Olmsted sent examples of flowers with it suggests that it was written to a woman and/or a botanist. The recipient was also apparently familiar with the fact that Olmsted had a farm on Staten Island and might well have visited it.

    Anne Charlotte Lynch fulfills all of these conditions, and more. She moved to Hartford, Connecticut, with her mother soon after the death of her father in 1819, and lived there until she went to Albany in 1831 to attend the Female Academy there. When Olmsted attended Miss Rockwell's School in Hartford in the fall of 1828, Anne Lynch was also a student there, and years later she recalled leading him to school by the hand. Moreover, she had visited Olmsted at his Staten Island farm at least once—on May 15, 1853. Of that occasion Olmsted wrote his father: "We had a very pleasant visit last Sunday from Miss Lynch. I like her much and shall try to be intimate with her. She is acquainted with all the distinguished people and her taste is highly cultivated, though her verses are as dull as anybody else's except Mrs. Hemans & Mrs. Sigourney and the rest of that sort. I've read several pages of it and retained presence of mind." This letter was apparently part of Olmsted's cultivation of her. After he moved to New York City in the spring of 1855 and was all the more anxious to improve his connections in the city's "literary republic," he frequently attended her salon.

    Charles Loring Brace, who wrote Olmsted that the recipient of this latter had returned from Europe, probably had no childhood acquaintance with Anne Charlotte Lynch. His family did not move to Hartford until the year after she went to Albany, and she did not live in Hartford again; but by early 1852 he had come to know her in New York. He also wrote Olmsted about her activities, and to such an extent that at one point Olmsted reprimanded him for dwelling on her rather than discussing other matters that interested him more at the time.

    Anne Lynch had toured Europe for several months in the latter part of 1853, returning before January 1, 1854. Also, most of the letters she wrote that were reproduced in her *Memoirs* contain the same salutation (unusual for him) that Olmsted uses in this letter—"My Dear Friend" (Laura Wood Roper, *FLO: A Biography of Frederick Law Olmsted* [Baltimore and

London, 1973], p. 7; FLO to CLB, Feb. 8, 1853, above; FLO to JO, May 19, 1853; FLO to JO, July 7, 1855; Vicenzo Botta, ed., *Memoirs of Anne C. L. Botta, Written by Her Friends. With Selections from Her Correspondence and from Her Writings in Prose and Poetry* [New York, 1894], pp. 250–52).

2. Olmsted and his brother had intended to travel beyond Texas to Oregon via Mexico, but were unable to find companions for the potentially dangerous trip through Mexico. Instead, they spent the winter traveling on horseback in Texas and visited Mexico only briefly, with a former Texas Ranger as a guide (JHO to Sophia Stevens Hitchcock, Aug. 13, 1854, William Page Papers, Detroit Institute of Art, Detroit, Mich.; *JT*, pp. 273–355).
3. John Hull Olmsted.
4. Olmsted and his brother had recently completed a three-week trip to the coast through the lower valley of the Guadalupe River. In "A Tour of the Southwest" number nine, which he wrote at this time, he described further the beauty of that region in the spring:

> During the last three weeks I have made a very delightful tour of observation in the lower valley of the Guadalupe. The scenery was often beautiful, and the weather voluptuous with the first warm breath of Spring. The prairies, which had generally been burnt over during the Winter, were just new-clothed in their most agreeable garb of close, short grass, exactly the color of luxuriant young wheat; a few modest and pretty flowers only jeweling the smooth and even verdure. In the valleys of the streams where we usually bivouacked at night, the wild plum was blossoming in abundance, sometimes filling the air with agreeable odor; the willow and elm were swelling their buds and breaking out in curling leaflets. The frogs were piping of the happiness of renewed life under the decay of the tangled rushes, and birds that sing at no other time of year, seemed to be attracted by the whiteness of our tent and gathered in flocks on the branches over it, so as to wake us at daybreak every morning by their sprightly and sportful notes.

5. *Sophora secundiflora,* commonly called frijolito or frijolillo (*Forty Years*, 1: 111, n. 1).

New-York Daily Times, April 24, 1854

A TOUR IN THE SOUTHWEST.

NUMBER EIGHT.

THE REFUGEES FROM EUROPEAN DESPOTISM IN TEXAS.

Special Correspondence of the New-York Daily Times.

San Antonio de Bexar, March, 1854.

Previous to 1848, the European emigration to Texas was largely composed of the least intelligent and poorest class of the German and Germanic-French population. Many were paupers, and some were petty criminals, whom lenient magistrates handed over unpunished to the Emigration Company,[1] satisfied to rid their country of them. There were among them, however, many bold and enterprising young men, some of whom were induced, by special offers, to strengthen and encourage the emigration. There were also a few who accepted the offers of the company merely from love of liberty and discontent with the political and social evils of their native land.

In 1847 the Emigration Company failed. In 1848 the German people burst from the grasp of their masters, but, caught with fair words and perjury, were again held to the ground.

Since then the emigration to Texas has included a remarkable number of high-minded, intellectual and cultivated people. I should judge a considerably larger portion of these than the emigration to the North. A few of them are voluntary emigrants; many have fled to save their lives, having been condemned to death as traitors; many more have been driven to seek a new country from the destruction of their property, or from having all means of obtaining an honest and honorable livelihood obstructed, on account of their acknowledged political opinions, by the management of the police.

Few of this class have been able to bring with them any considerable amount of property, and it is wonderful how they are generally able to sustain their intellectual life and retain their refined taste, and more than all—with their antecedents—to be seemingly content and happy, while the necessity of supporting life in the most frugal manner by hard manual labor is imposed upon them.

One evening, at a log house, after the most difficult and beautiful music of the noblest of German operas, and the dearest and most patriotic hymns of the fatherland had been sung, there were gentlemen, some of whom had had the rank of noblemen, waltzing to gay music with two ladies, each of distinguished beauty, grace and accomplishments. One of the company observed to me, "I think if some of our German tyrants could look upon us now, they would be a good deal chagrined to see how we are enjoying ourselves, for there is hardly a gentleman in this company whom they have not condemned to death or to imprisonment for life."[2]

I have visited one gentleman,[3] the taxes on whose estate, previous to 1848, were not less than $10,000. He had enjoyed unusual advantages of education, even for a wealthy German, and had resided several years in England, in France and in Italy. He had been led to adopt and to publicly express Democratic political views, and, on the breaking out of the Revolution he was called upon by the people to head the first movement in that part of Germany in which he lived. He obeyed the call, tearing himself from his weeping wife on the very day of a deep family bereavement, separating himself from nearly all his relations and former friends, vainly striving to lose a private grief in the enthusiasm of a momentous public struggle. Three months' fighting, and a popular constitution was yielded by their Duke. But soon came Prussian bayonet and reaction, and he was forced to flee. With the moiety of his fortune which he was able to take with him, he purchased a farm in Texas. He has now a comfortable house, a small library, and an excellent musical instrument, and his wife and children are all with him.

He employs no hired laborers on his farm. His two sons work with him till 11 o'clock in the forenoon in Summer, and till 12 in Winter. In the afternoon they are engaged in study. During the last year they have cultivated sixty acres of land, raising 2,500 bushels of corn, besides some wheat, tobacco and cotton. His sons are as fine pictures of youthful yeomen as can be imagined, tall, erect, well-knit, with intelligent countenances, spirited, ingenuous and gentlemanly.[4] In speaking of his circumstances, he simply regretted that he could not give them all the advantages of education that he had himself had, but he added that he would much rather educate them to be independent and self-reliant, able and willing to live by their own labor, than to have them ever feel themselves dependent on the favor of others. If he could secure them here, minds free from prejudice, which would entirely disregard the conclusions of others in their own study of right and truth, and spirits which would sustain their individual conclusions without a thought of consequences, he should be only thankful to the circumstances which exiled him.

One morning in the mountains, we met two herdsmen, riding in on fiery mustangs, at a dangerous gallop among the rocks, searching for cattle. We halted, and were presented to them. One was a doctor of Philosophy from Berlin, the other a baron of ancient and honored name.[5] The latter invited us to call at his "castle," which was appropriately placed on a prominent rocky elevation in the vicinity. We were there received with the most cheerful hospitality and refined courtesy by his lady, who served us lunch, consisting of jerked beef, corn-bread and tin goblets of hot *bouillon*. The baronial residence

VIEW OF SISTERDALE

was made of logs, and had been built entirely by the hands of its owner. The larger part of it he was obliged yet to use as a barn, and the "family apartments" were separated from this by a partition composed partly of deer-skins and partly of calico. The logs were plastered with mud however, the outside door fitted tightly, and, though all the furniture and upholstery was of household manufacture and of the most rude and rustic description, the only essential comfort wanting was—room. This was now the more noticeable from the presence of a late addition to the family, a fine healthy baby, which the Baroness assured us weighed nearly twice as much as children at its age usually did in Germany. There was not the slightest indication of a repining spirit.

It is a strange thing, the like of which, I think will occur to one hardly anywhere else than in Texas, to hear teamsters with their cattle staked around them on the prairie, humming airs from "Don Giovanni," or repeating passages from Dante and Schiller as they lay on the ground looking up into the infinite heaven of night, or to engage in discussions of the deepest and most metaphysical subjects of human thought, with men who quote with equal familiarity, Hegel, Schleiermacher, Paul and Aristotle, and who live in holes in the rock, in ledges of the Guadalupe, and earn their daily bread by splitting shingles.

A gentleman,[6] much beloved by the people of his native district for his benevolence and generosity, who has been President of an important institution for the elevation of the working classes, for several years a member of the Chamber of Deputies, and in 1848, of the National Assembly of Prussia, arrived here a short time ago. I saw him to-day with a spade working on the road-side, a common laborer, earning a dollar a day. This occupation will be but temporary, nor is he under the absolute necessity of engaging in it. He simply prefers it to idly waiting for more satisfactory duties to be offered him.

Another gentleman[7] I have seen to-day, highly accomplished as a scholar, able to converse in six languages, an author; in 1848 the President of one of the Provincial Assemblies of Germany; since then, two years in prison, and finally escaping in the night and coming safely to Texas, where he supports by his labor a large family. I never saw a man more cheerful, strong in faith, and full of boundless hopes and aspirations for the elevation of all mankind, (including Africans.) I have had the no small blessing of being in his company most of the time for several days; not the slightest evidence of disappointment, dejection, or anything of bitterness have I seen in him.

I have never before so highly appreciated the value of a well-educated mind, as in observing how these men were lifted above the mere accident of life. Laboring like slaves (I have seen them working side by side, in adjoining fields), their wealth gone; deprived of the enjoyment of art, and in a great degree of literature; removed from their friends, and their great hopeful designs so sadly prostrated, "their mind to them a kingdom is," in which they find exhaustless resources of enjoyment. I have been assured, I doubt not with sincerity, by several of them, that never in Europe had they had so much satisfaction—so much intellectual enjoyment of life as here. With the opportunity permitted them, and the ability to use it, of living independently by their own labor—with that social and political freedom for themselves which they wished to gain for all their countrymen, they have within themselves means of happiness that wealth and princely power alone can never purchase or command.

But how much of their cheerfulness, I have thought, may arise from having gained during this otherwise losing struggle to themselves, the certain consciousness of being courageously loyal to their intellectual determinations—their private convictions of right, justice, and truth.

Truly, it has seemed to me, there may be a higher virtue than mere resignation, and our times may breed men as worthy of reverence as the martyrs of past ages.

What have not these men lost—voluntarily resigned—that mean and depraved and wicked souls are most devout to gain. And for what? For the good of their fellow men—they had nothing else to gain by it. For their convictions of truth and justice. Under orders of their conscience. In faithfulness to their intellect. And they have failed in every earthly purpose, but are not cast down—are not unhappy. What shall we think of those from whom life was also taken—who as cheerfully and bravely gave their life also?

I was looking at some portraits of gentlemen and ladies—the gentlemen decorated—in a room here, the other day. "Those are some of my relatives that remain in Germany." "And who are these?" I asked, pointing to a collection on the opposite wall, of lithograph and crayon-sketched heads. "These are some of my friends. That one—and that one—and that one—have been shot; that one—and that one—are in prison for life; that one—poor fellow—is in Siberia, and that one—he has been made to suffer more than all the others, I am afraid."

I once, when in Germany, met an American clergyman, who, I have since seen it said in the papers, has been sent to Asia, to teach the Hindoos Christianity; and he was good enough to inform me that all the German Republicans were mischievous, cut-throat infidels; who well deserved to be shot, hung, and imprisoned for life; and that I very much wronged those who were doing this for them, in my feelings about it. He had dined, only the day before, with several of the higher classes, with a number of Prussian and Austrian officers, and he never met with more gentlemanly and kind-hearted men. When I mentioned the fact that one of these officers had, a few days before, knocked down upon the pavements, with a blow of his fist, an aged laboring man, for coming, guiltlessly, into the street with red stockings on,[8] he presumed that he had thought it his duty to do so; harsh measures had to be used to support the laws when the people were so exceedingly depraved. I believe he did not alter my feelings about it, very much; but I confess that these refugees in Texas have taught me something.

"Hate?"—said one of them—"hate? we do not hate. It was with injustice, imposture, oppression, degradation and falsehood, we struggled. We did and do not hate our enemies; they are the growth and the natural fruit of the system which they sustain, and we are only sorry for them. We have no personal enemies. It is an insane enmity that B―― has, because the police killed his wife, and he has never recovered from it; so he still talks of revenge. A healthy mind can have no hatreds. We fought with men because they stood for ideas; but it was the ideas we fought against, not the men."

YEOMAN.

Olmsted wrote this letter in late March 1854, after his return from Sisterdale around the twenty-seventh of the month.

1. The Society for the Protection of German Immigrants in Texas (also called the *Mainzer Adelsverein*), which was organized in 1844 by a group of German noblemen led by Prince Carl of Solms-Braunfels to direct German emigration to Texas (Rudolph L. Biesele, *The History of the German Settlements in Texas, 1831–1861* [Austin, Tex., 1930], pp. 66–110).
2. This event took place at the home of Edouard Degener during Olmsted's first visit to the German settlement of Sisterdale in early February 1854 (*JT*, pp. 196–98).
3. Edouard Degener (1809–1890), born in the duchy of Brunswick, the son of a rich banker whose business he inherited. With the advent of the Revolution of 1848, Degener supported the movement for a republic, served twice in the legislative body of Anhalt-Dessau, and was a member of the first German national assembly, which met in Frankfort in 1848. With the failure of the revolution, he emigrated to the United States in 1850 and settled at Sisterdale. During the Civil War he was imprisoned for several months by Confederate authorities for his Unionist sentiments. During Reconstruction he was a member of the Texas constitutional conventions of 1866 and 1868, and served in the U.S. House of Representatives from April 1870 to March 1871 (Adolf E. Zucker, ed., *The Forty-Eighters: Political Refugees of the German Revolution of 1848* [New York, 1950], p. 286; *BDAC*).
4. Hugo and Hilmar Degener, aged fourteen and fifteen at the time of Olmsted's visit. Both were killed on August 10, 1862, at the Battle of the Nueces, when Confederate forces caught and decimated a group of German men attempting to escape to Mexico in order to fight for the Union (*JT*, p. 196; Guido A. Ransleben, *A Hundred Years of Comfort in Texas: A Centennial History. Revised and Enlarged*... [San Antonio, Tex., 1954], p. 94; Robert W. Shook, "The Battle of the Nueces, August 10, 1862," *Southwestern Historical Quarterly* 66, no. 1 [July 1962]: 31–42).
5. August Siemering, born in Brandenburg in 1830, was the schoolmaster at Sisterdale at this time. He had studied and been a teacher in Berlin. Olmsted's reference may, instead, be to Ernst Kapp (1808–1896), a scholar and geographer and uncle of Friedrich Kapp. He received a Ph.D. from the University of Bonn in 1828 and in 1831 became professor of a gymnasium in Minden, Westphalia. Between 1831 and 1846 he wrote several works on geography. He was imprisoned during the Revolution of 1848 and emigrated to the United States in 1849, settling at Sisterdale in January 1850. The baron that Olmsted mentions was Baron von Westphal (Alexander J. Schem, ed., *Deutsch-Amerikanisches Conversations-Lexikon*..., 11 vols. [New York, 1869–74], s.v. "Siemering, August"; Hermann Seele, *The Cypress and Other Writings of a German Pioneer in Texas*, trans. Edward C. Breitenkamp [Austin, Tex., and London, 1979], p. 109; Samuel Wood Geiser, "Chronology of Dr. Ernst Kapp [1808–1896]," *Southwestern Historical Quarterly* 50, no. 1 [Oct. 1946]: 296–300; R. L. Biesele, *German Settlements*, pp. 171–72).
6. Unidentified.
7. Olmsted is probably referring here to Adolf Douai. Much of the description is accurate: Douai was a scholar and author and knew several languages. He also had a large family that he supported by his own labor on the *San Antonio Zeitung*. He possessed the strong faith and aspiration for the elevation of mankind that Olmsted describes. Since he accompanied Olmsted and his brother on their first trip to Sisterdale, he is the only German in West Texas of whom Olmsted could truly say that he had been "in his company most of the time for several days." The part of the description which does not fit Douai is that dealing with the man's role in the German revolution of 1848. That discrepancy could well be due to a difference between the

account that Douai gave Olmsted in 1854 and the version that he set down in his autobiography years later. In any event, Douai was simply a delegate to the provincial landtag of Saxe-Altenburg, and not the president of the body (although he did claim in his autobiography to have been chairman of the Finance Committee). Moreover, he did not spend two years in jail, although he was imprisoned three times, for a total of twelve months, during the period 1848-51; and he did not escape from jail. Olmsted apparently thought that Douai had escaped from jail just before immigrating to the United States, however, since he made that assertion in his "Appeal for Funds for the *San Antonio Zeitung*" of early October 1854 (Adolf Douai, "Autobiography," pp. 41-42, 46, 56-57).

8. The incident that Olmsted describes here must have taken place during his tour of Germany with Charles Loring Brace and his brother, John, in the summer of 1850. German authorities had recently put down the revolutions of 1848 and were still vigilantly watching for signs of insubordination. They apparently interpreted the wearing of red clothing—the color adopted by the revolutionaries—as a gesture of defiance.

New-York Daily Times, May 13, 1854

A TOUR IN THE SOUTHWEST.

The Nebraska Question in Texas—Position of Gen. Houston—How it Affects the Slaveholding Interest.

Special Correspondence of the New-York Daily Times

San Antonio de Bexar, Texas,
Tuesday, April 18, 1854

The Nebraska excitement[1] scarcely reaches Texas. The intelligent large planters are generally gratified and grateful to Senator Douglas for his unexpected and gratuitous offer, but consider it of doubtful value to themselves in particular, because the opening of Nebraska to slave-settlers would bring its lands in competition before immigrants with those in Texas, and most wealthy Texans are extensive land-owners and speculators as well as slave-owners. For this reason they are reconciled to the vote of Houston[2] against the measure, and the absence of Rusk[3] from the Senate when the vote was taken.

The poorer class of Americans know little about the matter, and are indifferent. The Germans alone are led to think and reflect. To assist them, you will be surprised to learn that a translation of Mr. Seward's speech in the Senate[4] has been extensively circulated under the frank of Gen. Houston.

"*Der alte Fuchs!*" (the old fox!) I heard one of them exclaim, as he observed this significant circumstance.

There is a difference in the political sentiment of the people of the

North and the South, with which, during all my extended tour, I have been more and more painfully impressed.

Patriotism at the North is much more generous and national in its application than it is at the South. There are evident indications of this in the action and speeches of public men, particularly on any subject in which the most jealous and sensitive inquisitiveness can suspect a danger of overlooking all the possible rights of the States in their individuality. But in the general conversation of the people in public affairs, it is much more manifest. When it is a question of internal policy, you never hear it discussed, except as to how the interests of the South are to be affected. The North is looked upon with a constant jealousy. Her prosperity is considered to have been in some way obtained at the expense of the South, and there is constant reference made to the supposed efforts of Northern people to *overreach* the South. Ninety-nine people out of a hundred at the South talk of Northern statesmen and politicians, as only our extreme Anti-Slavery agitators represent those of the South, as cunning Yankee tricksters in politics.

Southerners are patriotic, intensely patriotic, but *the South* is not patriotic. The patriotism of Southerners, in proportion to its intensity, is concentrated. It centres between a man's heels. The patriotism of the Northern people is broad and generous; it is national, and centres at Washington. I speak of patriotism as a sentiment—an interior spring of the mind, influencing its determinations independently of assignable reasons. The North feels towards the South as if it were a part of itself—honors it and glories in it, and sorrows for it and with it, as bone of its bone and flesh of its flesh. The South loves the North as its business partner, and cares for its glory and success only so far as it is reflected upon itself, and accrues to the honor, safety, and wealth of itself.

The dissolution of the Union, as an economical measure, has never been conceived of by a Northern mind. The extremists of the North have urged that union with the South, under certain circumstances, made the North responsible for the iniquity of the laws of the South, growing out of its determination to sustain and perpetuate the institution of Slavery; they have, therefore, attacked the Constitution of the Union as morally wrong. They have gone further; they have declared that because it was wrong it was not binding, and they have acted consistently in this, that while they repudiate for themselves a share in the wrong, they decline to use the privileges which it confers upon them. They refuse to vote. They are politically disarmed. As a power of the North, opposed even upon moral grounds to the purposes of the South, they are practically non-combatants.[5]

But the men of the South, who, when the North has been suspected of a disposition to restrict them in the employment of certain means of improving their property—means of doubtful constitutional integrity, of doubtful morality, and of evident national inexpediency—have advocated, and labored to effect, a secession of the Slave States. Such men suffer themselves, and are suffered by others, not merely to act politically, but to occupy positions of great honor and influence.

Examine the proceedings of the Conventions of these factionists,[6] and you will find that they are as impracticable, as fanatical, and as unfit for meddling with public affairs, as the most insane Abolitionist. They are certainly the counterparts of the extreme Anti-Slavery men of the North, except that the latter profess to be influenced by moral arguments, and they only by rage and selfishness—partriotic selfishness.

Suppose that instead of the heroic General Pierce,[7] of New-Hampshire, the equally heroic General Pillow,[8] of Tennessee, or General Quattlebum,[9] of South Carolina, had been our President, would his own party in the North itself have been gratified—would any one have thanked him for his generosity, and considered it as a peculiar expression of his love for the Union, had he chosen for his Secretary of War that very brave and talented citizen of Massachusetts, Theodore Parker?[10] Theodore Parker has not expressed hostility to the Union more strongly than Jefferson Davis.[11]

If a Southern President had turned out a Virginian, at a time when his severe labors were nearly approaching an honorable conclusion, and had put in his place a citizen of Ohio, who should immediately destroy a great part of the results obtained by the labor of his predecessor, the subserviency to party power in our country might let it pass without indignation; but if the new appointee to the directorship of the Census of the United States[12] had been the editor of the *Emancipator,*[13] or even the gentlemanly, cautious and moderate Anti-Slavery editor of the *National Era,*[14] no one will believe that it would have been hailed anywhere at the North as a most appropriate, suitable, and broadly patriotic appointment.

The reputation of Mr. DeBow, the present Commissioner of the Census, as an extremist of the Slavery school of politics, is not less notorious than that of Mr. Garrison or Dr. Bailey among the Anti-Slavery agitators, and his private sentiment of enmity towards the North and devotion to the peculiar interests of the South, are so strong that I have heard him spoken of by one of his friends as in a condition approaching insanity on the subject.

President Pierce, on his acquisition of office, almost immediately removed certain of the Territorial Judges in whose Courts the legality of holding slaves is expected to be tried. I think there were three such removals of Judges on what were supposed to be, of course, merely party grounds; an action of the Executive power unprecedented, with but two excusable exceptions, in the history of our Government.[15] Suppose that the remaining Judges were all Northern men, and that the President should have proposed to fill the vacancies he had thus created with Northern men—men having a private pecuniary interest, if it were possible, in the contraction of the market for slaves, as all slaveholders have in its extension—would it have met with general approval at the North; would it have been considered at the South as a wise, suitable and just proceeding? But the counterpart of this was the action of our President; and it passed entirely unnoticed at the North, and the patriotism of the South was in no way ashamed to accept it as proper and common-place.

I do not wish to dampen the patriotism of the North. I hope that love for our whole country, and a spirit of justice and severe good faith, may, if possible, be strengthened as a ruling influence in our politics, by the present excitement. But I trust that the conviction will not be lost, after the excitement occasioned by this Nebraska plot shall have subsided, that it is not safe to carry the spirit of conciliation so far as to give the ultraists of the South all those offices and opportunities for effecting their purposes which they most desire, while those of correspondingly extreme Northern views are excluded from the slightest direct political power.

Congress and the General Government will always "bear watching" in their action upon questions into which Slavery enters as an important element of consideration, for another reason, the value of which is scarcely at all appreciated at the North. No strong opposition to the designs and wishes of the South can ever have been made by individuals at the North from pecuniary considerations. Anti-Slavery principles improve no man's property. But there is not probably a single Southern member of Congress or Cabinet Secretary or departmental functionary, who has not a direct pecuniary interest in strengthening, enlarging and perpetuating the institution of Slavery. Any vote to weaken, restrict or decrease the permanence of Slavery, given by a Southerner, must be given solely from considerations of the general good—from patriotism and in good faith, in opposition to his immediate private pecuniary interests. For example, the introduction of Slavery into Nebraska will so much enlarge the field of slave labor, as to probably increase the demand for slaves sufficiently to add 5 per cent to the value of each—in the same way that when the field of commerce was enlarged by the discovery of gold and the consequent immigration in California, the general value of ships was increased some twenty per cent. The owner of a ship of the value of $50,000 thus became $10,000 richer in a few months. The arch rowdy of our country,[16] to gain the confidence of the South, some years since boasted in the Senate that he was the owner of a considerable number of slaves, having acquired them by his marriage. Suppose them to be one hundred in number—at the late current prices they may be considered to be of the value of $800, on an average, each. He gains then $4,000 directly, by the passage of his Nebraska bill. Indirectly, by gaining power for the general slave property interest, for future operations, his private pecuniary advantage is much greater.

I know a gentleman in Kentucky who owns nearly one hundred slaves, which pay him a very small interest on their value. He told me he would have sold them this Winter to go South, but he believed if a Slave State could be obtained on the Pacific coast, as he had reason to hope there might be in two years from this time, slave property would be increased in value nearly one hundred per cent., and he should continue his investment in that anticipation.

It will be evident that this gentleman could well afford to give $50,000 to effect the passage of the Nebraska bill, the ratification of the Gadsden Treaty, the construction of the Southern Pacific Railroad, and the annexation of the Walker Republic[17] as slave territory to the United States. I know of one other Southern gentleman who makes no secret that he has spent $40,000 during the last year, in furtherance of these schemes, and considers it a good investment.

Consider the immense power which these speculators have when the patronage of the Federal Government is placed in their hands. Honorable and honest speculators and officers though they be, are they to be expected to know "no North, no South," in the disposition of this patronage?

It is true that but a small proportion of the people of the South have this personal interest in wresting power from the North, but this small proportion have the *money power*, and the ignorance and stupidity of the poorer class at the South is so great that it possesses the means of almost absolute control of public opinion. It has been generally noticed by editors at the North how falsely and incompletely the newspapers with which they exchange at the South represent the public sentiment of the North on the Nebraska business. Hon. John M. Botts, of Virginia, also justly complains of this, in his letter on the subject in the *National Intelligencer*.[18] It has come within my knowledge that the promise of a considerable job of work, which had been given to a poor but worthy young printer, has been lately retracted, because there was issued from his office a newspaper of small local circulation, into which articles of the Daily Times and other Northern papers, indicative of the general sentiment of the North, had been copied, though without editorial endorsement; and another printer is to have the work, because he publishes a paper in which only the views of *Arnold* Douglas[19] and others of that sort have been placed before the people. Censorship of the press is a tyranny of European despotism from which we are happily exempt. "*Non nobis*," etc.[20]

YEOMAN.

---

1. A reference to the controversy stirred up by the Kansas-Nebraska Bill, which Senator Stephen A. Douglas of Illinois introduced on January 23, 1854, and which the Senate passed on March 4. House action on the bill began on March 21 and was climaxed by a debate on the floor of the House that lasted from May 8 until the bill's passage on May 25. President Franklin Pierce signed the bill into law on May 30 (Robert W. Johannsen, *Stephen A. Douglas* [New York, 1973], pp. 415, 428–34).
2. Sam Houston (1793–1863), the hero of the Texas war for independence and at this time a U.S. senator from Texas (*DAB*).
3. Thomas Jefferson Rusk (1803–1857), a leader in the Texas war for independence and thereafter an advocate of annexation to the United States. He was a U.S. senator from Texas from 1846 until his death (ibid.).
4. A speech delivered in the Senate on February 17, 1854, in which New York senator William H. Seward attacked the Kansas-Nebraska Bill's abrogation of the Missouri Compromise (Allan Nevins, *Ordeal of the Union*, vol. 2, *A House Dividing, 1852–1857* [New York and London, 1947], p. 140).

5. A reference to the Garrisonian abolitionists, who combined pacifist doctrines of nonresistance and "no government" with their demands for the abolition of slavery. William Lloyd Garrison offered the classic statement of their refusal to engage in political activity in the "Declaration of Sentiments" that he drew up for the New England Non-Resistance Society in 1838:

> As every human government is upheld by physical strength, and its laws are enforced virtually at the point of the bayonet, we cannot hold any office which imposes upon its incumbent the obligation to compel men to do right, on pain of imprisonment or death. We therefore voluntarily exclude ourselves from every legislative and judicial body, and repudiate all human politics, worldly honors, and stations of authority. If *we* cannot occupy a seat in the legislature or on the bench, neither can we elect *others* to act as our substitutes in any such capacity.

(Wendell Phillips Garrison and Francis Jackson Garrison, *William Lloyd Garrison 1805–1879: The Story of His Life Told by His Children*, 4 vols. [New York, 1885–89], 2: 230–34; Peter Brock, *Radical Pacifism in Antebellum America* [Princeton, 1968], pp. 113–69.)

6. A reference to the response by Southern extremists to Northern opposition to the expansion of slavery as expressed in the Wilmot Proviso and in Northern efforts to block enforcement of the Fugitive Slave Law of 1850. The second meeting of the Nashville Convention in November 1850 was the occasion for several speeches advocating secession, although that body finally called for a future Southern rights convention instead. A more recent gathering that Olmsted probably had in mind was a South Carolina state convention of May 1852 that affirmed the state's right to secede, although declaring secession to be inexpedient at the time. During this period, meetings of states' rights parties that advocated secession were also held in Mississippi, Georgia and Alabama (Harold S. Schultz, *Nationalism and Sectionalism in South Carolina, 1852–1860* [Chapel Hill, N.C., 1950], pp. 26–42; Philip M. Hamer, *The Secession Movement in South Carolina, 1847–1852* [Allentown, Pa., 1918], pp. 38–60, 139–43; Robert R. Russel, *Economic Aspects of Southern Sectionalism, 1840–1861* [Urbana, Ill., 1924], pp. 73–78; FLO to CLB, Nov. 12, 1850, *Papers of FLO*, 1: 358–62).

7. Franklin Pierce received a political appointment as brigadier general in the U.S. Army at the beginning of the Mexican War, and raised a regiment of 2,500 men. In late May 1847 he embarked with them for Vera Cruz, and then directed a three-week march to join the forces of Winfield Scott at Puebla, 150 miles inland. On the march, Pierce commanded his troops in two sharp, if brief, encounters with Mexican troops. During the rest of the campaign to capture Mexico City, however, military glory eluded him. At the beginning of his first real battle, that of Contreras, his horse shied at the artillery fire and fell, giving Pierce a wrenched knee and painful internal injuries. A subordinate officer then assumed command of his brigade, and a rumor went through the army that the change of command was due to a cowardly failure by Pierce to lead an advance. The suspicion remained, and Pierce's injuries—coupled with the onset of diarrhea—kept him from demonstrating courage or military ability during the rest of the campaign. In the presidential canvass of 1852 the Whigs revived the old charges of cowardice, which made Pierce compare unfavorably with the Whig candidate, his old commander, Winfield Scott (Roy Franklin Nichols, *Franklin Pierce, Young Hickory of the Granite Hills* [Philadelphia and London, 1931], pp. 147–67, 209).

8. Gideon Johnson Pillow (1806–1878), who gained notoriety as a "vain, ambitious, quarrelsome, and unsuccessful soldier." Appointed as a brigadier general (later major general) in the Mexican War by President James K. Polk, his former law partner, Pillow fought a series of battles under General Winfield Scott that were followed by angry quarrels with Scott himself. Pillow played a leading part in the Nashville Convention of 1850 that formulated Southern demands—in the face of Northern personal-liberty laws—that all parts of the Compromise of 1850, including the Fugitive Slave Law, be enforced. He opposed the demands made for secession by the more radical delegates to the Convention, however (*DAB*).

9. Paul Quattlebaum (1812–1890), South Carolina soldier, politician and industrialist. In 1836, as captain of a South Carolina militia company fighting the Seminole Indians in Florida, he nearly captured the Seminole chief Osceola, and did capture much of the chief's ceremonial clothing, including a "handsome head-gear of beautiful ostrich-plumes." This exploit gained him considerable popularity in South Carolina. In 1843 he became a brigadier general in the South Carolina Militia and held that command for ten years. Unlike Pierce and Pillow, he did not fight in the Mexican War. Quattlebaum was active in politics, serving in the South

Carolina House of Representatives from 1840 to 1843 and in the state senate from 1848 to 1851. He was an ardent supporter of nullification and in time became a secessionist and a signer of the South Carolina Ordinance of Secession (Paul Quattlebaum, *Quattlebaum, a Palatine Family in South Carolina* [Conway, S.C., 1950], reprinted from the *South Carolina Historical and Genealogical Magazine* 48, no. 2 [April 1947]: 84–87).

10. In his many speeches and sermons against slavery, Theodore Parker consistently invoked the "higher law" argument that it was a man's duty to obey the law of God, not that of man. Accordingly, he attacked the Fugitive Slave Law of 1850 and even the U.S. Constitution itself. In his first sermon on slavery in 1841, he stated a conviction that he would repeat many times in the next two decades: "I know that men urge in argument that the Constitution of the United States is the supreme law of the land, and that it sanctions slavery. There is no supreme law but that made by God; if our laws contradict that, the sooner they end or the sooner they are broken, why, the better" (Henry Steele Commager, *Theodore Parker* [Boston, 1936], pp. 205ff.).

11. After the death of John C. Calhoun in 1850, Jefferson Davis became the leader of the "Southern Rights" faction of the Democratic party in the U.S. Senate; as such, he opposed the Compromise of 1850. In 1852, after serving only two years of his Senate term, Davis resigned in order to run for governor of Mississippi as the Democrats' anti-Compromise or "Resistance" candidate against Henry S. Foote, the candidate of the Union party, which was an alliance of Whigs and pro-Compromise Democrats. Davis himself did not call for the immediate secession of the South as a response to the unsatisfactory nature of the Compromise of 1850 and its enforcement in the North, but the Mississippi Resistance party, under its earlier gubernatorial candidate, John A. Quitman, did call for secession, having been formed for that purpose (Hudson Strode, *Jefferson Davis*, vol. 1, *American Patriot, 1808–1861* [New York, 1955], pp. 203–34, 222–25).

12. In March 1853, Franklin Pierce appointed James D. B. DeBow (1820–1867), a Louisiana Democrat and Southern nationalist, as secretary of the U.S. Census in place of Joseph C. G. Kennedy (1813–1887), a Pennsylvania Whig. Although DeBow did not make great changes in the work already done under Kennedy's direction in designing the form of the census of 1850, he had been an outspoken critic of Kennedy's work (Otis Clark Skipper, *J. D. B. DeBow: Magazinist of the Old South* [Athens, Ga., 1958], pp. 69–76; *DAB*).

13. The *Emancipator* was the organ of the American and Foreign Anti-Slavery Society, and was edited by Joshua Leavitt. Olmsted's mention of the *Emancipator* in this place was probably a mistake: his naming of William Lloyd Garrison in the following paragraph indicates that he was probably thinking instead of the *Liberator* (*DAB*).

14. The editor of the *National Era* was Gamaliel Bailey (1807–1859) (ibid.).

15. Olmsted is referring to the attempt by Franklin Pierce to control the three-man supreme courts of the Oregon and New Mexico territories by removing two members of each court and replacing them with his own appointees. When Pierce submitted the names of his replacements for the Oregon court on March 15, 1853, the Senate delayed its decision and on the next day considered the matter in secret executive session. Apparently in response to assertions by some senators that the president did not have the power to remove territorial judges for no cause, Senator George Badger of North Carolina submitted a resolution which called for Senate recognition of the power of the president "to remove a Territorial judge from office although appointed for a term of four years, and although there may be no power of removal reserved to the President by the law creating such office." On April 4 the Senate approved the Badger resolution by a vote of 25 to 9. By April 8 the Senate had approved Pierce's replacements for the four men he had removed from the Oregon and New Mexico courts, as well as for two men he had removed from the court of the Territory of Minnesota. As Olmsted observes, Northern newspapers hardly took notice of this proceeding (See U.S., Congress, Senate, *Journal of the Executive Proceedings of the Senate of the United States of America* [Washington, D.C., 1887], 9: 65, 67, 73, 74, 81, 84, 89, 90, 95, 126, 128, 129, 131, 132, 142, 143, 145, 147, 149, 155, 156, 160, 166).

16. The "arch rowdy of our country" was Senator Stephen A. Douglas (1813–1861), author of the Kansas-Nebraska Act—as Olmsted's reference later in the paragraph to "his Nebraska bill" indicates. Douglas's biographer reveals that, at least prior to his marriage in 1847, the senator showed little of gentlemanly manners or social grace: "Deficient in elegance, his bearing contained 'a dash of the rowdy.' His manners were described by some as downright coarse.

Informal and careless of his dress, Douglas smoked cigars, drank whiskey, and worst of all, chewed tobacco, the one 'bond of brotherhood among all western men'." After the death of his first wife, Martha Martin, in January 1853, Douglas neglected his apperance and increased his drinking, and it is probably to his conduct in that period that Olmsted especially refers.

Martha Martin was the daughter of Colonel Robert Martin, one of the wealthiest planters in the upper Dan River region of North Carolina. As a wedding present, Martin offered the couple a cotton plantation he owned in Mississippi, complete with its slaves. Douglas declined, suggesting that the colonel transfer the property in his will instead. When Martin died in 1848, Martha inherited the plantation of over 2,500 acres and over 100 slaves. Martin's will ensured that Douglas could not inherit the slaves from her: they were to pass to her children, or, if she died without issue, they were to be freed and colonized in Liberia. Douglas, however, was to serve as manager of the property for his wife, and was to receive 20 percent of its annual income (R. W. Johannsen, *Stephen A. Douglas*, pp. 206–11, 381, 451).

17. The American adventurer William Walker (1824–1860), who is best known for his conquest of Nicaragua in 1855 and the establishment of a short-lived republic there. Olmsted's reference here is to Walker's brief 1853 conquest of Baja California and Sonora, Mexico, where he proclaimed an independent republic (*DAB*).
18. John Minor Botts (1802–1869), a Virginia Whig and U.S. congressman from 1839 to 1843 and from 1847 to 1849. At this time he was practicing law in Richmond, Virginia. Botts was a strong opponent of secession and of the Southern Rights Democrats. In a letter of February 11, 1854, to the *National Intelligencer,* he attacked the Kansas-Nebraska Bill as "the most mischievous and pernicious measure that has ever been introduced into the halls of Congress" (*DAB*; *BDAC*; "On The Nebraska Question. A Letter From Mr. Botts," *National Intelligencer*, Feb. 16, 1854, p. 2).
19. A play on Douglas's full name, Stephen Arnold Douglas, suggesting that he was a traitor with a traitor's name.
20. Part of the title, "Non Nobis, Domine," of Psalm 115 (which is given in Latin in the Episcopal *Book of Common Prayer*); it means "not unto us" and is the first phrase of the Psalm, which begins, "Not unto us, O Lord, not unto us, but unto thy name give glory, for thy mercy, and for thy truth's sake."

New-York Daily Times, May 18, 1854

A TOUR IN THE SOUTHWEST.

NUMBER TEN.

German Immigrants of the Middle Class in Texas—Education at the South.

Special Correspondence of the New-York Daily Times

San Antonio de Bexar, April, 1854.[1]

In a previous letter[2] I have described to you the exceedingly honorable character supported by those German people of Texas who, in Europe, enjoyed the luxuries and advantages of education and wealth, and who have been driven to emigrate hither by persecutions of the police, and other misfortunes arising from their political views. These form a remarkably large number of the recent emigrants. The great mass, however, consists of young men of the middle and lower orders of society, who, if they had remained in Germany, would have been liable to be reduced, by the various restrictions and taxes on business and by the oppressive guild-laws of the handicraftsmen, to live almost hopelessly in the condition of laborers struggling against starvation. Many of these have been educated with care and in the midst of considerable comfort, but are wholly unprovided with capital.

This class of immigrants find immediate employment on the farms here, at such a rate of wages that, in from two to four years' time, they can always themselves become landholders, and be wholly independent of others— at least, for a mere personal livelihood. I have often found such young men clubbing together, either for the purchase or rent of land; and a picture of the condition of a family of this class, with a single man in partnership, established on a farm of their own, four years after immigration, I have given in a previous letter. The small number of women that immigrate occasions many bachelors to be their own housekeepers. Frequently, however, as soon as they have obtained the necessary means, they send to Germany for the betrothed, whom they have been obliged to leave there, to come and join them.

I am writing from a camp in the mountains. Near us there are several of these young Germans, who have either bought or rented or squatted upon land, which they cultivate and live upon, in small cabins or huts, alone, or in partnership with one another. There are four living together in one cabin. Two of them are mechanics, and earn a dollar and a quarter a day in the employment of the wealthier farmers; the others rent and work together a piece of land—the capital of the four being combined in the purchase of horses, cattle and swine, which, with their increase, are cared for and employed in their labor by the agriculturists.

Many of these young men, either with a little capital that they have been able to bring with them, or which they have earned by labor here, or with borrowed capital, become tradesmen, and I have not been in a single town in Texas in which I have not found at least one of these German shop-keepers established. Owing to their frugal manner of living and their habitual exactness of calculation and close attention to their business, the German tradesmen almost invariably make money rapidly. As soon, however, as they have acquired sufficient capital, instead of extending their business, they commonly sell out to new comers, and purchase land and stock and settle as farmers and graziers. I know one who six years ago commenced keeping a store in a small country town, with a capital of only three hundred dollars, who now owns several thousand acres of land, besides town houses which he rents, and other property, which altogether must be worth considerably more than twenty thousand dollars. He lives on a farm with a wife he had left in Germany from want of ability to bring her with him when he emigrated, and I have lately seen him among his hired laborers, guiding a plow with his own hands, no less industrious than when seven years ago he solicited employment as a laborer for himself.

It is the same with mechanics; as soon as they have earned sufficient capital—often in two years after their arrival—they become farmers, laboring on their own land. Those who remain long in the towns, seldom do so in the station of journeymen, but rent or build themselves shops or take contracts for work themselves, and rapidly accumulate property. I know a house-painter—a trade for which there is very little employment in this country—who arrived here only two years since. In a little more than a year he paid out of his earnings for a very comfortable house, half of which he occupies himself and the other half rents for over 10 per cent. interest on the capital invested in the whole, and he has just completed building a very handsome stone house, also, I presume, paid for out of his earnings at his trade, which he has rented at $35 a month.

There is another important class of immigrants who come here from Germany—small farmers and tradesmen—who, though they have hitherto been able to live comfortably and happily, have not in the old country been able to increase their fortune materially, and who are unable to leave their families in comfortable circumstances, or to find honorable and lucrative employment for their children. This class usually bring with them a small capital, with which they immediately purchase land and stock for farming.

I lately spent a night with a family of this class of the immigrants who arrived in the country last Fall, and who had been settled only about two months.[3]

Their house, although built merely for temporary occupancy, until

ERNST KAPP'S HOUSE IN SISTERDALE

they could spare time and money for one more comfortable, was a very convenient, long, narrow log cabin with two rooms, each having a sleeping loft over it, two halls, or rooms open at the ends, and a corn-crib. The cooking was done outside by a camp-fire, but with utensils brought from Germany, and peculiarly adapted for it. A considerable stock of furniture was stored in the halls, yet in the boxes in which it had been imported. The walls of the two rooms had been made tight with clay, and they were furnished with doors on hinges. (No man who has traveled much on the frontier will look upon these indications as trivial.) Our supper was cooked and served to us on china, on a clean tablecloth, in one of these rooms, skillfully and nicely. A sofa occupying one side of the room had evidently been made by the women of the family after the building of the cabin. On the walls there were hung a very excellent old line engraving of a painting in the Dresden Gallery, two lithographs and a pencil sketch, all glazed and framed with oak.

The family consisted of several middle-aged and elderly people, a young man, a young lady, and four very sweet, flaxen-haired children. They were all very neatly dressed, the head-dresses of the females being especially becoming and tidy. They were courteous and affable, and the tones of their voices were amiable and musical. One of my traveling companions was a German, and our conversation with them was left entirely to him. He went away however after supper, to call on one of the neighbors. An hour or two later, as I returned to the house, after looking to our horses, one of the elder women spoke to me in German; I could not understand, and she called to the young lady, who came before me, and bowing in a very formal manner, addressed me in these words: "Sire, will you to bed now go, or will you for rest, wait?" I replied that I would at once go to bed, if she pleased. She bowed and walked before me till opposite the open door of the second tight room, in which a candle had been placed, and pointing to it, said: "There, Sire." There were three single beds in our sleeping-room, all extremely clean, and we were provided with washing apparatus and other bed-chamber luxuries very unusually found, even in the "best hotels," in the Southwest. The walls of the room, too, were adorned with some good engravings and some paintings of religious subjects, of ordinary merit.

The head of this family had been a tradesman in a small town in Bavaria, where also he had owned a little farm. He had evidently been able to live there with considerable comfort. He could not, however, see any way in which he might provide for his family, so that he could leave them without great anxiety at his death. But now, if this farm should be divided among his children, all of them could, by honest labor, be sure of obtaining, come the worst, sufficient food and raiment and shelter, and in no case would they be dependent on the favor or kindness of public functionaries for the privilege of laboring for their living.

"Only one thing," said the mother, "we regret. It is that our children, who have so well commenced their education in Germany, cannot here continue it."

In Prussia every child is legally *obliged* to attend school.[4] This forced education is, without doubt, often felt by the poor man as a tyranny, preventing him from enjoying for a time that assistance in his labor for the support of his family which his children are capable of giving him. It has also been speciously urged that the child, being forced against its will to go to school, would resist his education, proceed with it as slowly as possible, and gain comparatively slight advantage from it, that the children altogether would be less well educated than if education were made, as in our Northern States, cheap but optional. The argument is fallacious, because, under all systems, *the child* is equally forced "unwillingly to school." It is only the peculiarity of the Prussian, that the State claims the right and exercises it (not as a duty to the child but to itself), of preventing the parent from withholding, from selfish motives, an education from his child.

I am glad to say that the Prussians, and all Protestant Germans here, seem by no means to undervalue the advantages of Education, as a security for the continued safety and welfare of the State. There is a general desire that a law similar to that of Prussia should be enacted by the Legislature of Texas; —that well-prepared teachers should be employed, and adequate school-houses and apparatus for teaching be supplied, and that all the children in the State should be compelled to prepare themselves for the future exercise of citizenship, either by the use of these free means or such other as their parents may be able and willing to provide for them.

Every one sees the danger, under a democratic system of government, of allowing the mass of the people to grow up in ignorance and unenlightenment of mind. In countries cursed with aristocratic institutions, like the Southern States and Prussia, the danger to be apprehended by the privileged classes from the education of the oppressed classes is greater than that which arises from their ignorance. In Prussia it is attempted to steer between both dangers, and by making the teachers functionaries, dependent for their living on the goodwill of the aristocracy, to compel them, while they educate the minds of the people in a low but useful degree, to *misinstruct* them, by habituating their minds to the idea of the rightfulness and the necessity of their submission to tyranny. The attempt has failed.

At the South, instead of providing means and compelling the education of the degraded class, to that degree which shall make them most useful as laborers and artisans—finished tools of their masters—the plan is adopted of wholly denying the means of education, and preventing the child of the degraded from even educating himself so far as he is disposed to; barring, restricting, and interrupting the natural development of his mind. This, undoubtedly, has its effect on making the relation of the masters and their people less dangerous.

It has, however, this great difficulty, even immediately. The large majority of the aristocratic class is itself poor and ignorant, and this part, having equal political rights, nominally, with those who reap the advantage of the degradation of the lower class, danger arises from their ignorance and unenlightenment. See the difficulty manifest now in Mississippi, where the poor and ignorant people, unwilling to submit to a tax, refuse to allow the debts of the State to be paid; in consequence of which the credit of the State has fallen so low, that works essential to its future prosperity cannot be carried on for want of means.[5]

The education of the children of this ignorant aristocracy, is therefore, as every one perceives at the South, a matter of vital necessity. The degraded laboring class (slaves) however, constitute so large a proportion of the whole population, and so large a part of the land is reserved by their owners for the application of their labor, that the poor and ignorant moiety of the population is so scattered, and forced into such a vagabond method of life, that it is entirely impracticable to provide adequate means for educating them. The degree of this difficulty experienced is evident in the results exhibited by statistics, showing the proportion in which the smallest measure of education is possessed by the aristocratic class of the Southern States, and the whole people of the Free States, respectively. While there is but one in several hundred of the people of the North that are not able to sign their names to legal documents, in most of the Southern States the proportion is one in from seven to twenty.[6]

A merchant in Western Texas tells me that a majority of his customers are Germans. Among these, in seven years' dealings with them, he has never found a man unable to write his name; a very common thing to find among the Americans with whom he has occasion to do business.

As the eastern part of Texas is to have, for an unlimited time, a planting aristocratic state of society, with slave labor, and the west—under the effect of the German immigration—will be a farming, democratic and free labor community, here will eventually arise a difficulty in adapting a school system suited to both sections, which can only be solved by a division of the State.

There is throughout the State, a much stronger disposition to give the means of some education to all its *white* children, than I have seen manifested anywhere else at the South. The present Executive, a native of that old pedagogue State, Connecticut, has done much by his personal and official influence to encourage this disposition, and the late Legislature constructed a fund for general educational purposes, of the sum of two million dollars.[7]

YEOMAN.

---

1. In this letter, Olmsted says that he was writing "from a camp in the mountains," which was probably the camping-place in Sisterdale, north of San Antonio, where he and his brother spent a week during their second trip to the area in March 1854. They returned to San Antonio in late March, and Olmsted probably dated and mailed the letter before setting out on April 1 for a two-week trip to Mexico (*JT*, pp. 222, 273).
2. "A Tour in the Southwest" number 8, *New-York Daily Times*, April 24, 1854, above.

3. Olmsted stayed with this family during his first trip to Sisterdale, in company with his brother and Adolf Douai, in February 1854. He described the experience in *Journey Through Texas,* and said the place was on the Cibolo River some thirty miles north of San Antonio and near a settlement, probably that of Boerne (*JT,* pp. 187–90).
4. School attendance had been compulsory in Prussia since the Rescripts—royal orders—of 1716 and 1717 (M. E. Sadler, "The History of Education," in *Germany in the Nineteenth Century: Five Lectures* . . . , 2d ed. [Manchester, England, 1912], p. 107).
5. In 1830 the state of Mississippi chartered the Planters' Bank and subscribed two-thirds of its authorized capital of three million dollars. To finance the venture the state sold two million dollars in bonds, but stopped paying interest on them in 1841. Within ten years those desiring state assistance for railroad construction sought to strengthen the state's credit by securing resumption of payment of interest on the Planters' Bank bonds. In the fall of 1852, however, the voters of Mississippi defeated such a proposal, which amounted to repudiation of the debt represented by the bonds (Benjamin U. Ratchford, *American State Debts* [Durham, N.C., 1941], pp. 105–8).
6. While the figures on illiteracy in the seventh census bear out Olmsted's assertion concerning the states of the slaveholding South, where the proportion of adult white illiterates in the total white population ranged from 1 in 7 to 1 in 22, the figures for the "whole people of the North" were not as strikingly superior as he claims. The proportion of adult illiterates in the whole population of the free states ranged from 1 in 14 to 1 in 107. If one counted only the native-born adult illiterates in the total population (assuming free blacks to be native-born), all of the New England states had fewer than one such illiterate for every 100 inhabitants: 1 in 118 in Rhode Island, 1 in 273 in Maine, 1 in 287 in Connecticut, 1 in 336 in New Hampshire, 1 in 510 in Vermont and 1 in 534 in Massachusetts (U.S., Census Office, 7th Census, *The Seventh Census of the United States: 1850. Embracing a Statistical View of Each of the States and Territories* . . . *J. D. B. DeBow, Superintendent of the United States Census* [Washington, D.C., 1853], pp. xxxiii, lxi).
7. The governor of Texas at this time was Connecticut-born Elisha Pease (1812–1883). In response to his urging, the Texas legislature in January 1854 created a permanent school fund with two million of the fifteen million dollars in U.S. Bonds that the state received from the federal government in the Texas boundary settlement of 1850 (Ernest Wallace, *Texas in Turmoil, 1849–1875,* The Saga of Texas Series [Austin, Tex., 1965], p. 40; *DAB*).

New-York Daily Times, May 27, 1854

FROM THE SOUTHWEST.

Indian Troubles on the Texan Frontiers—Inefficiency of Measures for their Suppression.

Special Correspondence of the New-York Daily Times

San Antonio de Bexar, Monday, April 17, 1854

We crossed the Medina in returning from a trip to the Rio Grande, last Saturday morning, and hesitated whether we should not turn from our road and follow it up to the ranch of an Irish gentleman, who has one of the largest flocks of sheep in Texas, which he had invited us to look at.[1] Preferring, however, to spend Sunday in town, we fortunately concluded to postpone our visit.

The next morning (yesterday) a messenger came into the city with the information that during the night the ranch had been visited and plundered by Indians, who had also killed two of the shepherds. In the course of the day a party was formed to go in pursuit of the Indians.

This morning a woman came into the city with the information that yesterday a party of Indians came to her house, which is about sixteen miles from here, and called for meat and drink, and as soon as they had obtained it, shot her husband, killing him at once, and knocked her down by a blow upon her head with the butt of a rifle, and left her for dead, while they caught the children, of which there were four, the oldest a girl of fourteen. She recovered sufficiently to run from the house and escape through some thick bushes which grew near it. She heard for a long time the shrieks of the children, but whether they were killed or taken into slavery by the savages she cannot tell.[2]

On the Rio Grande, and at other exposed points on this frontier, there have lately been a number of Indian outrages, but none perhaps so bold and frightful as this.

The absurd inefficiency of our national system of managing the Indian tribes is horribly apparent in these occurrences. *Theoretically,* there are no Indians allowed to come within some hundred miles of where these tragedies were enacted, except a few tribes, small in numbers and peaceable and friendly in disposition, with whom an agent of the Government, to make sure of their good behavior, is constantly living.

To keep the savage Indians at a distance from the settlement, there is a cordon of military posts which are greatly valued by the people on the frontier on account of the excellent market they offer for corn, beef, and so on. What the pioneers would do without the soldiers to provide for, Heaven knows. These posts are all called forts, though they are generally mere camps, with a log hospital, magazine and quartermaster's store-houses—the soldiers living in tents. At one of them which we visited last week, there are two hundred men, admirably dressed, drilled and disciplined. There are some settlers immediately around this fort. Within a month these settlers have had their cattle killed and their horses stolen by the Indians. The Indians have even ventured into the stable of the post, and succeeded—though one of them was supposed to have been shot by the sentry—in taking off three of the Government's horses.[3]

At Fort Duncan[4] there are four'hundred men—infantry and artillery. They are in admirable condition for marching upon Mexico, but within a fortnight the Indians have stolen the beef from under their guns, and attacking a forage party, killed the beast the commanding sergeant was upon with an arrow, cut four mules from the wagon and escaped unharmed.

On the Mexican side of the Rio Grande we saw a mule which was worth about $60, but which the rider said he had bought of an Indian for $5,

The Journey through Texas, 1854

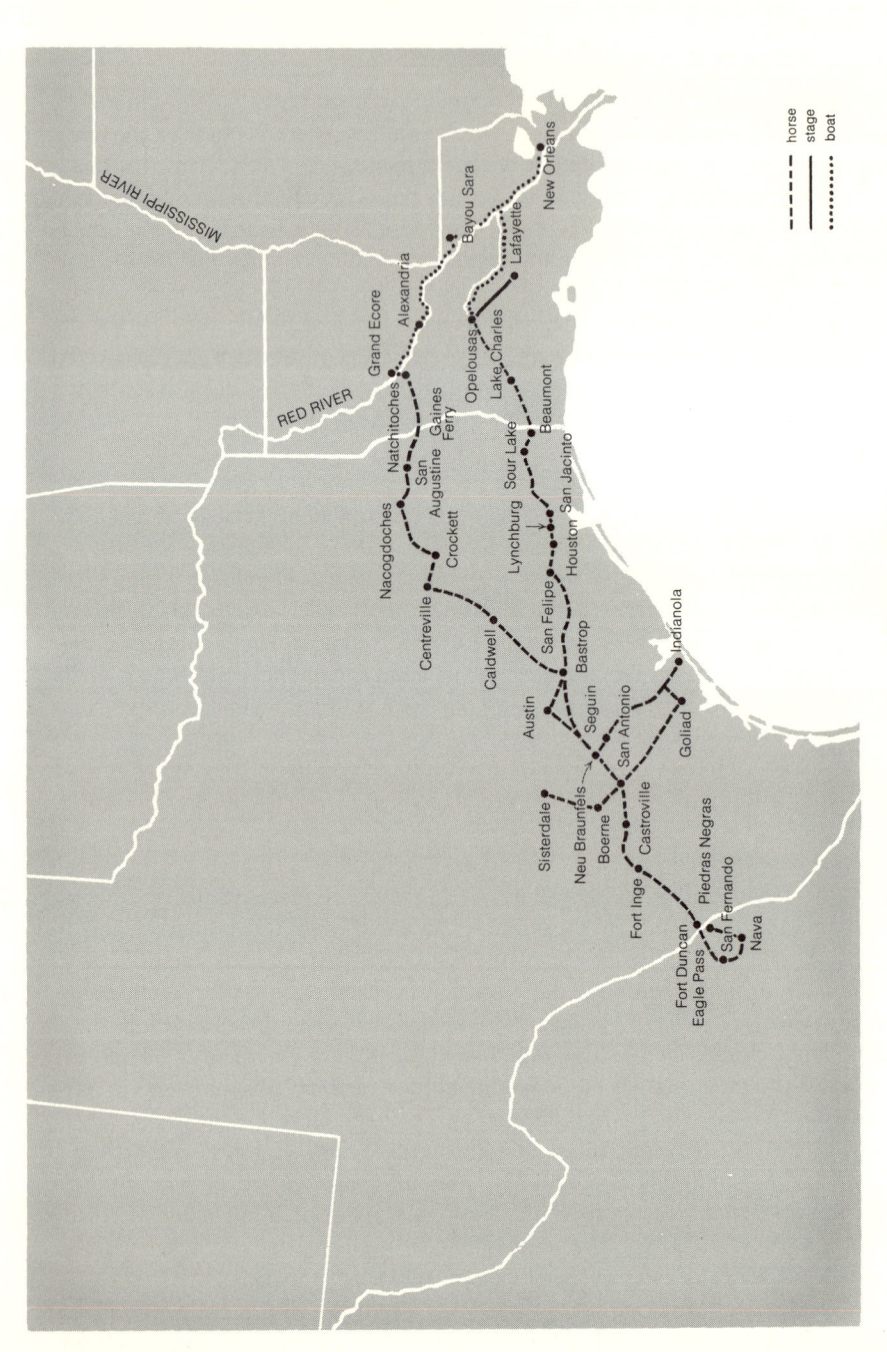

and which our guide recognized as being one that had been stolen from an American settler a few weeks ago.

The last murder by the Indians was committed sixteen miles from here yesterday evening. I do not know what time it was that the woman who escaped arrived here. It was about 9 o'clock when I saw two Germans very hastily saddling their horses, strapping on each a blanket, and filling their pockets with bread. They told me what had occurred, and I asked where they were going.

"To hunt the Indians. There is a company making up; will you join us?"

"No."

"Lend me your Colt, then?"

"Yes; here it is."

"Loaded?"

"Yes."

"All right. We shall start as soon as a company gets together on the plaza."

I walked into the plaza an hour afterwards, and found my German friend very impatiently waiting, with two or three others, who were all talking of the business as if it were a frolic they were anxious should begin. There, too, was a Government Indian agent, guessing what Indians it had been, and very patiently waiting for certain preparations to be made for pursuing them. At noon, the German came home to dinner in extreme vexation. Some soldiers had been ordered to join them, and they had not got ready yet. There are four companies of infantry in camp near the city. I walked to the plaza again after dinner. There were still the small crowd of Indian agents, volunteers and idlers, smoking and talking, waiting, and *making preparations*.

About 3 o'clock this afternoon a squad of soldiers rode by my window, and I followed them to the plaza. Here they joined a number of citizens, and waited half an hour, everybody inquiring of everybody else what they were waiting for now. Finally, the Indian agent remarked that he did not see that there was anything else to wait for, and they had better go. A Mexican led off as a guide, and they trotted calmly out of town.

The soldiers were not exactly in parade equipment. Most of them wore flannel shirts, without coats. The only part of their uniform they retained, was the pantaloons and the fatigue cap. They were infantry soldiers, but had been for this occasion mounted. They each carried a blanket, a haversack of provisions, and a canteen. I asked the corporal why they did not take muskets or rifles like the volunteers? "They'd be too lumbersome, Sir; we have all got Colts." A couple of pickayune Spanish mules, led by a Mexican mounted on another, followed the detachment with rations roped on to their backs, and a buffalo robe, and apparently a tent for the Indian agent to sleep in.

It was 3½ o'clock when the pursuit commenced. When the prisoners are brought in, I will tell you.

My German friend, who had been ready on the parade-ground at half past 9, fully armed, equipped and rationed for a forced march of several days,

THE MILITARY PLAZA IN SAN ANTONIO

had left the plaza before the soldiers came. Whether he had given it up in despair, or had in his impatience ordered himself to advance before the company, as a scouting party, I do not know.

It is my private opinion that if there had been ten New-York firemen scattered over the ten miles square around San Antonio, when that poor woman came in this morning, they would in some way or other have heard of it, and got together and been twenty miles on their way to rescue the children before the detachment had drawn its rations.

April 18.—They found the dead bodies of three of the children in the house. The Indians are supposed to be Comanches, the most formidable of American savages.[5] Could it have been the mere gratification of the love of cruelty and bloodshed that they had in view in these murders? It seems hardly possible. How else can their conduct be explained?

A month ago we were about making a trip through the Bandera Pass, which is at the head of the Medina valley, near which these occurrences have taken place, but were deterred by accounts of Indian disturbances. According to the account sent to the newspapers by some people who belong to a faction of the Mormons, and who are squatting in the Pass this Summer, they had been annoyed by the Indians killing their cattle, and formed a company to attack them. They stole upon the Indians, surprising them in camp, fired a volley upon them, killing several as they believed, though they found no dead bodies. The Indians fled, and they took as booty what they left behind. We afterwards learned from a German who lives in that vicinity, that there was in the Pass an old Indian burying ground, and he believed that the Indians had come to visit it, and had found that the graves had been opened and the bones of their fathers scattered by the whites, and that if they really committed any depredations at all, at that time, it was in revenge for this outrage on their feelings. The most they had done was to shoot some oxen.

It seems to me probable that the present massacres have been made by the Indians in retaliation of the attack then made upon them by the whites.

YEOMAN.

1. The ranch, on the San Geronimo Creek, of Bryan V. Callaghan, a San Antonio merchant and native of Cork, Ireland (*JT*, p. 294; *San Antonio Ledger*, April 20, 1854, p. 2; Ellis A. Davis and Edwin H. Grobe, eds., *The New Encyclopedia of Texas*, 4 vols. [Dallas, Tex., 1929?], 3: 1547).
2. Olmsted describes here the Indian attack on the ranch of James Forrester outside San Antonio on April 16, 1854. A somewhat different version of the event appears in *Journey Through Texas*, page 294. Local newspapers reported that Mrs. Forrester reached San Antonio at 2:00 A.M. on the seventeenth, and that a party of a dozen men immediately set out in pursuit of the murderers. A second, larger group made the leisurely preparations for departure that Olmsted describes (*San Antonio Ledger*, April 20, 1854, p. 2).
3. This was Fort Inge, eighty miles west of San Antonio, which Olmsted and his brother reached on April 3, the third day of their trip into Mexico (*JT*, pp. 285–86, 299).
4. Fort Duncan was on the Rio Grande opposite the Mexican town of Piedras Negras (ibid., pp. 314–15).
5. In *Journey Through Texas*, Olmsted reported that the opinion that the attack on the Forrester ranch had been the work of Comanches came from the Lipan Indian chief Castro. He volunteered to assist in tracking the Comanches, but when the trail began to indicate that the marauders were Lipans, he escaped in the night with the horse belonging to the leader of the search party. Castro then took his tribe to the open plains and carried on depredations for over two years.

    This series of events added drama to Olmsted's recollections of the last day of his trip back to San Antonio from Mexico. Near Castroville he and his brother were overtaken by Castro and several braves, who surrounded them but offered no violence. Castro announced that he was on his way to San Antonio to see the Indian agent there, in an attempt to gain permission to conduct raids into Mexico to steal horses and mules for the Americans. After riding seven miles, the Indians stopped at Castroville to drink at the local grocery. Olmsted later concluded that this was Castro's final reconnoitre before starting warfare on the whites, and that "probably our scalps were only saved to us by the hankering of the brutes for a parting draught of whisky" (ibid., pp. 290–95; *San Antonio Ledger*, April 27, 1854, p. 2).

New-York Daily Times, June 3, 1854

A TOUR IN THE SOUTHWEST.

NUMBER TWELVE.

Probable Division of Texas into Five States—The German Settlers.

Special Correspondence of the New-York Daily Times

Texas, April, 1854.

When the Republic of Texas was annexed as a State to the United States, it was the expectation that it would eventually be so divided as to make five States, giving to the slave property interest the advantage of ten additional votes in the National Senate. A provision in the Act of Annexation renders it optional with the people of Texas to separate their territory from time to time into as many States, not exceeding five, as may each contain a population equal to the number required by our fundamental law for the construction of a State by special act of Congress.[1]

It has been generally expected that a separation of Texas into two States would soon be made. It has been supposed that Trinity River would be the division, and in anticipation of the event, that part of the country lying east of this stream is universally designated as Eastern Texas, and that beyond its right bank is distinguished with equal exactness as Western Texas.

A sectional, political jealousy of a very strong nature exists between these two sections of the State, which has its basis in a covetousness of the people of each to obtain as much as possible [of] the patronage and credit and the use of the Commonwealth property of the entire State, before it shall be divided for their own part of it.

This jealousy, which amounts with many of the people to a bitter animosity, has been greatly increased during the last two sessions of the Legislature by alleged breaches of faith on the part of the majority who represent the interests of the East.

The Pacific Railroad project, which proposes to carry the road through Northern Texas,[2] is looked upon by the people of the West with no favor. If constructed as proposed, they consider that the road will be rather an injury than a benefit to them. To the East, however, it would be of incalculable advantage. To carry the bill, which offered to donate to the road an immense amount of State property as an inducement to foreign capitalists to undertake its construction, it is alleged, and universally believed in the West, that the Eastern members pledged themselves to vote for the so-called Loan bill,[3] the passage of which would have insured the construction of certain internal roads which have been undertaken and are grievously needed by the West. The Pacific Railroad bill became a law; the Loan bill was subsequently defeated by Eastern votes. The people of the West, generally, consider themselves, to use their own phrase, as having been *sold* in the transaction, and are in consequence intensely exasperated.

Yet no public demonstration of this feeling is made, and in the legislative debates you may see nothing reported by which any distinct division of interests between the two sections of the State is proclaimed. Only the vehemence and rhetorical emphasis with which it is denied, except in the lapses of excitement, betray it. The hope is expressed and the intention avowed that Texas may long remain one great, united, powerful State, retaining the undoubted advantage it has in the united strength of all parts acting together, and that distinction, consequence and power it holds as the greatest State in the Territorial area of the Union.

And these declarations on the part of the political leaders in the Legislature and elsewhere, are sincere. The intention of a speedy division of the State into two has been abandoned. It is now the purpose to endeavor by all possible means to continue the State in its unity, until, at least, the time arrives when it may be divided at once into five States.

The main reason for this change of purpose, I have no doubt is this:

A majority of the citizens of the whole of Western Texas are Mexicans and Germans, who have no attachment to the institution of Slavery, and whose interests would lead them to look with disfavor upon the continued filling up of the country by slave laborers. It is possible that the further introduction of slaves into the new Western State would be prohibited, or that it would be required that all slaves subsequently introduced into the country, should be educated and held subject to be made free after their labor should have paid their value and the expenses of their support and education.

The great Territory of what has been known as Western Texas would thus be made attractive to free emigrants, and would probably increase in population more rapidly than the East.

I will give the opinion upon this point of a very intelligent gentleman, who has lately himself come hither from Germany, and who for two years before his emigration had an opportunity, in the way of his business, of conversing with several thousand persons intending to leave that country for the United States. The objection of the existence of Slavery, he informs me, is constantly made by them to Texas, as a destination, and he has not the least doubt the immigration would be increased more than one hundred per cent., if Slavery were legally forbidden, or henceforth excluded from Western Texas.

Should, therefore, a division of the State be now made at Trinity River, as has been generally anticipated, it is probable not only that two Senators, not particularly devoted to the perpetuation of Slavery as the prime interest of their constituents, would be added to Congress, but that Western Texas would increase in population so rapidly as to secure the right to redivide itself once, if not twice, before the East would be able to do so. Thus it might happen that, instead of the Slave States gaining power by the annexation of Texas, they would have actually given to Freedom six Senatorial votes, while they themselves gained but four.

Of course the slave owners of the East, and the slave owners and those ambitious to become slavemasters in the West, will now be sufficiently careful not to let their minor quarrels touching railroads and such unimportant means of wealth, interfere with their paramount interest in the stability of the value of negroes.

It seems to them now probable that the State of Texas will remain one, casting but two votes in the Senate, until its population is sufficiently large to permit a division of it into five States. It may then be expected that one entirely inland State will be formed, its northern boundary being New-Mexico and Kansas; its eastern boundary Arkansas and Louisiana. If the Pacific Railroad is constructed through this, as is the Texas project, it will be settled extensively by slave planters throughout its whole length. If this scheme fails, it will for a long time be very sparsely settled, except in the East, between the Red River and the Trinity, which is now being more rapidly taken possession of by slave owners than any other part of the present State, and will soon be a rich and populous planting district. The Southern boundary line of this State will be carried where it is necessary to effect the desired division of votes.

Four States may be conveniently constructed of the remaining Territory; each having a front (as town-lot speculators would say) on the sea-shore. The first between the Sabine and the Trinity, the second and third between the Trinity and the Guadalupe, the division between them being probably the Brazos, above San Felipe de Austin and the Colorado below; and the fourth, between the Guadalupe and the Rio Grande.

This last State to be west of the Guadalupe, as far as I have been able to judge from the prevailing sentiment of the people, is likely to enter the Union, nominally, as a Slave State, because it will not be thought right to destroy the value of their property in slaves, which immigrants to the Territory have brought with them while Slavery was legal. But the further introduction of slaves will be prohibited, and such will be the public feeling that this prohibition will be enforced, as a similar prohibition of the State of Georgia never has been. Slaves which have previously been brought into the country will be likely to be held, subsequently to the formation of the State, subject to great amelioration of their condition, and to education, and the earliest practicable scheme of emancipation which can be carried out without a practical confiscation of the property of their owners in them. The political position of the State will be generous and broadly Democratic, and it will be virtually an acquisition to the number and the power of the Free States.

Although the time at which this may occur is still many years distant, and circumstances may seem to entirely change the aspect of affairs, I give my opinion that this is the prospect from *present indications*, with distinctness, because I have formed it with care, and because it is a subject of great interest to all those who look from elsewhere towards Western Texas as a desirable country for their future residence. Among the grounds for my opinion are the following:

A very large majority of the present population of the territory described (which I should have observed compares in its area with the State of

Proposed Division of Texas into Five States

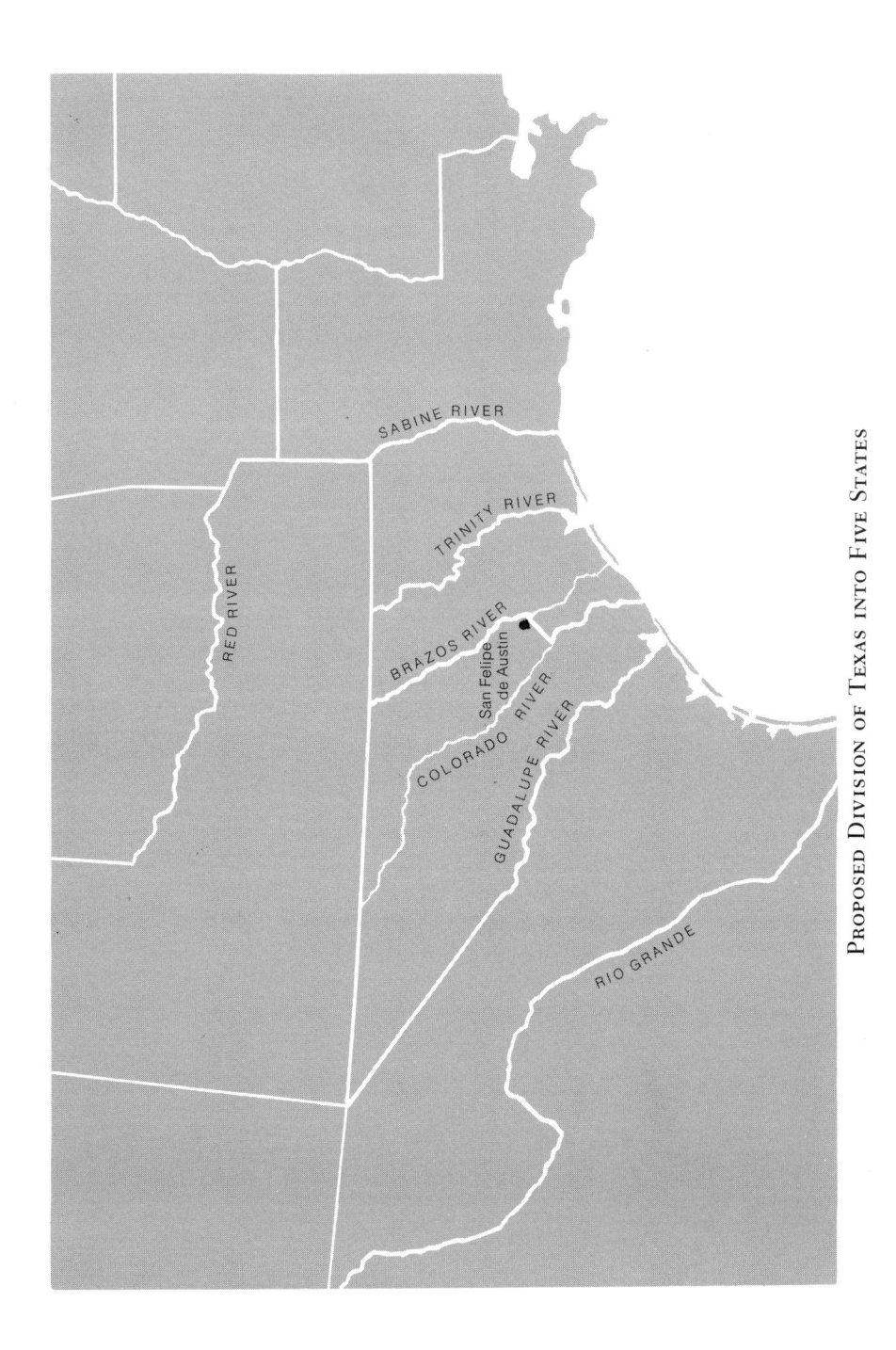

New-York) are men who have been, or now are, accustomed to hard labor with their own hands, for the support of themselves and their families. The proportion of this class to that of the slaves, and of slaveholders or whites from Slave States, is much more likely to be increased than lessened in the future. Consequently, the majority of the laborers in the State are likely to be freemen, and these free laborers will not only not be slaves, as is the case with a majority of the laborers in Delaware and Maryland, but they will be *voting citizens*, looking out sharply for their own interests.

And it is only by especial laws, onerous in their execution upon the rest of the community, that Slavery can be sustained. Especially will this be the case here, where the facilities for the escape of negroes from Slavery are greater than anywhere else at the South, and the people at large are already heavily taxed for the apprehension of fugitives. Neither the Mexican nor the German population is at present regarded and treated by the Anglo-American Texans with that respect for their rights and regard for their interests and opinions which might be likely to conciliate their political friendship.

A variety of circumstances will tend to render slave property insecure in this frontier territory, except at the expense of kindness or relaxation of discipline, which will interfere materially with its profits, and bring its results more directly in unfavorable contrast with those of competitive labor. This is already very perceptible.

The larger the population of free laboring proprietors, the smaller will be the proportion of land open to occupation by slave-owners and their property. But a small part of the country is attractive to planters, from its natural adaptation to their purposes. Much of this is already settled upon by Germans. The vicinity of free laboring families, I have shown in my letters on the "Industry of the South," in the *Times,* is everywhere considered objectionable, as demoralizing (to discipline) and otherwise interfering with the profit of working slaves, by their owners.

The territory not adapted to planting consists of mountains, with narrow valleys, suitable for the fields of small farmers, and the steadings of sheep ranges; and of great prairies, intersected and divided by arid plains and thorny thickets, and deficient in wood and water. A large part of these are well adapted to grazing purposes, and especially to wool-growing.

Experiments indicate that much of the land is remarkably well adapted to vineyards, and that the manufacture of wine, to which many of the Germans are accustomed, will be profitable.

In one part of the territory, there are several abundant water-courses, with rapid streams, unnavigable, and readily dammed at frequent intervals. On the banks of these streams are inexhaustible quarries of the most easily-worked stone, suitable to building purposes, that I have ever seen, equal to the Caen stone of France, superior to the Portland stone of England, more like the Leith stone, of which Edinburgh is built, than any other I remember, but superior to it in softness and fineness. Sand, lime and clay, are also here found in abundance. Bituminous coal, iron, copper and lead, have been found in the mountains. On the one hand of these streams are the most productive cotton lands in the world; on the other is an unsurpassed wool-growing region.

The Germans find the climate very favorable to their health, and not inimical to vigorous labor.

Taking these natural circumstances into consideration, in connection with the character of its present population, especially of that part of it derived from Germany, it seems probable that the State must be one of very varied industry, and that the habits and the interests of the people will generally be opposed to the continuance of a degrading labor system among them. It must be remembered that the Mexican population within the territory is large and increasing, and that it is a dark-colored, mixed race, including often no small proportion of African blood, so much so that it requires the eye of an expert to distinguish many of those held as slaves, on account of their color, from others among the Mexicans who are constitutionally eligible to the highest offices. The Mexicans have no repugnance, but rather the contrary, to equality and the closest intimacy with negroes. But the intelligence, the enterprise, and the peculiar habits of mind which are the effects of early industrial training, that exist as most important elements in the Germans, as well as the rational regard for liberty, as a right of man, which they generally have, is wanting in the degraded Mexicans.

There are no capitalists among the Germans, but they will inevitably gain wealth much more rapidly than the Anglo-Americans, though it will be by productive industry rather than *speculation*. They are cautious but patient, industrious and persevering in whatever they undertake. They contrast remarkably with the American Southerners in this respect. Southerners are rarely enterprising, but they are adventurous. Their business must be magnificent and attended with excitement and grand glory, or they sleep over it. A German will speculate patiently for years on a half acre of vines in which he can work before breakfast, while he finds it hard to earn his living by the rest of his day's labor. If wine is to be profitably made in Texas, this poor German settler will be the one to demonstrate it, to find how it is to be profitably made and to make it. So it will be of Wheat and Barley and Rice; so of Olives, of Indigo and of Tea; of the Fig, the Palm and the Agave. So it will be especially of all kinds of manufacturing and mining, and of various enterprises, to success in which Southern American proprietorship and Slave labor has never yet been found adequate.

I have found the Germans everywhere remarkably contented and satisfied with their success and their prospects. Their success and contentment is every year increasing the emigration, and I see no reason why it should not continue growing larger, year after year, for an indefinite time. The present residents have proved the climate to be unexpectedly favorable to the health of

Northern Europeans. They have proved that there is an abundant reward for labor to be obtained from the soil, and a large interest to be had on the employment of capital. They have demonstrated that cotton can be cultivated to greater advantage by free white laborers than with negro slaves, and at present prices with great profit. They have demonstrated that the climate is not destructive to energy and industry in white men, as is so frequently asserted, and they do not at present seem at all likely to fall into those indolent and inefficient habits which so generally characterize the Anglo-American settlers. With the latter, emigration certainly does seem to tend strongly towards barbarism. It is not so with the patient and industrious, but genial German. This is seen, as I have often shown in my letters, in the comfort which even the poorest Germans contrive to secure in their homes, so much more than the generality of Americans in Texas.

There is, then, I conclude, in Western Texas, a most favorable territory and a promising basis of character for a prosperous, wealthy, healthy-minded, and happy community, and a great, free, independent state. And such a State, self-governed by such a people, I hope to live to see here.

YEOMAN.

1. The joint resolution of Congress of March 1, 1845, annexing Texas to the United States provided that "New States, of convenient size, not exceeding four in number, in addition to said State of Texas, and having sufficient population, may hereafter, by the consent of said State, be formed out of the territory thereof, which shall be entitled to admission under the provisions of the federal constitution." In any state so formed north of the Missouri Compromise line (latitude 36°30′ N) slavery was to be forbidden, but south of that line the Missouri Compromise did not apply; instead, the people of the states seeking admission were to decide whether or not to allow slavery. The Compromise of 1850 considerably reduced the size of the territory affected by this provision and set the present western and northern boundaries of Texas, the northernmost boundary being the Missouri Compromise line (Henry Steele Commager, ed., *Documents of American History*, 9th ed. [New York, 1973], nos. 165, 174).
2. In 1853, after various other attempts, the Texas legislature moved to encourage the construction, across the state, of a link in a transcontinental railroad. It created a corporation called the Mississippi and Texas Railroad and ordered the governor to call for bids for the construction of a railroad from the eastern border of Texas to El Paso. The anticipated route of the railroad was from Shreveport, Louisiana, to El Paso, Texas, along the thirty-second parallel. The company that would be awarded the contract for construction was to receive twenty sections of land for every mile of road completed. The project had progressed no further by the time Olmsted wrote this letter because the governor did not open the bids until August 1854 (St. Clair G. Reed, *A History of Texas Railroads, and of Transportation Conditions under Spain and Mexico and the Republic and the State* [Houston, Tex., 1941], pp. 96–100).
3. Olmsted is probably referring to a bill passed by the Texas legislature in response to a proposal made by Governor Elisha Pease in his message of December 1853. He proposed that the state lend money for the construction of railroads and for other internal improvements, drawing from its school and university funds, and from other funds set aside for charitable and benevolent purposes (*Texas State Gazette* [Austin], Dec. 27, 1853, pp. 3–6).

JOURNEY THROUGH TEXAS AND THE BACK COUNTRY: 1854

New York Daily Tribune, June 3, 1857

THE SOUTHERNERS AT HOME

NO. I

From the Journal of a Northern Traveler on Horseback.

WESTERN MISSISSIPPI

I commenced my ride on the east bank of the Mississippi at Bayou Sara. Back of the town is a long hill, at the top of which is the old French village of St. Francisville—a collection of decaying, shanty-like houses, and with a few new, comfortable and handsome mansions.

A group of men at the tavern stared at me as if it were rare for a stranger to pass, and one of them got upon a horse and soon afterward joined me on the road.

Not from a particularly social disposition, however, for he scarcely returned my nod and replied not a word to my salutation, but with a frowning curiosity examined closely my clothing, horse and equipment. Following his example, I discovered a pistol thrust into the watch-fob of his pantaloons. His countenance was such as made me wish that I had been provided myself with a weapon if we were to travel far in company. I asked: "Can you tell me how far it is to Woodville, Sir?"

"I don't know."

"Have you no idea of the distance?"

"You won't get beyond there to-night."

"Can I be sure of getting there before dark?"

"No place for you to stop this side of there, I reckon."

"You can't tell me about how many miles it is there?"

"No."

Gradually I got the better of his taciturnity. He told me the land in the vicinity was owned by "big-bugs." It used to be thought " 'bout the richest sile God Almighty ever shuck up," and was called the "gardying of the world." But it was now much deteriorated. He had not lived here many years, but it had grown manifestly less productive under his observation. He pointed out the residences of several of the large Hemipterae aforesaid, mentioning their specific names and the number of negroes they possessed, always sneeringly. He himself was overseer for "one of the biggest kind of bugs," who was now in Paris. He generally spent the Summer at Saratogy, or Newport, or Paris, "some of them Northern places."

Suddenly reining off at a fork of the road, he said, without turning his

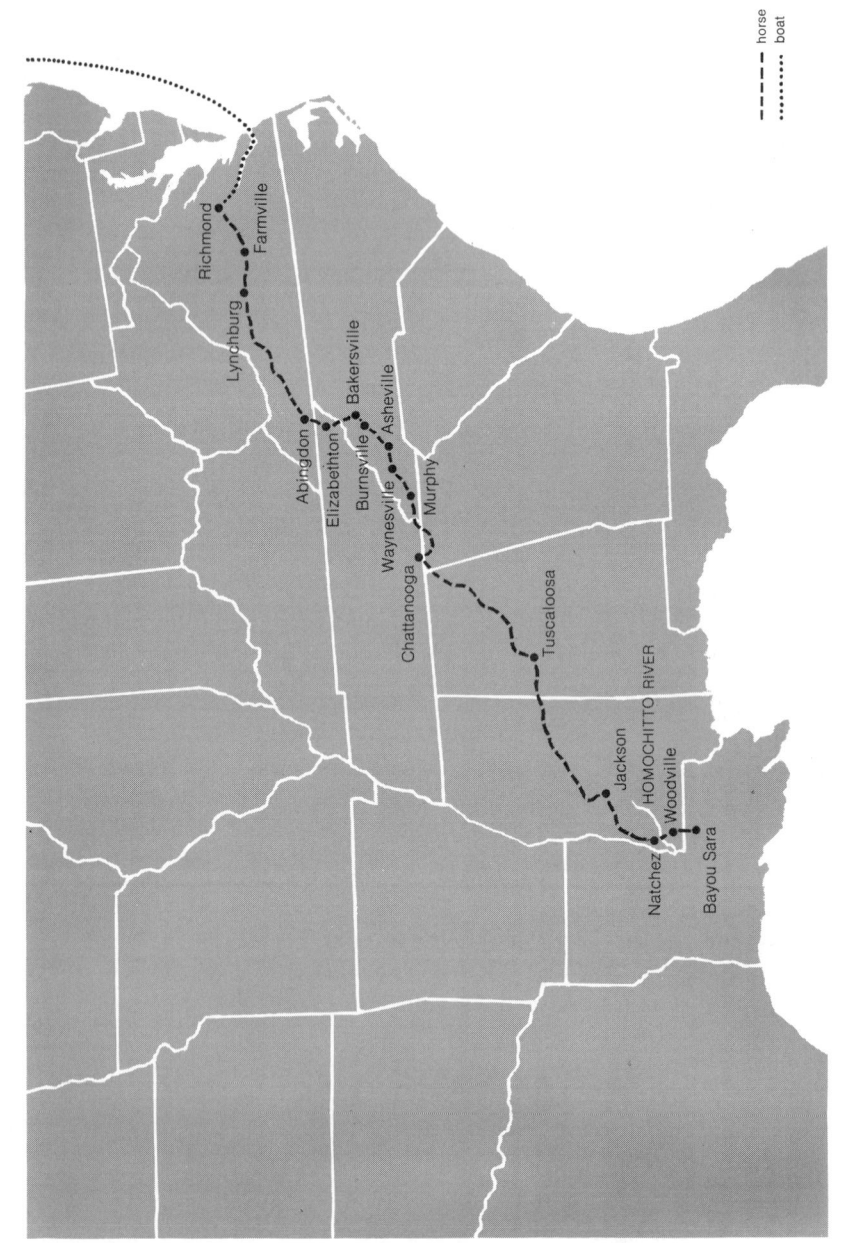

The Journey through the Back Country, 1854

face at all toward me: "If you are gwine on to Woodville, that's your road—this is mine," and rode off, making no reply to my good bye.

Neither at the telegraph station at Bayou Sara, nor at several shops in which I afterward inquired, could I get any exact information about the road to be pursued to Natchez, or the distance to Woodville, which appeared by the map to be the first town upon the proper course. Afterward I made inquiry of twelve different persons, perhaps half of them negroes, whom I met or passed on the way. It was only by pertinacious questioning I could get any of them to give a guess at the distance, in miles; some thought it twenty, some thirty—none gave a number between these. The stupidity of the more brutalized slaves is often described by saying that they cannot count above twenty. I suspect a great many of the whites are but little more educated. This experience with regard to distances, at any rate, is very common. It is rare to find in the plantation districts a man, white or black, who can give you any clear information about the roads or the distances between places in his vicinity.

Coming from the flat coast country, I found the landscape pleasing, though rather tame in its features. For some miles about St. Francisville it has an open, suburban character, with a style of residences indicating rapidly accumulating wealth and advance in luxury among the proprietors. For twenty miles to the north of the town there is on both sides a succession of large sugar and cotton plantations. Much land still remains uncultivated, however. The roadside fences are generally hedges of roses—Cherokee and sweet brier. They are planted first by the side of a common rail fence, which while they are young supports them in the manner of a trellis; as they grow older they fall each way, and meet together finally, forming a confused, sprawling, slovenly thicket, often ten feet in breadth and four to six feet high. Trumpet creepers, grape-vines and cat-briers, and, in very rich soil, cane, grow up through the mat of roses, and add to its strength. It is not so pretty as a stiffer hedge, yet very agreeable, and the road being sometimes narrow, deep and circuitous, delightful memories of England were often brought to mind.

There were frequent groves of magnolia grandiflora, large trees, and every one in blossom. The magnolia does not, however, mass well, and those groves were much finer, which also were not unfrequent, where the beech, elm and liquidambar formed the body, and the magnolias stood singly out, magnificent chandeliers of fragrance. The cucumber magnolia, with a large leaf extremely beautiful at this age of the year, was less frequently seen.

The soil seems generally rich, though much washed off the higher ground. Young pine trees, and other indications of impoverishing agriculture, are seen on many plantations. The cultivation, however, is directed with some care to prevent this.

The soil is a sandy loam, so friable that the negroes, always working in large gangs, superintended by a driver with a whip, continued their hoeing in the midst of quite smart showers, and when the road had become a poaching mud.

Once only did I see a gang which had been allowed to discontinue its work on account of the rain. This was after a very heavy thunder-shower, and the appearance of the negroes whom I met crossing the road back to their field, from the gin house, to which they had retreated, was remarkable.

First came, led by an old driver carrying a whip, forty of the largest and strongest women I ever saw together; they were all in a simple uniform dress of a bluish check stuff, the skirts reaching little below the knee; their legs and feet were bare; they carried themselves loftily, each with a hoe sloping over the shoulder and walking with a free powerful swing, like Zouaves on the march. Behind came the cavalry, thirty strong, mostly men, but some women, two of whom rode astride, on the plow mules. In the rear of all a lean and vigilant white overseer on a brisk pony. The men wore small blue Scotch bonnets, the women handkerchiefs, turban fashion, or nothing at all on their heads.

The slaves generally of this district appeared uncommonly well—doubtless because the wealth of their owners has enabled them to select the best from the yearly exportations of Virginia and Kentucky.

The plantation residences were generally of a cottage class, well shaded by trees, and sometimes with quite extensive and tasteful grounds, usually obtained by trimming out the natural groves.

An old gentleman, sensible, polite and communicative, a capital sample of the planters, who rode a short distance with me, said that many of the proprietors were absent, and some of the plantations had dwellings only for the negroes and the overseer. He called my attention to a field of cotton which, he said, had been ruined by his overseer's laziness. The negroes had been permitted at a critical time to be too careless in their hoeing, and it was now impossible to recover the ground thus lost. Grass grew so rampantly in this black soil that, if it once got a good start ahead of you, you could never overtake it. That was the curse of a rainy season. Cotton could stand drouth better than it could grass.* The inclosures are not often of less than a hundred acres. Fewer than fifty negroes are seldom found on a plantation; many muster by the hundred. In general the fields are remarkably free from weeds and well tilled.

I arrived shortly after dusk at Woodville, a well-built and pleasant court town, with a small but pretentious hotel. Court I judged was in session, for the house was filled with guests of somewhat remarkable character. The landlord was indifferent, and, when followed up, inclined to be uncivil. At the breakfast-table there were twelve men beside myself, all of them wearing black cloth coats, black cravats and satin or embroidered silk waistcoats; all, too, sleek as if just from a barber's hands, and redolent of perfume, which really had the best of it with the kitchen fumes. Perhaps it was because I was not in the regulation dress that I found no one willing to converse with me, and could obtain not the slightest information about my road, even from the landlord.

I might have left Woodville with more respect for the excess of decorum if I had not, when shown by a servant to my room, found two beds in it, each of which proved to be furnished with soiled sheets and greasy pillows, nor was it without much perseverance and bribery that I succeeded in getting them changed on the one I selected to take. A gentleman of embroidered waistcoat took the other bed as it was, with no apparent reluctance, soon after I had effected my private arrangements. One washbowl and one towel, which had previously been used by some one else, was expected to answer for both of us, and would have done so but that I now carried a private towel in my saddlebags. Another requirement of a civilized household existed in connection with the hotel, only in an indecent form. A servant, when I inquired for it, confidentially advised me to follow the other gentlemen to the open stable-yard.

The bill was excessive, and the hostler, who had left the mud of yesterday hanging all along the inside of Belshazzar's legs, and who had put the saddle on so awkwardly that I resaddled him myself after he had brought him to the door, grumbled, in [the] presence of the landlord, because I gave him no larger gratuity than a dime.

As I was riding out of the village, I met a middle aged man, wearing a shabby black suit and a dirty white cravat, perhaps a clergyman. He reined up across the road, so as to stand directly before me, and when I turned to pass, lifted his hands as if he would seize my bridle, at the same time asking abruptly but drawlingly, and in the monotonous, whining tone of a fatigued invalid: "Where did you get that horse?"

"In Texas, Sir."

"Did you ride him all the way from Texas?"

"I rode to Opelousas and then came by steamboat."

"Came where by steamboat?"

"To Bayou Sara."

"Belong in Bayou Sara?"

"No, Sir."

"Don't belong about here, do you?"

"No."

"Belong in Opelousas?"

"No, Sir, I belong in New-York."

"In New-York—long way from home arn't you?"

"Yes."

"Yes; Don't belong in Texas then?"

"No, Sir."

"What was you a doin' there?"

"Traveling."

"What did you come here for?"

"I am on the road to Natchez."

"Going to Natchez?"

"Yes."

"Yes—You'll take boat, there I reckon; sell your horse, won't you?"

"No, Sir, I intend to ride home to New-York."

"To New-York! It's a long way to New-York, arn't it? Well, it's a right good chunk of a horse for a journey; what you reckon he's worth?" &c.

I tried several times to pass him, and finally did so, with some apology for my haste, to which he paid no attention, but after my back was turned upon him, calling out, "Nigger dog?"[1]

"No, Sir," I replied, with a smile; then recollecting the sort of men I had seen at the Hotel, I turned to look at him again, but his next question, made in the same stupid, good-natured tone, and a look in his wooden face, removed all suspicion.

"Didn't you hear of no revivals, 'spose, along?"

"No, Sir,—rather the other way."

"I 'spose—Seems like there was a general holdin' up don't it? Bretherin ought to pray more. Smart sprinklin' o' Baptists, I expect, in Texas?"

I turned away again to conceal my emotions, and answered as soon as I could.

"I should think not, where I was best acquainted."

"Heap o' Methodist bretherin there, ain't ther?"

"More of the Methodists, I believe."

He returned to my side.

"Skuss o' Baptists, then, in Texas?"

"Yes, Sir, so I heard at San Antonio. In that town I understood there were no Baptists."

"Nary Baptis—humph—sharp is she?"

"Rather."

"Expect you don't want to sell her?"

"No, Sir."

"Expect you wouldn't take her weight in gold for her?"

"I don't know but I would. But good morning, Sir; I must jog along."

"Don't reckon to be partin' with her then?"

"No, Sir." I rode on, and he followed me.

"I should like to keep her for you, if you wanted to leave her."

"I thank you, Sir; I do not."

He walked along by my side. At length I asked what he would give for her.

"Oh, I did not expect you wanted to sell her."

"I did not, Sir; but I would like to know what you would be willing to give for her."

"I reckoned perhaps you'd like to leave her behind, if you could be sure of leaving her in good hands—if you could have some one that would take an interest in her. I wan't thinking of buying your dog. Don't know but I'd give ye a dollar for her."

"I would not sell her, Sir, for fifty."

He turned and left me without another word.

This man's voice was a most exasperating, drawling whine. I noticed the same in the next man I conversed with this day. Among the lowest class of the Southerners the nasal tone is quite as common and intense and painful as in the worst of the New-Englanders. It is not as often found among the middle and more educated class at the South as in New-England, however; but more or less of negro tones and idioms are common to all Southerners—even the most educated. The Yankee of the stage and of *Punch*, whom I never saw in New-England, I first met with in perfection in real life in South Carolina. Long, dry and dead hair and open mouth; slow, harsh, nasal utterance, and a vigilant, peering, sinister eye; wearing a narrow, swallow-tailed, snuff-colored coat, with brass buttons, short waistcoat and loose pantaloons, very short at top and bottom. Pork and molasses, generally called a New-England dish, I saw eaten for the first time, on land, in Mississippi.

The Mississippians and the Southerners generally are remarkably deficient in the kind of curiosity which characterizes the New-England Yankee; but an endless questioning without purpose, merely as an expression of social disposition, is a very common experience among the better sort of uneducated people. I do not think that I ever met with anything which I believed to have an impertinent basis or intention in any Southerner. Pure rudeness or surliness is another thing, and is more commonly met with by far in Mississippi than in any other country in which I have traveled.

*"Fine Prospect for Hay."—While riding by a field the other day which looked as rich and green as a New-England meadow, we observed to a man sitting on the fence, "You have a fine prospect for hay, neighbor." "Hay! that's *cotton, Sir,*" said he, with an emotion that betrayed an excitement which we cared to provoke no further; for we had as soon sport with a rattlesnake in the blind days of August as a farmer, at this season of the year, badly in the grass.

All jesting aside, we have never known so poor a prospect for cotton in this region. In some instances the fields are clean and well worked, but the cotton is diminutive in size and sickly in appearance. We have seen some fields so foul that it was almost impossible to tell what had been planted.

All this backwardness is attributable to the cold, wet weather that we have had almost constantly since the planting season commenced. When there was a warm spell, it was raining so that plows could not run to any advantage; so, between the cold and the rain, the cotton crop is very unpromising. * *

The low flat lands this year have suffered particularly. Thoroughly saturated all the time, and often overflowed, the crops on them are small and sickly, while the weeds and grass are luxuriant and rank.

A week or two of dry hot weather will make a wonderful change in our agricultural prospects, but we have no idea that any sort of seasons could bring the cotton to more than an average crop.

Hernando (Miss.) Advance, June 22, 1854

This is the first of a series of letters by Olmsted entitled "The Southerners at Home," which appeared in ten instalments in the *New York Daily Tribune* between June 3 and August 24, 1857. The first half of the letter appears in similar form in *Back Country,* pages 11–16, while the last half is the only passage of any length that Olmsted left out of *Back Country.* The letter describes the beginning of his journey in the back country of the South, in May 1854, and is therefore presented at this place in the volume.

1. Olmsted's unwelcome companion had turned his attention from Olmsted's horse to his dog, Judy, a bull-terrier that he acquired in Centreville, in eastern Texas, soon after beginning his Texas journey (*JT,* p. 93).

Appeal for Funds for the *San Antonio Zeitung*

[c. October 1854][1]

The statements made in this paper are extracted or condensed from a letter of Dr. A. Douai, dated San-Antonio, Texas, September 4th 1854. Their accuracy and authenticity is certified to by Mr. Olmsted of New York who spent the last winter in Western Texas and made it his business to inform himself reliably upon the subject to which they relate.

Dividing the settled portions of the state of Texas with three sections—the first, between the Sabine and Trinity Rivers, the second, between the Trinity and the Guadalupe and the third, between the Guadalupe and the Rio Grande, the following classification of inhabitants may be made.

	Eastern Texas	Central T.	Western T.	Total
Whites Born in the Free States	8,000	7,000	10,000	25,000
Whites Born in the Slave States	66,000	32,000	40,000	138,000
Germans & Other Europeans	8,000	6,000	11,000	25,000
Mexicans	none		25,000	25,000
Negroes	32,000	18,000	35,000	85,000
Indians	2,000	1,000	7,000	10,000

Somewhat definite indications may be drawn from this classification, of the number of persons in Western Texas whose interests will be found in a few years to be opposed to the extension of Slavery and in favor of a free state between the Slave states on the gulf and the republic of Mexico.

All classes of the population of Western Texas are increasing rapidly except the Indians. The direct German immigration continues in an increasing ratio to that of the Americans. The whole Mexican population is opposed to slavery and opposed to the settlement of slaveholders in the country (while it is friendly to all other immigrants.) So distinctly is this the case that in two counties where the slaveholders were most powerful, all the Mexican residents have been driven from their homes and expelled [from] the counties by Lynch-law process.[2] All the male Mexican population is entitled to vote on arriving at mature age.

Among the German population there is a universal repugnance to slavery and a disinclination to its introduction or further extension in the country. But the majority of the German population being more or less dependent for employment or patronage on the slaveholders, who are the sole capitalists of the country, are timid, irresolute and conservative in their actions and expressions on the subject. They are forced to realize every day however that their ultimate interests are opposed to the Slave-labor system. A considerable part of the German population will be entitled to vote in from two to four years.

The Germans and Mexicans together form about 2/15 of the present white population. A strong party has lately been formed among the Germans, distinctly and avowedly hostile to the extension of Slavery. It includes in it many brave men who previous to the revolutions of 1848 had gained European reputations as Statesmen, Lawyers, Scholars, Merchants and Proprietors; many of whom now support their families solely by their manual labor, and are made directly cognizant of the degradation of labor effected by the presence of Slavery.

Of the American-born population, more than three quarters is non-slaveholding, but even more than the Germans, is subject to the moral rule of the slaveholders. "This," says Dr. Douai, "may at anytime become otherwise. They may find out how different are their interests from those of the slaveholders. But it seems that the impulse, the issue, the beginning, must be made by us foreigners. In vain we have expected till this day, their initiating the matter, and now that we have started the movement, laid the foundation of a Free party, we find that there is something to be hoped from that quarter."

A convention of about 140 Germans from all parts of the state was held at San Antonio on the 17th of May last, at which it was resolved that Slavery should be considered an evil to the country: that, nevertheless, legal rights of property in slaves should be respected and not violently or suddenly destroyed; *but* that, in legislation, it were better policy to take measures for the gradual and quiet extinction of the evil than for its perpetuation and extension.[3]

No strong demonstration against these resolutions was made by the American press or people until more than a month after their publication: then one Rossy, a baptized Jew, formerly a representative from Comal County and notoriously a political speculator, denounced them and the new Free party (so called) in the American papers. A considerable part of the German population of San Antonio & New Braunfels were induced to take sides with Rossy against the movement.[4] Immediately that this was known by the slaveholders and that large class of ruffianly characters who congregate in these frontier towns, their constrained excitement burst forth with great violence. Public threats of *lynching* the leaders of the Free party were made, and it is believed that it was only because they speedily found that they could not rely upon the support of the "reactionary" Germans for extreme measures, and that the Free party was too strong to be easily conquered in a fight, that these threats were not executed. A great many Germans, however, were appalled by the violence of the slaveholders and their allies. The "San Antonio Zeitung," a German paper which had published the Resolutions against the perpetuation of slavery and which sustained the views of the Convention, was in danger of being broken up; many subscribers feared to take it and countermanded their subscriptions and many stockholders expressed their dissatisfaction with the editor.

This paper is owned by a large company of small share-holders. It was started about two years ago. The editorship had then been unanimously conferred upon Dr. Douai, a man admirably qualified, brave, discreet and amiable, as well as highly cultivated in all respects. He had then but lately arrived in Texas, having only escaped from prison within the year. Under his management, the Zeitung was very popular among the Germans and very successful, its subscription list soon becoming larger than that of any other of the 57 newspapers published in the state, with one exception. Notwithstanding extraordinary expenses it has paid 5 per cent. per annum on the capital invested, the editor himself receiving a salary of $600. on which he supports a large family and an aged father, formerly a clergyman in Europe and educated in luxury, in a city where the expenses of living are as great as in New York.

During the late excitement Dr. Douai offered his resignation to the directors, assuring them that he would remain in no situation where he was not perfectly free to express his convictions in accordance with his own discretion on any subject whatever. Forthwith, an attempt was made to have this resignation accepted and to employ Rossy as editor. It was found that there were three parties among the directors, a Free party, a Moderate or Quietist party and a Slavery party. It was finally resolved that on the 17th of September the paper should be sold, so as to make it wholly dependent on the public patronage—but not to the highest bidder, but to the bidder who should be on the whole most agreeable to the stockholders.[5]

Dr. Douai, urged thereto by many of the directors, issued a Circular to all Germans in Texas on the subject, requesting the assistance and support of all who were in favor of practicing the rights of free thinking, speaking and voting on the subject of the extension of Slavery.[6] On the 4th September he says, "At the time I write it is beyond doubt that the Zeitung can be sustained (by subscriptions) and continued in its free spirit and speech—can even speak more freely than before, finds a public where it had none before and will find many friends among *Americans* as soon as it shall be published half in English and half in German. *This shall be done*, as soon as I become proprietor."

Dr. Douai had ascertained that a majority of the stockholders would sell the paper and office to him on certain terms which he was prepared to offer, in preference to anyone else. (Advices since received announce that this has been done.)

Dr. Douai is poor and his party is poor. To enable him to carry on the paper and increase its influence as proposed, he requires a loan for one year of at least $340.00.

He writes to the friends of free speech at the North, who are not poor, in conclusion: "Well. Help us to save our paper founded so hardly by my one and half years work without just recompensation—endangered now and for ever if I cannot become its proprietor. Help us to save it from the hands of these Slaveholders and Hunkers who will get possession if I cannot myself, or if because of that little debt, and the want of paper and materials, I should be obliged to sell it again to the highest bidder."

It is proposed to raise a fund to sustain free speech and to advocate the propriety and expedience of forming an ultimately free state in Western Texas.

---

1. This description of conditions in West Texas and appeal for support of Adolf Douai's *San Antonio Zeitung* was drawn up by Olmsted and his brother, John, on the basis of Douai's letter to John of September 4, 1854, which Douai wrote in response to a request for information that Olmsted had sent to Charles Riotte from Chattanooga, Tennessee, in July 1854.
2. This claim, drawn from Douai's letter of September 4, 1854, appears to be an exaggeration. During the summer and fall of 1854, however, there were nativist meetings in several Texas cities, including Bastrop and Matagorda, at which calls were made for the expulsion of Mexicans from Texas. At a gathering in Austin in October a committee was appointed to execute the order to "drive them forth as pariahs from our midst." Olmsted had information on movements to expel Mexicans from at least two counties—Matagorda and Guadalupe. In his "A Tour in the Southwest" number 9, written in March 1854, he related that "at a meeting of the citizens of Matagorda County, last Summer, it was formally resolved that no Mexican should be allowed to remain in the County after a certain date." In August 1854, at a meeting in Seguin, Texas, a committee was appointed and charged with preventing the movement of any more Mexicans into Guadalupe County. Douai mentioned this incident in a letter to the Olmsted brothers, describing how a printer with the *Seguin Mercury* had been fired and told to leave the county because of his persistent opposition to "all attempts to disfranchise and drive out the Mexican population of that county" (William Darrell Overdyke, *The Know-Nothing Party in the South* [Baton Rouge, La., 1950], p. 30; "A Tour in the Southwest" no. 9, *NYDT*, May 12, 1854; Adolf Douai to FLO and JHO, Feb. 9, 1855; "The Rio Grande Commissioner," *Austin Intelligencer and Echo,* n.d., scrapbook, p. 18, John L. Haynes Collection, Barker Library, University of Texas, Austin).
3. The convention held in San Antonio on May 14-15, 1854, for the purpose of defining the position of progressive Germans on a series of political, social and religious issues was instigated by an organization called *Der Freie Verein,* which had been formed in Sisterdale, Texas, in November 1853. The founders of the *Verein* included men who became Olmsted's friends during his visit to Sisterdale with Adolf Douai in February 1854—among them, Ernst Kapp, Julius Dresel, August Siemering and Edouard Degener. Representatives of several German settlements, societies and clubs attended the meetings in San Antonio in May 1854, which coincided with the meeting there of the second annual German *Saengerfest.* The "platform" drawn up by the convention defined positions on a number of issues, expressing what Douai later described as "social-democratic" ideology. Concerning slavery, the platform declared: "Slavery is an evil, the abolition of which is a requirement of democratic principles; but, as it affects only single states, we desire: a. That the federal government abstain from all interference in the question

of slavery, but that, if a state resolves upon the abolition of the evil, such state may claim the assistance of the general government for the purpose of carrying out such resolve" (Rudolph L. Biesele, "The Texas State Convention of Germans in 1854," *Southwestern Historical Quarterly* 33, no. 4 [April 1930]: 247-55; Adolf Douai, "Autobiography," pp. 113-14; *JT,* pp. 191-200).

4. The *San Antonio Zeitung* published the San Antonio platform in German on May 20, 1854, and six days later the *Neu Braunfelser Zeitung* carried the response of the conservative Germans there. The author (who signed himself "R") was presumably Alexander Rossy. He protested vigorously against the platform, and especially against the slavery plank. The same issue of the *Neu Braunfelser Zeitung* carried a protest against the San Antonio platform by 135 residents of Neu Braunfels.

   The controversy spread beyond the German community in June, when attacks were made on the platform by the *San Antonio Western Texas* and the *Austin Texas State Gazette.* On June 24, in a letter published in the latter, Alexander Rossy declared that the bulk of the German settlers were indifferent to the issues discussed in the San Antonio platform, and characterized those who had drawn up the platform as "designing men" and "political babies." Later in the month, Germans attending mass meetings in Neu Braunfels and Lockhart rejected any suggestion of disturbing the institution of slavery (R. L. Biesele, "The Texas State Convention of Germans," pp. 255-61).

5. Douai described these developments more fully in his letter to John Hull Olmsted of September 4, 1854. The starting point, he wrote, was Alexander Rossy's letters in the English-language press attacking the San Antonio platform and those who wished to form a political party on the basis of it:

   > As soon as the slaveholders and their partisans learned, that there was a division of opinion and sentiments among the Germans, and that in New Braunfels and San Antonio a considerable part of German population expressed themselves in favor of Mr. Rossy: on a sudden their excitement, long constrained and retained, burst forth and became violently loud. For some time the press and many Americans spoke aloud of lynching the new party—no word was too mean for them as to be applied to these daring men; the "San Antonio Zeitung" seemed to be in danger of being broken up, many anxious subscribers gave up their subscriptions and Know Nothingismus lifted its head in several Texan counties against that foreign born revolutionary German people. Now you know too well the true spirit of slaveholders as to ignore, that we new party formers would have been smashed into atoms, had the slaveholders and their partisans felt strong enough to do so. The only reason why Lynch law was not proclaimed, but the excitement subsided very soon is: They could not in any way rely on a strong majority for themselves, they feared their adversaries and had better to acquiesce in threatening and flattering.
   >
   > Under these circumstance the question arose: Shall we continue the "San Ant. Zeitung?" This paper, you know, was started by a company of shareholders. Many of them uttered their dissatisfaction with the paper. I found for the first time a great many strong opponents against the tendency of the "Zeitung" and not many steadfast friends. I resolved on giving back to my committents the Editorship (formerly deferred unanimously on my person) and begged them in a general meeting of the stockholders to be released. Forthwith a party formed, which intended to give the Editorship to Mr. Rossy. But some weeks afterwards, when this party had measured their number, means and significance with the other party that sustained myself—they gave it up and left the field to my friends. Then a third party rose, willing to make the "Zeitung" theirs and subservient to a number of office hunters, railroad schemers and middle party men; this third party excited very soon the hatred both of Freemen and Hunkers. In a second meeting of shareholders it was resolved to sell the printing office and the newspaper in order to make it dependent on the sole public patronage. Now my friends insisted on me, that I should make a proposal of becoming myself proprietor and I did so—although sacrificing much indeed.

6. In his letter to John Hull Olmsted of September 4, 1854, Douai wrote the following about his circular:

   > I circulated a letter of which you find a copy inclosed, summoning all those Germans in Texas who are opposed to the extension of slavery and in favor of protecting the rights of our population—the rights of free thinking, speaking, voting—which now are trampled upon by slaveholders in many places—and in favor of sustaining a free party paper in West Texas—

to help me by sending me subscriptions and their powers of attorney or proxies in order to secure my buying the property of press and "Zeitung."

A Few Dollars Wanted to Help the Cause of Future Freedom in Texas

[c. October 1854][1]

Texas, by the terms of the joint resolution of annexation may be & probably ere long will be, divided into *five states*. There are reasons to hope that one or two of these states may be *secured to free labor* & real republicanism. The same system that is relied upon to preserve *Kansas*—the organized introduction of free laborers—has already been silently at work in the Western part of Texas. That region (between the Colorado and Mexico) is suited to be worked by whites, being not a cotton or sugar planting, but a grazing district.

A German Emigration Company *has thrown* in upon it, on a merely economical system, 7,000 free Germans[2] all of whom nearly are dependent on their own arms for a livelihood—and almost all of whom appreciate the inevitable antagonism with slave labor. Their numbers have been swollen by about 4,000 individual German emigrants, making altogether 11,000 intelligent men whose interests and ideas conflict with those of slave-holders.

Besides those there are 25,000 Mexicans annexed with the country—voting citizens—all of one mind against slavery.

One fifth the American population are Northern born men, and but a very small part of the remainder are actual slaveholders.

Altogether it is thought that the interests and secret wishes of a large majority of the inhabitants there are opposed to slavery.

Could this people be brought to feel their power and act together, this part of Texas, to be set off into one or two states, would with great certainty, become free.

A year ago, a free German paper was firmly established, which has cautiously but firmly advocated these ideas. It has gradually got to be considered so dangerous by slave owners that an effort has been made to buy out and silence the paper. Upon this, the Editor has determined to purchase the paper of its proprietors (stock holders) and to secure himself an entirely free position. To enable him to do this he has written to a personal friend here to aid him to the amount of $350.

Unable himself to give the entire sum, the writer asks such as are disposed to help sustain & further this free influence to contribute towards it. He is himself cognizant of these facts and knows this Editor to be a man of great strength & beauty of character & of perfect integrity—admirably adapted to his precise position.

This assistance given *now* in a quiet way may ultimately prove of infinte importance.

To Dr. Adolph Douai, Editor of the "San Antonio Zeitung"

The undersigned[3] have contributed the amounts below and beg you to accept them to be used at your discretion in furtherance of the rights of free labor and the enlightenment as to their true future, of the free laborers of Western Texas.

H. H. Elliott,	$25.00
C. L. Brace,	5.00
H. W. Beecher,	5.00 paid
Bowen M'Namee & Co.,	10.00 paid
S. B. Chittenden,	10.00 paid
S. T. H.,	5.00 paid
W. M. Neill,	10.00

To be returned to Fred L. Olmsted, Southside, Staten Island, N.Y.

1. Olmsted and his brother, John, circulated this appeal in response to requests for assistance made to them by Adolf Douai during September 1854. On September 7 Douai wrote to John Hull Olmsted, asking him to take steps to pay Douai's debt of $220 to the New York firm of Wells & Webb for type, and to purchase some $130 worth of additional type and paper. In return, he offered to send John Hull Olmsted a draft for the total expense, payable in one year. On September 18 he wrote again, repeating his request and reporting that on the previous day the stockholders of the *San Antonio Zeitung* had voted to sell him the paper and its printing office.
  The Olmsted brothers decided to try to raise the money as a gift rather than as a loan. They probably began to circulate this appeal during the first week of October, at the same time that John Hull Olmsted wrote to other potential contributors. By early November the Olmsteds had collected $230 for the *Zeitung* (Adolf Douai to JHO, Sept. 18, 1854; JHO to ?, Oct. 4, 1854; JHO to Isaac Clinton Collins, Oct. 5, 1854; Adolf Douai to "Dear Friend!," Nov. 17, 1854; FLO to JO, Dec. 31, 1854).
2. Presumably a reference to the colonization activities of the *Mainzer Adelsverein*, or "Society for the Protection of German Immigrants in Texas," which was organized in 1844 and brought about the settlement of Neu Braunfels and several other German communities during the next decade (R. L. Biesele, *German Settlements*, pp. 66ff.).
3. The contributors were Henry Hill Elliott, brother of Charles Wyllys Elliott; Charles Loring Brace; Henry Ward Beecher; the New York silk goods firm of Bowen, M'Namee & Company; Simeon B. Chittenden (b. 1814), a New York dry goods merchant and brother of the Hartford dry goods merchant Henry Abel Chittenden, whom the Olmsted brothers knew; and, probably,

William Neill, a brother-in-law of Charles Loring Brace (*NCAB*, 13: 465–66; *The New-York City Directory, for 1853–1854. Twelfth Publication* [New York, 1853], p. 85 [see Spear 1000]; Alvan Talcott, comp., *Chittenden Family: William Chittenden of Guilford, Connecticut, and His Descendents* [New Haven, Conn., 1882], pp. 72, 126, 127; FLO to JHO, Feb. 16, 1847; FLO to Samuel Cabot, Jr., July 4, 1857, n. 9, below).

CHAPTER V
THE LITERARY REPUBLIC
1854–1855

FROM OCTOBER 1854 to the end of 1855, Olmsted was engaged in two quite different undertakings. One was his literary career, which at first took the form of writing *A Journey in the Seaboard Slave States*. He also continued to write letters to the *New-York Daily Times* on topics of concern to him; the letter published here addresses the problem of training and disciplining seamen. In April 1855 his literary activity expanded as he left Staten Island for Manhattan to become a partner in the publishing firm of Dix, Edwards & Company and managing editor of *Putnam's Monthly Magazine*. His letters to his father, his partner Arthur T. Edwards, and his assisting editor Parke Godwin tell of his work as a publisher. They give his views on such questions as payment to English publishers for the right to reprint their works in America and the position the *Monthly* should take on current political issues. The letter to his half-sister Bertha describes his approach to travel and travel-writing, and contains one of his earliest statements of the concept of "unconscious influence," which was to play so important a role in his later views on character formation and the nature of the creative process.

In this period, Olmsted also became increasingly active in the free-soil movement. His letters to Edward Everett Hale in this chapter describe his earliest association with the New England Emigrant Aid Company, while his letters to James B. Abbott chronicle his purchase of the mountain howitzer that he sent to Kansas in October 1855 for the defense of free-state settlers.

New-York Daily Times, October 18, 1854

THE ARCTIC

Lessons Concerning Means of Security
on Ocean Steamers.

Widely calamitous accidents, like this of the *Arctic,*[1] always have their good consequences in stimulating research, discovery and invention, and thus in constantly diminishing the liability of their recurrence. In the multitude of counselors there is wisdom, and all should be encouraged to make public any means to prevent collisions at sea that may occur to them. That the general excitement may be usefully directed, however, it is well to show the impracticability which is sure to characterize the great majority of these suggestions.

Whenever a disaster occurs to any of our great modern machines of locomotion, it is the first impulse of most persons to blindly blame their speed, as the cause of it. This is generally found upon investigation to be an error. The loitering sloops and slow coaches of our fathers murdered a larger proportion of their passengers than our clipper ships, steamers and railroads. I have been an extensive traveler, and it is my experience that the fastest conveyances, whether steamers, railway trains, or mail coaches, are the safest and surest. This is not because mere speed is in itself an element of safety in all cases (it is so sometimes), but because the same enterprise and skill which obtains speed is most likely to secure safety along with it. As to railroads, I believe that the absence of a healthy and sufficient competition is the prime cause of accidents. I believe that it is perfectly practicable to run our trains regularly at sixty miles an hour, and with greater safety than they are now run at fifteen or twenty. And on steamboats, every Western traveler will bear witness that it is the *cheap* third rate craft, whose owners are liars, and whose officers ruffians, that most frequently burst, burn, snag and sink. In all our public conveyances, whether on land or sea, the great danger arises from *a false economy in wages.*

As to what has been libelously termed the "murderous speed" of the *Arctic,* you have already shown how it may be that the safety of those on board a steamer is in proportion to the impetus, and consequently the speed, with which she comes in collision with the class of vessels she is most likely to meet on the Banks.[2]

Another advantage arising from speed in a fog has been thus far overlooked by the public, so much indeed that one conservative soul insists that the steamers should always stop entirely when they encounter a fog. To whom it might not probably be a sufficient answer that if they did so, it is probable that instead of the chances (not more than one in ten thousand) of a collision, and the then further chances to the passengers of drowning, there would be the almost inevitable certainty of their starving to death. For on the "Banks" and in the Gulf-stream *there is always fog.* At the same time, I am told, it is calculated that on an average, in the usual sailing track between here and Europe, there are *seventy* square miles of free water for every vessel at any given time. I have myself been sixty days afloat at one time when no other vessel came within sight of the one I was in.[3] Suppose the passage across the foggy region is made by a steamer by running thirteen miles an hour in twenty-four hours; is not the danger of a collision to all parties less than if she remains forty-eight hours in the fog by running at half speed? If the *Arctic* had been running 13 1/10 miles an hour instead of 13 (if that was her exact speed while in the fog), she would have escaped the collision with the *Vesta*[4] just as certainly as if she had been going at less speed than she was, while in the latter case the danger of her collision with other vessels would have been increased. I have myself seen a collision between two large vessels escaped by a hair's-breadth, which would inevitably have occurred and probably sent aloft some hundred souls, if the speed of either had been in the slightest less than it was.

A large vessel will be generally less damaged by coming in contact with a small one, if the former is sailing rapidly, than if she is sailing slowly, and as the course of small craft can usually be more easily changed, and they can be handled more rapidly, it is their business to keep out of the way of large craft. This is less the case, however, when the larger craft is a steamer. High speed on a steamer, while it increases her own safety, adds to the danger of small craft before her, because within the time she is running the distance at which objects are perceptible in the usual fog on the Banks, it is not possible to materially vary the position of the small craft, or to alter the course or check the speed of the steamer. And now a word about *fog signals*.

I have hardly taken up a newspaper since the loss of the *Arctic* was announced, that I have not seen the firing of cannon recommended, or taken for granted to be the best means of warning to vessels to get out of the way of the steamer in a fog; yet it would seem that a moment's consideration of the narrative of events, would have shown the absurdity of the suggestion. Immediately after the danger occasioned by the collision was discovered to be imminent, the *Arctic* began and thereafter continued till the moment at which she was submerged, to fire cannon. And we can but envy the fate of that one

THE WRECK OF THE *Arctic*

Hero—and tearfully congratulate rather than commiserate his father—who, amid the general devilish cowardice of the wretched crew, went down doing his duty, a true man—the utmost end of a man fulfilling.[5] Perhaps yet, it may be found that this was not lost—perhaps some vessel *was* attracted toward the sinking steamer by this firing, and arriving near where she disappeared after all the boats had left, perhaps she has picked up some of those persons, still floating, whose loss we now deplore. For this is always understood to be the object of cannon-firing at sea, when no other is apparent, to attract vessels, not to warn them off. Cannon firing is a signal of distress.

Yet, in connection with this recommendation of cannon firing, a really practical suggestion, though not quite original, has been made. It is to give notice of the *course* of the firing vessel by varying the number and rapidity of the discharges. This may be applied to other means of warning by noise, as for instance to the steam whistle. I see no sufficient objection to a general law requiring all steam vessels to be provided with the most powerful steam whistles or trumpets, and that these shall be used at certain, *fixed, frequent* intervals in fogs, in such manner as shall signal within hearing of them the course pursued by the steamer. Thus one blast, ten seconds in length, might mean North; two of ten seconds, East; three, South; one of ten seconds, followed by one of five seconds, N.E.; one of ten seconds, one of one second, and one of five, N.N.E.; two of ten seconds, one of one second, two of five seconds, E.S.E.; and so on. A *short,* a *moderate,* and a *long* blast would constitute the *letters,* and sixteen words could be very plainly and quickly spelled with them. Perhaps eight would be all that would be desirable, and the system might be still further simplified with advantage. Experiments may be usefully made to obtain a more powerful or penetrating noise than that of the ordinary whistle now in use. There must be an absolute requirement that such signals shall be frequently repeated in fogs by the steamers, else the annoyance they will occasion to passengers will prevent their being used. It is probable that such blasts of the steam-whistle could be heard and clearly distinguished on board any sailing vessel within an eighth—perhaps a quarter—of a mile of a steamer. It would only be otherwise when the sailer was to windward of the steamer in a gale, and unless the former were scudding, the danger of a collision would be small, because of the slow progress of the steamer to windward.

It is extremely improbable that any fog signals can be used that will serve to warn off steamships. The rumble and dash of the engines and paddles drowns all exterior noises. Let any one consider what a terrifically loud crash there must have been when the bows of the *Vesta* were stove against the broad side of the *Arctic*—thick plates of iron and heavy timbers breaking up like glass—and consider that this crash was imperceptible to many in the *Arctic,* and by others was thought to be merely the dash of a little heavier than ordinary wave, and the impracticability of giving warning to a steamer at any distance will be better appreciated. Therefore it is that sailing vessels, in a fog, must look out for themselves against a steamer, and a steamer must provide for her own safety by running with sufficient speed to crowd off or run down anything afloat in their way.

And therefore, again, it is proper that the law positively require that the best possible fog signals should be constantly used by a steamer when running in a fog, and make the officers of the deck responsible with their lives, for any loss of life that may occur from their neglect to employ them. The occasional tolling of a bell—the only signal now in ordinary use—is by no means sufficient. I do not remember any instance of *two steamers* ever having come in collision at sea before this of the *Arctic* and *Vesta,* and it is fortunate that the danger is so small, for I know not in what direction to look for any practicable means of lessening the liability of its occurrence, except by increased, incessant and responsible vigilance on the part of the officers and men.

The danger of running ashore—much greater than that of collision with other ships, in the vicinity where the *Arctic* and the *City of Philadelphia*[6] were lost, I am not considering. To avoid collisions, the great requisite is vigilance—in a fog, a *good look out, forward and aft, alow and aloft.* To save shipwreck the great requisite is *science.* The master who, when running at full speed, has put his craft ashore, stem-on, after a passage only from Cape Clear to Cape Race, must be thought not properly educated for the duties that have been culpably devolved by the owners upon him, or else he has not been adequately supplied with instruments.

The loss of property alone, in the foundering of the *Arctic,* would have been a matter of public regret. The first plain lesson (even if there had been no more deplorable loss) would have been that hereafter all ships destined to carry valuable cargoes or which were themselves of great value, should be provided, as was the *Vesta,* with permanent, watertight bulk-heads, dividing the hold into several close apartments. Here the smaller vessel with damage which, but for this provision, would have been far more quickly fatal, proceeds at once upon her way towards a safe port, where she arrives safely and speedily,[7] while the poor *Arctic,* after two or three hours' steam and hand-pumping, is claimed by the irresistible sea. It is probably within the selfish interest of the underwriters to make this element of safety rapidly become a general one. But if they do not soon take measures for this purpose, the law should again be employed—all vessels unprovided with bulk-heads should be taxed sufficiently to make it the interest of their owners to provide them, and all vessels in the regular passenger traffic should be required to be furnished with them, as they now are with lifeboats.

But it is wrong any longer to talk of the dreadful loss of life which is now sending a shudder of bereavement through half the civilized world, as the result of the accident which sunk the *Arctic.* By the proper use of the means at hand the passengers and crew might all have been saved after the accident occurred.

It is doubted, I know by some, if the *Arctic* was provided with all the *derniers resorts,* which are required by law. I judge that she was so,[8] but whether or not, should be ascertained by a searching and pitiless legal inquisition, and though I have the most heartfelt condolence for Mr. Collins,[9] and sympathize fully in the national gratitude to his enterprise and energy, I hope if the owners are found guilty of neglect in this particular, the utmost penalty of the law will be enforced. Provisions to secure life in the event of the loss of ships are much less neglected now than they have formerly been, but yet they are so much more than is reasonable or just to passengers. I have never seen but one vessel in which printed instructions were placed before passengers, how to behave, where to place themselves, and what to do in a dangerous emergency. It should be known on the steamers that when it is best to take to the boats, the officers will certainly inform the passengers, that in that case, *such a boat* will be manned by the first officer and such a number of his watch, and will take on board, for instance, *the passengers having their berths in the starboard main cabin;* that such another boat will be commanded by the boatswain, and will take on board the *second-cabin passengers;* such another by the second officer, and that it will be reserved for the *engineers and firemen;* and so of the rest. And it should be well understood that the officers will shoot down the first man, passenger or otherwise, who attempts to occupy another boat to that for which he is detailed, and that in the event of a fatal accident to any of the boats the proper crew of that boat will be immediately divided into so many squads as there are boats remaining, by their boat's officer and such squad be directed to which other boat they shall attach themselves; if then it is necessary to leave any behind more than volunteer, that it shall be decided by lot who they are to be.

It was not the result of the accident I have said—that which we are now mourning. It arose as far as the accounts received at the period at which I write, would indicate, from the want of *common* morality, common *manliness* on the part of the crew and from the absence of proper discipline. Is Capt. Luce[10] to blame for this lack of discipline? It is no time yet to allow a direct answer to this question to be in one's mind.

The commanders of these great packet steamers have two such divided and distinct classes of duties expected of them that it is hardly possible they can satisfactorily perform both. As far as my own observation goes, the British steamer commanders, who do not succeed as well as the Americans in gaining the admiration and friendship of their passengers, and who, I believe, are themselves no better seamen or navigators, do maintain a better, more exact and *orderly* discipline in their ships. The seamen and servants work with less spirit and rapidity, perhaps, but they work more by rule and routine and they are consequently more to be depended upon. Discipline does not mean forced or frightened obedience as too many young officers suppose; discipline means *system*. And I say that on the English steamers the seamen work more as a part of a system, of which their officers are another part, and in the American, more as individuals led or driven together by their officers, though this is less so on the Collins line than any other.

I maintain that our whole merchant marine, in this respect, is deeply, radically, disgracefully, demoralized. The very small number of Native American seamen, so far from being the brave, generous, heroic men they are poetically and romantically described to be, are the very meanest, most reckless, dastardly and despicable class of men ever allowed to be long at liberty in the world. Why? Because the seamen in American ships (I do not mean in American alone) are so treated that it is impossible for them to retain self-respect and decent, orderly, *gentlemanly* habits of mind; and, therefore, no American whose disposition and character is good, will go to sea unless he is unusually fortunate in his ships, and has the hope held before him of rapid preferment. I do not believe there is one native seaman in a hundred, who is not a helpless drunkard when on shore, and always shipped in an intoxicated condition when he goes to sea. And there are even a smaller number who do not always fear and hate their officers when at sea, obey them from fear more than from a regard to their contract or from the effect of a decent discipline, and desert them whenever they dare to, if their selfish interests or instincts direct it. And all this is even more true of the foreigners who have been long in our service (with frequent exceptions in the seamen of Northern Continental Europe), with the additional disadvantage that they are more ignorant, less cultivated intellectually, and consequently more desperate in villainy, more cowardly, and more unreasonable and uncontrollable in times of danger.

While our Commerce has increased with amazing rapidity, our number of native seamen has probably hardly increased at all in the last ten years. Consequently wages have nearly doubled for first rate, able seamen, and many a ship goes to sea half manned, and with a crew composed of desperadoes and sots, too mean to live ashore, and only made to do ships' duty by a constant irritating and brutalizing system of working up[11] and bullying on the part of the officers.

What wonder their character becomes slavish and even diabolical!

This difficulty is increasing yearly. It is already a great drawback upon the successful progress of our commercial supremacy. Is there no help for it—no remedy? In the present excitement let reflection be directed to this also. I am only satisfied that the remedy will not tend to make seamen less men and more slaves, less rationally orderly, and more machine-like. Meantime the discipline of these great steam packets should be *educational* as well as sufficient for the trip. The crews, as much as possible, should be in the permanent service of the lines. They should be brought under as perfect *habits* of disciplined control as are ever the crews of our men-of-war. Contrast the conduct of the crew of the *Somers,* when she was lost off Vera Cruz,[12] with that of the *Arctic.* The brig capsized and sunk, and the crew were left swimming with some drifting wreck of spars, sufficient only partially to support them; but they were loyal to their duty and their contract, and had confidence in their officers. Disciplined order was immediately restored, and directions were given for the assistance of the weaker and poorer swimmers, and for other purposes; which were obeyed implicitly, and without a moment's hesitation, by men struggling for life under far more desperate circumstances than those of the *Arctic* at the time the boats left her and the raft was crowded upon and broken up.

F.L.O.

Staten Island, October 15

1. The *Arctic* was a 284-foot, 2,794-ton, wooden-hulled paddle-wheel steamship launched in 1850 by the New York–based New York and Liverpool United States Mail Steamship Company, which was also known as the Collins Line. The ship was noted for its luxury and speed, and in 1852 made a record eastward crossing of the Atlantic of nine days and seventeen hours.

        On September 24, 1854, the *Arctic* collided with the much smaller, iron-hulled French steamer *Vesta* in dense fog fifty miles southwest of Cape Race, Newfoundland. The collision sheared off the bow of the *Vesta,* but her watertight compartments kept her from sinking and enabled her to reach St. John's, Newfoundland, safely. In contrast, the *Arctic* rapidly filled with water, lost power and sank within three hours; 359 lives were lost. Among the dead were many prominent New Yorkers. News of the tragedy reached New York on October 11 and produced a reaction of shock and grief. During the next few days much of the popular response turned to anger as later reports described how members of the crew, along with some men among the passengers, had seized the lifeboats and left women and children to drown.

        Olmsted had been concerned about the lot of merchant seamen ever since his voyage to China in 1843, and in December 1851 had published an article in the *American Whig Review* in which he described his own experience of the heartless and brutal treatment of the *Ronaldson*'s crew by its officers. In that article he proposed a program for training merchant seamen and suggested ways to replace the "brutalizing tyranny" on merchant ships with "new elements of confidence, good temper, and sobriety of feeling" among officers and men. The *Arctic* tragedy aroused his concern once more, and in this letter to the *Times* he again suggested ways to educate men for service in the merchant marine and to secure proper discipline on board ship.

        On October 20, 1854, the *New-York Daily Times* published two letters that were critical of Olmsted's letter on the *Arctic* of October 18, one of which was from Daniel Tracy, the superintendent of the New York Sailors' Home. Tracy declared that the U.S. Navy and merchant marine had no superiors in terms of discipline and that, as a rule, the crews of American ships were "used kindly and humanely." He challenged Olmsted's claim about the drunkenness of the seamen on American ships, asserting that only one of fifty was a helpless drunkard while on shore, and that on an average only three of the one hundred residents of his Sailors' Home were such. The difficulty of finding good crews was due, he believed, to the rapid expansion of commerce and the luring away of many good seamen to the California gold fields. He added that while writing his letter he had spoken with several captains and mates who had been to sea for over twenty years, all of whom characterized Olmsted's sweeping assertions as "*without foundation in truth*—in other words, as utterly and shamelessly false."

        Olmsted replied with a letter, as long as his first one, that appeared in the *Times* on October 24. He defended his basic points and supported them with quotations from various sources, including articles in the *Sailor's Magazine,* a publication of the American Seamen's Friends Society, which operated the New York Sailor's Home. His rebuttal was so thorough that it caused his brother, John, to comment to their father, "He used rather too heavy metal on such a man I think but am very glad the subject is stirred."

        At the beginning of his reply to Tracy, Olmsted did admit that he had written his first letter hastily and that the assertions that most displeased Tracy were indeed "too sweeping." Those statements, he explained, he "did not wish or expect to be understood literally." Having granted that much, Olmsted went on to assert the fundamental accuracy of his first letter. First, he cited his qualifications, declaring that my own opportunities of observation have not been quite contemptible, that I have sailed in American and foreign craft of all classes, more than forty thousand miles; that I have been intimately associated with seamen at home and abroad, at sea and on shore, and that I am experimentally acquainted with the benefits to them growing out of the excellent system of the New-York Sailor's Home; and—as Captain Tracy thinks it important to inquire—I am an American born; though (if one more irrelevant word may be excused) as far as possible from being a *Know-Nothing.*

Tracy had stated that there was virtually no opportunity for rapid advancement in the merchant marine: most men who became captains, as he said, "come in at the 'hawsehole' and work their way aft." It took six years to be rated as an able seaman, and at least six years after becoming mate to advance to captain. This situation did not impress Olmsted, who responded:

I say that when a young man has to "come in at the hawse-holes," and spend six years, first as the inferior and then as the equal, and all as the mate and most closely-confined associate of such crews before he can look for any promotion—that if he is not "demoralized, radically, deeply, disgracefully," it is a miracle. If he is not brutalized by the treatment that such a crew have to endure to force them to the necessary labor for the crack passages which our ships are all striving to make, I do not know what will brutalize a man.... Why, if *interest* combines with duty to make officers treat their crews as if they were not composed purely of brutes, do they not do it? Because these officers are brutes themselves, made brutes by their own six years or more of suffering under this same brutal system.

To emphasize the prevalence of brutality, Olmsted quoted Richard Henry Dana's description, in *Two Years Before the Mast,* of the angry and arbitrary flogging of one of the crew, and said that he had once asked several seamen if they had seen instances of worse treatment. "They all agreed that they had," Olmsted reported, "and some said they had had worse on their last voyage." As for himself, Olmsted added, referring to his experience with Captain Warren Fox on the *Ronaldson,* "I have seen a man more barbarously used than this, and I have heard similar blasphemy on board a ship the Captain of which had the reputation on shore of being an uncommonly humane and pious man." The flogging described by Dana indicated the common mode of relations between officers and crew, Olmsted concluded:

The Captain is supreme—a perfect despot, holding the crew subject to his authority, not for certain reasonable purposes, alone, but subject to his good pleasure, to his passions and whims; as slaves, as horses, and cattle. And the majority of their crews *are* slaves. They subject themselves to this slavery, because they are too mean, too sensual, too spiritless, too little able to command and restrain themselves, to be, or do anything else. Between land-sharks and boarding-house keepers, and merchants and shipmasters, they are bought and sold....

As the majority of men are constituted there is a moral necessity for this brutalizing system, as long as the service is without any sort of *educational system.* That there is no absolute necessity for it is proved by the success of those few shipmasters whose moral nature has been strong enough to carry them, with live hearts and clear heads, through the present brutalizing ordeal of forecastle and petty official slavery.

(Alexander Crosby Brown, *Women and Children Last: The Loss of the Steamship Arctic* [New York, 1961], pp. 15, 20, 26, 43–50, 67–84, 213–14, 219–20; [Frederick Law Olmsted], "A Voice from the Sea," *American Whig Review* 14 [Dec. 1851]: 525–35; "The Arctic's Lessons," *NYDT,* Oct. 20, 1854, p. 1; Daniel Tracy, "The Character of Sailors—Reply to FLO," ibid.; "The Arctic. Character and Treatment of American Seamen—Rejoinder of F.L.O.," ibid., Oct. 24, 1854, p. 2; JHO to JO, Oct. 25, 1854.)

2. "The Loss of the *Arctic*" (*NYDT,* Oct. 12, 1854, p. 4).
3. Presumably a reference to Olmsted's voyage to China in the summer of 1843, when according to the journal he kept, the crew of the *Ronaldson* sighted no ships during the sixty-four days before raising Java Head on August 8 (*Papers of FLO,* 1: 147).
4. A 250-ton, 152-foot screw-propeller steamer built in 1853 and owned by the firm of Hernoux et Compagnie of Dieppe (A. C. Brown, *Women and Children Last,* pp. 47–48).

5. Stewart Holland, a young engineer, fired the *Arctic*'s signal cannon once a minute after the collision and was last seen at his post when the ship sank. Isaac Holland, assistant sergeant-at-arms of the United States Senate, remarked on learning of his son's death: "Better a thousand times that he should perish in the manly discharge of his duty, than have saved a craven life of such cowardice and selfishness as marked the conduct of many of the crew" (ibid., pp. 80–81, 157).
6. The *City of Philadelphia*, an iron-hulled propeller steamer of the Inman Line, ran aground near Cape Race, Newfoundland, only two weeks before the sinking of the *Arctic* (ibid., p. 138).
7. After jettisoning cargo and rigging and repairing the forward bulkhead, the *Vesta* steamed slowly to St. John's, Newfoundland, where it arrived safely on September 30, 1854 (ibid., pp. 130–32).
8. The *Arctic* did carry a large number of life preservers and the six lifeboats required by federal law, but these boats could have carried only 180 of the ship's 282 passengers and 153 crew members to safety (ibid., pp. 67–70, 214, 219).
9. Edward Knight Collins (1802–1878), founder and general manager of the New York and Liverpool United States Mail Steamship Company. His wife, son, daughter, and brother-in-law died in the tragedy (ibid., pp. 18–20, 110, 156–58, 201).
10. James C. Luce (1805–1879) had assumed command of the *Arctic* in 1850. Luce survived the sinking by clinging to a piece of one of the *Arctic*'s paddle boxes until he was rescued by the French ship *Cambria*. He lost his eleven-year-old son in the sinking of the *Arctic* and never went to sea again. For the rest of his career he was an inspector for the Great Western Marine Insurance Company (ibid., pp. 34, 90–91, 105–10, 173–79, 202–3).
11. *Working up* was "keeping men at work on needless matters, beyond the usual hours, for punishment" (William H. Smyth, *The Sailor's Word-Book: An Alphabetical Digest of Nautical Terms*... [London, 1867], s.v. "working up").
12. On December 8, 1846, the U. S. Navy brig *Somers* capsized during a squall while maintaining a blockade of the Mexican coast (*New York Daily Tribune*, Dec. 31, 1846, p. 1).

To John Olmsted

Southside November 7th [1854]
Tuesday—Election day

Dear Father

As I was returning from town yesterday evening—cold, damp & windy—coming to the foot of Vanderbilt's Avenue, I was tucking in the blankets & buffalos—making myself into a mummy. Mr. Seaman drove up from behind to pass me, startled Bell,[1] who jumping, probably loosened the breeching in some way so the "avalanche"[2] shot in to him, terrified him—runaway.

I kept him in the middle of the road a few moments, going at a jumping gallop—was trying to get myself loose of my wrapping when he kicked in the dash board and jerked the reins out of my hands. They are short reins, but I am much ashamed of it.

He immediately afterwards ran off the bank. It is a kind of causeway you remember with trees planted near the road and a space of 10 feet between them and a stone wall. The carriage did not upset though I supposed it would any moment, or catch & be pulled to pieces either on the trees, or the wall. It jumped from one side to the other but did not catch or throw me out. The curtains were buckled down fore and aft. Just east of the hay scales, you remember, the trees run out & the space between them & the wall narrows; also there is here a large old apple tree with branches low crossing the space. I saw this before me and was sure that we should fetch up. I threw up the front seat and lay myself down in the bottom as the safest position. As we came to the apple tree, away went the top and every thing higher than the dash board. One of the seats was thrown out and several of the miscellaneous articles. But the waggon righted & came out onto the fair road, swinging round the corner at the hay scales. I knew the toll gate was close before us & that we should probably fetch up against it. I kicked out the hind seat, threw myself over the back, my feet tripped & I could not recover, but I held on with [one] hand & let my self down as near the ground as I could & let go and immediately got up, uninjured. Waggon was going through the gate & a woman was fainting with fright.

I went back & picked up the things. Mr. Seaman drove up and took me in. At Wandell's, the waggon makers opposite Judge Emerson's,[3] we found the waggon & Bell quietly feeding in the stable. He had been turned round at Osgood's hill by someone trying to stop him & finally caught by Wandell.

Running gear of the waggon uninjured, box frame somewhat broken, top left under & in the apple tree all broken & torn to smash—no value; shafts broken; horse, a little cut in the shoulder, not lame this morning.

I borrowed a saddle & rode home immediately. This morning I find myself stiff & sore down the back and right side & right knee slightly sprained, pantaloons spoiled. Glad it's no worse.

The ground has been so hard—no rain yet to penetrate—that I have not thought it best to take up the trees. It is so hard to get them out without breaking the rootlets when the soil is baked, & have been waiting in hopes of a storm.[4] Today, we have begun on trees to be delivered on the island, to be sent up this P.M. that the wagon &c. may be brought back from Wandell's. We have been principally engaged on fences & in painting the last week.

Saturday morning I went up to N.Y. Collected $105 for Douai & with $15 before collected, & borrowing some from myself, paid $140 on account of Douai.[5] Last night we heard from Seward[6] who invites me to call on him next week in New York.

In P.M. Saturday called on Mr. Bateman[7] at the St. Nicholas. He gave me an order for two to the play in the evening & invited Brace. I went with Brace & his wife.[8] The play was Young America[9]—with Ellen as newsboy. It is very touching and good. Charley was much interested & we all had a good crying spell. Without regard to age, Ellen Bateman is one of the best actresses I ever saw—no stage manner, but a perfect natural child. She is now ten years old, her sister twelve.

Bateman said if I thought best he would, after fulfilling his engagement, give a benefit to the Children's Aid Society.[10] He says he has picked up a

ELLEN BATEMAN AS THE NEWSBOY IN *Young America*

great many ragamuffin boys in the street and given them a start for an honest life & some of them are now men of wealth & standing at the West.

Sunday morning he came down here with me bringing Kate. Ellen was a little unwell & they did not think it prudent for her to go out & her mother stayed to keep her company. We liked Kate very much & she & her father both seemed very much to enjoy being in the country. It is really very wonderful how little injured she has been by this life. 5 years now in which she has been on the stage 5 nights out of six probably when not travelling. Yet she is so simple & child like as you could wish—very sensible & well bred, too, & with less bad habits than usual. Her mother seems to be an uncommonly fine & sensible woman. They have never been in a theater except their mother was with them.

You probably saw the paragraph I wrote for the "Times" about them last week.[11] I wrote it almost entirely on conjecture, but Bateman says it is quite true in all points, only they have scarcely given any instruction to the children at all in acting & only tried to give them a clear understanding of the meaning & spirit of their parts & left the posturing & delivery & gesture &c. to their instinct.

Bateman gave me all the particulars of his fight in California.[12] He was informed that the editor was armed & expecting to meet him in the street. When he went out, therefore, he took a revolver with him to defend himself—having previously made his will &c. The editor saw him coming, crossed the street with a friend & came up to him. When he stopped before him, Bateman raised his arm & with one blow knocked him down. His friend fired at Bateman, who then drew his own revolver & all three fired several shots.

He says the newspaper accounts here were all furnished by the editor & his friends & were very false. The court held him justified & the citizens as an expression of their approbation presented the children with $1,000 on their benefit night. The law-suit, loss of time &c. altogether cost him a very great sum.

Yesterday I drove them up. We found Ellen sick abed with Panama fever, Dr. Marcy attending her.[13] As the bills were posted with a large lithograph of "Ellen Bateman as the Newsboy" it was a predicament. After a capital lunch in their parlor I went with Mr. Bateman to the theater[14] to make arrangements for a change of pieces & to cast the new ones.

While waiting for some actors who had to be sent for, he took me all over "behind the scenes"—explained all the machinery &c. from the ventilator to the basement. There is an immense & most complicated amount of it. The guards against fire are most excellent. A company was rehearsing on the stage & I was introduced to several of them, very clever, simple, light & kind hearted people they seemed to be. Wonderfully affected and demonstrative of pity &c. at Ellen's illness.

I am at a little loss about voting this P.M., but believe I shall go the clean Whig ticket, except the member of Congress—for which I shall support the Soft candidate, the regular Whig being a Hunker & the Independent having I suppose no chance.[15] Dr. will vote against Raymond.[16]

Your affectionate son,

F.L.O.

Dr. thinks this air is not good for Bell & wishes you would send down if you like for Mary.

1. "Belshazzar," the stallion that Olmsted bought in Beaumont, Texas, in May 1854 at the end of his journey through Texas and rode on his journey in the back country (*JT*, p. 379; *BC*, p. 36).
2. A Texas corruption of *ambulance*, which referred to a wagon equipped with springs (Mitford M. Mathews, ed., *A Dictionary of Americanisms on Historical Principles* [Chicago, 1951], s.v. "avalanche").
3. William Emerson (1801–1868), Olmsted's Staten Island neighbor and the older brother of Ralph Waldo Emerson, was judge of the Richmond County Court of Common Pleas. Emerson later represented Olmsted in the bankruptcy proceedings resulting from the failure of Dix, Edwards & Company (Benjamin K. Emerson, *The Ipswich Emersons. A.D. 1636–1900. A Genealogy of the Descendants of Thomas Emerson of Ipswich, Mass.* . . . [Boston, 1900], pp. 176, 264–65; Dorothy V. Smith, *Staten Island: Gateway to New York* [Philadelphia, 1970], p. 220; William Emerson to FLO, Oct. 1, 1857).

THE LITERARY REPUBLIC: 1854-1855

4. Olmsted began to expand the orchards on his Staten Island farm when he moved there in 1848. After his trip to England in 1850 he imported 5,000 pear trees and samples of a variety of trees and shrubs as the basis of what he hoped would be a large and varied nursery business (FLO to FJK, Dec. 21, 1850, Aug. 5, 1851, and Oct. 17, 1852).
5. Olmsted was collecting money to support the *San Antonio Zeitung*, Adolf Douai's free-soil newspaper.
6. William H. Seward (1801-1872), then a Whig senator from New York (*DAB*).
7. In this passage, Olmsted describes the Bateman family, one of the most popular theatrical groups of the time. Head of the family was Hezekiah Linthicum Bateman (1812-1875), Baltimore-born actor and theater manager. His wife was Sidney Frances Bateman (1823-1881), daughter of an English comic actor, Joseph Cowell, who emigrated to the United States and settled near Cincinnati. In 1839, following a short acting career, Sidney Frances married Bateman and thereafter devoted herself to educating their daughters, training them in acting, and writing plays. The two outstanding child prodigies of the Bateman family were the girls Olmsted mentions in this letter—Kate Josephine Bateman and Ellen Bateman. They made their New York debut in 1849 in scenes from Shakespeare's *Richard III,* in which four-year-old Ellen played Richard and six-year-old Kate played Richmond. P. T. Barnum soon hired them to appear at his Museum and in 1851 he took them on a widely acclaimed tour of the British Isles. Then followed a highly successful tour of the United States from 1852 to 1854. In addition to scenes from Shakespeare, their repertoire included contemporary sentimental, comic and melodramatic pieces. At the time of this letter, the Batemans were living at the St. Nicholas Hotel at 515 Broadway (*DNB*, s.v. "Bateman, Hezekiah Linthicum," and "Bateman, Sidney Frances"; *Notable American Women,* s.v. "Bateman, Kate Josephine"; Enid Eleanor Adams, *Our Bateman Ancestry, Compiled for Robert Edwin Bateman* [Victor, Idaho, 1971], pp. 197-99).
8. Charles Loring Brace and his wife, Letitia Neill Brace (1822?-1916).
9. *Young America; Or, The New-York News Boy,* a drama written by Sidney Frances Bateman and first presented in San Francisco in April 1854 (Sidney Frances Bateman, "The 'Prize Drama' Correspondence," *Daily California Chronicle,* June 23, 1854, p. 2; George R. MacMinn, *Theatre of the Golden Age in California* [Caldwell, Idaho, 1941], pp. 462-63).
10. The New York philanthropic organization of which Brace was the executive secretary. One of its major programs was the "placing-out" system by which it settled vagrant city children in farm households in the West (Miriam Z. Langsam, *Children West: A History of the Placing-Out System of the New York Children's Aid Society, 1853-1890* [Madison, Wis., 1964], pp. 21-32).
11. In the unsigned article "Parental Schoolmasters," published in the *New-York Daily Times* of November 1, 1854, page 1, Olmsted described the education of the Bateman children by their parents as follows:

> As an exemplification of the power which a patient and affectionate teacher has over the youthful mind, nothing can be more instructive than the Bateman children. They were, of course, naturally *clever,* and possessed an aptitude for acting. This is obvious in the greater spirit and abandon with which they play those characters most natural to them; such as the "Young Couple" and the "Spoiled Child," in which they always give the highest delight to their audience, not as prodigies, but as themselves—simple, happy, careless children. But in Shakespeare characters, such as *Shylock* and *Hamlet,* which they cannot be supposed to at all adequately comprehend, and yet in which they actually rival many assuming tragedians of mature experience of mankind, it is clearly *art* we admire, and must be the result of laborious study. And this, a stranger cannot help thinking, must have been at the expense of an unnatural maturity—always painful, and almost always followed by fatally pernicious consequences. Such, however, a friend who has had an opportunity of an intimate acquaintance with them, assures us is not the case; off the stage they are fully as artless, frolicsome and *childlike* as any children of their age. They are, perhaps, a little behindhand with their Geography and "Ciphering," but are as fond of toys, sugar-plums, and of people who like them and can play with them, as Eliza and Sarah Smith, who share alternatively the honors of the "head of the class," at the ward school. Their parents have always been their teachers, and their system of instruction, *with reference to its results,* has been as judicious as it has been sufficient. The secret of its success we believe to lie in making their studies as easy, attractive, and as *agreeably associated* as possible. The extent and reliability of their memory is really the most marvelous circumstance of their success,

although few probably ever think of it. We understand that they have committed to memory the most of the immense amount of words they must have learned by *rote* while sitting on their father's knee or in their mother's lap—repeating, not from the book, but from their teacher's voice. Their lessons have always been made short, but very frequently repeated, and always in alternation with cheerful recreation. The path before them is made as attractive to them as possible; they are led in it by affection and never driven by authority. Let parents heed the lesson.

Olmsted might have seen the Bateman sisters perform *Young Couple* in Richmond, Virginia, on December 21, 1852, while he was visiting the city (*Richmond Enquirer,* Dec. 21, 1852, p. 2).

12. Olmsted describes here Bateman's fight with Frank Soulé (1810–1882), editor of the *Daily California Chronicle,* which occurred on June 30, 1854. The Batemans had sponsored a playwriting contest to obtain the best three-act drama about life in California with parts suitable for Kate and Ellen. The $1,000 prize was awarded to Sidney Frances Bateman for her play *The Mother's Trust; Or, California in 1849,* which she had submitted anonymously. Mrs. Bateman's donation of the prize to a local orphanage failed to placate Soulé, who upon learning the identity of the winning author, accused her of plagiarizing from the book *All's Not Gold That Glitters; Or, The Young Californian,* written in 1853 by Emily Bradley Neal Haven (G. R. MacMinn, *Theatre of the Golden Era in California,* pp. 464–69; "The Prize Drama for the Batemans," *Daily California Chronicle,* June 22, 1854, p. 2; "To the Twenty-one Victims," ibid.; "Stop Thief!," ibid., June 30, 1854, p. 2; James Nisbet, "Freedom of the Press—Brutal Outrage," ibid., July 1, 1854, p. 2; Richard H. Dillon, Introduction to *Annals of San Francisco . . . With the Continuation Through 1855, Compiled by Dorothy Huggins. Being a True Facsimile of the Celebrated Original Works First Published in 1855 and 1939 Respectively . . .,* by Frank Soulé, John H. Gihon and James Nisbet [Palo Alto, Calif., 1966], pp. xviii–xix).

13. Erastus Edgerton Marcy (1815–1900), a leading homeopathic physician, was treating Ellen Bateman for malaria (Rossiter Johnson and John Howard Brown, eds., *The Twentieth Century Biographical Dictionary of Notable Americans* [Boston, 1904], s.v." Marcy, Erastus Edgerton").

14. The Bateman children were appearing at Niblo's Garden, located at the corner of Prince Street and Broadway (*NYDT,* Nov. 1, 1854, p. 4; John A. Kouwenhoven, *The Columbia Historical Portrait of New York: An Essay in Graphic History . . .* [Garden City, N.Y., 1953], pp. 198, 347).

15. The election of 1854 in New York offered a bewildering array of parties and candidates to the voters. Olmsted intended to vote primarily for Whig candidates, partly because of the strong anti-Nebraska stand taken by the party: its platform condemned the Kansas-Nebraska Act, praised the New York senators and congressmen who opposed its passage, and declared that the act's repeal of the Missouri Compromise freed the Whig party from the obligation of supporting any further compromises with slavery. Olmsted intended to vote for Myron Clark (1806–1892), the gubernatorial candidate of the Whig and Anti-Nebraska parties (which had merged platforms and tickets) and also the candidate of the Free Democracy and Prohibition parties. Clark opposed the expansion of slavery and the Kansas-Nebraska Act, and was the leader of the state's prohibition forces. Running with Clark for lieutenant governor was Henry J. Raymond, editor of the *New-York Daily Times,* who had the endorsement of all the parties supporting Clark except the Free Democrats. Raymond's nomination particularly offended Horace Greeley, who had hoped to run on the Whig ticket for either governor or lieutenant governor.

Although Olmsted planned to vote for most of the Whig slate, he could not support the congressional candidate in his district, Henry W. Vail, whom he dismissed as a "Hunker." That term was originally used to characterize the more pro-Southern faction of the New York Democratic party, whose differences with the antislavery "Barnburners" had by this time split the state party. Olmsted tended to give a broader meaning to the term, applying it to anyone who supported the Fugitive Slave Law, expansion of slave territory, or the use of federal officials to protect property in slaves.

Olmsted also decided not to vote for Gabriel P. Disosway, whom he calls an "Independent," and who was a Whig running on the Anti-Nebraska ticket against Henry W. Vail, the official fusion candidate of the Anti-Nebraska and Whig parties. Predictably, Olmsted did not intend to vote for the Know-Nothing candidate, William W. Valk—who carried the district—or for Daniel B. Allen, the candidate of the "Hard" or "Hunker" faction of the Democratic party. It was unusual for him to vote for a Democrat, especially since the "Soft," or "Barnburner," faction of the Democratic party in 1854 adopted a much milder position than

usual on the slavery issue. The "Soft" delegates voted down a declaration strongly condemning the Kansas-Nebraska Act and adopted instead a "cunningly worded resolution declaring the repeal of the Missouri Compromise inexpedient and unnecessary, yet rejoicing that it would benefit the territories and forbidding any attempt to undo it." This caused nearly half of the delegates to bolt the convention, after which they ran anti-Nebraska candidates on a Free Democracy ticket. Olmsted chose, however, to vote for the "Soft" candidate, Connecticut-born and Yale-educated Frederick William Lord (1800-1860). Lord had practiced medicine in Sag Harbor, Long Island, for fifteen years and in 1846 had retired to Greenport, Long Island, where he lived as a gentleman farmer and cultivated fruit and ornamental trees. Although running as a Democrat in 1854, he had been a Whig member of the Thirtieth Congress (1847-49) and was to be a delegate to the Republican National Convention in 1860 (DeAlva Stanwood Alexander, *A Political History of the State of New York*, 2 vols. [New York, 1906], 2: 126-27, 184-204; Robert Sobel and John Raimo, eds., *Biographical Directory of the Governors of the United States, 1789-1978*, 4 vols. [Westport, Conn., 1978], 3: 1082-83; *BDAC*, s.v. "Lord, Frederick William," and "Valk, William Weightman"; *NYDT*, Nov. 7, 1854, p. 3; ibid., Nov. 9, 1854, p. 1; ibid., Nov. 10, 1854, p. 1).
16. That is, John Hull Olmsted was not going to vote for Henry Raymond for lieutenant governor.

To Bertha Olmsted and Sophia Stevens Hitchcock

[Early 1855]

Dear Bertha[1]

I have a mission for war & fighting you know & now comes your turn for a blow up. If you can afford to spend an hour or two writing a letter we can afford to spend a franc or two to read it or to have you spend it for us. So be a little more careless about it and put the time you spend in thinking about it into thinking about something else & the time you spend in writing about it in writing about something else and at the end of the quarter send in your bill. There are not less than a dozen of us and twouldn't be more than a shilling apiece if every letter came double postage because you didn't leave out some one thought or fact & I have no doubt the collective thoughts and facts thus obtained quarterly, would be worth at least 1/6 apiece to us.

Don't bother yourself so much about times and seasons; write when you conveniently can and feel like it and mail when it's handy to do so. If the letter comes sooner than we expected of course it gives us *unexpected* pleasure and if [it] does not come so soon as we should like it, then we are all the gladder to get it when it does come. We have had but one letter from you since you got out that was not filled on the first page altogether, generally a part and sometimes the whole of the second, with explanations and apologies and reasonings and conjectures on these two topics, which, though Father may think it best to humor for the sake of giving you training in preciseness & economy, he is bored by, I venture to say, as much as any body else.

Recollect that Paris is no further from New York—Hartford, that is—than Geneseo was when you were a child and Uncle Owen[2] lived there, and that nobody has any more reason to be anxious about you than if you were at the Reverend Mrs. James Gordon Abbott's in New York,[3] & write what is pleasant and easy and beneficial to yourself and when it is easy and pleasant & most comfortable to yourself and don't think anybody's going into mourning if we don't hear from you by a particular steamboat or that anybody will faint away if three letters come at once.

There's no use in giving directions as to who shall and who shan't read your letters; you ought to know that. If you particularly request that any one shall not be shown to Mr. Smith, Father will be very careful to give it to him by mistake, that he may understand, as he will be sure to do, if he is not a goose, that you would like to correspond with him confidentially & knowing Father's habits of mind have taken that way to tell him so without any impropriety. But as in this case he will of course be impudently mistaken, so you will be if you write any particular show letters. They are the very ones that will stick at Litchfield or that Tot will get to play great conflagration with[4] and Mr. Smith will call and forget to ask whether you have been heard from lately, entirely from bashfulness; and just the time when you have missed three steamers running will be the time Mr. Smith will have accidentally noticed what steamers have been coming & will have, before he knows it, have asked *what* has been heard from you by them & Dr. Bushnell & Tom Beecher and Mrs. Dolly Ducklegs will be calling just after your last show letter, after having been saved three weeks for some such people, will have been dispatch'd to Litchfield for little Fanny to take the initiatory lessons in Lamplightology with, and when you haven't been heard of for three weeks & when last heard from had just been invited by the Marquis of Chandos to attend a fete champetre and were debating whether you should accept because it would be Saturday & you were afraid you might not be back before sundown & wouldn't be in a proper state of mind to put on clean linen for Sunday.[5]

And by the way, don't you begin to see yet that very few people, that are not very wicked people in other respects, ever drink wine or go to balls from bad motives? They go to enjoy themselves, but the essence of enjoyment is not selfish, it is in the opportunity of contributing and assisting to the enjoyment or pleasure of others. That is, after the first childish excitement of coming out is past.

Having cut off your right & left flanks, I don't mind allowing that the body of your letters is very pretty reading & indicates a very charming, sensible young woman, who is under very good circumstances for her improvement & making a very good use of them. Descriptions of the old school and the scholars and the teachers and servants & hangers on—clear, vivid, and picturesque & truthful as Villette[6] and a good deal more amiable and healthy. But the account of the present state and condition of the friend & chaperon[7] was better than anything else, and so exactly described her, directly & incidentally, as to show keener powers of insight into human nature & natural phenomena than the writer had before been suspected of.

Did you read the article a month or two since in the "Revue de deaux (meaning two (2)—I don't know the exact orthography) Mondes," on American women?[8] Look it up. My impression is that none of those much flattered authoresses could have written so clever [a] picture of "Miss Stevens,"[9] as yours. I jumped up & down 19 times and cracked the chimney of the lamp when I came to the result of her experience as an artist and good sense as a woman upon the vexed question of whether man (kind) is by nature a nocturnal or a dié-tetic animal.

Equally with her I have half burst the fetters of heathen custom; rising about the fifth hour of day light and devoting the intervening time till cheering night lights up her lamps to eating, drinking & getting ready. About 9 P.M. I get to work & between that & bedtime invariably accomplish much more than when rising before light I devote the day to labor. I protest against your unwarranted interferences with the sweet counsels of nature. Better drink cold tea than destroy genius—better waste the morning feu de (da di des) bois[10] than burn the midnight oil in vain for want of nature's restorative potion in proper place, time & dose. Take it easy & pursue your bent; that's the great secret of mental health.

You are not so young as you think you are. Mary[11] is of another sort and develops slowly and silently, people do not recognize her & therefore do not recognize you & you do not recognize yourself to be so old as you are. You are not a child but a particularly smart young woman and you are in danger of not taking those responsibilities upon yourself that belong to you.

I have lately received a physiological & philosophical principle that commends to my conviction—as consistent with my recollections of myself & others & of my every day observation very strongly—that reflection lays dormant while acquisition of data is made a business of. The acquisition of knowledge interferes with the development of wisdom. The learned *scholars* are always great fools (unless persons originally of quite extraordinary *capacity*). Be careful therefore not to carry childhood or the proper time for healthily receiving *instruction* so far on in life as to interfere with *education,* the drawing out of your private endowments. Don't let women & men have the entire construction of your rules & motives & ideas, but let what God gave *you* in particular, have fair play.

Don't let them shut you up much. German & French & dancing & music & History can very possibly be learned more rapidly, easily & perfectly at Paris than elsewhere, but they can be learned—& that well enough—in New York or Hartford or London or San Francisco. Therefore, what time and strength you can not give to other things in Paris, give to them. But there are other things to be attained and learned in Paris that are not to be anywhere but Paris, and there are certain things to be learned at Madame Le Duc's[12] that are not to be anywhere else in Paris, and they are more valuable possibly than language or graces or anything to be obtained from professors or books on history. I suspect you have by this time got the best of them, so I will tell you as summer approaches do you insist upon *going out.* If Madame will not let you, cut your cable. Make sure that by some means or other you get out.

Emerson and J. R. Lowell have both been decrying the value of foreign travel;[13] and if everybody travelled as they travelled and as nearly all do travel in these days, they were right. Shakespeare knew better and in his days it was impossible to travel as people do & will now. The great advantage of travel should be, that by it, habits of mind, which do not originate in the will & individual needs, wants and temperament, but in the warping & moulding effect of rigid circumstances, *may* be, and if it is best they should be, will be, if one please, warmed & melted away. Therefore keep home warm in your affections & your recollections, but not in your habits. And the great key to good in foreign travel is to place oneself in situations & circumstances, where one will be most liable to *accidents.* I don't mean disagreeable accidents. To place oneself where (I mean) one does not know *what to expect next.* You want to learn French—the professor & book are valuable accessories but the accidental, *inci*dental & unconscious method of receiving instruction, such as you have in a French family, is the best way to arrive quickly at perfection. You want to study *the* French; they are not to be understood by the study of their legislation & courts and theatres & newspapers but by seeing them incidentally, in the street, in the shops, in the *families,* through the window before you are up in the morning, in the bread and butter and eggs & milk they give you for your money. If there is no plaster in the bread; no hairs in the milk, if the eggs are fresh & cream rises on the milk, and for a proportionate measure of money you do not get these things so in New York, your respect for the French should rise & you should try to see what were the influences lying back of government, whether legal or of custom or in religion (that is to say, Theology, for religion is the same everywhere) that have caused it.

What traveller, what philosopher or historian can tell me or has told me, without evident falseness of bigotry, what effect, on the whole, the Democratic revolutions of the last hundred years have had on the minds of the French people at large. Who knows whether they have been benefitted or injured by them, elevated or debased in character; who gives me an opinion entitled to respect on the subject? No one—no one has leisure & the right kind of industry to enquire into that matter rightly. It is not to be ascertained in Paris or but partially there & with difficulty. Paris *does not* constitute France: the fact that it rules France & with travellers passes for France is a speaking one—affords a strong indication of what France is—that's all.

But worse, Louis Napoleon[14] & his Court, the Army, the officials, the police, the savants, the actors, the newspapers, the Diplomatique, the gentlemen & ladies that are able to hope to procure tickets to the Prefect's ball, the men who keep the shops, the workmen & the gamins, the flower women & the grisettes & the rest—all the interesting people do not begin to make up Paris. Add all your professors & esses, the servants & the omnibus drivers & conductors, the guides, commissionaires, washwomen, artists, doorkeepers, priests, nuns & performers and all you are likely to see while merely searching for pleasure or moving for business and convenience & you after all know very little, see very little of the people of Paris. A majority of the people of Paris are in back somewhere, or are the wives & children of the shop keepers & workmen & adventurers &c. How are you to see these & to learn by seeing them what is essentially good & essentially bad in Paris—for it is their habits and ideas & hopes and fears that will teach it to you, far more than all the rest.

You will learn it by accident—all you can do is to put yourself in the way of accidents. Strolling the streets without an object leads you unconsciously to it. Looking for nothing, cast your eyes down by accident & you will see gold. And this is not true of information alone. The best thoughts come to us unawares; not by study; that is, not directly by study. But if entirely without study, you will not have knowledge enough or strength enough to pick up the gold you stumble upon. But don't let study be the end—only the means. Get provisions on board & use the charts others have prepared, but don't neglect voyages of discovery yourself. It is in the streets & parks, on the bridges & in the omnibuses, in the placards and in the street cries, as much—ten times more—you are to learn as in the classes, at the theatre, in the newspapers & from the professors.

I want you by all means, also, if you can in any way accomplish it, to get out into the country, & when you are there try hard to put yourself in the way of having relations with something beside other *ruralists* merely; try to find (by accidents) what the real people of the country are—the men who are planting beets & thatching cottages and whittling sabots & the women who are tethering cows & carrying water and who go out whitewashing & cleaning house. You will never see much of such people when you try to, but you must travel or live or stroll or have a passion for something else which incidentally, when you don't expect, will bring you against such people.

The great accomplishment & acquirement or development of grace of endowment in yourself to be got in Paris above America is not language or manner or any sort of information, but appreciation of beauty and of excellence, more especially in fine arts. This you ought to be in particularly good circumstances for—make the most of them. But the way to make the most is not to go to work methodically, unless indeed you find both the sense of beauty & the talent to reproduce it already unusually developed in you & you determine to become an artist. But the way is to go as often as you can without making it really tiresome to the Louvre[15]—stroll through, look at the pictures, just as you feel like doing, without *trying* at all, for some time at any rate, to appreciate what you are told is best, but just trying to enjoy yourself in fact, trying or being careful that you don't go so much & study & try to see beauty so much as to make it secretly a bore to you. What you want is to unconsciously & incidentally cultivate your eye & the eye of your mind & heart. It will come when you don't know it, this appreciation of excellence, never fear. Go occasionally to the Luxembourg & see the modern paintings.[16] Go to Versailles[17] (go there ten times at least before August.) You will be most pleased & interested with them probably for some time, but gradually you will see nearly all of them are poor trash and the old, dark, smokey, shadowy blotches of blues and browns & dull reds in the Louvre that at first you would not accept as presents if it were with the condition that you must have them hung up in your bedroom—they will have grown in some way attractive to you & when you begin to wonder in what way, then go to Sophy & ask her to go with you & tell you what she likes & why she likes it. Then read Ruskin[18] & anything else you please—anything you can read on the general subject without boring yourself. The only thing that I saw in the Louvre that I would walk a mile to see again was Murillo's Virgin.[19] But half of it or more was shut off when I was there.

Make it a point, as often as it is not out of your way, to go past the antique statues, & as much as convenient when in the garden let your eyes rest on the casts—especially one of the serpent & lion or tiger[20] which is superb & if you want to know what present to get for me, that's it & whenever you find it in plaster or in bronze in miniature let me know & if I can cheat myself in any way I'll put you in funds for it.

One other thing to be particularly acquired & cultivated in Paris—a delicate & refined taste (of the table) & the art of cooking. Ask yourself "what is it that makes this & that better than the nearest thing like it I am accustomed to" & get as much into the kitchens as you can.

Practice your eye also as much as you can make convenient by accident and also with intent, on architecture. Lounge about the (can't remember the market place, quaint old carved domestic architecture) and about Notre Dame.[21] And whenever you are approaching the Hotel de Ville[22] keep your eye upon it—it is a delightful thing to remember—rather than upon the flower market & the washing boats & baths—Plenty of flowers in Hartford & washerwomen and bathing tubs & seines, but nothing in America to help one's growth in Beauty as the Hotel de V. (Hotel Devil we might well have punned on it once.)

Mrs. Cranch is a nice woman, very. I'd be glad to have you know her. They are very poor, very cultivated, very amiable & happy people. Tell Mr. Cranch you know me.[23] Make much of Mr. Spring,[24] too—the best hearted man in the world, but with no pertinacity of mind, only of soul. But cut the American world in Paris & see the French. Try to make French friends. Don't be bashful or careful or cowardly, only modest.

My dear Mrs. Sophie Hitchcock

How-dy do? hope I see you [well]; much obleeged—quite smart considerin' &c.

What I want to say to you is, wouldn't it be a good thing for you to write for Putnam or Harper's magazine?[25] Fred Perkins[26] is working editor of

THE HOTEL DE VILLE, PARIS

Putnam now & I suppose would be disposed to have you well paid for old acquaintance sake wouldn't he? They usually pay $5 a page. Harper's pay still better for a certain class of articles, as I judge from hints that have been given to me, & they are such articles as you could get up, I should think, if you once get the right idea, very easily. Harper is not quite so respectable as Putnam & I have always thought I wouldn't write for it—so long as they constantly reprint articles from the English magazines & give no credit. But when such men as Ripley & Curtis[27]—one the best critic & the other the most promising story teller in the country—are regularly occupied upon it, it does not become small people to stand on dignity.

What you want to do for Harper is to write some lively narratives or Life Sketches & send with them piquant *illustrations*—anything that is really new—new in Paris as well as here. I am sure you could strike some rich vein in Paris that has not been opened.

If you have seen Harper, you have seen, at times past, sketches in Paris, street & café sketches. They were not very good. I suppose Dick Tinto[28] furnished them. They were not of narrative or continuous interest enough & the illustrations were too much in the Charivari style[29] & that of the light French literature—looked too like copies not from nature but from other woodcuts, & the writing was too spotty & there was too great an exertion to point a moral at frequent intervals.

The Porte Crayon[30] sketches are nearer what are wanted, but are too affected & too evidently made for the purpose. The French country & country town & Paris atelier stories in Household Words[31] are the right sort of thing (and are delightful & interesting in themselves, aside from their market value.) Something in the style of the Philosophe sur le roof—translated as "the attic philosopher in Paris,"[32] a bad translation of the title but capital of the book, would do. (And that also is most delightful reading & if you haven't, get it for your own comfortation—good Sunday reading.)

Some of your earlier letters to the Tribune[33] (were very good there &) would almost do, wanting incident and picturesque points for illustration. Your later letters in the Tribune were bad, strained and too interjectionary & affected a great deal. You are not successful in rhapsodies, which is perhaps strange. The letter on Rambouillet & the one on Dinner parties at M. Bossange's[34] was very good. But search for a voice of your own both in matter & style—for a single article or two or three—some sort of an account of your Pensionat—what you call it—I should think would do very well, with all its surroundings & historical reminiscences of Madame & some ghost stories & recollections of Gascony by the old nurse or cook & the going to Church & hither & thither & one thing & another, that might splice in handsomely to give variety and shadow & opportunity for illustration. For something of this sort that suited the market, & with cuts original & clever in style & subject, I have no doubt they would pay *very handsomely.*

It will do you good once in a month or two to spend a few days on such a thing as a vacation from your regular work. If you feel like making the trial, send to me & I will certainly get something done with it. If Harper should decline, as I don't believe he would, I can at all events get it in the Times[35] at $5 a column without the cuts—that at the worst, so it wouldn't be absolutely wasted. Send a small instalment or sample to start with & let me try.

Yours Affectionately

Fred.

Putnam does not want sketches (illustrations).

The original is in the possession of Terry Niles Smith. Internal evidence indicates that Olmsted wrote this letter in early 1855—probably in February or March—while he was living and writing at his Staten Island farm, and before he moved to New York in mid-April to engage in the publishing business as a partner in Dix, Edwards & Company.

1. Bertha Olmsted, Olmsted's half-sister.
2. Owen Pitkin Olmsted (1794–1873), Olmsted's uncle, who had lived in Geneseo in western New York (*Olmsted Genealogy*, p. 60).
3. Mary Olmsted (1832–1875), Bertha's sister and Olmsted's half-sister, had attended the Reverend Gorham D. Abbot's Collegiate Institute for Young Ladies in New York during the academic year 1846–47 (Abbot Collegiate Institute for Young Ladies, *Catalogue of the Abbot Collegiate Institute for Young Ladies... Gorham D. Abbot, Principal* [New York, 1853], p. 25; *Olmsted Genealogy*, p. 60).
4. That is, any letters that Bertha intended for effect would not reach the people she wanted most to impress: they might be misplaced at the Litchfield home of cousin Frances Olmsted Coit

(1829–1907), for example, and not be read by John Hull and Mary Perkins Olmsted, who lived on Staten Island, and whose infant son, John Charles, was affectionately called "Tot." At one point during the summer of 1855, for instance, John Hull Olmsted wrote his father, "I have expected Bertha's last from Litchfield instantly but have not received it" (*Olmsted Genealogy*, pp. 109, 154; JHO to JO, July 8, 1855).

5. A series of playful references by which Olmsted predicts the fate of Bertha's "show" letters. That is, by the time friends inquired about her activities in Paris, Bertha's descriptions of events and society might have been sent to Litchfield to be read to Fanny Coit (b. 1852), the infant daughter of Olmsted's cousin Frances. Horace Bushnell was the family minister, and Thomas Kinnicut Beecher (1824–1900) had been principal of Hartford High School from 1848 to 1852. "Lamplightology" refers to *The Lamplighter*, a popular sentimental novel by Maria Susanna Cummins published in 1854 (*Olmsted Genealogy*, pp. 109, 155; *Papers of FLO*, 1: 72–74, 329–30; *DAB*, s.v. "Cummins, Maria Susanna").

6. A novel by Charlotte Brontë (1816–1855), first published in 1853 under the pseudonym Currer Bell. The central character in *Villette* is a young Englishwoman teaching at a girls' school in Brussels (Sir Paul Harvey, ed. and comp., *The Oxford Companion to English Literature*, 3d ed. [Oxford, 1948], s.v. "Villette").

7. Bertha was living in Paris with Sophia Stevens Hitchcock, a friend of the Olmsted family whose husband, Stephen W. Hitchcock, had died in 1852 (*Papers of FLO*, 1: 91–93).

8. Emile Montégut, "Scènes de la vie et de la litterature americaines. 1. le roman de moeurs. *The Lamplighter*, Boston et Londres, 1854," *Revue des deux mondes*, 2d ser., 8 (Oct.–Dec. 1854): 876–911. The "much flattered authoresses" to whom Olmsted refers were Maria Susanna Cummins; Harriet Beecher Stowe; Elizabeth Claghorn Gaskell, author of the novel *Cranford* (1853); Elizabeth Wetherell (pseudonym for Susan Bogert Warner), best known for her novel *The Wide, Wide World* (1850); and the Brontë sisters, Ann, Charlotte, and Emily.

9. Sophia Stevens Hitchcock (1826–1892).

10. That is, wood fire. As the words in parentheses indicate, Olmsted was not sure of the correct article to use in this expression, or indeed what the forms of the possessive article "de" were in French.

11. Mary Olmsted, Olmsted's half-sister.

12. The proprietor of the *pension* at which Bertha and Sophia Stevens Hitchcock were living in Paris (Bertha Olmsted, manuscript chronology of European travel, n.d., Olmsted Papers).

13. In an unsigned article entitled "Fireside Travels" in the April 1854 issue of *Putnam's Monthly*, James Russell Lowell (1819–1891) reminisced about discussions he had had with a friend in Rome. In those talks, he recalled, he had argued that "a man should have travelled thoroughly round himself and the great *terra incognita* just outside and inside his own threshold, before he undertook voyages of discovery to other worlds." He also declared that it was to know things, and not men, that one needed to travel, and that "the wisest man was he who stayed home, that to see the antiquities of the old world was nothing." Lowell later included this piece in his collection of essays, *Fireside Travels*, first published in 1864.

Olmsted's reference to Emerson is probably to the passages in the essay "Self-Reliance" that deplore traveling and assert that "it is for want of self-culture that the superstition of Travelling, whose idols are Italy, England, Egypt, retains its fascination for all educated Americans," and that "Travelling is a fool's paradise" because it holds out false hopes of becoming intoxicated with beauty and losing one's sadness. Emerson first published the essay in 1841 in his first collection of essays. Many editions of the volume were published thereafter, including an English edition with an introduction by Thomas Carlyle in 1853 and an American edition in 1854 ([James Russell Lowell], "Fireside Travels. Cambridge Thirty Years Ago. A Memoir Addressed to the Edelman Storg in Rome," *Putnam's Monthly* 3, no. 16 [April 1854]: 379–80; *DAB*).

14. Charles Louis Napoleon Bonaparte (1808–1873), emperor of France from 1852 to 1870 (*EB*).

15. The Louvre, built as a fortress in the thirteenth century, had become the French national museum of art in 1793. At the time Olmsted wrote this letter, the Louvre was being enlarged according to plans prepared by the architect Ludovico Visconti (David H. Pinkney, *Napoleon III and the Rebuilding of Paris* [Princeton, 1958], pp. 80–82).

16. The collection of paintings at the Luxembourg Palace, which in 1818 had been made a national museum for the display of works by living French painters and sculptors.

17. The palace of Versailles, where most of the paintings were of French historical scenes and personages.

18. John Ruskin (1819–1900), the English art critic whose *Modern Painters* Olmsted had read and admired in 1849 (*Papers of FLO*, 1: 283, 323–25).
19. Probably the *Madonna of the Rosary* or *Vierge au Rosaire*, painted c. 1645–50 by Bartolome Esteban Murillo, in the Louvre (August Liebmann Mayer, *The Work of Murillo Reproduced in Two Hundred and Eighty-seven Illustrations, With a Biographical Introduction* [New York, 1913], pp. 5–10 and plate 25).
20. *Lion et Serpent*, a life-size bronze statue in the Jardin des Tuileries near the Louvre, done in 1835 by Antoine-Louis Barye (Stuart Pivar, *The Barye Bronzes* [Woodbridge, Suffolk, 1974], pp. 4–11).
21. Probably Les Halles, the central market place of Paris, in a neighborhood with many houses with ornately carved façades dating from the sixteenth and seventeenth centuries; and the cathedral of Notre Dame on the Ile de la Cité (Jacques Silvestre de Sacy, *Le Quartier des Halles*... [Paris, 1969], pp. 80–286; Thomas Forester, ed., *Paris and Its Environs: An Illustrated Handbook* [London, 1859], pp. 138–43; Jean Pierre Babelon, Michel Fleury and Jacques de Sacy, *Richesses d'art du quartier des Halles: Maison par maison* [Paris, 1967], pp. 5–9 passim).
22. The Hotel de Ville, seat of the municipal government in Paris, which was completed in 1628 and burned in 1871.
23. Christopher Pearse Cranch (1813–1892), Unitarian minister, painter, critic and poet. In 1843, after a decade in the ministry, he married Elizabeth de Windt. With her encouragement and a small independent income, he turned to landscape painting. In 1846 the Cranches went to Italy to study art; they were accompanied by George W. Curtis, through whom Olmsted probably met them. They returned to America for the years 1849–53 and spent the next decade in Paris (*DAB*).
24. Marcus Spring (1810–1874), a New York commission merchant, philanthropist and social reformer. He contributed funds for the establishment of both Brook Farm and the Fourierist North American Phalanx at Red Bank, New Jersey. He was a director of the North American and one of the leaders of the group that left that community in 1853 to found the Raritan Bay Union (*Papers of FLO*, 1: 385, n. 12; Maude Honeyman Greene, "Raritan Bay Union, Eagleswood, New Jersey," *Proceedings of the New Jersey Historical Society* 68, no. 1 [Jan. 1950]: 4–8, 10–14, 19; Eric R. Schirber, "The End of an Experiment: The Decline and Final Dissolution of the Phalanx," *Monmouth Historian* 2 [Spring 1974]: 32–34).
25. *Putnam's Monthly Magazine of American Literature, Science, and Art*, edited by Charles F. Briggs (1804–1877), was first published in January 1853. Publication of *Harper's New Monthly Magazine*, edited by Fletcher Harper (1806–1877), began in June 1850 (Frank Luther Mott, *A History of American Magazines*..., 5 vols. [Cambridge, Mass., 1938–68], 2: 383–92, 419–28; *DAB*, s.v. "Briggs, Charles," and "Harper, Fletcher").
26. Frederic Beecher Perkins (1828–1899), author, editor and librarian, who lived in Hartford, Connecticut, before moving to New York City c. 1854. Sophia Stevens Hitchcock had presumably been acquainted with him in 1848–51, when she was living with the Olmsted family and teaching at the Hartford High School. It was during those years that Olmsted was courting Perkins's sister, Emily. In 1854 Perkins became an editor of the *New York Daily Tribune* and in the following year he served as managing editor of *Putnam's Monthly* prior to the purchase of that journal by Dix, Edwards & Company. He was the father of the social reformer Charlotte Perkins Gilman (*DAB*; *Yale Obit. Rec.*, 4th ser. 9 [June 1899]: 611; JHO to Bertha Olmsted, Jan. 28, 1855; *Papers of FLO*, 1: 91).
27. George Ripley (1802–1880), editor of the literary department at *Harper's Monthly*, and George W. Curtis, occupant of the "Editor's Easy Chair" of that journal (*DAB*).
28. Olmsted is probably referring to the series of illustrated articles entitled "Life in Paris. By an American," which appeared in *Harper's Monthly* between 1852 and 1854. "Dick Tinto" was the pseudonym of Frank Boott Goodrich (1826–1894), the American journalist and playwright who was then living in Paris. Although Goodrich was writing a series of articles on France for the *New-York Daily Times*, there is no evidence that he wrote the articles in *Harper's Monthly* (*DAB*).
29. That is, in the style of *Le Charivari*, a daily journal of politics, literature and the arts, published in Paris.
30. Beginning with "The Virginia Canaan," which appeared in the December 1853 issue of *Harper's Monthly*, David Hunter Strother (1816–1888) published a series of unsigned articles on life in the South. These essays were collected and published as *Virginia Illustrated, by Porte Crayon*, in 1857 (*DAB*).

31. *Household Words,* a weekly magazine founded in 1850 by Charles Dickens and edited by him until 1859. After c. September 1854 the American edition of the magazine was published by Olmsted's friend Joshua A. Dix. During the time that Olmsted was a partner in Dix, Edwards & Company, that firm published the American edition. Olmsted's reference in this letter indicates that he was acquainted with the contents of the magazine before he became professionally concerned with it.
32. Emile Souvestre, *An Attic Philosopher in Paris; Or, A Peep at the World from a Garret. Being the Journal of a Happy Man* (New York, 1854).
33. Sophia Stevens Hitchcock's series of thirty-nine letters for the *New York Daily Tribune,* entitled "An American Woman in Paris," appeared between December 2, 1853, and December 2, 1854 (*New York Daily Tribune,* Dec. 2, 5, 15, 16 and 28, 1853; Jan. 5, 11, Feb. 13, 24, 25, March 3, 9, 11, 15, 22, April 7, 14, May 11, 24, 29, June 5, 6, 8, 10, 17, 21, July 15, 22, Aug. 23, 24, Sept. 14, 26, 27, 28, Oct. 10, Nov. 22 and Dec. 2, 1854).
34. Olmsted is referring to "An American Woman in Paris" number 16 ("The Merino Sheep of Rambouillet") and number 17 ("Breakfast at Rambouillet"). "M. Bossange" is Hector Bossange (1795–1884), a French bibliographer and bookseller whom Bertha Olmsted and Sophia Stevens Hitchcock visited in Paris (*New York Daily Tribune,* March 22, 1854, p. 6; ibid., April 7, 1854, p. 6; JHO to Bertha Olmsted, Jan. 28, 1855; *Dictionnaire de biographie francaise . . .* [Paris, 1933–59], s.v. "Bossange [Les]").
35. The *New-York Daily Times.*

To JOHN OLMSTED

Boston, March 13th—Tuesday night [1855]

Dear Father

We reached New York Thursday night before eleven.[1] Friday morning Curtis gave his decision in the negative,[2] "entirely," he said, "on personal grounds, which no one but himself could appreciate." I invited him to dine with me the same day at Fischer's in Barclay St.,[3] which he did, and professed the strongest friendship for us and interest in the Magazine and offered to assist in every way; not only by furnishing frequent articles but by reading and giving opinions on manuscripts and advising on all points—only no regular duties.

The next morning I called on Dr. Bellows[4] with Dix.[5] Sunday, Dix and his wife[6] at the island[7] with me. Monday, Dix had an interview with Godwin,[8] who finally agreed in a very handsome manner to be our friend, furnish the book criticisms, foreign notices &c. at a certain price, furnish other articles as they were wanted, all subject to rejection, and to give advice, examine manuscripts &c. And I called on Dana[9] who was also very friendly and ready to do anything he could, said he could not write much but would advise and look at manuscripts. He told me he had stopped off Mrs. Hitchcock,[10] because he saw that she had written herself out. Her first were excellent—the last poor. He accepted an invitation to meet Godwin & Curtis with us, some early night after our return.

I am just at this moment inclined to take the responsibility of editing the Magazine myself with the stated assistance of these three men. I should require the assistance of a scholarly proof-reader and I should probably take up my residence in New York. If I should do so it would be with the intention only of taking the position temporarily until a capable and satisfactory editor in chief could be obtained, that is for a year perhaps. By that time, I hope the personal reasons of Curtis might be removed.

We came by Fall River, here, last night. This morning I walked several miles to see Lowell[11] but he had gone from home, probably on a lecturing tour, to be absent a month. I then called on Dr. Gray[12] and afterwards on Dr. Parker.[13] Tomorrow we are to meet Longfellow[14] and Prof. Felton[15] at Dr. Gray's. Dix goes in the morning to Dedham to see Edmund Quincy.[16] He is now calling on some of the editors. Thursday I shall go to Concord to see Emerson[17] & afterwards to Andover to call on Mrs. Stowe.[18] We have then an agreement to meet Curtis at Providence.

Your affectionate son

Fred.

1. Olmsted and Joshua A. Dix had been traveling through New England in order to visit past and potential contributors to *Putnam's Monthly*, which the firm of Dix & Edwards recently had acquired from its founder, George P. Putnam (F. L. Mott, *History of American Magazines*, 2: 419–31).
2. George W. Curtis had been an assistant editor of *Putnam's Monthly* since 1853. In March 1855, Dix, Edwards & Company invited him to become the new editor, replacing Charles F. Briggs. Curtis declined the position, probably because he was then occupying the "Editor's Easy Chair" at *Harper's Monthly* and, as a popular lecturer, was absent from New York for extended periods of time. He did agree, however, to act in an advisory position and review manuscripts submitted for publication. Years later, Olmsted described the result of the decisions of Curtis and Charles A. Dana mentioned in this letter: "Curtis and Dana were the editors, behind the door," he recalled. "They were carefully concealed. All editorial correspondence was in the third person. I was rather the Secretary of the editor. I never appeared as the editor, but only as the broker between the editor and the contributor, printers, etc." (G. W. Curtis to William D. O'Connor, March 9, 1855, Papers of Dix, Edwards & Co., Houghton Library, Harvard University, Cambridge, Mass.; FLO to Mariana Griswold Van Rensselaer, Sept. 23, 1893; F. L. Mott, *History of American Magazines*, 2: 419–23; Laura Wood Roper, "'Mr. Law' and *Putnam's Monthly Magazine*: A Note on a Phase in the Career of Frederick Law Olmsted," *American Literature* 26, no. 1 [March 1954]: 88–90; Gordon Milne, *George William Curtis & the Genteel Tradition* [Bloomington, Ind., 1956], pp. 70–79).
3. Probably the "French ordinary in Barclay Street," where Olmsted often ate supper with his friend Charles A. Dana. Describing the scene to his father, he wrote: "The company consists of a dozen Frenchmen, two Frenchwomen, Mr. Dana of the Tribune and one or two irregulars. Generally half a dozen courses well cooked with little or no dessert but apples & cheese" (FLO to JO, April 27, 1855).
4. Henry W. Bellows (1814–1882), minister of the Unitarian Church of All Souls in New York City and founder and editor of the *Christian Inquirer*. Although Bellows apparently did not assist with *Putnam's Monthly* or contribute to it, he soon became an important friend and ally of Olmsted's. He supported Olmsted's work as designer and architect-in-chief of Central Park

and in 1861 convinced him to become the general secretary of the U.S. Sanitary Commission, of which Bellows was president (*DAB*).

5. Joshua A. Dix.
6. Julia Rogers Dix, whom Dix had married in 1854 (*NCAB*, 5: 306).
7. Olmsted was still living on the farm at Southside, Staten Island.
8. Parke Godwin (1816–1904), editor and author, had joined the staff of the *New York Evening Post* in 1836. In 1853 he became political editor of *Putnam's Monthly* and remained in that position after the magazine was purchased by Dix, Edwards & Company. The most important essays Godwin published in *Putnam's Monthly* during Olmsted's association with the firm include "America for the Americans" (*Putnam's Monthly* 5, no. 29 [May 1855]: 533–41), "The Kansas Question" (ibid. 6, no. 34 [Oct. 1855]: 425–33), "The Coming Session" (ibid., no. 36 [Dec. 1855], pp. 644–49), "Calhoun on Government" (ibid. 7, no. 37 [Jan. 1856]: 90–100), "The Real Question" (ibid., no. 40 [April 1856], pp. 428–34), "The Political Aspect" (ibid. 8, no. 43 [July 1856]: 85–94), and "The Late Election" (ibid., no. 48 [Dec. 1856], pp. 647–54) (see John Raymond Wennersten, "A Reformer's Odyssey: The Public Career of Parke Godwin of the *New York Evening Post*, 1837–1870," [Ph.D. diss., University of Maryland, 1969], pp. 214–15; and F. L. Mott, *History of American Magazines*, 2: 422–23).
9. Charles A. Dana (1819–1897), assistant editor of Horace Greeley's *New York Daily Tribune*, contributed criticism of French and German literature to *Putnam's Monthly*. After Dix, Edwards & Company purchased the magazine in 1855, he became an editor (*DAB*; F. L. Mott, *History of American Magazines*, 2: 419–25; FLO to Mariana Griswold Van Rensselaer, Sept. 23, 1893).
10. Sophia Stevens Hitchcock's last essay in the "American Woman in Paris" series appeared in the *New York Daily Tribune* on December 2, 1854.
11. James Russell Lowell (1819–1891) was a valued contributor to *Putnam's Monthly* (a portrait engraving of him appeared as the frontispiece of the December 1854 issue), and Olmsted undoubtedly hoped he would continue to write for the magazine. It does not appear that Lowell did so. At the time of Olmsted's visit, Lowell was absent on a lecture tour of the Midwest (*DAB*; Martin Duberman, *James Russell Lowell* [Boston, 1966], p. 143. Lowell's known contributions to *Putnam's Monthly* include "The Fountain of Youth" (*Putnam's Monthly* 1, no. 1 [Jan. 1853]: 45–49), "Our Own, His Wanderings and Personal Adventures" (ibid., no. 4 [April 1853], pp. 403–8; no. 5 [May 1853], pp. 533–35; and no. 6 [June 1853], pp. 687–90); "Fireside Travels. Cambridge Thirty Years Ago. A Memoir Addressed to the Edelmann Storg in Rome" (ibid. 3, no. 16 [April 1854]: 379–86; and no. 17 [May 1854], pp. 473–82); and "A Moosehead Journal, Addressed to the Edelmann Storg at the Bagni di Lucca" (ibid. 2, no. 11 [Nov. 1853]: 457–69).
12. Asa Gray, botanist and professor of natural history at Harvard.
13. Probably Theodore Parker.
14. Henry Wadsworth Longfellow (1807–1882), the American poet, had published "The Warden of the Cinque Ports" in the first issue of *Putnam's Monthly*. He remained a frequent contributor during its years of ownership by Dix, Edwards & Company. The poems Longfellow published in the magazine while Olmsted was a partner include "Oliver Basselin" (*Putnam's Monthly* 5, no. 29 [May 1855]: 457–58), "Victor Galbraith" (ibid. 6, no. 31 [July 1855]: 25), and "My Lost Youth" (ibid., no. 32 [Aug. 1855], pp. 121–22).
15. Cornelius C. Felton (1807–1862), classicist and president of Harvard College from 1860 until his death. In 1852, 1853 and 1854, Felton delivered a series of lectures on ancient and modern Greece at the Lowell Institute in Boston. Olmsted may have wanted Felton to publish these lectures in *Putnam's Monthly* (*DAB*).
16. Edmund Quincy (1808–1877), abolitionist author and editor, had published his novel, *Wensley, A Story Without a Moral*, in serial form in *Putnam's Monthly*. During Olmsted's association with the magazine, Quincy contributed "Kingsley's Poems" (*Putnam's Monthly* 7, no. 41 [May 1856]: 532–39; see George W. Curtis to Joshua A. Dix, May 4, 1855, Papers of Dix, Edwards & Co.; *DAB*).
17. The editors of *Putnam's Monthly* attempted to persuade Ralph Waldo Emerson to publish in their magazine (George W. Curtis to Joshua A. Dix, July 25, 1855, Papers of Dix, Edwards & Co.).
18. Harriet Beecher Stowe.

"Plan of Weekly Magazine"

[Spring 1855]

These views I have heard expressed in conversation by several ladies & gentlemen of high literary standing repeatedly during the last six years—but nothing has been done.

To bring the subject to more practical consideration and discussion I will now propose a plan for a periodical.

It shall be published weekly and be of a form similar to the London "Examiner,"[1] "Atheneum"[2] & "Spectator,"[3] the Leader[4] & the Economist[5] or the late New York "Literary World"[6] and shall be of a size that may be sold with profit at the News Rooms and Railroad Stations at 5 or 6 cents a number.

1. Each number shall have a department of contemporary history in which the news of the week shall be given concisely but with clearness and with great care to have the probably true particulars sifted from the probably false, accompanied with a small but penetrating & suggestive running commentary.

2. Each number shall have a department of entertaining reading matter; popular but of a very high character such as that which distinguishes the Household Words.[7] Philosophical topics treated in an entertaining manner will be suitable for this department and it is hoped that some of our philosophers & professors may be induced to drop the stiff dignity which unfortunately habitually distinguishes them as a class in our country & meet the people recreatively in this department. Faraday is a regular contributor for Household Words[8] & no other is more amusing or instructive to the immense audience of that weekly.

3. Leading articles on topics of Statesmanship, Metaphysics, Moral Philosophy, Truths of History, Public Affairs, Social Reforms, Legal & Legislative Improvements, the Progress of Man, &c. These articles to be written not by the editor solely by any means, but by general or special contributors (of any country) the only restriction being the requisite value of thought & excellence of composition and an absence of very strong objection on the editors' part to the views presented.

4. Regular contributions from the corps of writers to be interested in the periodical—these articles to be of the same character as the leading editorials but to [be] presented to the public as individual views, the periodical to be responsible neither for the opinions, the reasoning or the spirit of them further than that they be manly and worth reading.

5. Open columns—for correspondents, on all subjects; for new opinions & suggestions & discussions by persons of any creed or doubt in Theology, Mental Philosophy &c. To be absolutely open to all, as far as possible, whether orthodox or outcast, Puseyist[9] or Pagan.

6. Articles on Art & Science, Fine Arts & Esthetic subjects, & Poetry, by regular or chance contributors. But regular contributors on the Arts, on

THE LITERARY REPUBLIC: 1854-1855

Music & on Fine Arts to be engaged so that carefully studied & instructive articles of this class shall appear at regular intervals, as for instance on Architecture, Painting, Sculpture, Inventions, discoveries and advancements in Chemistry, Geology, Astronomy &c. twice a year, on Music once a month &c. Esthetic commentaries and criticisms on events of current interest, items of intelligence on Scientific & Esthetic subjects.

7. *Reviews* of the most thorough and impartial character. Literary Intelligence & Literary discussions. Reviews of public documents & of speeches.

8. Selected articles of important import, illustrative of the present State of Society, the progress of opinions, or otherwise of a suggestive & meaning character, mainly from foreign journals.

9. Concise information in answer to enquiries.

10. Observations on the state of trade, on commerce, the markets &c.

11. Statistical information.

The original is a fragment in the Olmsted Papers. The editors have tentatively dated the document as having been written in the spring of 1855, since it was at that time that Olmsted became actively involved in the publishing business and began working as managing editor of *Putnam's Monthly*. The "Plan of Weekly Magazine" was written on notepaper that Olmsted used for nearly two years: the earliest surviving letter written on that paper is to John Olmsted, October 21, 1853, and the latest is a draft of his letter to Arthur T. Edwards of August 7, 1855. Olmsted presumably drew up the proposal for the consideration of his partners in the firm of Dix, Edwards & Company: at least, a letter he wrote Dix in the fall of 1856 indicates that the firm was considering the publication of a weekly magazine at that time.

This proposal is presumably a version of the plan for a weekly "Commentator"—a cross between the *Westminster Review* and the *New York Tribune*—that Olmsted had discussed with friends in the early 1850s and referred to specifically in his letter to Charles Loring Brace of December 1, 1853 (above). While Olmsted did not implement the plan during the time between 1855 and 1857 that he was in the publishing business, he did see it come to fruition in the next decade. It took the form of *The Nation*, which he attempted unsuccessfully to launch in the summer of 1863. The magazine began publication in the summer of 1865 under the editorship of Edwin L. Godkin, who was to have been Olmsted's assistant editor and in whose hands he left the enterprise when he went to California in September 1863 (E. L. Godkin to FLO, May 9, 1863; FLO to Mary Perkins Olmsted, May 9, 1863; FLO to Charles Eliot Norton, Sept. 12, 1863, Charles Eliot Norton Papers, Houghton Library, Harvard University, Cambridge, Mass.; FLO to Joshua A. Dix, Wednesday night [probably Oct. 29, 1856], Papers of Dix, Edwards & Co.).

1. The *Examiner, A Sunday Paper on Politics, Domestic Economy, and Theatricals*, founded by Leigh Hunt and John Hunt in 1808. John Forster edited the *Examiner* in 1855 (*DNB*, s.v. "Hunt, James Henry Leigh," and "Forster, John").
2. The *Athenaeum, A London Literary and Critical Journal*, founded by James Silk Buckingham in 1828. William Hepworth Dixon was its editor between 1853 and 1869 (*DNB*).
3. The *Spectator, A Weekly Journal of News, Politics, Literature, and Science*, founded in 1828 by Robert Stephen Rintoul (*DNB*).
4. The *Leader*, founded in 1849 by Thornton Leigh Hunt in cooperation with George Henry Lewes (*DNB*; Henry Richard Fox Bourne, *English Newspapers: Chapters in the History of Journalism*, 2 vols. [London, 1887], 2: 250, 313).
5. The *Economist*, a weekly "political, commercial and free-trade journal," founded in 1843 and edited by James Wilson (*DNB*).
6. Publication of the *Literary World* began in New York in February 1847. Evert Duyckinck, its first editor, hoped to make the journal an organ of American literature. Its publishers, Osgood

and Company, were dissatisfied with this goal, however, and replaced Duyckinck with Charles Fenno Hoffman in April 1847. Duyckinck and his brother George purchased the *Literary World* in October 1848 and served as its editors until 1852, when the magazine ceased publication following a fire (F. L. Mott, *History of American Magazines,* 1: 766–68; Perry Miller, *The Raven and the Whale: The War of Words and Wits in the Era of Poe and Melville* [New York, 1956], pp. 188–89).

7. *Household Words,* conducted by Charles Dickens between 1850 and 1859.

8. There is no evidence that the natural philosopher Michael Faraday (1791–1867) himself wrote articles for *Household Words,* but Dickens did borrow Faraday's lecture notes and arranged for Percival Leigh to write at least two articles, "The Chemistry of a Candle" and "The Mysteries of a Tea-Kettle," from them. Although best known as a comic writer and contributor to *Punch,* Leigh had been trained as a doctor and retained a strong interest in scientific subjects. He wrote at least six scientific pieces for *Household Words* (Edgar Johnson, *Charles Dickens: His Tragedy and Triumph,* 2 vols. [New York, 1952], 2: 708–9, 1132; *DNB*; [Percival Leigh], "The Chemistry of a Candle," *Household Words* 1, no. 19 [Aug. 3, 1850]: 439–44; idem, "The Mysteries of a Tea-Kettle," ibid. 2, no. 34 [Nov. 16, 1850]: 176–81; Anne Lohrli, comp., *Household Words, a Weekly Journal 1850–1859, Conducted by Charles Dickens: Table of Contents, List of Contributors and Their Contributions Based on the Household Words Office Book in the Morris L. Parrish Collection of Victorian Novelists, Princeton University Library* [Toronto, 1973], s.v. "Leigh, Percival").

9. That is, a follower of Edward Bouverie Pusey (1800–1882), Regius Professor of Hebrew at Oxford and the leader of the "Oxford Movement" in the Church of England. He sought to counteract the spread of rationalism and doctrinal laxity by reasserting the true doctrines of the Church of England, which he found in the patristic writings of the early church fathers and in the teachings of seventeenth-century Anglican divines (*DNB*).

To JOHN OLMSTED

New York May 28th 1855

Dear Father,

I have been looking for you every day for about a fortnight past.

I had to borrow the money I let mother have on Saturday of Parke Godwin, as our bank was dry and Edwards[1] was abed with a dysentery. I thought I should be able to return it the same day but have received nothing.

The Magazine sold a trifle more last month than it had for a month or two previously. No additional numbers of any consequence were ordered and our first printing is not quite exhausted. The number seems to have created no sensation, nor is much note taken of the change, except in connection with the "America" article[2] which has been reprinted very extensively. A translation of it with notes appeared last week in the Staats Zeitung. The Express[3] and the New Orleans Crescent have had long Editorial commentaries upon it, condemning it, and a great many papers expressing satisfaction. By the way, how is non-enfranchising the adult foreign-born citizens to send their children to the free schools? How will any of the Know Nothing proposed measures remedy the evils you complain of? I think they will rather tend to increase them.

THE LITERARY REPUBLIC: 1854-1855

The June number, I sent you with the names of the writers of most of the articles. The authors of those not marked were Elliott & Rose Terry.[4] I think the number is a very capital one. Briggs,[5] the old Editor, wrote us it was better than any that had preceded it (since the Magazine was started). We have materials for the July number, which will, I think, make it fully as good a one, if not better. We have about 40 accepted articles on hand and half a dozen engaged to be written by persons of ability, on special subjects. There is no doubt that there will be a great improvement in the quality of the Magazine, which cannot fail, I hope, to improve its circulation, sufficiently to return on capital.

The best writers seem already to have acquired confidence that we can be depended upon to do our duty strongly & boldly and that the Magazine is to be more than ever the leading magazine and the best outlet of thought in the country. This is more than half the battle. If we can get the writers, there is little fear but that we shall get the readers. It is generally understood that we have capital enough at command and shall pay generously & promptly, and the consequence is that we are now declining every day manuscripts that we should have accepted during the first month.

If we had capital enough, we could engage immediately in the Book publishing business extensively. As many as eight books have been offered us. We have agreed to publish this "Twice Married," when it is completed in the Monthly. Have you read it? From this on, the manuscript is said to be much better than what has gone before, & it is thought the best description of New England people—the best enletterment of their talk—ever published. Who is the author? Philleo, a lawyer of Hartford?[6] Stewart, a member of Parliament formerly—the author of the criticisms on Forrest & others in the Tribune,[7] which have made a good deal of talk & been much admired by some—wished us to publish a small popular book of similar matter. Actors of Our Time it might be called. We have concluded to decline it because we did not wish to use the capital which we might need for the Monthly or other more important purposes. Godwin has two books on the tapis[8] which we shall be glad to publish & probably shall, tho Putnam has long been a personal friend of his and we shall not urge it.[9] Our English publisher offered to sell us a copyright of a new Life of Goethe,[10] to be published simultaneously here & in London. Declined. A small book of Letters of a Lady from the Salt Lake City & descriptive of the tour thither we may probably publish in the fall.[11] She was the wife of the U.S. Commissioner, & we have some of the matter accepted for the Monthly.

Our Editor's[12] incognito is still perfectly preserved. I think no one suspects who he is.

I believe that I never told you that we bought of McElrath[13] the whole back stock of Household Words. It was a big lot and costs something but leaves room for a large profit on all we can sell, and the sale though small is constant & rather likely to increase. Edwards found it necessary to get a book-keeper, a very dry, trusty sort of man he seems to be. His salary is $800 a year & we discharge at the end of this month, the young man he had depended upon to assist him, but who proved incompetent. His salary has been at $400.

Our offices & packing rooms have been reconstructed & put in good order & are now quite pleasant & convenient. Dr. Moffat has also painted my room last week, and I find it very pleasant & a capital place to work for the city.[14]

I got on finely with my book,[15] last two weeks.

Was at the farm yesterday. Things looking finely, especially the trees, but a great pity the orchard has not yet been manured or tilled—the men having all been engaged about the house, hedge, road &c. I hope it will be this week but there is "heaps" of other work that needs doing. The doctor[16] looks blue & thinks all the time about selling off land or house to pay for his improvements. Mary better than usual and babies fine.[17] Really the young one begins to look flesh and bloody. The garden is particularly satisfactory; thanks to Louis.

Tom Day must be a paltry vulgar man. Nothing could be in worse taste than his notice of the Monthly[18]—but it was not only in bad taste. I would write to him about it if I were not pretty sure that if he attempted to correct his impertinence he would make matters worse. The Courant seems to me to have become much poorer than ever under his administration. It is positively bad now—before, it was mainly negatively good. Flippancy is worse than dullness. The tone of the paper is constantly insulting to its readers. The Editor takes the patronizing position of a schoolmaster or clergyman towards them. The Times is far more gentlemanly.

When shall I see you? You will stay with me, will you not? I can make you tolerably comfortable, if you can get up so high. It is quite cool & quiet here.

Your affectionate son,

F.

1. Arthur T. Edwards.
2. The article "America for the Americans" by Parke Godwin in the May 1855 issue of *Putnam's Monthly*, which vigorously attacked demands made by the nativist American or "Know Nothing" party that all foreign-born citizens be prohibited from holding office and that immigrants be required to pass a naturalization period of up to twenty-one years before being permitted to vote. Godwin warned that it was dangerous to proscribe and set apart any group in that way, and argued that it was by the exercise of political rights than men learned to value and respect them. The present naturalization period of five years was long enough to prepare immigrants for responsible citizenship, so long as adequate pains were taken during that time to educate and prepare immigrants for their future responsibilities ("America for the Americans," *Putnam's Monthly* 5, no. 29 [May 1855]: 533–41).
3. Olmsted's references here are to the *New-Yorker Staats-Zeitung* and to the *New York Morning Express*, which published an editorial on May 2, 1855, attacking the *Putnam's* article "America for the Americans."
4. Charles Wyllys Elliott, author of *Cottages and Cottage Life* (1848) and a student of Andrew Jackson Downing, wrote the essay "About Barns." Rose Terry (1827–1892) of Hartford was

the author of "The Mormon's Wife," which appeared in the June issue of *Putnam's Monthly* (*Papers of FLO*, 1: 384, n. 2; memorandum by Calvert Vaux (Nov. 1894), Calvert Vaux Papers, New York Public Library, New York; *Notable American Women*, s.v. "Cooke, Rose Terry"; "About Barns," *Putnam's Monthly* 5, no. 30 [June 1855]: 629-31; "The Mormon's Wife," ibid., pp. 641-49).

5. Charles F. Briggs, author and editor, had edited *Putnam's Monthly* from its founding in January 1853 until it was purchased by Dix, Edwards & Company in March 1855 (*DAB*; F. L. Mott, *History of American Magazines*, 2: 419-26).

6. Dix, Edwards & Company published *Twice Married: A Story of Connecticut Life* in 1855. Its author was Calvin W. Philleo (1822-1858), a Hartford lawyer and *litterateur*. He also contributed "Stage-Coach Stories" to *Putnam's Monthly* and published articles in *Harper's Monthly*, *Atlantic Monthly*, and *Graham's Magazine* (C. W. Philleo to Joshua A. Dix, Sept. 29, 1857, Papers of Dix, Edwards & Co.; David H. Van Hoosear, *The Fillow, Philo, and Philleo Genealogy. A Record of the Descendants of John Fillow, A Huguenot Refugee from France* [Albany, N.Y., 1888], pp. 113-14; "Twice Married. My Own Story," *Putnam's Monthly* 5, no. 27 [March 1855]: 313-20; no. 28 [April 1855], pp. 409-20; no. 29 [May 1855], pp. 541-44; no. 30 [June 1855], pp. 578-87; 6, no. 31 [July 1855]: 85-91; no. 32 [Aug. 1855], pp. 181-92; and no. 33 [Sept. 1855], pp. 239-50; "Stage-Coach Stories," ibid. 3, no. 13 [Jan. 1854]: 80-94; no. 14 [Feb. 1854], pp. 212-19; no. 17 [May 1854], pp. 505-13; no. 18 [June 1854], pp. 595-608; and 4, no. 20 [Aug. 1854]: 175-85).

7. William Stuart (pseudonym for Edmund O'Flaherty) (1821-1886), English-born journalist and theatrical promoter. After serving briefly in Parliament he immigrated to the United States in 1854 to avoid prosecution for fraud. In 1855 Stuart wrote a series of reviews for the *New York Daily Tribune* in which he criticized performances by Edwin Forrest (1806-1872), a noted Shakespearean actor (*Appleton's Cyc. Am. Biog.*, s.v. "Stuart, William"; *DAB*, s.v. "Forrest, Edwin"; William Stuart, "Edwin Forrest. By Stuart. From the *New York Tribune*, 1855," scrapbook of newspaper clippings, New York Public Library, New York City).

8. That is, "on the carpet," or ready to go.

9. George P. Putnam (1814-1872) had published Godwin's *Vala, A Mythological Tale* (1851) and *The Putnam Home Cyclopedia. A Hand-Book of Universal Biography* (1852). Dix, Edwards & Company published Godwin's *Political Essays* in 1856 (*DAB*, s.v. "Putnam, George Palmer").

10. Probably *The Life and Works of Goethe: With Sketches of His Age and Contemporaries, from Published and Unpublished Sources*, by George Henry Lewes, which was published in London by D. Nutt in November 1855 and in Boston by Ticknor and Fields in 1856. It became the standard English-language biography of Goethe and was republished numerous times (*DNB*).

11. Dix, Edwards & Company published Mrs. Benjamin G. Ferris's *The Mormons at Home: With Some Incidents of Travel from Missouri to California, 1852-3. In a Series of Letters* (1856). Benjamin G. Ferris served as secretary of Utah Territory from 1852 to 1853 ("Life Among the Mormons," *Putnam's Monthly* 6, no. 32 [Aug. 1855]: 144-48; no. 33 [Sept. 1855], pp. 262-66; no. 34 [Oct. 1855], pp. 376-81; no. 35 [Nov. 1855], pp. 501-5; and no. 36 [Dec. 1855], pp. 602-7; Orson F. Whitney, *History of Utah* ..., 4 vols. [Salt Lake City, Utah, 1892-1904], 1: 506-7).

12. George W. Curtis.

13. Thomas McElrath (1807-1888), publisher and business manager of the *New York Daily Tribune* from 1841 to 1858. When Arthur T. Edwards was looking for a partner in the publishing field, McElrath recommended Joshua A. Dix as "attentive and industrious as well as intelligent and prompt." At the time of this letter, Dix, Edwards & Company had just begun publishing a monthly edition of Charles Dickens's popular weekly *Household Words*, and the partners hoped to sell back issues for a profit (*NCAB*, 3: 456-57; Thomas McElrath to A. T. Edwards, Feb. 12, 1855, Papers of Dix, Edwards & Co.).

14. Olmsted was residing in a building owned by Dr. William B. Moffat, located at 335 Broadway (*The New-York City Directory, for 1854-1855. Thirteenth Publication* [New York, 1854], p. 501 [see Spear 1004]; *Trow's New-York City Directory... For the Year Ending May 1, 1856* [New York, 1855], p. 587 [see Spear 1008]).

15. *Seaboard Slave States*.

16. John Hull Olmsted.

17. Mary Perkins Olmsted and her children, John Charles and Charlotte Olmsted.

18. Thomas Mills Day (1817-1905) of Hartford, whose two youngest sisters Olmsted had courted in the mid-1840s, had become proprietor and editor of the *Hartford Courant* in January 1855.

In an editorial on May 22, the *Courant* noted the growing popularity of *Putnam's Monthly Magazine* and praised it, saying that it had a "higher flight than the Knickerbocker, or even Harper." It then went on to disagree with the views expressed in the "America for the Americans" article in the May issue of *Putnam's*, asserting that immigrants benefited from being disfranchised during their first years in the United States, since they were then freed from "temptations of the demagogue" and were better able to concentrate on economic improvement without exciting the antipathy that arose when they held the balance of power.

What seems to have excited Olmsted's disapproval was the personal tone of comments that Thomas Day included in the editorial. In a very familiar way he noted, concerning *Putnam's Monthly:* "We are pleased to learn that one of our Hartford boys has become part owner, and that another is engaged upon literary labors connected with the Magazine." The first of these "Hartford boys" was Olmsted and the second was Frederic Beecher Perkins, who was "working editor" and editorial writer of the monthly at this time. Day then went on, even more familiarly, to object to a review in the May issue of *Putnam's* of D. W. Bartlett's *American Agitators and Reformers*, which he assumed Perkins had written. The review began by noting that Bartlett seemed to "divide the world into men, women and the Beecher family," since three of the fifteen or twenty people he included were Beechers, and ended with a confession by the author that he had little sympathy for Bartlett's "worship of personalities." As a general rule, he observed, "good men do not like eulogy and notoriety, and bad men do not deserve them—while the public is rather nauseated with celebrities of all sorts."

In his editorial in the *Courant*, Day responded to what he viewed as Perkins's disrespectful treatment of his older, more eminent, relatives: "There is rather an irreverent use of the Beecher family, in the editorial notes upon Bartlett's Agitators, that smacks of Fred. 'Tis an ill bird that fouls its own nest.' 'Good men do not like eulogy and notoriety.' We take the liberty to doubt *that.*"

Part of Olmsted's disapproval of Day's editorial may have stemmed from his fear that Hartford readers would think that he, rather than Perkins, was the "Fred" referred to in it (*Papers of FLO,* 1: 242, 284, 285; *Yale Obit. Rec.,* 5th ser. 6 [June 1906]: 528–29; Thomas Day Seymour, *The Family of the Rev. Jeremiah Day of New Preston* . . . [New Haven, Conn., 1900], p. 21; *Putnam's Monthly* 5, no. 29 [May 1855]: 547; "Putnam's Magazine," *Hartford Daily Courant,* May 22, 1855, p. 2; George W. Curtis to William D. O'Connor, Jan. 28, 1855, Papers of Dix, Edwards & Co.).

To Parke Godwin

July 12 [1855]

My Dear Godwin

I saw Duggan[1] last night; he has not yet written, and I told him he need not, on Wallace,[2] for us.

Do you feel like giving us a very comprehensive and thorough built article for September on the State of our politics? If so, go ahead. We have had nothing you know in the Monthly on the recent developments of the Kansas question; so if you please make that the back-bone. We shall be prepared and willing to lose a thousand Southern subscribers if the article commands the attention and respect most of your articles have. So with all possible justice, charity and courteous tone to the feeling of the South, say just what you think about it.

If you think September is not quite the best time for us to come out with this, postpone it till October or later and give us anything else you please for September. Recent Filibustering[3] and what is to be looked for, might serve for a short article. I incline to think however that September will be as good a time as any for us to deliver our fire at the "Conventions" cowards.[4]

 Yours Truly

Fred. Law Olmsted

The original is in the Bryant-Godwin Collection, Manuscripts and Archives Division, Rare Book & Manuscripts Division, The New York Public Library, Astor, Lenox and Tilden Foundations, New York City.

1. Peter Paul (or Paul Peter) Duggan (d. 1861), Irish-born portraitist who did illustrations for some of the journals published by Dix, Edwards & Company. Among these were illustrations for two series in the *Schoolfellow* during 1856—"About New York" and Olmsted's "Visit to a Chinese School." Duggan also did three illustrations for Olmsted's *Seaboard Slave States*.
  Duggan emigrated to the United States c. 1810 and by 1855 was a professor at the New York Free Academy of Design. In 1856 poor health forced him to retire and he soon moved abroad—first to London and then to Paris (*Dictionary of Artists in America*, s.v. "Duggan, Peter Paul or Paul Peter"; [Frederick Law Olmsted], "Visit to a Chinese School," *Schoolfellow: A Monthly Magazine for Boys and Girls* 8 [1856]: 120–24, 162–64, 194–97; *SSS*, pp. 387, 415, 423).
2. The American literary, art and legal critic Horace Binney Wallace (1817–1852). Godwin, who had known Wallace when both were students at Princeton, wrote the article for *Putnam's Monthly*. It was a discussion of Wallace's life and a review of a posthumous volume of his writings published in 1855 entitled *Art, Scenery, and Philosophy in Europe. Being Fragments from the Portfolio of the Late Horace Binney Wallace, Esq., of Philadelphia* (*DAB*; [Parke Godwin], "The Late Horace Binney Wallace," *Putnam's Monthly* 6, no. 33 [Sept. 1855]: 267–76; George W. Curtis to Joshua A. Dix, Aug. 23, 1855, Papers of Dix, Edwards & Co.).
3. During the summer of 1855 two rival groups from the United States were engaged in filibustering activities in Nicaragua. One was led by a Texan, Henry L. Kinney, who proposed to colonize an extensive tract of land to which he had acquired title. Letters of his that were published in American newspapers in early 1855 indicated that he intended to take over the government of the country. The Pierce administration moved to halt Kinney's scheme, and courts in Philadelphia and New York ordered him to appear before them. On June 6, 1855, however, he and a group of associates secretly left New York for Nicaragua. A month earlier, the filibuster William Walker—who had established a short-lived republic in northern Mexico in 1853—launched an expedition from San Francisco to conquer Nicaragua. By the time of this letter he was well on his way to success (Allan Nevins, *Ordeal of the Union*, vol. 2, *A House Dividing, 1852–1857* [New York and London, 1947], pp. 368–69, 372–74, 405–8).
4. Probably a reference to the American Party National Convention that met in Philadelphia in early June 1855. The convention resisted the demands of its antislavery members and adopted a platform that deplored agitation of the slavery issue by the other parties and called for maintenance of existing laws on the subject (ibid., pp. 398–99).

To Arthur T. Edwards

August 7 [1855]

My Dear Sir

 I did not suppose that you would, upon reflection, be willing to leave the views which I understood you to express last night unrepudiated.

I hold that merely as a matter of money-making, a man can never afford to do what is not right—that he can never afford to sink his principles, that when he has money in his pockets that rightfully belongs to another man he can not afford to keep it there however temporarily inconvenient it may be to him. To pay it and however convenient it may be to his creditor to dispense with it—consistently of course with the practical requirements & customs of commerce.

Perhaps Dix & I misunderstood you in thinking you expressed ideas contrary to these. But I think it more probable that in the heat of discussion you allowed yourself to use arguments which if they had been addressed to you would have made you indignant and angry as they did me.

We were all wrong. The discussion should have been avoided altogether or should have been carried on in entirely different manner.

The question of the right of the owners of Household Words to a payment from us is one upon which I am willing to admit an honest and reasonable difference of opinion may obtain. You are mistaken in supposing that upon this point I have much feeling. I should not stand out if you and Mr. Dix disagreed with me in a practical question depending upon it.

The question of our duty from courtesy is another one, and upon this too I should yield to a majority.

The question of expediency is still another and one upon which a difference of opinion might with propriety exist and upon which, if I stood one to two, I could yield my position with no ill grace.

These questions might all have been indefinitely deliberated upon before our first payment. After that payment and the letter which accompanied it, I think our conclusion can not be reconsidered until there is some material change in the circumstances, without a sacrifice—I will not say of principle—but of self respect and business character.

I think that upon reflection you will agree with [me] up to the last point.

If Bradbury & Evans' letter can be considered as a sufficient circumstance to exonerate us from what we should otherwise have been obliged to do, there would be no need to discuss the matter further.

My opinion has always been that it would not, even if we were assured that the apparent impertinence of that letter was real and intentional.

But upon reflection, I have not thought that it was so. Others, whose judgment I suppose to be better than mine upon it, have not, and I had thought that you yourself expressed the opinion to me in conversation that the objectionable phrase was a mere rapid business expression with no ungracious intention towards us.

But if we should not so conclude and if we could feel that the supposed impertinence of Messrs. Bradbury & Evans through their clerk exonerated us from what we should otherwise consider obligations in honor and courtesy, I really believe that it would be bad *policy* for us, looking at it from a mere dollar and cent point of view, to take advantage of it. I think it would be better for us, if we could, to pocket the petty insult and retain and sustain the position in which we first placed ourselves, as long as possible.

I think so because it seems to me that it is necessary to do so to sustain the reputation we aspire to of a liberal and gentlemanly publishing house. I do not wish to obtain such a character by the smallest neglect of punctilious accuracy and the closest economy, but by always acting and deciding, as if it were instinctively, on a certain broad sentiment, the sentiment which Jesus expresses as doing unto others as we would be done by—not Quixotically, but simply and fairly.

I say that I would do as a matter of policy, but I must do simply as a matter of comfort. I have seen enough of business as ordinarily conducted to detest it. If I thought that which is usual was necessary I am quite sure that I would prefer to starve or to commit suicide in some less painful manner, most certainly would rather be a poor laboring man than to have any part in it.

But we know that it is not necessary even to success; experience shows that those who are in the most haste to get rich are the most likely to be tript up and to leave beggarly families. The most liberal are the richest merchants now in New York, though there are no doubt several exceptions.

Why is it so? Mainly because they gradually obtain reputations and characters that draw the best and safest and most profitable kind of business to them. Because the honestest men find more pleasure and comfort in dealing with them than with men who are merely technically honest and "cheap."

In the publishing business such a character must be of far greater value than in business in general, because publishers deal with a class of men that often have very little business talent or taste for driving bargains or making money by financial good *management*. On this ground I at once gave way to you when you objected to Dr. Hunter's[1] proposal and before you offered the additional reason of the danger of being compromised in libel suits.

If Mr. Bancroft should apply to me for information as to the London publishers, the mere want of ready and cordial good grace on the part of Messrs. Bradbury & Evans in replying to our note would be a sufficient ground with me for not recommending them as a house with which it would be agreeable for him to correspond & they may in consequence lose a very valuable republication.

But I should mention to him as a circumstance much in favor of his addressing a certain other publishing concern that it had paid Mr. Hurlbert *liberally* for a service that he not only had no legal claim upon them for but that he performed without any purpose of benefitting them and which he did not even expect any remuneration of them for. So also I should speak well of the publisher who has continued up to this time to make semi-annual remittances to Mr. Brace for his "Hungary," published four years ago—a remittance made precisely as if there were a legal necessity of it, in a simple business like form.[2]

The opinion of Bradbury & Evans or of Mr. Dickens or of any one else who is informed of our remittances to them *may*, very likely, never be worth a postage stamp to us, but it *may* also be more profitable simply as an advertisement than any other investment we could make. And if our business is at all points carried on in that spirit, I am not only sure that it will be far more confortable but I am confident that in the long run it will be more profitable.

You agree with me I know on the general principles I have enunciated. If we differ it is as to whether they apply to this particular case.

You will excuse me if I say that *to me* it seems obviously absurd when by simply reprinting and distributing "Household Words" we make $3,000 a year, to say that we are under *no obligations to those who furnish it to us*. Yet I know that there is somehow a difference of opinion upon this among sensible & honest men and as a member of the community, I am willing to waive my opinion & to remain under obligations to the Englishmen, because of the impracticality of paying my individual share.

So if a majority of the firm disagreed with me, I should & could not insist upon their paying what they felt no need to pay. I should then remain under personal obligations to the English proprietors, not without the hope of in some way, bye and bye, making them some suitable acknowledgement if not remuneration.

Then as to regard for our reputation. To acquire the respect of others we must have self respect. Now I feel at once that I can not withdraw at least for the present from the position in which we have placed ourselves without wounding my self respect—not even though that position exposes us to insults from Bradbury & Evans. And this feeling is strong prima facie evidence that our reputation would be compromised if we did have it. It would hardly lessen this evidence if this feeling could be argued away, for very few men would take the trouble to argue the matter, but would form an impression at once, unfavorable to us, which it would be difficult to remove.

It was for this reason I suppose that I was myself rather impatient of argument yesterday.

I hope in any discussing we may have hereafter we shall all keep our good nature without losing our frankness.

Yours truly,

Fred. Law Olmsted.

Olmsted wrote this letter the day after he and Edwards had an argument on the question of the obligation of their firm to pay foreign authors and publishers for material they republished in the United States. The particular issue involved was whether to make further payments to Bradbury & Evans, English publishers of *Household Words,* for the right to publish an American edition of the magazine. Dix, Edwards & Company had recently forwarded its first payment, £30, to Bradbury & Evans, and for its pains had received a curt reply that the amount was too small. This annoyed Edwards, who apparently wanted to respond by discontinuing the payments.

In the heated discussion between the partners of the American firm that occurred on the afternoon of August 6, 1855, Edwards understood Olmsted to assert the "absolute *moral right*" of foreign authors to a percentage of the sale of their works, while Edwards maintained that such payments were "an act of *courtesy rather than of right.*" Olmsted's recollection of the argument was rather different: he recalled that Edwards said such things as "In carrying on a business a man must sink his principles sometimes," "I don't believe in taking money out of our pockets to give to those rich Englishmen," and "We cannot always afford to do what is right etc."

Apparently, Joshua A. Dix, the third partner in the firm, informed Edwards soon after the altercation that he had offended Olmsted. In response, Edwards wrote Olmsted that evening in an attempt to mollify him. "I have learned with great regret," he wrote, "that I had both wounded your feelings, and at the same time left an impression upon your mind in regard to my sentiments in the copy right question which if true would reflect most unpleasantly upon my honor." He assured Olmsted that he was not "inclined to use an argument fitted to quiet a highwayman's conscience in dealing with *any question,* no matter how trivial its import."

Edwards then discussed the question of making payments to Bradbury & Evans. He objected to sending them further payments, he said, not because they were rich, but because they had been uncivil. "What I meant to convey," he explained, "was that I do not like the curt letter we received from Bradbury & Evans, in which they did not show even an appearance of common civility in replying to our courteous letter enclosing £30, but showed very plainly that they thought it small business in us in not sending a larger sum. I consider that we did them a favor, and the only return was a surly intimation that we might bring a larger offering the next time."

In his reply to Edwards's letter of August 6, presented here, Olmsted relinquished the absolute moral stance that Edwards had accused him of assuming the previous day, and argued instead that expediency dictated making payments to Bradbury & Evans, because of considerations of the firm's reputation and future success (A. T. Edwards to FLO, Aug. 6, 1855; FLO to "My Dear Sir" [A. T. Edwards], draft letter, n.d. [Aug. 7, 1855]).

1. Possibly the writer William T. Adams (1822–1897), best known for his "Oliver Optic" stories for young adults. One of several pseudonyms he used was "Clingham Hunter, M.D." "Dr. Hunter" evidently proposed that Dix, Edwards & Company publish something that Olmsted felt was in poor taste. He thought the firm should reject "Hunter's" proposal for that reason alone, because of the effect it might have on the firm's reputation among literary men (*DAB,* s.v. "Adams, William Taylor").

2. Olmsted was especially concerned that Dix, Edwards & Company develop among English publishers a reputation as a fair and honest firm. He hoped that these publishers would urge English authors to consign advance copies of their works to the firm for publication and distribution in the United States. As a way of demonstrating the importance of a firm's reputation, Olmsted states here that if the American historian George Bancroft (1800–1891) sought his advice in choosing an English publisher for a volume of his *History of the United States,* he could cite the liberality of Longman, Brown, Green, and Longmans, English publishers of William H. Hurlbert's *Pictures of Cuba* (1855), or of Richard Bently, who issued the English edition of Charles Loring Brace's *Hungary in 1851.* Similarly, Olmsted argues that unless Dix, Edwards & Company earned the desired reputation, English publishers would discourage authors from dealing with the firm.

William H. Hurlbert (1827–1895), journalist and author, joined the staff of *Putnam's Monthly* in 1855 as "critic of painting, sculpture, musical and dramatic matters, and foreign literature." In addition, he contributed "What Cheer" to the July 1855 issue of the magazine (*DAB,* s.v. "Bancroft, George," and "Hurlbert, William"; W. H. Hurlbert to Joshua A. Dix, May 4, 1855; Papers of Dix, Edwards & Co.; see also FLO to Joshua A. Dix, Aug. 3, 1856, below).

To Edward Everett Hale

10 Park Place
August 23 [1855]

My Dear Hale

Our friend Douai is in a corner again, the muster of the Sierra Nevada filibusters at San Antonio[1] having been taken advantage of to overawe his party.

His subscribers neglect to pay up, believing that his paper will be interrupted by Lynch law process. His advertising patrons have been forced to discontinue their important assistance to his financial position.

Vexatious law suits and other contrivances for embarrassing him have been instituted.[2] He would undoubtedly have been lynched if he was not too brave & too well prepared for them. For fourteen days a strong armed guard was maintained at his printing office, & he sleeps in it well armed every night.[3]

He is unable in consequence to meet his note for type & ink, due here this week for $150.[4] I have given my honor that it shall be paid & shall prevent legal proceedings against him, if entirely out of my own pocket.

He writes as if overpowered & despairing—expects to quit & come North. I want to encourage him to stay & maintain the position he has gained & if he will, he must be sustained.

I suppose you will be helping them to *arm* in Kansas, which is a better thing & I don't want to divert anything from it.[5] So I won't ask you to assist me now with this, but I want, if you have it, that letter from Douai which I gave you. I am going to try to tax the peace people, whose consciences won't let them contribute for arms—& want that letter to send to Gerrit Smith.[6]

I want mightily to go to Kansas myself this fall or next winter: if I find it possible to leave my business so long as will be necessary, perhaps I may—particularly if it comes to fight. I should like to know what you anticipate there.

I can't well write a word to you without much emotion even now,[7] but I am anything but a miserable or even a dissatisfied man & most sincerely.
    Your friend,
                                                            Fred. Law Olmsted

---

The original is in the New England Emigrant Aid Company Papers, Manuscript Department, Kansas State Historical Society, Topeka, Kansas.

1. Presumably a reference to a volunteer company of Texas Rangers under the command of Captain James H. Callahan that was formed in San Antonio in the summer of 1855 to protect the Texas border against Indian attacks (Walter Prescott Webb, *The Texas Rangers: A Century of Frontier Defense* . . ., 2d ed. [Austin, Tex., 1965], pp. 146–47; William J. Hughes, *Rebellious Ranger: Rip Ford and the Old Southwest* [Norman, Okla., 1964], p. 120).
2. Olmsted must have drawn some of this information from a letter from Adolf Douai to him of August 12, 1855, that has not survived. Some of the information comes from Douai's letter to Olmsted of August 4. In that letter, Douai reported that several leading San Antonio merchants had stopped advertising in the *Zeitung* and that he had lost one-sixth of his subscribers. He said that his ex-partner, I. M. Riedner, was working to destroy his credit by spreading rumors that he was on the verge of bankruptcy and claiming that he was "sold to the Northern Abolitionists," receiving free paper from them and serving their purposes for pay (Douai to FLO, Aug. 4 and 26, 1855).
3. In his autobiography, Douai described this incident as follows:

> In the middle of 1855 a band of 12 pro-slavery rowdies rode to San Antonio and boasted that they would lynch me and throw my press in the river if the citizens of the town did not do it. Immediately 12 turners with loaded guns occupied the roof of the house which stood entirely isolated. My old father . . . barricaded the entrance to the house and

collected a small arsenal of weapons. As an old soldier he seemed to get young again. The rowdies stayed away when they reconnoitered the situation. (Adolf Douai, "Autobiography," pp. 118-19.)

4. Douai owed the New York type founders Wells & Webb $150 for type (Adolf Douai to JHO, Sept. 4, 1854, and Aug. 4, 1855).
5. At this time Eastern supporters of the free-soil cause in Kansas, led by members of the New England Emigrant Aid Company, were raising money to supply Sharps rifles and other arms to the free-state settlers in the territory. They began their activities after fraudulent voting by Missourians in the election of May 30, 1855, produced a proslavery territorial legislature. By the time Olmsted wrote this letter, two hundred Sharps rifles had been purchased and efforts were being made to raise money for one hundred more. Olmsted became active in the cause in September, when James Burnett Abbott, officer of a Kansas free-state militia company, was in New York attempting to raise funds (William H. Isely, "The Sharps Rifle Episode in Kansas History," *American Historical Review* 12, no. 3 [April 1907]: 551-56; FLO to J. B. Abbott, Oct. 7, 1855, n. 1, below).
6. Gerrit Smith (1797-1874) of Peterboro, New York, a wealthy philanthropist and leading figure in both the abolitionist and peace movements. He was one of the founders of the Liberty party and a vice-president of the American Peace Society. The violence of the proslavery forces in Kansas so angered Smith that a few months after Olmsted wrote this letter he was contributing large sums to send free-state settlers to the territory and to provide them with arms. He also urged resistance to federal authorities there on the grounds that they were aiding the cause of slavery (*DAB*; Ralph Volney Harlow, "Gerrit Smith and the John Brown Raid," *American Historical Review* 38, no. 1 [Oct. 1932]: 32-38).
7. Hale's wife, the former Emily Baldwin Perkins of Hartford, Connecticut, had been engaged to Olmsted for a short time during the summer of 1851, following a long courtship. Soon after the public announcement of the engagement, however, she broke it off. She then left Hartford to avoid the gossiping that ensued and went to visit friends in Worcester, Massachusetts. There she attracted a circle of admirers that included Hale. She was immediately taken with him, and a serious courtship developed. Hale proposed to her in May 1852 and they were married the following October (Jean Holloway, *Edward Everett Hale: A Biography* [Austin, Tex., 1956], pp. 96-101; *Papers of FLO*, 1: 89-91).

To Parke Godwin

[September, 1855]

Dear Godwin

The "Kansas"[1] is excellent—puts the main issue plainly, strongly and straightforwardly. We are all well satisfied & ready to stand by it.

I have suggested a couple of verbal exchanges. If I was to criticize it, I should say that the distinction between the "greater part of the slaveholders" (observe the #) and the propagandists and fire-eaters was hardly sufficiently presented or sustained.[2] Could not some expression of respect for the character of the better & more conservative class of Southerners be introduced with good effect—& some expression of regret that they do not exercise more influence—or cannot—in politics.[3] Men like your Savannah friend.

Two Southerners that I have seen within a few days tell me that they believe most educated men at the South desire that there should be no further extension of slave territory—that Kansas should be a free state—are afraid of the propagandists & would be glad to rebuke them.

Such men are, I suppose, most of our subscribers at the South & we should encourage them to speak out—though we know they dare not.

A distinct denial of any desire or purpose to interfere with Slavery in the *states* should be appended to or in some way introduced in the last paragraph.[4]

Yours Truly

Olmsted

Don't fail to go to Syracuse.[5] You will be much wanted.

The original is in the Bryant-Godwin Collection, New York Public Library.

1. An article by Parke Godwin entitled "The Kansas Question," which appeared in the October 1855 issue of *Putnam's Monthly* (vol. 6, no. 34, pp. 425–33).
2. A reference to a section of the article in which Godwin described the change that had taken place in the South's view of slavery. From an inherited evil soon to be abolished, slavery had become an institution good in itself and "the natural relation between the two races":

    > With this change in opinion, from despairing lament or feeble apology to positive vindication, came a corresponding change in tactics, from defense to aggression. While the greater part of the slaveholders accepted the glorifying view of their system, merely as a politic reaction against the bitter reproaches of the civilized world, or as a pleasant *couleur de rose* dream-land, into which imagination might escape from the too painful reality, there were others, more daring spirits, with whom argument was action, and of whom it might be said—
    >
    > ——Straightforward goes
    > The lightning's path, and straight the fearful
    >   path
    > Of the Cannon ball.
    >
    > Without caring a whit for the right or wrong, the good or evil of slavery or of anything else, and animated mainly by an insatiable thirst for power and gain, they found it exceedingly convenient to adopt the philanthropic theory. They eagerly embraced the premises, and more eagerly shot to the conclusion. Slavery is a good thing, a desirable thing, a benefaction and heaven's blessing to all concerned, and *ergo*, ought not to be restricted, but diffused! (Ibid., p. 430.)

3. Godwin apparently did not make the changes in this passage that Olmsted suggested.
4. This paragraph of the letter is on a separate sheet of paper. Godwin did not add the disclaimer that Olmsted suggested.
5. On July 18, 1855, the New York state committees of the Whig and Republican parties agreed to hold their state conventions in Syracuse on September 26. As anticipated, this resulted in a fusion of the two parties: the Whigs joined the Republican convention and the combined delegates adopted the Republican platform, with its strong stand against the Kansas-Nebraska Act (Glyndon G. Van Deusen, *Horace Greeley: Nineteenth-Century Crusader* [Philadelphia, 1953], pp. 198–99).

THE LITERARY REPUBLIC: 1854–1855

To JAMES B. ABBOTT

Address: James Burnett Abbott, Esq.,[1]
Lawrence, K.T.

                                89 Moffat's Building New York[2]
                                        September 17 [1855]

My Dear Sir
    Little has been done here yet, except in the arrangements of preliminaries. Tonight I had a little meeting in my room. Greeley, Field, Priestly, Elliott, Perkins,[3] made out a list of names, and tomorrow one or two paid collectors will be employed to call personally with a short circular note to the effect that the Kansas settlers need immediate assistance, and urging that liberal contributions be made, which will be taken charge of and used under their directions by their authorized agent.[4] I hope in a week from this to have a fund sufficient to purchase for you 100 _____.[5]
    It is thought best that the way in which the money is to be used should not be mentioned. It is for the Kansas settlers, with whom I am in correspondence, to direct that, and I keep my own counsel.
    Will you please write me, authorizing me to act as agent (in your place), and also another paper directing me how to use any money that may come into my hands for you (until further orders).[6] Also, please write the names of your contributors in New York, & the amounts contributed by each.
    God speed the right.
    Yours truly

                                              Fred. Law Olmsted
                                              Care Dix & Edwards
                                              10 Park Place

The original is in the James Abbott Collection, Manuscript Department, Kansas State Historical Society, Topeka, Kansas. This letter and the two succeeding letters in this volume from Olmsted to Abbott (October 4 and 7, 1855) were published in "The Abbott Howitzer—Its History" (Kansas State Historical Society, *Collections of the Kansas State Historical Society,* 17 vols. in 16 [Topeka, Kans., 1881–1928], 1–2 [1875–81]: 223–24).

1. James Burnett Abbott (1818–1879) moved to Kansas from Connecticut in 1854 after a varied career in manufacturing. Territorial Governor Andrew Reeder appointed him as one of the judges of returns of the election for a territorial legislature on May 30, 1855, but Abbott resigned when the board of judges accepted as legal the ballots of large numbers of Missourians who crossed into the Territory in order to vote for proslavery candidates. Soon after, Abbott joined one of the militia companies that free-state settlers began to form in response to the proslavery sympathies of the legislature. In July 1855 he went to Boston to secure one hundred Sharps rifles for his militia company. The officers of the New England Emigrant Aid Company, under whose auspices he had moved to Kansas, promptly purchased the rifles for him. He then began a tour of the East in an effort to raise funds for an additional one hundred rifles. On

August 17 he arrived in New York, where Olmsted became one of his most active assistants. Abbott secured money for seventeen rifles and then returned to Kansas, leaving Olmsted in charge of raising money in New York for one hundred more rifles.

    Abbott continued to be active in the free-state militia, and in November he commanded his company in the rescue of Jacob Branson from the proslavery sheriff Samuel J. Jones—an event that touched off the "Wakarusa War" of late 1855 (ibid.; *The United States Biographical Dictionary. Kansas Volume* . . . [Chicago and Kansas City, 1879], pp. 11–14; W. H. Isely, "The Sharps Rifle Episode," pp. 551–56; J. B. Abbott to Amos A. Lawrence, Sept. 1, 1855, in the possession of Phillip Rutherford).

2. The Moffat Building at 335 Broadway.
3. Horace Greeley; the lawyer and legal reformer David Dudley Field (1805–1894); Charles Wyllys Elliott; and Frederic Beecher Perkins. The "Priestly" to whom Olmsted refers was probably John Priestley (d. 1872), a New York paper manufacturer and grandnephew of the scientist and philosopher Joseph Priestley. He is probably the "Priestly" with whom Olmsted reported discussing politics on New Year's Day, 1850, in the midst of the sectional crisis that produced the Compromise of 1850. At that time Olmsted described Priestley as the editor of the *American Whig Review*. This may have been the case, since James D. Whelpley, who became editor after the death of the founder, George H. Colton, in 1848, became involved during the next year in projects for the commercial exploitation of Honduras that caused him to leave the *Review*. Although his successor has been identified as George W. Peck, the evidence is not conclusive. In any case, Priestley could well have served as an assistant editor. The offices of his paper company and those of the *Review* adjoined each other at 118 and 120 Nassau Street. Priestley may also have been one of the editors of the *Review* when it accepted and published Olmsted's article "A Voice from the Sea," which appeared in the December 1851 issue. Another earlier connection between Olmsted and Priestley is indicated by the fact that Priestley had sold paper to Adolf Douai. Priestley later assisted Olmsted in his unsuccessful attempt in the summer of 1863 to launch the weekly journal that finally appeared two years later as *The Nation*. Priestley became a member of the Century Club in the first year of its existence, 1847, and in 1866 (seven years after Olmsted became a member) sponsored the membership of the architect Henry Hobson Richardson, whose mother was a granddaughter of Joseph Priestley (F. L. Mott, *History of American Magazines*, 1: 750–51; The Century Association, New York, *The Century, 1847–1946* [New York, 1947], p. 398; ibid., "Report of the Board of Management of 'The Century,' for 1872" [New York, 1873?], pp. 11–13; *Doggett's New York City Directory, for 1850–51* . . . , p. 407 [see Spear 988]; ibid., appendix, p. 21; *DAB*, s.v. "Richardson, Henry Hobson"; FLO to JO, Jan. 4, 1850; A. Douai to FLO and JHO, March 28, 1855; FLO to Mary Perkins Olmsted, June 29, 1863; information on John Priestley supplied by Andrew Zaremba, librarian, The Century Association).
4. The appeal ran as follows:

    We are appealed to by the free settlers in Kansas for assistance. They are threatened with prosecutions and persecutions under the unjustifiable laws recently enacted there by Missourians claiming to be the legislature of Kansas. They need money for their defense. We ask you for contributions which will be handed their accredited agents.

    C. W. Elliott, Paul Babcock, L. Draper, J. E. Williams, Robert Gilchrist, E. A. Stansbury, Thomas Fessenden ("A Historical Relic," *Topeka Daily Capital,* Jan. 8, 1884.)

5. That is, 100 Sharps rifles.
6. On September 19, 1855, Abbott, while still in New York, wrote Olmsted as follows:

    Having been appointed an agent by the Friends of Freedom and actual settlers of Kansas, to solicit subscriptions for the purpose of obtaining arms, ammunition &c. to prevent if possible the further outrages and depredations by Missouri maurauders, and having remained here as long as consistent with my duties at home, therefore I wish you to act in my place and solicit subscriptions for the above object, and purchase Rifles or howitzers ammunition &c. and forward the same to me or such persons as may be selected to rec[eive] the same after my return. I would recomend you to advise with Messrs D. D. Field, H. Greely and such other Gentlemen as they may think best as to the true mode of carrying on this enterprise.

He directed Olmsted to send all packages via F. A. Hunt & Company, St. Louis, Missouri (J. B. Abbott to FLO, Sept. 19, 1855, James Abbott Collection).

To JAMES B. ABBOTT

Moffat's
October 4 [1855]

My Dear Sir

I can delay writing to you no longer, although I have nothing to communicate at all satisfactory.

The whole fund now at my command is less than $350. I shall try a few days longer in hopes to make it up to at least $400 before I make my purchases.

With regard to the objects for which I shall use it, I shall probably act as I indicated to you in my last conversation. I have the advice of a veteran officer and I shall in a few days send you a letter of military advice which I shall receive from him for you. He entirely agrees with the view I took of your position. You have as many S's[1] as you can use to advantage. For the bulk of your arms, the old fashioned pieces would really be better than S's. This he says, with the highest opinion of S's for especial service. I shall therefore probably either send you an h. or m.[2] & some things that will be of peculiar value under certain circumstances which are not unlikely to occur in a defensive position.[3]

By this mail I shall send a valuable book.[4] It is out of print, but I hope to obtain several copies which are in private hands. The pencil marks are to be disregarded, but the ink marks you are advised to observe carefully.

Yours truly

O.

The original is in the James Abbott Collection, Kansas State Historical Society.

1. For "Sharps rifles."
2. Probably for "a howitzer or mortar."
3. Presumably a reference to the six swords, five hand grenades and fifty rockets that Olmsted later said he sent with the mountain howitzer to Kansas. War rockets, with warheads of shot or shell, were generally fifteen inches long with a weight of six pounds, or seventeen inches long with a weight of fifteen pounds. They could be fired from a tripod or from a prone position. In the latter case, which would have been the most likely form of their defensive use in Kansas, the rockets would travel near the surface of the ground for one hundred yards or more and then "rise more or less, become deflected and rush about in a most destructive manner" (FLO to F. G.

Adams, Dec. 24, 1883, quoted in FLO to James B. Abbott, Oct. 7, 1855, n. 3, below; Warren Ripley, *Artillery and Ammunition of the Civil War* [New York, 1970], pp. 345–47).

4. The book that Olmsted sent Abbott may have been the *Manual of the Patriotic Volunteer, on Active Service, in Regular and Irregular War,* by the English adventurer Hugh Forbes, an edition of which was published in New York in 1854 by the Society of Universal Democratic Republicanism. This seems likely, since Forbes was probably the man Olmsted later said he consulted "who, under Garibaldi and others, had had part in a good deal of guerrilla defensive warfare in Europe" and who encouraged him to buy a mountain howitzer. Forbes had taken part in the military campaigns of Garibaldi and his allies during 1848–49 and came to the United States around 1855. He found some employment as a translator for the *New York Tribune,* and might have made contact with Olmsted either through Horace Greeley or through some member of the community of émigré European republicans in New York, which provided such allies for Olmsted in his free-soil activities as William Montague Browne and Friedrich Kapp.

In 1857 Forbes served as drillmaster for the forces that John Brown was gathering at Tabor, Iowa, and agreed to write a manual of arms for Brown. A year later he gravely embarrassed Brown's supporters by informing some Republican congressional leaders of the plan to conduct raids into the South to free slaves and produce slave insurrection (FLO to F. G. Adams, Dec. 24, 1883, quoted in FLO to James B. Abbott, Oct. 7, 1855, n. 1, below; Richard J. Hinton, *John Brown and His Men; With Some Account of the Roads They Traveled to Reach Harper's Ferry,* rev. ed. [New York and London, 1894], pp. 145–52; Stephen B. Oates, *To Purge This Land with Blood: A Biography of John Brown* [New York, Evanston and London, 1970], pp. 200–201, 211–13, 248–50).

To James B. Abbott

New York
October 7, 1855

My Dear Sir

I wrote you three days ago, and sent by same mail a little book, which I think will be useful.

I have ordered and unless my arrangements fail shall have ready for shipment on the 10th the instrument I proposed to purchase for you,[1] and with it 25 shell and 25 canister cartridges & all necessaries except powder, which you had better order from St. Louis. The necessary quantity for these cartridges will be of coarse powder, 12 lbs, and perhaps ¼ that of rifle powder, for charging the shells. I shall send you by private conveyance, if possible, instructions for charging &c. so clear that I think you will have no difficulty to use the instrument with the best effect, if there should unfortunately be occasion.

One discharge of it at musket range is considered equally effective with a simultaneous fire of one hundred muskets—while its moral effect in producing consternation & panic upon an enemy, especially of undisciplined men, is far greater. If you can use it properly, as I doubt not you will, it is worth a dozen field pieces.

MOUNTAIN HOWITZER PURCHASED BY OLMSTED FOR THE DEFENSE OF LAWRENCE, KANSAS

  It will come by the under ground,[2] via Chicago & [*Peneach*],[3] as agreed.
  Yours truly
Acting Commissioner

The original is in the James Abbott Collection, Kansas State Historical Society.

1. The "instrument" that Olmsted purchased was a mountain howitzer—a light field gun designed to be transported in sections by pack animals. He described his role in a letter of December 24, 1883, to F. G. Adams, secretary of the Kansas State Historical Society, in response to receiving a copy of the society's *Collections* containing his letters to Abbott:

> My observations in the Slave States, of which I had published an extended record, led me to feel strongly the importance of organized emigration and I had been as active as I could afford to be in drawing attention to the subject and aiding schemes for the purpose. In consequence of these schemes a larger number of emigrants had been drawn from New England and New York to Kansas when in September, 1855, Mr. J. B. Abbott, as their representative, called on me to represent that they were in need of arms to defend themselves against men seeking lawlessly to make Kansas a Slave State. He gave me a letter recommending him and his object from the Hon. A. A. Lawrence, which I retained and herewith send you. I took some trouble to satisfy myself as to the facts and send you another letter on the subject addressed to me by Mr. Theodore Dwight—President of an Emigrant Aid Society in New York and representing 3000 emigrants then already established in Kansas.
>   I aided Mr. Abbott in obtaining subscriptions to a fund for obtaining rifles until, as

I reckoned, the number of 350 had been provided. It then occurred to me that as the emigrants we wished to aid had mostly settled in communities; as they proposed to act in the form of a militia organization and simply for the purpose of self defense against enemies much more accustomed to border frays with small arms than themselves, it might be better that they should be provided with some other weapon in addition to the rifle. I sought counsel with a man who, under Garibaldi and others, had had part in a good deal of guerrilla defensive warfare in Europe and he strongly sustained my suggestion.

Making inquiries as to what might be available, I visited the New York State Arsenal and there found a mountain howitzer which I ascertained did not belong to the State but to a private owner. Friends soon provided means for its purchase together with fifty rounds of canister and shell with time fuses; five hand grenades; fifty rockets and six swords. With a view to ease of handling and transportation in carts, these things were shipped in ten packages (five casks and five packing-cases). It was supposed by the seller that the goods were going on board ship and had been so packed with a view to landing in boats on some foreign coast. Care was taken to favor this presumption and to prevent their actual destination from being ascertained. It is of interest that the only man to whom I confided the arrangement for this purpose and who personated the ship-master supposed to receive the goods from me was afterwards an officer of high rank in the Southern Confederacy.

With the goods was sent carefully studied advice for practice with canister and shell; for the use of rockets; for the defense of houses with hand grenades and for preparing substitutes for hand grenades from means likely to be available in new settlements.

The entire outfit, including freight paid to Kansas city, involved an outlay of $480. (FLO to F. G. Adams, Dec. 24, 1883, History Cannon File, Manuscript Department, Kansas State Historical Society, Topeka, Kans.)

Olmsted's accomplice in the purchase of the howitzer was probably William Montague Browne (1823–1883), an Anglo-Irish newspaperman whom he met c. 1855. Browne is the only friend of Olmsted's from this period whose correspondence with him has survived and who played an important role in the Confederacy. Browne immigrated to the United States in 1851 or 1852, and around the time of this letter was writing editorials on foreign issues for the *New York Journal of Commerce.* Olmsted could have met him, then, as a member of the "literary republic" of New York. At this time Browne was also friendly with friends of Olmsted's who were actively engaged in free-soil and antislavery agitation: in a letter to Olmsted after the Civil War, Browne sent warm greetings to their mutual friend Friedrich Kapp. Moreover, a man with an Irish accent would have been a good person to impersonate a ship's captain who was going to deliver the howitzer to a "foreign shore." Browne's accent would have helped to allay any suspicion that the gun would be sent to Kansas.

Further evidence of the friendship between Olmsted and Browne is the fact that Olmsted offered Browne a position on the staff of Central Park during its early years. Browne chose instead to remain a journalist. In the spring of 1859, in reward for his strong support of James Buchanan, he was made editor of the *Washington Constitution,* the recognized organ of the Buchanan administration. Browne's activities as a doughface Democrat did not chill his friendship with Olmsted immediately, however. In June he agreed, at Olmsted's request, to recommend that August Nette, a friend of Charles Riotte, be made collector of customs at San Antonio. (Riotte had arranged that if this were done, he would become assistant collector and receive part of the collector's salary.)

By the end of 1860, relations between the two men had become strained, with Olmsted accusing Browne of being "wrong," "unjust" and "insolent" for expressing the pro-Southern sentiments found in the *Constitution.* Browne replied to Olmsted's criticism in a friendly manner, but staunchly defended his position. If the South could not find justice in the Union, he declared, she must seek it by secession. On January 31, 1861, Browne threw in his lot with the Confederacy, publishing the last issue of the *Constitution* and moving to Georgia. He soon secured a high position in the Confederate government; as soon as Robert Toombs was appointed secretary of state, Browne became the assistant secretary and took over much of the work of the department. Thereafter he became increasingly close to Jefferson Davis, who appointed him interim secretary of state in March 1862. In April 1862 Davis made him an aide-de-camp on his military staff with the rank of colonel of cavalry. In that role Browne performed many tasks for Davis and in April 1864 assumed the post of commandant of conscription in Georgia, being charged with enforcing the central government's conscription laws in the face of obstructive tactics by Georgia's states'-rights governor, Joseph Brown.

It was not until nearly two years after the end of the Civil War that Browne attempted to resume his friendship with Olmsted. On February 19, 1867, he wrote that the war had left him ruined—his house and possessions devastated by a Union cavalry raid, himself exhausted and his wife incurably ill. He assured Olmsted that the war had done nothing to diminish "the sincere, cordial, friendship which I have felt for you for many years." He then went on to ask for assistance in securing a loan with which to buy farm implements and mules for working a cotton plantation that a friend had offered to let him use. Olmsted was in no mood to resume cordial relations with a man who he must have felt had betrayed his adopted country. He wrote Browne a scathing reply, chiding him for his "rebellion" and deploring the persistent rebel spirit described in letters he received from the South. Browne replied, earnestly denying what Olmsted's informants told him of the mistreatment of Northerners, Southern Unionists and freedmen. This exchange marked the virtual end of the friendship, and correspondence, of the two men (E. Merton Coulter, *William Montague Browne: Versatile Anglo-Irish American, 1823–1883* [Athens, Ga., 1967], pp. 1–11, 78–79, 82, 92, 98, 104; Rembert Patrick, *Jefferson Davis and His Cabinet* [Baton Rouge, La., 1944], pp. 101–2; W. M. Browne to FLO, June 14, Nov. 14 and Dec. 10, 1860 and Feb. 19 and March 7, 1867; Charles Riotte to FLO, June 1, 1860).

2. On October 24, Olmsted shipped the howitzer to Benjamin Slater in St. Louis, a warehouseman who acted as forwarding agent for the New England Emigrant Aid Company. From St. Louis, the howitzer went to the company's forwarding agent in Kansas City, J. Riddlesbarger. A group of free-soil settlers from Lawrence transported the gun from there to Lawrence.

Early in November, Abbott wrote Amos A. Lawrence about his plans for the howitzer and the effect produced by the arrival of the first group of one hundred Sharps rifles. He said that he was awaiting the arrival of

> a few rifles which I bought in Philadelphia and am looking every day for ____ which was to be sent from New York on the 10th October. This last I shall probably leave at Lawrence, where it can be better guarded, more readily manned, also more liable to be wanted than at any other point in the Territory, yet I do not believe that it will ever be necessary to fire a gun. In the fact that they are here will preclude the necessity for their use—the arrival of your 100 Rifles on the 1st Monday of October, the day of the election called by the (Missouri) legislature, had a most wonderful and magical effect on the Missourians, who came out to vote. The first noticeable change produced by the discovery of so many deadly weapons in town was that of bringing the voice down to a soft whisper from what was before more in accordance with a low, coarse, bullying desperado. Also, there seemed to be a remarkable change in the features from the high rum color to a light pale and through the day after this occurrence you would have mistaken them for gentlemen they were so affable and polite. Perhaps Dr. Cabot could explain the principle of this change.

(FLO to J.B. Abbott, Oct. 24, 1855, James Abbott Collection; Samuel A. Johnson, *The Battle Cry of Freedom: The New England Emigrant Aid Company in the Kansas Crusade* [Lawrence, Kans., 1954], p. 59; J. B. Abbott to A. A. Lawrence, Nov. 3, 1855, in the possession of Phillip Rutherford.)

3. Editors' reading of the word in the original.

To Edward Everett Hale

New York, October 23 [1855]

My Dear Hale,

I called at the Tribune Office with your note & enclosures & Greeley not being in left it with Dana[1] for him. I have called several times since but have not been able to see Greeley, nor has he apparently done anything in consequence of my request, though Dana says he intended to.

I have also seen Raymond[2] who thinks "it is not our case" to make the most of the free-soil prospects in Kansas, because if you give people the impression that there are great probabilities of its being made free they will say, "Then what the devil are you making such a fuss about it for"—& go back to old parties.

To which I haven't any quite satisfactory reply.

Have you?

I am writing now while I wait to have my ammunition boxed up. My shipment has been detained day after day till this time by the failure of contractors to furnish *fuses* for shells. I was determined not to pay them for anything until they gave me *everything,* lest they should be tricky. I believe it will go this afternoon—a 12 pound howitzer, 24 shell & 24 canister cartridges. After paying for everything I shall have a balance left of 30 or 40 dollars—which belongs to the military organization of Kansas, virtually.

I think I will send it to St. Louis to be expended for powder for them. I don't like to send powder from here—& have had the cartridges packed without it.

I am exceedingly busy or I should have replied to your letter sooner. One of my partners[3] is at the West. We are *organizing* a new Children's Magazine—a Junior Put[4]—and my book[5] is slowly printing—to be published in December. The printer's devils haunt me—tight market without & some shinning[6] to be done, which is dreadful punishment to a contemplative man.

Please send your manuscript[7] to "Dix & Edwards for the editor of Putnam's Monthly."

Yours truly,

Fred. Law Olmsted.

Rev. Ed. Hale

The original is in the New England Emigrant Aid Company Papers, Kansas State Historical Society.

1. Charles A. Dana.
2. Henry J. Raymond.
3. Joshua A. Dix (see FLO to JO, Nov. 8, 1855, below).
4. The children's magazine, or "junior *Putnam's,*" was the *Schoolfellow* (see FLO to JO, Nov. 8, 1855, below).
5. *Seaboard Slave States.*
6. That is, borrowing or attempting to borrow money (M. M. Mathews, *Dictionary of Americanisms,* s.v. "shinning").
7. "The Spider's Eye," one of Hale's earliest pieces of fiction, which the editors of *Putnam's Monthly* accepted for publication by January 17, 1856. It appeared, unsigned, in the July 1856 issue (vol. 8, pp. 11–18; FLO to E. E. Hale, Jan. 17, 1856, New England Emigrant Aid Co. Papers).

THE LITERARY REPUBLIC: 1854-1855

To Parke Godwin

[c. October 1855]

My Dear Godwin

We are very glad you undertake the Calhoun,[1] but after striving to manage the material engaged purposely for December we can not without making the number very strong meat make place for it. We will try to do so if you particularly wish us to but would prefer postponing it to January, when it would be made the first article probably.

Would not this on the whole be better? We shall be glad if you think so.

But at any rate—I need not say, we shall be glad to have it & to have it as thorough and distinct for Democracy as possible. Display the real fundamental theory of Government according to Calhoun without the modifications required by temporary & existing things, & place the Democratic theory by its side. That's what is wanted.

Of course we will pay you your own price, if it is for a year's labor.

Yours Truly

F. L. O.

The original is in the Bryant-Godwin Collection, New York Public Library.

1. An article entitled "Calhoun on Government," which Parke Godwin wrote in response to the publication of *The Works of John C. Calhoun,* edited by Richard R. Crallé (*Putnam's Monthly* 7, no. 37 [Jan. 1856]: 90-100).

To John Olmsted

89 Moffats Building
November 8 [1855]

Dear Father,

I *am* overworked certainly very much but I am not unusually unwell. I am afraid I cannot come to Hartford until my book[1] is in type, which I hope will be before Thanksgiving. Dix was gone for a fortnight on our business at the West which gave me unusual labor, besides the unusual labor of correcting proofs, &c.

I begin to print with some fifty pages at the end unfinished—calculating to write them up while the bulk of it was being set. But I have not yet had time to write a page of it. It is to be sure partly in my own hands: a good deal of my time having been occupied in re-touching the early part—particularly the historical sketch of the political economy of Virginia, which I deem very important and very valuable.

To get myself clear of all other distractions I have been engaging myself to go to the island to spend some days in which to write up my narrative conclusion every day—for the next day—since Dix got back a week or more since, but am everyday detained by some absolute constrainment. I can't, as I might usually, make a clerk do some of my work because they are so extremely engaged at the office. Edwards has hardly left, or either of the clerks or porter, before 12 midnight at night for some weeks—being engaged chiefly in folding & wrapping advertizing circulars, &c.

As for my book I am much worried by its bulk. It seems likely to run to two volumes of good size & Dix says will have to be sold at $2.50—which is enough, I apprehend, to ruin a great circulation. I am going to own it myself, paying the firm a percentage for publishing. If it fails the loss is mine; if it has large sale, I get the lion's share of profits.

This ponderosity becomes a goblin of botheration to me. Reputation or notoriety it can not fail to give me—not perhaps friendship but respect, I think. For while I strike right & left and strike hard I do so respectfully and with the grace of sincerity. The style of the heavier parts of the book will I think be considered good. I am certain that I have gained much power in that respect while writing it.

I have said some unpleasant things from a sense of duty. I thought they ought to be said & nobody else appeared to be ready to say them. If they are true they will now make their way—if not, it will be discovered.

Henry Barnes[2] was here night before last. He has a daughter a month old. Brace spent last night with me. He has taken a house in town for the winter.

I borrowed $300 of Patten the other day while Edwards was waiting to hear from you. He was very cold. Edwards speaks confidently of the future & so far as I am judge with reason, but he is tight driven now & we greatly need more capital to take proper advantage of our opportunities. If another good man should offer with capital, we should not decline. What we most want besides capital is a salesman traveller. None of us can be spared from station duties, while we find personal presence in the exterior markets of the greatest value.

I rather regret we have undertaken the Child's Magazine.[3] It will need much capital & labor to make it very valuable or honorable to us.

Mrs. Kirkland[4] will be the editorial contributor & Charles Elliott & Miss Terry[5] regular contributors. Aid from Godwin & others is also engaged. All to be well paid.

I mean now to go to the island Saturday & hope to stay down some days—having proof sheets sent me at night to be returned in the morning.

I said my health was not very bad. It is no way different from usual, but I have got excessively fatigued lately, as if I was going out at the knees (from going upstairs so much I suppose) & I grow thin & pale some, I suppose from lack of sleep. For I can't help writing very late now—& don't sleep after nine at latest. During the day I am too subject to interruptions to write absorbingly. Sam Brooks of Cheshire—Linda's boy[6]—was in today. Is looking for a French teacher—woman—for Mrs. LeConte.[7] How are you all?

Your affectionate son,

Fred.

1. *Seaboard Slave States.*
2. Albert Henry Barnes, a classmate of John Hull Olmsted at Yale, was a Presbyterian minister in Lawrenceville, Pennsylvania (*Yale Obit. Rec.,* 2d ser. 8 [June 1878]: 302).
3. *Schoolfellow: A Monthly Magazine for Boys and Girls,* which Dix, Edwards & Company purchased from Evans & Dickerson in 1855.
4. Caroline M. Kirkland (1801–1864), the popular writer, agreed to become contributing editor of the *Schoolfellow* on November 6, 1855. Dix, Edwards & Company evidently intended to alter the character of the magazine, for Miss Kirkland asked Dix to inform her "*how* you wish the new periodical to differ from it." In 1857, in an effort to forestall bankruptcy, the firm sold the *Schoolfellow* to D. Austin Woodworth, who merged it with the *Youth's Cabinet* (*DAB*; C. M. Kirkland to [J. A. Dix], Nov. 6, 1855, Papers of Dix, Edwards & Co.).
5. Rose Terry.
6. Samuel Hull Brooks, Olmsted's first cousin, was the son of Linda Hull Brooks (1796–1865), the sister of Olmsted's mother (*Papers of FLO,* 1: 202, n. 2).
7. Abigail Anna Brooks Le Conte (c. 1818–1879), Samuel Brooks's sister and Olmsted's cousin (ibid., p. 274, n. 16).

To JOHN OLMSTED

89 Moffat Building
Sunday, December 9, '55

Dear Father

Since the receipt of your last letter, from which I understood that you would be willing if it appeared quite necessary to the proper publication of my book to advance payments on its cost,[1] I have not written because I have been expecting to go to Hartford to talk about it.

I thought Edwards would go to Boston & see if he could [get] a Boston house to take hold with us in the publication. He has no other business there however until the close of the month & deems it advisable, as I believe it is, that before making such a proposition, he should be furnished with a fair, clean proof of the greater part of the book—if not the whole of it.

In a week or ten days the stereotyping, I should now judge, would be completed: then will be some delay to complete the electrotyping of the last cuts. But of the first 150 pages we are ready to order the press-work immediately.

Edwards is anxious I should make definite arrangements before we begin that. I have asked him to put on paper his proposition for me to offer you & I will send it as soon as he does so. If it would really give you much trouble or inconvenience to accept this, I don't want you to do it. I don't doubt that I could easily make such an arrangement as I proposed to you, with someone here—Barney or Judge Emerson & Dudley Field[2]—for there can be little doubt that the book will pay eventually 20 per cent. on cost of publication, I should think. The only objection I have to doing so is the exposition to them that would be necessary of our want of capital—& of my private want of capital.

But considering that as a matter of business entirely—I want for my private purposes outside of the business, a small sum of money, outside of the partnership business, I mean, and a little outside of all business.

There is a certain kind of private advertizing of myself to be done in connection with the issue of my book which I don't want to feel so cramped in doing as I do. There is a sort of literary republic, which it is not merely pleasant & gratifying to my ambition to be recognized in, but also profitable. It would for example, if I am so recognized & considered, be easy for me, in case of the non-success of this partnership, to get employment in the newspaper offices or other literary enterprises at good wages—to make arrangements for correspondence if I wished to travel, & so on.

To take & keep a position as a recognized litterateur, as a man of influence in literary matters, I need at the time of the publication of my book to be able to spend a little more than I like at this juncture to draw out of our partnership bank. And I hate, as Edwards expects of me, to be running in debt to tailors & cobblers & cooks.

Only the first four-page sheet of the original letter is in the Olmsted Papers in the Library of Congress. Since Olmsted filled the fourth page and did not close the letter, it is probable that the letter originally contained other pages that have not survived.

1. Because they anticipated that the *Schoolfellow* would lose money in its first year of publication, Dix and Edwards decided that the firm could not issue *Seaboard Slave States* unless Olmsted paid the printing costs. On November 24, 1855, Olmsted asked his father to loan him $500 to pay the printer (FLO to JO, Nov. 8, 1855 (above), and Nov. 24, 1855).
2. That is, if his father could not lend him the money, Olmsted might be able to borrow it from Hiram Barney (1811–1895), a New York City lawyer, from William Emerson or from David Dudley Field ("Obituary Record. Hiram Barney," *NYDT*, May 20, 1895, p. 2).

CHAPTER VI
EUROPEAN INTERLUDE
1856

LITTLE HAS SURVIVED of whatever Olmsted wrote describing his travels in Italy, Austria and Germany in the spring of 1856 and his residence in London during the summer and fall of that year. The first letter in this chapter gives some indication of his response to Italy, and particularly to the architecture of Rome. The letter to his partner Joshua A. Dix relates his experiences in the literary world of London, especially with William M. Thackeray and the circle of editors of *Punch*. The other letters in the chapter deal with concerns of longer standing. Those to the *New-York Daily Times* and to James Elliot Cabot reflect Olmsted's continuing preoccupation with the question of the South and slavery, while the unusually personal letters to his half-sister Bertha reveal as much of his feelings about life and love as any he ever wrote.

TO JOHN OLMSTED

[March] 27, 1856

Dear Father,

We were not quite so near Genoa as I thought when I ended my last letter to you, however we reached there during the morning and before we could get a permit to land, the weather had become fine and we had a capital day ashore and enjoyed ourselves very much.

During the night we ran calm[ly][1] to Leghorn, where we landed, paying nine francs ([*three for*] permit and six for boats) soon after noon.[2] We rode to the English Cemetery,[3] a beautiful place, and looked for an hour or more for the grave stone of Mr. Brush, but could not find it.

We had a delightful sail along the moonlighted mountain coast, the sea as calm as a mill pond and the air softer than anything, arriving early next morning at Civita Vecchia[4]—six days from Marseilles—& gladly exchanged the Bosphorus for the top of a little diligence.[5]

The road to Rome, though the scenery was monotonous, was not uninteresting & the ride was very pleasant. I shall go on using superlatives of pleasure if I diarize Rome.

Most things disappointed [*my*] expectations at the first glance. Rome is smal[*ler an*]d drearier and uglier in its whole outside [*than I*] should have thought & thus far in pictures [*I have*] seen nothing that would pay you for crossing [*the*] street.

It is otherwise with the marbles,[6] and St. Peter's, poor as it seemed at a distance & mean as [*compared*] to my anticipations, still in some particularities, quite profounded me as I approached [*the*] front closely & though exceedingly different f[*rom*] all I had imagined, astonished and regularly [*awed*] me.[7] Three or four times indeed I have been [*back &*] felt in a dream.

The nature about Rome [*is far finer than I had known and I have never seen anything like it. In fact,*] where I am disappointed in my imaginations, I am not less in[*terested &*] instructed & every day more & more gratified.

I was born for a traveler. I do enjoy it exceedingly & I had no idea I could get so much out of such a hasty journey.

Bertha & Sophie are both more than they used to be—than we had imagined.

Bertha says I can't write any more for this mail.

---

1. The italicized material in brackets in this letter presents the editors' reading of words partially lost in a worn and torn fold in the manuscript.
2. Olmsted and his half-sister Mary had sailed from Marseilles to Genoa and then to Leghorn, or Livorno.
3. The English cemetery at Leghorn was the burying ground for Protestant travelers who died while in central Italy (John Murray, pub., *Handbook for Travellers in Central Italy* . . ., 8th ed., [London, 1874], p. 198).
4. Civitavecchia, forty-five miles west of Rome, was the principal port for central Italy.
5. That is, Olmsted and his party left the *Bosphorus,* a 350-ton bark on which they had sailed from Marseilles to Civitavecchia, and took a public stagecoach (*Lloyd's Register of British and Foreign Shipping* . . . [London, 1856], s.v. "Bosphorus").
6. Presumably Olmsted is referring to the famous Greek and Roman statuary in the Vatican Museum.
7. Olmsted recalled the effect of the square in front of the basilica of St. Peter's, designed by Michelangelo, with its great enclosing colonnade, when, many years later, he undertook to design the campus of Stanford University in California. He made it clear to Leland Stanford that the California climate required an approach that was quite different from the one traditionally adopted in the East:

> If we are to look for types of buildings and arrangements suitable to the climate of California it will rather be in those founded by the wiser men of Syria, Greece, Italy and Spain. You will remember in what a different way from the English methods, the spirit of which we have inherited, the open spaces about nearly all buildings that you have seen in the South of Europe to which throngs of people resort, have been treated. In the great "front yard" of St. Peter's, for example, not a tree, nor a bush, nor a particle of turf has been made use of. This is not because Michael Angelo and his successors have been blind to the beauty of foliage and verdure in suitable places. (FLO to Leland Stanford, Nov. 27, 1886, Stanford University Archives, Palo Alto, Calif.)

To Bertha Olmsted

Glasgow
June 18th, 1856

Dear Bertha;
    I am very sorry that I did not answer your letter immediately as I fully intended to. And I have meant to every day since. Not that I have anything of consequence to say. You acted with courage & I don't doubt rightly, i.e. conscientiously.[1] You do not give me the slightest clue to the reason or process of the sudden conviction. Probably you could not. Instinctive or unexplainable convictions generally have greater weight, & rightly so, than deliberate conclusions of judgment in determining a good hearted person's action in love. Yet I have felt very sad to see the love of such a man as Bartholomew repulsed, partly from sympathy with him, no doubt, but also from general apprehensions which I suppose are foolish. But the fact is I feel that Bartholomew is one of the very few men I have ever known both in woman's society & out of it, who do not attempt to be and can not be imposters. Most men do their courting, instinctively it seems, by a steady imposition. Bartholomew is the same to men that he is to women; he has no capacity to hide his faults or deficiencies & never attempts it. They stick out, but his virtues are other men's manners & are

Edward Sheffield Bartholomew

therefore realized at their true value slowly. Therefore it was important to him, peculiarly so, that he should have full and long opportunities of revealing himself unconsciously or purposelessly to you.

As I said I don't think it necessary that we should know the reasons of a conviction to act upon it—it is the state of mind (heart) that settles the question. But then it troubles me that the state of mind or conviction on which you acted decisively was but one day old, while as you say your instinct or unreflective "dreams" (state of mind) had all been for weeks previously of an opposite character. You had received no new light, no new fact, no closer observation, no experience of incompatibility of character had occurred; it must have been a sudden reflection or a mere wave of the impulse, a wave of reaction which invariably follows a new state of the mind, under which you acted.

I have been much troubled by reflections of this sort—added to the deepest sympathy which I have for Bartholomew—which I would have for any man under similar circumstances, but peculiarly for one of his character. However, though I don't know you very well, I have more confidence in your good sense than I would have in most girls'. You have some deficiencies of constitution & are badly diseased in one faculty, but I don't see that these difficulties could have operated in the present case; so finally I bring myself to believe that it is most probable you have, by whatever process, done what was best, what was most judicious under the circumstances. It is only another case of unfortunate attachment, for which you are in no way responsible. It happens every day. God knows why. It is the most melancholy thing in the world.[2]

I came from London to Birmingham a week ago, staid with Field[3] over Sunday & Monday, & Tuesday to Edinbro'. Three days of business moderately successful there & then here. I return to Edinbro' tomorrow & to London Tuesday or Wednesday (17th—18th). Sad place this Glasgow, more vice & poverty; crape hat bands; long, severe faces, white cravats & black coats, rags, squalor, drunkenness & riot than I ever saw elsewhere. It is worse than Rome or Naples on the outside. Bad faces & bad manners. They raise good people here at great expense.

Your affectionate brother

The original is in the possession of Terry Niles Smith.

1. A reference to Bertha's refusal of a proposal of marriage by the sculptor Edward Sheffield Bartholomew. Olmsted had reservations about the way that Bertha reached her decision, as he made clear to his half-sister Mary on June 9, shortly after receiving the letter from Bertha to which this letter is the reply:

> It's as plain as anything coming through a letter can be that Bertha has acted not, as she supposes, from a sudden revelation of herself, but from one of those unaccountable freaks to which all women, but especially all women of fine organization, are subject in love

matters and the probabilities are very great that twenty years hence she will look upon it as the one dreadful accident of her life.... You must understand that I don't find fault with Bertha at all for acting on her immediate present conviction, but a little more experience would teach her to be more cautious in receiving sudden convictions, a little doubtful of her ability to reason so rapidly to a conclusion of so much importance. (FLO to Mary Olmsted, June 7, 1856, in the possession of Terry Niles Smith.)

2. Olmsted's sympathy and concern for Bartholomew stemmed in part from his own painful experience in 1851 when Emily Perkins broke off her brief engagement to him. He may also have recalled his keen disappointment when in 1846 Emily's cousin Elizabeth Baldwin refused to allow him to correspond with her, leaving him "right smack & square on dead in love with her, beached and broken backed." Drawing on these experiences, Olmsted was deeply worried about the effect that Bertha's refusal would have on Bartholomew: "I should not be much surprised if Bartholomew, supposing he understands Bertha as she meant he should, should be made insane. He is just the man to be ruined by it. I hope that he will hope. If he does you'll see something great in his studio next winter. But he may take it the proud way, which is the worst of all & makes a man a devil. At any rate you may be sure he is about as well worth praying for as any man above ground this summer. I should be greatly relieved to hear that he was dead." In fact, Bartholomew died within two years. His health was already poor, due to the toll taken by a severe case of small pox in 1848 and a subsequent hip infection that left him permanently lame (ibid.; Susan Underwood Crane, "Edward Sheffield Bartholomew," *Connecticut Quarterly* 2, no. 3 [July–Sept. 1896]: 203–14; *Papers of FLO,* 1: 11, 65–67).
3. Alfred T. Field, Olmsted's friend and former neighbor on Staten Island, who in 1854 had returned to his native England to take charge of his family's hardware business in Birmingham (*Papers of FLO,* 1: 342, n. 11).

New-York Daily Times, July 10, 1856

HOW RUFFIANISM IN WASHINGTON AND KANSAS IS REGARDED IN EUROPE

To the Editor of the New-York Times:

Edinburgh, (Scotland)
Thursday, June 19, 1856

The position of an American traveling in Europe is just now a most unpleasant one. In railway carriages and other public places when he is not known as an American, he is obliged to hear language applied to his country which it is difficult to allow to pass in silence, and yet which he cannot deny to be just. The most that he can do is to repudiate the disgrace for himself personally, and his section or his State. And this he finds exceedingly difficult to do satisfactorily. Every American citizen is part sovereign of his country, and responsible for the actions of its Government. Every American citizen is and feels himself in a peculiar sense a foreign Minister of his country, a representative of its sovereign. When civilization is outraged in the Senate of his country,[1] can he refuse to explain or defend the stigma attaching to himself thereby?

In society, when one is known to be an American, the studied avoidance of reference to his country is more expressive than the strongest denunciation of the barbarism that has lately reigned in its high places.

One is met by men whom he has formerly known as admirers and lovers of his country and its Government, with expressions of sadness and disappointment. "I have lately been compelled to admit," said one of the founders of the Reform Club,[2] but a man of too liberal views to be ranked among the present Whigs, to me, "I have lately been compelled to admit that the experiment of extreme liberalism in America has failed. In its material results merely it has succeeded wonderfully, but its effects on society are evidently the reverse of favorable to the progress of civilization and Christianity. Even your legislators are murderers and ruffians of the worst stamp; your Government plots civil war, and encourages robbery and piracy in order to give strength and stability to an institution in itself barbarous, and which has in all nations heretofore lost ground just as fast as Christianity and civilization have advanced. Your law system, admirable and superior in many respects to ours, as it is, is apparently powerless to punish crime of the most heinous character, when the guilty parties are men of station and wealth."

It is useless to reply to such allegations that it is but to part of our country they apply. Foreigners cannot understand our nice distinctions between local and federal responsibility. Besides, Washington and Kansas are federally and not locally self-governed. All is charged to the Republican system.

Rarely do we find a friend who is willing to understand late events as favorably to our political principles as the editor of the *North British Daily Mail*, a leading Scotch newspaper,[3] who thus reflects upon them:

> To those who admire the political institutions of the United States, the free and enterprising spirit of the citizens of the Republic, their noble self-taxation (exceeding in amount all other public burdens) for purposes of education alone, whilst we even in Scotland are grumbling in our miserly hearts at the proposal of a penny per pound, the respectability secured to labor, the boundless means of industrial development, and the various characteristics in which the political and social condition of that great nation is superior to our own, there is something inexpressibly painful and disappointing in the present state of its affairs and future prospects. We refer not, to its irritated and hostile relations to ourselves;[4] these are probably but the temporary result of internal maladies, that are far more worthy of consideration. What a scene of anarchy, of outrage, of bitterness, and division, is presented in the interior of the Republic! The protection afforded to noon-day murder in the capital, the introduction of Lynch law into the Senate House, the intolerance of free discussion, the deadly broils between an Anti-Slavery and a Pro-Slavery Party in Kansas, and an infamous war of extermination waged against unoffending Indians in Oregon, present such a

combination of elements as can only remind one of "the beginning of the end." Whilst empty and heedless stump orators are boasting of the glorious position of the Federal Republic, it is treading over the crust of a volcano; whilst they are reveling in brilliant visions of future destiny, it is advancing rapidly to the brink of a precipice. Whatever may be the fortune or the fate of the United States in their national capacity, one cannot but observe and regret at least the practical predominance of a spirit which is totally at variance with the principles of their Constitution and with ideas which we well know to prevail in American society. A man is shot in one of the hotels of Washington with impunity, because he is only a poor Irishman;[5] others are hunted and killed like wolves, because they are only Indians;[6] a Senator is felled with a bludgeon in the Senate House, because he is only a friend of negroes; and a town is destroyed, and a whole Territory given over to organized violence, because they are only inhabited by some citizens who wish to found a Free State![7] Where, in such acts, is any trace of that freedom, equality and humanity, which form the basis of the Republic, and ought to be its chief glory? The most wretched despotism that has sprung from the dregs of Spanish rule in the New World could do nothing worse than is now being done in the United States; and when a great nation thus departs from its fundamental principles, common sense as well as all history assure us that either a speedy reaction must set in, or that the political system must fall into ruin and dissolution.

At the root of all this disorder in the United States is the question of Slavery. Mr. Herbert, the murderer of the Irish waiter, is protected and screened by the Southern party, because killing a slave or a low Irishman is in their opinion no murder. Mr. Sumner was beaten with a club by Mr. Brooks because he made a speech in support of Freedom and against Slavery. The town of Lawrence is destroyed because it is inhabited by a "Free-State" Party. The present civil war in Kansas has its origin entirely in the breach of the Missouri compromise at the instigation of the Slave States. The grand object of the struggle is to convert Kansas into a Slave Territory, not by fair votes, but by violence, by dragoons and cannon, and by ruffianism. And it is important to observe that of these proceedings of the Pro-Slavery Party Mr. President Pierce is the strenuous abettor and supporter. The Democratic Party finds it necessary to identify itself with all the vilest outrages of the "nigger-drivers." Even Mr. Buchanan, to whom the Northerners looked for greater impartiality and dignity of mind than have been displayed by other Democratic candidates for the Presidential chair, has adopted, since his return to the States, all the demands of the slave interest.[8]

On the Continent, I assure you, that Republicanism has lost prestige most seriously from the events to which I allude. The German and French Republicans meet an American with melancholy or scornful and averted faces. "The Austrian Government has been guilty of no greater or meaner crime," said one, "than your Government in its method of extending Slavery, if we may believe the newspaper accounts of the recent movements in Kansas." It is true. The Austrian tyranny works secretly, but straightforwardly and with avowed purpose. The American, with false pretences of impartiality, connives at and encourages measures which naturally and inevitably lead on to the ruin or murder of those whom it has chosen to make its enemies, and, then, indirectly, shields from justice and apologizes for the murderous banditti it has employed.

YEOMAN

The text presented here is taken from the *New-York Daily Times,* July 10, 1856.
1. A reference to the caning of Senator Charles Sumner of Massachusetts on the floor of the U.S. Senate by Congressman Preston Brooks of South Carolina on May 22, 1856.
2. The Reform Club was founded in 1836 as a mutual gathering place for British Radicals and Whigs in order to "form a central and national focus for the liberal element in politics" (Norman Gash, *Politics in the Age of Peel: A Study in the Technique of Parliamentary Representation, 1830-1850* [London, New York and Toronto, 1953], pp. 403-11).
3. Robert Somers (1822-1891), who from 1849 to 1859 was the editor of the *North British Daily Mail,* a newspaper published in Glasgow (*DNB*).
4. Central America was a source of irritation between Great Britain and the United States during the presidency of Franklin Pierce. In 1854 an American warship leveled Greytown on the Mosquito Coast—a British protectorate—because of the wounding of an American citizen in disorders there, and in 1855 the seizure of Nicaragua by the American adventurer William Walker strengthened British fears of American expansionism in the Caribbean. In 1856 the British reinforced their West Indies fleet and supplied arms to Costa Rica for the overthrow of the Walker republic in Nicaragua. The situation came to a head in May 1856 when Pierce officially recognized the Walker republic. At the same time Pierce broke off discussions with the British minister in Washington, John F. T. Crampton, who had angered Americans by recruiting soldiers in the United States to fight for the British in the Crimean War. Conciliatory gestures by both governments soon eased the tensions between the two countries (Harry C. Allen, *Great Britain and the United States: A History of Anglo-American Relations, 1783-1952* [New York, 1955], pp. 434-48).
5. On May 8, 1856, Philemon Thomas Herbert (1825-1864), an Alabama-born U.S. congressman from California, shot and killed an Irish waiter, Thomas Keating, at Willard's Hotel in Washington. The murder took place during a brawl that was said to have started after Herbert struck Keating for refusing to serve him breakfast without a direct order from the hotel management, the regular time for serving breakfast being past. The murder trial did not occur until July; the jury, after forty-five minutes of deliberation, acquitted Herbert on grounds of self-defense (*NYDT,* May 9, 1856, p. 4; and July 26, 1856, p. 1).
6. A reference to the "Yakima War" of 1855-56, which resulted from efforts of the U.S. government, following the separation of the Oregon and Washington territories in 1853, to settle the Indians of Oregon Territory on reservations (Ray H. Glassley, *Pacific Northwest Indian Wars* [Portland, Ore., 1953], pp. 109-42).
7. A reference to the "sacking" of Lawrence, Kansas Territory, the central town of the antislavery settlers, on May 21, 1856. The town was not destroyed, although its two chief buildings—the Free State Hotel and the house of Charles Robinson, agent for the New England Emigrant Aid Company—were burned, the presses of two newspapers—the *Herald of Freedom* and the *Kansas Free State*—were destroyed, and there was much looting (David M. Potter, *The Impending Crisis, 1848-1861* ..., ed. and completed by Don E. Fehrenbacher [New York, 1976], pp. 208-9).
8. James Buchanan (1791-1868), who had been ambassador to England during Franklin Pierce's administration, returned to the United States in April 1856. On June 2 the Democratic National Convention made him its presidential candidate and adopted a platform that supported the Compromise of 1850 and the Kansas-Nebraska Act and opposed congressional interference with slavery in the territories (*DAB*).

EUROPEAN INTERLUDE: 1856

To Joshua Augustus Dix

Brighton, Sunday August 3d, 1856

My Dear Dix,
    I thank you much for your letter of 15th or thereabouts of August.[1] You should have written me in that way before.

    If I were very sensitive, perhaps I should feel it an indignity to be stationed in London, as a branch of a commercial house of which I am one of the three original heads and to be continuously addressed by the signature of the house itself as if I were a very young, undisciplined clerk, whom it was necessary to constantly caution not to be too self confident, rash & speculative, to be strenuously constrained from involving those who employed him in dangerous risks, & so on.

    If I were in the habit of going ahead in proud stubborn blindness, if I disdained to consult you in matters of importance or neglected to advise you of what I was about, if I habitually exhibited an absurd confidence in my own judgment & business capacities; a little delicate reproof or attempt to constrain me might be proper & useful. But the contrary of this to a fault, is my character, so much so that both you & Dana[2] said (& I do not doubt Edwards[3] felt) that it would be the chief obstacle to my success in England.

    You will remember also my answer to you, & you will see that events have justified my expectations of myself. But if anything could have paralyzed all the elements of success in my character & habits, it would have been just such letters as you have been sending me & the want of such full free & honest advices as your letter, at last received, contains.

    To be frank with you, the manner in which you have treated me is inexcusable. How do you judge me? You have had good opportunities of knowing me, my weaknesses & foibles. You know my prevailing motives & tendencies with regard to our business. Am I the man among us most inclined to extravagant expenditures, to inconsiderate movements, to rash & dangerous speculations? If I were, you might be justified not only in constantly cautioning me, but even in trying to put some absolute barrier on the career in which my folly could drag you.

    But at the worst, if I were your youngest & silliest clerk, would it not be a childish & undignified thing to write me, "We have perfect confidence in your integrity & docility to the extent, *in an emergency,* of twenty five pounds! But do be careful." This, in almost exactly these words, is what you have written me, only in two consecutive sentences, instead of one.[4]

    Don't think that I attach too much importance to this. In my own mind I put the best construction upon it and do not allow it to interfere with my cordial & friendly cooperation with you, I hope, at all.

    Certainly, if I see an opportunity to make a purchase for a hundred pounds, that I should in any case be likely to make without waiting for your advice, I shall not be prevented by your general orders from not making it. The probability of it is about the same as of your buying a paper mill without previously asking my consent.

The only absolute safety you can have against such pranks might be secured by advertising in the Atheneum[5] that Dix, Edwards & Co. of New York would not be held responsible for the purchases of any of their partners to any amount exceeding 25 pounds unless consent in writing of the majority of the partners was produced by the individual offering to purchase.

With regard to the blocks purchased by Mr. Low, I will simply say that until [you expressed] something like a private apology in your letter—at least a private reservation—you have been persistently unjust & uncivil to me. If you did not agree with the ideas written by Mr. Edwards and in some cases at least recorded on the books of the partnership, you should have been more prompt with your reservation and have given equal dignity to it.

Remarks on this subject came to me in nine successive letters, all in the same strain, & no notice has ever been taken of my replies. I think you have acted throughout in a most absurd way.

I maintain & sincerely believe, 1st—that I was not responsible for the purchase. 2d, that it was a judicious one. (If you had been content to wait to hear my notions I should have made it so, but) before you knew or had any idea what the blocks were, Edwards wrote me in an angry manner, that he should sell them as soon as they arrived & he did not doubt we should lose $500 on them. You paid no attention to any request of mine with regard to them. Edwards even neglects a business order about them. Excuse me however for touching a sore spot, as it seems to be [to] all of us.

But let me say here that I think when you wish to advise me upon such points as how to write a friendly letter or any other topic of deportment or morals, it would be as well to do it in your private and not your collective capacity. As I can not be advised with before these treatises are indited, I prefer not to be held responsible for their record as the views of the firm in the copybook.

But, to have done with joking and growling, I want you—you, Dix—to write me sometimes in the way not only of the details, but of a general survey of our business, especially as relates to the English department of it. Recollect that in the few days after we began to consider it possible to do any English business, before I left, we talked very little about it & that little had reference entirely to the where & how of obtaining books on commission, not at all to the manner in which they should be dealt with & how this business should connect with the general business.

I suppose & act upon the supposition that Low has the general direction of this branch, as you have of the manufacturing, but that you, because of your previous experience with it at Putnam's,[6] look after it in its relation & connection with the general business & superintend & advise with Low. If so, I think you ought to write me more about it, not in its details as he does, but in its general drift. I have frequently intimated that I somewhat doubted if it would be best to solicit or even to take consignments from any & everybody. Low sometimes seems to be arguing against me, but neither you nor Edwards have apparently discussed it at all & I doubt if you have got my idea.

If I should come home, the whole subject could be so much more satisfactorily debated and a broad policy distinctly entered upon so much more confidently & judiciously by all, that I don't want to undertake to do it by correspondence. But I need every day to know your purposes & preparations better than I do.

This dull season, Putnam falling off alarmingly, Schoolfellow dragging,[7] lots of projects apparently lost sight of, the numerous speculations ready for launching in the autumn, and finally this English experiment,[8] in the success of which *our honor* is more at stake than in all the rest (because it involves the fulfillment of promises & our worthiness of the *trust* of others more than the rest.) All these make the next six months the grand crisis of our business. I would prefer to restrict rather than enlarge the requisitions upon your labor, discretion & capital. I hope you will look out before November to have a sufficiently numerous & capable company of clerks & porters to relieve you from petty & unimportant occupation of your time. The business will be so large & varied that its mere superintendence with the proper deliberation & discussion upon new projects, the consideration of questions of taste & invention, & the conduct of important correspondence will certainly require all your time & talent. I think too that Low, at the outset, will have more than he can do to make the best of the materials already secured to him for the English book department. Six months ago it was, as you then told me, chiefly of consequence to get some consignments. Now the only thing comparatively is to dispose of those which have been got.

I don't well know what you think. What you say seems to be said rather with the purpose of encouraging me than as a spontaneous expression of your business judgment. But I tell you that if, with my present knowledge, I had to demand what I would take in England when I came here, it would be just about what I have succeeded in getting. If you understood all I mean by this without knowing more of the grounds of my judgment, I don't suppose you would at all agree with me.

I do not believe it is desirable that I should stay in London another day for the avowed purpose of gaining consignments from other houses. I should not from my own impulse at present solicit another house to consign. What I chiefly hope to do in the next year is to unobtrusively obtain the friendship and confidence of the publishing *body* for our house. To convert the present confidence of those who consign to us into a really active friendship, to make them desirous to serve us, and if we are to be (I hope not) considered here as the rivals of Bangs,[9] to make them our partisans, to make them do our advertising, blow our trumpets, sound our praises, vindicate our character & advantages.

If Welford[10] considers us in opposition to him, I would not ask that he should do anything better for us than to go on in the way he began. I cautioned him not so much from policy as self respect. If we much exceed the expectations of our present consignors, we may leave the battle in their hands. A year or two hence we shall not find people waiting to be solicited to consign to us. They will be soliciting us to undertake to do for them what we have done for Bradbury & Evans, Parker & so on.[11]

If you will publish some books that will make themselves known here and sell heavily of such consignments [as] are already offered us, Mr. Welford will have done us the greatest service possible by giving his friends an opportunity of reaction from injustice and suspicion.

There is much other reason why for a year to come every effort should be made (consistently with dignity) on your side, & why I should be comparatively quiet & indifferent with regard to further consignments. There are many publishers—of good books too—whose consignments would be an injury to us at present.

Punch[12] I should be very glad to have you take as I have proposed—from the influence it would indirectly have on our position here. But I would not like to have you risk any financial embarrassment for it. *Punch* is owned & conducted by a club or association of its contributors together with the publishers & Joyce,[13] who is the Secretary & Treasurer. Mark Lemon is the editor.

I dined with them all at Thackeray's the other night—Mark Lemon, Thackeray, Shirley Brooks, Leigh, Tom Taylor, Leech, Horace Mayhew. I need not say they are good men as well as jolly fellows, *all active, productive minds and connected with various other good things as well as Punch*. At the dinner, whereat were also Bayard Taylor, Hurlbert & Story, Bradbury & Evans were markedly polite to me—each of them, & Joyce, asking me to drink with them, &c.[14]

The idea was suggested that some sort of American correspondence with Punch might be practicable. Who would be the man for that? The set dine together weekly at Bradbury & Evans & at their dinner their business is arranged & under the vinous warmth the good things sprout. It is this which has kept Punch alive so long, without doubt.

You ask how I like the Schoolfellow. Judging from the July number, I do not like it as a whole & I am not satisfied with any part of it—except Duggan's street scenes,[15] which are good. But you have not one real genius for children at work for it. Neither Dana nor you, nor Miss Terry nor Elliott[16] have the proper qualities for its editor. And any one of you *alone* would do better than you all unenthusiastically and inharmoniously combined. There is nowhere sufficient personal responsibility and absorption in it.

My China story was completed and carefully & intelligibly arranged & laid *altogether* wherever you found a part, at three o'clock in the morning of the day I left New York. How do you suppose I can re-complete it without knowing *where* the interruption occurs? How could you have printed the illustrations (as per advertisement of contents) when the matter illustrated was wanting?[17]

EUROPEAN INTERLUDE: 1856

Tell Dana he will do me a kindness if he will go to [Staten] island sometime as you do & visit John. The poor fellow is so lonely & gets so blue there.

Is Curtis to be married this summer? Give my love to him.

Yours cordially,

Fred. Law Olmsted

Send me early copies of Godwin & Greeley.[18] I may get them reviewed. Does not Curtis want me to get the basis of an article on modern English dramas & comedies? What are they? Hurlbert goes on triumphantly. He will have the material to distill monthly volumes, for ten years, on his return.

The original is in the Papers of Dix, Edwards & Company, Harvard University.

1. Olmsted must have meant the "15th or thereabouts of July," for he dated this letter precisely and internal evidence indicates that he wrote it soon after August 1, 1856.
2. Charles A. Dana.
3. Arthur T. Edwards.
4. Olmsted was bristling at the personal criticism he had received in a letter from his partners, Dix and Edwards, in response to a bill they received amounting to £ 116/16 for 152 woodcuts and electrotypes that had been purchased in England by Sampson Low, Jr. (1822–1871), a London literary agent employed by Dix, Edwards & Company. Low was the son and partner of the English publisher Sampson Low (1797–1886), whose firm was marketing *Seaboard Slave States* in England. Olmsted considered the younger Low to be "a capital sort of fellow" and wanted to leave the British business of Dix, Edwards & Company in his hands. Dix and Edwards, however, were distressed by Low's purchase of the plates and made their displeasure clear to Olmsted:

    > *We cannot imagine the reason for making such a purchase* as we were particular in instructing you not to make purchases without consulting us in regard to them, except in the single instance of Bentley's woods. *There is no earthly use to which we can possibly put them, and when they arrive we shall if possible sell them for what they will fetch.* Here we have more than $750 invested in stock that is of no use to us. We cannot use them in the Schoolfellow, as we find it necessary to have cuts made for the articles to be published. You are well aware that we have not sufficient capital to permit us to invest a dollar of it in stock that may not be made available immediately, *and we must insist that there should be no more purchases on our account without our consent.* We shall instruct Messrs. Low & Co. to draw on us and shall honor their draft in this instance, but expect it to be the last that is made on us for any purchases. We can use our money to better advantage here.
    >
    > *Do not think of purchasing any stereotype plates no matter how low they are offered to you.* It will not do for us to incur any obligations whatever that we cannot promptly meet and *it is because we cannot place our funds in this way that we write as urgently as we do.*

    (*DNB*, s.v. "Low, Sampson"; FLO to JO, c. Feb. 1, 1856; Dix, Edwards & Co. to FLO, April 30, 1856.)
5. The *Athenaeum, A London Literary and Critical Journal*, then edited by William H. Dixon (*DNB*).
6. Dix had been a clerk in the office of George P. Putnam (see FLO to JO, March 13, [1855], n. 5, above).
7. John Hull Olmsted had informed his brother that Dix, Edwards & Company was earning little profit and that sales of *Putnam's Monthly* "had fallen off alarmingly" (JHO to FLO, July 10, [1856]).

389

8. That is, the attempt of Dix, Edwards & Company to become the agents for selling the publications of a number of British publishing firms in the United States.
9. Bangs Brothers and Company, a New York book dealer, had previously employed Sampson Low, Jr., as its agent in London (FLO to JO, c. Feb. 1, 1856).
10. Charles Welford (1815–1885), a partner in the firm of Bartlett & Welford, New York importers of foreign books (George Templeton Strong, *Diary of George Templeton Strong*, ed. Allan Nevins and Milton Halsey Thomas, 4 vols. [New York, 1952], 1: 12, n. 2).
11. That is, if Dix, Edwards & Company proved successful as American agents for Bradbury & Evans and John William Parker (1792–1870), other English publishers would request similar relationships with the firm (*DNB*, s.v. "Parker, John William").
12. The humorous magazine *Punch*, founded by Mark Lemon (1809–1870) and Henry Mayhew (1812–1887) in 1841 (*DNB*).
13. William Joyce, an engraver for *Punch* (William M. Thackeray, *The Letters and Private Papers of William Makepeace Thackeray: Collected and Edited by Gordon N. Ray*..., 4 vols. [Cambridge, Mass., 1945–46], 2: 396, n. 134).
14. The dinner that Olmsted attended was one that Thackeray gave annually at his home for those associated with *Punch*. They included William Bradbury and Frederick Evans, its publishers; William Joyce; C. W. Shirley Brooks (1816–1874), an editor; Percival Leigh, a frequent contributor; Tom Taylor (1817–1880), a writer who later became an editor; John Leech (1817–1864), artist and caricaturist; and Horace Mayhew (1816–1872), one of the editors. Americans at the dinner included Bayard Taylor (1825–1878), author of numerous travel books and a contributor to *Putnam's Monthly;* William H. Hurlbert; and the sculptor William Wetmore Story (1819–1895).

    At this dinner, Olmsted experienced an embarrassing moment that he related years later to his son, Frederick Law Olmsted, Jr. He arrived at the dinner dressed in white tie and tails, only to find the others dressed less formally in black tie. Thackeray immediately noticed his *faux pas* and called out, "Here comes Olmsted, in a *white* stock" (Laura Wood Roper, *FLO: A Biography of Frederick Law Olmsted* [Baltimore and London, 1973], p. 116; *DNB; DAB;* Bayard Taylor, *Life and Letters of Bayard Taylor,* ed. Marie Hansen-Taylor and Horace E. Scudder, 2 vols. [Boston, 1884], 1: 320–21; idem, *At Home and Abroad: A Sketch-Book of the Life, Scenery, and Men* [New York, 1860], pp. 416–21).
15. Paul Peter Duggan contributed illustrations for the series in the *Schoolfellow* entitled "About New York," one episode of which appeared in the July 1856 issue (see FLO to Parke Godwin, July 12, 1855, n. 1, above).
16. Charles A. Dana, Rose Terry and Charles Wyllys Elliott.
17. Olmsted's story "Visit to a Chinese School." The *Schoolfellow* advertised that it would publish the story in five parts, but only three appeared—in the April, May and June issues of 1856 ("Yeoman" [Frederick Law Olmsted], "Visit to a Chinese School," *Schoolfellow* 8 [1856]: 120–24, 162–64, 194–97).
18. In 1856 Dix, Edwards & Company published Parke Godwin's *Political Essays* and Horace Greeley's *A History of the Struggle for Slavery Extension or Restriction in the United States from the Declaration of Independence to the Present Day. Mainly Compiled and Condensed from the Journals of Congress and Other Official Records, and Showing the Vote by Yeas and Nays on the Most Important Divisions in Either House.*

EUROPEAN INTERLUDE: 1856

To James Elliot Cabot

Worleys Hotel[1]
London
August 6th, 1856

J. Elliot Cabot Esq.[2]
Boston

Dear Sir
    Your letter of February 18th was forwarded to me from New York and reached me sometime since while I was traveling on the continent. Will you pardon me for having, while still traveling, postponed for so long a time to reply to it.
    I thank you very much for taking the trouble to express to me the good opinion you have been able to form of my book on the Seaboard Slave States.
    You encourage me to publish further on the subject. The business which detains me in Europe at present engrosses my whole time. My brother, however, is arranging my notes on Texas & the Mexican frontier and they will be published I hope in October. I may be able to prepare a third volume for publication next spring.
    I expect to be laughed at for picking at this vein so long, but there is such a general ignorance of the real condition of the different classes of the South and the sources of trustworthy information are so few that I think I am warranted in giving the fullest details of my personal observations.
    I am sorry that I can not agree with you with regard to the character of the Southerners. I have met very few who were open to argument in any direction by which any measure looking to the gradual extinction of Slavery would be demanded. Until some new economical element acting on the case arises, I am utterly hopeless of the South's moving for its own relief, in any other direction than emigration or importation. I have no doubt there are broad schemes for both these purposes, which only wait the election of Mr. Buchanan to be distinctly avowed & vigorously urged by the representative minds of the South.
    I am Dear Sir
    Very gratefully & truly yours

Fred. Law Olmsted

The original is in the Houghton Library, Harvard University, Cambridge, Massachusetts.

1. Probably the lodging house of John Worley at 15 New Cavendish Street, Portland Place (*Post Office London Directory, 1856...*, p. 1492).
2. James Elliot Cabot (1821–1903), of Boston, was a brother of Samuel Cabot, Jr., and a brother-in-law of Edmund Dwight, Jr., with both of whom Olmsted corresponded while promoting his

scheme for free-labor colonization in Texas during 1857. At the time of this letter, J. Elliot Cabot was assisting his brother Edward in his architectural firm, having abandoned the legal profession after two years of practice. He had also studied natural science at several German universities in 1841–43. In 1848 he had accompanied the naturalist Louis Agassiz on his expedition to Lake Superior, and a number of the illustrations that Agassiz published in later works were drawn by Cabot from material gathered at that time. In 1857 Cabot married Elizabeth Dwight, daughter of Edmund Dwight, and spent most of the next two years on an extended honeymoon in Europe. He spent part of the 1860s again working in his brother's architectural firm, and part of the 1870s teaching philosophy and logic at Harvard College. A close friend of Ralph Waldo Emerson, he spent much time between 1876 and 1882 assisting the philosopher in his work. After Emerson's death in 1882, Cabot edited an eleven-volume edition of Emerson's works and wrote the authorized biography (Lloyd Vernon Briggs, *History and Genealogy of the Cabot Family, 1475–1927* . . . [Boston, 1927], pp. 693–96; James Elliot Cabot, . . . 1. *Autobiographical Sketch*. 2. *Family Reminiscences*. 3. *Sedge Birds* [Boston, 1904], pp. 5–60; T. W. Higginson, "Memoir of James Elliot Cabot," *Proceedings of the Massachusetts Historical Society*, 2d ser. 20 [Dec. 1906]: 526–33).

To Bertha Olmsted

10 Crown Street
3 September night, [18]56

Dear B,

I received enclosed from Mr. B.[1] from New York. He has not been here.

This letter, I must tell you, confirms a feeling I have before in some slight way expressed to you about B. Do you not feel in it the revelation of a different man than that you have known as Mr. B? As I said I do not know another man who could have written with so much real dignity of soul & so little false pride, so much honest & unconscious humility. Men do not often appear to men in this way. It is the bubbling up of the suppressed goodness & humanity of a soul that has been somehow hardly dealt with.[2] All that is disagreeable in the nature of the man has been forced to the outside in defense of the interior and uneducated & ordinarily-and-at-will inexpressible refinement, delicacy & tenderness. It is the antipodes of the French ideal of man, that in which all the possibility of refinement, grace, amiability, *tact* of a soul is spun by the most laborious machinery into thread & woven into a garment which is always worn or only taken off to be washed in excessive trials of the temper. Return it me sometime.

Read the articles about Cayenne prisoners[3]—especially note that the alleged facts offered from the French government in extenuation are proved to be falsehoods. Remember that today Louis Napoleon feels so strong that he & his wife & baby, lounge about on the rocks and sands & through the dark woods of Biarritz unattended & so much assured that they are not known by strangers or the peasants from common people. And yet & yet philosophers, poets and statesmen & private gentlemen of no name or position different from father for instance, because they had been appointed to offices by the Republic which this man swore to support & defend with his life & because, when he was not, they were faithful to their oaths & refused [to] acknowledge his treason as a holy right—these men are thought safe nowhere but & in no circumstances but in chains in the pestilential climate of Cayenne on the "Island of Despair," half starved & treated altogether like galley slaves. A few—something like a tenth of these gentlemen still surviving—the safety of ——France requires it. Noble monarch, sweet empress, darling little cherub! There are other wives & little ones in France, not so happy—nay, there can be no happiness even at Biarritz for these never-tiring murderers.

Read also the account of himself by a German revolutionist in Household Words,[4] beginning I think in July—& still continuing, & see who even in cool blooded Prussia are the Reds—the blood-men. Remember how rarely we get even the smallest glimpse of this side of the story. What interests are engaged at any cost to maintain *order*. Yours & mine for instance. Only justice & mercy, only conscience demand of us not to subject our minds to the slavery forced on our hands & tongues in all Europe.

The original is in the possession of Terry Niles Smith.

1. Bertha's suitor, Edward S. Bartholomew. In October, Bertha wrote to Sophia Stevens Hitchcock the following description of Bartholomew's letter and her response to the first part of this letter from Olmsted to her:

> Soon after I wrote you last, I received a letter from Fred enclosing one to him from Mr. B. It was written about the eighth of July & had been sent to America & back to England. It was in reply to a letter Fred had written him after my decisive letter, and was a free confiding to him of his state of mind. It spoke of his sufferings at the result of affairs—his first despair—afterwards settling down to a sort of resignation which was after all nothing but a state of faintly hoping, still clinging to the hope he was not willing to give up. He spoke most delicately of me—of the suffering expressed in my last letter—of his regret at the pain he had caused me. Fred wrote only a line or two about it—asking me if I did not see something in that letter, which disclosed a noble delicate nature; what one would not perhaps discover in intercourse with the man, because all that was disagreeable & uncouth had been brought to the outside by untoward circumstances. It confirmed entirely his former opinion of the man. He knew of no man capable under such circumstances of showing such a noble spirit—&c. &c.
>
> This letter startled me out of the quiet that I had begun to settle into.... For several days I was turning & twisting in all the images that had entangled me before.... Then your letter came, & at once I settled down into more than former quietness & assurance. It is strange how exactly contrary is your influence over me from Fred's. I have great faith in Fred's sincerity as well as confidence in his judgement—& though he does not seek directly to influence me I can't but be acted upon by what I know to be his opinions. But your opinions are always exactly opposite to his—your judgement completely contradictory to his—and even if I were really in love, such strong expressions as you use, such confidence as you seem to have in the judgements you have formed of the man could not but influence me greatly, knowing as I do the opportunities you have for judging clearly. (Bertha Olmsted to S. S. Hitchcock, Oct. 5, 1856, Page Papers, Archives of American Art, Smithsonian Institution, Washington, D.C.)

2. Bartholomew had endured physical suffering and financial privation during his early years as a sculptor, and he felt that recognition of his ability had been slow in coming. He was always shy and something of a recluse, and his constantly poor health, combined with his driving sense of how little time he had to realize his artistic ambitions, apparently made him difficult at times. Soon after his death an old friend wrote of him as follows:

> Bartholomew possessed an extremely nervous and impatient spirit, that became morbid the instant he was ill. He was not without faults. He would often do and say things of which he would instantly repent and sorely for months, but I never knew a man of more spotless purity of motive, or of more sterling rectitude of heart. He was ever ready to do a kindness to any person, friend or enemy, who might ask for it. True, he was impetuous, and terrible in his passion sometimes, but a kind and considerate word would melt him to tears. (S. U. Crane, "Edward Sheffield Bartholomew," pp. 212-13.)

3. A reference to the penal colony on Devil's Island in Cayenne, French Guiana, where the most outspoken critics of Napoleon III and his Second Empire were transported. On August 25 and 30, 1856, the *Times* of London carried letters by the French historian and socialist Louis Blanc describing the harsh treatment of political prisoners at Cayenne (S. C. Burchell, *Imperial Masquerade: The Paris of Napoleon III* [New York, 1971], pp. 146-47, 345).

4. An unsigned four-part series describing the experiences of an officer in the revolutionary army of Baden during 1849 in the defense and surrender of the fortress of Rastadt and his subsequent six-year imprisonment. The author was Otto Julius Bernhard von Corvin-Wiersbitzki (1812-1886). A member of the Prussian nobility, though of Hungarian descent, he was educated in the cadet schools of Potsdam and Berlin and from 1830 to 1835 served as a lieutenant in the Prussian army. He then left the army and became a writer, primarily of history, living first in Frankfort and then, after 1840, in Leipzig. He was in Paris when the Revolution of 1848 broke out in Germany, and soon joined the revolutionary army of Baden. He commanded the troops defending the Rhine side of the city of Baden against the Prussians and then retreated to the fortress of Rastadt, where as chief of the general staff of the defenders, he directed the defense of the fortress and negotiated the terms of its surrender. A Prussian military court condemned him to death, but his sentence was commuted to ten years' imprisonment. He spent six years in solitary confinement at the prison at Bruchsal before being released in October 1855. He then went to England, where he was active in literary circles (Veit Valentin, *Geschichte der Deutschen Revolution von 1848-49...*, 2 vols. [Berlin, 1930-31], 2: 532-34; *Meyers Grosses Konversationslexikon...*, 6th ed., 24 vols. [Leipzig and Vienna, 1902-13], 4: 303-4; A. Lohrli, *Household Words*, s.v. "Corvin-Wiersbitzki, Otto Julius Bernhard von"; "The Last Days of a German Revolution," *Household Words* 14, no. 333 [Aug. 9, 1856]: 75-81; "Condemned to Death," ibid., no. 335 [Aug. 23, 1856], pp. 140-44; "Beating Against the Bars," ibid., no. 336 [Aug. 30, 1856], pp. 147-54; "Six Years in a Cell," ibid., no. 338 [Sept. 13, 1856], pp. 205-13).

To Bertha Olmsted

Southside[1]
Sunday 2nd November, [18]56

Dear Bertha

I am deeply touched by your letter (from Munich). It was very wrong to neglect writing to you from London. I was very much busy of course before leaving London, after your letter last received there came, and when writing to father I postponed writing you until I could do you more justice.

EUROPEAN INTERLUDE: 1856

Can you not understand that you make a larger demand upon me—a demand more difficult for me to meet than anybody or anything else? Because I must wrest myself so entirely from my daily habit—from my ordinary subjects of thought—because you are so far from me and don't know me and are liable to mistake me. You give me the position towards you of an adviser if not an instructor—a position I have to no one else, being to all others a disputant, a counsellor on equality, or a master. So to others I habitually speak without fear—knowing that what I say carelessly, wrongly, exaggeratedly, is to be tryed and the wrong and overplus to be neutralized by another prejudice and will, or, speaking with authority to my business people, that it is for myself, for my own success or failure, I speak. You appeal directly to my conscience, my common sense. My conscience is a healthier one than yours, my education & knowledge is broader and more valuable than yours. But your common sense—tact and instinct—is better, safer, than mine. It only should be clearer, freer, bolder and directer in commanding your action than it is. I respect it & have more confidence in it than you have yourself. And when you are concerned lest I should not have liked what you have written me, as you tell me, you place me in a position to yourself which you ought not—which I have no right to take.

What I shall most like to see is evidence of any sort of your own independent individuality. I want you to differ with me, to fight me, and to conquer me. To write what I do not "like" and to make me like it. But I did like what you wrote—at least I respected it, and accepted it. I think perhaps I have more faith in you & more respect for you than you for yourself. You must learn not to be so easily influenced by others, by me or anyone else, & to be superior to moods. The chief use of friends is not to be priests and kings to us—not to advise us or command us but to help us, equally by sympathy and by opposition, to find out clearly and confidently, our own judgment and our own instinct, taste, genius, inspiration, love appetite, antipathy & repugnances. The sum of all is God revealing Himself to us each individually & faith is the courage to accept and abide by this individual revelation. To be true to ourselves, our healthy selves, is to be true to God, in whose image we are created. Do & follow that which you *most* continually & confidently feel right & best—most satisfactory for yourself. Then however wrong in particulars you will be right in drift.

You speak of the peculiar curse of travelling. Yet this like all others you can & apparently do turn to blessing. Do you [not] believe that indignation and abhorrent perception of evil, of that which is contemptible & hateful, is just as good for us, just as necessary to our health as admiration and longing for that which is truly admirable & good?

I am afraid you will find Sophy in a tight place—wanting your sympathy and help.[2] Don't think you cannot help her. I hear *all* the family are strongly opposed to her marrying Mr. P. That Simon[3] has (indignantly) refused to assist him to obtain a divorce. How nearly right their idea of P. may be, you can judge better than I, but I suspect they are influenced more by ideas of "what people will think," "how strange," an idea that P. is unorthodox & [a] far

395

from respectable vagabond than any real judgment of his character with some reference to his husband qualities.

This at all events was the case at London. Mrs. S. thought it "unsafe." It would not be recommended as a model match perhaps in a boarding school lecture room. My first impression was good. P. is a man who must have a wife. S. is a woman who must have a husband. Each would suit the other better than most anyone else.

I have heard nothing of or from Bartholomew since I wrote you. It seems to me you will have been apart from each other so long, when you meet again, that a new strangership will have been established. So you will meet with less embarrassment & emotion & more naturally & satisfactorily than you have imagined. Don't take anybody's advice with regard to him. Judge for yourself, and follow your own good sense in your intercourse with him. Don't be thwarted by modesty or any other form of fear but carry out courageously what is best. It is hard to judge—hard to decide what one does think. I too am finding it so. It is to overcome that hardness & be & do positively that we live.

Yours affectionately

F.

The original is in the possession of Terry Niles Smith.

1. Olmsted wrote this letter soon after returning from England. "Southside" is the section of Staten Island where his farm was located.
2. Sophia Stevens Hitchcock, Bertha's companion in Europe during 1854, 1855 and 1856, who had become increasingly involved with the American painter William Page (1811–1885), then residing in Rome. Page's young second wife, Sarah Dougherty Page, had left him for an Italian count in the fall of 1854, the arrival in Rome in July 1853 of Page's three daughters by his first marriage (aged nineteen, seventeen and fifteen) having created a situation she could not abide for long. Sophie Hitchcock arrived in Rome with Bertha in December 1855 and soon began to study drawing with Page. Their intimacy increased, and by the time of this letter she and Page had decided to marry, although she and her friends were still trying to keep their plans secret. In June 1857 Page returned to the United States to divorce his wife and in October he and Sophie were married outside Rome (Joshua C. Taylor, *William Page: The American Titian* [Chicago, 1957], pp. 139–40, 156–58; *DAB*; Bertha Olmsted to S. S. Hitchcock, Oct. 5–10, 1856, Page Papers; Bertha Olmsted to S. S. Hitchcock, Nov. 15, 1856, Page Papers).
3. Simon Stevens, brother of Sophie Stevens Hitchcock (*DAB*, s.v. "Stevens, Benjamin Franklin").

CHAPTER VII
FREE-SOIL CRUSADE
1857

THE YEAR 1857 marked the height of Olmsted's efforts to promote free-labor colonization in the Southwest. This was also the most intense period of his writing about the South. The letters to Edward Everett Hale in this chapter indicate his plans early in the year and show how he tried to use his newly published book, *A Journey Through Texas,* to promote the immigration of free-soilers to that region. His letters to Samuel Cabot, Jr., tell the story of his involvement with the New England Emigrant Aid Company in planning the establishment of colonies in Texas and in seeking sources of men and money for the project. The chapter also contains the introduction and supplement that he wrote for the American edition of *The Englishman in Kansas: Or, Squatter Life and Border Warfare,* by the English newspaper correspondent Thomas H. Gladstone. These include Olmsted's most thorough-going condemnation of Southern violence and the threat it posed to free institutions wherever slavery existed. The supplement to *The Englishman in Kansas* also records his assessment of the implications of the sectional policies of the Buchanan administration and of the Supreme Court's ruling in the Dred Scott case.

To EDWARD EVERETT HALE

92 Grand Street[1]
New York
January 10, '57

My Dear Hale,

I shall send you herewith a copy of my "Journey in Texas," &c.[2]

Brace tells me that in Boston last week he saw someone from Kansas who said it was a common thing for the more zealous fighting free soilers there to talk of "taking Western Texas next." I have a constantly improving conviction that that is the thing to be done next—that it can be done easily and that when it is done, the process of bringing the South to its senses will be very rapidly accelerated. Be sure that once surrounded, slavery will retreat upon itself & free soil will be advanced with a rapidity that will soon become frightful & Randolph's prediction of the masters running away from the slaves will be realized,[3] as soon as the concentration & the competition of free-labor is experienced.

I have said nothing directly about it in the book but much to lead men to think about it & with the greatest sincerity to induce immigration of Yankees thither.

Is there any inexpensive way in which I can get my book into the hands of the Kansians? I would like to supply some hundred copies at cost to any agency by which that would be effected. My purpose being to encourage attention to Texas among the right sort of men & to diffuse information about the country.

My brother John was for[ced] to leave the country again last week & this time goes with his family all—to Havana en route for Italy—to reside permanently—having given up all hope of being able to live in this climate. He has been rapidly declining in these two months past. I much fear I shall never see him again.

"Republicanism," so far as I can judge, is steadily gaining ground in New York, since the election.

How can I get copies of "Texas" to the newspapers in Kansas? By mail best probably. Can you tell me the proper address?

Yours very truly,

Fred. Law Olmsted

The original is in the New England Emigrant Aid Company Papers, Manuscript Department, Kansas State Historical Society, Topeka, Kansas.

1. At this time Olmsted was residing at 92 Grand Street on Manhattan (*Trow's New York City Directory... For the Year Ending May 1, 1858* [New York, 1857], p. 635 [see Spear 1015].
2. *Journey Through Texas* was available in proof sheets at this time (FLO to E. E. Hale, Jan. 17, 1857, New England Emigrant Aid Co. Papers).
3. John Randolph of Roanoke made this comment in a speech in the U.S. House of Representatives opposing a bill to tax coarse woolens used by slaveowners to clothe their slaves. Randolph cited Patrick Henry's warning that under the Constitution the federal Congress had the power to abolish slavery in the states and would do so. Randolph declared: "The first step towards this consummation so devoutly wished by many is to pass such laws as may yet still further diminish the pittance which their labor yields to their unfortunate masters, to produce such a state of things as will insure, in case the slave shall not elope from his master, that his master will run away from him" (Henry Adams, *John Randolph* [Boston and New York, 1899], pp. 278–79).

FREE-SOIL CRUSADE: 1857

To Edward Everett Hale

92 Grand St.
New York
January 30 /57

My Dear Hale,

Is there not an objection to Emigrant Society's sending slips about Texas.[1] It would at once expose the object, which I think it very desirable to conceal.

I would have a note addressed to the editors (& any others) from some well-known gentlemen in whom they would have confidence as Republican leaders, saying in effect, "It is deemed desirable for the Republican cause that the facts (& ideas) given in these pages, should have general currency. You will do a good thing if you will, from time to time, as you may find it convenient, insert portions of them among the selected matter of your paper."

In the beginning and until some respectable nuclei are established, it is best no distinct organization for Texas should exist, or if it is necessary it should be secret & those who are recruited should only know of it as a commercial business.

What I want now is to influence a few hundred New Englanders to go thither voluntarily, convinced that their reports would soon draw all necessary additional immigration. The first thing is to counter-act the opinion that the region is doomed to be subject to all the evils of a slave holding country (which I say it can not be). 2d, to let it be known that it is attractive, wholesome & profitable for free-labor.

Yours faithfully

Fred. Law Olmsted

The original is in the New England Emigrant Aid Company Papers, Kansas State Historical Society.

1. Olmsted was in the process of preparing some 239 sets of pages from *Journey Through Texas* to send to editors in the North with a plea that they publish some of the material to keep interest alive for the time when a concerted attempt to settle Texas with free-labor farmers could be made. Apparently, Hale undertook to send a hundred sets of the pages, along with a cover letter, to editors in New England. Hale's letter ran as follows:

    Dear Sir,

    If you have read Mr. Olmsted's striking book on Western Texas, I am sure you have been impressed, as I have, with the amazing opportunities thrown open to settlers there, & the very encouraging prospect for making a free state there by the quiet introduction of capital & settlers.

    In the present condition of Kanzas it is impossible to make any public movement for this purpose—indeed I do not think it would be well, were it possible, but a few of us are desirous of preparing the public mind in New England for some future action, & of opening the eyes of our people to the immense advantages of emigration to Texas. We have obtained therefore a hundred copies of some sheets of Olmsted's book which we are circulating through the country.

Following this, Hale ended each letter with one of two paragraphs:

[1] I send one to you—can you not see that one of your editors shall make such extracts from it from time to time this summer as may attract attention towards so interesting a country.

[2] I send to you therefore by this mail some attractive passages from Olmsted's book in slips, hoping that you will be willing at your convenience to publish parts of them or all of them in your paper this summer. Call attention to them in any form you please so you do not excite jealousy at a distance by giving the impression that there is a concerted plan for New England emigration into Texas. As there is no such plan it would be a pity that the free state men there should incur any odium from a suspicion of it.

I am sure that you will thus do a good service in the good cause & you will especially oblige.

Yrs. truly

By February 26, Hale had sent slips and letters with the second ending to eight editors in New England, and slips with letters with the first ending to eighteen others (FLO to E. E. Hale, Feb. 4, 1857, New England Emigrant Aid Co. Papers; letterpress book, vol. 2, Edward Everett Hale Papers, Manuscripts and History Section, New York State Library, Albany, N.Y.).

To Edward Everett Hale

New York, February 19th. /57

My dear Hale

To-day I encountered by the luckiest chance the man of all others for you to see from West Texas: an American in whose judgement you may have more confidence than any other I know. He assisted Douai, edited the paper once in his absence, wrote for & proof-read his English department, stood by him in the most dangerous crisis—in this wise. The Vigilance Committee sent a six foot major to him with a subscription paper on which all the other merchants' names of the town stood for $50 each, for a fund nominally to pursue fugitive slaves & reward the captors. This man—Ulrich is his name—politely declined. The major then told him that he was known to sympathize with the abolitionizers & it would not be safe for him to remain long in those parts. Ulrich immediately answered that it would not be safe for the major to remain long on his premises and if he ever showed his face within his store again he would be put out, that he would welcome an attempt on the part of the major's party to expel him from San Antonio & he would be very willing to leave if he could not force the major to.[1]

I believe Dr. Douai finally quarrelled with him, as he would have done with you or I, if we had been there I suspect—Ulrich counselling a more discreet tone. Only one friend remained after Ulrich, Riotte.[2] He is a merchant & perilled much in his friendship for the doctor. You would perhaps consider him cowardly or over-careful, but he told me today in a manner that I felt to be genuine that if there should ever be a contest for a free-state with a chance of success—if it should come to fighting—he should be ready to spend his fortune & if necessary his life, for freedom.

He was one of the men Dr. Stillman spoke of in connection with the Unitarian church project. He seems to have had no definite plan about it, but says he would like a good powerful, attractive preacher but none of the "old-fogy Christianity." I imagine he thinks a man of Parker's[3] views & habits would draw in the Germans & Americans disgusted with the ranting, canting, Hard-Shell, Baptist & cataleptic Methodist sort of thing.

I saw him but a few minutes but I got without asking for it one pleasant bit of information. Within a year he says a hostility to Slavery has become much more decidedly evident among the Mexicans about San Antonio & often gets forcible expression. He had heard a poor white from the South, also, lately exclaim, "We don't want any more of these damn'd niggers moving into these parts," & he thinks that feeling is gaining among them. He describes some encouraging symptoms among the Americans of the better class. One man, a slaveholder, born a Missourian, to whom he had lent my "Seaboard Slave States," on returning it, confessed he thought Western Texas should be made a free-state & he wished it were possible. If there were any chance of success he would be one to favor a movement for it.

Ulrich promises to come to Boston—particularly in the course of a fortnight. If possible, I will come with him.

I showed him the notice of my book which I had just found, in the Advertiser,[4] which much gratified him. He said he wished he could send some copies of it to land-owners at the West (Texas). Can you send me some copies—one or two?

I have had a letter from an illiterate man in Rhode Island who has determined to go to Texas.

The book sells very well & I get letters almost daily indicating much interest in the subject.

Yours cordially

Fred. Law Olmsted

The original is in the Sophia Smith Collection, Smith College, Northampton, Massachusetts.

1. In a letter to Olmsted of October 28, 1854, Douai elaborated on this incident:

> You know Mr. Enoch Jones, the S.A. & Mex. Gulf Railroad Contractor; his partner is Mr. Ulrich, an old native of Pensilvania, a northern (Seward) Whig like Jones himself and a steadfast enemy of slavery. The slaveholders were raising funds in order to establish an insurance company against losses of negroes (the two legged property was running away to Mexico on a large scale); they went with their safeguard from house to house, to slaveowners and non-slaveowners and extorted money. When Mr. Ulrich refused to give one cent for the purpose, he was threatened by Major T. Howard, U.S. Indian Agent and leader of the slavery party, with expulsion from the town. Mr. Ulrich's courage stopped this impudence

somewhat; he excited his friends to come to his aid—and the adversaries did not feel strong enough.

During the fall of 1854, Douai was looking anxiously for someone to read and correct his English articles and translations, and could find few men who were both literate in English and sympathetic with his views. One of his main reasons for having an English proofreader was to spare himself the embarrassment of having the proslavery English-language press hold up to ridicule the clumsiest examples of his English prose. In November he secured the assistance of Joseph Ulrich, but the results were unsatisfactory: "With a noble ardor and diligence he revises my articles," Douai wrote of Ulrich, "but from the fact that just those passages he corrected, have attracted the plump, gross, ridiculous invectives and critics of the 'Western Texas,' while it was not the same case with others, have aroused in me the opinion, that Mr. Ulrich is not entirely the man for it" (Adolf Douai to FLO, Nov. 17 and Dec. 7, 1854).

Ohio-born Enoch Jones (1802–1863) was a dam and canal contractor, manufacturer, merchant and an incorporator and director of the San Antonio and Mexican Gulf Railway. Joseph Ulrich was his partner in a general merchandise store in San Antonio and they later made joint investments in San Antonio land. George Thomas Howard (1814–1866) was at this time a government contractor in San Antonio (*The Handbook of Texas*, 3 vols. [Austin, 1952–76], 3 [*Supplement*]: 453; Books of Deeds, Bexar County Courthouse, San Antonio, Tex., vol. S-1, pp. 170–71; vol. S-2, pp. 296–97; vol. U-1, p. 59; Frederick Charles Chabot, *With the Makers of San Antonio: Genealogies of the Early Latin, Anglo-American, and German Families with Occasional Biographies* . . . [San Antonio, Tex., 1937], pp. 318–20, 344–45).

2. Charles Riotte.
3. The Unitarian minister Theodore Parker.
4. A review of Olmsted's *Journey Through Texas* in the *Boston Daily Advertiser* of February 18, 1857. The *Advertiser* was edited by Hale's father, Nathan Hale. The review combined praise of Olmsted's writing with enthusiasm for the great attractiveness of Texas for free-labor settlers:

Olmsted's Journey through Texas

It is now a year or more since that we called attention more than once to Mr. Frederic Olmsted's journey through the sea-board slave States, which is by far the most valuable book we have on slavery and the Southern social system. That book will gradually assume the position of a standard book of reference among all persons, of whatever opinions, whose interest in slavery or in anti-slavery is more than a pretence. Mr. Olmsted promised, at that time, to follow up that book by an account of his observations in Texas; and this promise he has now fulfilled.

We are so ignorant of the resources of this immense country of ours, that it will fairly surprise most readers in the sea-board States, to be told by a careful observer, not given to undue enthusiasm, that we have within our own limits, an American Italy, unrivalled for climate, unless the old Italy rivals it, of the most luxurious beauty and of the richest soil conceivable. Such in fact is the region known as Western Texas, for which we made the Mexican war. Most readers will be even more surprised when they learn that this inviting region is still open to settlement in its most attractive parts. The only considerable emigration which it has yet attracted is that of a very considerable body of Germans,—some of them men of the first intelligence and of high accomplishments.

The Rio Grande river forms the western boundary of this attractive region;—on the western side of that river are the dominions of the Republic of Mexico. Such vicinity of a foreign power, which does not tolerate the institution of slavery, and does not restore fugitive slaves, renders it almost impossible for slave-holders to retain their people in Western Texas. This fact has materially checked emigration thither from the South, although the soil is eminently fitted for the cultivation of cotton, and this crop is profitably raised by the labor of free men.

Mr. Olmsted gives a most fascinating account of his experiences in this region among the German settlers and others. He also passed over the frontier into Mexico, and we have a curious chapter of Mexican experience. His adventures in crossing and recrossing Eastern Texas shows us what the eastern part is of that empire State. Simply as a book of travels the volume is to the last degree interesting; but, as in its predecessor, there is an amount of statistical and other information which makes it an indispensable book for students, merchants and statesmen.

We copy an account of a German village, New Braunfels, in Texas.

FREE-SOIL CRUSADE: 1857

Then followed "An Evening Far from Texas," from *Journey Through Texas,* pages 143–47 (Jean Holloway, *Edward Everett Hale: A Biography* [Austin, Tex., 1956], pp. 10, 100).

To Edward Everett Hale

321 Broadway February 20 /7

My Dear Hale

I wrote you yesterday of Ulrich.[1] I had a longer interview with him today.

Touching the sect of the preacher wanted he says he cares nothing, only that he should be able to talk simply, forcibly and in a manner to make rough men of strong good sense, respect godliness. He has observed of the frontiersmen, though sound hearted & honest & reverent, that they hold the general clerical Christianity in great contempt. He himself was born, bred, & still holds with some loyalty with the faith & practices of the Hicksite Quakers.

They have a Presbyterian Church in San Antonio, which is trying to build a meeting house. The congregation numbers about 200—of which only one man is "of any account." He is the elder & has both pluck & piety. About the time of his taking the office of elder he had publicly said something, of Governor Bell,[2] which the Governor then at Austin had regarded as insulting & for which he threatened dire punishment. Governor Bell soon came to San Antonio, whereupon the elder bought a revolver & for several successive days dogged the Governor, placing himself in his way, taking care the Governor should be informed who he was, & for the avowed purpose of provoking him to attack. As elder of the Church he thought it would not be best to act except on the defensive. Our Hicksite friend considers this the only respectable embodiment of Presbyterianism in West Texas.

A Baptist clergyman caused it to be advertized that he would preach in a school house in San Antonio on a certain Sabbath day & proposed to form at that time the nucleus of a Baptist Church. He did not receive sufficient encouragement, however. Meeting with no hospitality, he was obliged to fasten the horse which he had ridden from Austin to the school-room window & sleep himself in the school-house. He mentioned this unpleasant circumstance to the brethering as rayther discouraging in his sermon, yet he was allowed to buy fodder for his horse again of the Mexicans Sunday night & next morning he was met riding east very early & on a stranger's asking him how far it was into San Antonio, he replied, "Damn San Antonio!" So the warm river runs all winter thro' the town for nothing still, as far as the Baptists are concerned.

A Lutheran clergyman has lately organized a church among the Ger-

403

mans.[3] He is a good man and laborious & has begun at the right end by establishing a good child's school. An Agent of the Boston Christian Aid Society (?) some time ago visited San Antonio & the Lutherans had commissioned Ulrich to ask aid for their church of this Society. They are very poor & the clergyman poorly supported.

The Presbyterians expect to pay their preacher $1200 a year. He supposes a Unitarian clergyman could get as much, but will make no promises until he returns & consults with friends.

Ulrich himself was once a working printer & it is in his plans, when he has made a little more money in his business (in two or three years he says) to give it up & establish a paper himself. English & German, for he speaks German perfectly, his parents having been "Pennsylvania Dutchmen."

He has thought much of building a cotton mill at San Antonio himself. Cotton, power, building material & labor all cheap, he says, & a capital & peculiar market over the border. Good fertile farm land—cotton land—within 20 miles of San Antonio is now from $1. to $5 an acre. 20 miles further West, it is not generally worth over $1. & much can be bought for less. He owns large tracts himself & he says the largest land-owner in Texas, Maverick,[4] is well inclined to free-soil & perhaps would act confidentially to obtain northern immigration. Maverick, who has been in the Senate of Texas, has spoken to him strongly in favor of a free-state.

Many Missourians have been in West Texas this winter looking at land, some evidently merely speculating on the prospect of a stampede of Slave-holders from Missouri if Kansas comes in free. Since it has been anticipated that Kansas would be free, the idea that West Texas might be so has generally been given up & an increased slave holding immigration is anticipated—not merely from Missouri, but of Kentuckians & all others who would otherwise have moved to Missouri or Northern Arkansas.

On the other hand, lately a good many people have come among them from Illinois—for stock raising.

A wealthy old gentleman called on me today—said he had read my book & it had occurred to him that the best thing he could do with his sons was to send them to West Texas to be stock-farmers. He wanted advice about it.

Yours faithfully

Fred. Law Olmsted.

Ulrich spends next week in Philadelphia. The week after, if especially desirable he will come to Boston. He offers to stay a week longer than he had intended & give one whole week to anything we want of him.

The original is in the Sophia Smith Collection, Smith College.

1. Joseph Ulrich.

2. Peter Hansborough Bell (1808–1898), governor of Texas from 1849 to 1853 (*DAB; BDAC*).
3. The Lutheran clergyman Phillip Friedrich Zizelmann arrived in Texas in the fall of 1851 and attempted to found a church in San Antonio. He was unable to gain adequate support for his project, but was able to support himself by starting a school. He left San Antonio in the summer of 1852 following a severe illness and soon after founded a Lutheran church in Fredericksburg, Texas. He returned to San Antonio in October 1856 and began the process that led to the formal organization of St. John's Lutheran Church in December 1857 (August L. Wolff, *The Story of St. John's Lutheran Church, San Antonio, Texas...* [San Antonio(?), 1937], pp. 11–28).
4. Samuel Augustus Maverick (1803–1870) of San Antonio moved to Texas in 1835, played an active role in the movement for independence, and was a respected figure in the affairs of the republic and state thereafter. During his lifetime he amassed landholdings of some 385,000 acres (*NCAB*, 6: 466; *Yale Obit. Rec.*, 2d ser. 1 [July 1871]: 18–19).

American Editor's Introduction to *The Englishman in Kansas*

Having been requested to edit and introduce an American edition of this English book, I have thought I could best serve a public purpose by examining and setting forth its value and purport as evidence and intelligent European commentary upon the present exciting questions of our politics.

Mr. Gladstone,[1] a kinsman of the distinguished ex-chancellor of the Exchequer of England, visited Kansas, at a moment of interest in its history, and in the history of our country. His opportunities of obtaining trustworthy information were good, and he appears to have used them calmly and diligently. As a foreigner, with claims of friendship, or even acquaintance, upon no one in the territory, except Colonel Sumner,[2] who, as the military representative of the federal authority, was respected by both parties, he occupied a neutral position in their warfare.

Going back of these circumstances, I find that Mr. Gladstone arrived in New York near the beginning of the year 1856, with the ordinary motives of an English traveler of his class. From all I can learn of those who knew him here, his testimony on any subject should be received with particular respect. He is thought to observe closely and accurately, to study carefully, and to be slow in expressing the conclusions of his judgment. He is not known to have had, at this time, more knowledge of, or interest in, American politics, than is common among English conservative gentlemen—about as much, that is to say, as is common among us with regard to the affairs of Sweden or Brazil.

He proceeded, very soon after his arrival, to Washington, and thence further south, and, during the winter, enjoyed the hospitality of South Carolina and Mississippi. In the spring he continued his journey through Missouri, and so, finally, to Kansas, arriving at Leavenworth city on the 21st of May.

THE PAPERS OF FREDERICK LAW OLMSTED

THE

ENGLISHMAN IN KANSAS:

OR,

Squatter Life and Border Warfare.

BY

T. H. GLADSTONE, ESQ.,

AUTHOR OF THE LETTERS FROM KANSAS IN THE "LONDON TIMES."

WITH AN INTRODUCTION,

BY

FRED. LAW OLMSTED,

AUTHOR OF "A JOURNEY IN THE SEABOARD SLAVE STATES,"
"A JOURNEY THROUGH TEXAS," ETC.

NEW YORK:
MILLER & COMPANY, 321 BROADWAY,
LATE DIX, EDWARDS & CO.
1857.

TITLE PAGE FROM *The Englishman in Kansas*

Our whole country was then hotly engaged in the presidential canvass. So great was the tumult in Kansas, and such was the temptation upon our editors and newsmongers to disallow or exaggerate the conflicting reports of its condition, according as their influence was likely to be favorable, or otherwise, to the success of one or another candidate, that it became, and has continued to be, very difficult for a cautious mind, not possessing private means of information, to form a confident judgment, first, as to the reality or extent of the alleged calamity of Kansas, and second, as to the absolute or relative culpability of either of the contending parties.

Readers, who have been accustomed to hear the "disturbances" in Kansas spoken of only as such as are "incidental to all new settlements," will, perhaps, be inclined to set down this calmly observant traveler as an impostor, or a romancer, when they find him describing the condition of the territory, upon his arrival, as "a holiday of anarchy and bloodshed." Readers at the South, who have been accustomed to rely for contemporary history on Southern newspapers, or on those of the North in which information is given in a form adapted to the Southern market, may question if he were in his right mind when they find him testifying that: "among all the scenes of violence I witnessed, the offending parties were invariably on the pro-slavery side."[3] Those who have seen nothing inconsistent with the official assurances of our late president, in the rapid humiliation of his three successively appointed governors, will hardly believe that the sympathies of an impartial, dispassionate, but justice-loving Englishman, could have been so immediately engaged, on his arrival in the territory, for the Free-state party, as is implied by this narrative, unless his mind had been previously prejudiced against their opponents.

He had been in intercourse, almost from the moment of his landing in America, chiefly with Southern minds. He came to Kansas fresh charged from Southern social influence. And yet, before he had met a single avowed free-soiler in the territory, he evidently had a most painful impression of the injustice, tyranny, and persecution to which the majority of the actual settlers were subjected, and was well convinced that the pro-slavery party, and the influence of the South, acting through the federal government, was wholly to blame for this.

"But, surely," some indignant "democrat" will ask, "he would not have us suppose that the truth about Kansas has been monopolized all along by one party; that the black republican newspapers have been all right, and the rest all wrong?" This may have been the case without any advantage in veracity of character to those who told the truth. It may have happened that nothing could have served their purpose better than the truth. Certainly, if that purpose was to be served by proving a desperate determination on the part of the administration to establish slavery in Kansas, if necessary, at any cost of justice and humanity, and of our reputation with the world as a civilized people, nothing could have answered it better than what Mr. Gladstone, carefully studying the facts upon the ground, was led to consider the truth. He attributes the most honorable conduct, in all respects, as good citizens, to the Free-state party in the territory, while it would be difficult to describe a people more unfit to exercise the rightful privileges of citizenship than those whom he represents to be engaged, under the patronage of the federal authorities, in persecuting that party.

Such a contrast between the character of the emigrants from the Slave States and of those from the Free—both being, not many generations back, of the same origin and blood—would, indeed, be incredible, if there were not anterior reason to expect in the former a special proneness to violence, and a distrust, or habitual forgetfulness of law and civilized customs under exciting circumstances.

Such a dangerous quality—gravely dangerous, wherever this policy of so-called squatter sovereignty, involving, as it does, squatter warfare, shall be tried; and ten-fold grave to us of the North, since the recent decision of the Supreme Court,[4]—such a dangerous quality is inbred and with every generation growing more established in the character of the citizens of the South. It is so from the inexorable force of circumstances—thus:

The title to property in slaves is derived at no remote period, from certain vindictive and lawless barbarians, who, having overpowered an enemy, considered his life as forfeited, and if they spared it, did so from no regard to the abstract right or sacredness of life, or any motive of humanity, but simply for the purpose of enjoying the profits of his labor. His labor and abject submission to all their demands upon him was the price of his life, and with this understanding he was transferred to America. At first the only persons so held were "Black-a-moors," and all Black-a-moors in the country were so held and considered, and only by terror of death, legalized and insured by legislation and military force, continued to be held in the requisite habit of subordination for profitable labor, by their purchasers and inheritors. Hence, exceptional laws, exceptional customs, and hence, irresistibly, a defection from the usual sentiment of the sacredness of human life, as far as the negro was concerned. But as the negro is, after all, really a human being, whatever affects him, inevitably affects all human beings associated with him. Thus arises a peculiar influence which must produce and reproduce peculiar qualities among people nurtured in a slaveholding community.

Hence, however our Southern fellow-citizens may continue to talk, and sentimentalize, and clothe themselves under ordinary circumstances in accordance with the customs, literature, laws and religious maxims of the rest of the civilized world, it is an inevitable effect of their peculiar institution to diminish in them that constitutional and instinctive regard for the sanctity of human life, the growth of which distinguishes every other really advancing people just in proportion to their progress in the scale of Christian civilization. Mr. Gladstone is not the first traveler whose studies among them have taught us this; nor is it necessary to assume the truth of his testimony to prove that there is this essential difference between the people of the Free and the Slave states. In what community, uninfluenced by slavery, could such a record be made, of recklessness unrestrained in regard to the life of its citizens, as the following, which is taken from the *Louisville Journal* (June, 1854), and was suggested by the "Mat Ward case,"[5] in which case, again, the alleged murderer was presently allowed to go free.

There have been scores of notorious cases of murder and *acquittal* in this city. There was the case of Kunz who killed Schaffer. Kunz, hearing that Schaffer had spoken lightly of a member of his family, went to his coffee-house and cursed him. Schaffer picked up a small stick and went around the counter as if to strike Kunz, whereupon the latter thrust a deadly weapon into his breast and killed him. *He was tried and discharged without punishment.* There was the case of Delph who killed his uncle, Reuben Liter. Delph armed himself deliberately, and went to the upper market-house to meet Liter. He met him, sought a quarrel with him, and shot him dead on the spot. The quarrel was about a prostitute. *Delph was tried and acquitted by a jury.* There was the case of Croxton who killed Hawthorn. Hawthorn was in a coffee-house, sitting in a chair, drunk and asleep. Croxton struck him on the head in that condition with a brick-bat, and killed him. *He was acquitted by a jury.* There was the case of Peters who killed Baker. In Natchez, a long time before, Baker, in a fight, had wounded Peters, and made him a cripple. Peters being thus disabled, Baker supported him. The latter, after about a year, became very poor, and discontinued his bounty. Thereupon, Peters pursued him to this city, rode in the night in a hack to his house, sent the hackman to inform him that a gentleman and friend wished to see him on business, and when Baker came out and stood at the window of the hack, shot him dead instantly. *Peters was acquitted by the jury* and lived here for some years afterwards—long enough indeed to murder or try to murder a prostitute, upon whose bounty he subsisted. There was the case of the Pendegrasts, who killed Buchanan, a schoolmaster. The elder Pendegrast, with two of his sons and a negro, went to Buchanan's school-house with loaded guns and killed him, without giving him a chance for his life. *The jury gave a verdict of acquittal.* There was the case of Shelby who killed Horine in Lexington. The two dined at the same public table, and, upon Horine's going into the street, Shelby demanded of him why he had looked at him in such a manner at the table. Horine answered that he was not aware of having looked at him in any unusual manner. Shelby said—"You did, and if you ever do it again, I will blow your brains out. I don't know who you are." Horine responded—"I know you, and suppose a man may *look* at you, if your name *is* Shelby." At that, Shelby struck him with his fist, and without any return of the blow, and without any display of a weapon by Horine, for he was unarmed, Shelby shot him dead. Shelby was indicted, but *the jury found no verdict against him.* There was the case of Harry Daniel, of Mount Sterling, who killed Clifton Thompson. Daniel and Thompson were lawyers, and brothers-in-law. Thompson made some imputation upon Daniel in open court. Daniel drew a pistol and shot him dead in the presence of judge and jury. Thompson had a pistol in his pocket but did not draw it. *Daniel was acquitted by a jury.*

Similar cases might be cited by the volume in which public sentiment, finding its expression in the action of a jury, is proved to be constantly triumphant over all laws and ecclesiastical formulas in justifying homicide when it results from the quick and vehement anger of an undisciplined intellect. This is the natural consequence of the lurking danger everywhere present at the South, by which its citizens are compelled to hold themselves always in readiness to chastise, to strike down, to slay, upon what they shall individually judge to be sufficient provocation or exhibition of insubordination.

Southerners themselves may, perhaps, affirm that they are unconscious of this sense of insecurity, and this habit of preparation. But every habit breeds unconsciousness of its existence in the mind of the man whom it controls, and this is more true of habits which involve our safety than of any others. The weary sailor aloft, on the lookout, may fall asleep; not the less, in the lurch of the ship, will his hands clench the swaying cordage, but only the more firmly that they act in the method of instinct. A hard-hunted fugitive may nod in his saddle, but his knees will not unloose their hold upon his horse. Men who live in powder-mills are said to lose all conscious feeling of habitual insecurity; but visitors perceive that they have acquired softness of manner and of voice.

If a laborer on a plantation should contradict his master, it may often appear to be no more than a reasonable precaution for his master to kill him on the spot; for, when a slave has acquired such boldness, it may be evident that not merely is his value as property seriously diminished, but the attempt to make further use of him at all, as property, involves in danger the whole white community. "If I let this man live, and permit him the necessary degree of freedom, to be further useful to me, he will infect, with his audacity, all my negro property, which will be correspondingly more difficult to control, and correspondingly reduced in value. If he treats me with so little respect now, what have I to anticipate when he has found other equally independent spirits among the slaves? They will not alone make themselves free, but will avenge upon me, and my wife, and my daughters, and upon all our community, the injustice which they will think has been done them, and their women, and children." Thus would he reason, and shudder to think what might follow if he yielded to an impulse of mercy.

To suppose, however, that the master will pause while he thus weighs the danger exactly, and then deliberately act as, upon reflection, he considers the necessities of the case demand, is absurd. The mere circumstance of his doing so would nourish a hopeful spirit in the slave, and stimulate him to consider how he could best avoid all punishment.

But how is it in a similar case at the North? I have seen it. "I am sorry," says the farmer; "I am sorry you have such a bad temper, John. I can't afford to have you live with me, if you have not more respect for yourself and for me, than to play the blackguard. I will pay you what I owe you, and then we will part—part friends, if you please, for I bear no malice." And John goes, ashamed of himself, and with a sensible resolution to acquire a better self-government. The man who would knock John down, under these circumstances, especially if John were the weaker man, or taken at disadvantage, from behind, or with a weapon, would live without the respect, the confidence, or the affection of his neighbors. He would be called a vindictive, irritable, miserable old fool.

Mark the difference at the South. The same man would be called, and, perhaps, rightly, a brave, generous, high-toned, and chivalric gentleman. And, perhaps rightly, I say, for the impulses which would lead him, in the instant, and without reflection, to act decisively, that is, perhaps, to kill, and, at all events, to very cruelly hurt his fellow-being, and that without the smallest regard to fairness, it is not impossible might have been based on a generous sense of his duty to the public, and a superiority to merely selfish considerations. Thus slavery educates gentlemen in habits which, at the North, belong only to bullies and ruffians.

But, "planters sleep unguarded, and with their bedroom doors open." So, as it was boasted, did the Emperor at Biarritz,[6] last summer, and with greater bravery, because the assassin of Napoleon would be more sure, in dispatching him, that there would be no one left with a vital interest to secure punishment for such a deed; and because, if he failed, Napoleon dare never employ such exemplary punishment for his enemies as would the planters for theirs. The emperors of the South are the whole free society of the South, and it is a society of mutual insurance. Against a slave who has the disposition to become an assassin, you find his emperor has a body-guard, which, for general effectiveness, is to the Cent garde[7] as your right hand is to your right hand's glove.

It is but a few months since, in Georgia, or Alabama, a man treated another precisely as Mr. Brooks treated Mr. Sumner[8]—coming up behind, with the fury of a madman, and felling him with a bludgeon; killing him by the first blow, however, and then discharging vengeance by repeated strokes upon his senseless body.* The man thus pitifully abused had been the master of the other, a remarkably confiding and merciful master, it was said—too much so; "it never does to be too slack with niggers." By such indiscretion he brought his death upon him. But did his assassin escape? He was roasted, at a slow fire, on the spot of the murder, in the presence of many thousand slaves, driven to the ground from all the adjoining counties, and when, at length, his life went out, the fire was intensified until his body was in ashes, which were scattered to the winds and trampled under foot.[9] Then "magistrates and clergymen" addressed appropriate warnings to the assembled subjects. It was no indiscretion to leave doors open again, that night.

Will any traveler say that he has seen no signs of discontent, or insecurity, or apprehension, or precaution; that the South has appeared quieter and less excited, even on the subject of slavery, than the North; that the negroes seem happy and contented, and the citizens more tranquilly engaged in the pursuit of their business and pleasure? Has that traveler been in Naples?[10] Precisely the same remarks apply to the appearances of things there at this moment. The massacre of Hayti[11] opened in a ball-room. Mr. Cobden[12] judged there was not the smallest reason in the French king's surrounding himself with soldiers the day before the hidden virus of insubordination broke out and cast him forth from his kingdom. The moment of greatest apparent security to tyrants is always the moment of their greatest peril. It is true, however, that the tranquillity of the South is the tranquillity of Hungary and of Poland; the tranquillity of hopelessness on the part of the subject race. But, in the most favored regions, this broken spirit of despair is as carefully preserved by the citizens, and with as confident and unhesitating an application of force, when necessary to teach humility, as it is by the army of the Czar, or the omnipresent police of the Kaiser. In Richmond, and Charleston, and New Orleans, the citizens are as careless and gay as in Boston or London, and their servants a thousand times as childlike and cordial, to all appearance, in their relations with them, as our servants are with us. But go to the bottom of this security and dependence, and you come to police machinery, such as you never find in towns under free government: citadels, sentries, passports, grape-shotted cannon, and daily public whippings of the subjects for accidental infractions of police ceremonies. I happened myself to see more direct expression of tyranny in a single day and night at Charleston, than at Naples in a week; and I found that more than half the inhabitants of this town were subject to arrest, imprisonment, and barbarous punishment, if found in the streets without a passport after the evening "gun-fire."[13] Similar precautions and similar customs may be discovered in every large town in the South.

Nor is it so much better, as is generally imagined, in the rural districts. Ordinarily there is no show of government any more than at the North: the slaves go about with as much apparent freedom as convicts in a dockyard. There is, however, nearly everywhere, always prepared to act, if not always in service, an armed force, with a military organization, which is invested with more arbitrary and cruel power than any police in Europe. Yet the security of the whites is in a much less degree contingent on the action of the patrols than upon the constant habitual and instinctive surveillance and authority of all white people over all black. I have seen a gentleman, with no commission or special authority, oblige negroes to show their passports, simply because he did not recognize them as belonging to any of his neighbors. I have seen a girl, twelve years old, in a district where, in ten miles, the slave population was fifty to one of the free, stop an old man on the public road, demand to know where he was going, and by what authority, order him to face about and return to his plantation; and enforce her command with turbulent anger, when he hesitated, by threatening that she would have him well whipped if he did not instantly obey. The man quailed like a spaniel, and she instantly resumed the manner of a lovely child with me, no more apprehending that she had acted unbecomingly than that her character had been influenced by the slave's submission to her caprice of supremacy; no more conscious that she had increased the security of her life by strengthening the habit of the slave [of subservience] to the master race, than is the sleeping seaman that he tightens his clutch of the rigging as the ship meets each new billow.

The whole South is, in fact, a people divided against itself, of which one faction has conquered, and has to maintain its supremacy. The "state of siege" is permanent. Any symptoms of rebellion on one side, or of treachery on the other, cannot safely be left to the slow process of civil law; every white man is expected to deal summarily with them, and in such a manner as to pervade with terror, cowardice, and hopelessness all the possibly disaffected; and in many districts, where the contagion of a bold or hot brain would be most dangerous, the life of the whole white population is that of a "vigilance committee," every man and woman grim-faced for a possible ferocious duty.

There is no part of the South in which the people are more free from the direct action of slavery upon the character, or where they have less to apprehend from rebellion, than Eastern Tennessee. Yet, after the burning of a negro near Knoxville, a few years ago,[14] the deed was justified as necessary for the maintenance of order among the slaves, by the editor of a newspaper (the *Register*), which, owing to its peculiarly conservative character, I have heard stigmatized as "an abolition print." "It was," he observed, "a means of absolute, necessary self-defense, which could not be secured by an ordinary resort to the laws. Two executions on the gallows have occurred in this county within a year or two past, and the example has been unavailing. Four executions by hanging have taken place, heretofore in Jefferson, of slaves guilty of similar offenses, and it has produced no radical terror or example for the others designing the same crimes, and hence any example less horrible and terrifying would have availed nothing here."[15]

The other local paper (the *Whig*), upon the same occasion, used the following language:

"We have to say, in defense of the act, that it was not perpetrated by an excited multitude, but by one thousand citizens—good citizens at that—who were cool, calm, and deliberate."

And the editor, who is not ashamed to call himself "a minister of Christ,"[16] presently adds, after explaining the enormity of the offense with which the victim was charged—"We unhesitatingly affirm that the punishment was unequal to the crime. Had we been there we should have taken a part, and even suggested the pinching of pieces out of him with red-hot pincers—the cutting off of a limb at a time, and then burning them all in a heap. The possibility of his escaping from jail forbids the idea of awaiting the tardy movements of the law."

How much more horrible than the deed are these apologies for it. They make it manifest that it was not accidental in its character, but a phenomenon of general and fundamental significance. They explain the paralytic effect upon the popular conscience of the great calamity of the South. They indicate that it is a necessity of these people to return in their habits of thought to the dark ages of mankind. For who, from the outside, can fail to see that the real reason why men, in the middle of the nineteenth century, and in the centre of the United States, are publicly burned at the stake, is one much less heathenish, less disgraceful to the citizens than that given by the more zealous and extemporaneous of their journalistic exponents—the desire to torture the sinner proportionately to the measure of his sin. Doubtless, this reverend gentleman expresses the uppermost feeling of the ruling mind of his community. But would a similar provocation have developed a similar and equally tumultuous, avenging spirit in any other nominally Christian or civilized people? Certainly not. All over Europe, in every free-state—California, for significant reasons, temporarily excepted[17]—in similar cases, justice deliberately takes its course; the accused is systematically assisted in defending or excusing himself. If the law demands his life, the infliction of unnecessary suffering, and the education of the people in violence and feelings of revenge, is studiously avoided. Go back to the foundation of the custom which thus neutralizes Christianity, among the people of the South, which carries them backward blindly against the tide of civilization, and what do we find it to be? The editor, who still retains moral health enough to be suspected, as men more enlightened than their neighbors usually are, of heterodoxy, answers for us. To follow the usual customs of civilization elsewhere would not be safe. To indulge in feelings of humanity would not be safe. To be faithful to the precepts of Christ would not be safe. To act in a spirit of cruel, inconsiderate, illegal, violent, and pitiless vengeance, must be permitted, must be countenanced, must be defended by the most conservative, as a "means of absolute, necessary self-defense." To educate the people practically otherwise would be suicidal. Hence no free press, no free pulpit, nor free politics, can be permitted in the South, nor in Kansas, while the South reigns. Hence every white stripling in the South may carry a dirk-knife in his pocket, and play with a revolver before he has learned to swim. "Self-preservation is the first law of nature."

I happened to pass through Eastern Tennessee shortly after this tragedy, and conversed with a man who was engaged in it—a mild, common-sense native of the country. He told me that there was no evidence against the negro but his own confession. I suggested that he might have been crazy. "What if he was?" he asked, with a sudden asperity.

What if he was? To be sure; what if he was? In fact, he was not burned because he deserved it; nor, if we consider, because he was believed by his rulers to have committed the offenses charged upon him. It was not a question of evidence, of morality, but of expediency—simply, of self-preservation. His life depended not upon a conviction of his guilt, in the minds of his judges, but upon the opinion which the subject people of the county were likely to have about it, the same necessity requiring this jury of his peers to be degraded, cunning, and suspicious. To make them sure that their rulers are a strong and hard-hearted race, quick, sure, and terrible in their vengeance, was the object. It was a question no more of justice than of mercy, to the victim used in accomplishing the object.

Is it incredible that men, nurtured in communities whose most conservative and respectable classes, whose very professional teachers feel themselves justified in taking part in such barbarity, upon such grounds, should have been found, by Mr. Gladstone, guilty of purely barbarous conduct towards a people whose patient and self-controlling habits were so new to them that they could only ascribe them to a slave-like cowardice? Evidently, to the invaders of Kansas, it must have seemed a merciful treatment of those they had been taught to consider their enemies, when they fell into their hands, merely to hang, or shoot, and scalp them, without torture.

"No people," it has been said, "are ever found to be better than their laws, though many have been known to be worse." If, in the following advertisement, which was recently published in North Carolina, the proper-names and technical phrases were suitably changed, and it were presented to us by a traveler as coming from the Sandwich Islands, would it not strike us that it had been rather premature to class the natives of those islands among the Christian nations of the world?

> STATE OF NORTH CAROLINA, JONES COUNTY.—*Whereas,* complaint upon oath hath this day been made to us, Adonijah McDaniel and John N. Hyman, two of the Justices of the Peace of said county, by Franklin B. Harrison, of said county, planter, that a certain male slave belonging to him, named Sam, hath absented himself from his master's services, and is lurking about said county, committing acts of felony and other misdeeds. These are, therefore, in the name of State, to command the said slave forthwith to surrender himself and return home to his master; and we do hereby require the Sheriff of said County of Jones to make diligent search and pursuit after the said slave, and him having found, to apprehend and secure, so that he may be conveyed to his said master, or otherwise discharged as the law directs; and the said Sheriff is hereby authorized and empowered to raise and take with him such power of his county as he shall think fit for apprehending the said slave; and we do hereby, by virtue of the Act of Assembly, in such case provided, intimate and declare that if the said slave, named Sam, doth not surrender himself and return home immediately after the publication of these presents, that *any person may kill and destroy the said slave, by such means as he or they may think fit, without accusation or impeachment of any crime or offense for so doing, and without incurring any penalty and forfeiture thereby.*
>
> Given under our hands and seals the 29th day of September, A.D., 1856.
>
> A. McDANIEL, J. P. [SEAL]
>
> J. N. HYMAN, J. P. [SEAL]
>
> $100 REWARD.
>
> I will give Fifty Dollars for the apprehension and delivery of said boy to me, or lodge him in any jail in the State, so that I get him, or ONE HUNDRED DOLLARS FOR HIS HEAD.
>
> F.B. HARRISON.[18]

May not the most conservative of us soon be obliged to consider less what we can do and suffer to retain the fellowship, than what we can do to guard against the sinister influences upon our own politics and society, of contiguous States, under the laws of which there is still the liability of such an exposition of constitutional barbarism? What is to be expected of such seed but such bitter fruit as that of Kansas, under the heat of Squatter Sovereignty?

The supreme judicial authority of the same State has declared that it would be preposterous, while the intention of holding the slaves in their present subjection was maintained, to consider it a crime for a white man to shoot a woman attempting to escape from the ordinary chastisement of indocility. It was decided (in the case of the State *vs.* Mann), by Justice Ruffin, "essential to the value of slaves, as property, to the security of the master, and to the public tranquillity," that such recklessness with human life should be unrestrained by the law.†[19]

Let the reader who thinks there must be "two sides" to this story of Kansas, and that Mr. Gladstone has chosen to give his countrymen but one of them, remember that the necessity which has made the South thus exceptional among civilized States, in its law, must have made the people of the South much more exceptional among civilized mankind in their habits and character. Mr. Gladstone demonstrates but one consequence—that one which, being defended and apologized for by the President of the United States, has most injured the reputation of democratic institutions throughout the world.[20] The world should recognize the fact that the disgraceful condition of Kansas, the atrocious system, which the federal government of the United States has been forced to countenance in Kansas, is the legitimate fruit of despotism, not of free government.

There are, however, many other characteristics of the people of the South which have had their origin in this necessity, which we of the North—since the absence of slavery is likely hereafter to depend on a local ordinance, since slavery is officially intimated to be national, and all opposition to slavery declared to be "sectional"—cannot afford to overlook. Would to God we had "nothing to do with it." But, as a Southern-born man said to me, lately, "It is a white man's question." Shall we hereafter exercise our rights as citizens of the United States, which are simply our natural rights as men, only by favor of Sharps rifles and in entrenched villages?[21]

It is, for instance, the foundation of that peculiar political cooperativeness and efficiency which we see in the people of the South. Nothing is safe if the slaves rise. Towards any party or measures, therefore, which, however indirectly, militate in the least against the everlasting subordination of the slave race, they act, as they do towards the slaves themselves, with the self-preserving instinct of a community always prepared for the attacks of a savage enemy. Hence, the intensity and completeness with which they give themselves up to any political purpose in which an increase of wealth, and, consequently, of stability in power, is involved for the slaveholding body. They engage in it as in war, and hold ordinary rules of morality and social comity to be suspended till they have gained their ends.

Their orators are wont to boast that they belong to a military people. What are termed the military qualities of the South are, again, the natural effects of this inherited watchfulness and readiness to meet, instantly and decisively, with cruelty and bloodshed, the first symptoms of insubordinate disposition on the part of their slaves. These military qualities are, in fact, not such as are most valued for modern armies—individual staunchness, patience, and endurance of character, contributing to combined concentrativeness, precision, and mobility—but rather those of the feudal ages, or of savage warriors, the chief being mere belligerent excitability, readiness of resort to arms, an idolatrous estimate of the virtue of physical courage, and an insane propensity of that kind which leads Indian braves to amuse or disgust their visitors, as the case may be, by "scalp-dances" and monotonous recitative of their glorious achievements, past and prospective. A government of force is ordinarily a government of threats and gasconading ostentation. The subject must continually know that the master is confident in his strength.

We are well instructed by Humboldt,[22] that the only worthy purpose of the student of history is to learn the influence which different circumstances have had on the development of character in mankind. Doubtless, slavery has not wholly failed of good effects upon the character of our fellow-citizens of the South. I do not now inquire what those effects are, because such an inquiry is not pertinent to the subject of this book. In the conduct of those who represent the influence of slavery in Kansas, only the worst qualities which it is possible for men to acquire have hitherto been displayed. Even the measurable success with which they have, to this moment, maintained their conquest, is due to no good judgment, energy, or bravery of their own, but is evidently entirely dependent on what, to such observers as Mr. Gladstone, must be the most incredible and inexplicable circumstance in the whole sad business—the encouragement they receive in their villainy from the democratic party of the Free-states, and the constant countenance, supplies, reinforcements, and patronage of the federal administration. Withdraw this; let the oppressed citizens generally feel that it would be right, and proper, and lawful to deal with their present rulers as they have been dealt with by them, and the savages would disappear from the land as the more manly Indians have before them, and then the present scandal of Kansas would be lost in the natural peace, order, and prosperity of a society, no member of which need have aught to fear but from his own folly, nor aught to hope but from his own industry, as surely as the fire-blackness of its winter prairies is submerged in the green flood of its spring.

Is it unpatriotic to thus show the incompatibility of slavery with good citizenship?

The people of the South are "my people." I am attached to them equally as to those of Massachusetts or Pennsylvania. My blood and my fortune are equally at their service. I desire their prosperity as I do that of no other people in the world. I look upon slavery as an entailed misfortune which, with the best disposition, it might require centuries to wholly dispose of. I would have extreme charity for the political expedients to which it tempts a resort.

But it seems to me now, that such inexcusable scoundrelism in our common matters, as has been shown in Kansas, should make us consider if charity has not been carried too far; if the forbearing, and apologetic, and patronizing disposition towards everything in the South, or of the South, or for the South, is not as much calculated to bring us into difficulty as the reckless and denunciatory spirit attributed to the abolitionists. Have not thousands of our Northern people so habituated themselves to defend the South that they have become as blind to the essential evils and dangers of despotism as if they were themselves directly subject to its influence?

In the South itself, there has been for many years a school of fanatics, who maintain that slavery is essential to a high form of civilization; who, in their selfish anxiety to maintain it, have trained themselves to think that its influence is wholly ennobling and refining, christianizing and civilizing. These views are so flattering to the predominant bad propensities developed by slavery that they are propagated with a zeal and a success like that of the immediate followers of Mahomet. The characteristic vices of the middle ages are unearthed and enshrined under the name of chivalry, and the youth of our country is taught to reverence a reckless, blundering, and blood-thirsty buccaneer as a "second Washington," and a silly, romantic, swaggering poltroon, who can talk wickedly of women and wear a graceful feather, as "the Marion of Kansas."[23]

Against this gospel no one dare contend with a spirit and boldness at all comparable to that of its apostles. Books, periodicals, and newspapers, are interdicted, if they maintain the faith which was universal among its friends in the South when our Union was formed. However calm and respectful their manner, they are denied the service of the United States mails;[24] those who receive them are denounced as abolition traitors; gentlemen who acknowledge themselves to privately hold similar opinions, and who are on terms of friendship with their authors, feel obliged to "discountenance" them. "If I should express my real opinions," said one, himself a large slaveholder, "it is not unlikely I should be mobbed and my life placed in jeopardy by men who never have owned and never will own a single negro."

Nay, have we not recently seen that, for a mere act of customary politeness to a political opponent, and of respect to a high official of our national government, Mr. Aiken, of South Carolina, the wealthiest citizen and the largest slave-owner of that state, has been denounced and insulted, as guilty of a "gross wrong" to his constituents?[25] There is no "democratic paper" in all the South, believes the editor of the South Carolina *Times*,[26] that has not condemned the act; no paper which has approved of it. In all the South, not one editor still lives to sympathize with the instincts of a gentleman of the old school. So complete is the success of the new gospel of slavery in its own country.‡

At the North, we have not only "public documents" sent us by the ton, but many self-styled democratic newspapers, which follow, as near as can be thought discreet for propagandists, in the same course—denying the evils of slavery, apologizing for them, or, with astounding impudence, in the case of these Kansas barbarisms, charging them upon the persecuted and long-suffering victims, whom, also, they hold up to scorn, as "traitors" and "abolitionists." The most successful journal in the service of the administration here in New York, is not satisfied thus negatively to serve the purposes of the slavery fanatics, but takes the aggressive against freedom, daily arguing "the universal failure of free society,"[27] earnestly combating "the wide-spread delusion that Southern institutions are an evil, and their extension dangerous," and

418

diligently advocating the claims to universal adoption of a system, living under the influence of which Jefferson declared the citizen "must be a prodigy who retained his morals and manners undepraved;" which Patrick Henry testified to be "at variance with the purity of our religion;" which Mason[28] held "to produce the most pernicious effects on manners," and calculated to draw "the judgment of heaven upon a country;" which Franklin termed "an atrocious debasement of our nature," and "a plan for the abolition" of which Washington declared to be "among his first wishes."

When the Supreme Court finds slavery to have been considered a national institution by these statesmen in the construction of our constitution;[29] when this opinion, at variance with every impression we have received from our fathers, is welcomed with cheers and congratulations in the North, as by the State Democratic Convention of Connecticut;[30] when nearly all the newspapers of the South, and one quarter of those at the North, express nothing but satisfaction with the criminality of the late administration in Kansas; nothing but charity or admiration for the savages nurtured by slavery to fight its battles; nothing but sneers and maledictions for the grand results of free government manifested in the patient, orderly, and industrious character of their victims; when with the ruling, though minor party, of our citizens, freedom and the "Rights of man" are subjects only of ridicule—slavery only of apology or laudation; when foreigners find border-warfare the most interesting subject of observation on our continent; when the subjects of every crowned head in Europe are pointed to Kansas for a caution against dreams of self-government; when our army is used as a reserve force for bands of robbers,[31] while they murder the sons, and ravish the daughters, and devastate the property of our dearest friends and neighbors, and all in the service of slavery, is it not reasonable to believe that there is greater danger of our forgetting the evils which the people of the South suffer from slavery than of our overlooking the advantages which they claim to enjoy from it?

*"There are tender souls," says Mr. Elliott, in the "New England History,"[32] "who feel that after death the good alone live, and should only be spoken of, and this, in a degree, is true;" but "it is safest, it is more manly, to see men fairly, as they are, whoever they are, alive or dead." The late Mr. Brooks' character should be honestly considered, now that personal enmity toward him is impossible. That he was courteous, accomplished, warm-hearted, and hot-blooded, dear as a friend, and fearful as an enemy, may be believed by all; but, in the South, his name is yet never mentioned without the term gallant or courageous, spirited or noble, is also attached to it, and we are obliged to ask, why insist on this? The truth is, we include a habit of mind in these terms which slavery has rendered, in a great degree, obsolete in the South. The man who has been accustomed, from childhood, to see men beaten when they have no chance to defend themselves; to hear men accused, reproved, and vituperated, who dare not open their lips in self-defense, or reply; the man who is accustomed to see other men whip women without interference, remonstrance, or any expression of indignation, must have a certain quality, which is an essential part of personal honor with us, greatly blunted, if not entirely destroyed. The same quality, which we detest in the assassination of an enemy, is essentially constant in all slavery. It is found in effecting one's will with another man by taking unfair advantage of him. Accustomed to this in every hour of their lives, Southerners do not feel magnanimity and the "fair-play" impulse to be a necessary part of the quality of "spirit," courage, and nobleness. By spirit they apparently mean only passionate vindictiveness of character, and by gallantry mere intrepidity.

†"Such service as is required of a slave, can only be expected of one who has no will of his own; who surrenders his will in implicit obedience to that of another. Such obedience is the consequence only of uncontrolled authority over the body; there is nothing else which can operate to produce that effect. The power of the master must be absolute to render the obedience of the slave perfect."—2. DEVEREUX'S N. C. Rep., 263.

‡The argument with which the South Carolina *Times,* in the article referred to, disposes of the claim of courtesy, strikingly sustains the opinions I have expressed, that it is to an habitual precaution against insubordination of the slaves that we are chiefly to attribute the peculiar customs and manners of the South. Speaker Banks is an opponent of the extension of slavery—not an abolitionist in the political sense; "but," says the *Times,* "we regard him as beyond the pale of a refined courtesy—excluded by his own acts. If incurable fanaticism be a merit, Speaker Banks has it. If inexpiable treason be a virtue, Speaker Banks can claim it. To prove this we need only repeat what we have said before. Mr. Speaker Banks avows sentiments that lead directly, and lead inevitably, to insurrection, rapine, and murder! He boldly proclaims himself an enemy to the South—to the institutions of the South."

Olmsted's reference to the Dred Scott decision early in this introduction indicates that he began writing it soon after March 6, 1857. A later quotation of an excerpt from a North Carolina newspaper article that appeared in the *Liberator* of April 10, 1857, suggests that he completed the introduction just before starting work on the supplement to *The Englishman in Kansas,* which he dated April 10, 1857.

1. Thomas A. Gladstone.
2. Edwin Vose Sumner (1797–1863), colonel of the First U.S. Cavalry and commander of Fort Leavenworth in Kansas Territory in 1856 (*DAB*).
3. Thomas A. Gladstone, *The Englishman in Kansas; Or, Squatter Life and Border Warfare... With an Introduction, by Fred. Law Olmsted...* (New York, 1857; rpt. ed. with an introduction by James A. Rawley, Lincoln, Neb., 1971), p. 64.
4. The decision of the U.S. Supreme Court in the Dred Scott case on March 6, 1857.
5. A reference to the murder trial of Matthew Flournoy Ward (1826–1862) in Hardin County, Kentucky, in April 1854.
    Ward killed William H. G. Butler, the schoolmaster of his younger brother, William, who had been guilty of distributing chestnuts to some of his friends while at school. The boys ate the nuts and threw the shells behind their desks, and when Butler discovered

what had happened, he whipped William Ward and called him a liar for denying the claim of one of the boys that they had eaten the nuts after class began. Matt Ward resented the imputation that his brother was a liar, and set out to exact an apology from Butler. Ward was slight of stature and suffered badly from rheumatism, and was physically no match for Butler. Accordingly, he purchased two pistols loaded with buckshot before confronting the schoolmaster. He then proceeded to the school in company with his brother Robert, who was armed with a bowie knife in order to prevent any interference by the assistant schoolmaster. At the school, Ward demanded an apology, which Butler refused to make before explaining the whole incident. Ward called him a scoundrel and a liar, to which Butler replied with a blow to the face. Ward then thrust his pistol to Butler's chest and shot him fatally. At the end of the murder trial, the jury quickly found Ward not guilty. The trial attracted widespread attention in the Eastern press, in part because of the social prominence of Ward's family in the Louisville region and in part because of the eminence of the lawyers for the defense, including John Larne Helm, the ex-governor of Kentucky, and John J. Crittenden, the venerable U.S. senator from that state.

The article from the *Louisville Journal* that Olmsted quotes appeared in the *New York Herald*. The italics in the quotation were added by Olmsted (*NYDT*, April 27, 1854, pp. 1, 2, 8; ibid., April 28, 1854, p. 3; ibid., April 29, 1854, pp. 3, 8; "A Horrible Record," *New York Herald*, July 4, 1854, p. 2).

6. Napoleon III of France, who vacationed at the resort of Biarritz in southwestern France during August and September of 1856.
7. The Hundred Horse Guards, created in 1854 by Napoleon III for his own service (*NYDT*, May 24, 1854, p. 2),
8. A reference to the caning of Massachusetts senator Charles Sumner by South Carolina representative Preston L. Brooks in the U.S. Senate chambers on May 22, 1856. Brooks died on January 27, 1857.
9. Unidentified.
10. Olmsted had visited Naples in April 1856. Its ruler was the cruel and despotic Ferdinand II (1810–1859), King of the Two Sicilies. After popular uprisings in 1849, Ferdinand instituted a reign of terror and confined thousands of citizens in prisons. In 1856 France and England appealed to him unsuccessfully to relax the severity of his rule (*EB*).
11. Probably a reference to the slave revolt in Haiti that began on August 22, 1791, while many planters were at a ball in Cap François, as described in Charles Wyllys Elliott's book *San Domingo* (1857).
12. Richard Cobden (1804–1865), British statesman.
13. In Charleston, South Carolina, no Negro or person of color was permitted to be on the streets at night without a ticket from his owner or employer authorizing him to be there. This applied to the period between the beating of tattoo by the City Guard—at nine o'clock in the evening between September 20 and March 20, and at ten o'clock the rest of the year—and the beating of reveille thirty minutes before sunrise. Both free blacks and slaves were subject to fines if found on the streets after tattoo, and slaves, with the consent of their owner, could also receive from five to nineteen lashes (Charleston, S.C., Ordinances, etc., *A Digest of the Ordinances of the City Council of Charleston from the Year 1783 to Oct. 1844* . . . [Charleston, S.C., 1844], pp. 90, 96).
14. A reference to the burning of a slave near Dandridge, Jefferson County, Tennessee, on June 19, 1854. The man was the only slave of a farmer named Elijah Moore, and lived with Moore, his wife, and his wife's sister, Jane Lotspeech. According to the slave's confession, he developed a passion for Miss Lotspeech and made advances to her, which she rejected. When he persisted, she reported his actions to Moore, who threatened to whip him. On the night of June 14, the slave murdered Moore and his wife in their bed with an axe, then subdued Miss Lotspeech, raped her, and killed her. He made his escape by lying on the bottom of a canoe and drifting down the French Broad River, which ran near the Moores' farm. On the eighteenth he was apprehended and confessed to the murders, his captors securing the confession "by screwing his fingers and then his hands in a vice until all the bones were mashed, (and other treatment which cannot be mentioned in print)." His captors then tied him to a tree, built a pile of pitch pine around him, and burned him to ashes in the presence of a thousand or more persons ("Murder and Burning to Death in Tennessee," *New York Daily Tribune*, July 4, 1854, p. 6; "Negro-Burning," ibid., July 11, 1854, p. 4).
15. This statement appeared in the *Knoxville Register* of June 25, 1854, as a letter from Dandridge,

Tennessee, from a friend of the editor's, and not as a statement by the editor himself. The letter was quoted in full in the *New York Daily Tribune* article "Murder and Burning to Death in Tennessee."

16. The editor of the *Knoxville Whig* was the eccentric William Gannaway ("Parson") Brownlow (1805–1877), a Methodist clergyman and editor of the *Whig* from 1849 to 1861. Although he was an ardent Unionist, Brownlow strongly defended the institution of slavery and denounced abolitionists, warning that they wanted to set off a bloody rising of the slaves (*DAB;* E. Merton Coulter, *William G. Brownlow: Fighting Parson of the Southern Highlands* [Chapel Hill, N.C., 1937], pp. 94–95).

17. The transiency of population and temptations offered to criminals by the great amount of wealth constantly circulating on the California mining frontier in the early 1850s produced waves of lawlessness that were met in many places by the organization of vigilante groups. This was true not only in the mining camps but in San Francisco as well. In 1851 and again in 1856, vigilance committees undertook to expel criminals from that city and to punish the perpetrators of major crimes when the courts and officers of the law appeared incapable of acting effectively (Rodman W. Paul, *California Gold: The Beginning of Mining in the Far West* [Cambridge, Mass., 1947], pp. 204–9; Josiah Royce, *California, from the Conquest in 1846 to the Second Vigilance Committee in San Francisco; A Study of American Character* [Boston and New York, 1886; rpt. ed. with an introduction by Earl Pomeroy, Santa Barbara, Calif., 1970], pp. 344–66).

18. This excerpt from a North Carolina newspaper appeared in an article entitled "Spirit of Slavery" in the *Liberator* of April 10, 1857, page 1. It was not reprinted by any New York newspaper around this time, which suggests that the *Liberator* was Olmsted's source. Olmsted added the italics in the body of the excerpt and rendered the phrase "one hundred dollars for his head" in capitals instead of the regular-sized type used by the *Liberator*.

19. The passages that Olmsted quotes in the text and in his footnote are from the decision by Thomas Ruffin (1787–1870), associate justice of the North Carolina supreme court in 1829 in the case of The State *versus* John Mann. The defendant was appealing a conviction in a lower court for shooting and wounding a slave he had hired, as she attempted to escape from him to avoid a whipping. Ruffin ruled that the man who hired a slave had the same absolute authority over the slave as did the owner. Following the passage that Olmsted quoted in his footnote, Ruffin went on to observe that although this state of affairs was repugnant to the "principle of moral right," it was necessary wherever slavery existed: "There is no remedy. This discipline belongs to the state of slavery. They cannot be disunited, without abrogating at once the rights of the master, and absolving the slave from his subjection. It constitutes the curse of slavery to both the bond and free portions of our population. But it is inherent in the relation of master and slave." (*DAB;* North Carolina, Supreme Court, *Cases Argued and Determined in the Supreme Court of North Carolina. From December Term, 1826, to June Term, 1834... By Thomas P. Devereux*..., 2d ed., 4 vols. [Raleigh, N.C., 1851], 2: 263–68).

20. The consequence of southern law and habits to which Olmsted refers was presumably the imposition on the territory of Kansas of a proslavery legislature elected by fraud and violence and then recognized and upheld by President Franklin Pierce as the legitimate governing body of the territory. Pierce persisted in his support of the "bogus" legislature despite warnings of territorial governor Andrew H. Reeder about the extent of election frauds in Kansas.

For Olmsted's observations on how the ensuing violence affected European views of American governmental institutions, see "How Ruffianism in Washington and Kansas is Regarded in Europe," pages 381–84 above (T. H. Gladstone, *Englishman in Kansas*, pp. 1–3; Allan M. Nevins, *Ordeal of the Union*, vol. 2, *A House Dividing, 1852–1857* [New York, 1947], pp. 385–86, 416–18; James D. Richardson, *A Compilation of the Messages and Papers of the Presidents, 1789–1897*..., 10 vols. [Washington, D.C., 1896–99], 5: 355, 358–59).

21. This passage indicates the seriousness with which Olmsted viewed the Dred Scott decision, President James Buchanan's approval of it, and Franklin Pierce's attack, in his last annual message (December 2, 1856), on antislavery agitation as sectional and disruptive of the Union.

Olmsted anticipated that the next step by the Buchanan administration and the Supreme Court would be to declare that since the right of property in a slave was "distinctly and expressly affirmed in the Constitution" (as the Dred Scott decision had held), citizens had the right to take slave property wherever they wished in the United States. This was the same concern expressed by Abraham Lincoln in his "House Divided" speech of June 17, 1858, in which he predicted that the Supreme Court would soon declare that no state had the power to exclude slavery from its limits. "We shall *lie down* pleasantly dreaming that the people of *Missouri* are on the verge of making their State *free,*" he warned, "and we shall *awake* to the *reality,* instead, that the *Supreme* Court has made *Illinois* a *slave* State."

Basing his judgment on the experience of Kansas, Olmsted believed that if this final step in the nationalizing of slavery took place, slaveholders would carry their slaves to free states and then demand the same severe legislation—the suppression of freedom of the mails and of speech and press—that the "bogus" legislature of Kansas had authorized. Where those demands were successful, residents would be able to exercise their natural rights of free speech "only by favor of Sharps rifles and in entrenched villages," as was already the situation in Kansas (J. D. Richardson, *Messages and Papers of the Presidents,* 5: 397-407; Don E. Fehrenbacher, *The Dred Scott Case: Its Significance in American Law and Politics* [New York, 1978], pp. 485-87).

22. Friedrich Heinrich Alexander Humboldt (1769-1859), the German naturalist and traveler, and author of the multivolume treatise on the physical world, *Kosmos.*
23. The statements to which Olmsted refers here have not been located, but the "second Washington" was probably the ex-senator from Missouri, David Rice Atchison (1807-1886), who exerted strong pressure on Stephen A. Douglas to put forward the Kansas-Nebraska Bill and afterward took a leading role among the Missouri "border ruffians" operating in Kansas.

The "Marion of Kansas" was probably Henry T. Titus (1815-1881), a Floridian who was one of the most active and picturesque of the proslavery military chieftains in the territory. Descriptions of his braggadocio and physical appearance suggest that he is the man Olmsted had in mind: he wore a full beard and often sported an ostrich feather in his hat (*DAB,* s.v. "Atchison, David Rice"; Alfred Jackson Hanna and Kathryn Abbey Hanna, *Florida's Golden Sands* [Indianapolis and New York, 1950], pp. 171-85; *New York Daily Tribune,* Dec. 13, 1856, p. 7).
24. After 1835, a "virtual censorship of the mails crossing the Mason and Dixon line" was in effect (Clement Eaton, "Censorship of the Southern Mails," *American Historical Review* 48, no. 2 [Jan. 1943]: 267).
25. When the Thirty-fourth Congress met in mid-December 1855, no party had a majority of seats. Two months of angry debate ensued before the Republican Nathaniel P. Banks of Massachusetts was chosen over William Aiken (1806-1887) of South Carolina by a vote of 103 to 100. Aiken then followed House tradition by escorting Banks to the Speaker's chair, for which action he was subjected to the criticism to which Olmsted refers (A. M. Nevins, *Ordeal of the Union,* 2: 412-15).
26. The *South Carolina Times* was a newspaper published in Columbia, South Carolina, between 1854 and 1857.
27. Presumably a reference to the strongly proslavery *New York Journal of Commerce,* edited by Gerard Hallock. Olmsted was so disgusted with the *Journal*'s defense of the Fugitive Slave Act of 1850 that he referred to the paper as the "Journal of Cotton" (Frank Luther Mott, *American Journalism: A History, 1690-1960,* 3d ed. [New York, 1962], pp. 181-82, 352; FLO to Charles Loring Brace, Jan. 11, 1851, *Papers of FLO,* 1: 367).
28. George Mason (1725-1792) of Gunston Hall, Fairfax County, Virginia, a leading figure in the revolutionary movement in his state, author of the Virginia Declaration of Rights in 1776 and one of the most active members in the Constitutional Convention of 1787. Though he was a slaveholder, opposition to slavery was a consistent feature of his public career (*DAB*).
29. A reference to the Dred Scott decision.
30. Olmsted's statement here appears to be inaccurate and exaggerated. The Connecticut Democratic state convention met on February 18, 1857, well before the Supreme Court announced the Dred Scott decision, and the proceedings of the convention as described in the newspapers do not indicate any discussion of the issue. However, the *Hartford Daily Courant* of March 14, 1857, did announce that a resolution welcoming and supporting the decision had been passed by the Democratic convention of Connecticut's fourth congressional district when it met to nominate its candidate for congressman. It was probably this action that Olmsted had in mind. The *Courant*'s report is of questionable accuracy, since the fourth district convention met two to four days before the Supreme Court announced its decision, and no mention of the resolution approving the Dred Scott decision appeared in local Democratic newspapers. According to the *Courant,* which was probably Olmsted's source, the resolution read as follows: "Resolved,

that the recent decision of the Supreme Court of the United States, declaring the Missouri Compromise null and void, because unauthorized by the Constitution, is a most gratifying confirmation of the views and doctrines of the Democratic Party on this long-disputed question, and affords additional reason for faith and confidence in its principles" (*Hartford Daily Times,* Feb. 18, 1857, p. 2; ibid., March 10, 1857, p. 2; *Hartford Daily Courant,* March 14, 1857, p. 2).

31. Olmsted's reference must be, not to the regular army in Kansas, but rather to the role of the territorial militia in the "sack" of Lawrence of May 21, 1856. In early May, the Douglas County grand jury issued indictments against a number of free-state men living in Lawrence, and the U.S. marshal called for a large citizen's posse to help him serve his warrants. To assist in the process, territorial governor Wilson Shannon enrolled members of a number of proslavery military organizations into the territorial militia, including more than four hundred men under the command of Jefferson Buford of Alabama. Also in the marshal's posse were units commanded by B. F. Stringfellow, members of the Platte County Rifles under David R. Atchison, and other groups, including the Lecompton Guards and the Doniphan Tigers. These forces invested Lawrence on May 20, and remained outside the town the next day while the federal marshal served warrants and made several arrests. The marshal then disbanded his posse, and the proslavery sheriff of Douglas County, Samuel J. Jones, immediately summoned the whole force to assist him in serving writs in the town. So it happened that many of the men who pillaged the town of Lawrence were members of the territorial militia that had, moments before, been under the command of a federal officer (A. M. Nevins, *Ordeal of the Union,* 2: 434–37; Walter L. Fleming, "The Buford Expedition to Kansas," *American Historical Review* 6, no. 1 (Oct. 1900): 44–47).

32. A reference to a two-volume study published in 1857 by Olmsted's friend Charles Wyllys Elliott, *The New England History, from the Discovery of the Continent by the Northmen,* A.D. 986, *to the Period when the Colonies Declared their Independence,* A.D. 1776.

Supplement by the American Editor
to
The Englishman in Kansas

April 13, 1857.

All the federal offices in Kansas continue to be filled by the ringleaders of the conspiracy against free-labor.[1] Some of them are guilty directly in their own persons, and all are guilty indirectly, as conspirators and abettors, before and after the fact, of the murder of citizens whose only offense was a confession that they preferred that slavery should not be established in the territory. Let the reader not slight this statement. It would be a disgraceful and wicked thing for one to make such assertions without adequate ground of perfect conviction of their truth. If undeniable or if convincing testimony of their truth is readily within his reach, no man who respects himself, and who would live with a clear conscience, can fail to regard them gravely, anxiously, indignantly.

It is a simple, undeniable, indefensible fact, that the new President of the United States not merely still refrains from executing justice in Kansas, but also that he has renewed and extended the countenance, patronage, honors, and friendship of the government to men who regard it as a merit and a matter of boasting that, for a political purpose, they have shot, in cold blood, and in the back, citizens of several independent, sovereign free states, of whom they knew no harm but that they intended to vote against the establishment of slavery in territory belonging to those states, and of which they were residents and land-owners.

With a possible exception in the new secretary,[2] there is no man now in Kansas recognized by our federal government, including its judicial branches, to have any official authority there, who is not a notorious plotter and probable pledged conspirator to prevent an honest action of the law of Squatter Sovereignty, as it is defined by the President and all its friends.

There are plenty of Free-state men from the North, capable and respectable, who have always belonged to the Democratic party, and who supported Mr. Buchanan in the hope that he would be just to Kansas, but not one such has been appointed to office.

The Hon. R. J. Walker has been selected to succeed Governor Geary, who resigned his office, either because, as his enemies say, he considered his life in danger from the Proslavery faction, or, as his friends say, because the President refused to sustain him in taking any measures inclining towards justice.[3] Governor Walker has been recently known to the public chiefly for his efforts to have a railroad built from his state of Mississippi through a district at present occupied chiefly by non-slaveholding farmers in Texas, and thence a thousand miles across a desert country to that portion of California which is nearest to the cotton-soils of Sonora, and which it is thought might be made a slave state even without this assistance.[4] He asserts that he desires to have the free-soil party in Kansas treated with fairness.[5] He is the only one at present holding office for Kansas, who has ever made this profession. He remains yet in Washington, attending to some necessary private business: he is a business man, and was a subscriber for one million dollars' worth of the stock of the Grand Southern California Railroad Company. Nevertheless, it is thought he may take a look at the territory in May.

Under a process of law, which the President recognizes as constitutional and valid, many good citizens, accused of resistance to the tyranny of an organization made by the Missourians for the purpose of establishing slavery in Kansas, have been torn from their families, and held in unwholesome confinement until some died and all were greatly impoverished.[6] Of the many hundred boasting robbers and murderers of Free-state settlers, none yet are punished or even rebuked by the officers appointed to execute justice in the name of the majesty of the people of the confederate states.[7]

The body of men who were last year appointed by the partisans of slavery for the purpose of preventing the success of any movements unfavorable to the establishment of slavery in the territory, and whose acts for that purpose are laws to the President of the United States and all those whom he appoints to office, have recently pretended that they were willing to give an opportunity to the people of the territory to indicate, by a vote, what they demanded in their government.[8] The instrument of this pretension—just now warmly commended by the Northern friends of Slavery extension, because it is the first act of this body which assumes to be intended to carry out their petted principle of Squatter Sovereignty—is the same which ex-Governor Geary vetoed on the ground of the absurd inconsistency of its provisions with its alleged purpose. It provides for a census of the citizens of the territory who were resident in it, on the 15th March, when no emigrants from the Free states would be likely to have recently become resident, but when, as it has now been made manifest, multitudes would have just come in by land from Missouri. From the census thus taken by officials, every one of whom is a sworn enemy of freedom, a voting list is to be made up, which is to be revised by sworn friends of slavery. The territory is then to be formed into nineteen voting districts, the size, and shape, and relations of which, to each other, and to Missouri, are to be determined by men who are ashamed of nothing which has been done to subdue the free-soil party of the territory in the last two years. The number of delegates who are to represent the people of each district, is to be proportionate to the population returned by the special census. This proportion, not very difficult for a business man to ascertain, is to be declared by the Governor and Secretary, appointed by the President, and as this is the only duty connected with the election assigned to the governor, it is evident that the "Legislature" had some misgivings that the friends of Mr. Buchanan, in the Free states, were speaking the truth when they declared that he was disposed to do the fair thing with Kansas.

Finally, the votes are to be taken, not by ballot, but *viva voce,* by vocal declaration, so that the slavery party may not be voted against by one man who is not willing to make himself known as a free-soiler to the land-officers, who are to settle disputed claims—and there are comparatively few claims which are not disputed—these land-officers being all men committed to, and identified with, the conspiracy, to establish slavery on the soil of Kansas. The inspectors of election are to be men similarly pledged or sworn to disregard the rights of the free-soilers, and by such trusty hands, the vote is to be recorded, and returned. The whole process, in short, is in the hands of the same unscrupulous miscreants, who have been protected in every crime of which the reader has read in this book, by the present federal judiciary. It has been often reported, of late, that the scandalous laws enacted last year by the Legislature, established by Missouri in the territory, have been repealed under the conciliatory policy of the session of this year. Certain laws which it would have been impracticable to attempt to execute, have been repealed.[9] It yet remains a legal felony for any man in the territory to order a book, such as this, for instance, to be sent to him. Any one who offers to receive a free-soil newspaper, is liable to five years imprisonment. No conscientious free-soiler is eligible to sit upon a jury; and, in general, no practicable means of harassing, persecuting, and silencing, those who would act effectively against the establishment of slavery in the territory, are left unprovided for.

And, yet, it is very plainly declared by Governor Walker, after long consultation with the President, pending his acceptance of the governorship, that he will attempt to carry out these laws, and force the people to accept this tyrannical usurpation of authority as a constitutional republican government. He believes, we are told, that it will be impossible to establish slavery in Kansas, because of its ungenial climate,[10] (though it is milder than that of Virginia) therefore we are to believe that he will not lend himself to the schemes of his old friends, who have shrunk from nothing to conquer those who are opposed to its establishment, and if the foolish people from the North will only kiss the hand that smites them, and lie quietly under the heel that crushes them, he has confidence that he will restore peace and order in the territory.

What of their rights as men and as citizens? What of justice? What of squatter sovereignty? What of the honor and faith of the nation? Not one word.

The hope that constitutional liberty can be maintained in America, now rests on the integrity of the independent state governments in declaring, demanding, and securing the rights of their citizens.

It is impossible, if the policy of the new administration is to be judged from present symptoms, that the thinking citizens of each state in which men can yet afford to think freely, should not before long ask themselves:

"What are the delegated, and what the reserved rights of this state? Why should it remain in union with others for whose convenience and satisfaction its citizens are forced to relinquish, on common ground, their fundamental rights—rights, the free use of which is essential to the preservation of a decent and civilized state of society? Is it from a craven devotion to political tranquillity we allow these rights to be suppressed, systematically, formally, and year after year, and administration after administration, suppressed? Is it from pride in holding our state part of a Great Nation? Have we no patriotic duty but to keep men of our own party in office?

"What is the value of the federal constitution to us, if, in our territories, more than half our people can be deprived of the rights to which those who made the Constitution declared all men, everywhere, to be justly entitled, and which they fought a long, desperate, and bloody war to secure?"[11]

It is the crime of a coward and not the wisdom of a good citizen to shut his eyes to the fact, that this Union is bound straight to disastrous shipwreck, if the man at the helm maintains his present course.

The prophetic mind of Jefferson, unconsciously but clearly described the process by which we have suffered ourselves to be brought to our present perilous condition.

> Is this the kind of protection we receive in return for the rights we give up?
> Our rulers will become corrupt, our people careless. A single zealot may commence persecutor, and better men be his victims. It can never be too often repeated that the time for fixing every essential right on a legal basis is while our

rulers are honest, ourselves united. From the conclusion of this war, we shall be going down hill. It will not then be necessary to resort every moment to the people for support. They will be forgotten and their rights disregarded. They will forget themselves but in the sole faculty of making money, and will never think of uniting to effect a due respect for their rights. The shackles, therefore, which shall not be knocked off before the conclusion of this war, will remain on us long; will be made heavier and heavier till our rights shall revive or expire in a convulsion.*

   The time to guard against corruption and tyranny is before they shall have gotten hold on us. It is better to keep the wolf out of the fold, than to trust to drawing his teeth and talons, after he shall have entered.†

*Notes on Virginia. London, 1787, p. 269.
†Ibid., p. 197.

Olmsted wrote this supplement in the context of discussions of the future of Kansas that arose following the resignation of territorial governor John W. Geary on March 4, 1857, and President James Buchanan's appointment of Robert J. Walker as his successor on March 26. The *New York Daily Tribune* published several editorials between the latter date and April 13 that were critical of the administration's policy toward Kansas and deplored the continued dominance of proslavery interests in the territory. The subject matter and tone of this supplement indicate that Olmsted read those editorials and drew directly from them.

1. Olmsted seems to have based this assertion particularly on an editorial in the *New York Daily Tribune* of April 6, 1857. The section of the editorial that most directly parallels Olmsted's statements is as follows:

    All the appointments recently made for Kansas by the new President are of the most active, bitter, unscrupulous leaders of the Pro-Slavery faction—Whitfield, Emory, Woodson, Ransom, &c. While not one man who was previously known as sympathizing with the Free-State movement in Kansas has ever been appointed to any post whatever by either Pierce or Buchanan, the men who planned and consummated the gigantic fraud and usurpation of March 30, 1855, have been and are the dispensers of Federal patronage in Kansas, and themselves the recipients of the most desirable offices. Some of them have led marauding bands of Missourians in their repeated invasions of Kansas; Federal officers are known as having themselves fired at and killed unarmed Free-State men, but no one was ever removed or publicly rebuked by his superiors for such slight misdemeanors.

    The *Tribune*'s particular reference was to the appointments made by President Buchanan for Kansas posts on April 1: John W. Whitfield and Daniel Woodson as register and receiver of the Delaware Land District, at Doniphan; Fred. Emory as register of the Western Land District, at Ogden; and Epaphroditus Ransom as receiver of the Osage Land District, at Fort Scott (*New York Daily Tribune*, April 6, 1857, p. 4; Daniel Webster Wilder, *The Annals of Kansas... New Edition. 1541-1885* [Topeka, Kans., 1886], p. 160).
2. The new secretary of Kansas Territory, Frederick Perry Stanton (1814-1894), was appointed by President Buchanan on March 26, 1857, and took the oath of office on April 2. At the time of his appointment he was practicing law in Washington, D.C., after serving for a decade as a congressman from Tennessee. He had been a strong advocate of the rights of the South during the congressional debates over the Compromise of 1850, but during the debate on the Kansas-Nebraska Bill had expressed the view that it offered no practical advantage to the South, since slavery could not exist in either territory (*DAB*; D. W. Wilder, *Annals of Kansas*, pp. 159, 160).
3. John W. Geary (1819-1873) had been appointed governor of Kansas Territory by President

Franklin Pierce in September 1856. He quickly put an end to the violence of armed bands that had kept the territory in turmoil since the previous spring. In December, however, he antagonized the proslavery territorial officials and legislature by urging them to repeal the most proscriptive of their laws inhibiting freedom of speech and press, and by vetoing a bill that would have put the state-making process securely in the hands of the proslavery faction. By February, Geary had become increasingly concerned about threats of violence made against him by proslavery partisans, but when he asked the commander of federal troops at Fort Leavenworth for two companies of dragoons for protection, the general refused his request. Frustrated by lack of administration support and fearful for his own safety, Geary submitted his resignation on March 4 (to take effect March 20) and soon left Kansas for the East (*DAB*; D. W. Wilder, *Annals of Kansas*, p. 156).

4. The new governor of Kansas Territory, appointed by President Buchanan on March 26, was Pennsylvania-born Robert J. Walker (1801–1869), one of the major figures in the Democratic party. He was connected by marriage to the leading families of Pennsylvania, but his brilliant economic and political career was based in Mississippi, where he had moved in 1826. He engaged in extensive land speculations and railroad and mining promotion and served as U.S. senator from Mississippi from 1836 until his appointment as secretary of the treasury by James K. Polk in 1845. He supported James Buchanan for the presidency in 1856, but Southern opposition prevented him from securing the post of secretary of state. He accepted the offer of the governorship of Kansas, after some hesitation, because of his party's need for a man of standing in that post who could keep the Democratic party united at the same time that he resolved the controversies raging in the territory.

For several years Walker had been the most active business promoter of a southern transcontinental railroad line. In 1852 he secured a charter from the New York legislature for the Atlantic & Pacific Railroad Company, authorizing the issuance of a hundred million dollars in capital stock. To encourage other investors, Walker subscribed for ten million dollars of stock. At the same time, he engaged in negotiations with the Mexican government for a right of way across northern Sonora state. Those efforts were superseded by the Gadsden Purchase of 1853. In 1853 the Texas legislature created a charter for construction of the Texas section of a transcontinental railroad, to be called the Mississippi and Texas Railroad. In 1854 Governor Elisha Pease awarded Walker and his associates the contract for constructing the road, but in November of that year the governor refused to accept the stocks offered by Walker's group as the $300,000 deposit required by the state before construction could begin. In the meantime, Walker's adversaries within the Atlantic & Pacific had exposed the precariousness of the finances of that corporation and further weakened his position. Always resourceful, Walker then subsumed the virtually defunct Atlantic & Pacific under the charter of another Texas railroad he had acquired, the Texas Western (*DAB*; James P. Shenton, *Robert John Walker: A Politician from Jackson to Lincoln* [New York and London, 1961], pp. 129–33; St. Clair G. Reed, *A History of Texas Railroads, and of Transportation Conditions under Spain and Mexico and the Republic and the State* [Houston, Tex., 1941], pp. 98–101; Robert R. Russel, *Improvement of Communications with the Pacific Coast as an Issue in American Politics, 1783–1864* [Cedar Rapids, Iowa, 1948], pp. 96–97, 128–29).

5. In his letter accepting his appointment as governor of Kansas Territory, Walker declared "that the actual *bona fide* residents of the Territory, by a fair and regular vote, unaffected by fraud or violence, must be permitted, in adopting their State Constitution, to decide for themselves what shall be their social institutions" (*New York Daily Tribune*, April 1, 1857, p. 5).

6. Olmsted must have had in mind two different groups of free-state settlers who were imprisoned during 1856. The first consisted of seven men arrested in May after a grand jury issued indictments of treason against the leaders of the free-state movement. Those imprisoned were the free-state "governor," Charles Robinson, arrested in Lexington, Missouri, on May 10; George W. Brown, editor of the *Herald of Freedom*, and Gaius Jenkins, arrested on May 14; George W. Smith and George W. Deitzler, arrested in Lawrence on May 21; and John Brown, Jr., and Henry H. Williams, arrested on May 31. Brown and Williams were members of a free-state militia group, the Potawatomie Rifles, that had marched to support the town of Lawrence against the federal marshal and his posse on May 21, and were therefore accused of treasonable resistance to the territorial government. All of these men were held in prison until September, at which time they were freed on bail.

A much larger group of free-state men was arrested as the result of Governor

Geary's pacification of Kansas. On September 11, in his inaugural address, Geary ordered that armed groups disband or leave the territory. Two days later, at Hickory Point, Jefferson County, a free-state group from Lawrence attacked an entrenched proslavery band that had recently attacked the free-state settlement of Grasshopper Falls and was expected soon to join with other bodies of proslavery guerillas that were, despite Geary's proclamation, moving against Lawrence. In the Hickory Point encounter, one proslavery man was killed. Immediately after the fight, 101 men of the free-state force were arrested by federal troops, while no proslavery men were taken. Judge Sterling G. Cato of the territorial supreme court then indicted all 101 men on a charge of first-degree murder and refused them bail. Their situation was graphically set forth in a letter signed by 98 free-state prisoners, dated October 19, that was published in the *New York Daily Tribune* of November 3, 1856, on the eve of the presidential election. The prisoners stated that one of their number, William Bowles, had died after being refused medical treatment by all the doctors in the proslavery town of Lecompton to whom they had appealed for assistance. A large portion of the prisoners' statement was quoted by T. H. Gladstone in *Englishman in Kansas*. A number of the Hickory Point prisoners were freed after their trial in late October, but at least nineteen received five-year sentences for manslaughter (D. W. Wilder, *Annals of Kansas*, pp. 118-23, 136-37; James C. Malin, *John Brown and the Legend of Fifty-Six* [Philadelphia, 1942], pp. 25-26, 183-85; T. W. Gladstone, *Englishman in Kansas*, pp. 311-15; "Voices from the Political Prisons of Kansas," *New York Daily Tribune*, Nov. 3, 1856, p. 6; John H. Gihon, *Geary and Kansas. Governor Geary's Administration in Kansas. With a Complete History of the Territory. Until June 1857 . . .* [1857; rpt. ed., Freeport, N.Y., 1971], pp. 140-47).

7. Even during the period of Geary's pacification of Kansas, few proslavery men were arrested, and the justices of the territorial supreme court, Sterling G. Cato and Samuel D. Lecompte, consistently released on bail those who were brought before them. The most flagrant example of the judges' determination on this score was Lecompte's treatment of Charles Hays, who was accused of killing a free-state man, David Buffum, near Lecompton on September 16, 1856. Governor Geary visited the dying man and directed Cato to record his statement and his identification of Hays as his murderer. When a grand jury indicted Hays for first-degree murder, Lecompte released him on bail. This action outraged Geary, and he ordered federal marshal I. B. Donalson to rearrest Hays. The marshal refused to do so, and resigned his post rather than carry out the governor's order. Geary then had Hays arrested by an officer of the militia, whereupon Lecompte promptly released him on a writ of *habeas corpus* (D. W. Wilder, *Annals of Kansas*, pp. 138, 143).

8. That is, on February 14, 1857, the proslavery territorial legislature had passed a bill—which governor Geary vetoed and the legislature then passed over his veto—defining the process for holding a constitutional convention and submitting a constitution to Congress in order to gain statehood. The legislature provided that a census of inhabitants should be carried out on March 15 by the county sheriffs—who owed their appointments to the legislature—and their deputies. The sheriffs then were to file lists of qualified voters in the various counties. County commissioners—again, appointees of the legislature—would then choose judges of elections, and on the third Monday in June 1857, the authorized voters would elect members of a constitutional convention to meet at Lecompton in September. The constitution drawn up at that time would be submitted to Congress without being presented to the voters of the territory for approval. The *New York Daily Tribune* of April 6, 1857—clearly an important source for Olmsted's statement—said the following of the procedure leading up to the constitutional convention: "The census is to be taken, the voting lists first made up, then revised, and the districts laid off, and the votes canvassed entirely by the creatures of the bogus Legislature—every one intensely Pro-Slavery. The Free-State men have no voice in the premises from first to last, nor are the Federal officers allowed any real power in the premises" (Allan M. Nevins, *The Emergence of Lincoln*, vol. 1, *Douglas, Buchanan, and Party Chaos, 1857-1859* [New York and London, 1950], pp. 137-38).

9. An editorial in the *New York Daily Tribune* of April 9, 1857, dealt with this issue, pointing out that the Kansas legislature had repealed only two pieces of legislation among the acts it had passed to suppress antislavery agitation: it had repealed a test oath for voters and section 12 of chapter 151 of the territorial laws, "An Act to Punish Offences against Slave Property," which had made it a felony, punishable by a minimum of two years at hard labor, for any free person to make a statement or circulate a written document asserting that persons did not have the right to hold slaves in the territory.

The test oath that the legislature repealed was part of chapter 66, section 11, of the territorial laws, which provided that if the right of a person to vote was challenged, he should take an oath before a judge of election to sustain the Fugitive Slave acts of 1793 and 1850, and also to sustain the Kansas-Nebraska Act, with its specific abrogation of the Missouri Compromise. The legislature left intact, however, its requirement that all territorial legislators and officers take such an oath.

Despite the repeal of these two sections of the territorial laws, as the *Tribune* editorial pointed out, it was still a felony, punishable by a minimum of five years at hard labor, to circulate or help publish any document that was "calculated to produce a disorderly, dangerous, or rebellious disaffection among the slaves in this Territory, or to induce such slaves to escape from the service of their masters, or to resist their authority." The *Tribune* also noted that no person with antislavery beliefs was permitted to be a member of a jury sitting in a case involving a violation of any part of the "Act to Punish Offences against Slave Property" (Kansas Territory, *The Statutes of the Territory of Kansas; Passed at the First Session of the Legislative Assembly, One Thousand Eight Hundred and Fifty-Five...* [St. Louis, Mo., 1855], pp. 332-33, 715-17).

10. Walker made the clearest statement of his "isothermal line" theory of the natural limits of slavery expansion in his inaugural address as territorial governor of Kansas, which he delivered at Lecompton on May 27, 1857:

> There is a law more powerful than the legislation of man, more potent than passion or prejudice, that must ultimately determine the location of slavery in this country; it is the isothermal line, it is the law of the thermometer, of latitude or altitude, regulating climate, labor and production, and as a consequence, profit and loss.... It is this same great climatic law now operating for or against Slavery in Kansas: if, on the elevated plains of Kansas, stretching to the base of the American Alps—the Rocky Mountains—and including their eastern crest, crowned with perpetual snow, from which swoop over her open prairies those chilling blasts, reducing the average range of the thermometer here to a temperature nearly as low as that of New England, should render Slavery unprofitable here, because unsuited to the tropical constitution of the negro race, the law above referred to must ultimately determine that question here, and can no more be controlled by the legislation of man, than any other moral or physical law of the Almighty. (*NYDT*, June 6, 1857, p. 1.)

11. Although Olmsted was not yet ready to join the small group of Northerners who preferred to dissolve the Union rather than submit to the actions of an increasingly proslavery national administration, he is suggesting here that a continuation of the course indicated by unwavering presidential support for the "bogus" proslavery legislature in Kansas and by the Dred Scott decision was unacceptable to him. In this passage he is referring, indirectly, to the Massachusetts Disunion Convention held in Worcester, Massachusetts, in January 1857, and led by William Lloyd Garrison, Wendell Phillips and Thomas Wentworth Higginson. That gathering proposed a national disunion convention, and its supporters soon collected six thousand signatures calling for such a gathering in July 1857 (Tilden G. Edelstein, *Strange Enthusiasm: A Life of Thomas Wentworth Higginson* [New Haven and London, 1968], pp. 199-201).

To Samuel Cabot, Jr.

92 Grand St., New York
29th June 1857, Monday night

My Dear Doctor,

I received your request concerning the German pamphlets too late to attend to the matter before to-morrow.[1]

Please to consider that I am always glad to make myself of service to the Society in such matters, when there is an opportunity here.

The conversation with Colonel Ruggles[2] which Dr. Webb[3] was to report to you has been a cause of a good deal of concern in my mind. I should like to know, as soon as convenient to you, what has passed between you since.

In this conversation the Colonel seemed to take a little different position from that in which we had previously understood him to be standing. His property and the information he had previously given us I consider of comparatively little value, but the moral power of having his name associated with the operations of the Society I consider to be of great importance & I think it probable that he possesses information which in some future juncture would be of the greatest service to us. Chiefly, however, the reflections started by the conversation I had about it with Dr. Webb lead me to a point which I wish we had discussed more fully and with regard to which, now I have fully deliberated upon it, I should be relieved to know that you share my convictions.

I am very strong in the belief that an organization formed for the purpose of speculating in land, by or in connection with machinery for enlisting & facilitating the transit of emigrants, would do nearly every thing which we wish to have done, at least for some time to come, even though those engaged in it were entirely indifferent to the higher purpose of the N.E.E.A. Society. There would probably never be a question of yielding to the wishes of such men as Colonel Ruggles—men I mean whose objects were purely commercial—when it would not be discreet to do so (as far as the public could be informed) for the purpose of abating suspicion or misleading opposition to the purposes *we* should have in view. I want the matter to be so arranged that not only such "National Democrats" as Colonel R., but hot slave-holders in Texas, and especially very conservative merchants in New Orleans, may be made to work with us with all their might.

I have stated the point broadly in hopes that you will let me know how far you agree or differ with me, and also, so far as practicable, how it is likely to be regarded by the Society. I do not mean to ask you to define a plan at all—only to say how far this principle is likely to be regarded when the time comes for forming a plan.

Of course I depend upon convincing the *outside* members that the greatest liberality of dealing with the emigrants will in the end be the truest economy—or, if we do not succeed in convincing them, of coming so near it that they will be overruled by the majority, which I would take care to always have composed of those who will keep the political and benevolent purpose uppermost.

Oblige me, my dear doctor, by writing me fully and frankly on this subject. It is becoming evident to me that if I engage myself in this business at all it will have to be exclusively, with all my heart & strength. The happiness of my life will depend on the movement's being very broadly and deeply successful. I want the preliminary steps to be taken with great care and long-sightedness.

The more I contemplate it, the more momentous does the work we propose to engage in appear to me to be. I fully believe that only adequate wisdom is needed to make the duty we assume to ourselves as eventful as that of the Convention of 1776.

I confess to you I have a dread of Dr. Webb's going through Neosho.[4] His purpose will be sure in some way to leak out (he being known as the Secretary of the Society) and I consider it of the utmost importance that the views of the Society in that direction should not at present be suspected.

At least, if the Society is to operate openly and as, in the case of Kansas, with a hurrah, let it not do so without the fullest consideration, and when it begins, let it do so with a demonstration of real power—but if it is to operate silently by counter-mining the silent enemy, let the silence be absolute—from the beginning, absolute, absolute.

I pray the Doctor to be cautious to the last degree. (over)

My best regards to your wife.

Yours very truly

Fred. Law Olmsted

P.S.

That you may understand the grounds of the plan on which I should wish to work and for which I should be best able to work zealously, I will copy from my reply to the letter I read you from Lord Goderich[5] my remarks on what I deem a misapprehension of his.

> It might be desirable, but it is not at all necessary in my judgment, to accomplish the purpose of establishing a barrier to the progress of Slavery Westward, that the immigrants to the frontier should be persons of trustworthy anti-slavery principles. I believe there is no part of the Slave States, where, if by any means, a sufficiently large number of persons, willing and able to get their living by agricultural labor, could be brought to reside, slave-labor would not very soon be withdrawn, unless as an exceptional luxury with the very rich who had been from childhood accustomed to the service of slaves. But where slave-labor has been long established & all the habits & customs of the people of all classes are inter-woven with it, poor free laborers will seldom enter into competition with the capital & talent which is interested in making the best market for slave labor. * * *.[6] If free-laboring people [however][7] would go to Texas [West] in complete village communities, so as to be independent of employment under slave holders' capital, and of the services of slaves to themselves, neither slaves nor slaveholders would ever come near them. A few such communities once successfully established along the frontier line [of slavery] would without any purpose in the minds of those who composed them, completely prevent the progress of Slavery Westward. Nay, by a law which is every day becoming more clearly established, such communities would, surely, however slowly, move up upon & drive back slavery.

The original is in the New England Emigrant Aid Company Papers, Military Historical Society Collection, Special Collections, Mugar Memorial Library, Boston University, Boston, Massachusetts (hereafter cited as NEEA Co. Papers, BU).

1. Cabot had sought Olmsted's assistance in distributing a pamphlet to German immigrants arriving at Castle Garden in New York harbor. The pamphlet, *Wegweiser für Ansiedler im Territorium Kansas,* was published in May 1857 by the New England Emigrant Aid Company and the Massachusetts State Kansas Committee. The author was Karl Kob, whom the Emigrant Aid Company was about to send to Kansas to found the *Kansas Zeitung* (see FLO to Samuel Cabot, Jr., June 30, 1857, below; Samuel A. Johnson, *The Battle Cry of Freedom: The New England Emigrant Aid Company in the Kansas Crusade* [Lawrence, Kans., 1954], pp. 13–14; Karl Kob to Samuel Cabot, Jr., May 30, 1857, NEEA Co. Papers, BU).
2. Daniel Ruggles (1810–1897), born in Barre, Massachusetts, graduated from West Point in 1833 and was stationed primarily in Wisconsin until 1845, when he was moved to Texas. He fought in the Mexican War and advanced his rank to brevet lieutenant colonel. He was stationed in the Indian Territory from 1849 to 1851, in Texas from 1852 to 1856, and at the time of this letter was serving on courts martial. On May 15, 1857, in a meeting with the executive committee of the New England Emigrant Aid Company, Ruggles had given "an interesting account of certain portions of Texas to which he is desirous of directing immigration." A few days later he sent the committee a communication about purchasing land and founding settlements in Texas.
    During the Civil War, Ruggles fought with the Confederacy, becoming a major general and commander of the Department of the Mississippi in 1863 and commissary-general of prisoners in 1865 (*Appleton's Cyc. Am. Biog.;* George Washington Cullum, *Biographical Register of the Officers and Graduates of the U.S. Military Academy at West Point, N.Y., From Its Establishment, March 16, 1802, to the Army Re-Organization of 1866–67 . . .* , 2 vols. [New York, 1868], 1: 440; U.S. Military Academy, West Point, Association of the Graduates, *Twenty-Eighth Annual Reunion . . .* [Saginaw, Mich., 1897], pp. 88–89; Minutes of the Executive Committee of the New England Emigrant Aid Co., May 15 and 22, 1857, New England Emigrant Aid Co. Papers).
3. Thomas Hopkins Webb (1801–1866), the secretary of the New England Emigrant Aid Company (S. A. Johnson, *Battle Cry of Freedom,* pp. 13–14; *The Biographical Cyclopedia of Representative Men of Rhode Island* [Providence, R.I., 1881], s.v. "Webb, Thomas Hopkins, M.D.").
4. Webb traveled to Kansas in July 1857 and apparently intended to go on to the Indian Territory south of Kansas and perhaps to northern Texas, where the New England Emigrant Aid Company was thinking of buying land. Warnings of the danger of malaria deterred him, however (T. H. Webb to Samuel Cabot, Jr., July 30, 1857, NEEA Co. Papers, BU).
5. George Frederick Samuel Robinson (1827–1909), second viscount Goderich, the son of Frederick John Robinson (1782–1859), first viscount Goderich and first earl of Ripon, who held many important offices and served briefly as prime minister after the death of George Canning in 1827.
    In a letter of May 5, 1857, to Olmsted, Lord Goderich offered three reasons for his decision not to assist in the proposed attempt to secure emigrants from England for the settlement of West Texas. First, such settlers would be in danger of harassment from proslavery men like the Missouri "border ruffians in Kansas"; second, few English farmers were then seeking to emigrate, and most potential emigrants were "Town Artisans & labourers without capital." Additional capital would be necessary, and since it could come only from dedicated opponents of slavery, it would be necessary to make public the true purpose of the movement—that is, to stem the westward spread of slavery by means of a barrier of free-soil settlements; third, and this appears to be the "misapprehension" that Olmsted sought to dispel in his reply to Goderich, there was the danger that unless English emigrants were carefully chosen for their antislavery views, they might become proslavery once they reached Texas. Goderich explained his view as follows: "I am sorry to say that I am convinced that a careful selection of the Emigrants would be necessary in order to secure their being really friends to free labour, when they were settled in their new country," he wrote Olmsted,

> as I fear that many Englishmen would have no objection whatever to "keep their own nigger," any more than your countrymen. In this opinion those whom I have consulted also agree, indeed the idea was first suggested to me by a friend; & if it be true, as I cannot doubt it is, the fact constitutes the strongest objection to any attempt at sending out emigrants

from hence. If they joined the Southerners, they would be greatly worse than useless, and if, by careful selection, security were taken against that danger, there would be most serious risk that harm rather than good would still be done to the cause we are anxious to promote; as, if the notion once got abroad in the United States that a reinforcement of picked Englishmen were being sent out to aid the Free State Party in occupying Texas, it would surely raise a storm throughout your country, dangerous to the friendly relations of the two nations, and highly injurious to the Free State Party itself. (Lord Goderich to FLO, May 5, 1857; see also *DNB*.)

6. At this point Olmsted uses asterisks to indicate that he has left out a portion of his letter to Lord Goderich.
7. The bracketed words in this part of the quotation were presumably added by Olmsted in his letter to Cabot in order to clarify the meaning of what he had written to Goderich.

To SAMUEL CABOT, JR.

From the office of the Evening Post
Tuesday P. M., June 30th 1857

Dear Sir,

I find that no distribution of circulars or pamphlets is allowed at Castle Garden.[1] It is possible however that I may succeed by some subterfuge or round-about method in accomplishing it.

Mr. Kapp,[2] the President of the German Republican Association has promised to see Mr. Garrigue, President of the German Society and Commissioner of Emigration,[3] and I shall trust to their judgment to affect the best distribution.

With regard to the number, to be used here, it strikes me that 1000 is much too small a quantity for a free general distribution, and too large for a private, personal distribution. I will send you 2000, however, and advise further after hearing from Mr. Garrigue.

I am yet not able to ascertain satisfactorily about the navigable quality of the Red River above the raft.[4] Land travel for our district nearly always commences I suspect from Port Caddo.[5] The passage once made through the raft has closed again.

A most attractive account of the upper region, & the most particular, I have found, is in "DeBow's Resources." *"Texas–Red River."*[6]

Yours very truly,

Fred. Law Olmsted

The original letter is in the New England Emigrant Aid Company Papers, Boston University.

1. Castle Garden, near the Battery on Manhattan, was the disembarkation point for immigrants entering the United States via the harbor of New York.

2. Friedrich Kapp.
3. Rudolph Garrigue, president of the *Deutsches Gesellschaft der Stadt New York* and ex-officio member of the New York State Board of Commissioners of Emigration (Robert Ernst, *Immigrant Life in New York City, 1825–1863* [New York, 1949], p. 29; *Jahres-Bericht der Deutschen Gesellschaft der Stadt New-York, Erstattet vom Berwaltungsrath am 22 Februar 1856* [New York, 1856]).
4. The Red River raft was a two-hundred-mile stretch of the river in which a series of dams had been formed by trees washed downstream. The raft flooded the nearby country and blocked access to the thousand miles of navigable river upstream. It began above Natchitoches, Louisiana. A channel was cleared through the length of the raft under the direction of Henry Shreve between 1833 and 1838, but efforts to clear out the raft permanently met with constant frustration. By the early 1850s, clearing efforts were concentrated on keeping a narrow channel open through the raft. It was not until 1880 that the raft was cleared out and the river was opened permanently for navigation (Florence L. Dorsey, ... *Master of the Mississippi: Henry Shreve and the Conquest of the Mississippi* [Boston, 1941], pp. 164–78, 194–203; Henry Sinclaire Drago, *Red River Valley: The Mainstream of Frontier History from the Louisiana Bayous to the Texas Panhandle* [New York, 1962], pp. 96–108).
5. Port Caddo, Texas, on Lake Caddo, thirty miles northwest of Shreveport, Louisiana (*JT*, map facing p. 42).
6. James D. B. DeBow, *The Industrial Resources, Statistics, &c. of the United States, and More Particularly of the Southern and Western States,* 3d ed., 3 vols. (1854; rpt. ed., New York, 1966), 3: 338–40.

To Samuel Cabot, Jr.

92 Grand Street
July 4th, 1857

My Dear Doctor

I have just received your favor of July 2d.

"A good plan of action in a matured form" implies fuller knowledge and consideration than is yet possible. I have written in various directions for information and in about a month's time, I shall be glad, if you will allow me, to propose a plan for provisional movements at least.

Mr. Dresel,[1] one of the few determined, avowed and laboring freesoilers of Western Texas has been here this week and I have had much conversation with him. Two successive bad crops—entire failures—a recurrence of Indian troubles, robberies and murders, an increased and more general ruffianism and barbarism on the part of the Americans, the total cessation of immigration of Germans, the increasing demoralization of those resident and the entire abandonment of hope of a free state, are exceedingly discouraging circumstances.[2] On the other hand, however, it is to be considered that the crop-failures have damaged the Slave-holders as much as the Germans, that there has been very little American immigration, and that the landowners have been greatly disappointed and are now in a condition of mind to resort to expedients they would have scorned a few years ago, or to sell at low prices. And that there seems to have been some reaction among thinking men from that fanaticism which effected the expulsion of Douai.

I think we should now find the large majority of Germans against us in any movement which was suspected to have a free state as one of its objects, because they consider the last movement in that interest to have been ill-judged and harmful to them, they have made up their minds to Slavery, consider a free state utopian, & desire to make the best of what is inevitable;—I mean that we should, if such a purpose was suspected at the outset, have their opposition to it. Secretly and at heart it may be understood that all Germans are opposed to slavery.[3] It is more their natural character, than of any other people in the world—not by any means excepting the English.

These things I am inclined to consider essential to forming a free-state in Western Texas. An organization for land-speculation and the collection and assistance (by means of agents in Europe) of emigrants or colonists, with a cash capital at the outset of not less than $100,000. 2d, that this organization has not the aim to make a free state, but merely a community of freemen. 3rd, the co-operation, cordially, fully and extensively, of certain large landowners in Texas who are probably *at present* pro-slavery partisans.

If the charter under which the organization operated could be granted by the Texas or the Louisiana legislature and the head quarters of the Company appear to be, not at New York as you suggest, but at New Orleans or San Antonio, I should consider its power for good certain to be three times as great as would otherwise be the case.

These questions, however, are for the future. The Red River project is one which requires to be defined to a certain extent, more immediately.

Assuming that the pro-slavery party expect ever to make a slave-state West of Arkansas and between Kansas & Red River, it may be reckoned upon with confidence that they will take the earliest possible opportunity to throw that country open to settlement. For the following reasons: An extensive movement of Slaveholders & slaves is certain to take place from Missouri during the next two years. This movement will most naturally and cheaply take a Southwesterly course; i.e. into Neosho, if that territory is open to it. If the organization of that territory is delayed two years, this emigration will not only have passed by & be lost, but Missouri will have become much more practicable for emigrants to cross from the free-states—both on account of the retreat or the defection of the resident ruffians and by the progress of rail-roads and free-state settlers on routes leading across Missouri towards Neosho. Secondly, because every month's delay increases the free-soil force on the Northern border of Neosho—Kansas—and sets free the men and the capital which have together conquered Kansas to freedom.

For these reasons, and because also of the very clear intimations of Governor Walker & because I see in various quarters indirect efforts to prepare the public mind for it, I think it may be considered to have been determined on the part of the administration to throw open Neosho as soon as practicable to slave-holding settlement.[4] (It must be our congressional policy to postpone it as long as possible and to insist on Squatter Sovereignty & that as well guarded as possible when it must come. It must be fought off till next spring at any rate, that the Southerners do not have the advantage of the open Red River entrance, when the Missouri & Ohio are closed to us).

If Neosho is to open to settlement on preemption,[5] next summer, is it possible to secure it for freedom? Is it worth while to undertake to do so by organized emigration?

These questions I do not feel able to answer with confidence at present, but there are two points upon which I have made up my mind.

1st. If it is to be done, the bulk of emigration to be relied upon must be composed of Germans and not of New Englanders. New England and all the East has been pretty severely dragged for emigrants lately. A reaction to the emigration furore is probable. Stimulating emigration from New England is going to be unpopular with our conservative & rich & patriotic old gentlemen and old women—ministers, doctors & lawyers especially. Better keep these on our side.

German settlers for Neosho must be composed in about equal measure of those who have had some experience in the country & of newcomers. One Yankee to five Germans will be sufficient to give the latter courage and unity to oppose Slavery actively, with arms, should arms become necessary.

2dly. If at any time in the next ten years, Neosho should become a free-state, it will very soon be the most profitable field of free-labor in the union. I should like what I say to be remembered—though anyone who looks at the map, seeing its waters, it relations to the East, West and South, and considers the advantages of its climate, the variety of its productions, which is to be immensely greater than that either of Kansas or Texas, the variety, extent and accessibility of the mineral resources which the most superficial observations have already disclosed, any one must at once perceive that no free state or territory has half the attractiveness which it would possess. It has every advantage of Kansas with the addition of much more navigable and mill-power water, better soils,[6] more wood, & more mineral wealth, more valuable forage, and a climate, which while equally healthy, permits the growth of cotton and figs and almonds and pecan nuts & olives, is acceptable to camels, cashmere goats, alpacas & Llamas (as our own & the Kansas climate is not), and (in the South), allows sheep, horses & neat-stock to be reared with no more than three weeks' winter foddering or shelter being required for their perfect health and improvement.

If Neosho should become a free state there will be some large towns in it: probably one or two of the largest interior towns on the Continent. These will be the market towns not only of Neosho but of the great Continental pastoral region lying west of the 100° of longitude. One of these towns will be on the Arkansas. Another or others on the Red River or its tributaries, probably.

FREE-SOIL CRUSADE: 1857

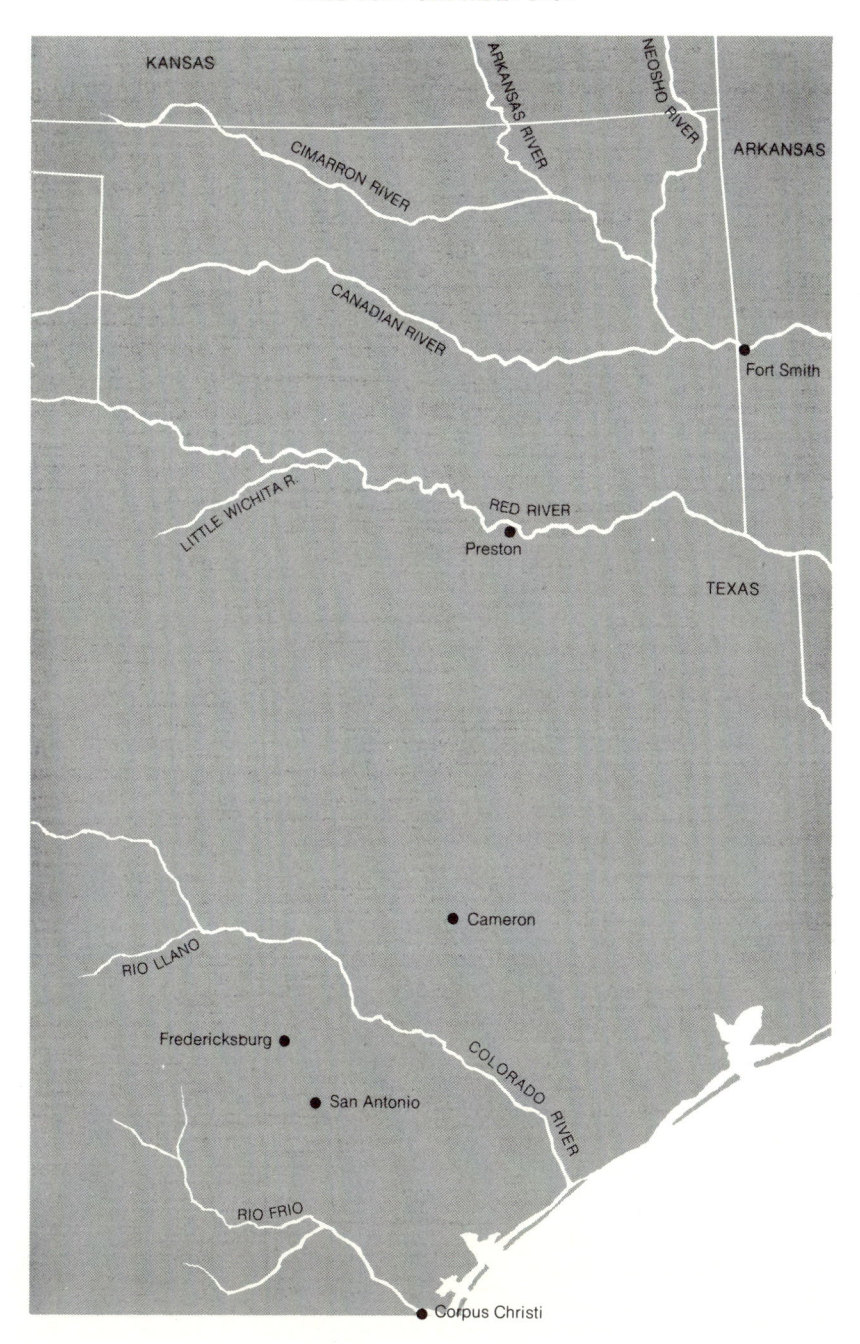

FREE-SOIL TEXAS AND NEOSHO

If Neosho becomes a free state, Northern, & especially Northwestern, Texas will not be a regular Slave-holding community. That part of Northern Texas lying to the west of the counties at present occupied by Slave-holders is not likely in the event of Neosho's becoming a free state, to be settled upon by them: it is likely to be attractive to free-laborers and to capital.[7] Land can not be bought at present in Neosho, but land can be bought in that part of Texas referred to, and at very low prices, as low perhaps as 30 cents an acre. It is not possible to settle free soilers in Neosho at present, but it is possible to settle them in that part of Texas on the opposite side of the river. If Neosho becomes a free state it is certain to have intimate & important commercial relations with Western Texas. An important town in that vicinity is likely to be established—and even if Texas adjoining remains a Slave State, as likely to grow on her side [of] the river as the other (vide Louisville & St. Louis & their rivals New Albany and _____). Consequently here is a good place to speculate.

Also, if we are to fight for Neosho, it will be of great service to have a quiet unobserved post in that South-Western quarter. It may also be of great value to have established an entrance for emigration by Red River before that object is suspected.

Suppose that land can be bought here at 50 cents an acre, that 20,000 acres should be bought; 2,000 reserved for town lots, alternate lots to be given away to tradesmen, mechanics &c. for a while—9,000 acres to be offered to colonists in Germany in farms of say 100 acres each, at $1.00 an acre payable in five years after occupation, with interest at __ per cent, payable annually after the first year, with mortgage security on the farms and improvements; 1,000 acres to be given to old, free soil, experienced, German, Texan frontiersmen & frontier farmers; 1,000 to Yankee farmers (from Kansas), $5,000 to $10,000 [to] be expended in mills, cotton-gins, school-houses &c. & in payment of agents, advertising in Germany &c. Within a year I think there would be established a colony of 500 souls, the foundation of a town made and the speculators would have some 1,900 acres of "town lots," 7,000 acres of agricultural land still to dispose of to new-comers, and notes safe for $9,000—mills, school-houses &c. Capital invested so far $20,000.

It is the opinion of Mr. Dresel that land in the part of Texas towards which we are looking has not yet been taken up; if it has not, it may be bought at 25 cents an acre (& certain fees)—that being the value of Texas landwarrants, of which the Rail Roads will have plenty to be disposed next winter.

Of the value of the town lots & farm-lots you are better able, from your Kansas observation, to judge than I am. 500 Germans however never fail to draw 500 after them & no frontier farmer was ever long satisfied to own no more than 100 acres around his "improvements."

This suggestively with reference to the Land Trust Company.

The fact that you state with reference to the navigable condition of upper Red River was mentioned by me to Dr. Webb.[8] I have written to a cotton merchant at New Orleans and to the Post Master at Preston to ascertain what may be depended upon.

I have written to the Cotton Supply Associations of Liverpool and Manchester and engaged Mr. W. Neill,[9] who sails next Wednesday to urge the subject on their attention. Mr. N. is a cotton merchant. I have also written fully to Lord Goderich requesting his influence with these associations to be used to favor our scheme. I should be glad to see Mr. Padelford[10] & could probably supply him with some important facts & arguments.

Yours Very Truly

Fred. Law Olmsted

The original is in the possession of Phillip Rutherford. The letter of Cabot to Olmsted of July 2, 1857, to which this letter is a reply, has not survived, but it presumably contained a request by Cabot that Olmsted propose "a good plan of action in a matured form" for a scheme of creating a free-soil colony in northern Texas. Olmsted had already discussed the idea with members of the executive committee of the New England Emigrant Aid Company. He had visited Boston sometime between mid-May and mid-June, and on June 19 the executive committee had authorized the "Texas Committee" of Samuel Cabot, Jr., Thomas H. Webb and Martin Brimmer to employ Olmsted and others to gather advice and help to select land for purchase.

The Emigrant Aid Company responded quickly to the plan that Olmsted outlined in this letter. On July 8, Charles J. Higginson reported to Samuel Cabot, Jr., that he had talked with Charles G. Nazro, president of the Boston Kansas Company, which had been chartered in March 1857, and of which Higginson was one of twelve directors. That company had $10,000 to invest, and Higginson asked Cabot: "Why might not Olmsted's scheme for a settlement on the Southern border of the Indian Territory be proposed to them?" Since the Emigrant Aid Company could not expect to have funds available for a Texas venture for several months, Higginson suggested that the Emigrant Aid Company propose to the Boston Kansas Company that when Olmsted went to Texas he should invest from five to six thousand dollars of their money in land and the rest in a mill or other "improvement." To engage their interest, he proposed to read to them Olmsted's letter of July 4, 1857, to Samuel Cabot, Jr., beginning with "Suppose that land can be bought here at 50 cents an acre" (page 440 above). Higginson then proposed various ways that the two groups could merge their interests in the project once the New England Emigrant Aid Company began to use its own funds: the Boston Kansas Company could transfer to the Emigrant Aid Company one quarter of its interest in Texas property, it could repay the Emigrant Aid Company up to $2500 for expenses incurred in fostering the undertaking, or it could turn the whole property over to the Emigrant Aid Company and receive stock for the whole amount expended. "If it seems as if we were working too cheaply," Higginson concluded, "having perhaps none of the profit, it must be remembered that quick action is, according to Olmsted & Douai, a great element of profit, & that we cannot act now, having no money, & besides, Olmstead & all of us will be learning a good deal in the course of the year & shall be able to judge whether to strike, with new funds or those released from Kanzas, to the North or South of this proposed settlement" (C. J. Higginson to Samuel Cabot, Jr., July 8, 1857, in the possession of Phillip Rutherford; FLO to Samuel Cabot, Jr., Sept. 14, 1857, below; *The Act of Incorporation and By-Laws of the Boston Kansas Company, Boston, Mass.* [Boston, 1857], pp. 3-6, in Baker Library, Harvard Business School, Cambridge, Mass.; "Charles G. Nazro," *Boston Transcript*, July 8, 1895; Minutes of the Executive Committee of the New England Emigrant Aid Co., June 19, 1857, New England Emigrant Aid Co. Papers).

1. Probably Julius Dresel (1816-1891?) of Sisterdale. His liberal political views and activities caused him to leave Germany in late 1848, and he was presumably a member of the *Freie Verein* of Sisterdale, which issued the call for the meeting in San Antonio in May 1854 of the state convention of Germans that drew up the radical San Antonio platform (Rudolph L. Biesele, "The Texas State Convention of Germans in 1854," *Southwestern Historical Quarterly*

33, no. 4 [April 1930]: 247–55; Gustav Dresel, *Dresel's Houston Journal: Adventures in North America and Texas 1837–1841, Translated from a German Manuscript and Edited by Max Freund* [Austin, Tex., 1954], pp. xxv–xxvi; *An Illustrated History of Sonoma County, California*... [Chicago, 1889], pp. 506–7; "Appeal for Funds for the *San Antonio Zeitung,*" n. 3, p. 317 above).

2. The extent of Olmsted's discouragement about securing German assistance for the free-soil movement in Texas is indicated by a passage in an installment of his "Southerners at Home" series in the *New York Daily Tribune* that he wrote at about this time:

> I am sorry to say that, since the outbreak of the Know-Nothing pestilence, which was extremely rancorous in Texas, the German immigration has almost entirely ceased; and the discouragement of two failures of crops leaves little reason to expect its revival. The country will soon probably be occupied by the slave labor withdrawing from Missouri, and the German population, dispirited and dispersed, lose all its respectable qualities. A slaveholding country cannot support towns, and without towns or village communities the maintenance of varied, intelligent industry is impossible. The Germans will relapse to boors or progress to ruffians. ("The Southerners at Home" no. 6, *New York Daily Tribune,* July 11, 1857.)

3. An agent for the New England Emigrant Aid Company who toured Texas in early 1858 and visited Olmsted's friends in San Antonio found that, as Olmsted asserts, the Germans there were secretly and at heart opposed to slavery. "I find O. has not at all exaggerated," he reported to Cabot. "They were silenced but not convinced" ([H.R.S.] to "My Dear Friend" [Samuel Cabot, Jr.], March 9, 1858, NEEA Co. Papers, BU).

4. Olmsted had a suspicion, apparently shared by the leaders of the New England Emigrant Aid Company, that Robert J. Walker, whom President Buchanan had appointed as territorial governor of Kansas in March 1857, intended to work for the creation of a slaveholding state in the Indian Territory south of Kansas. In his letters to Cabot, Olmsted called this area "Neosho"—meaning not only the valley of the Neosho River in the eastern part of the Indian Territory, but the whole region between Kansas and Texas (A. M. Nevins, *The Emergence of Lincoln,* 1: 145).

The "very clear intimations" by Walker that Olmsted refers to were probably the references to the Indian Territory in his inaugural address, delivered at Lecompton, Kansas Territory, on May 27, 1857:

> Upon the south Kansas is bounded by the great southwestern Indian territory. This is one of the most salubrious and fertile portions of this continent. It is a great cotton growing region, admirably adapted by soil and climate for the products of the South, embracing the valleys of the Arkansas and Red River, adjoining Texas on the south and west, and Arkansas on the east, and it ought speedily to become a State of the American Union.... It is essential to the true interests, not only of Kansas, but Louisiana, Texas and Arkansas, Iowa and Missouri, and the whole region west of the Mississippi, that this coterminous Southwestern Indian Territory should speedily become a State, not only to supply us with cotton and receive our products in return, but as occupying the area over which that portion of our railroads should run, which connect us with New Orleans and Galveston, and by the Southern route to the Pacific. From her central position, through or connected with Kansas, must run the Central, Northern and Southern routes to the Pacific, and with the latter, as well as with the Gulf, the connection can only be secured by the Southwestern Territory becoming a State, and to this Kansas should direct her earnest attention, as essential to her prosperity. (*NYDT,* June 6, 1857, p. 1.)

5. The Preemption Act of 1841 permitted a squatter to take up public land before it was surveyed, and to purchase 160 acres at the minimum price of $1.25 an acre before public auctions for the area were held.

6. Here Olmsted appended a footnote citing a description by Randolph Barnes Marcy of the country along the road that he opened in 1849 between Fort Smith, Arkansas, and Sante Fe. The road ran westward through heavy timber for 180 miles before emerging onto the plains (U.S., War Department, ... *Exploration of the Red River of Louisiana, in the Year 1852; by Randolph B. Marcy, Captain Fifth Infantry U.S. Army*..., H.R. Exec. Doc., 33d Cong., 1st sess., 1853–54, p. 111).

7. Here Olmsted appended a footnote citing Marcy's description of the country along a road running

west from Fulton, Arkansas, on the Red River, to the Rio Grande, and passages by J. D. B. DeBow on the suitability of west Texas to wool-growing and on the fertility of the Red River valley (ibid., pp. 113-14; J. D. B. DeBow, *Industrial Resources,* 3: 338, 340).
8. Thomas H. Webb, secretary of the New England Emigrant Aid Company.
9. William Neill (b. c. 1823), brother-in-law of Charles Loring Brace and senior member of the cotton mercantile firm of Neill Brothers & Company, which he and his brother Henry established in New York and Mobile in c. 1856. By 1857 Henry had moved to London and established the firm's main office there (*New Orleans Times-Democrat,* Sept. 13, 1906, p. 5; *New Orleans Picayune,* Sept. 13, 1906, p. 7).
10. Seth Padelford (1807-1878) of Providence, Rhode Island, a vice-president of the New England Emigrant Aid Company who was about to go to England and intended to work while there to increase British interest in supporting free-labor colonization in Texas (*The Biographical Cyclopedia of Representative Men of Rhode Island,* s.v. "Padelford, Seth"; FLO to Samuel Cabot, Jr., July 26, 1857, n. 1, below).

To the Secretaries of the Cotton Supply Associations of Manchester And Liverpool[1]

New York, July 6th, 1857.

To the Secretary of the Cotton Supply Association
Sir

My attention having been directed for some years past to the cotton producing regions of the North American Continent, I take leave to present certain views I have formed for the consideration of your association.

Under the stimulus of high prices, valuable contributions of cotton are obtained from various other parts of the world than the United States; measures may be taken by which this auxiliary supply will be much increased. After much research and several costly experiments however, it yet remains very questionable if any where else in the world, an equal value of cotton-wool can be obtained from a given expenditure of labor, as in that part of the North American Continent lying between the thirtieth and the thirty sixth parallels of latitude. No where else are the same meteorological conditions found which here prevail, nor is [it] to be expected that by any exercise of human ingenuity they will be obtained.

The amount of labor engaged in the production of cotton within the region thus favored does not exceed that of one strong man to a square mile. If one half the agricultural population of Europe was transferred to this region it would not be at all densely populated and the laborers would probably be better paid in producing cotton at 1½ d. a pound, than they are at present. An adequate supply of labor only is needed to increase the supply of Cotton from North America, tenfold. It is for the interest of those whose capital is invested in Slaves that the impression should prevail that the cultivation of cotton is impracticable by means of any other than negro slave labor, a monopoly of supplying which in the United States they enjoy. After extended and exact inquiry, having spent a summer in the cotton districts for the purpose, I am certain that this is not the case. There are exceptional, malarious and pestilential regions but in the largest part of the present Cotton producing region of the United States the labor of men of the English or Teutonic races will produce more cotton, man for man, in a life time, than of those of the African race.

I would suggest to your association therefore, that inquiry be made with regard to the practicability of increasing the supply of cotton by inducing free laborers to engage in its cultivation in the South Western territories of the United States. There are here vast tracts of suitable soil, as yet unoccupied by planters, and in which the political and social circumstances that prevent the introduction of free laborers elsewhere exist, if at all, in a very limited degree.

Three years ago the Governor of the State of Texas[2] told me that the cotton crop of the United States might be doubled on the land as yet unoccupied in that state alone. There are millions of acres of this land in the vicinity of which Slavery does not exist in a form to prevent their occupation by free labor. There is nothing in the laws, nor, under discreet direction, need there be anything in the prejudices of the people, to prevent free settlers occupying this land. Large tracts of it can be procured at from two to six shillings (sterling) an acre. If a large free emigration were directed to them they would rapidly increase in value several hundred per cent. This increase in value would prevent the subsequent immigration of Slave-holders upon them. In Comal County in Texas within the last ten years, three thousand Germans have settled. Since they have been well established as a community, no slave proprietor has settled among them and such as were previously settled in the vicinity have been induced to employ free-laborers in occupations for which they would otherwise have purchased more Slaves. The Germans were thus engaged in the cultivation of cotton, and in one year, they produced, without previous experience or the usual conveniences, 800 bales, which I was informed, by the Merchant who purchased it, was superior in quality to any slave grown cotton he had ever seen.

Some further information on this subject may be gathered from my narrative of a Journey in Texas, a copy of which I take leave to send you by my friend Mr. William Neill of the house of Neill Brothers and Company, Cotton Merchants, to whom I have also communicated more fully my views of the measures which might be taken to increase the supply of cotton from the United States.

If your association should be disposed to prosecute the enquiry I have suggested I would gladly give any assistance in my power—coming to England for the purpose, if it should be thought desirable. I have recently seen two of the largest Cotton Spinners of America[3] and am able to give you assurance of an effective co-operation on their part with any judicious movement to direct free laborers to increase cotton production in America. If you should think it well to send an agent to examine the regions available for this purpose, as I would venture to earnestly recommend, it would give me pleasure to accompany him upon the journey, and to assist in obtaining all desirable information. It would be best to leave New York in September, and as most of the country to be examined would have to be traversed on horseback, three months time should be allowed for the journey. The expenses of the tour need not exceed £200, and my personal services would be gratuitous to your association.

It is desirable that this subject should not at present be publicly discussed.

The original of this letter has not been located. The text presented here is that published by Percy W. Bidwell in "The New England Emigrant Aid Company and English Cotton Supply Associations: Letters of Frederick L. Olmsted, 1857." The editors have, however, omitted the frequent and uncharacteristic underlining of words that appears in Bidwell's rendering of Olmsted's letter, and which was probably added later by another hand (*American Historical Review* 23, no. 1 [Oct. 1917]: 115–17).

1. In early 1857 British cotton spinners were apprehensive about finding adequate supplies of cotton to meet the rapidly increasing demand for their products. They had been unable to secure sufficient increase in the production of Indian cotton, and sectional controversy in the United States made them fearful that supplies from the South might soon be disrupted. On April 21, representatives of cotton manufacturing interests met in Manchester to form the Cotton Supply Association. A month later the executive committee of the association met with representatives of the Liverpool Chamber of Commerce and the Liverpool Cotton Brokers' Association, but failed to win the cooperation of either group. The strength of the association remained in Manchester, although it had a handful of supporters in Liverpool (Arthur W. Silver, *Manchester Men and Indian Cotton, 1847–1872* [Manchester, England, 1966], pp. 76–87).
2. Elisha Pease.
3. Probably Amos A. Lawrence (1814–1886), a leading Massachusetts cotton textile manufacturer and merchant and the treasurer and financial mainstay of the New England Emigrant Aid Company, and Patrick Tracy Jackson, Jr. (1818–1891), junior partner in one of the leading cotton-spinning firms of Massachusetts, Charles H. Mills & Company. Jackson's father, Patrick Tracy Jackson (1780–1847), was one of the leading figures in the development of textile manufacturing in the state. Jackson married Charles Loring Brace's first cousin Susan Loring (1823–1895) (*DAB*; Charles Henry Pope and Katharine Peabody Loring, eds., *Loring Genealogy*... [Cambridge, Mass., 1917], pp. 166–68; Edmund Dwight, Jr., to FLO, July 12, 1857; information on Jackson's partnership supplied by John W. Lozier; John Sherman Brace, *Brace Lineage*..., 2d ed. [Bloomsburg, Pa., 1927], p. 104).

To SAMUEL CABOT, JR.

Address: Dr. S. Cabot, Jr.
(N.E.E.A. Society)

New Haven, July 26th, 1857.
(Morris Cove)

Dear Sir

I extremely regret the circumstance which so long delayed my receipt of your letter of 16th July,[1] to which I now reply.

Enclosed I send you a copy of the draft of communication addressed by me on the 6th July, severally, to the Cotton Supply Associations of Manchester, and of Liverpool.[2] These papers were taken out and would be delivered in person to the Secretaries of the associations, by Mr. William Neill, one of our largest Cotton merchants, dealing with Manchester, and the editor of a weekly Cotton circular, much quoted by the English journals. Mr. Neill sail'd from New York on the 8th. You will perceive that my object has been thus far to secure a proper consideration of the subject, and that in these papers I have treated it simply in the Cotton Supply aspect. By the same mail however I addressed letters to individuals, with whom I have had a little correspondence, previously, treating of the political and moral bearings of the project, stating the general principles on which I thought it would be best to proceed; fortifying my suggestions and statements with documents and in two instances—to Lord Goderich M.P. from the West Riding and C. Fowell Buxton M.P.,[3] who has much influence in Manchester—requesting that the proposal of my letters to the Cotton Associations meet with due consideration. I addressed a short note also (continuing a conversation I had last autumn on the agricultural capabilities of the United States) to the editor of the *Times*.[4] Colonel Hamilton,[5] who has the most encouraging view of the project, promised me to write to Lord Stanley[6] and friends at Liverpool by the following steamer's mail.

I trust that what has been thus done (previous to my receiving any intimation that you had thought of soliciting money in England) will have prepared the ground favorably to Mr. Padelford's arrival. It is a most fortunate circumstance that a competent person will be present to meet objections and take advantage of various circumstances in the discussion, if one should occur, in which facts likely to be familiar to Mr. P. will tell happily.

With regard to the proposal to be made by Mr. Padelford, if any, and the information most desirable to be furnished, he will of course be guided by circumstances, but unless met with much greater favor than I can anticipate, I may venture to say that I am confident in the judgment that it would not be best to urge much more at present than careful enquiry, in some such manner as I have done in my letters. We shall find, I apprehend, a strong influence against us in East India and other colonial interests, and also in a narrow patriotism. From Lord Goderich's letter to me, I am sure that the American political relations of the project should be kept out of sight as much as possible in England.[7] The name of the N.E.E. Aid Society should not at present be mentioned, because the Society has a certain political notoriety and English gentlemen will generally feel it to be their duty not to listen to a proposal which seems likely to connect their names with the internal political affairs of [a] foreign government. This is not only somewhat reasonable but with the class represented by the *Times*, it happens now to be a fashion. They may be drawn into it gradually, as they gain knowledge of the true character of the society, perhaps, but the dread of lending their aid even indirectly to what might turn out to be a merely political scheme (in the narrow sense), would be likely to prevent their giving the subject a fair hearing. Everybody knows who has had to do with Englishmen, that it is peculiarly true of them, that it is the first step which costs. The great point at first is to get them to listen. If they will go so far this autumn as to send out an agent to obtain information, I shall feel quite sure of our leading them from that to the most valuable co-operation [...][8]

I enclose papers put into my hands last night by Mr. Kapp[9] which must be used with discretion. I promised to return them in course of the week. They contain offers to sell lands of the choicest unimproved character in the vicinity of the northernmost German settlements of Texas[10] and precisely in the line we wish to occupy and evidently at unusually low prices. I think some encouragement should be offered to the owners, who are Scotchmen—the merchants mentioned in my book at Neu Braunfels, who bought the free labor cotton.[11] I know that they have made their land investments with great care. I have another offer of choice, selected lands in the same region and to the northward of it, 20,000 acres at 90 cents an acre. Another of 2,000 acres same district, selected lots at 50 cents or one half in alternate lots, for nothing, on condition of occupation within three years: another of 2 leagues on the Brazos, Milam County (6,000 acres), $1.50 an acre, another on the Nueces 35 miles north of Corpus Christi, 20,000 acres, in one body, at $1.00 an acre. Large tracts of cotton land can be best got, however, by dealing with the Railroad companies.

I am obliged to close suddenly and will probably write further by next mail.

Yours respectfully,

Fred. Law Olmsted

Olmsted wrote this letter at Morris Cove, near New Haven, Connecticut, where he was writing *Back Country*. The original of the letter has not been located. The text used here, from which at least one section is missing, is that published by Percy W. Bidwell in "The New England Emigrant Aid Company and English Cotton Supply Associations: Letters of Frederick L. Olmsted, 1857." As in the previous letter, the editors have omitted the uncharacteristic underlining of words that appears in Bidwell's published version (*American Historical Review* 23, no. 1 [Oct. 1917]: 115–17).

1. In his letter to Olmsted of July 16, 1857, Cabot reported on a meeting of the Executive Committee of the New England Emigrant Aid Company on July 15 with Seth Padelford, who was about to depart for England. Padelford agreed to do what he could in England to further the Company's plan to promote free-labor cotton culture in Texas. It was agreed that Padelford should present a statement "showing as thoroughly as the facts will allow that a comparatively small outlay of money judiciously applied can be made the means of inducing free-labor to apply itself to the culture of cotton, show that it is better than slave labor, in that field, both because it is *free*, & intelligent, & because it can command a supply of labourers limited only by the labouring population of the Northern States & of Europe." The Executive Committee agreed that Olmsted was the best man to write such a piece, and asked Cabot to approach him about doing so. Cabot also asked Olmsted if he would be able to go to England to promote the cause there, and whether, if he went to England, he could also carry out his plans to go to Texas for the purpose of buying land for settlement by free-labor farmers under the auspices of the New England Emigrant Aid Company. Cabot was confident that the Texas enterprise would soon meet with considerable success. The hoped-for money from England would make it possible for

the process to begin while the Emigrant Aid Company's funds were still tied up in Kansas. "Then in a few months," Cabot wrote,

> we shall have large sums of money set free in Kansas which can be applied to aid in this same object. We shall from the fact (when known) that we are acting, induce a large emigration from Kansas through the confidence which the settlers there feel in our Company & the friendly feeling which they have toward us. At first we must of course act in secret—but, I think when the ball on a hill begins fairly to move, the knowledge that our Company is acting will accelerate the motion and crush out old, rather than rouse new opposition. (Samuel Cabot, Jr., to FLO, July 16, 1857.)

2. FLO to the Secretaries of the Cotton Supply Associations of Manchester and Liverpool, July 8, 1857, above.
3. Charles Fowell Buxton (1823-1871), member of the House of Commons from Newport (*DNB*).
4. John Thadeus Delane (1817-1879), editor of the *Times* of London (ibid.).
5. James Alexander Hamilton (1788-1878) of Dobbs Ferry, New York, lawyer and politician, third son of Alexander Hamilton and father of Eliza Hamilton Schuyler. At the height of his political career he was an intimate of several leading figures in the Democratic party, played an important role as an ally of Martin Van Buren during the formation of Andrew Jackson's cabinet in early 1829 and served three weeks as interim secretary of state in March of that year. In 1840 he changed his allegiance to the Whig party and later became a Republican. He carried on an extensive correspondence with political leaders in the United States, England and Continental Europe. In addition to assisting Olmsted in his free-labor cotton schemes in 1857, he worked during the following year with Charles Loring Brace and others to form the Vine Growers' Association, which promoted the emigration of German viniculturists to Missouri.

    Only a few weeks after he wrote this letter, Olmsted received assistance of another sort from Hamilton. In early September 1857 Hamilton wrote and was the first to sign the most influential of the petitions submitted by Olmsted's friends urging his appointment as superintendent of Central Park. It was the signature of Washington Irving—Hamilton's neighbor and the second man to sign the petition—that in the end secured Olmsted's approval by the park commissioners (ibid.; James A. Hamilton, *Reminiscences of James A. Hamilton; or, Men and Events, At Home and Abroad, During Three Quarters of a Century* [New York, 1869], pp. 421-22; FLO, "Passages in the life of an Unpractical Man," an autobiographical fragment; FLO to CLB, Dec. 1, 1853, n. 16, above).
6. Edward George Geoffrey Smith Stanley (1799-1869), fourteenth earl of Derby (*DNB*).
7. Lord Goderich to FLO, May 5, 1857. Goderich warned that "if the notion once got abroad in the United States that a reinforcement of picked Englishmen were being sent out to aid the Free State Party in occupying Texas, it would surely raise a storm throughout your country, dangerous to the friendly relations of the two nations, and highly injurious to the Free State Party itself. I feel the danger of such a proceeding very strongly" (see FLO to Samuel Cabot, Jr., June 29, 1857, above).
8. At this point Bidwell omitted a portion of the letter. In an explanatory footnote he wrote: "Here follows a criticism of the work of an English traveller, Robert Russell (*North America, its Agriculture and Climate*, Edinburgh, 1857), which Olmsted feared might exert an unfavorable influence on the English attitude toward the colonization scheme. He also sketches his plans for a third volume of the series *Our Slave States*, which appeared in 1860 under the title, *A Journey in the Back Country*." The criticism of Robert Russell that Bidwell deleted was probably similar to the one that Olmsted published in the section of *Back Country* entitled "The Question of Cotton Supply," which he very likely had already written by the time he wrote this letter (P. W. Bidwell, "Letters of Frederick L. Olmsted, 1857," p. 116, n. 5; *BC*, pp. 337-55).
9. Friedrich Kapp.
10. Presumably the German settlements on the Rio Llano, a hundred miles north of San Antonio.
11. See *Journey Through Texas*, page 146.

FREE-SOIL CRUSADE: 1857

To Samuel Cabot, Jr.

New Haven, August 18th /57

My Dear Sir

After dispatching a letter to you yesterday I received yours of 12th.

I wrote to you saying that you could not depend on me, for the purpose of freeing myself from any thing like an engagement to you—or rather that you might not be disappointed hereafter if I should not be able to meet your expectations of me. I have not determined not to go on your business, my heart is in it, but I am under the necessity now, much more than I have been, of making a permanently lucrative disposition of myself. I shall be closely engaged for a month or more to come. My eyes have failed lately & I have lost a fortnight in writing in consequence. So I shall not immediately form determined plans. Probably I shall come to Boston as you wish, to see you early in September.

I at present incline to think that Texas should be considered as a secondary & entirely subordinate field and that all possible capital, study, forecasting & statesmanship, should be given immediately to Neosho. I believe a coup de main will be attempted there and it is better that New-England be depopulated than it succeed. Anything & everything can be suspended, if not sacrificed, to gain that position. I am disposed to think therefore that whatever is done in Texas should be done chiefly with reference to Neosho. The *chief* object of large (general) operations in Texas, at this time should be, to gain the land-interest & revive the German Anti-Slavery party.

The Kansas Zeitung,[1] has been well noticed in the Tribune; I don't know about the German press of New York—will enquire; you can send some copies to Mr. Kapp[2] & I will call on him, & see that [it] is noticed & seconded in the Post & Times.

I hope to hear of your success with the Land T. Comp.[3] soon.
Yours Very Truly

Fred. Law Olmsted.

The original is in the possession of Phillip Rutherford.

1. Publication of the *Kansas Zeitung,* edited by Karl Kob on the initiative and with the support of the New England Emigrant Aid Company, began in Atchison, Kansas, in July 1857 (Karl John Richard Arndt, *German-American Newspapers and Periodicals, 1732–1955: History and Bibliography...* [Heidelberg, 1961], p. 152; Kansas State Historical Society, *Collections of the Kansas State Historical Society,* 17 vols. in 16 [Topeka, Kans., 1881–1928], 1–2 [1875–81]: 181).
2. Friedrich Kapp.
3. For "Land Trust Company" (see FLO to Samuel Cabot, Jr., July 4, 1857, above).

To Samuel Cabot, Jr.

New York, September 14th, 1857

Dr. S. Cabot.
N.E.E. Aid Soc.
My Dear Sir,

  From the tenor of your last communication I infer that it is not probable that your Society would wish me to make the journey in Neosho and Texas at this time, as was proposed in June.

  I have to-day received notification of my appointment to the office of Superintendent of the Central Park of New York, with a request that I would enter upon the duties of the office immediately. I have determined to do so to-morrow and therefore relinquish the intention I have hitherto had to visit you this week.

  It is unnecessary to assure you of the very deep interest I have in the scheme of free colonization, Southward from Kansas. My duties at the park will occupy my time & mind very closely for some time to come, but I wish as far as possible to be allowed to actively co-operate with you in your great work.

  Since I saw you I have taken a good deal of pains to obtain information regarding Neosho, and the result is the highest possible estimate of its attractiveness to Northern settlers. I earnestly advise you to send a judicious person to carefully survey the ground, especially the Southeastern part, from the Arkansas to the Red River, adjoining Arkansas. It is my impression, from a great variety of indications, that no part of the United States ever offered greater natural attractions (as respects productiveness & salubrity) than this part of Neosho. I would urge the importance of early steps in this direction. An expenditure of a great treasure of money and life would be justified to establish firmly a respectable colony of brave and careful New Englanders, South of the Arkansas river near the State line. It is my conviction, however, that if Neosho is thrown open, and it is undertaken to prevent its becoming a slave state, during the next two years, success can only be secured by the aid of a transatlantic organization for directing German emigrants directly thither. I mean the organization of an extensive system of agencies & canvassing—with inducements similar to those offered by the Illinois Central R.R.,[1] and carefully systematized, cheap & comfortable facilities of transit.

  I have been disappointed in the receipt of information from Texas. I believe Dr. Douai has been more fortunate and he will translate for you a letter from Mr. Riotte,[2] of which I can only say the author is deserving of the highest confidence and the warmest sympathy for his personal sacrifices for the principles of free men.

  I enclose a letter giving some important information with regard to Red River. The information with regard to the wheat producing qualities of the soil of Northern Texas, is [*however incredible it may seem,*][3] not to be disregarded. I have received numerous confirmations of it & I am inclined to believe that Southern Neosho & Northern Texas may become the most productive wheat districts *in the world*. There are tolerably authentic statements of 50 bushels of wheat of the heaviest description having been produced here to the acre, with the rudest frontier cultivation. At the same time North *Eastern* Texas & South eastern Neosho have apparently *unequalled* cotton-growing advantages.

I have received a reply to my communication to the Manchester Cotton Association,[4] which I enclose. I also send you a letter from Lord Goderich[5] which I have this day received. I beg for various reasons that your Society will give very early attention to this subject and that you will soon return this letter with some advice about a reply. The matter should not be allowed to drop. A well defined scheme should be presented to our English friends, as soon as practicable, but in the mean time they must not be allowed to lose sight of the importance of the subject both materially & philanthropically. Col. James Hamilton[6] wrote me last week that he contemplated making a trip to Europe soon (in a few weeks, I judge). "Should I do so," he says, "I will certainly employ all the time I may be on the other side to impress influential persons with my views of the advantages of your project. It is a glorious one & if successful would be of infinite service to both countries." Col. H's facilities of reaching influential persons both political & mercantile in England are of the best, & the opportunity should not be lost. If you are ready to do anything or to propose anything definitely, & will write me soon, I will take a day to visit Col. H. at his residence, to consult with him & give him all the information likely to assist his purpose, which I can obtain.

The Kansas Zeitung has been well noticed in the German papers here, & several copies are taken in New York. From what I hear, I infer that it is conducted with remarkable good judgment, and is likely to be very useful.

Be kind enough to show this letter & its enclosures to Dr. Douai, with warm regards.

I shall always esteem it an honor and a favor to be entrusted with any duty for your Society in New York.

Faithfully Yours

Fred. Law Olmsted.

The original is in the possession of Phillip Rutherford.

1. The Illinois Central Railroad used a variety of inducements to promote settlement along its route from Chicago to Cairo, Illinois. It sold land on credit at low interest rates on condition that the purchaser carry out certain improvements during the first six years; thus, by the end of that time, which also marked the time period for payment, one half of the land would be fenced and under cultivation. The Illinois Central also sold whole town sites to promoters at low prices and was the first railroad to attempt to stimulate and direct immigration from Europe by stationing agents there (Paul Wallace Gates, *The Illinois Central Railroad and Its Colonization Work* [Cambridge, Mass., 1934], pp. 130, 159, 188).
2. Charles Riotte.

3. Olmsted drew a line through the words in brackets.
4. Olmsted to the Secretaries of the Cotton Supply Associations of Manchester and Liverpool, July 6, 1857, above.
5. George Frederick Samuel Robinson, second viscount Goderich (see FLO to Samuel Cabot, Jr., June 29, 1857, n. 6, above).
6. James Alexander Hamilton.

To Samuel Cabot, Jr.

92 Grand St., October 22d, 1857.

My Dear Doctor Cabot,

I have begun writing an article which I intend for the "Atlantic Monthly" based on Weston's "Progress of Slavery," which I consider the most respectable book which has been published in my time in the United States. As he has publickly referred to the chances of occupying Neosho by free men, I mean to treat that point frankly, and confidently, and especially advertise the advantages which milder climates offer to emigrants.[1]

Please write me if Dr. Webb[2] has returned & if he brings any further information regarding the country.

Write me also if your Society[3] "still lives," & how you feel & what you expect in Boston—Kansas-ward and politically, if you have time.

I have further letters from England intimating great interest in the Neosho project, but I take it any movement is at present out of the question.

Everything is black & blacker in New York.[4] Slavery has nothing to gain however by the present condition of things.

Yours most cordially

Fred. Law Olmsted.

The original is in the possession of Phillip Rutherford.

1. Olmsted did not publish the article to which he refers here, and no identifiable draft of it has survived. The book that he praises was *The Progress of Slavery in the United States*, by George Melville Weston, which was published in 1857. The reference to Neosho came at the end of the preface of the book and read as follows:

> Unless the acquisition of Cuba shall precipitate a struggle for the possession of that island, it is the opinion of the author, of the soundness of which the reader must judge, that free emigration to warmer climates should be directed to the Southwest, immediately to Missouri and Kansas, but soon to Arkansas, with a view to the Indian territory behind

Arkansas, to New Mexico, and to Northern Texas; and that, when slavery is surrounded upon its southwestern frontier, it will be time enough, and until then utterly useless, for any purpose of extinguishing it, to invade it in Virginia and Kentucky.

That peculiar combination of warmth and moisture required in the production of cotton, is found in large portions of Arkansas, which are now entirely unoccupied, and in the Indian Territory beyond it. The overwhelming preponderance of the white race in Northern Texas, in Arkansas, except immediately on the Mississippi and Red River bottoms, in Southwestern Missouri, and in Kansas, renders it easy to exclude the negro slave from this admirable and extensive cotton region. Free labor is therefore invited to enter upon the cultivation of a great staple of commerce, the profits of which have been so long monopolized by slavery. The production of cotton, now at length made possible for the free agriculturists of the United States, will prove a mine of wealth in their efficient and thrifty hands.

George Melville Weston (1816–1887), like Olmsted, played a role in providing the Republican party with a critique of slavery and slave society. Like Olmsted, he was of seventeenth-century New England stock, his ancestor John Weston having immigrated to the Massachusetts Bay Colony in 1644. His grandfather, Captain Nathan Weston, settled at Augusta, Maine, in the 1780s, after which he represented that town in the Massachusetts General Court and later served in the state senate and executive council. Weston's father, Nathan, was a judge in Maine for thirty years, serving on the state supreme court as an associate justice from the beginning of Maine's statehood in 1820 to 1834 and as chief justice from 1834 to 1841.

George Weston graduated from Bowdoin College in 1834, then studied and practiced law. He was appointed county attorney for Kennebec County in 1839 and 1842, and from 1840 to 1844 edited the *Augusta Age,* the leading Democratic newspaper in the state. Soon after 1844 he moved to Bangor, Maine, where he engaged in business and did editorial work for the *Bangor Democrat.* He was an outspoken critic of the Kansas-Nebraska Bill, and his role in the opposition led to his appointment in 1855 as claims commissioner for the state of Maine in Washington. While holding that post he served for a time as editor of the *Republic,* a daily newspaper created by Francis P. Blair and others to strengthen the influence of former Democrats in the Republican party. The *Republic* was published from 1857 to 1859.

During the years he spent in Washington, Weston published a series of pamphlets concerning the growing sectional crisis. They included *The Poor Whites of the South; The Federal Union. It must be Preserved. No. 1; Southern Slavery Reduces Northern Wages; Will the South Dissolve the Union?;* and *Who Are Sectionalists?*—all published in 1856—and *Disunion—Its Remedy,* a speech published in 1860. In 1857 Weston published his major work on slavery, *The Progress of Slavery in the United States.* In 1862, Weston gained part interest in the *Washington National Republican,* but in 1863, the same year that Olmsted left the U.S. Sanitary Commission to manage the Mariposa Estate in California, Weston sold out his interest in the paper and turned to a business career in land and lumber in Bangor, Maine.

Weston played no role in public affairs during Reconstruction, but in 1876 he wrote a letter to the *Boston Globe* attacking the demonetization of silver that had taken place in 1873–74. The letter attracted widespread attention, and Weston elaborated his views in a series of articles. In 1876 he was appointed secretary of the U.S. Monetary Commission, a post he held until 1879. He wrote many of the papers included in the commission's report. In 1882 Weston published his major work on monetary policy, *Money.* From that year until his death he served as librarian of the U.S. Senate and continued to promote his views on the silver question (James William North, *The History of Augusta, From the Earliest Settlement to the Present Time* ... [Augusta, Me., 1870], pp. 500–505, 952–56; Bowdoin College, *General Catalogue of Bowdoin College, 1794–1916* [Brunswick, Me., 1916], p. 93; Eric Foner, *Free Soil, Free Labor, Free Men: The Ideology of the Republican Party Before the Civil War* [New York, 1970], p. 167; *National Republican,* Feb. 12, 1887, p. 1; *Bangor Daily Whig & Courier,* Feb. 14, 1887, p. 3).
2. Thomas H. Webb, secretary of the New England Emigrant Aid Company, who had traveled to Kansas on business for the company during the summer of 1857 and returned in October (T. H. Webb to Charles J. Higginson, Oct. 12, 1857, NEEA Co. Papers, BU).
3. The New England Emigrant Aid Company.
4. A reference to the effects of the Panic of 1857.

To Samuel Cabot, Jr.

> 92 Grand St.
> New York
> October 27 [1857]

My Dear Dr. Cabot
    I have just received your favor of yesterday and am glad to hear of Dr. Webb's safe return[1] and of your encouragement from Kansas.
    I am satisfied that the movement Westward of European and New England or Atlantic emigrants will be very great next year & probably for some years to come. The advantages in climate etc. are so great that I do not believe it will want a large expenditure to coax it Southward, either towards Arkansas or Texas. For the South to undertake to occupy Neosho next summer is to surrender Missouri, to greatly endanger Arkansas, and to weaken Texas.
    The hard times will make Mr. Buchanan reluctant to recommend the railroad projects which are a necessary part of Walker's Neosho scheme and it is altogether such a hazardous thing to attempt, as the South is situated, that in my opinion, it will be given up for the present. Yet the longer it is postponed, if it is ever to [be] opened to settlement, the better the chances of the North will be. And this they must see.
    Walker's project of slicing off the Southern half of Kansas to add to the Indian territory,[2] I take it will be given up, without doubt, since the election has shown the free soil strength there.[3]
    Have you noticed how weak Arkansas is in Slave population? Less than one to a square mile, or half the proportion to area of Missouri in 1850: and the increase very slow, showing that the natural drift of emigration Neosho-ward is very weak.
    I am very much puzzled to know how to treat the matter in the article intended for the Atlantic Monthly.[4] Mr. Underwood[5] writes me that they can not get it into the December number, and that for the January number it must be ready 1st December—that is before the President's message is out. Between that and January something will have turned up to show the Southern designs, probably, and our policy must be re-shaped to meet them.
    Do you think there would in any case be any harm in showing the strength of Northern emigrating movement and the consequent requirement of the North for Neosho, and the weakness of the South and its inability to make use of Neosho, if it opened to Slavery? At the same time showing the great fertility & attractiveness of Neosho and the consequent probability of a rush thitherward from the North, as soon as it shall be opened?
    Is there any chance of my seeing General Pomeroy[6] here?
    You speak of preparations to settle "the Neosho"—if Walker's project proceeds. I hope you don't mean the Neosho river country merely. That will take care of itself. You should concentrate everything between the Arkansas

and the Red River. One of the first things to be done is to get a clever resident correspondent at Van Buren[7]—a spy and shipping agent. Van Buren is a St. Louis in futuro.

Do you see rumors that the missionaries among the Choctaws are to be expelled or ought to be expelled for their unsoundness on the goose?[8] Trusty men can probably be found among the missionaries from whom important information, if not secret assistance, can be obtained.

Excuse these abrupt suggestions. I am extremely occupied.

With best regards to Dr. Webb—to whom I should be gratified, if he could find time to write a little of any new facts he got about Neosho.

I am, my dear doctor,
yours most cordially

Fred. Law Olmsted

The original is in the possession of Phillip Rutherford.

1. Thomas H. Webb, who had been in Kansas.
2. The editors have found no evidence of such a scheme by territorial governor Robert J. Walker. For at least a year after Olmsted wrote this letter, however, the leaders of the New England Emigrant Aid Company continued to anticipate a move by the Buchanan administration that would open the Indian Territory to settlement and keep it secure for slavery. For instance, Cabot wrote in this vein to his brother in September of 1858:

   The South with the northern Democrats to back her, is busily, though quietly, laying a train which she thinks will blow the Anti-Slavery folks sky-high before they know what is coming. Last winter during the heat of the Congressional contest an article was inserted into one of the Territorial bills whereby the Indian agents are clothed with full powers to decide what white men may be admitted into the Indian Reserves & to expel any one whom they may choose; in accordance with which the Agent of the Reserve south of Kansas, between it & Texas, has proclaimed & published that no d____d Abolitionist will be permitted to come or remain in any part of that Reserve, & at the same time he is permitting slave-holders with their slaves to come in freely, take land & build houses, cultivate farms &c. The intent is evidently to get so strong a hold there, that when they are ready, the Reserve may be purchased from the Indians & the mask thrown off, & the Free-state men defied. But "L'homme propose et Dieu dispose." The outrages of the slave power have created a spirit which they do not count upon, especially in Kansas, there are thousands of men, as I am assured by those from among their midst, well able to know, who are burning for the contest & only wait as they say to hear the Boston bell strike, to go on & take possession of that country, peaceably if they are allowed, but forcibly if they must. This state of things is known to but few, & it is best that it shl'd not be known, it is high time that Freedom should use some of the silence, & secrecy, so well understood by her opponent, & countermine till she has the power in her own hands. If we win in 1860 Slavery dies, surely, though perhaps slowly. (Samuel Cabot, Jr., to James Elliot Cabot, Sept. 20, 1858, NEEA Co. Papers, BU.)

3. In the elections for a territorial legislature in Kansas on October 5 and 6, 1857, two of the three counties south of the Kansas River—Douglas and Shawnee—returned Republican majorities, and territorial governor Robert J. Walker's proclamation of October 19, declaring the proslavery majority returned for Johnson County to be fraudulent, added that county to the list (*NYDT*, Oct. 13, 1857, p. 4; and Oct. 27, 1857, p. 4).
4. Olmsted was in the process of writing an article for the *Atlantic Monthly* based on George M. Weston's *Progress of Slavery in the United States* (see FLO to Samuel Cabot, Jr., Oct. 22, 1857, n. 1, above).
5. Francis Henry Underwood (1825–1894), one of the leading promoters of the *Atlantic Monthly*,

which first appeared in November 1857 with James Russell Lowell as editor and Underwood as assistant editor (*DAB*).

6. Samuel Clarke Pomeroy (1816–1891), financial agent of the New England Emigrant Aid Company and a general in the free-state army, the Kansas Volunteers, for which he had raised a company of men in Iowa (*DAB;* Samuel A. Johnson, *The Battly Cry of Freedom: The New England Emigrant Aid Company in the Kansas Crusade* [Lawrence, Kans., 1954], pp. 55–57; William H. Isely, "The Sharps Rifle Episode in Kansas History," *American Historical Review* 12, no. 3 [April 1907]: 558, no. 1; information supplied by Larry Jochims).

7. Van Buren, Arkansas, which is situated on the Arkansas River in the far-western part of the state a few miles below Fort Smith.

8. The missionaries on the Choctaw reservation in the Indian Territory south of Kansas. The expression "sound on the goose question" originated in Kansas during the mid-1850s; it meant to be a reliable supporter of slavery (M. M. Mathews, *Dictonary of Americanisms,* s.v. "goose").

APPENDIXES

I Calendars of Olmsted's Newspaper Letters on the South
   "The South," *New-York Daily Times,* February 16, 1853, to February 13, 1854
   "A Tour in the Southwest," *New-York Daily Times,* March 6 to June 7, 1854
   "The Southerners at Home," *New York Daily Tribune,* June 3 to August 24, 1857

II Annotated Itineraries of Olmsted's Southern Journeys, 1852–1854

III Chronology of Frederick Law Olmsted, 1852–1857

I
CALENDARS OF OLMSTED'S NEWSPAPER LETTERS ON THE SOUTH

"The South"
New-York Daily Times

Number	Date	Also printed in *Seaboard Slave States*:
1	February 16, 1853	
2	February 19, 1853	40–47
3	February 25, 1853	24–29, 113–25
4	March 4, 1853	94–98, 190–93
5	March 10, 1853	101–12
7	March 17, 1853	
8	March 30, 1853	
9	April 5, 1853	
10	April 8, 1853	
11	April 13, 1853	
12	April 20, 1853	149–52
13	April 23, 1853	152–61
14	April 28, 1853	
15	May 4, 1853	308–15
16	May 10, 1853	317–31
17	May 14, 1853	351–55
18	May 19, 1853	338–51
19	May 24, 1853	357–59, 360–67
20	May 27, 1853	355–57, 368–75
21	May 31, 1853	376–78, 380–84, 386–88, 393–95
22	June 7, 1853	395–402
23	June 11, 1853	419, 462–86
24	June 14, 1853	

In "The South" series, no letter numbered 6 or 31 was published, and the numbers 30, 44 and 45 were inadvertently used twice.

459

APPENDIX I

Number	Date	Also printed in *Seaboard Slave States*:
25	June 16, 1853	454–61
26	June 21, 1853	
27	June 30, 1853	
28	July 8, 1853	
29	July 13, 1853	21–26, 418–20, 430–32
30	July 21, 1853	432–39
30	July 27, 1853	466–72
32	August 9, 1853	472–78
33	August 13, 1853	405–9, 448–49
34	August 19, 1853	
35	August 26, 1853	
36	September 1, 1853	549–56, 557–59
37	September 10, 1853	559–65, 568–73
38	September 14, 1853	578–81, 593–98
39	September 22, 1853	658–59, 660–62, 687–88
40	October 6, 1853	663–64, 665–68, 669–72
41	October 24, 1853	659–60, 674–81
42	November 3, 1853	673–74, 682–86

		Also printed in *Back Country*:
43	November 9, 1853	187–96
44	November 21, 1853	72–76, 80–86
45	November 26, 1853	76–80, 88–93
44	December 3, 1853	135–41
45	December 28, 1853	141–46, 152–56
46	January 12, 1854	
47	January 26, 1854	
48	February 13, 1854	

"A Tour in the Southwest"
New-York Daily Times

Number	Date	Also printed in *Journey Through Texas*:
1	March 6, 1854	46–52, 55–57
2	March 15, 1854	55, 62–64, 66–67, 115–18, 119–21
3	March 21, 1854	77, 80, 82, 84–85, 88, 123–24, 125–26
4	March 23, 1854	89, 91, 97–108
5	March 31, 1854	110–15, 121–23
6	April 4, 1854	135–37, 138–47

CALENDARS OF OLMSTED'S NEWSPAPER LETTERS ON THE SOUTH

Number	Date	Also printed in *Journey Through Texas*:
7	April 14, 1854	169–72, 177–81
8	April 24, 1854	191, 196–97, 198–200
9	May 12, 1854	232, 233–35, 237, 240–41, 244–47, 253–54
(unnumbered)	May 13, 1854	
10	May 18, 1854	
(unnumbered)	May 27, 1854	294–95, 298–99
11	May 31, 1854	215–21
12	June 3, 1854	
13	June 7, 1854	274–75, 278–81, 284, 285–88

"The Southerners at Home"
New York Daily Tribune

Number	Date	Also printed in *Back Country*:
1	June 3, 1857	11–17
2	June 10, 1857	17–25
3	June 20, 1857	25–27, 28–34
4	June 23, 1857	34–40
5	July 4, 1857	41–54
6	July 11, 1857	177–86
7	August 1, 1857	196–204
8	August 8, 1857	164–77
9	August 10, 1857	205–12
10	August 24, 1857	212–20

II

ANNOTATED ITINERARIES OF OLMSTED'S SOUTHERN JOURNEYS

1852–1854

Introduction

The compilation of accurate itineraries of Olmsted's travels is a difficult task. A major cause of that difficulty is the fact that Olmsted took considerable care to disguise the identities of the people and places he visited during his travels. He made this clear in a passage in *Back Country* that he wrote in reply to J.D.B. DeBow's attack on him for abusing the hospitality of his hosts:

> There are numbers of men in the South for whom I have a warm admiration, to whom I feel grateful, whose respect I wish not to lose. There are others for whom I have a quite different feeling. Of a single individual of neither class have I spoken in these three volumes, I believe, by his true name, or in such a manner that he could be recognized, or his home pointed out by any one who had not been previously familiar with it and with him, being, as a rule, careful to so far differ from the actual order of the events of my journey in narrating them, that facts of private life could not be readily localized.[1]

As Olmsted asserts in this statement, he gave the names of only those persons he met in passing and about whom he had nothing negative or controversial to report. Among these were J. Seguine and Mr. Wallace of the Great Dismal Swamp; Mrs. Barclay near Fayetteville, North Carolina; Mr. Peabody in Columbus, Georgia; Henry Clay's son James in Lexington, Kentucky; Mrs. Stoker and Mr. Strather between Natchitoches, Louisiana, and San Augustine, Texas; the immigrants Julius Froebel, Mr. Ujhazy and Ottomar von Behr (in a footnote added after von Behr's death), and G. W. Kendall, editor of the *New Orleans Picayune*, in the San Antonio region; and John Woodland, whose services as a guide in Mexico Olmsted wished to recommend. He also revealed the identity of Adolf Douai (calling him "the German editor, Dr. Douai"), with whom he spent a good deal of time in San Antonio and during his travels to the

Sisterdale settlements. Although he reported that he had deep discussions with Douai, he revealed none of the antislavery editor's opinions.

In this group, the most interesting example of Olmsted's avoidance of unfavorable comments about persons whose names he revealed is the case of Mr. Strather. In the passage in which he identified Strather, Olmsted gave a glowing description of his house and hospitality. But in another section, summing up various experiences in East Texas, he gave—without mentioning the name of his host—a damning description of his house, family and fare.[2]

As for men from whom Olmsted received extensive hospitality and whose farms or plantations he described at length, he usually referred to them by letters that were to some extent correct: "Mr. C." for Charles Benedict Calvert, "Mr. D." for Edouard Degener, and "Mr. T." for Gustav Theissen. In two cases the initials are correct, but not for the man's last name: "Mr. R." for Richard Taylor, and "Thomas W." for Thomas W. Gee. Richard J. Arnold is a special case: Olmsted referred to him as "Mr. A." in the letters in "The South" series, but changed the name to "Mr. X." in *Seaboard Slave States*.

It should also be noted that while Olmsted frequently gave names or initials of persons he encountered in the first two volumes of his writings about the South, he seldom did so in *Back Country*, where the names he gave were almost certainly fictitious. This suggests that J.D.B. DeBow's criticism led him to be more cautious than he had been previously.

Part of Olmsted's method of disguising the identities of those he visited was to offer only meager descriptions of the personal characteristics and domestic surroundings of those with whom he stayed the longest. His omission of such details is unfortunate, since it was just such considerations of domestic amenity and taste that greatly concerned him as a social commentator. The information he did provide concerning the plantations he visited was primarily agricultural—crops grown and amount harvested, acreage, amount of livestock and number of slaves. This material enables the modern-day researcher to identify some of these places from the manuscript census. So far as the editors can tell, Olmsted did not attempt to mislead his readers with intentionally false statements.

Another problem encountered in preparing such itineraries is the fact that Olmsted did not always make clear whether he actually visited a place he described, or simply learned about it through conversation. One such instance is his discussion of North Carolina fisheries in *Seaboard Slave States*, pages 351–55. He could not have visited the Currituck Bay region at the point in his narrative that the discussion occurs. He could conceivably have done so during his time in the Great Dismal Swamp region, but there is no indication that he did. Also, his statement "If I owned a yacht, I think I would make a trip to Currituck next summer, to witness this Titanic dentistry," suggests that he had not witnessed the process of clearing out underwater stumps that he describes at length. Therefore, the editors have not included a visit to that region in these itineraries.

ITINERARIES OF OLMSTED'S SOUTHERN JOURNEYS: 1852-1854

Olmsted's chief means of disguising where and when a particular event occurred was to place it out of order in his narrative, or in a section of general discussion. In such cases he did not claim that he was presenting events in the actual order of their occurrence. Instead, he simply described a place he visited without describing his route to and from it, and left the reader to draw his own conclusions. For instance, his description of a visit to a "free-labor farm"—probably that of Nathaniel Crenshaw, a Quaker who had freed his slaves and made no secret of his opposition to slavery—appears in *Seaboard Slave States* immediately after Olmsted's visit to Thomas W. Gee. In fact, Crenshaw's farm was near Richmond, and Olmsted visited it more than a week before he went to Gee's. By placing the description of the free-labor farm where he did, Olmsted suggested to the reader that it was somewhere in the vicinity of Petersburg and thus helped hide Crenshaw's identity.

Olmsted's disguising of the location of two other plantations he visited—those of Richard Taylor and Meredith Calhoun—is even more misleading. In *Seaboard Slave States* his description of Taylor's plantation follows his discussion of the area around Opelousas, Louisiana, and the Red River region. Since it is the last plantation described in the book, there is no indication of where he went after visiting it. By this means, Olmsted suggested that the plantation was far from its actual site: Taylor lived twenty miles north of New Orleans, and Olmsted visited him before he went up the Red River.

The most remarkable of Olmsted's attempts to conceal the time and place of a visit was his treatment of Meredith Calhoun's plantation on the Red River. He had good reason to be circumspect, since in his account of the plantation he described the whipping of a slave girl.

In his letters in "The South" series and in *Back Country,* Olmsted presented the description of Calhoun's plantation as part of a general discussion of slavery that followed the conclusion of his account of his travels. In the book he did add a statement that the plantation was on a tributary of the Mississippi, accessible only by steamboat, and that its 1,000 slaves made up one fifth of the population of a county where blacks heavily outnumbered whites. He then inserted the chapter in which the material appears, entitling it "The Property Aspect of Slavery," between a chapter describing a trip through southern Mississippi, ending twenty-five miles below Vicksburg, and one describing a trip across northern Mississippi, beginning at Vicksburg.

This arrangement has confused careful scholars as well as casual readers of *Back Country*. For instance, Charles S. Sydnor assumed that the plantation was in Mississippi and cited Olmsted's description of it more than thirty times in his study of slavery in that state.

It has also been confusing to readers that the description of the Calhoun plantation appears in the volume that apparently deals with Olmsted's ride through the back country of the eastern South after the journey through Texas with his brother in early 1854. Only those who take note of the dating of the chapters, and who know that the material in the second and third chapters of *Back Country* originally appeared in five letters near the end of "The South" series in the *New-York Daily Times* in November and December of 1853, would know that Olmsted visited these places during his first southern journey. In his admirable edition of *Cotton Kingdom,* Arthur Schlesinger, Sr., apparently assumed that the first three chapters of *Back Country* had been arranged in the order of their occurrence. As a result, he misdated the beginning of the third chapter of *Back Country*—which appears in *Cotton Kingdom*—as 1854, though the actual date was 1853.

An additional problem arises from Olmsted's use of datelines in his accounts. Sometimes the date he gave was for the day an event occurred, and other times it indicated when he wrote the passage. Moreover, the day of the week and the day of the month he gave in his private letters do not always match. For instance, the date in his letter to Charles Loring Brace of Thursday, December 22 [1852] is incorrect, since the 22nd was a Wednesday. In such cases, he usually appears to have given the correct day of the week and the wrong day of the month. In this case the letter should probably be dated Thursday, December 23, 1852. Another apparent instance of Olmsted's mistaking the day of the month is his letter to Frederick Kingsbury dated February 26, 1853. He must instead have written it—at least in large part—on Sunday, February 27, since it describes events that occurred on that day. For these reasons, the dates given by the editors in the itineraries sometimes differ from those that Olmsted supplied.

For the creation of a full itinerary, it is necessary to have adequate information in some form. The information provided in Olmsted's newspaper letters and books, supplemented by private letters and entries in John Olmsted's journal recording his receipt of letters from the South, makes possible a fairly complete itinerary of the first southern journey up to the point where Olmsted left the train forty miles east of Memphis on his return trip. After that, all we know is that he completed his journey back to New York by public transportation "along the eastern base of the Appalachian Chain in the upper parts of the States of Mississippi, Alabama, Georgia, the Carolinas and Virginia...."[3]

In the book *Journey Through Texas,* prepared by John Hull Olmsted, the frequent and apparently accurate indication of the dates on which events occurred greatly simplifies the task of drawing up an itinerary for that part of Olmsted's second southern journey. His ride alone through the back country from Bayou Sara, Louisiana, to Richmond, Virginia, however, presents greater problems. It is possible to give a good account of his itinerary from Bayou Sara to Jackson, Mississippi, but his travels from there to Chattanooga, Tennessee, during the next three weeks can be reconstructed only in a general way. From there to Richmond his narrative is sufficiently detailed to permit a fairly full accounting of his movements.

In the itineraries that follow, firm dates are given in roman type; tentative dates are italicized.

1. *BC*, p. 400.
2. *JT*, pp. 64–66, 115–17; for the original account of the visit, which contains elements of both descriptions in the book, see "A Tour in the Southwest" no. 2.
3. "The South" no. 44, *NYDT,* Nov. 21, 1853, p. 2.

First Southern Journey
1852–1853

1852

December 10	Arrives in Washington after a 12-hour trip from New York (*SSS,* p. 5; "The South" no. 1).
December 13	Visits Charles Benedict Calvert's 2,000-acre estate, Riversdale, just outside the District of Columbia in Prince George's County, Maryland (*SSS,* pp. 6, 11; "The South" no. 1, above, n. 2).
December 16	Travels by steamboat from Washington to Acquia Creek, Virginia, and by train to Richmond, Virginia (*SSS,* p. 16).
December 16–26	Makes Richmond his base for short excursions to nearby plantations and farms ("The South" no. 10).
December 21	Visits the James River farm of a slaveholder (*SSS,* p. 40; "The South" no. 2).
December 22	Spends the night with Quakers Nathaniel and John Bacon Crenshaw on Nathaniel's free-labor farm, Rocouncy, six miles north of Richmond (FLO to CLB, Dec. 22, 1852, above, n. 1).
December 26 or 27	Journeys to Petersburg, Virginia, where he visits Abner Leavenworth, Frederick Kingsbury's uncle (FLO to FJK, Oct. 17, 1852, above, n. 8; FLO to FJK, Feb. 26, 1853; JO Journal).
December 28	Takes the train south to visit Thomas W. Gee near Stony Creek in Sussex County. Hires a horse and loses his way. Spends the night at "Mr. Newman's" ("The South" no. 14; *SSS,* p. 59; "The South" no. 2, above, n. 6).
December 29	Arrives at Gee's 1,400-acre tobacco plantation. Dines with Gee. Returns to Petersburg ("The South" no. 2, above, n. 6; *SSS,* pp. 91–93).

APPENDIX II

1853

January 2 — Travels by train and steamboat to Norfolk, Virginia (*SSS*, p. 306; *Norfolk and Portsmouth Herald*, Jan. 5, 1853, p. 2).

January 4–6 — Visits the Dismal Swamp area south of Norfolk (*SSS*, pp. 149–53).

January 4 — Drives to Deep Creek at the head of the Great Dismal Canal (*SSS*, p. 159).

January 5 — Calls upon James Seguine, a New York merchant residing in Norfolk County and a relative of Olmsted's Staten Island neighbor Stephen Seguine. Also meets George T. Wallace, who holds slaves in partnership with Seguine and began reclaiming farmland from Dismal Swamp in the 1840s (U.S., Census Office, 7th Census, *7th Census 1850. Virginia* [Washington, D.C., 1850], schedule 2, Norfolk County, p. 235; Charles Frederick Stansbury, *The Lake of the Great Dismal* [New York, 1925], pp. 63–66).

January 6 — Returns to Norfolk (*SSS*, p. 316).

January 7 — Leaves Norfolk by ferry and takes the train from Portsmouth to Weldon, North Carolina. Proceeds by stagecoach to Gaston, North Carolina. Misses the train there and stays overnight (*SSS*, p. 316).

January 8 — Arrives in Raleigh, North Carolina (FLO to JO, Jan. 10, 1853).

January 14 — Leaves Raleigh on a stagecoach and spends the night at Mildred Barclay's house, 26 miles south of Raleigh (*SSS*, pp. 326–27; U.S., Census Office, 7th Census, *7th Census 1850. North Carolina* [Washington, D.C., 1850], schedule 1, Cumberland County, p. 107).

January 15 — Visits a piney-woods farm and turpentine works. Travels to Fayetteville, North Carolina (*SSS*, pp. 328, 336; "The South" no. 19).

January 17 — Visits a cotton factory at Fayetteville (JO Journal; *SSS*, pp. 356–57).

January 18 or 19 — Takes a steamboat down the Cape Fear River to Wilmington, North Carolina. Proceeds by boat and train toward Charleston, South Carolina (*SSS*, pp. 368, 374–76).

January 19 or 20 — Dines at Marion Court House, South Carolina, and

	observes slaves during the stagecoach journey across South Carolina ("The South" no. 22; *SSS,* pp. 380, 381, 384, 386–90).
January 20 or 21	Transfers to train and arrives in Charleston (*SSS,* pp. 393–94, 404).
January 27	Journeys by boat from Charleston to Savannah, Georgia (*SSS,* p. 405; JO Journal).
January 27–28	Visits an old acquaintance at or near Savannah ("The South" no. 23).
January 29	Rides south to Richard Arnold's Bryan County plantation, White Hall (*SSS,* pp. 409, 416).
January 30	Attends a "cracker" church service ("The South" no. 25; *SSS,* p. 428).
January 31	Tours Arnold's 2,200-acre rice plantations (Joseph Karl Menn, "The Large Slaveholders of the Deep South, 1860" [Ph.D. diss., University of Texas, 1964], pp. 556–57; "The South" no. 24, above, n. 6).
February 1	Returns to Savannah (*SSS,* p. 546).
February 2	Arrives in Columbus, Georgia, after a 24-hour journey by train and stagecoach (JO Journal; *SSS,* pp. 546–47).
February 2–4	During his stay in Columbus, visits the garden of George Henry Peabody, a Connecticut-born horticulturist and merchant who owns a general store in Columbus (*SSS,* p. 548; Louise Ware, *George Foster Peabody: Banker, Philanthropist, Publicist* [Athens, Ga., 1951], pp. 1–3, 6).
February 5–12	Arrives in Montgomery, Alabama, after a day's journey from Columbus. Visits frequently with Jefferson F. Jackson, a college friend and classmate of Frederick Kingsbury (FLO to FJK, Feb. 26, 1853, above, n. 6; *SSS,* pp. 547, 549).
February 12	Leaves Montgomery, traveling by steamboat down the Alabama River. During a stopover, explores Selma, Alabama (*SSS,* pp. 549–50).
February 13	During a stopover, visits Claiborne, Alabama (*SSS,* pp. 550–51).
February 14	Arrives in Mobile, Alabama (JO Journal; *SSS,* pp. 565–66).

APPENDIX II

February 16, 17 or 18	Takes an overnight trip by steamboat and train from Mobile to New Orleans (*SSS*, pp. 568, 578; "The South" no. 37).
February 17, 18 or 19	Arrives in New Orleans.
February 23	Arrives at Richard Taylor's plantation, Fashion, 20 miles north of New Orleans, late at night after a trip by steamboat (FLO to CLB, Feb. 23, 1853; *SSS*, p. 656; FLO to FJK, Feb. 26, 1853, above, n. 2).
February 24	Tours Taylor's 1,200-acre sugar plantation ("The South" nos. 39 and 40; *SSS*, pp. 658–62; FLO to FJK, Feb. 26, 1853, above, n. 2).
February 25	Is driven back to New Orleans by one of Taylor's slaves ("The South" no. 41).
February 26	Makes reservations on steamboat bound up the Red River but discovers it will not leave that day as scheduled. Dines with Thomas Levingston Bayne, a college friend of Charles Loring Brace's (*SSS*, pp. 603–4; FLO to FJK, Feb. 26, 1853; FLO to CLB, Feb. 23, 1853, above, n. 5).
February 27	Goes visiting with Bayne, presumably seeing a plantation and quadroon friends of Bayne's, as planned (FLO to FJK, Feb. 26, 1853).
March 2	Leaves New Orleans by steamboat.
March 4 or 5	Arrives at Grand Ecore, Louisiana, just above Natchitoches. Stays in a hotel at Natchitoches (*SSS*, p. 624).
March 6	Walks in countryside near Natchitoches and observes slaves belonging to a Creole planter (*SSS*, p. 629).
March 7	Journeys, probably by stagecoach, to Meredith Calhoun's plantation on the Red River at present-day Colfax, Louisiana (*SSS*, p. 634; "The South" no. 44, above, n. 2).
March 8	Tours Calhoun's 15,000-acre cotton plantation and meets him ("The South" nos. 44 and 45; *BC*, pp. 72, 76, 92; "The South" no. 44, n. 2, above).
March 9 or 10	Returns to Natchitoches, probably to retrieve baggage that had mistakenly been sent up river before his departure from New Orleans ("The South" no. 44; FLO to FJK, Feb. 26, 1853).

March 10	Boards a steamboat whose destination is New Orleans. Observes the plantations belonging to blacks on the Cane River (*SSS*, pp. 620, 633).
March 12	Arrives back in New Orleans (*New Orleans Daily Picayune*, March 13, 1853).
March 15	Departs by steamboat for Vicksburg, Mississippi ("The South" no. 44).
March 17	Arrives in Vicksburg and spends the night on a wharf boat (*BC*, p. 125).
March 18	Finds that flooding caused by heavy rains will prevent him from making a tour of plantations in the Yazoo River region. Travels by steamboat to Memphis, Tennessee ("The South" no. 44).
March 20	Arrives in Memphis and spends the night there (*BC*, pp. 125–27).
March 21	Leaves Memphis, heading east by train for 40 miles. Transfers to a stagecoach and travels all night (*BC*, pp. 128–30, 135, 145).
March 22	A washed-out bridge interrupts the trip. Spends the day and night at the home of a northern Mississippi slaveholder (*BC*, pp. 135, 141).
March 23	Observes his host's 20 slaves beginning their day's work. Resumes trip by stagecoach. Plans to complete his journeys by traveling through the upcountry sections of Mississippi, Alabama, Georgia, the Carolinas and Virginia (*SSS*, p. 362; *BC*, pp. 142, 151–52, 156; "The South" no. 44).
April 6	Arrives back at Staten Island, New York (JO Journal).

Second Southern Journey
1853–1854

1853
November 10   Begins journey to the South with his brother, John Hull Olmsted (JO Journal).

APPENDIX II

November 11	Stays overnight in Baltimore, Maryland (*JT*, p. 1).
November 12	Takes the train to Cumberland, Maryland and proceeds to Wheeling, Virginia (*JT*, pp. 1–3; JO Journal).
November 13	Spends the day in Wheeling and leaves on a steamboat after midnight (*JT*, pp. 4–5).
November 15	Arrives in Cincinnati, Ohio (*JT*, p. 5).
November 17	Travels by stagecoach to Lexington, Kentucky (*JT*, pp. 10–11).
November 18	In Lexington, visits Ashland, the home of deceased Whig party leader Henry Clay (*JT*, pp. 17–18).
November 19	Goes by train to Louisville, Kentucky, and passes through Frankfort (*JT*, p. 19; JO Journal).
November 20 or 21	Meets George Prentice, editor of the *Louisville Daily Journal*, and Charles W. Short, an eminent botanist (FLO to CLB, Dec. 1, 1853, above, nn. 2 and 5).
November 22	Abandons his plans to travel by overland route. Is driven 2 or 3 miles to Portland, Kentucky, below the falls of Ohio, where he boards a steamboat (*JT*, p. 23; *Louisville Daily Times*, Nov. 23, 1853, p. 3).
November 24	Disembarks at Smithland, Kentucky, and eats Thanksgiving dinner there. Boards stern-wheel steamboat bound for Nashville, Tennessee (*JT*, pp. 26–27).
November 28	Arrives in Nashville (JO Journal; *JT*, p. 28).
November 28 and 29	Dines and spends much time in conversation with John Hull Olmsted's Yale classmate, Samuel Perkins Allison (JO Journal; FLO to CLB, Dec. 1, 1853, above, n. 7).
November 30	Leaves Nashville by boat (*JT*, p. 37; FLO to CLB, Dec. 1, 1853).
December 2	Arrives at Smithland and boards a steamboat bound for New Orleans (*JT*, p. 37).
December 6 and 7	During long stopovers for refueling, observes slaves picking cotton on river plantations, one of which is near Fort Adams, Mississippi (*JT*, p. 42).
December 8	Arrives in New Orleans (*New Orleans Commercial Bulletin*, Dec. 9, 1853, pp. 2, 3; *JT*, p. 42).

ITINERARIES OF OLMSTED'S SOUTHERN JOURNEYS: 1852–1854

December 10	Boards steamboat to go up the Red River (*JT*, pp. 43–44; JO Journal).
December 12	Low water detains him at Alexandria (*JT*, p. 44).
December 14	Leaves steamboat at Grand Ecore and drives 4 miles to Natchitoches (*JT*, p. 44).
December 15	Purchases horses and a mule for the saddle trip through Texas. Meets his guide, "B.," who is a Northern man but an old settler of Texas. "B." proceeds to San Augustine, Texas (*JT*, pp. 45–46).
December 16	Attempts to visit the plantation of a local gentleman. Becomes lost and dines at a log cabin (*JT*, pp. 46–52, 53; "A Tour in the Southwest" no. 1).
December 19	Leaves Natchitoches with John to begin the saddle trip. Spends the night at Nancy Stoker's, in Sabine County, Louisiana, halfway between Natchitoches and the Sabine River (*JT*, pp. 54–55, 60; U.S., Census Office, 7th Census, *7th Census 1850. Louisiana* [Washington, D.C., 1850], schedule 1, Sabine County, p. 106).
December 20	Eats lunch with a fox-hunting gentleman and rides in the rain across the Sabine River into Texas at Gaines Ferry. Spends the night at the home of "Mr. Strather"—probably Walter Strother, who was approximately fifty years old and owned 27 slaves and real estate valued at $5,000 (U.S., Census Office, 7th Census, *7th Census 1850. Texas* [Washington, D.C., 1850], schedule 1, Sabine County, p. 323; ibid., schedule 2, Sabine County, p. 387; *JT*, pp. 62–63, 65; "A Tour in the Southwest" no. 2).
December 21	Is detained at Mr. Strother's by a storm (*JT*, p. 65).
December 22	Rides 25 miles through the storm to San Augustine (*JT*, p. 67).
December 23	Meets his guide, "B.," and attempts to find suitable horses for the trip (*JT*, pp. 72–73; JO Journal).
December 26	Leaves San Augustine and rides 18 miles. Spends the night in a log cabin (*JT*, pp. 75–76).
December 27	Arrives in Nacogdoches and camps for the night 5 miles beyond town (*JT*, pp. 78, 80).
December 28	Crosses the Angelina River and camps approximately 25 miles from Nacogdoches (*JT*, pp. 80–81).

APPENDIX II

December 30	Crosses the Neches River and enters Houston County (*JT*, p. 82).
December 31	Rides through Crockett and camps beyond it (*JT*, pp. 83–84).

1854
January 2	Camps on bottom land beyond the Trinity River (*JT*, pp. 89, 91–92).
January 3	Loses his route but arrives in Centerville. Spends the night at an inn and is given a bullterrier named Judy by the innkeeper (*JT*, pp. 92–95).
January 4	Rejoins the regular road to San Antonio and, after buying venison from a herdsman, camps in the woods near the prairie (*JT*, p. 95).
January 5	Probably crosses the Brazos River at the old Mexican post of Tenoxtitlan. Spends the night in a cabin belonging to the son of a Northern man. First encounters a "norther," the strong north wind, accompanied by intense cold, that blows across Texas in the autumn and winter (*JT*, pp. 97–102).
January 6	Arrives in Caldwell and stays overnight (*JT*, pp. 102–3, 107).
January 7	Continues onward in the norther and spends the night in a log cabin (*JT*, pp. 108, 121–23).
January 9	Arrives in Bastrop. Guide, "B.," leaves, planning to rejoin him in San Antonio (*JT*, pp. 109, 131; JO Journal).
January 9 or 10	Arrives in Austin in the evening (*JT*, pp. 110–11; JO Journal).
January 9–13	Visits sessions of the Texas legislature several times (*JT*, p. 113).
January 14	Leaves Austin. An accident with a saddle forces him to spend the night at Manchac Spring (*JT*, pp. 129, 130–31, 133).
January 15	Passes through San Marcos and camps in a live-oak grove (*JT*, pp. 134–36; "A Tour in the Southwest" no. 2).
January 16	Arrives in the German town of Neu Braunfels. Visits the Protestant clergyman and stays overnight at the inn (*JT*, pp. 138–46).

ITINERARIES OF OLMSTED'S SOUTHERN JOURNEYS: 1852–1854

January 17	Arrives in San Antonio, where he boards at a German inn (*JT*, pp. 147–50, 167; JO Journal).
January 19	The guide, "B.," who had rejoined him, departs for the North. Tries to find a group leaving for Mexico and talks with Julius Froebel, a scientist and German immigrant who commands a wagon train. Is encouraged to consult a naturalist living near Neu Braunfels—probably Otto Friedrich (1800–1880) (*JT*, pp. 165–66; Adolf E. Zucker, ed., *The Forty-Eighters: Political Refugees of the German Revolution of 1848* [New York, 1950], p. 294; Samuel Wood Geiser, *Naturalists of the Frontier . . . with a Foreword by Herbert Spencer Jennings* [Dallas, Tex., 1937], pp. 138–39, 323).
January 27	Leaves San Antonio. Encounters a norther and spends the night in the inn at Neu Braunfels (JO Journal; *JT*, pp. 167–69).
January 28	Attempts unsuccessfully to visit Otto Friedrich at Neu Wied, near Neu Braunfels. Spends the day with Rev. L. C. Ervendberg, a Protestant minister. Ervendberg is a director of the Western Texas Orphan Asylum at Neu Wied and president and the only professor of the school West Texas University (*JT*, pp. 169–71; Rudolph L. Biesele, *The History of the German Settlements in Texas, 1831–1861* [Austin, Tex., 1930], pp. 115, 134, 212–13, 216–17).
January 30	Learns that the naturalist has no definite plans to visit Mexico. Leaves Neu Braunfels and stops at Seguin (*JT*, pp. 181, 183).
January 31	Leaves Seguin at dusk. Stays overnight at a cabin occupied by German settlers (*JT*, pp. 183–84).
February 1	Arrives back in San Antonio (*JT*, p. 187).
February 3	Accompanies the German editor Adolf Douai on a trip to the mountains. Spends the night with a German family living on the Cibolo River (*JT*, pp. 187–88).
February 4	Arrives at the German settlement Sisterdale, and meets Baron von Westphal and either August Siemering or Ernst Kapp. Lunches with the baron and dines with Ottomar von Behr. Stays overnight with Gustav Theissen (*JT*, pp. 191–94; R. L. Biesele, *German Settlements*, pp. 173, 215; Hermann Seele, *The Cy-*

APPENDIX II

press and Other Writings of a German Pioneer in Texas, trans. Edward C. Breitenkamp [Austin, Tex. and London, 1979], pp. 111-15; "A Tour in the Southwest" no. 8, above, n. 5).

February 5	Calls upon several settlers of Sisterdale. Meets Edouard Degener and spends the night at his home (*JT*, pp. 194-96; "A Tour in the Southwest" no. 8, above, n. 3).
February 6 and 7	A norther causes him to remain at Degener's home (*JT*, p. 196).
February 8	Leaves Sisterdale (*JT*, pp. 200-201).
February 9	Arrives back in San Antonio (JO Journal).
February 14	Sets out on a trip to the Gulf coast of Texas. Rides only 12 or 14 miles (*JT*, pp. 227-28).
February 15	Rain mixed with snow confines him to camp (*JT*, pp. 228-29).
February 16	Rides to the Guadalupe River and camps out beneath magnificent trees (*JT*, p. 229).
February 17	Meets and talks with an old black couple. Arrives at Seguin and camps near San Geronimo Creek (*JT*, pp. 229-32).
February 18	Remains in camp because of rain (*JT*, p. 232).
February 19	Passes Mount Capote, rides through prairie lands and probably camps in the bottom lands of the Guadalupe (*JT*, pp. 232-34).
February 20	Reaches Gonzales and camps nearby (*JT*, pp. 235, 237).
February 21	Rides 20 miles across the prairie and camps by a brook (*JT*, p. 238).
February 22	Enters a more wooded area and camps by a creek (*JT*, pp. 238-39).
February 23	Arrives at Victoria and spends the night beyond the town with the family of a slaveowning planter (*JT*, pp. 240-43, 245).
February 24	Rides through the driving rain to Lavacca and stays overnight (*JT*, pp. 245, 247-50).
February 25	Crosses the Chockolate River. The horses and mule become mired in the swampy grounds. Extricates

	them and proceeds to Indianola (JO Journal; *JT*, pp. 251–52, 254).
February 27	Gives up his intention of visiting Corpus Christi and other coastal towns. Leaves Indianola at noon and spends the night with a family living near the Chockolate River (*JT*, pp. 255–56).
February 28	Arrives back in Victoria and remains overnight (*JT*, pp. 258–59).
March 1	Crosses the Guadalupe River by ferry and camps by Manahuila Creek (*JT*, pp. 260–61).
March 2	A norther strikes his camp. Rides to Goliad and visits the old mission there (*JT*, pp. 261–62; JO Journal).
March 3	Camps near a bog where a flock of geese stampedes the horses (*JT*, pp. 267–69).
March 4	Passes through Helena (*JT*, p. 270).
March 5	On his way back to San Antonio, visits two ranches owned by Mexicans (*JT*, pp. 271–72).
March 6 or 7	Arrives back in San Antonio (JO Journal).
March 13	Leaves San Antonio with John Hull Olmsted on his second excursion to the mountains. Takes the old Fredericksburg road and loses the trail (FLO to [Anne Lynch], March 12, 1854; *JT*, p. 209).
March 14	Encounters difficulties in crossing the Guadalupe River and camps on its banks with a German mechanic (*JT*, pp. 210–12).
March 15	Spends the night near the Currie's Creek settlement (*JT*, p. 213).
March 16	Fights a prairie fire (*JT*, pp. 213–22).
March 16–23	Spends a week in camp interviewing the settlers and collecting agricultural information (*JT*, p. 222).
March 24	Begins the trip back to San Antonio via the Comanche Spring road (*JT*, p. 222).
March 26	Spends the night in camp and is almost taken for a horse thief by a settler (*JT*, p. 222).
March 27	Arrives back in San Antonio (JO Journal).
April 1	Sets out from San Antonio for a trip across the frontier to Mexico. Rides to Castroville, on the Medina River (*JT*, pp. 273, 275–76).

APPENDIX II

April 2	Continues and probably spends the night at Dhanis (*JT*, pp. 278–80).
April 3	Reaches the military outpost Fort Inge (*JT*, pp. 284–85).
April 4	Visits an Indian camp 3 miles north of Fort Inge. Procures a guide, John Woodland, for the trip to Mexico (*JT*, pp. 288, 290, 303, 305).
April 5	Accompanies two officers en route to their posts on the Rio Grande (*JT*, pp. 303, 306–8).
April 6	Arrives at Fort Duncan and its neighboring town, Eagle Pass. Crosses the Rio Grande and enters Piedras Negras, where he obtains a Mexican visa. Talks to a runaway slave. Spends the night at Eagle Pass (*JT*, pp. 314–15, 322–24, 337).
April 7	Crosses the river and rides 30 miles to San Fernando. Remains overnight with a French family (*JT*, pp. 338–39, 342–45, 350–53).
April 9	Continues south through Morelos and San Juan to Nava. Stays in the mansion of Don Tomas Cantu (*JT*, pp. 353–55).
April 10	Returns to Piedras Negras (*JT*, p. 355).
April 11	Rides toward the Texas settlements and camps in the desert (*JT*, p. 355).
April 12	Parts company with his guide, John Woodland, probably at Fort Inge (*JT*, p. 355).
April 14	Reaches Quihi and stays overnight with a German family from Hanover (*JT*, p. 290).
April 15	Leaves Quihi and encounters a group of armed Lipan Indians, but the ride continues without incident. Decides to return to San Antonio rather than visit a ranch on the San Geronimo. Arrives in San Antonio (*JT*, pp. 290, 293–94; "A Tour in the Southwest" unnumbered).
April 24	Begins return trip from San Antonio (*JT*, p. 356).
April 26	Passes through Neu Braunfels (JO Journal).
April 28	Camps near Bastrop (*JT*, pp. 357–58).
April 29	Enters a district populated by wealthy German farmers (*JT*, p. 358).
April 30	Rides 22 miles from the Colorado to the Brazos River.

	Spends the night with a family from Maine (*JT*, p. 358).
May 1	Crosses the Brazos at San Felipe by ferry. Camps on the edge of the prairie (*JT*, p. 360).
May 3 or 4	Arrives in Houston (*JT*, pp. 360, 362–63; JO Journal).
May 6 or 7	Leaves Houston and passes through Harrisburg. Reaches San Jacinto (*JT*, pp. 364, 366–67; JO Journal).
May 9	Stays overnight with a former Kentuckian who owns one of the largest stock farms in the area (*JT*, pp. 367, 373).
May 10	Passes through Liberty and the bottom lands of the Trinity River (*JT*, pp. 374–75).
May 12	Rides through Sour Lake (*JT*, pp. 375–76; JO Journal).
May 13	Beyond Beaumont, the horses and mule become mired. Returns to Beaumont (*JT*, pp. 376–79).
May 14	Sells his mule and exchanges horses (JO Journal; *JT*, p. 379).
May 15	Leaves Beaumont. Heads toward the Sabine River but frequently loses his way. Stays overnight at a house where a drover is also a guest (*JT*, pp. 381–82).
May 17	Takes a ferry across the Sabine River to Louisiana. Rides to the Big Woods (*JT*, p. 391).
May 18	Journeys to Lake Charles (*JT*, pp. 392, 394).
May 19	Spends the night at the home of an Italian-French immigrant, "Old Man Corse" (*JT*, p. 395).
May 20	Stays overnight at "Jacques Beguine's" house (*JT*, p. 400).
May 21	Remains overnight at the house of a French-speaking Dutch family approximately 15 miles west of Opelousas, Louisiana (*JT*, pp. 401, 405).
May 22	Arrives in Opelousas (*JT*, p. 405; JO Journal).
May 23	Possibly makes a short trip to Lafayette, Louisiana (*SSS*, p. 589).
May 24	Leaves Opelousas on a steamboat. During a stopover in Washington, Louisiana, attends a Creole ball (JO Journal; *JT*, p. 406; *SSS*, pp. 639, 642–46).
May 26	After 24 hours of travel by steamboat through "al-

APPENDIX II

ligator bayous," reaches the Mississippi River. Parts from John Hull Olmsted, who continues on to New Orleans and New York by water. Rides from Bayou Sara, Louisiana, to Woodville, Mississippi (*JT,* p. 406; *New Orleans Commercial Bulletin,* May 29, 1854, p. 3; JO Journal; *BC,* pp. 11, 16).

May 27	Is refused lodging at the first house at which he stops. Stays overnight with one of the poorer slaveholders of the area (*BC,* pp. 20–21).
May 28	Crosses the Homochitto River and arrives in Natchez, Mississippi (*BC,* pp. 33, 34, 36).
May 29	Stays overnight with a German farmer (*BC,* p. 41).
May 30	After a 30-mile ride, is refused lodging at three houses. Stays overnight at the home of an overseer on the plantation Evermay, owned by the Benjamin Smith family, in Claiborne County, Mississippi (*BC,* pp. 42–44; Introduction, above, n. 25).
May 31	Probably begins to turn eastward in his journey. Stays overnight with a family from Maryland (*BC,* pp. 158, 161–62).
June 1	Stops overnight at a large, comfortable house (*BC,* pp. 164–65).
June 2	Proceeds to Jackson, Mississippi (*BC,* pp. 62, 159).
June 3 and 4	Is detained in Jackson because of illness (JHO to JO, June 15, 1854; [Frederick Law Olmsted], "Filibusterism and Other Matters in Mississippi," *NYDT,* June 14, 1854, p. 4).
June 5	Proceeds by an indirect route east toward Tuscaloosa, Alabama. Lodges at the home of a man known to his family as "Doctor" (*BC,* pp. 158, 167).
June 6	Spends the night with a planter who employs Indian labor (*BC,* pp. 170, 174–75).
June 7	Stays overnight with a "slaveholding abolitionist," whom he calls "John Watson," probably in Madison County, Mississippi (one of the few counties with a three-to-one slave/white ratio) (*BC,* pp. 197–98).
June 8	Lodges at the log cabin home of a tradesman's mother (*BC,* p. 196).
June 9	Spends the night with a nonslaveholding "poor white" family, probably in Winston County, Mississippi (a

	county whose white/slave ratio approaches three to one and which borders Noxubee County, in which the ratio is the reverse) (*BC*, pp. 197–98).
June 12–13	Arrives in Tuscaloosa and remains there at least one day in an unsuccessful attempt to procure cash (*BC*, pp. 425–26).
June 15	Enters a hillier section of Alabama north of Tuscaloosa. Dines with a slaveholder who is the local postmaster and owns a sawmill. Stays overnight with a farmer who grows cotton and owns a dozen slaves (*BC*, pp. 206–7).
June 16	Observes a family mining iron ore and talks with a miner, probably all in Walker or Jefferson counties, in the general vicinity of modern-day Birmingham, Alabama (*BC*, pp. 211–12).
June 17	Lodges with a slaveholder who raises cotton (*BC*, p. 213).
June 18	Rides only 8 miles before stopping at a nonslaveholder's house, where he remains overnight (*BC*, pp. 215–16).
June 19	Passes through a valley populated by poor farmers (*BC*, pp. 220–21).
June 21	Spends the night at the best farm that he finds in all the mountainous district (*BC*, p. 227).
June 23–27	Arrives in Chattanooga, Tennessee. Procures cash there only after a meeting of a bank's board of directors is called (*BC*, pp. 426–27; JHO to JO, July 3, 1854).
June 29	Leaves Chattanooga. Stays in a large, white house belonging to a Tennessee "squire" (*BC*, pp. 233–36).
June 30	Rides east and stays in a cabin that is not on the main road and is probably located in northwestern Georgia, southeast of Chattanooga (*BC*, pp. 221, 237–38, 240).
July 1–2	Visits the Tennessee copper-mining region in eastern Polk County (*BC*, pp. 242, 244).
July 3	Leaves the mining area (*BC*, p. 244).
July 4	Passes miserable huts, probably in North Carolina, before stopping for the night at the home of a slaveholding family (*BC*, p. 246).

APPENDIX II

July 5	Rides through Murphy, North Carolina, and spends the night near the Tomahila Mountains (*BC*, pp. 246–47).
July 6	Crosses the Tomahila Mountains (*BC*, p. 247).
July 8	Passes near Waynesville, North Carolina (*BC*, p. 249).
July 9	Spends the day ascending and descending Balsam Mountain (*BC*, pp. 252, 254–56).
July 11	Visits Asheville, North Carolina (*BC*, p. 251).
July 12	Rides until late in the evening. Spends the night in a log cabin (*BC*, pp. 257–58).
July 13	Proceeds toward Burnsville, North Carolina. Probably lodges at the residence of a slaveholder (*BC*, pp. 267–68).
July 14	Arrives in Bakersville, North Carolina, wishing to find the road north to Greensville, Virginia. Is advised to go to Elizabethton, Tennessee. Probably stays overnight with a nonslaveholder who believes slaves should be returned to Africa (*BC*, pp. 267–69, 271).
July 15	Travels to Elizabethton. Spends the night at the home of a man of "superior standing" who hates slavery (*BC*, pp. 262–63).
July 17	Arrives in Abingdon, Virginia (*BC*, p. 273).
July 18	Stays overnight in a large, attractive house (*BC*, pp. 273–74).
July 19	Lodges at the log cabin of a nonslaveholder (*BC*, p. 276).
July 20	Spends the night at a boarded log cabin (*BC*, pp. 277–78).
July 22	Descends the eastern slope of the Blue Ridge Mountains (*BC*, p. 279).
July 23	Arrives in Lynchburg, Virginia (*BC*, p. 400).
July 24	Leaves Lynchburg in the morning and heads toward Farmville, Virginia. Becomes ill and sleeps until late afternoon. Is refused lodging at five houses and finally spends the night at a store (*BC*, pp. 400–404).
July 29	Arrives in Richmond, Virginia (*BC*, p. 279).
July 31	Takes a steamboat to New York (*BC*, p. 283).
August 2	Arrives at Staten Island, New York.

III
CHRONOLOGY OF FREDERICK LAW OLMSTED

1852–1857

1852

February 18 — Volume 1 of *Walks and Talks of an American Farmer in England* is published.

October — Volume 2 of *Walks and Talks* is published.

December 10 — Begins first journey through the South.

1853

February 16 — First letter of the series "The South" is published in the *New-York Daily Times*.

April 6 — Ends first southern journey.

November 10 — Begins second journey through the South with his brother, John Hull Olmsted.

1854

January 23 — Kansas-Nebraska Bill is introduced in Congress.

February 13 — Last letter of "The South" series is published.

March 6 — First letter of the series "A Tour in the Southwest" is published in the *New-York Daily Times*.

May 30 — Kansas-Nebraska Act is signed into law.

June 7 — Last letter of the series "A Tour in the Southwest" is published.

c. August 2 — Ends second southern journey.

October — Circulates appeal for funds for *San Antonio Zeitung*.

1855

March 30 — Proslavery, "bogus" territorial legislature is elected in Kansas.

APPENDIX III

April	Becomes a partner in the publishing firm of Dix, Edwards and Company and moves to New York City. Until January 1856, acts as managing editor of *Putnam's Monthly Magazine*.
October	Buys mountain howitzer and ammunition for free-state settlers in Kansas, acting as agent for James B. Abbott.
1856	
January	Publishes *A Journey in the Seaboard Slave States*.
February	Leaves for eight months in Europe on business for Dix & Edwards.
March 29	Last issue of the *San Antonio Zeitung* is published.
March–May	Travels on the Continent—from Paris to Marseilles, Nice, Genoa, Leghorn and Rome; then south to Naples, Pompeii and Amalfi; north to Florence, Venice and Trieste; and on to Vienna, Prague, Leipzig and Dresden.
May	Adolf Douai leaves Texas for Boston.
May 20	Lawrence, Kansas, is "sacked" by proslavery forces.
May 22	Charles Sumner is caned by Preston Brooks in U.S. Senate chambers.
May–July	Lives in London and attends to publishing matters. Socializes with circle of editors of *Punch*. Frequently visits parks in London and vicinity.
July 21–c. 29	Meets father and stepmother in Liverpool and travels with them back to London via Wales, Chester, Coventry, Kenilworth, Warwick, Stratford, Leamington, Oxford and Windsor.
c. August 7–20	Travels with family to Dresden via Ostend, Bruges, Ghent, Mechlin, Lièges, Aix-la-Chapelle, Cologne, Bonne, Coblenz, Bingen, Kastel, Hesse-Cassel, Frankfort, Leipzig and Dresden. Returns to London via Berlin and Hamburg.
September	New territorial governor of Kansas, John W. Geary, begins program of "pacification."
October	Returns to New York from England.
December	Writes "Letter to a Southern Friend."
1857	
January	Publishes *A Journey Through Texas*.
January	John Hull Olmsted leaves for Cuba and Europe in search of better health.

CHRONOLOGY OF FREDERICK LAW OLMSTED: 1852–1857

March 4	Governor Geary of Kansas resigns.
March 6	Dred Scott decision is announced by U.S. Supreme Court.
March–April	Writes introduction and supplement for American edition of T. H. Gladstone's *The Englishman in Kansas*.
March 26	Robert J. Walker is appointed governor of Kansas Territory.
April	Becomes partner in publishing firm of Miller & Company, with George W. Curtis and J. W. Miller.
May	Begins to work with New England Emigrant Aid Company to promote free-labor colonization in Texas and "Neosho."
June	Publishes American edition of *The Englishman in Kansas*. Withdraws as partner in Miller & Company.
June 3	First letter of the series "The Southerners at Home" is published in the *New York Daily Tribune*.
August 6	Publishing firm of Miller & Curtis fails.
August 12	Applies for post of superintendent of Central Park in New York City.
August 24	Last letter in "The Southerners at Home" series is published.
September 11	Appointed superintendent of Central Park.
November 24	John Hull Olmsted dies in Nice.

INDEX

Italic numbers indicate illustrations.

"A., Mr." *See* Arnold, Richard J.
Abbot, Gorham D. ("James Gordon Abbott"), 338, 344
Abbott, James Burnett (1818–1879), 24, 64, 363, 365–66, 369, 371
"Abbott Howitzer," 25, 366–72
Abingdon, Va., 482
Abolitionists, 85, 283, 286
Acquia Creek, Va., 92, 467
Adams, William T. [pseud. "Dr. Hunter"], 359, 361
Africa, 122, 166, 482
Agricultural practices: in England, 139, 140, 166, 171; in the North, 87, 101, 103, 115, 134, 137, 192; in the South, 86–92, 97–101, 103–4, 128–31, 134–37, 139, 140, 192–93, 199–200, 205, 257, 267, 309–10, 438, 444
Aiken, William, 418, 423
Alabama, 10, 33, 481; description of, 205–9; frontiersmen in, 155; slavery in, 183–85, 188, 411
Alexandria, La., 473
Allen, Anthony Benezet, 143
Allen, Daniel B., 336
Allen, Richard Lamb, 143
Allison, Samuel Perkins (1827–1858), 1, 236–37, 245, 472; FLO's encounter with, 16–17, 21, 29, 231, 232–36
Amazon River, 145, 233
American Agriculturalist (periodical), 143

American and Foreign Antislavery Society, 267, 287
American party. *See* Nativism; Know-Nothing party
American Peace Society, 363
American Seamen's Friends Society, 143, 329
American Whig Review, 329, 366
"Andover, Mrs." *See* Stowe, Harriet Beecher
Anjer, Java, 171
Anti-Nebraska party (N.Y.), 336
Antwerp, Belgium, 145, 147, 151
Apollyon, 208, 209
Arctic (ship), 322–31, *324*
Aristotle, 278
Arkansas, 404, 437, 454
Arnold, Louisa Caroline Gindrat (1804–1871), 161, *162,* 163
Arnold, Richard J. (1796–1873), *161, 162,* 163–64, 187, 464, 469; plantations of, 10, 13, 160–61, 163, 188, 191; slaves of, 167, 182, 186, 193–94, 255
Asheville, N.C., 482
Ashland (estate), 472
Association for the Religious Instruction of the Negroes (Liberty County, Ga.), 172–73
Atchison, David Rice, 423, 424
Athenaeum, A London Literary and Critical Journal, 350, 351, 386, 389

487

INDEX

Atlantic and Pacific Railroad Company, 429
Atlantic Monthly, 355, 452, 454
Austin, Tex., 317
Austin Texas State Gazette, 318
Austria, 262, 268, 383

Badger, George E., 287
Bailey, Gamaliel, 283, 287
Baker, Anthony Wayne (1826–1854), 10, 210, 212
Bakersville, N.C., 482
Baldwin, Elizabeth (1824–1912), 381
Baltimore, Md., 472
Bancroft, George, 359, 361
Bandera Pass, Tex., 298
Bangs Brothers & Company (publishers), 387, 390
Banks, Nathaniel P., 420, 423
Baptists, 164, 312, 401, 403
Barclay, Mildred ("Mrs. Barclay"), 463, 468
Barnes, Albert Henry, Jr. (1826–1878), 211, 212, 374, 375
Barney, Hiram, 376
Barnum, P. T., 102, 335
Bartholomew, Edward Sheffield (1822–1858), 379, 392, 394; relations of, with Bertha Olmsted, 71, 380, 393; relations of, with FLO, 379–80, 381, 396
Bartlett, D. W., 356
Bartlett & Welford (book importers), 390
Barye, Antoine-Louis: *Lion et Serpent,* 342, 346
Bastrop, Tex., 317
Bateman, Ellen (1844–1936), 102, 333, 336; ability of, 95, 332, 335
Bateman, Hezekiah L., 332, 333, 335, 336
Bateman, Kate Josephine (1843?–1917), 333; ability of, 95, 102, 335; education of, 335–36
Bateman, Sidney Frances, 335, 336. Writings: *The Mother's Trust,* 336; *Young America,* 332, 335
Bayne, Thomas Levingston (1826–1891), 203, 204, 211, 213, 214, 470
Bayou Sara, La., 307, 309, 311, 480
Beaumont, Tex., 334
Beecher, Henry Ward, 50, 320
Beecher, Lyman, 50, 115
Beecher, Thomas Kinnicut, 338, 345

Behr, Ottomar von, 18, 463, 475
Belfast, Ireland, 52, 204
Bell, Currer. *See* Brontë, Charlotte
Bell, Peter Hansborough, 403, 405
Bellows, Henry W. (1814–1882), 347, 348
Bentham, Jeremy, 238
Bently, Richard, 361
Bethels, for sailors, 142, 143
Biarritz, France, 392, 393
Bingen, Hesse-Darmstadt, 235, 238
Birmingham, Ala., 481
Birmingham, England, 139, 380
"Black Republicans," 407
Blacks, natural capacities of, 178, 181, 229, 259
———free, 15, 121–24, 204, 229; laws concerning, 125–26, 189, 197, 264, 269; in the North, 91, 100, 120, 123–24, 263–65; in the South, 118–21, 263–64
Blanc, Louis, 394
Blue Ridge Mountains, 136, 139
Boerne, Tex., 294
Bogue, David, 83
Bois de Boulogne (Paris), 156, 162
Bossange, Edouard, 114, 115
Bossange, Hector, 344, 347
Boston, Mass., 25, 60, 397, 401, 404, 452; compared to the South, 97, 119, 131, 411; FLO in, 347, 441, 449
Boston Christian Aid Society, 404
Boston Daily Advertiser, 65, 401, 402
Boston Kansas Company, 32, 441
Botta, Anne Charlotte Lynch. *See* Lynch, Anne Charlotte
Botts, John Minor, 285, 288
Bowen, M'Namee & Company (silk merchants), 320
Brace, Charles Loring (1826–1890), 33, 49–52, 51, 113–14, 320, 397, 448; as abolitionist, 5, 83, 84; biography of, 49–52; correspondence of, with FLO, 16, 17, 21, 22, 82, 204, 231, 236, 271, 274, 351; friends and relatives of, 56, 69, 94, 115, 236, 237, 443, 445; in Hungary, 6, 359, 361; mission work of, 120, 121, 212, 335; relations of, with FLO, 4, 5, 9, 72, 126, 266, 281, 332, 374
Brace, Letitia Neill (Mrs. Charles Loring) (1822?–1916), 52, 204, 332

488

INDEX

Brackenridge, Henry Marie, 107, 111
Bradbury, William, 388, 390
Bradbury & Evans (publishers), 22, 358–61, 388, 390
Briggs, Charles (1804–1877), 21, 54, 346, 348, 355
Brighton, England, 385
Brontë, Charlotte, 345; *Villette,* 338, 345
Brook Farm, 21, 346
Brooks, C. W. Shirley, 388, 390
Brooks, Linda Hull (aunt), 375
Brooks, Preston L., 26, 383, 384, 411, 419, 421
Brooks, Samuel Hull (cousin), 375
Brown, George W., 429
Brown, John, 26, 34, 368
Browne, William Montague (1823–1883), 368, 370–71
Brownlow, William Gannaway ("Parson"), 413, 414, 422
Bryant, William Cullen, 21, 63
Buchanan, James, 370, 384, 429, 454; administration of, 28, 30, 455; and Kansas, 424–25, 426, 427–28, 442; and slavery, 383, 391, 422
Bunyan, John, 209
Burnsville, N.C., 482
Bushnell, Horace (1802–1876), 4, 7, 8, 338, 345
Business ethics, 358–60
Butler, Andrew P., 26
Buxton, Charles Fowell (1823–1871), 32, 446, 448

"C., Mr." *See* Calvert, Charles Benedict
Cabot, James Elliot (1821–1903), 26, 377, 391–92
Cabot, Samuel, Jr. (1815–1885), 31–32, 66, 434, 435, 441, 442, 447, 448, 455; biography of, 52–53
Calhoun, John C. (1782–1850), 67, 177, 181, 287, 373
Calhoun, Meredith (b. c. 1805), 11, 222–23, 228, 229; plantations of, 216–30, 465, 470
California, 197, 233, 258, 284, 329, 334, 336, 351, 413, 422, 425
Callaghan, Bryan V., 294, 299
Callahan, James H., 362
Calvert, Charles Benedict ("Mr. C.") (1808–1864), 10, 106, 464; plantation of, 87, 88, 91–92, 467

Calvin, John, 83
Cane River (La.), 471
Cape Fear River (N.C.), 468
Carlyle, Thomas, 345; *Sartor Resartus,* 246, 269
Cartwright, Samuel, 110, 111, 181
Castle Garden (N.Y.C.), 434, 435
Castro (Lipan Indian chief), 299
Cato, Sterling G., 430
Cayenne, French Guiana, 392, 393, 394
Central Park (N.Y.C.), 1, 2, 12, 32–34, 50, 348, 370, 448
Central Railroad of Georgia ("Savannah and Macon Line"), 198, 202
Century Club, 366
Charivari (periodical), 346
Charleston, S.C., 97, 163, 194, 197, 201, 411, 412, 421, 468, 469
Chateau du Mick (Antwerp, Belgium), 91–92
Chattanooga, Tenn., 317, 481
Cherokee District (Ga.), 199, 200
Children's Aid Society (N.Y.C.), 50, 52, 94, 203, 204, 211, 212, 236, 237, 238, 332–33, 335
Chinese, 147, 170–71, 267; coolies, as free-labor force, 193, 197, 258
Christianity, 58, 100, 117, 142, 382
Cibolo River (Tex.), 475
Cincinnati, Ohio, 232, 234, 472
City of Philadelphia (ship), 326, 331
City Point, Va., 141, 143
Civitavecchia, Italy, 377, 378
Claiborne, Ala., 469
Claiborne County, Miss., 480
Clark, Myron, 336
Clay, Cassius M., 3, 232, 236
Clay, Eliza Caroline (1809–1895), 160, 163
Clay, Henry, 91, 472
Clay, James, 463
Cobden, Richard, 411, 421
Coit, Fanny (b. 1852), 338, 345
Coit, Frances Olmsted (1829–1907) (cousin), 344–45
Colfax, La., 470
Collins, Edward Knight, 327, 331
Collins Line, 327, 329
Columbus, Ga., 164, 201, 469
Commerce: in Great Britain, 97, 139, 145; in the North, 145, 146, 359; in the South, 13, 96–98, 116, 119,

INDEX

Commerce (*cont'd*)
144–47, 151–52, 156–58, 190–91, 197, 198, 201–2, 209, 435, 464
Compromise of 1850, 3, 5, 84, 92, 237, 287, 306, 384, 428
Connecticut, 6, 9, 124, 126, 293, 419, 423
Cook, Clarence, 54
Cooper, James Fenimore, 232
Cooper, Peter (1791–1883), 235, 238
Cooper Union for the Advancement of Science and Art (N.Y.C.), 238
Corn Laws (England), 138, 140
Corvin-Wiersbitzki, Otto von, 394
Costa Rica, 76–77, 384
Cotton supply, 443–48
Cotton Supply Associations of Liverpool and Manchester, 441, 445, 446
Cranch, Christopher Pearse (1813–1892), 342, 346
Cranch, Elizabeth de Windt, 342, 346
Crawford, Thomas, 95, 102
Creek Indians, 205
Crenshaw, John Bacon (1820–1889), 93, 94, 467
Crenshaw, Nathaniel Chapman (d. 1866), 10, 93, 465, 467
Crimean War, 237, 384
Crux, Thomas, 92
Cuba, 197, 233
Cumberland, Md., 472
Cumberland River, 16, 232, 253
Cumberland River Iron Works, 258, 267
Cummins, Maria Susanna, 345; *The Lamplighter*, 345
Currituck Bay (N.C.), 464
Curtis, George W. (1824–1892), 21, 23, 54, 57, 63, 343, 346, 347, 348, 353, 389; biography of, 53–56. Writings: *Lotus-Eating*, 54; *Potiphar Papers*, 54

Daily California Chronicle, 336
Dana, Charles A. (1819–1897), 21, 60, 63, 347, 348, 349, 371–72, 385, 388, 389
Dana, Richard Henry: *Two Years Before the Mast*, 330
Dante Alighieri, 278
Davis, Jefferson, 214, 283, 287, 370
Day, Thomas Mills (1817–1905), 354, 355–56

DeBow, James D. B. (1820–1867), 34, 283, 287, 463, 464; *The Industrial Resources, Statistics, &c. of the United States*, 435, 436, 443
Deep Creek, Va., 468
Degener, Edouard ("Mr. D.") (1809–1890), 18, 276, 280, 317, 464, 476; sons of, 277, 280
Delane, John Thadeus, 32, 304, 448
Democratic party, 30, 336, 383, 417
Deutsches Gesellschaft der Stadt New York, 436
Devereux, John, 114
Devereux, Thomas Pollock (1793–1869), 10, 113, 114; family of, 114
Devil's Island. *See* Cayenne, French Guiana
Dickens, Charles, 352, 359–60; as founder and editor of *Household Words*, 22, 56, 347, 352, 355
Dickinson, Daniel Stevens, 233, 237
Dick Tinto. *See* Goodrich, Frank Boott
Disosway, Gabriel P., 336
Dix, Joshua A. (1831–1894), 55, 94, 347, 348, 355, 372, 373, 374, 389; biography of, 56–57; family of, 347, 349; relations of, with FLO, 23, 51, 348, 351, 361, 385–86
Dix, Edwards & Company (publishers), 21, 54, 55, 56, 62, 334, 346, 347, 348, 349, 355, 357, 360, 361, 372, 375, 376, 389, 390; FLO's association with, 1, 20, 22, 23, 24, 72, 94, 322, 344, 351, 386, 389
Doherty, Hugh, 181
Don Giovanni (Mozart), 278
Douai, Adolf. *See* Douai, Karl Daniel Adolf
Douai, Karl Daniel Adolf (1819–1888): biography of, 57–61; as editor of *San Antonio Zeitung*, 18, 19, 20, 24, 25, 28, 64, 75, 314–20, 332, 335, 361–62, 363, 400–402, 437; *Fata Morgana*, 60; relations of, with FLO, 278, 280–81, 291, 294, 317, 450, 451, 464, 475
Douglas, Stephen A., 17, 281, 284, 285, 287–88, 423; family of, 288
Douglas County, Kansas Territory, 424, 455
Douglass, Frederick (1817–1895), 123, 126

490

INDEX

Downing, Andrew Jackson (1815–1852), 8, 354
Drapetomania (disease), 110
Dred Scott Decision, 28, 30, 407, 416, 419, 420, 422, 423
Dresel, Julius (1816–1891?), 18, 317, 436, 440, 441
Duggan, Peter Paul (or Paul Peter) (d. 1861), 356, 357, 388, 390
Duncan, Lucius Campbell (1801–1855), 210, 212; family of, 212
Duyckinck, Evert, 351–52
Dwight, Theodore, 369
Dwight, Timothy (1752–1817), 7, 8
Dysaesthesia Aethiopica (disease), 110–11

Economist (periodical), 350, 351
Edinburgh, Scotland, 94, 380, 381
Education, 292, 335; need for, 234–36, 244, 292–93
Edwards, Arthur T. (1828–1857), 22, 23, 55, 56, 352, 353–54, 355, 360–61, 374, 375, 376, 385, 386, 387; biography of, 62–63
Egypt, 171
Eliot, George, 238
Elizabethton, Tenn., 482
Elliott, Charles Wyllys (1817–1883), 23, 51, 232, 235, 236, 238, 353, 365, 366, 374, 388, 424. Writings: "About Barns," 354; *Cottages and Cottage Life,* 354; *New England History,* 419; *San Domingo,* 241
Elliott, Henry Hill (1805–1868), 320
Emancipator (newspaper), 283, 287
Emerson, Ralph Waldo, 21, 334, 340, 348, 349; "Self-Reliance," 345
Emerson, William (1801–1868), 55, 332, 334, 376
England. *See* Great Britain
Ervendberg, L. C., 475
European Republicans, 6, 235, 275–81, 381–84, 392–94. *See also* Browne, William M.; Degener, Edouard; Douai, Adolf; Dresel, Julius; Forbes, Hugh; Kapp, Friedrich; Riotte, Charles
Evans, Frederick, 388, 390
Evans & Dickerson (publishers), 375
Evermay (plantation). *See* Smith, Benjamin
Examiner (newspaper), 350, 351

"F., Mr." *See* Florence, Thomas B.; Fuller, Henry M.
Fairfax County, Va., 88, 89
Faraday, Michael, 350, 352
Farmville, Va., 82, 84, 482
Fashion (plantation). *See* Taylor, Richard
Fayetteville, N.C., 468
Federal government. *See* U.S. government
Felton, Cornelius C. (1807–1862), 348, 349
Ferdinand II (King of the Two Sicilies), 421
Ferris, Mrs. Benjamin G.: *The Mormons at Home,* 353, 355
Field, Alfred T. (1814–1884), 203, 204, 235, 238, 380, 381
Field, Charlotte Errington (c. 1817–1880), 203, 204
Field, David Dudley (1805–1894), 365, 366, 376
Five Points House of Industry (N.Y.C.), 94, 100, 103, 121
Florence, Thomas B. ("Mr. F."), 87–88, 92
Forbes, Hugh, 368; *Manual of the Patriotic Volunteer,* 367, 368
Forrest, Edwin, 353, 355
Forrester, James, 295–99; family of, 299
Fort Adams, Miss., 472
Fort Duncan, Tex., 295, 299
Fort Inge, Tex., 299
Fort Leavenworth, Kan., 405, 420, 429
Fox, Warren, 330
France, 72, 175, 340; government of, 246, 345, 392; people of, 239, 340, 392
Frankfort, Ky., 472
Franklin, Benjamin, 419
Franz Josef I (emperor of Austria-Hungary), 245, 246, 411
Frederick Douglass' Paper, 126
Fredericksburg, Va., 90
Free Democracy party (N.Y.), 336–37
Freedman's Bureau, 56
Free laborers, condition of, 124, 131–32, 229–30, 254, 256
Free-soil colonization, 18–20, 24–34, 138, 397–400, 431–56
Free Soil party, 5, 84
Freie gemeinden, 58, 61

491

INDEX

Freie Verein (Sisterdale, Tex.), 18, 317, 441
Friedrich, Otto, 475
Friends, Society of, 92, 93
Froebel, Julius, 463, 475
Fugitive Slave Act of 1793, 431
Fugitive Slave Act of 1850, 5, 84, 85, 286, 336, 423, 431
Fuller, Henry M. ("Mr. F."), 87–88, 92

Gaines Ferry, Tex., 473
Garibaldi, Guiseppe, 368, 370
Garrigue, Rudolph, 435, 436
Garrison, William Lloyd, 5, 50, 283, 286, 287, 431
Gaskell, Elizabeth Claghorn: *Cranford*, 345
Gaston, N.C., 468
Geary, John W., 28, 30, 425, 428, 429, 430
Gee, Thomas W. ("Thomas W."), 10, 102, 152, 464, 465, 467; family of, 102
Geneseo, N.Y., 337–38, 344
Geneva, Switzerland, 82, 83
Genoa, Italy, 377, 378
George P. Putnam and Company. *See* Putnam, George P., and Company
Georgia, 10, 20, 253; description of, 199–202; railroads in, 198–99; slavery in, 184, 188, 189, 193, 302, 411
German Republican Association (N.Y.), 435
Germans, 88, 279. *See also* Texas, West, Germans in
Germany, 279–80
Gindrat, Louisa Caroline. *See* Arnold, Louisa Caroline Gindrat
Gladstone, Thomas H., 405; *The Englishman in Kansas*, 1, 28–29, 34, 35, 397, 405, 407, 408, 414, 416, 417, 430
Gladstone, William, 405
Glasgow, Scotland, 97, 98, 146, 380
Gliddon, George R., 181
Goderich, Lord. *See* Robinson, George Frederick Samuel
Godwin, Parke (1816–1904), 21, 347, 349, 352, 353, 357, 374; biography of, 63. Writings: "America for the Americans," 354; "Calhoun on Government," 373; *Political Essays*, 355, 389, 390; "The Kansas Question," 363, 364; *Vala, A Mythological Tale*, 355
Goodloe, Daniel Reaves (1814–1902), 35
Goodrich, Frank Boott [pseud. Dick Tinto] (1826–1894), 343, 346
Gordon, William W., 198, 202
Gosport, Va., 143
Graham's Magazine, 355
Grand Ecore, La., 214, 470, 473
Gray, Asa (1810–1888), 50, 232, 236, 348, 349
Gray, Jane Loring (Mrs. Asa), 50, 236
Great Britain, 32, 53, 119, 138–39, 140, 145, 146, 171, 229, 230, 309, 384; FLO in, 7, 16, 55, 72, 103, 452; people of, 138–39, 157, 239, 241
Great Dismal Swamp, Va., 50, 93, 94, 113, 114–15, 143, 464, 468
Greeley, Horace (1811–1872), 232, 236, 238, 336, 349, 365, 366, 368, 371–72; *A History of the Struggle for Slavery Extension or Restriction in the U.S.*, 389, 390
Greensville, Va., 482
Greytown (Mosquito Coast), 384
Griscom, Thomas ("T. R. Griscom"), 106–7, 111
Guadalupe, Tex., 317
Guadalupe River (Tex.), 275, 476

Habersham, Robert, 163
Haiti, 411, 421
Hale, Edward Everett (1822–1909), 26, 27, 64, 322, 362–63, 399, 400; biography of, 64–66; family of, 64, 65. Writings: "How They Lived at Naguadavick," 66; "The People's Park" (sermon), 66; "The Spider's Eye," 65, 372; *Sybaris and Other Homes*, 66
Hale, Emily Baldwin Perkins (Mrs. Edward Everett) (1829–1914), 363
Hale, Nathan, 402
Halifax, Nova Scotia, 145
Halifax County, N.C., 10
Hallock, Gerard, 423
Hamilton, James Alexander (1788–1878), 33, 50, 51, 237, 446, 448, 451; family of, 448
Hampton Roads, Va., 141, 143, 145, 344

492

INDEX

Harper, Fletcher (1806–1877), 346
Harper, William ("Chancellor Harper") (1790–1847), 133, 140; *Memoir on Slavery,* 140
Harper's Monthly, 21, 22, 342–43, 346, 348, 355
Hartford, Conn., 4, 71, 274, 337, 339, 342, 373
Hartford Courant, 354, 355–56
Hartford Daily Times, 354
Hartford High School, 71
Harvard College, 236, 349
Havana, Cuba, 398
Haven, Emily Bradley Neal: *All's Not Gold That Glitters,* 336
Hawthorne, Nathaniel, 21
Hayfield (estate), 236
Hegel, Georg, 58, 278
Hemans, Felicia Dorothea (1793–1835), 274
Henry, Patrick, 398, 419
Herbert, Philemon Thomas, 383, 384
Higginson, Charles J., 32, 441
Hildreth, Richard, 268
Hitchcock, Sophia Stevens (Mrs. William Page) (1826–1892), 163, 339, 343–44, 346, 347, 396; "An American Woman in Paris," 347, 349; family of, 395, 396; relations of, with Bertha Olmsted, 22, 71, 338–39, 342, 345, 347, 378, 393, 395
Hoboken, N.J., 61, 77
Hoffman, Charles Fenno, 352
Holland, Stewart, 324–25, 331
Homochitto River (Miss.), 480
Hotel de Ville (Paris), 342, 343, 346
Houdon, Jean Antoine, 95, 101
Household Words (periodical), 22, 56, 344, 347, 350, 352, 353, 355, 358, 360, 393. *See also* Dickens, Charles
Houston, Sam, 281, 285
Howard, George Thomas, 400, 401, 402
Howe, Samuel Gridley, 60
Hugo, Victor, 235, 238
Humboldt, Friedrich, 61, 417, 423
Hungary, 411; revolution in, 6, 246
Hunkers, 265, 269, 317, 318, 334, 336
Hunt, F. A., & Company (St. Louis, Mo.), 367
"Hunter, Dr." *See* Adams, William T.
Hunt's Merchant's Magazine, 166, 171

Hurlbert, William Henry (1827–1895), 54, 359, 361, 388, 389, 390; *Pictures of Cuba,* 361

Illinois, 404
Illinois Central Railroad, 450, 451
Illiteracy, in the North and South, 124, 126, 255, 293, 294
Indiana, 264, 269
Indians, American, 205, 295–99, 314, 417; Lipans, 299, 478
Indian Territory, 3, 31, 442, 455
Ireland, 52, 132
Irish, 131–32, 157; in America, 88, 108, 110, 120, 200–201
Irving, Washington, 24, 448
Italy, 23, 176, 398

Jackson, Ellenor Noyes (1823–1887), 213, 214
Jackson, Jefferson Franklin (1821–1862), 10, 213, 214–15, 469
Jackson, Miss., 480
Jackson, Patrick Tracy (1780–1847), 445
Jackson, Patrick Tracy, Jr. (1818–1891), 445
Jamaica, 197
James River (Va.), 96, 98, 134, 141, 143, 144, 255, 467
Jardin des Tuileries (Paris), 346
Jefferson, Thomas, 67, 95, 101, 233, 251, 255, 419, 427; *Notes on the State of Virginia,* 255, 428
Jefferson County, Ala., 481
Jefferson County, Tenn., 413, 421
Jews, 88, 171, 186
Johnson, William Samuel, 114
Jones, Charles Colcock (1804–1863), 173, 180; "Moral Discipline and Culture of the Negroes," 173–77, 180, 181
Jones, Enoch, 401, 402
Jones, Samuel J., 25, 28, 366, 424
Jones County, N.C., 415
Joyce, William, 388, 390

Kansas-Nebraska Act, 2, 67–68, 271, 281–88, 336–37, 364, 384, 423, 428, 431
Kansas Territory: arming of settlers in, 64, 362, 366, 367, 368–72; as

INDEX

Kansas Territory (cont'd)
"Bleeding Kansas," 26, 30; "bogus legislature" of, 24, 25, 28, 30, 31, 56, 64, 422, 426, 430; disturbances in, 20, 24, 30, 356, 362, 363, 383, 399, 406, 423, 424–31; expansion of slavery in, 3, 28, 363–64, 404, 424, 440, 437, 442; free-soil movement in, 2, 53, 319, 363, 365, 366, 369, 372, 398, 407, 438, 448, 450, 454; politics in, 25, 31, 365, 382, 429

Kansas Zeitung, 434, 449, 451

Kapp, Ernst (1808–1896), 18, 280, 317, 475

Kapp, Friedrich (1824–1884), 59, 68, 77, 280, 368, 370, 435, 447, 449; biography of, 66–69; family of, 67

Keating, Thomas, 383, 384

Kendall, George W., 463

Kennedy, Joseph C. G., 287

Kentucky, 232–33, 237, 310; people of, 404

Kingsbury, Frederick (1823–1910), 3, 5, 49, 83, 84, 214; biography of, 69

Kirkland, Caroline M. (1801–1864), 374, 375

Know-Nothing party, 25, 330, 336, 352, 354, 442. *See also* Nativism

Knoxville, Tenn., 412

Knoxville Register, 413

Knoxville Whig, 413, 422

Kob, Karl, 434, 449; *Wegweiser für Ansiedler im Territorium Kansas,* 434

Kossuth, Lajos, 245, 246, 268

Koszta, Martin, 262, 268

Lawrence, Amos A. (1814–1886), 64, 369, 371, 445

Lawrence, Kansas Territory, 24, 28, 64, 365, 371, 383, 384, 430

Leader (periodical), 350, 351

Leavenworth, Abner (1803–1869), 69, 82, 84, 102, 113, 202, 204, 212, 467

Leavitt, Joshua, 287

Lecompte, Samuel D., 430

Le Conte, Abigail Anna Brooks, 375

Leech, John, 388, 390

Leghorn (Livorno), Italy, 377, 378

Leigh, Benjamin Watkins, 125

Leigh, Percival, 352, 388, 390

Leland Stanford, Jr., University, 378

Lemon, Mark, 388, 390

Les Halles (Paris), 342, 346

"Letter from a Southern Matron—The Domestic Aspect of Slavery" (*NYDT*), 193, 197

Leveson-Gower, Harriet Elizabeth Georgiana (Duchess of Sutherland), 256

Lewes, George Henry, 351; *The Life and Works of Goethe,* 353

Lexington, Ky., 472

Liberator (newspaper), 267, 287, 422

Liberia, 124, 126

Liberty County, Ga., 172–73

Lincoln, Abraham, 67, 76, 422

Lipscomb, Andrew Adgate ("A Native Southerner"), 168–69, 171–72, 175, 176; "The South and Slavery," 168–69, 171–72, 176

"Literary republic" of New York, 21, 23, 24, 376

Literary World (periodical), 350, 351–52

Liverpool, England, 32, 97, 445, 446

London, 339, 411; FLO in, 23, 25, 380, 385, 387

Longfellow, Henry Wadsworth, 21, 348, 349

Longman, Brown, Green, and Longmans (publishers), 361

Lord, Frederick William, 337

Loring, Susan (Mrs. Patrick Tracy Jackson, Jr.) (1823–1895), 445

Louisiana, 227, 239, 437; slave code in, 183, 185, 210, 211

Louis Napoleon. *See* Napoleon III

Louis Philippe, 6

Louisville, Ky., 232, 440, 472

Louvre (Paris), 341, 342, 345

Low, Sampson, Jr. (1822–1871), 386, 387, 389

Low, Sampson, & Co., 389

Lowell, James Russell (1819–1891), 21, 340, 348, 349; *Fireside Travels,* 345

Lowell, Mass., 146, 162, 200

Luce, James C., 327, 331

Lutherans, 403, 404

Luxembourg Palace (Paris), 342, 345

Lyell, Charles, 50

Lynch, Anne Charlotte (1815–1891), 50, 202, 203, 274–75

Lynchburg, Va., 482

494

INDEX

M'Curdy, Aldrich & Spencer (commission merchants), 113, 114
McElrath, Thomas (1807–1888), 56, 353, 355
Macon, Ala., 201
Madison County, Miss., 480
Mainzer Adelsverein. See Society for the Protection of German Immigrants in Texas
Maison Carrée ("Maison Quarrée") (Nîmes), 95, 101
Malay Archipelago, 166, 171
Manchester, England, 139; Cotton Supply Association of, 32, 445, 446, 451
Manufacturing, in the South, 89, 90, 96–97, 200–201, 258, 267
Marcy, Erastus Edgerton, 334, 336
Marcy, Randolph Barnes, 442
Marion Court House (S.C.), 468
Marseilles, France, 377, 378
Maryland, 88, 127, 205, 304, 480
Mason, George, 419, 423
Massachusetts, 109, 200
Massachusetts Disunion Convention, 431
Massachusetts State Kansas Committee, 434
Matagorda, Tex., 317
"Matt Ward Case," 408. *See also* Ward, Matthew Flournoy
Maury, Matthew Fontaine, 145, 151
Maverick, Samuel Augustus, 404, 405
Mayhew, Henry, 390
Mayhew, Horace, 388, 390
Medina River (Tex.), 294, 298
Melville, Herman: *Benito Cereno,* 21
Memphis, Tenn., 197, 215, 471
Mercer County, Ohio, 125
Merchant marine, 322–31; treatment of sailors in, 142, 327–30
Methodists, 312, 401
Mexicans, in West Texas, 301, 304, 305, 314, 315, 317, 319, 401, 403
Mexican War, 3, 237, 245
Mexico, 233, 357; FLO in, 275, 299, 463, 475
Michelangelo, 378
Milam County, Tex., 447
Mill, John Stuart, 111, 238
Miller, J. W., 23, 55, 57

Miller & Company (publishers), 23, 28, 55
Miller & Curtis (publishers), 32, 55
Mining, in the South, 97, 203, 481
Minnesota Territory, 287
Mississippi, 227, 250, 293, 307, 310; FLO in, 11, 33; people of, 313
Mississippi and Texas Railroad, 300, 302, 306, 429
Missouri, 33, 249, 404, 426, 437, 448, 454; people of, 24, 401, 404, 425
Missouri Compromise, 285, 306, 336–37, 383, 424
Mitchell, Elisha, 114
Mobile, Ala., 469, 470
Moffat, William B., 354, 355
Montégut, Emile: "Scenes de la vie et de la litterature americaines," 345
Monterrey, Mexico, 25, 76
Montgomery, Ala., 10, 201, 205, 206, 214, 469
Morel, Amos ("Robert") (slave), 182, 184–85, 187–88
Morel, Tom ("William") (slave), 182, 188
Mormons, 298
Morris, Adolphus, 93, 94
Morton, Samuel G., 181; *Crania Aegyptiaca,* 181
Mount Vernon (plantation), 90
"Mr. Newman," 467
Mulattoes, 121, 171, 228
Murillo, Bartolomé Esteban: *Madonna of the Rosary* (painting), 342, 346
Murphy, N.C., 482

Naples, Italy, 380, 411, 412, 421
Napoleon III (emperor of France), 26, 238, 245, 246, 340–41, 345, 392, 394, 410, 411, 421
Nashville, Tenn., 16, 232, 233, 236, 472
Nashville Convention of 1850, 286
Natchez, Miss., 311, 480
Natchitoches, La., 222, 473
Nation, 351, 366
National Era (periodical), 83, 259, 267, 283, 287
National Intelligencer, 107, 285, 288
Nativism, 25, 317, 318, 330, 336, 352, 354, 357, 442
Nazro, Charles G., 441

INDEX

Neill, Eliza, 203, 204, 211, 212
Neill, Henry M. (1838-1906), 203, 204, 210, 211, 443
Neill, William, 320, 321, 441, 443, 444, 446
Neill Brothers & Company (cotton merchants), 443, 444
"Neosho," 31, 433, 437-40, 442, 449, 450-52, 454-55
Nette, August, 370
Neu Braunfels, Tex., 17, 32, 447, 474, 475, 478
Neu Braunfelser Zeitung, 318
Neu Wied, Tex., 475
New Albany, Ind., 440
Newark, N.J., 61
New England, 8, 65, 111, 135, 176, 245-46, 348; emigration from, 138, 369, 399, 400, 438; people of, 239, 313, 353
New England Emigrant Aid Company, 24, 25, 31, 53, 60, 65, 66, 363, 365, 371, 399, 434, 442, 443, 445, 446, 448, 449, 452, 453, 455, 456; committees of, 53, 66, 441, 447; relations of FLO with, 3, 32, 34, 322, 397, 431-56
New England Non-Resistance Society, 286
New Jersey, 95, 106-7
New Mexico Territory, 287
New Orleans, La., 171, 204, 411, 437, 441; FLO in, 10, 209, 210-11, 212, 214, 470, 471, 472, 480
New Orleans Crescent (newspaper), 352
New York (city), 97, 98, 100, 109, 120, 121, 132, 142, 143, 145, 146, 298, 337, 339, 340, 343, 359, 437, 452; FLO in, 20, 332, 347, 348, 352, 354, 365, 368, 371, 467, 480, 482
New York (state); 8, 109, 116, 136, 230, 234, 236, 238, 336, 369, 398; compared with the South, 104, 116, 127, 128
New-York Daily Times, 9, 115, 171, 236, 241, 245, 267, 285, 336, 346, 449; FLO's writings for, 1, 7, 11, 12, 13, 14, 17, 20, 23, 26, 50, 67, 92, 94, 107, 110, 113, 170, 204, 209, 211, 269, 329-30, 333, 335, 344, 377, 466
New York Daily Tribune, 21, 59, 67, 236, 238, 344, 346, 347, 349, 351, 353, 355, 368, 371, 428, 430, 431, 449; FLO's writings in, 1, 7, 12, 33, 94, 442
New-Yorker Staats-Zeitung (newspaper), 352, 354
New York Evening Post, 21, 63, 349, 449
New York Journal of Commerce, 370, 418, 423
New York Literary World (periodical), 84
New York Morning Express, 352, 354
Niblo's Garden (theater), 334, 336
Nicaragua, 77, 285, 288, 357, 384
Nicholas I (czar of Russia), 411
Niles, William Woodruff, 71
Nonslaveholders, in the South, 125, 156-58, 187, 199, 242, 252-54, 268, 312-13
Norfolk, Va., 111, 128, 139, 142-43, 144, 145, 146, 151-52; FLO in, 120, 141, 149, 468
North: migration to the South from, 88-89, 92-93, 116, 118, 138-39, 401; people and institutions of, compared to the South, 91, 97, 100-101, 104, 106-9, 135, 229-30, 234-35, 241-42, 245-46, 282-85, 410
North, Christopher. *See* Wilson, John
North American Review, 65
"North and South. Impressions of Northern Society upon a Southerner," 241, 245
North British Daily Mail, 382, 384
North Carolina, 97, 127, 153-54, 197, 203, 251, 414, 415, 464; FLO in, 10, 33, 203, 204; people of, 152-53
Notre Dame, cathedral of (Paris), 342, 346
Nott, Josiah C., 181
Noxubee County, Miss., 481
Nueces, Battle of (1862), 280
Nuevo Leon, Mexico, 25

O'Flaherty, Edmund [pseud. William Stuart] ("Stewart"), 353, 355
Ogeechee River (Ga.), plantations on, 10, 159-61
Ohio, 109
Old Point Comfort Convention (1850), 147, 151
Olmsted, Bertha (1834-1926) (half-sister), 70, 345, 396; biography of,

INDEX

70–71; relations of, with Edward S. Bartholomew, 380, 381, 393
Olmsted, Charles John. *See* Olmsted, John Charles
Olmsted, Charlotte (1855–1908) (stepdaughter), 354
Olmsted, Denison (1791–1859) (cousin), 10, 114, 212
Olmsted, Frederick Law (1822–1903)
Biographical Information:
——education, 74, 346
——experience and theory of "unconscious influence," 322, 341–42, 380, 409–10
——farming activities, 83, 354
——free-soil colonization efforts, 26–27, 31–33, 53, 65, 68, 322, 397–404, 431–56, 485
——health, 374–75
——literary activities as editor and publisher, 20–23, 53–57, 62–63, 347–61, 363–64, 372–74, 385–90, 484–85
——purchase of arms for Kansas freestate settlers, 24–25, 65, 365–72
——relations with antislavery Germans in West Texas, 18–20, 24–25, 57–60, 68, 75–76, 275–81, 289–92, 314–20, 361–62, 400–404
——social reform activities and ideas, 6–9, 51–52, 83–85, 234–36, 237, 265
——superintendency of Central Park, 23–24, 450
——travels, general: during childhood, 348; to China, 170–71, 323, 329, 330; in Europe, 22–23, 279–80, 377–78, 484; in Great Britain, 23, 132
——travels, in the South: itineraries of, 9–11, 82, 93, 127, 164, 198, 211, 212, 213, 214, 215, 293, 463–81; FLO's comments on, 82, 203, 213
Landscape Designs:
——Riverside, Ill., 66
——Stanford University campus, 378
Writings:
——American editor's introduction to *The Englishman in Kansas,* 28–30, 405–24
——American editor's supplement to *The Englishman in Kansas,* 30–31, 424–31

——"The Arctic. Lessons Concerning Means of Security on Ocean Liners," 322–31
——*Cotton Kingdom,* 3, 12, 35, 466
——"How Ruffianism in Washington and Kansas Is Regarded in Europe," 26, 381–84
——"Filibusterism and Other Matters in Mississippi," 480
——*Journey in the Back Country,* 1, 12, 23, 33–35, 55, 171, 181, 230, 464–66; quotations from, 222, 223, 463
——*Journey in the Seaboard Slave States,* 14, 91, 92, 93, 101, 102, 110, 115, 126, 143, 152, 154, 163, 164, 170, 171, 187, 196, 197, 213, 214, 215, 401, 463–65; FLO's assessment of, 374; publication of, 1, 22, 72, 357, 372–76, 389; quoted, 163, 268, 464; responses to, 65, 266, 391; writing of, 11, 13, 20, 26, 354, 372–76
——*Journey Through Texas,* 17, 27, 34, 237, 267, 299, 448; publication of, 1, 12; responses to, 402; use of, to promote free-labor colonization, 31, 65, 397–99; writing of, 26, 28, 74, 391, 463–64, 466
——"Parental Schoolmasters," 333, 335
——"Real China, The," quoted, 170
——"South" series (*New-York Daily Times*), 12–17, 33, 81, 155, 304, 321, 459–60; FLO's comments on, 86, 93, 203, 209–10; responses to, 172, 269; writing of, 7, 13, 170, 212, 236, 245, 266, 267, 463–66
——"Southerners at Home" series (*New York Daily Tribune*), 17, 33, 271, 314, 442, 461
——"Tour of the Southwest" series (*New-York Daily Times*), 11–12, 17, 460–61, 463
——"Visit to a Chinese School," 357, 388, 390
——"Voice from the Sea," 366
——*Walks and Talks of an American Farmer in England,* 4, 9, 82, 83, 84–85, 93, 94; FLO's comments on, 82; publication of, 83
Olmsted, Frederick Law, Jr. (1870–1957) (son), 390
Olmsted, James (d. 1640), 7

497

INDEX

Olmsted, John (1791–1873) (father), 71, 72, 170, 203, 337, 338, 345; biography of, 71–73; family of, 20, 71, 73
Olmsted, John Charles ("Tot") (1852–1920) (stepson), 82, 83, 338, 345, 354
Olmsted, John Hull (1825–1857) (brother), 74, 82, 83, 203, 237, 334, 337, 354, 398; biography of, 73–75; correspondence of, 211, 317, 318, 329, 345; and FLO's business concerns, 21, 56, 389; in France, 72, 212; friends and classmates of, 10, 16, 49, 69, 210, 211, 231, 232, 375; and *Journey Through Texas*, 12, 26, 466; travels of, with FLO, 11, 281, 294, 299, 320, 471, 477
Olmsted, Mary (1832–1875) (half-sister), 22, 113, 339, 344
Olmsted, Mary Bull (Mrs. John) (1801–1894) (stepmother), 71, 352, 378
Olmsted, Mary Perkins (Mrs. John Hull) (1830–1921) (sister-in-law), 74, 82, 83, 273, 334, 345, 354
Olmsted, Owen Pitkin (1794–1873) (uncle), 338, 344
Opelousas, La., 311, 479
Oregon Territory, 287, 384
Osborne, James W., 114
Overseers, 100, 107, 110, 125, 130–31, 150, 217–18, 310

Padelford, Seth, 441, 443, 446, 447
Page, William (1811–1885), 395, 396
Pakenham, Richard, 181
Panic of 1857, 23, 453
Para, Brazil, 145
Paris, 212, 337, 343, 345, 346; FLO on, 210, 339, 340–42
Park, Mungo, 166, 170
Parker, John W., 388, 390
Parker, Theodore (1810–1860), 203, 204, 234, 283, 402; relations of, with FLO, 5, 21, 50, 348; views of, 237, 287, 401
Parkes, Josiah, 140
Paul, Saint, 278
Peabody, George Henry, 463, 469
Pease, Elisha, 294, 306, 429, 444
Pease, Lewis Morris, 93, 94, 100, 103
Pennsylvania, U.S.S., 143

Pentonville prison (England), 85
Perkins, Emily Baldwin (Mrs. Edward Everett Hale) (1829–1914), FLO's courtship of, 52, 64, 115, 346, 363, 381
Perkins, Frederic Beecher (1828–1899), 342–43, 346, 356, 365
Perkins, Mary Cleveland Bryant. *See* Olmsted, Mary Perkins
Perkins, Thomas F., 236–37
Petersburg, Va., 116, 119, 144–45, 146, 148, 465; FLO in, 10, 69, 110, 127, 141, 212, 467
Philadelphia, Pa., 97, 109, 119, 123–24, 151–52
Philleo, Calvin W., 353, 355
Piedras Negras, Mexico, 299
Pierce, Franklin, 283, 286, 287, 428, 429; administration of, 233, 357, 383–84; and Kansas, 25, 28, 283, 285, 422; and slavery, 30, 383, 416, 422
Pillow, Gideon Johnson, 283, 286
Planters' Bank (Miss.), 294
Poland, 411
Polk, James K., 286, 429
Polk County, Tenn., 481
Pomeroy, Samuel Clark, 454, 456
Port Caddo, Tex., 435, 436
Porte Crayon. *See* Strother, David Hunter
Portland, Ky., 472
Portsmouth, Va., 468
Powhatan, U.S.S., 143
Preemption Act of 1841, 442
Prentice, George Dennison, 11, 232, 236, 472
Price, William S.: "Moral Benefits of Slavery," 166, 171
Priestley, John (d. 1872), 365, 366
Prince George's County, Md., 467
Prohibition party (N.Y.), 336
Property, as stewardship, 231, 261–62
Proslavery apologists, 140, 171, 178–79, 183–84, 188–89, 265, 364, 418–20
Providence, R.I., 163, 348
Prussia, 69, 176, 292, 294, 393
Psalm 115, 288
Punch (periodical), 23, 313, 352, 388
Pusey, Edward Bouverie, 350, 352
Putnam, George Palmer, 21, 56, 63, 348, 353, 355, 389

498

INDEX

Putnam, George P., and Company (publishers), 82, 83, 93, 355
Putnam's Monthly Magazine, 56, 344, 346, 348, 352, 354, 355–56, 361, 372, 386, 387, 389; articles in and contributors to, 65, 342–43, 345, 348, 349, 352–53, 354–55, 356, 357, 364, 372, 390; editors of, 53–54, 60, 63, 346, 347–49, 355; FLO as editor of, 1, 2, 21, 22, 348, 351

Quadroons, 213
Quakers, *See* Friends, Society of
Quattlebaum, Paul ("General Quattlebum"), 283, 286
Quincy, Edmund (1808–1877), 348; *Wensley, A Story without a Moral,* 349

Raleigh, N.C.: FLO in, 132, 468; FLO's letters from, 111, 120, 125, 139, 143, 151
Randolph, John, 122, 125, 398
Rapides Parish, La., 11
Raymond, Henry Jarvis (1820–1869), 115, 197, 232, 236, 270, 334, 336, 337; relations of, with FLO, 9, 113, 372; and "The South" series, 50, 202–3, 210, 211–12, 266–67
Red Republicans, 235, 238, 393
Red River (of the South), 11, 222, 302, 435, 436, 440, 450; FLO's travels on, 10, 211, 213, 214, 215, 470, 473; and "Neosho," 31, 438, 455; people of, 210
Reeder, Andrew, 365, 422
Reform Club, 382, 384
Republican party, 61, 67, 364, 398, 453; 1860 national convention of, 337
Revolutions of 1848, 2, 6, 58, 238, 276, 280, 394
Revue des Deux Mondes (periodical), 339, 345
Reynolds, Lorin G., 198, 202
Richardson, Henry Hobson, 366
Richmond, Va., 93, 102, 146, 148, 150, 170, 247, 465; commerce of, 13, 119, 144; description of, 93, 94–98, 411; FLO in, 33, 92, 127, 194, 197, 336, 467, 482
Richmond Enquirer, 109, 111, 121

Richmond-on-Ogeechee (plantation), 159–60, 163
Riddlesbarger, J., 371
Riedner, I. M., 362
Rio Grande, 294, 299
Riotte, Charles, 25, 370, 450; biography of, 75–77; relations of, with Adolf Douai, 58, 60, 317, 400; relations of, with FLO, 18, 19, 64
Ripley, George (1802–1880), 60, 343, 346
Riversdale (plantation), 10, 88, 467; description of, 87, 91–92. *See also* Calvert, Charles Benedict
Riverside, Ill., 66
Robinson, Charles, 25, 28, 64, 429
Robinson, George Frederick Samuel (Lord Goderich) (1827–1909), 434, 435, 438; correspondence of, with FLO, 27, 32, 433, 441, 446, 451
Rochester Colored National Convention (1853), 264, 269
Rocouncy (farm), 10, 93, 467. *See also* Crenshaw, Nathaniel Chapman
Rome, 378, 380, 396
Ronaldson (ship), 329–30
Rossy, Alexander, 315, 316, 318
Ruffin, Edmund (1794–1865), 137, 140, 267. Writings: *Essay on Calcareous Manures,* 136, 140; "Southern Agricultural Exhaustion and Its Remedy," 267
Ruffin, Thomas, 415, 422
Ruggles, Daniel, 31, 432, 434
Rusk, Thomas Jefferson, 281, 285
Ruskin, John, 342, 346
Russell, Robert: *North America, its Agriculture and Climate,* 448
Russia, 229

Sabine County, La., 473
Saint Charles (steamboat), 213, 214
Saint Charles Hotel (New Orleans, La.), 210
Saint Charles Parish, La., 11
Saint Francisville, Miss., 307, 309
Saint John's Lutheran Church (San Antonio, Tex.), 405
Saint Louis, Mo., 368, 372, 440, 455
Saint Peter's Basilica (Rome), 378
Salisbury Plain (Wiltshire, England), 171

499

INDEX

San Antonio, Tex., 33, 298, 361, 362, 401, 437; churches in, 312, 401, 403, 404, 405; FLO in, 271, 275, 281, 288, 294, 297–98, 475, 476; Germans in, 17, 18, 19, 24, 314, 400, 441
San Antonio and Mexican Gulf Railroad, 75, 401, 402
San Antonio Convention (1854), 315, 317
San Antonio Platform (1854), 19–20, 59, 315, 316, 317, 318, 441
San Antonio Western Texas (newspaper), 318, 402
San Antonio Zeitung, 18, 57, 58, 59, 75, 280, 318, 362; FLO's support of, 19, 25, 60, 316, 317, 319, 320, 335
San Augustine, Tex., 473
San Francisco, Cal., 339, 422
San Geronimo Creek (Tex.), 299, 478
Savannah, Ga., 10, 156–58, 162, 194–96, 198, 201, 469
Savannah Republican (newspaper), 269
Scenery, descriptions of, 158–60, 163, 273–75, 309
Schiller, Johann, 278
Schleiermacher, Friedrich, 278
Schoolfellow (periodical), 357, 372, 374, 375, 376, 387, 388, 389, 390
Schuyler, George Lee (1811–1890), 237; family of, 50, 234, 237
Scott, Winfield, 83, 84, 237, 286
Secessionist conventions, 283, 286
Selma, Ala., 469
Seguin, Tex., 317
Seguine, James, 463, 468
Seward, William H. (1801–1872), 233, 237, 285, 332, 335
Shakespeare, William, 340
Shannon, Wilson, 25, 424
Sharps rifles, 24, 363, 365–66, 367, 371, 416
Shaw, Francis George (1809–1882), 55, 56
Short, Charles Wilkins, 11, 232, 236, 472
Siemering, August (1808–1896), 18, 277, 280, 317, 475
Sigourney, Lydia, 274
Sisterdale, Tex., 18, 19, 58, 277, 280, 290, 293, 294, 317, 441, 475, 476
Skinner, John Warburton, 211, 212
Slater, Benjamin, 371

Slaveholders, in the South, 84–85, 90, 130–131, 173, 206, 228–30, 239–40, 315
Slave labor, comparative expense of, 81, 92, 100–101, 104, 106–10, 116, 147, 257
Slavery, 124–25, 260–61, 267; abolition of, 180, 259, 262–63, 265, 270, 391; as civilizing and Christianizing institution, 118, 164–80, 190, 251–52; degradation of free labor by, 92, 116–17, 123, 150–51, 257; effect of, on society, 103–4, 148–51, 190–91, 239–40, 254, 260, 262, 407–20; expansion of, 17, 233, 250, 262–63, 284–85, 363–64, 381–84, 391, 416–17, 422–23; justification for, 84–85, 177–79, 260; need for Northerners' forbearance concerning, 81, 117–18, 131–32, 180, 246, 260–63, 363–64; paternalistic form of, 100, 153, 155, 161–62, 184–88
Slaves: amusements of, 120; breeding of, 258; clothing, food, and shelter of, 159, 217, 226, 248–49, 255; communication systems of, 122; condition of, 81, 179, 182–83, 188, 216, 226, 247–52, 261–62; condition of, compared to other groups, 100, 118, 131–32, 166, 249, 255, 256; corporal punishment of, 150, 219–22, 223, 227, 249, 255, 411, 412–13, 421; dependence of, on whites, 120, 122; domestic life of, 150, 174–76, 193–94, 210, 227; feelings concerning freedom of, 122–24; funerals and cemeteries of, 194–96, 197; illnesses of, 104–6, 110–11, 224–26; labor of, 101, 190, 191–92, 197, 218–19, 248, 309–10; laws affecting, 122, 179, 185–86, 189, 248; literacy of, 188, 252; morals of, 123, 126, 170, 203, 204, 227, 230; naming of, 187–88, 226; property of, 183, 184–85, 186, 189, 218; relations of, with free blacks, 121; relations of, with masters, 99–100, 239, 240, 248, 409–16; religion of, 164–80, 228–29; runaways among, 225; sale of, 183–84, 249–51; skilled, 182–83, 215
Slave trade, 34, 88, 205; laws regulating, 183–84, 188–89

500

INDEX

Smith, Benjamin, 37; family of, 37, 480
Smith, Gerrit, 362, 363
Smithland, Ky., 472
Society for the Protection of German Immigrants in Texas, 275–76, 280, 319, 320
Solms-Braunfels, Prince Carl, 280
Somers, Robert (1822–1891), 384
Somers, U.S.S., 328–29, 331
Sonora, Mexico, 425
Sophora secundiflora, 275
Soulé, Frank (1810–1882), 334, 336
South Carolina, 20, 140, 261, 264, 267–68, 313, 469
South Carolina State Convention (1852), 286
South Carolina Times, 418, 420, 423
Southern commercial convention(s), 13, 97–98, 144–47, 151–52, 190–91, 197
Southerners: beliefs and concepts of, 233–36, 282–85; characteristics of, 239–46; manners of, 95–96, 158, 201, 208, 213–14, 232–35, 241–45, 307–13, 407–20
Southern Literary Messenger (periodical), 256
Southern Pacific Railroad, 285
Southern Planter (periodical), 132, 139
Souvestre, Emile: *An Attic Philosopher in Paris*, 344, 347
Spain, 176
Spectator (periodical), 350, 351
Spring, Marcus, 342, 346
"Squatter sovereignty," 237, 407, 415, 425, 426, 438
Stanford, Leland, 378
Stanley, Edward George Geoffrey Smith, Lord, 446, 448
Stanton, Frederick Perry, 425, 426, 428
Staten Island, N.Y., 49, 72, 74, 83, 139, 143, 151, 170, 331, 347, 349, 374, 394, 396, 482; Tosomock Farm on, 83, 115, 335, 344, 354
State *vs*. John Mann, 415, 422
Stevens, Sophia. *See* Hitchcock, Sophia Stevens
Stier, Henry Joseph, Baron de, 92
Stillman, Dr., 401
Stoker, Nancy, 463, 473
Stony Creek, Va., 10, 467
Story, William Wetmore, 388, 390
Stowe, Harriet Beecher ("Mrs. Andover") (1811–1896), 15, 21, 50, 94, 113, 114–15, 121, 131–32, 345, 348; family of, 115. Writings: *Dred*, 115; *Uncle Tom's Cabin*, 83, 107, 121, 131, 132, 267
"Strather, Mr." *See* Strother, Walter
Strauss, David Friedrich (theologian), 58, 234, 237
Strother, David Hunter [pseud. Porte Crayon], 343; *Virginia Illustrated, by Porte Crayon*, 346
Strother, Walter, 463, 464, 473
Stuart, William. *See* O'Flaherty, Edmund
Sumner, Charles, 26, 76, 383, 384, 411, 421
Sumner, Edwin Vose, 405, 420
Sutherland, Duchess of. *See* Leveson-Gower, Harriet Elizabeth Georgiana
Syracuse, N.Y., 364

"T., Mr." *See* Theissen, Gustav
T'ai P'ing Rebellion (1850–64), 267
Taylor, Bayard (1825–1878), 388, 390
Taylor, Richard ("Mr. R.") (1826–1879), 11, 210, 214, 464, 465, 470; family of, 212, 214
Taylor, Tom (1817–1880), 388, 390
Tennessee, 232, 237, 412; FLO in, 33, 414
Terry, Rose (1827–1892), 353, 374, 388; "The Mormon's Wife," 354–55
Texas, 11, 30, 249, 306, 312, 314–15, 317, 319, 425, 438, 441, 450–51, 454; anticipated division of, 300–303, 306; free-soil movement in, 25, 27, 31, 32–33, 53, 66, 67, 392, 398, 399, 400, 402, 440, 441, 449; FLO in, 10, 75, 465; Germans in, 3, 18, 19, 20, 24, 447; legislature of, 294, 300, 306, 437. *See also* Texas, East; Texas, West
Texas, East, 271, 300, 464
Texas, West, 271, 300, 301–6, 317, 403, 404, 433, 437
——free-soil movement in, 3, 17, 19, 26, 27, 28, 271, 301, 302–6, 314–17, 319, 397–98, 401, 436–41
——Germans in, 305, 314; characteristics and attitudes of, 275–79, 288, 289, 290–91, 292, 305, 401; eco-

501

INDEX

Texas, West, Germans in (*cont'd*)
    nomic activities of, 305, 306, 315, 436–47; settlements of, 11, 17, 304, 403, 444, 448; and slavery, 20, 301, 315, 316, 442, 449, 488
Texas Rangers, 275, 361, 362
Texas Western Railroad, 429
Thackeray, William, 23, 388, 390
Thayer, Eli, 33, 65
Theissen, Gustav ("Mr. T."), 58, 464, 475
"Thomas W." *See* Gee, Thomas W.
Thoreau, Henry David: *Cape Cod,* 21
Times (London), 29, 32, 131, 132, 394, 446
Titus, Henry T., 423
Topeka Constitution (Kansas Territory), 25
Tract societies, 22, 142, 143
Tracy, Daniel, 329
Trees and shrubs, comments on, 95, 160, 163, 275, 309
Trinity River (Tex.), 301, 304
True American (newspaper), 3, 236
Turkey, 269
Tuscaloosa, Ala., 211, 480, 481
Tyler, John, 256
Tyler, Julia Gardiner, 256; "To the Duchess of Sutherland and Ladies of England," 256

Ujhazy, Mr., 463
Ulrich, Joseph, 400–404
Underwood, Francis Henry, 454, 455
U.S. Capitol grounds, 92
U.S. Census, 283
U.S. Congress, 96, 151, 246
U.S. Constitution: interpretations of, 67, 233, 251; principles of, 85, 383, 427
U.S. government: internal improvements by, 96; Kansas and, 407, 416; slavery and, 262, 263
U.S. Mint, Charlotte, N.C., 113, 114
U.S. Navy, discipline in, 141–42, 328, 329
U.S. Patent Office, Report of, 257
U.S. Postal Service, 164, 209
U.S. Sanitary Commission, relations of FLO with, 50, 237, 249
U.S. Senate, 382
U.S. Supreme Court, 28

Van Buren, Ark., 455, 456
Vandoeuvres Hamlet, Geneva, Switzerland, 83
Versailles, palace of, 342, 345
Vesta (ship), 323–26, 329, 331
Vicksburg, Miss., 215, 471
Virginia, 82, 89–90, 96, 109, 121, 124, 126, 127–51, 153, 251, 374, 427; agriculture in, 98–101, 104–5, 128–31, 134–37, 139; capitol of, 95, 101; FLO in, 10, 13, 20, 33, 94, 205; free blacks in, 118–19, 122, 123–24, 125–26; legislature of, 95, 101, 148, 152; people of, 88–89, 118, 122, 130–31, 145–47; railroads in, 92, 96, 144, 148–49; slavery in, 106–7, 109, 116, 124–25, 131, 150, 152, 251, 255, 310

Walker, Robert J., 429; as Kansas territorial governor, 31, 425, 426, 454, 455; and slavery issue, 427, 431, 437, 442
Walker, William, 288, 357, 384
Walker County, Ala., 481
Wallace, George T., 463, 468
Wallace, Horace Binney, 356, 357
Ward, Matthew Flournoy, 408, 420
Warner, Susan Bogert [pseud. Elizabeth Wetherell]: *The Wide, Wide World,* 345
War of 1812, 130, 133
Washington Constitution (newspaper), 370
Washington, D.C., 383, 405; agriculture near, 86–88, 92; characteristics of, 87, 89, 201, 382; FLO in, 10, 467; slave trade in, 88, 92
Washington, George, statues of, 95, 101, 102
Washington Territory, 384
"Watson, John," 480
Waynesville, N.C., 482
Webb, Thomas Hopkins (1801–1866), 432, 443; and New England Emigrant Aid Co., 433, 434, 440, 441; trip of, to Kansas, 452, 453, 454, 455
Weldon, N.C., 468
Welford, Charles (1815–1885), 387, 390
Wells & Webb (type founders), 320, 363
Wesley, John, 260, 267

502

INDEX

Westminster Review (periodical), 236, 238, 351
Weston, George Melville (1816–1887), 452, 453; *Progress of Slavery in the United States,* 452
Westphal, Baron von: family of, 277–78; FLO meets with, 18, 277–78, 280, 475
Wetherell, Elizabeth. *See* Warner, Susan Bogert
Whampoa Reach (Canton, China), 170, 267
Wheeling, Va., 472
Whig party, 364; relations of FLO with, 5, 84, 333, 336
White, Richard Grant, 54
White Hall (plantation). *See* Arnold, Richard J.
Whittier, John Greenleaf, 21
Wilkinson, James John Garth, 181
Williamson County, Tenn., 236–37
Wilmington, N.C., 468

Wilmot Proviso, 286
Wilson, John [pseud. Christopher North]: *Noctes Ambrosiannae,* 163
Winston County, Miss., 480
Wisclicenus, Gustave Adolf, 58
Woodland, John, 463, 478
Woodville, Miss., 307, 310–11, 480
Wykeham, William of (1324–1404), 242, 246

"X., Mr." *See* Arnold, Richard J.

Yakima War, 382–83, 384
Yale College (University) (New Haven, Conn.), 8, 10, 49, 69, 72, 114, 204, 211, 212, 214, 234, 236, 337, 375
Yazoo River (Miss.), 471
Youth's Cabinet (periodical), 375

Zizelmann, Phillip Friedrich, 405
Zollicoffer, Felix Kirk, 232, 237